Hands-On Novell® Open Enterprise Server for NetWare® and Linux

Ted Simpson

THOMSON
™
COURSE TECHNOLOGY

Australia • Canada • Mexico • Singapore • Spain • United Kingdom • United States

THOMSON

COURSE TECHNOLOGY

Hands-On Novell® Open Enterprise Server for NetWare® and Linux

by Ted Simpson

is published by Thomson Course Technology.

Managing Editor William Pitkin III	**Product Manager** Amy M. Lyon	**Developmental Editor** Lisa M. Lord
Production Editor Daphne Barbas	**Quality Assurance Coordinator** Christian Kunciw	**Technical Editor** David Mansheffer
Senior Channel Marketing Manager Dennis Williams	**Editorial Assistant** Allison Murphy	**Cover Design** Abby Scholz
Text Design GEX Publishing Services	**Compositor** GEX Publishing Services	

For permission to use material from this text or product, submit a request online at http://www.thomsonrights.com/
Any additional questions about permissions can be submitted by e-mail to thomsonrights@thomson.com

Disclaimer
Thomson Course Technology reserves the right to revise this publication and make changes from time to time in its content without notice.

ISBN-13: 978-1-4188-3531-6
ISBN-10: 1-4188-3531-5

Contents

TABLE OF
Contents

CHAPTER ELEVEN
Implementing and Securing Internet Services   437

CHAPTER TWELVE
Installing and Working with SUSE Linux   487

Introduction

Since the 1980s, Novell has been a leader in the development of LAN technology. The requirement for secure access to resources and services across LANs and the Internet has created a need for more powerful and complex network systems, but the variety of computer operating systems and network protocols can make it difficult to access and manage company information and services from different environments. In recent years, there has been a growing demand for businesses to use open-source systems and applications based on GNU licensing. With the open-source GNU licensing model, developers can use existing software to develop new applications, as long as they make the source code available, and businesses can take advantage of software developed by public institutions, such as government agencies and universities, without having to pay high licensing costs. Novell has responded to the demand for network systems that make it possible to integrate diverse operating systems and include support for open-source solutions with its new Open Enterprise Server (OES) product release. OES includes an updated directory system and a variety of network services designed to bring diverse computer environments and networks together so that they can work as one network, or what Novell calls "oneNet." In addition, Novell has continued its tradition of providing networking solutions by enhancing administrative utilities and strengthening its support of open-source software standards, including Linux, Apache Web Server, MySQL, and PHP/Perl.

To be competitive, companies and organizations need competent network professionals who can manage network environments consisting of Windows, Linux, and NetWare operating systems. Novell instituted the Certified Novell Administrator (CNA) and Certified Linux Professional (CLP) programs to help establish credibility for network administrators who have the knowledge and skills needed to set up and manage NetWare and Linux networking services. Appendix A lists the latest CNA and CLP exam objectives and maps them to the chapter and section of the book where they are covered. You can find more information on Novell certification options and testing at *http://education.novell.com*.

Hands-On Novell Open Enterprise Server for NetWare and Linux is intended to provide the concepts, skills, and hands-on experience you need to pass the Novell NetWare 6.5 CNA exam 50-686 and be able to use Open Enterprise Server to build network systems. In addition, this book includes many CLP exam objectives that address how to set up a Novell SUSE Linux Enterprise Server that can provide network services to both Windows and Linux clients. These skills, along with the CNA designation, will put you in a position to take advantage of the many opportunities in the rapidly growing and changing field of networked computing.

Novell Software Products Included with This Book

In 2005, Novell acquired the SUSE Linux company, a leading provider of Linux systems throughout Europe and the United States. This acquisition, along with Novell's long-standing commitment to open-source solutions, has made Novell a leader in the open-source software market. Today, Novell offers a variety of operating system products from the NetWare and SUSE Linux worlds. Following is a description of the NetWare and SUSE Linux software that have been included in this book:

- *NetWare 6.5 Open Enterprise Server*—The NetWare 6.5 Open Enterprise Server product included with this book is an evaluation copy that comes on two CDs. You can use these CDs to install NetWare on a server as described in Chapter 2.

- *SUSE Linux Enterprise Server 9*—The Open Enterprise Server product is included on a bootable DVD and includes version 9 of SUSE Linux Enterprise Server, which has been configured with Novell services such as eDirectory and iPrint. You can use this DVD to install SUSE Linux as described in Chapter 12.

Novell Software Products Licensing Information

The Novell software programs included with this book are evaluation versions licensed by Novell for temporary use (not to exceed five months) with the course book with which the software is provided. Use of the enclosed software programs is also subject to the terms of the applicable accompanying software license agreement ("License"). By using the software, you agree to be bound by the terms of the License.

The Novell Open Enterprise Server software DVD included with this book contains a full evaluation version of SUSE Linux Enterprise Server 9. To accommodate for this academic deliverable, the original software has been modified from CD to DVD and is distributed on an "as is" basis. Please note that this software is for classroom use only and is not to be used in a production environment. To download a fully functional, supported, and upgradeable version of SUSE Linux Enterprise Server and other Novell open-source products, visit *www.novell.com/downloads*.

For license information on the Novell software included with this book, please refer to the full license document at *www.novell.com/licensing/eula/oes/oes_1_english.pdf*.

Approach

I wrote this book to meet the Novell NetWare 6.5 CNA 50-686 exam objectives and to provide coverage of Open Enterprise Server, which also includes SUSE Linux Enterprise Server 9. One of the best ways to learn new technologies is by working with them, so this book includes many hands-on activities that enable you to apply concepts described in the chapters. The hands-on activities require access to NetWare, Windows XP, and Linux operating systems. The best way to gain experience with all these operating systems is through the use of virtual machines, which enable you to run other operating systems on a Windows XP desktop system, as described in Appendix C. If your Windows XP desktop computer has 1 GB RAM, you can use virtual machines to simultaneously run a NetWare 6.5 server and a Windows XP client on your desktop computer without needing multiple partitions or disk drives. With virtual machines, you can easily switch between a Windows XP and Linux client or between NetWare 6.5 and SUSE Linux Enterprise Server 9 servers. Depending on your lab configuration, there are three general approaches to performing activities in this book:

- *Individualized environment*—This environment requires student systems to have at least 1 GB RAM and a 1.5 GHz processor to run client and server systems simultaneously. In addition to the necessary computer hardware, this environment requires using VMware Player or VMware Workstation 5, described in Appendix C. A major advantage of this environment is that students can work outside the computer lab by storing their virtual computer files on removable media, such as USB hard drives.

- *Team environment*—In the team environment, you're assigned to a team of two students. Each team then designates one computer to act as the server and another computer to act as the client. The server computer should be dual-booting or use VMware to run NetWare 6.5 or Linux Enterprise Server 9. The client computer should also use VMware or be dual-booting so that it can run Windows XP or SUSE Linux 10. The team environment enables students to have full control of both their server and client computers.

- *Shared classroom server environment*—In this environment, the instructor installs a NetWare 6.5 OES server, and students are assigned areas of the server based on student numbers used when creating objects. The lab computer should be configured for multibooting so that students can switch between Windows XP, SUSE Linux 10, or SUSE Linux Enterprise 9 environments.

Your instructor will inform you what environment is being used and explain how to set up and configure your lab computer.

Intended Audience and Use

Hands-On Novell Open Enterprise Server for NetWare and Linux is intended for people who are getting started in computer networking and want to know about multiple network operating systems. To understand the material in this book, you should have a background in basic computer concepts and have worked with applications in the Windows environment. Although some Linux background is helpful, this book is intended to give you a basic introduction to Linux concepts and explain specific techniques in working with Linux. This book is intended for use in a classroom or an instructor-led training environment, but you can also use it with self-paced or Web courses where you work on your own server. If you're using a self-paced approach, you might want to download a copy of VMware (described in Appendix C) so that you can run NetWare and Linux servers along with a client on your desktop. For more information on VMware, visit *www.vmware.com*.

Chapter Descriptions

Chapter 1, "Introduction to Network Administration," introduces the role of networks in business environments, explains basic network system components—such as servers, clients, pathways, and protocols—and describes the network environment for this book's Universal AeroSpace case study. This chapter also gives you an overview of popular network certifications and introduces the Novell Open Enterprise Server product.

In **Chapter 2**, "Installing Novell NetWare 6.5 Open Enterprise Server," you learn how to plan for and perform a NetWare 6.5 OES installation, how to work with common NetWare console commands, and how to load and work with NetWare Loadable Modules.

In **Chapter 3**, "Working with the NetWare File System," you continue building the Universal AeroSpace network by learning how to design and create a network file system, based on Novell Storage Services. In addition, you learn how to back up the file system and create drive pointer mappings to ensure standardized access to data.

In **Chapter 4**, "Novell eDirectory Services," you begin building your version of the Universal AeroSpace network by installing client software, designing the eDirectory tree structure, and creating network objects.

In **Chapter 5**, "Creating and Securing User and Group Objects," you learn how to create groups, user accounts, and Organizational Role objects to give users secure access to the network. You also learn how to improve network security by setting up password restrictions, account restrictions, and intruder detection policies.

In **Chapter 6**, "Working with NetWare File System Security," you learn how to grant access rights to users and how to make trustee assignments to directories and files for users, groups, and containers in your Universal AeroSpace network. You also learn how to effectively use inherited rights to enable users to access and manage files and folders.

In **Chapter 7**, "Managing eDirectory Security and Operations," you continue working with trustee assignments, inherited rights filters, and administrative roles to grant effective rights through user, group, and container objects. You also learn how to delegate administrative functions to users and groups by using iManager roles, manage network time synchronization, and monitor eDirectory operations.

In **Chapter 8**, "Implementing and Maintaining Network Printing," you learn how to set up and maintain a network printing system that enables users to send output to network printers easily and reliably. You learn how to work with queue-based printing, Novell Distributed Print Services, iPrint, and the Internet Printing Protocol to plan and set up a network printing system. In addition, you learn basic troubleshooting techniques to identify and fix network printing problems.

Chapter 9, "Managing Desktop Environments with Novell Client," explains how to create login scripts to meet users' access needs and provide a standard set of drive mappings and desktop functions. In addition, you learn how to use ZENworks to configure and manage desktop policies for users and workstations.

Chapter 10, "Implementing Novell OneNet User Services," delves into Novell's oneNet strategy of allowing information and services to be accessed and managed from any computer with Internet access. You learn how to set up and use NetWare 6.5 utilities, such as iFolder, NetStorage, NetDrive, and Virtual Office, and see how to allow users to access network resources independently of client operating system or location.

Chapter 11, "Implementing and Securing Internet Services," covers the OES Internet delivery services, including Net Services and Web Services. You learn how to implement these services and secure them from unauthorized access and attacks. You also learn how to use Novell Certificate Services, firewalls, and antivirus software to protect data and services when users are accessing information across a public network.

In **Chapter 12**, "Installing and Working with SUSE Linux," you learn how to plan for and perform an installation of SUSE Linux Enterprise Server 9, which ships with Open Enterprise Server. You also learn how to use the YaST utility to view and change system configuration parameters.

Chapter 13, "Managing Linux Environments," introduces you to working in the Linux environment, including creating user accounts, working with command-line utilities, managing the file system, and assigning file system rights.

In **Chapter 14**, "Planning and Implementing Novell OES on Linux," you learn how to set up and configure Novell services, such as managing eDirectory objects, creating Linux-enabled user accounts, providing access to Windows-based clients, creating and using NSS volumes, and setting up iPrint.

Appendix A, "Certification Exam Objectives for Open Enterprise Server," maps CNA certification objectives to the chapter and section where information about the objective is covered. This appendix also lists the CLP objectives covered in this book.

Appendix B, "Integrating SUSE Linux Clients" describes how to set up a SUSE Linux 10 client for use with Novell Open Enterprise Server. This appendix includes SUSE Linux 10 installation, NetWare server administrative tasks, and iFolder client setup and introduces the new Novell Client for Linux product.

Appendix C, "Working with VMware Workstation 5," provides an overview of using VMware to set up virtual machines on your desktop. You learn how to create new virtual machines for NetWare 6.5 and Linux, configure virtual machine settings, and use the free VMware Player to run existing virtual machines.

Features

Hands-On Novell Open Enterprise Server for NetWare and Linux differs from other networking books in its unique hands-on approach and its orientation to real-world situations and problem solving. To help you understand how NetWare concepts and techniques are applied in real-world organizations, this book incorporates the following features:

- *Virtual machine technology*—Lab activities are designed to work with virtual machines so that you can set up a lab environment on your desktop computer.

- *Linux integration*—With the increased use of Linux in the workplace, this book provides opportunities to use the Linux operating system in each chapter's activities. Chapters 12, 13, and 14 and Appendix B focus on integrating Linux into network environments.

- *Hands-on activities*—Concepts are explained in the context of a hypothetical company (Universal AeroSpace) that casts you in the role of a student intern working for the network administrator. The hands-on activities are incorporated throughout the book, giving you practice in setting up, managing, and troubleshooting a network system. The activities give you a strong foundation for carrying out network administration tasks in the real world. Because of the book's progressive nature, completing the hands-on activities in each chapter is essential before moving on to end-of-chapter projects and subsequent chapters.

- *Chapter objectives*—Each chapter begins with a detailed list of the concepts to be mastered. This list gives you a quick reference to the chapter's contents and is a useful study aid.

- *Chapter summary*—Each chapter's text is followed by a summary of the concepts introduced in that chapter. These summaries are a helpful way to review the material covered in each chapter.

- *Key terms*—All terms introduced with boldfaced text are gathered into the Key Terms list at the end of the chapter. This list gives you an easy way to check your understanding of important terms.

- *Review questions*—The end-of-chapter assessment begins with a set of review questions that reinforce the material introduced in each chapter. Answering these questions ensures that you have mastered the important concepts. The review questions can also be used to help prepare for the CNA exam.

- *Case projects*—These projects are intended to make you think about the chapter concepts and how they can be applied to planning, designing, and troubleshooting network information systems.

- *Hands-on projects*—These projects give you the opportunity to reinforce and apply the chapter's concepts and techniques by building the Business Division for the Universal AeroSpace network on your own. Although each chapter's projects build on previous chapters, they are independent of the hands-on activities, meaning that you don't need to do the projects to complete hands-on activities in subsequent chapters.

- *Novell Open Enterprise Server software*—This book includes two CDs with an evaluation copy of NetWare 6.5 Open Enterprise Server and a bootable DVD with SUSE Linux Enterprise Server 9. For more information on these products and their licensing, refer to the previous section "Novell Software Included with This Book."

Text and Graphic Conventions

Additional information and exercises have been added to this book to help you better understand what's being discussed in the chapter. Icons throughout the text alert you to these additional materials:

Tips offer extra information on resources, how to attack problems, and time-saving shortcuts.

Notes present additional helpful material related to the subject being discussed.

The Caution icon identifies important information about potential mistakes or hazards.

Each Hands-on Activity or Project in this book is preceded by the hands-on icon.

Case project icons mark the end-of-chapter Universal AeroSpace projects, which are scenario-based assignments that ask you to independently apply what you have learned in the chapter.

The Example icon points out step-by-step instructions for procedures that aren't covered in hands-on activities but are common tasks that network administrators perform.

INSTRUCTOR'S MATERIALS

The following supplemental materials are available when this book is used in a classroom setting. All supplements are provided to the instructor on a single CD. You can also retrieve these supplemental materials from the Course Technology Web site, *www.course.com*, by going to the page for this book under "Download Instructor Files & Teaching Tools."

Electronic Instructor's Manual. The Instructor's Manual that accompanies this book includes:

- Additional instructional material to assist in class preparation, including suggestions for classroom activities, discussion topics, and additional projects.

- Solutions to all hands-on activities and end-of-chapter materials, including the review questions and case projects.

ExamView®. This book is accompanied by ExamView, a powerful testing software package that instructors can use to create and administer printed, computer (LAN-based), and Internet exams. ExamView includes hundreds of questions that correspond to the topics covered in this text, enabling students to generate detailed study guides with page references for further review. The computer-based and Internet testing components allow students to take exams at their computers, and they save instructors time by grading each exam automatically.

PowerPoint presentations. This book comes with Microsoft PowerPoint slides for each chapter. These slides are included as a teaching aid for classroom presentation, to make available to students on the network for chapter review, or to be printed for classroom distribution. Instructors, please feel free to add your own slides for additional topics you introduce to the class.

Figure files. All figures and tables in the book are reproduced on the Instructor's Resource CD in bitmap format. Similar to the PowerPoint presentations, they are included as a teaching aid for classroom presentation, to make available to students for review, or to be printed for classroom distribution.

LAB REQUIREMENTS

To do the case projects and set up your own version of the Universal AeroSpace network, you will be using your own dedicated NetWare server or be assigned to a NetWare classroom server and given a student reference number (an Admin user name preceded by your student number) and a data volume identified with your student number. If you're using a shared classroom server, your user account will have the necessary privileges to build your own network system by creating and managing network objects, such as users, groups, printers, and files, without affecting other students' use of the server. Your assigned data volume is the work area on the classroom server where you have been given all rights to create and manage files and directories so that you can complete the projects and activities. If you're doing the activities and projects on your own dedicated server, you need to use VMware as described in Appendix C or must have one computer designated as the NetWare server and a second computer to use as a client. You can also use VMware to run the NetWare or Linux server with the client on your desktop. For more information on VMware, see Appendix C and visit *www.vmware.com*.

Minimum Lab Requirements

Hardware:

- With a shared classroom server, each student system requires at least 256 MB RAM, an Intel Pentium or compatible processor running at 166 MHz or higher, and a minimum of 5 GB free space on the hard disk. The system needs to be able to dual-boot between Windows XP and SUSE Linux Enterprise Server 9. A CD-ROM drive is also important for loading software and performing certain activities.

- If you're using VMware to host dedicated server and client systems, each student system needs 1 GB RAM, a Pentium III processor running at 1.5 GHz minimum, and 10 GB free space on the hard drive.

- To set up a shared classroom server for NetWare 6.5, you need a classroom server with at least 1 GB RAM, an Intel Pentium III or higher processor running at 700 MHz or higher (Intel Pentium 4 1.2 GHz recommended), a minimum 8 GB hard drive (6 GB for the SYS volume and at least 500 MB for each student), a CD-ROM drive, a Super VGA or higher resolution display adapter and monitor, and a mouse.

Software:

- Windows XP Professional on each student system

- A copy of the Novell Open Enterprise Server DVD and CDs, which include both NetWare 6.5 and SUSE Linux Enterprise Server 9

In addition to the Novell software included with this book's CDs and DVD, additional software available as free downloads is recommended. Although the following software isn't required to complete the chapter activities, it will help enhance your learning experience:

- *SUSE Linux 10*—Appendix B includes information on installing and using Novell SUSE Linux 10 as a client system. You might want to use this appendix to perform a SUSE Linux 10 installation before Chapter 3. You can then use your SUSE Linux 10 system to perform many of the chapter activities. You can download a free copy of SUSE Linux 10 from *www.novell.com/products/suselinux/downloads/suse_linux/index.html*.

- *VMware Workstation*—VMware Workstation allows you to create and run other operating systems, such as Novell NetWare and SUSE Linux Enterprise Server 9, as applications on your Windows XP desktop. Appendix C provides information on installing and running VMware Workstation. You can download a 30-day evaluation of VMware Workstation at *www.vmware.com* and use it to create virtual machines for your NetWare and Linux servers.

- *VMware Player*—Although you can't use this product to create new virtual machines or install a new operating system, Appendix C describes how you can use it to run virtual machines created by VMware Workstation. You can download a free copy of VMware Player from *www.vmware.com*.

ACKNOWLEDGEMENTS

Although I have spent many hours rewriting this book for the Novell Open Enterprise Server product, it would never have been completed without the help of Course Technology management and staff, especially Amy Lyon, who directed and managed the project, and Will Pitkin, for his vision for the book and his persistence in working with Novell to obtain the latest information. I want to express my many thanks to my excellent editor, Lisa Lord, whose patient help and hard work, along with her mastery of technical jargon (also known as GeekSpeak) and the English language, brought life to the words in these chapters.

Credit for identifying technical problems with the hands-on activities goes to Christian Kunciw, Danielle Shaw, and Serge Palladino, who did an excellent job of checking each step and offering suggestions and alternative solutions. No book can be completed without all the work required to get it ready for printing. I feel fortunate to have had such an excellent production editor as Daphne Barbas to make sure this book was ready for publication. I take my hat off to the excellent reviewers—David Browne of Gibbs College-Livingston and COMPDAC, John Crowley of Bucks County Community College, Nina Milbauer of Madison Area Technical College, and Bert Nichols of Vatterot College—for their consistent hard work in ensuring that the content and activities would meet the practical demands of teaching NetWare concepts in the classroom environment. My thanks also to my excellent technical editor, David Mansheffer from Dunwoody College of Technology, who contributed so much to the technical content and applicability of the chapters and appendixes. I also owe a big thanks to Jason Novak for his technical help in keeping my computer running and helping me research information. I also want to thank the students in my advanced NetWare class, including Adam Stromquist, Timothy Bablick, Peter LeJeune, Jarret Hamilton, and Christopher Thompson, for their enthusiasm and perseverance in working with the new Novell software.

Finally, I want to thank my wife, Mary, who made many alterations in our schedule and helped keep me sane through the sometimes daunting challenges of meeting the ever-changing requirements that go with writing a book. I want to dedicate this book to my nephew, Eric Simpson, and my nieces, Kellie Thiele and Kari Simpson, who are growing up with computers as a standard part of their homes. By the time they get interested in networking, I'm sure the material in this book will be quite obsolete. As usual, I want to dedicate my writing efforts to my mother, Rosemarie (Ode), who although she's not a technical type, has a great depth of knowledge and wisdom about life and work.

1

INTRODUCTION TO NETWORK ADMINISTRATION

After reading this chapter and completing the activities, you will be able to:

♦ Describe the tasks performed by a Certified Novell Administrator and be able to differentiate among industry certifications

♦ Describe common network components and services

♦ Describe the features of Windows, SUSE Linux, and NetWare operating systems

To be competitive in today's rapidly changing information age, organizations and individuals need fast, reliable, and secure access to resources and services. Computer networks provide the information highway needed to connect people with information sources and services. As a result, computer networks have become one of the most vital parts of an organization's information system. As a network administrator, your job will be to ensure that users have secure and reliable access to the data and resources they need to perform their jobs. In this chapter, you learn about the hardware and software components that make up a network system as well as the tasks you need to learn to become a Certified Novell Administrator.

INTRODUCTION TO NETWORK ADMINISTRATION AND CERTIFICATIONS

Because of the key role network systems play in providing organizations with access to information and resources, people who can implement and manage network system environments are in high demand. Network administrative tasks can be divided into two major categories: network system management and network operating system management. Network system management includes tasks for implementing and maintaining the network pathway and protocols (described in the next section). Network operating system management involves working with the system software that provides users with the services and resources they have rights to access. Network operating system management tasks include the following:

- Installing server and desktop software
- Implementing and maintaining network services
- Creating and securing user accounts
- Performing software upgrades
- Managing and securing the network file system
- Installing and managing application packages

Since the beginning of microcomputer-based business systems in the early 1980s, Novell has been a leader in local area network (LAN) technology. Earlier versions of the Novell NetWare operating system excelled at offering rapid and secure access to file and print resources to a wide variety of locally attached computers. Today, Novell is developing products that help make many diverse network systems work as a single network. Novell uses the term **OneNet** to describe its strategy of developing products and services that help make diverse networks consisting of different hardware, operating systems, and applications, act as a single network. Novell's OneNet strategy is to simplify the complexities of managing and accessing networks and to increase an organization's capability to implement Internet applications by offering tools and solutions that work across different network environments.

To help ensure that people have the skills required to administer and troubleshoot network systems, Novell has established a number of certifications that have become industry recognized standards. Certifications consist of one or more exams taken at certified testing centers. In recent years, other companies and independent testing organizations have established additional certifications on specific products and computer networking skills. Table 1-1 lists several certifications that can enhance your employment opportunities in the network administration field.

Table 1-1   Common industry certifications

Certification	Vendor or Organization	Description
Certified Novell Administrator (CNA)	Novell	Consists of a single exam that signifies you have the knowledge and skills to perform common administrative tasks using Novell NetWare. This book focuses on covering the CNA objectives.
Certified Novell Engineer (CNE)	Novell	Consists of several exams that demonstrate you have the knowledge and skills to set up, troubleshoot, and maintain network systems using Novell operating system software and services.
Certified Linux Professional (CLP)	Novell	Consists of a single exam signifying that you have the knowledge and skills with Linux and Novell Nterprise Services to perform administrative tasks in a Linux-based network.
Certified Linux Engineer	Novell	Intended for administrators who need a more comprehensive knowledge of Linux to set up, troubleshoot, and maintain a Linux-based network system.

Table 1-1 Common industry certifications (continued)

Certification	Vendor or Organization	Description
Microsoft Certified Professional	Microsoft	This product-based certification shows you have achieved the knowledge and skills necessary to manage a particular Microsoft software product. Product-specific exams are available for Windows 2000 Professional, Windows XP, and Windows Server 2003.
Microsoft Certified System Engineer (MCSE)	Microsoft	Intended for professionals who design, implement, and troubleshoot an infrastructure for business solutions based on the Windows 2000 and 2003 platforms.
Microsoft Certified System Administrator (MCSA)	Microsoft	Intended for network administrators who manage and maintain a Windows-based network system using Active Directory.
Network+	CompTIA	Consists of a single exam showing that you have mastered network concepts, including cable systems, protocols, and essential network software services.

This book is intended to cover the knowledge and skills you need for CNA certification. In addition, this book gives you a basic background in SUSE Linux and Novell Open Enterprise Server to help build a base for taking the CLP certification.

The Certified Novell Administrator (CNA)

Novell has created a means for network administrators to demonstrate their competency at NetWare administration by passing a qualifying exam. Passing the exam earns a network administrator the designation of **Certified Novell Administrator (CNA)**, originally called the Certified NetWare Administrator. Novell developed the CNA program in 1992 to help define the role of network administrators in a NetWare environment. A CNA is considered qualified to be the network administrator of a network system using Novell products such as NetWare, GroupWise, and ZENworks. Because the Internet plays an important part in most networks, the new CNA program also requires administrators to have a basic understanding of Internet services and security. The program provides a standard of knowledge and performance that organizations can use to help ensure the quality of network administration and support.

> Novell expects CNAs to understand basic computer hardware, operating systems, and network systems, so in Chapters 2 and 12, you learn about computer hardware requirements for NetWare and Linux installations.
>
> **NOTE**

Current information on the CNA and other Novell certifications programs can be found on the Novell Education Web site at *http://education.novell.com*, which also includes a current list of test objectives for the CNA exam as well as other CNA-related information. The content of these programs and exams changes periodically, so it's a good idea to get the latest information from Novell before taking the CNA exam.

> As mentioned, CNA was originally Certified *NetWare* Administrator, and CNE was Certified *NetWare* Engineer. The name changes reflect a broadening of Novell's outlook and its product line.
>
> **NOTE**

As a CNA, your job will be to direct your organization's networking services and support to meet the processing needs of microcomputer users. To develop the CNA program, Novell researched the job duties of thousands of NetWare network administrators around the world to determine the common tasks that network administrators perform regularly. The sections that follow summarize Novell's research. They will help you understand the typical duties of a network administrator and give you an overview of the NetWare knowledge and skills you need to become a CNA.

Understanding NetWare Components and Commands

A NetWare administrator needs a solid foundation in the components of a NetWare network and how they interoperate. When a problem—such as the "File server not found" message—occurs on a computer attached to the network, network administrators must be able to troubleshoot the network and isolate the cause of the error by drawing on their knowledge of network components.

Just as a mechanic must learn how to use the tools for maintaining and repairing an automobile, a CNA must learn how to use the many NetWare commands and utilities to perform network maintenance and repair tasks, such as creating users, granting access rights, listing directory information, and working with printers. Starting with this chapter and continuing throughout the book, you learn how to use the commands and utilities that are a CNA's essential tools.

Supporting Client Computer Environments

The majority of computers attached to NetWare networks today run some version of the Windows operating system. As a CNA, you'll need to know how to install and configure the client software for attaching these computers to the network and establishing communications. With the rapid advances in microcomputer technology that require organizations to add new computers and replace existing ones each year, a main task of CNAs is installing and updating client software regularly.

In addition to Windows computers, your organization might also need to provide network support for Apple Macintosh and UNIX-based computers. Although Novell doesn't currently require a CNA to install client software on Macintosh and Linux operating systems, you'll need to be able to identify how NetWare software components enable UNIX and Macintosh computers to be attached to a NetWare network.

Managing Novell eDirectory Services

One of the most important features in NetWare 6.5 is Novell eDirectory Services, previously called Novell Directory Services (NDS). On a NetWare network, a user connects to the network itself rather than to a server (or group of servers). This requires a comprehensive, logical network design and tools for administering resources (such as disk space and printers) for the entire network. Novell eDirectory Services is the system that you, as a CNA, use to create, maintain, and administer the network design and resources. The logical network design is called the "directory tree." eDirectory is actually a database of information about the network and is built on the X.500 standard for a global network database. You learn about X.500 and eDirectory in detail in Chapter 4.

NOTE

Novell eDirectory Services is proving a useful network design and administration tool, and Novell is licensing eDirectory to other companies, such as Hewlett-Packard and SCO (Santa Cruz Operations), for use in their network operating systems and software products. Part of Novell's OneNet strategy has been to make eDirectory available for Windows Server 2003, Windows 2000 Server, Windows NT, and Linux operating systems. Using eDirectory on a variety of network operating systems makes it possible to access and manage servers using these operating systems as a single, uniform network.

Managing the Network File System

A network file system uses a directory structure to define how servers' data storage is organized. You might already know how a good directory structure on your computer's local hard disk makes it easier to run applications and access files. On a server, a good directory structure becomes even more important because many users share the same storage device. As a result, one of the most important tasks a CNA must undertake when installing a new server is planning and implementing an efficient directory structure to support users' processing needs. In this book, you learn the essential NetWare file system components as well as the design techniques for creating and maintaining a workable network directory structure.

Establishing and Maintaining Network Users and Security

NetWare has a sophisticated security system that enables network administrators to give users access to information yet protect special information from unauthorized access. To implement this security system as a CNA, you need to create a user account for each person who will access the network and then assign the appropriate security restrictions, such as passwords and other limitations, you think are necessary to protect user accounts from unauthorized access. In addition, to access files on the network, users need access rights to eDirectory objects and the directories and files they will be using. As a CNA, you'll assign these rights. In Chapters 5 through 7, you learn how to use NetWare utilities and commands to create users and assign the necessary rights to access eDirectory objects and the network file system. Because organizational structures change often, ongoing tasks for CNAs are adding and deleting users and modifying the rights assigned to users and groups.

Setting Up and Maintaining Network Printing

Perhaps one of the most complex and demanding tasks for a network administrator is creating and maintaining the network printing environment. Network printing has become an increasingly important issue on networks with sophisticated applications, such as desktop publishing and WYSIWYG ("what you see is what you get") word processors and spreadsheets. These applications require expensive laser and inkjet printers, which are often shared to control costs. As a CNA, you'll find that you need to upgrade your network printing environment often to support faster and more sophisticated printers and applications as they become available. In Chapter 8, you learn how to use the NetWare printing components and tools for installing and maintaining a network printing environment to meet your users' needs.

Loading and Updating Application Software

An ongoing and important job of network administrators is installing and upgrading application software packages that run on client computers. Whenever possible, you should install applications on the server so that they can be shared and maintained centrally. However, some applications don't run from a server, or they run more efficiently when installed on the computer's local hard drive. As a CNA, you need to be familiar with installing and configuring many different application software packages and know how to support these packages on the server or local computer.

A CNA must know how to obtain and install software upgrades as well as respond to user questions and problems. As a result, CNAs often find they need strong interpersonal skills to work with frustrated users. Yet another responsibility is policing copyright licenses of software to be sure your organization always has enough licenses to cover the number of users who are running the applications. This task is important because your company can be sued or fined if it's found in violation of copyright laws. To make a CNA's responsibility easier, some companies produce software that counts the number of users currently using a software package and does not allow more users than the number you have identified according to your software licenses.

Managing the Server and Monitoring Network Performance

A NetWare server has its own operating system and console commands that enable network administrators to control the server environment and includes special software called NetWare Loadable Modules (NLMs) for performing certain tasks or adding new services. Therefore, a CNA needs to spend some time each week at the server console using console commands and utilities to monitor server activity, add new services, and modify or configure existing services. You work with the NetWare 6.5 server console and NLMs in Chapter 2.

With the addition of users to the network, large printing loads, and the ever-increasing demands of high-speed computers for graphics applications, network performance can sometimes falter. As a CNA, you need to monitor your network system and server regularly to detect performance bottlenecks or problems and then determine whether additional hardware or configuration changes are necessary. In Chapters 2 and 12, you learn how hardware requirements play an important role in configuring a server's performance.

Developing and Implementing Network Security

Information is the lifeblood of an organization, and as a CNA, you'll be the guardian of the information stored on the LAN system. As a guardian of this information, you must be able to keep data secure and provide a means of recovering data in the event of a disaster. As shown in Figure 1-1, network security consists of several systems.

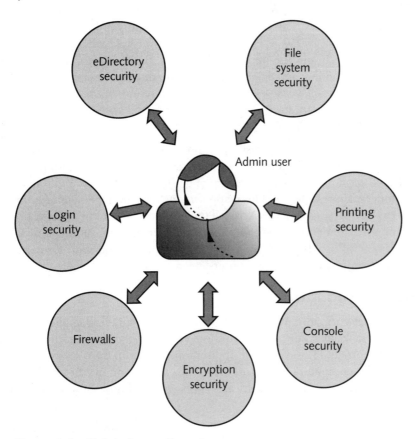

Figure 1-1 Network security systems

Login security is used to identify a person as an authorized user of the network by checking the user name and password against a database of valid user accounts stored in the eDirectory system. Effective login security requires user accounts to have secure passwords that are known only by the user. Novell eDirectory uses a highly encrypted password system that prevents intruders from acquiring user passwords during the login process or reading them directly from the server's hard disk. In Chapter 5, you learn how to increase the login security of user accounts by configuring password and login restrictions.

File system security uses trustee assignments to ensure that users can access or modify only data they're authorized to work with. In Chapter 6, you learn how to plan and set up file system security in a NetWare file system. In Chapter 13, you learn how to implement file system permissions in a Linux environment.

eDirectory security enables administrators to delegate administrative authority to other users. For example, with eDirectory security you can give administrative users the rights necessary to change user passwords in their departments. In Chapter 7, you learn how to use eDirectory security and administrative roles to assign users rights to perform administrative functions in the eDirectory tree.

Printing security makes it possible to control access to network printers and give certain users rights to manage selected printers. In Chapter 8, you learn how to use NetWare printing security to provide rights to network printers.

Console security involves keeping the server in a physically secure location as well as enabling certain security measures at the server console. In Chapter 2, you learn how to use console commands to increase the security of your server.

One of the benefits of implementing a LAN is providing access to data across the Internet. Although this function is important to an organization's operations, it also means exposing computers to security threats and virus attacks. As a result, an important task of a CNA is being able to implement encryption, firewalls, virus protection software, and other procedures to help eliminate the loss of data and user productivity caused by outside attackers gaining access to computers on the local network. In Chapter 11, you learn what a CNA needs to know about implementing encryption, firewalls, and virus protection software.

One of the worst nightmares a CNA can have is a server crash that results in losing all the network information stored on its hard drives. To prevent this catastrophe and let you sleep more easily, you need to be sure your server environment is as secure and reliable as possible. You also need a good backup system to restore all programs and data on your server after a major system failure.

Implementing and Maintaining User Services

With the rapid increase in communications and integrated computer applications, users need a simple and straightforward way to access and use these capabilities to increase their productivity. To help users make better use of new technologies, Novell has included a package called Virtual Office with NetWare 6.5. In Chapter 10, you learn how to deploy and configure Novell's Virtual Office system to help users access data across the Internet and use e-mail and other collaborative functions, including scheduling and calendaring.

Introduction to the Universal AeroSpace Corporation

Having practical experience with networks, such as through internships while you're a student, improves your chances of passing the CNA exam. In this book, you gain some practical experience with NetWare and SUSE Linux by playing the role of a student intern for the fictitious Universal AeroSpace (UAS) Corporation. By performing network administrative tasks related to this company's network, you'll learn how to apply network concepts and techniques that network administrators use. Universal AeroSpace is a small engineering firm founded in the mid-1980s to design and manufacture specialized parts for aircraft companies. The company's strength has been designing and manufacturing aircraft components using high-strength aluminum alloy materials. Last year, Universal AeroSpace was reorganized under new management. The organizational chart in Figure 1-2 shows the current company structure.

In 2001, the president of Universal AeroSpace worked to expand the corporation into other high-tech markets by actively pursuing a NASA contract. As a result of a proposal the Sales and Engineering departments drafted, the corporation was recently awarded a NASA contract to design and build specialized components for the new international space station. As a result, UAS has been expanding its operation, including hiring design engineers and office staff. One of the expansion priorities is installing a network information system that allows office staff and engineers to communicate and share computer resources using both the Windows and SUSE Linux environments. The new contracts require UAS engineers and office staff to travel frequently to aircraft and NASA facilities, making access to resources and information from the office and on the road necessary.

After working with an outside consultant to help analyze existing systems, management decided to install both NetWare and SUSE Linux network operating systems to meet the organization's diverse needs economically. Your assignment as a student intern is to work with the Universal AeroSpace IT personnel to learn the duties of a network administrator.

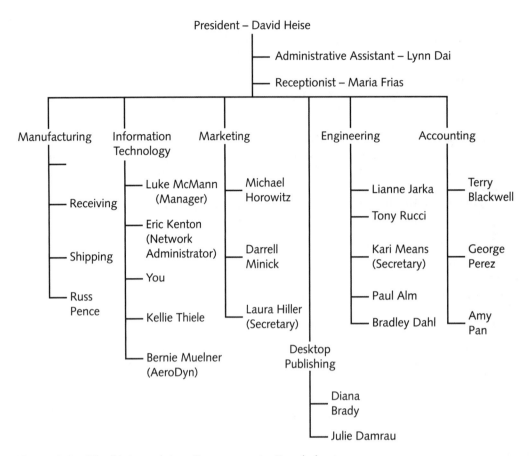

Figure 1-2   The Universal AeroSpace organizational chart

Company Tour

Figure 1-3 shows the layout of the UAS building with the current locations of computers and printers in each department. All office computers have Windows XP or SUSE Linux installed. Although several computers have attached printers, most printing is done to networked printers. The administrative computers are used to run accounting software and perform spreadsheet functions. The administrative assistant, Lynn Dai, and all department secretaries currently have Windows XP computers and laser printers used mostly for word processing. Diana Brady and Julie Damrau have powerful computers and laser printers for running the desktop publishing software needed to create and edit instructional manuals and sales material. Julie's computer has a DVD recorder shared with Diana for creating DVDs. Each salesperson has a Windows-based notebook computer with word processing and spreadsheet software to create documents and access the customer database system and cost sheets. Because the salespeople often need access to information while on the road working with customers, Novell's OneNet strategy will be important in providing solutions that give them access to their files and allow them to print documents when they're away from the office.

The Engineering Department is responsible for designing components that meet the buyer's specifications. Currently, the department has SUSE Linux installed on all desktop computers and two computer-aided design (CAD) systems attached to a shared plotter. Engineering files containing information the business staff needs to write contract agreements and documentation are shared. Most shared files are kept on the server, but certain large files are copied directly between computers.

As a result of the NASA contract, the company has expanded the Manufacturing Division by hiring more machine tool specialists and adding new computer-aided manufacturing (CAM) machines to fabricate parts and components. All computers in the Manufacturing Division are attached to the network system to share resources and communicate more easily.

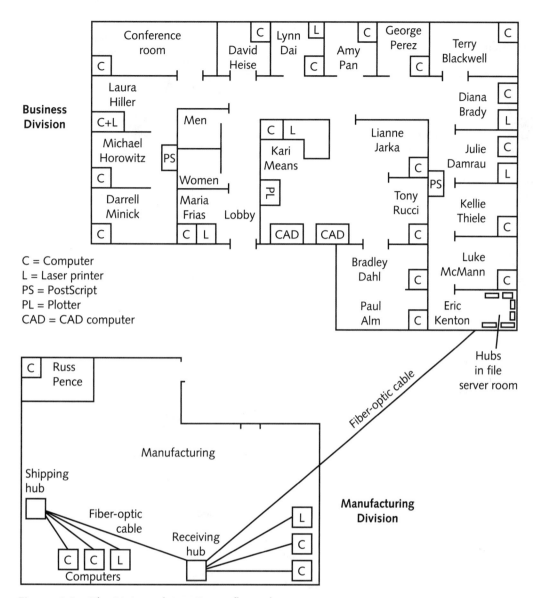

Figure 1-3   The Universal AeroSpace floor plan

The Information Technology Department is managed by Luke McMann and currently consists of a programmer/analyst, Kellie Thiele, and a network administrator, Eric Kenton. As a programmer/analyst, Kellie is responsible for network application services along with software development, configuration, and deployment. Eric's responsibilities as a network administrator consist of establishing and maintaining network users and security, implementing and securing the network file system, setting up and maintaining network printing, developing and implementing the backup and recovery system, supporting network communications, and managing the NetWare server and network performance.

INTRODUCTION TO NETWORK COMPONENTS

As shown in Figure 1-4, computer networks come in many shapes, sizes, and configurations. Networks can generally be categorized as local area networks, metropolitan networks, or wide area networks. **Local area networks (LANs)** are used to connect computers that are physically close to each other, such as those in the same building or office. LANs usually consist of a copper cable system that connects computers in the office or building to a central wiring hub. **Metropolitan area networks (MANs)** use fiber-optic or

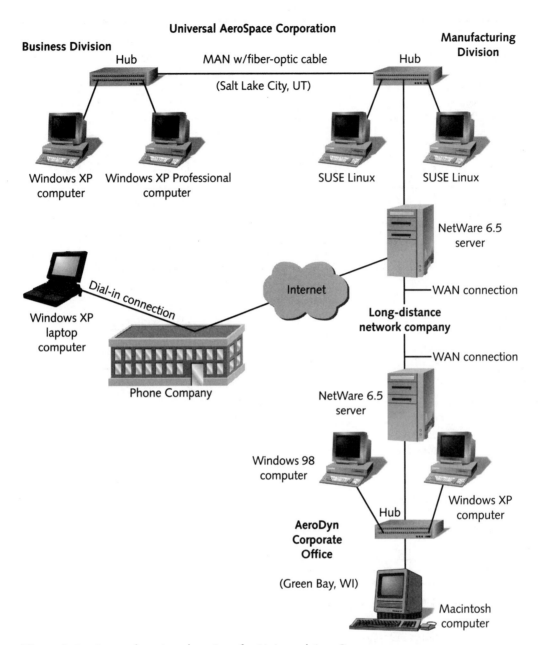

Figure 1-4 A sample network system for Universal AeroSpace

microwave towers to connect computers in the same geographical area, such as a city or county. **Wide area networks (WANs)** use carriers such as the phone system to connect computers over long distances, including across the country or even around the world. In the past, computer networks tended to be isolated entities owned and controlled by a specific company or organization. Many computer networks used proprietary systems that made it difficult to connect them to share information. Today, the Internet is breaking down these barriers with standards and technology that enable secure data transmission between almost every type of networked computer.

To become a CNA, you need to be familiar with the hardware and software components that make up networks so that you can select, implement, and maintain a network system that meets your organization's communication and processing needs. This section introduces the major hardware and software components that make up a LAN and explains how they can be applied in an organization. As shown in Figure 1-5, computer networks consist of three major types of components:

- The computer hardware and cable system
- Protocol software suites to control the communication process
- Software for accessing network resources and services

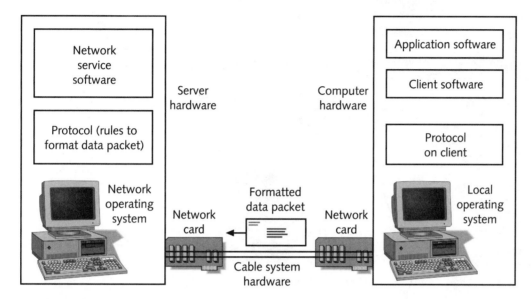

Figure 1-5   Network components

In a LAN, computer hardware typically consists of client computers, servers, and shared resources, such as printers and volumes. Software consists of the network operating system and services for providing network resources that client computers can access. Communication protocol suites, such as Transmission Control Protocol/Internet Protocol (TCP/IP), provide the rules and software that control data formatting and transmission. The following sections introduce you to these network components and explain how they are applied in an organization.

NOTE

For the CNA test, Novell identifies network components as servers, workstations (computers), peripherals, transmission media, and network interface cards. These detailed components are included in the major types of components covered in this chapter. Workstations and peripherals are examples of network entities. Servers are entities that provide network services, and transmission media and network interface cards are included in the network pathway component type.

Network Hardware Components

Hardware components are the most obvious parts of a network system because they can be easily seen. The hardware components of a typical network are shown in Figure 1-6. This section introduces each hardware component and the functions it performs on the network.

The Server

The first stop on your tour of network hardware is the network server, called a "NetWare server" in NetWare networks. Many who are familiar with minicomputers and mainframe computers tend to think of the server in terms of network control. In a LAN, however, a **server** is actually a servant of the network, responding to requests from computers for access to files and software stored on the server's disk system. With the exception of its disk system and typically large memory capacity, a server is similar to client computers on the network.

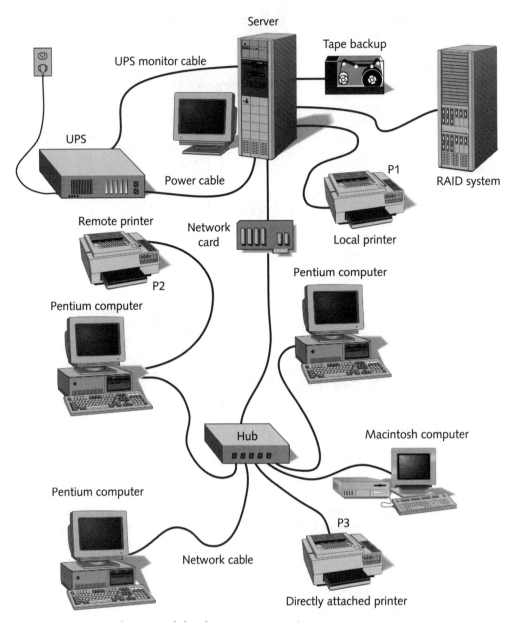

Figure 1-6   Sample network hardware components

Some servers are **nondedicated servers**, meaning they can function as a user's computer in addition to providing access to shared areas of the disk system. The server in Figure 1-6 is a **dedicated server**, meaning it can't be used as a client computer. This ensures better performance and eliminates the possibility of a user shutting down or restarting the server while others are still accessing it. To prevent unauthorized access to the server's hardware and software, most network administrators keep servers in separate rooms that can be secured.

The server shown in Figure 1-6 is a PC specifically designed to be a server (many vendors offer PCs designed for use as servers); it uses dual processors with 2 GB of memory and a high-capacity 400 GB RAID storage system. The redundant array of independent disks (RAID) storage system provides fault tolerance at the hardware level so that if one drive fails, the server can continue to provide information services using data from the other drives until the failed drive is replaced. On networks requiring file and print services, the server is specialized to provide high-speed disk access, whereas client computers require fast processors and high-resolution graphics.

Many networks use **client-server applications**, in which the server performs part of the data-processing function for the client by looking up and summarizing information from the database, and the client computer acts as an interface for the user. On networks using client-server applications, the server should be specialized to handle application processing.

Client Computers

Generally, each computer attached to the network for running user applications is called a **client computer**, which is where the actual processing of user software applications occurs. Adding memory or a faster processor to the server doesn't directly increase the speed of programs run on client computers. To increase user application performance, you must upgrade the client computer. The processing power of a client computer often equals or exceeds a server's speed. For example, in the sample network, the server contains a 1.2 GHz Pentium processor with lots of memory and disk space and a standard-resolution VGA monitor. The Windows-based computers contain 1.5 GHz Pentium processors with 512 MB of memory, 20 GB of disk storage, and high-resolution color monitors. Because most files and software are kept on the network server, the client computers can focus on processing speed and graphics resolution rather than on high-capacity disk storage.

Network Interface Card

A **network interface card (NIC)** is installed in each computer attached to the network, including the server. NICs can be wireless or attached to a cable system. As wireless standards and technology have improved, more organizations are implementing wireless NICs, especially for notebook computers or in rooms that don't have adequate cabling. A NIC allows the computer to be attached to the network system and is responsible for transmitting and receiving data packets on the network. A **packet** consists of hundreds to several thousand bytes of formatted data, framed with control bits identifying the source and target computers' addresses, called the **Media Access Control (MAC) addresses**. When it's manufactured, each NIC is assigned a unique address or serial number consisting of 12 binary digits. This binary number is referred to as the NIC's MAC address. When transmitting data, the network operating system sends a block of data to the NIC, which then waits for the network system to become available. When no other computers are using the network system, the NIC transmits the packet. The receiving NIC listens to the network and accepts any packets containing its MAC address. When a NIC detects its unique MAC address in the packet's target address field, it notifies the source computer that it has received a data packet. If no errors are detected in the packet, the NIC sends the packet to the OS software for processing.

Cable System

A network's cable system is the highway through which information travels from one computer to another. A **cable system** consists of the wiring that connects computers in the network. Just as getting onto a highway requires obeying certain traffic laws, sending information through the network requires each computer to follow a set of access rules. In the same way that gridlock can slow down or stop traffic on a highway, a network can also experience bottlenecks when the amount of information on the network exceeds the cable system's transmission capacity. One responsibility you will have as a network administrator is monitoring the network cable system for errors or performance bottlenecks. The cable system in Figure 1-6 shows a sample network that consists of twisted-pair cable similar to the cable that connects your telephone's handset to its base unit. In the sample network, twisted-pair cable runs from each computer in the network to a central connection box called a **hub** or **switch**, giving all computers equal access to the network system. A switch is a special type of hub that can direct packets of data out a specific port based on its destination computer instead of sending the packet out all ports, as with a hub.

Uninterruptible Power Supply

The box to the left of the server in Figure 1-6 is an **uninterruptible power supply (UPS)**, which contains batteries that supply temporary power to the server if the local power system fails. The UPS is an important piece of equipment for the server because it prevents data loss in a power outage or brownout. Because a power outage that occurs while many users are accessing the server is likely to result in lost data, never consider running a server without a UPS. When a UPS unit is not attached to the server, power interruptions could require restoring data from a backup tape to restart the server.

The UPS in Figure 1-6 contains an optional monitor cable that connects to a port on the server. This connection informs the server when the UPS is using battery power. This connection is also important in an extended power outage because it allows the server to close all files and takes itself offline automatically before exhausting the UPS batteries.

Tape Backup

The tape backup system in the network shown in Figure 1-6 consists of a digital audio tape (DAT) cartridge tape drive that can use Novell's Storage Management System (SMS) software or a third-party software package, such as ArcServe, Legato, or Veritas, to back up all data on the server automatically every night. At 1 a.m. each weekday morning, the tape backup software in the sample network copies all data to the tape cartridge. The network administrator then places the tape in the organization's fireproof vault for safe storage. A rotation system using several tapes allows each backup to be kept for at least one week, and one day's backup tape (for example, the tape made on Fridays) is stored off site in case of a disaster that wipes out the entire site.

Network Printers

Sharing printers on the network is often an important advantage of a LAN. Each client computer can send output to any network printer by directing the printed output to the print server; this output is then stored in a special directory called a **print queue**. After a computer has finished printing, the server directs the printout to the selected printer with special print server software. Printers can be attached and shared on the network in three different ways: as local printers, as remote printers, and as directly attached printers.

Notice that printer P1 shown in Figure 1-6 is attached to the server. This makes it a **local printer** because it's attached to the server's local printer port. Local printers have the advantage of working at high speeds and reducing network traffic, but have the disadvantage of limited locations in which they can be placed.

Printer P2, attached to a user computer, is controlled by the print server software, which enables users on any client computer to send output through the server to printer P2. Printer P2 is referred to as a **remote printer** because it's not directly attached to a printer port on the server. Remote printers can be located anywhere on the network where there's a computer. Performance problems and software conflicts with the computer can occur, however, when large print jobs are processed.

Printer P3 is a **directly attached printer** that has its own network card and is connected directly to the network cable system. This direct connection offers the benefit of independence from a computer without the loss of speed associated with a remote printer. For the highest possible level of performance, most network administrators attach high-speed printers directly to the network cable system.

Network Protocols or Rules

The network system's **protocol** defines the rules for formatting packets of data transmitted on the network cable system. The software used to implement a protocol is called the **protocol stack**. Although network cards are responsible for delivering data packets throughout the network system, the functions of the protocol stack include routing packets between different networks, verifying delivery, and requesting network services. Certain protocol stacks, such as IBM's Synchronous Data Link Control (SDLC), NetBEUI, and IPX/SPX, are called proprietary protocols because they are owned and controlled by a specific company. Other protocols, such as TCP/IP, are nonproprietary and are controlled by an industry organization consisting of vendors and users.

Because networks often need to support multiple protocol stacks for computers to communicate and access services using different operating systems, today's network operating systems are designed for multiple protocols. Common protocol stacks now include TCP/IP, SPX/IPX, and NetBEUI. In the following sections, you learn about these protocol stacks along with some of their advantages and disadvantages.

The TCP/IP Protocol

Transmission Control Protocol/Internet Protocol (TCP/IP) was first developed in the 1960s to support communication among mainframe computers in government agencies and educational institutions. Like SPX/IPX, TCP/IP is responsible for formatting packets and then routing them between networks by using IP. The IP protocol is more sophisticated than IPX in fragmenting packets and routing them over WAN links, such as those used when connecting to the Internet. The TCP/IP specifications were developed and are still maintained by an independent agency, the Internet Access Board (IAB). Because TCP/IP was developed to connect a large number of independent organizations, it was designed to support communications between diverse computers and operating systems. TCP/IP consists of four major layers for transmitting and receiving data, as shown in Figure 1-7.

Application Layer
This layer includes network services along with client software.
Transport Layer TCP/UDP services This layer is responsible for getting data packets to and from the application layer by using port numbers. TCP also verifies packet delivery by using acknowledgments.
Internet Layer This layer uses IP addresses to route packets to their appropriate destination network.
Network Layer This layer represents the physical network pathway and the network interface card.

Figure 1-7   TCP/IP layers

Moving from the bottom up in Figure 1-7, the network layer provides the communication pathway consisting of network cards and drivers. The Internet layer, or IP, is responsible for routing packets between networks. The transport layer consists of both the TCP and User Datagram Protocol (UDP) services and is used to handle packet flow between systems. Both transport services use port numbers to identify the sending and receiving of applications. For example, a Web server typically uses port 80, but the File Transfer Protocol (FTP) server defaults to port 21. Both TCP and UDP perform the service of a messenger by delivering packets to the correct application based on the port number. One of the major differences between TCP and UDP is delivery notification. When using UDP, the sender is never notified whether the packet has been delivered successfully. Although UDP's lack of delivery notification can cause transmission errors, it has the advantage of providing faster service for delivering small, intermittent messages. In addition to the basic services of UDP, the TCP transport service guarantees the delivery of packets by sending and receiving acknowledgments. With this acknowledgment system, the sender and receiver can establish a window for the number of packets to be acknowledged. This windowing capability offers better performance because each packet does not need to be acknowledged individually before another packet is sent. The application layer represents a network service, such as a Web server or an FTP server, that processes client requests and returns information via the transport and network layers.

NOTE Because of the popularity of the TCP/IP protocol stack for LANs and WANs, starting with NetWare 5, Novell has added the capability to use only TCP/IP for its network clients and services. Older versions of NetWare required administrators to support IPX for access to NetWare servers and TCP/IP for Internet access. By eliminating IPX, network administration and support are simplified and more efficient.

In TCP/IP, each computer attached to a network is called a host and is assigned a unique address. Routers connect independent networks and transfer packets from one network to another by using an IP network address, which enables packets to be sent over different routes and then reassembled in the correct sequence at the receiving station. IP addresses consist of 32-bit binary numbers, expressed as four bytes separated by periods using a method called **dotted decimal notation**. Each IP address in dotted decimal notation contains network and host components, as shown in Figure 1-8.

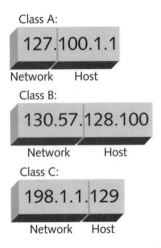

Class A:
127.100.1.1
Network   Host

Class B:
130.57.128.100
Network   Host

Class C:
198.1.1.129
Network   Host

Figure 1-8   Sample IP addresses

The network component of an IP address identifies the network cable system and is the same for all computers on the same network. The **host** component represents a device attached to the network and must be unique for each network entity on the cable system. Notice how the dotted decimal addresses are divided into three major classes. In a Class A address, the first number represents the network cable, and the last three numbers represent devices or computers attached to the network. In a Class B network, the address is split in half, with two numbers identifying the network and two the hosts. Class C addresses are intended for smaller networks with only one number reserved for the host computers. Setting up and working with IP addresses is an essential part of today's network administration. In Chapter 2, you learn how to assign an IP address to your NetWare 6.5 server during installation.

Novell Proprietary Protocols

The Sequential Packet Exchange/Internetwork Packet Exchange (SPX/IPX) protocol suite is the Novell proprietary system that manages routing and formatting NetWare packets on the network. To communicate, IPX must be loaded on each network client and server. Each client and server must also have network card driver software (described in the "Network Software Components" section) loaded to transmit the packets. IPX and the network card driver are brought together during client installation with a process called **binding**. SPX works with IPX to ensure successful delivery of data packets by using special control and acknowledgment packets from the receiver that inform the sender if any data packets need to be retransmitted. Some applications use a combination of SPX/IPX to ensure successful delivery of data packets.

NOTE The IPX protocol used by NetWare was first developed by Xerox in the late 1970s and later adopted by Novell for use in its networking products. It provided automatic addressing for network components, instead of the manual addressing used by TCP/IP.

NOTE

Because TCP/IP has been supported as a primary protocol since NetWare 5.0, most organizations are moving away from SPX/IPX to avoid supporting multiple protocols.

Besides IPX/SPX, Novell provides **NetWare Core Protocol (NCP)** as one of the languages that applications can use to access services on NetWare servers. The Novell client is designed to take advantage of all the services available through NCP. You learn more about installing and configuring the Novell client in Chapter 4. In addition to NCP, NetWare 6.5 servers support other application protocol languages, including HTTP, the Windows file service, and the Network File System (NFS) for UNIX. You learn more about these application protocols in Chapter 3.

Microsoft Proprietary Protocols

NetBEUI is the Microsoft protocol stack integrated into Windows products. Of the three protocols described in this section, NetBEUI is the smallest, fastest, and easiest to use. It also has the fewest features, so it's more limited in large networked environments because it doesn't support the network layer needed to route packets between networks. As a result, NetBEUI is limited to communicating with other computers attached to the same network cable system. Because it doesn't have the overhead of providing routing functions, it's extremely small and fast, making it ideal for small networks of 10 to 50 devices.

NetBIOS is the protocol many Windows-based applications use to communicate with applications running on other client and server computers. Allowing client applications to communicate with each other without needing a centralized server is often referred to as peer-to-peer networking. Although NetBIOS was originally developed to be used with NetBEUI, as a result of the popularity of peer-to-peer applications, other protocol stacks (including IPX/SPX and TCP/IP) provide support for NetBIOS. For this reason, an organization can use NetBIOS to allow computers to run peer-to-peer applications while accessing services from NetWare file servers.

Just as NCP is the proprietary language certain Novell applications use to request services from a NetWare server, the **Server Message Blocks (SMB)** protocol is the language many Microsoft clients use to request services from Microsoft servers. SMB provide a standard, well-defined way for servers and clients to communicate.

Network Software Components

A network's software components are perhaps the most difficult to understand because they aren't physical objects. In the network configuration shown in Figure 1-9, the network software components can be divided into five major categories: NIC drivers, protocol stacks, client software, network services, and the network operating system. Figure 1-9 shows how these software components are combined to enable computers and servers to communicate on the network. In the following sections, you learn what role each software component plays in a LAN.

Network Interface Card Drivers

Each server and client workstation must have a NIC to attach it to the cable system and to communicate on the network. A **network interface card (NIC) driver** is software containing instructions that enable the computer's processor to control card functions and interface with the application software. Periodically, card manufacturers release new versions of driver software to fix bugs or offer compatibility with new applications. As a result, one responsibility of a network administrator involves updating application and system software. Figure 1-9 shows a sample network configuration.

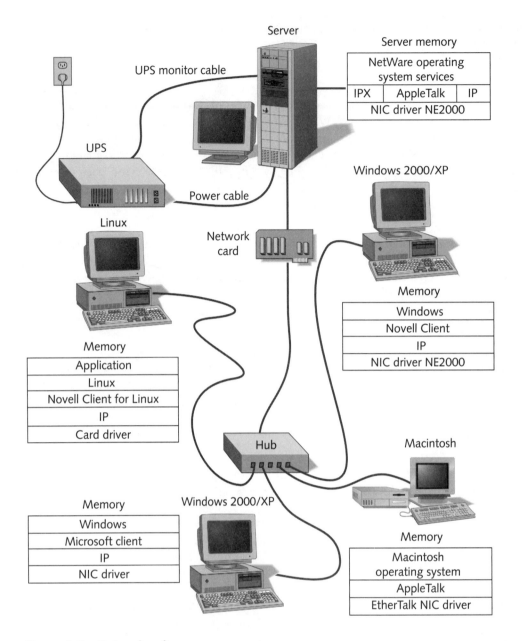

Figure 1-9   Network software components

Activity 1-1: Identify Network Adapter Properties on a Windows Client

Time Required: 5 minutes

Objectives: Identify network components and describe their functions.

Requirements: A Windows XP computer system

Description: Bradley Dahl has been having problems with his computer getting network error messages. Eric Kenton has decided to verify that Bradley's computer is using the same NIC settings as the other computers in the Engineering Department. In this activity, you simulate Eric Kenton's task of comparing Bradley's NIC settings by using My Network Places and Control Panel to document the settings of your network card. You then compare your findings to those of another student.

1. If necessary, start your computer and log on to your Windows system as Administrator.

2. Document your network adapter settings:

   a. Right-click **My Network Places**, and then click **Properties**.

   b. Right-click **Local Area Connection**, and then click **Properties**.

   c. Click the **Configure** button.

   d. Click the **Driver** tab, and record the driver date information here:

   _____

   e. Click the **Resources** tab, and record the IRQ (interrupt) and memory range here:

   _____

   f. Click **Cancel** to return to the Network Connections window.

3. Close the Network Connections window.

4. Compare your network adapter settings to those of your lab partner's, and document any differences here:

   _____

5. Log out.

Network Services

All network services require client and server software. The client software runs on the user's computer and provides a connection between the application and the service running on the server. Client software requires the following components:

- A desktop OS, such as Linux, Windows 2000/XP, or Macintosh OS X, to control local devices and run application software

- Driver software to control the NIC

- Requester and protocol software programs to format and send requests for network file and print services to the server; the requester program works closely with the computer's OS to examine requests and provide access to network services

The network in Figure 1-9 shows Novell Client sending IP-formatted requests via its card driver through the cable system to the NetWare server. The Macintosh computer has an EtherTalk driver so that it can use the same cable simultaneously to send requests to the server with the AppleTalk protocol. The capability to support different types of client operating systems is one of the strengths of the NetWare server.

With NetWare 6.0, Novell introduced the **Native File Access Pack (NFAP)**. NFAP enables diverse clients to communicate directly with a NetWare server by using their native protocol. For example, by using NFAP, Windows clients can access shared files from a NetWare server by using its native client protocol. Using NFAP makes setting up clients and accessing basic NetWare file and print services easier. In Chapter 3, you learn how NFAP is used to access file services on a NetWare 6.5 server. In the following activity, you document the client software components on your desktop computer.

ACTIVITY

Activity 1-2: Documenting Client Software Components

Time Required: 10 minutes

Objective: Identify client software components.

Requirements: A Windows XP computer system

Description: The network administrator wants you to document the configuration of the TCP/IP network software component on the new computers to be installed in the Marketing Department. In this activity, you learn how to view the software components of a Windows XP system.

1. Start your computer and log on to your local Windows computer with your assigned Windows administrator user name and password.

2. Right-click **My Network Places**, and then click **Properties**.

3. Right-click **Local Area Connection**, and then click **Properties**.

4. Right-click **Local Area Connection**, and then click **Properties** to open the Local Area Connection Properties dialog box shown in Figure 1-10.

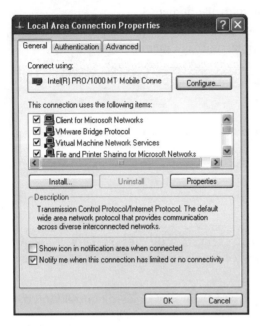

Figure 1-10   The Local Area Connection Properties dialog box

5. Record the number of items listed under "This connection uses the following items":

   _____

6. Click the **Internet Protocol (TCP/IP)** component, and then click the **Properties** button.

7. Record the TCP/IP settings for IP address and DNS server:

   _____

   _____

8. Click **Cancel** to return to the Local Area Connection Properties dialog box, and then click **Cancel** again.

9. Close the Network Connections window. When you're finished, log off your system.

The server component consists of the computer hardware and network operating system software needed to run network services and provide access to resources. Common network services include the following:

- *Security services*—These services are necessary to protect data from unauthorized access. Several types of security services are available in Novell, including login security, file system security, eDirectory security, encryption security, and firewall security. Each type of security is covered throughout this book. For example, in Chapter 2, you learn how to secure the server console. In Chapter 5, you learn how to implement login security. Chapters 6 and 7 cover file system and eDirectory security, and Chapter 11 deals with firewalls, encryption, and virus protection.

- *Directory services*—These services store information about network objects in a hierarchical database called the directory. With Novell's eDirectory service, network objects—such as users, groups, computers, printers, applications, and configuration information—are stored in containers. Containers are arranged in a hierarchical tree structure similar to the way folders are arranged on a disk drive. In Chapter 4, you learn about directory services in general and eDirectory in particular.

- *Message services*—These services are used to transfer e-mail messages and event notifications between client computers and servers. Messaging can be configured as part of Novell's Virtual Office product.

- *File services*—These services enable client computers to access and save data on a shared file system. In Chapters 3 and 6, you learn how to set up and secure the NetWare file system, and Chapter 13 explains how to implement file system security on a Linux server.

- *Print services*—These services allow printers to be attached to the network system and used by client computers. In Chapter 8, you learn how to set up, secure, and maintain a network printing system that supports both local and Internet printing.

- *Application services*—These services assist in running programs, such as spreadsheets, word processors, and database systems, by performing certain processing functions for client computers. Chapter 9 describes how to set up a client computer environment to support network applications.

INTRODUCTION TO NETWORK OPERATING SYSTEMS

The **network operating system (NOS)** is the software that controls network services and provides access to shared resources on the server computer. Historically, a major function of a network operating system has been to provide file and printer services to client computers. As a result, the server can be enhanced with specialized hardware and software to improve performance, security, and reliability beyond what can be expected from a desktop operating system, such as Windows 2000 Professional or Windows XP. The NOS is specialized to maximize use of the server's hardware by including the following features and services:

- *Performance*—A server's performance is determined by how fast it can respond to requests for data from client computers. Therefore, the major factors affecting a server's performance are its capability to keep frequently used information in memory, the speed of its disk system, and the speed of its processor unit.

- *Fault tolerance*—Fault tolerance is the system's capability to continue operating satisfactorily when there are errors or other problems. The server environment is designed with different levels of fault tolerance so that it can continue server operations despite physical errors on the disk drives or controller cards.

- *Security*—Security (preventing unauthorized access to information on the server) is one of the most important responsibilities of a network administrator. An NOS has features you can use to meet the security needs of your organization's users and data. For example, login security requires all users of the system's resources and services to supply a valid user name and optional password before being given access to the network. In addition, the optional intruder protection system, described in Chapter 5, can be used to lock out a user's account if someone exceeds the number of login attempts you have set.

- *Trustee assignments*—Trustees are objects such as users and groups that are given permission to use or manage resources. You use trustee assignments to assign privileges, called trustee rights or permissions, to network users allowing them to access data and perform certain functions on the network.

- *Client support*—An NOS should be able to support many types of client computers so that a network can integrate diverse computing environments. For example, you learned how the NetWare operating system enables Apple Macintosh users to share files with Linux and Windows-based computers.

As shown in Figure 1-11, today's NOSs can be defined as peer-to-peer or network-centric, depending on how they are designed.

Peer-to-peer systems enable client computers to communicate and share data with each other without the need for a dedicated server computer. In a peer-to-peer network, computers are organized into units called **workgroups**. Workgroups make it easer for users to find shared resources because administrators can group computers by department. Windows 98, Windows 2000 Professional, and Windows XP are designed as peer-to-peer operating systems. The main advantage of peer-to-peer systems is their capability to implement low-cost networks by saving the expense of dedicating a computer as a server. In addition, peer-to-peer systems let users in workgroups share data files and communicate easily with each other. In theory, this reduces the burden on the network administrator by placing more responsibility for data sharing in the hands of users.

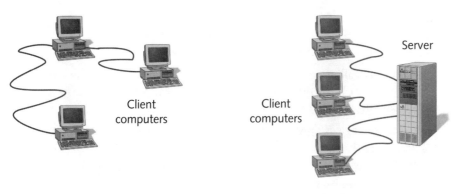

Peer-to-peer network
- Data stored on client computers
- Client computers *can* access data on other client computers

Network-centric system
- Data stored on server
- Client computers *cannot* access data on other client computers

Figure 1-11   Types of network operating systems

However, large peer-to-peer networks can be difficult to administer because shared data can exist in several locations, making data more difficult to retrieve, secure, and back up.

Network-centric systems dedicate one or more computers to act as servers and handle requests from client computers. A server authenticates users through a login process that enables them to access resources and services across the network. Network-centric systems use a directory service so that all systems can access a common database that includes user account information. These systems offer the following advantages:

- Centralized administration
- Single user login to gain access to all resources on the network
- Use of specialized server hardware and software to increase performance and reliability

Because of these advantages, network systems today are based on network-centric operating systems that rely on a directory service to make network objects and services available throughout the network. Common network-centric systems include Novell NetWare, SUSE Linux, and Windows 2000/2003. The following sections introduce the features of these directory services and network operating systems.

Directory Services

Directory services play a major role in today's network-centric operating systems by providing a central store of information about network objects that all servers on the network can share. The concept of a directory service has been around since 1988 when the X.500 specifications for the standard directory service model was released by the Open Systems Interconnection (OSI) organization. You learn more about the X.500 standard in Chapter 4. Two major goals of a directory service are to allow a single-user login and to provide centralized administration. A single-user login means that users have to submit their user names and password only once for access to resources on any server that's part of the directory system. When a user logs in to a directory service, a server in the directory tree authorizes the user by validating the user name and password in the directory. After these credentials have been validated, the user can access resources and services on any server he or she has the rights to use.

Centralized administration is made possible by giving an administrative user account rights to add, delete, or change objects in the directory system. Because the directory service contains configuration information on all network objects, users can modify the configuration of any network object they have administrative rights to.

Two major directory services are in use today: Novell's eDirectory and Microsoft Active Directory. Both directory services store information in network objects that are grouped into containers called organizational units and then organized into a hierarchical structure called a tree. In addition, both services support Lightweight Directory Access Protocol (LDAP), which is used to exchange information between directory services. The following sections introduce these directory services and explain some differences between them.

Novell's eDirectory Service

Novell used many of the X.500 standards to release its first directory service, called Novell Directory Services (NDS), in the early 1990s. Since that time, Novell has enhanced its directory service, renaming it as eDirectory with the release of NetWare 6.0. As you learn in Chapter 4, eDirectory stores network objects in a tree structure. Users log in to a directory tree, which enables them to access resources on all servers in that tree where they have been given rights. Administrative user accounts can be given rights to manage objects in any container of the tree. Containers in the tree are organized into Organization and Organizational Units, as shown in Figure 1-12.

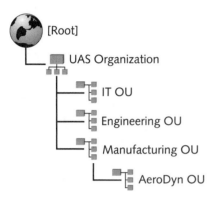

Figure 1-12   The Novell eDirectory tree

Some features of Novell's eDirectory include the following:

- eDirectory can run on multiple OS platforms, including NetWare, Linux, Windows NT, Windows 2000 Server, and Windows Server 2003. This capability allows networks consisting of multiple systems to act as one network by providing a single-user login and centralized administration.

- Portions of the eDirectory database, called partitions, can be placed on other servers in the network easily, which makes it possible for the network environment to be scalable. You learn how to partition eDirectory replicas between servers in Chapter 4.

- eDirectory trees offer high performance and reliability for large networks consisting of millions of objects.

- eDirectory has been in use for more than a decade, making it a mature directory service.

- eDirectory works independently of the Domain Name Service (DNS), allowing DNS to be dedicated for Internet services.

- eDirectory supports the LDAP standard to allow exchanging information with other network systems.

Microsoft Active Directory

Microsoft Active Directory, first introduced in Windows 2000, is a domain-oriented directory service that builds on the Microsoft domain system used in Windows NT. In Active Directory, network objects and servers are grouped into domains with servers classified as domain controllers or member servers. Domain controllers share a copy of the directory database for the domain in which they're located. Member servers don't have a copy of Active Directory domain objects; instead, they use the domain controller to look up information about network objects or validate user access. Domains are then organized into a forest that consists of one or more trees, as shown in Figure 1-13.

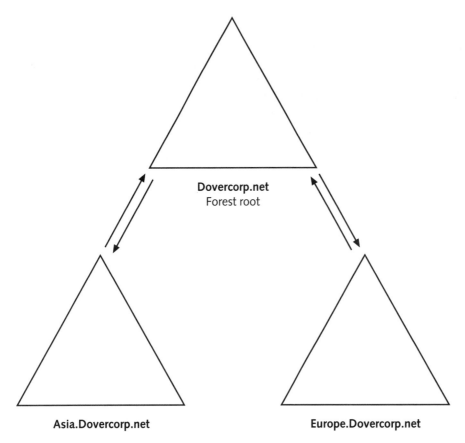

Figure 1-13   An Active Directory forest

Users log in to a forest, which allows them to access any shared resources on the servers in that forest they have been given right to. Some differences between Active Directory and eDirectory include the following:

- Active Directory allows Windows client computers using Windows XP or Windows 2000 Professional to be members of Active Directory. Being a member of Active Directory allows users to log on to the domain and makes it possible for administrative users to manage client computer data and configuration from a centralized site.

- Active Directory is a proprietary system that doesn't run on other OSs except Windows 2000 Server and Windows Server 2003.

- Active Directory requires servers to be upgraded to domain controllers to store a copy of the domain database, which is a more complex process than adding a partition to a Novell eDirectory server. After a server has been promoted to a domain controller, it can't be renamed. Removing the Active Directory database requires demoting the server to a member server.

- Active Directory relies on the use of DNS to find domain controllers.

Novell NetWare

Novell NetWare has been a leader in microcomputer-based NOSs, starting with NetWare 2 in the early 1980s. Because Novell was not in the business of producing desktop operating systems and application software, NetWare was designed from early versions to integrate with different desktop systems. NetWare has a proven history in providing high-speed, reliable, and secure network operating system environments for file and printer sharing. Today, Novell offers a wide range of NOS products and services that help organizations implement secure, high-speed network systems in a variety of client environments. In this section, you learn about the major versions of NetWare and the latest product features.

NetWare Versions

Although NetWare 6.5 is now Novell's flagship NOS, earlier versions of NetWare are highly stable network platforms that network administrators still depend on for consistent performance.

The primary difference between NetWare 3.0 and later versions is the introduction of Novell Directory Services (NDS), which was upgraded in NetWare 6.0 to become eDirectory. Both NetWare 2.0 and NetWare 3.0 had a flat database, called the bindery, that stored information about network objects, such as user, groups, and printers. A separate bindery database was stored on each NetWare 2.0 or 3.0 server, requiring users to have an account on every server containing resources they needed to access. Although the bindery system worked well in networks of one or two servers, when networks began to include a dozen or more servers and hundreds of users, maintaining user accounts on multiple servers became a bottleneck for administration. With the bindery, users had to log in to each server because the bindery database was not shared among servers.

NetWare 3.0 was server-centric, meaning each server managed its network objects individually. NetWare 4.0 and later are network-centric, meaning that all network objects are stored and administrated through a centralized directory database system (NDS, later called eDirectory). Following is a brief summary of some important enhancements in NetWare versions.

Features introduced with NetWare 4.0 include the following:

- Novell Directory Services (NDS) is an immensely scalable directory service that can support more than a million objects on the network. NDS is shared among all servers, so users logging in can do so from any computer and be recognized.

- NetWare Administrator, a Windows graphical administration utility, is the network administrator's main tool for managing the network; the enhancements include a Windows version, a configurable toolbar, and the capability to manage multiple networks simultaneously.

- NetWare Client 32 is a client software product that integrates with Windows 98 through XP and provides enhanced access to network services, including printing, application management, and administration.

Features introduced with NetWare 5.0 include the following:

- The ConsoleOne administrative tool is a Java-based utility that performs most administrative functions from a variety of OS environments, including Windows, the NetWare server console, and Linux systems.

- X Windows GUI server console interface enables administrators to run GUI-based server applications, including ConsoleOne.

- Novell Distributed Print Services (NDPS) allows network-attached printers to be shared and managed using Novell Client or the Internet Printing Protocol (IPP). In Chapter 8, you learn how to use NDPS to set up shared printers on a network.

- TCP/IP is the default protocol for communications to the NetWare services. Previously, the SPX/IPX protocol was necessary to communicate with NetWare services.

- Novell Storage Services (enhances volume and disk management) are available for user data volumes only.

New features of NetWare 6.0 include the following:

- The OneNet strategy to make data access and network administration independent of computer operating systems and network configurations

- New OneNet administrative utilities, such as iManager, Remote Manager, and iMonitor, that enable administrators to manage the network through a Web browser, independent of client OSs or network configuration

- Provides the following OneNet tools to enable users to access data via a Web browser, independent of client OSs or network configuration:

  - NetStorage Service, which allows access to network files from remote locations using a Web browser

  - iFolder service, which enables mobile computers to synchronize files with a central server automatically

  - Native File Access Protocol, which allows non-Novell clients to access a NetWare server's shared directories and files

- Internet Printing Protocol, which makes it possible to use and manage network printers across the Internet

The NetWare 6.5 network operating system includes all the features of NetWare 6.0 plus the following new features:

- Upgraded version of the iManager utility that enables network administrators to perform most administrative tasks, such as creating users and groups, through a Web browser

- Virtual Office client environment that makes it easier for users to access and use NetWare services

- New pattern-based installation options that enable you to create specialized and task-oriented servers, such as a server that's specialized to support Web applications

- New open-source development tools to help programmers develop applications without the cost of proprietary software development tools

Novell Open Enterprise Server

Open Enterprise Server is Novell's latest version of the NetWare 6.5 NOS combined with SUSE Linux 10. Enhancements released with Open Enterprise Server include the following:

- NetWare 6.5 operating system

- SUSE Linux 10 (described in the following section)

- Nterprise Services for Linux that enable the SUSE Linux 10 server to use Novell's eDirectory service and other Novell services, including iFolder, iPrint, NetStorage, and Virtual Office

The features of Novell Open Enterprise Server are discussed in more depth in subsequent chapters. The many added improvements, the acknowledged stability, and the increased need for Internet services in the industry will lead many organizations to upgrade their NetWare servers to Open Enterprise Server's NetWare 6.5. In Chapter 2, you learn how to install NetWare 6.5 on your computer.

Novell SUSE Linux 10

The Linux OS is based on UNIX and was first developed in the early 1990s at the University of Helsinki in Finland by a student named Linus Torvalds. Torvalds studied a freeware version of UNIX called Minix and used his knowledge to develop a new OS he named "Linux." UNIX was developed for use on large-scale computers, but Linux was designed for use on microcomputer-based systems. Because Linux was developed under the General Public License (GPL), the source code is freely available, so developers can modify the Linux system to meet their needs.

Linux is proving to be a viable enterprise-wide NOS that can help organizations reduce costs yet still provide robust and secure network services. As a result of this track record, there's a growing demand for Linux in almost every area of the IT industry, including Web servers, e-mail servers, application servers, and user desktops. To meet the growing demand for Linux services and support, Novell and other leading vendors are bringing many new services and support to the Linux environment. In Chapter 14, you learn about the growing demand for Linux and how Novell is helping meet these demands by providing services, support, and certification.

Most IT professionals agree that Linux and the open-source movement have changed the landscape of the IT industry. According to the market research firm IDC (*www.idc.com*), Linux is projected to grow at a compounded annual rate of 14% through 2007. An important part of the Linux growth is the use of open-source licensing, which enables developers to build systems using open-source software without paying royalties or other fees, as long as they release their source code with their product. Using open-source products offers the following benefits: lower total cost of ownership (TCO), reduced capital investment, and increased reliability and uptime compared to existing systems. In addition, many IT professionals agree that open-source products offer more flexibility and faster, cheaper application development.

When Torvalds developed Linux, he produced only the Linux kernel and a few utilities to manage it. Because Linux is distributed using the GPL license, other developers have created their distributions of Linux by adding their own utilities and applications that run on the Linux kernel. The following are some of the more common Linux distributions:

- SUSE Linux
- Red Hat Linux
- Mandriva Linux
- Turbolinux
- Slackware Linux
- Debian GNU/Linux
- Fedora Core 3

Novell bought the SUSE distribution of Linux in the spring of 2004 and has since added many services and utilities to enhance the use of SUSE Linux in NOS environments. Because of its GPL license and many free utilities and applications, SUSE Linux makes an ideal NOS for use in small and medium businesses. In addition, the reliability and performance of the SUSE Linux distribution make it an ideal choice for large enterprise network systems. In Chapter 12, you learn about the Novell SUSE Linux distribution and see how to install SUSE Linux on your computer.

Windows Server 2003

Windows Server 2003 provides client computers with centralized and fault-tolerant high-speed access to data. The advantages of this product are that it offers centralized management of multiple servers through the familiar Windows environment and supports access to TCP/IP and NetWare servers and mainframe computers. In addition, it supports a sophisticated directory service called Active Directory. Active Directory has many of the same features found in Novell's eDirectory service, such as a hierarchical database of all network objects that's shared by all servers in a domain. Another advantage is its usefulness as an application server (a server that runs the server portion of client-server applications). Many vendors offer client-server applications designed to run on this OS. Many network administrators use NetWare as their main NOS for file and print services and use Windows Server 2003 systems as application servers.

CHAPTER SUMMARY

- ❑ Industry certifications play an important part in allowing organizations to find and hire qualified network technicians, administrators, and engineers. Some popular networking certifications include the Novell CNA and CNE certifications, the Microsoft MCP, MCSA, and MCSE certifications, and the CompTIA Network + certification.

- ❑ To set up and manage a network, you need to be familiar with the services and components that make up a network system, including client computers, servers, volumes, printers, cabling, network cards, and protocols. Client computers run the application software and use client software to make requests for file services, print services, messaging services, and application services. Server computers provide network services to clients.

- ❑ A network protocol stack consists of software that formats and routes data packets between servers and clients. Because the client computer operating systems on a network can use different protocols, network administrators often need to support multiple protocol stacks on a NetWare network. Common protocols supported in NetWare servers include TCP/IP, IPX/SPX, and NetBIOS.

❑ Network operating systems can be classified as peer-to-peer or network-centric.

❑ In peer-to-peer networks, a computer can be both a client and a server, allowing it to share data and resources with other computers. Although peer-to-peer networks are flexible and easy to set up, they can be difficult to administer because of the lack of centralized control.

❑ Network-centric systems use centralized servers to authenticate user login requests and are geared toward providing network services to other clients rather than running application software, thus allowing better performance and security.

❑ Directory services provide centralized storage for information on network objects and resources that's shared among all servers that belong to the directory system. The major directory services in use today are Microsoft Active Directory and Novell eDirectory.

❑ Active Directory has the advantage of being widely used by developers and small to medium networks, whereas eDirectory provides a more scalable system that allows networks to integrate diverse environments consisting of Linux, Windows, and NetWare servers.

❑ The most common network operating system products in use today include Novell NetWare, Linux, and Windows Server 2003.

Key Terms

binding — A process that connects protocol stacks to the LAN card driver.

cable system — The wiring that connects computers in the network.

Certified Novell Administrator (CNA) — An administrator who has passed the CNA certification test; the objectives for this test are covered in this book.

client computer — The computer system that requests network services and accesses resources, such as shared files, printers, applications, or communication systems.

client-server applications — Applications that rely on software residing on both the client computer and the server.

dedicated server — A network server that can't be used as a client computer.

directly attached printer — A printer that's connected directly to the network cable system.

dotted decimal notation — IP addresses consisting of 32-bit binary numbers, expressed as four bytes separated by periods.

host — The part of an IP address that represents a device attached to the network and must be unique for each network entity on the cable system.

hub — A central connecting point for computers attached to a star topology network.

local area networks (LANs) — A high-speed communication system consisting of cables and cards (hardware) along with software that provides a means for different types of computers to communicate and share resources over short distances, such as within a single building or room.

local printer — A printer attached to the server computer.

Media Access Control (MAC) addresses — The binary hardware address of a network interface card. Each card is given a MAC address during manufacture, which it uses to send and receive data packets.

metropolitan area networks (MANs) — Networks that use fiber-optic or microwave towers to connect computers in the same geographical area.

Native File Access Pack (NFAP) — A protocol that enables diverse clients to communicate directly with a NetWare server by using their native protocol.

NetBEUI — A Microsoft nonrouting protocol stack commonly used on Windows.

NetBIOS — A standard protocol developed by IBM and used by Windows to find computers on the network by broadcasting the computer's name.

NetWare Core Protocol (NCP) — A protocol NetWare uses to access services on a NetWare server.

network-centric — A network operating system, such as NetWare 6.5, in which server functions run on a designated computer.

network interface card (NIC) — The network adapter that attaches a computer to the cable system.

network interface card (NIC) driver — The software driver that the operating system needs to communicate with the NIC.

network operating system (NOS) — The software that runs on servers to provide services to the network.

nondedicated server — A server that can also be used as a network client.

OneNet — Novell's strategy of making multiple networks that consist of diverse clients and services work together as one network.

packet — A formatted set of bits transmitted across the network.

peer-to-peer — A network operating system in which a computer can be both client and server.

print queue — A storage area used to hold print jobs.

protocol — A set of rules that define a communication procedure between computers.

protocol stack — Software that's responsible for formatting and routing packets of data between network devices.

remote printer — A printer that's attached to another client computer.

server — A computer that provides one or more network services.

server-centric — A network system in which users must log in to a central server to access network services.

Server Message Blocks (SMB) — The proprietary Microsoft protocol that clients use to access network services.

switch — *See* hub.

Transmission Control Protocol/Internet Protocol (TCP/IP) — The protocol commonly used to format and route packets between computers; also used on the Internet.

uninterruptible power supply (UPS) — A backup power system that uses batteries to supply continuous power to a computer during a power outage.

wide area networks (WANs) — Networks that use carriers such as the phone system to connect computers over long distances.

workgroups — Units consisting of one or more computers used to share data in a peer-to-peer network.

REVIEW QUESTIONS

1. Which of the following items is a pathway component? (Choose all that apply.)
   a. client computer
   b. TCP/IP
   c. hub
   d. network interface card

2. Which of the following protocols is used by computers to communicate across the Internet?
   a. TCP/IP
   b. SPX
   c. NetBIOS
   d. IPX

3. Novell's OneNet utilities work only with NetWare 6.0. True or False?

4. You log in to a Novell network and log on to a Windows XP computer. True or False?

5. NetWare uses the _____ service to store user names and passwords.
   a. security
   b. eDirectory
   c. file system
   d. application

6. A(n) _____ computer accesses network services, such as shared files and printers.

    a. server

    b. peer-to-peer

    c. client

    d. NOS

7. Which of the following protocols does Windows use to find a computer's address by broadcasting its name on the network?

    a. TCP/IP

    b. SPX

    c. NetBIOS

    d. IPX

8. Which of the following services works with client computers in running application software?

    a. file service

    b. application service

    c. messaging service

    d. directory service

9. Which of the following Novell services enables mobile computers to synchronize files with a central server automatically?

    a. iFolder

    b. iManager

    c. IPP

    d. NFAP

10. Which of the following is a feature of eDirectory? (Choose all that apply.)

    a. a domain-oriented structure

    b. specialized domain controllers

    c. capability to run on a variety of operating systems

    d. objects grouped into containers called Organizational Units

11. Operating system software that provides network services is referred to as the

    _____ .

    a. client

    b. NOS

    c. daemon

    d. DOS

12. Which of the following systems allows client computers to perform server functions?

    a. peer-to-peer

    b. network-centric

    c. NOS

    d. X.500

13. Directory services are used with peer-to-peer operating systems. True or False?

14. When using NetWare 6.5, _____ provides a global database of user and other network objects.

    a. Active Directory

    b. the NOS

   c. the eDirectory service

   d. NDS

15. A _____ provides rules used to communicate between computer systems on a network.

   a. protocol

   b. topology

   c. NIC

   d. media type

16. Which of the following networks consists of a fiber-optic or microwave link between buildings in the same city?

   a. WAN

   b. MAN

   c. LAN

   d. SAN

17. How would you configure a user's Windows computer to prevent him or her from having to log in to both Novell and the local computer?

   a. Install the Novell client.

   b. Remove the Novell client.

   c. Create a local user name with the same password as the NetWare user name.

   d. Remove the local user account.

18. _____ is a proprietary protocol owned by Novell.

   a. NetBEUI

   b. NetBIOS

   c. IPX

   d. TCP/IP

19. _____ application services are often part of database systems in which client computers make requests for specific data records from database services running on a server.

   a. Server-centric

   b. Clustering

   c. Peer-to-peer

   d. Client-server

20. Computers in Microsoft peer-to-peer networks are organized into logical units called _____ .

   a. forests

   b. domains

   c. workgroups

   d. trees

CASE PROJECTS

CASE
PROJECTS

Case Project 1-1: Designing a Network System for the Wiggerts Heating and Air-Conditioning Company

The Wiggerts Heating and Air-Conditioning Company, headquartered in Duluth, Minnesota, is a supplier and installer of heating and air-conditioning systems throughout the Midwest. In addition to supplying heating and air-conditioning equipment to dealers and stores, the company offers installation and repair services. Given the information shown in Figure 1-14, diagram the network hardware components needed to connect all computers to a centralized server with a star-based network topology.

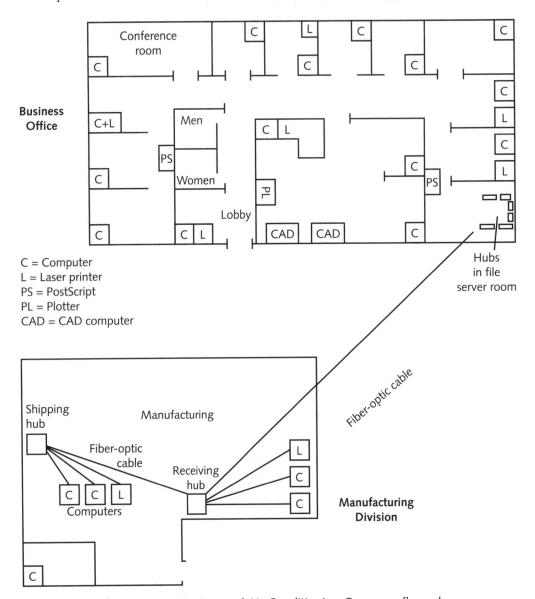

C = Computer
L = Laser printer
PS = PostScript
PL = Plotter
CAD = CAD computer

Figure 1-14 The Wiggerts Heating and Air-Conditioning Company floor plan

What other hardware components would you recommend be included on the network server?

Case Project 1-2: Selecting a Network Operating System for the Wiggerts Heating and Air-Conditioning Company

CASE PROJECTS

Identify the network operating system you think would meet this organization's needs in the most economical way, and include your reasons for selecting it.

2

INSTALLING NOVELL NETWARE 6.5 OPEN ENTERPRISE SERVER

After reading this chapter and completing the activities, you will be able to:

♦ Identify the requirements for installing NetWare 6.5

♦ Perform a NetWare 6.5 Open Enterprise Server installation

♦ Identify and be able to use basic NetWare console commands

♦ Monitor server health and performance

As networks grow, installing new servers and upgrading existing servers are ongoing processes that network administrators need to perform. Although your primary responsibility as a network administrator will be setting up and maintaining the network environment, to become a CNA you also need to know how to plan for and perform a basic NetWare 6.5 installation. In addition, in this chapter you learn how to use NetWare console commands and remote management utilities to manage your NetWare 6.5 Open Enterprise Server environment.

PREPARING FOR NETWARE 6.5 INSTALLATION

As described in Chapter 1, Novell's NetWare operating system has a long history of providing high-performance, reliable network services since the early 1980s. NetWare 6.5, the latest version of the NetWare kernel included in Novell's Open Enterprise Server distribution, continues to provide support for all Novell services and offers a wide range of development tools and utilities. Before performing a NetWare 6.5 Open Enterprise Server installation, you need to be prepared to supply information that the installation procedure requires and should be familiar with NetWare 6.5 hardware requirements and installation options. In this section, you learn the hardware requirements and the information for configuring the server and software components correctly.

NetWare 6.5 Hardware Requirements

Essentially, NetWare 6.5 consists of an OS kernel (Server.exe) that provides core NetWare server services to the network and a software bus that allows other modules containing specialized services and control functions to be loaded and unloaded, as shown in Figure 2-1.

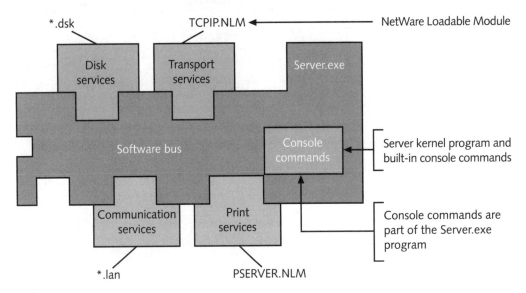

Figure 2-1   NetWare 6.5 architecture

In addition to providing basic core NetWare services and support for loadable modules, the NetWare 6.5 kernel has been designed to support Java applications and provide Internet services using HTTP. These capabilities require additional system resources, such as processor speed and memory, that weren't needed in earlier NetWare versions. Because of its modular design, the hardware requirements needed to run NetWare 6.5 vary based on the number of modules and services to be loaded and the number of users logging in. The minimum hardware environment for installing a NetWare 6.5 server is shown in Table 2-1 along with the hardware recommended to satisfactorily support an average-size network environment.

Table 2-1   NetWare 6.5 hardware requirements

Component	Minimum	Recommended
Processor	Pentium II or AMD K7	Pentium IV
Memory	512 MB	1 GB

Table 2-1   NetWare 6.5 hardware requirements (continued)

Component	Minimum	Recommended
Disk	500 MB DOS 2 GB free for SYS volume	500 MB plus 1 MB for every megabyte of RAM to allow for memory dumps (for example, 1.5 GB if you have 1 GB of RAM) 4 GB for SYS volume plus additional space for company data storage
Monitor	Super VGA	Super VGA
CD ROM	Standard CD Drive	Bootable CD drive

In addition to the hardware requirements, if you're installing NetWare 6.5 into an existing eDirectory tree, the eDirectory tree must be version 8.6 or later (see Chapter 4) and contain no NetWare server versions before NetWare 4.11. NetWare 6.5 also supports multiple processors to increase server performance. When using multiple processors, at least two Pentium III 700 MHz processors or later are recommended.

The NetWare 6.5 installation process consists of four major phases:

- Installation startup
- Initial installation
- Pattern selection
- Server configuration

Each phase requires entering or recording certain information. In the following sections, you prepare for the installation process by learning what information is required in each installation phase. Figure 2-2 is a sample NetWare Server Installation Planning form that you can use to help guide you through obtaining information for a successful NetWare 6.5 Open Enterprise Server installation.

Installation Startup Phase

When the installation process starts with the **installation startup phase**, you need to select the installation language and regional settings. The regional settings include the country, code page, and keyboard. Depending on your location, you might need to change the default settings shown on the NetWare Server Installation Planning form. After accepting the NetWare 6.5 and JReport runtime license agreements, you need to select whether you want to perform a default or manual installation. For most installations, you should select the manual installation to better control the installation settings. The last step in the installation startup phase is to prepare the NetWare boot partition as described in the following section.

NetWare Boot Partition

On a NetWare server, disk storage space is divided into two or more separate areas called partitions (see Figure 2-3).

NetWare Server Installation Planning Form

Server Hardware

Computer make and model: _____

Processor1: _____ Clock speed: _____

Processor2: _____ Clock speed: _____

RAM: _____

Installation Startup Options

Language: _____ (English)

Country: ____(001 USA) Code page: _____(437 U.S. English) Keyboard: _____ (U.S.)

Installation type: Default or Manual

Boot partition size: _____ (default 500 MB)

Initial Installation Information

Server ID: _____

Disk controller type: _____ Model: _____

NetWare driver: _____

    Drive 1 capacity: _____ Drive 2 capacity: _____

Network interface card 1: _____ Driver: _____

Network interface card 2: _____ Driver: _____

SYS partition size: _____ Location: _____

Pattern Selection Information

Server installation type: ____ Custom ____ Basic ____ Premigration

Preconfigured server: _____

Custom components to install:

    _____ _____

    _____ _____

    _____ _____

Server Configuration

Server name: _____

Server IP address: ____.____.____.____ Subnet mask: ____.____.____.____

Use DNS server: Yes or No ____ DNS IP address: ____.____.____.____

    Host name: _____ Domain name: _____

    Using IPX? Yes or No____ If Yes, complete the IPX information below.

    IPX frame type and network address: _____ _____

Time zone: _____

eDirectory tree name: _____ (new or existing)

Server eDirectory context: _____

Admin user name and password:

License type: _____ # Users: _____ Location: _____

Novell Modular Authentication Services: NDS

    _____

    _____

    _____

    _____

Figure 2-2   The NetWare Server Installation Planning form

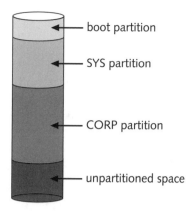

- boot partition
- SYS partition
- CORP partition
- unpartitioned space

Figure 2-3   NetWare 6.5 disk partitions

The boot partition is a file allocation table (FAT)–formatted partition used to start the computer by loading Novell DOS, which loads the NetWare Server.exe software kernel (shown previously in Figure 2-1) along with disk drivers stored in the boot partition. After the Server.exe kernel is loaded, Novell DOS is removed from memory. The boot partition is also used to store memory dumps if the server should crash because of a hardware or software driver problem. To be used for memory dumps, the boot partition must have enough space to store the contents of the server's RAM. The boot partition is quite small; usually 500 MB is enough to store the server and driver files needed to boot the NetWare OS. To store a memory dump, if your server has 1 GB of RAM, for example, a boot partition of 1.5 GB is recommended. After creating the boot partition, the remainder of the disk space on the drive is then reserved for NetWare partitions, as shown in Figure 2-3. NetWare partitions are organized into storage pools, from which logical storage areas called volumes are created. You learn more about partitions, storage pools, and volumes in Chapter 3. All NetWare servers require a SYS volume of at least 2 GB for a minimal system. If you plan to install many of the OneNet services described in this book, you need to have a SYS volume of at least 4 GB. To prevent the SYS volume from being filled up with user data, the network administrator then creates additional partitions to hold company data volumes.

Initial Installation Phase

After the boot partition is created, the installation program copies the necessary system files into the boot partition and then starts the **initial installation phase** by loading the NetWare Server.exe kernel. During the initial installation phase, the NetWare 6.5 kernel is used to load the disk and LAN drivers and create the SYS volume.

Disk Driver Information

NetWare 6.5 disk drivers are modular, with separate drivers called **Host Bus Adapters (HBAs)** to manage the controller cards and **Custom Device Modules (CDMs)** that work with the HBAs to control the individual storage devices attached to the controller card. Disk controllers that don't have HBAs and CDMs included with NetWare need to have their NetWare drivers loaded from a floppy disk or CD supplied by the manufacturer before they can be used with NetWare. NetWare 6.5 includes HBAs and CDMs for Intelligent Drive Electronics (IDE) controllers that can handle most IDE and Enhanced IDE (EIDE) type and drives. Servers supporting a small number of users and devices can use IDE disk controller cards. Larger servers that support more storage devices, such as large hard drives, CD-ROMs, and tape backup systems, however, often use SCSI controllers because they have higher speeds and support a wider range of devices than IDE controllers. For example, to ensure better speed and expansion capability, Universal AeroSpace selected a SCSI disk controller for its server. UAS is planning to expand its storage devices in the near future, and SCSI controllers will support additional high-speed disk drives and a planned optical disk system for archiving engineering designs.

In addition to the type of controller, you should identify the make and model on the NetWare Server Installation Planning form to be sure that the correct driver is selected during installation. NetWare 6.5 can detect many popular IDE and SCSI disk controllers that Novell has tested. Therefore, to make installation simpler, when selecting a SCSI disk controller for a server, check to see that the disk controller you select is included with NetWare. In most cases, you can best ensure this by purchasing controller cards that are NetWare 6.5 certified. Before installation, you should identify the disk system components and drivers to be used on your server and then document them on your NetWare Server Installation Planning form.

Network Interface Cards

To communicate with other devices on the network, a server needs at least one network interface card (NIC). Additional NICs can be installed to allow access to the server from multiple network cable systems. When multiple NICs are installed in a server, the server acts as a router, passing packets of data through network cable systems, as shown in Figure 2-4.

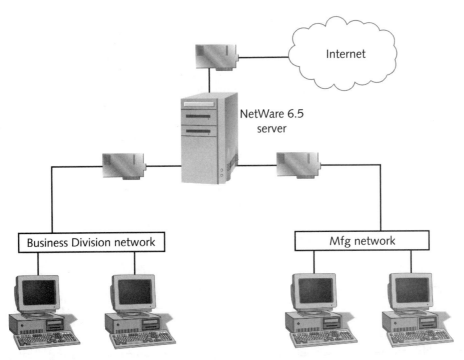

Figure 2-4   Multiple NICs installed in a server

To access NICs, NetWare requires a driver to be identified during NetWare installation. As a result, before installing NetWare on the server, you need to identify the make, model, and configuration for each NIC on your server. To make installation easier, NetWare contains drivers for many popular NICs. As with disk controllers, one of the best ways to be sure a driver for your network card is included with NetWare is to purchase a card that has been Novell certified. You also need to supply the hardware configuration for the card, which can consist of an interrupt, a Direct Memory Access (DMA) channel, an input/output (I/O) port, and a memory address. You can configure the card by using special software or by placing jumpers or setting switches on the card itself. The NetWare Server Installation Planning form has a space for filling in the make, model, and driver information.

NetWare System Partition

The next step in preparing for server installation is defining the amount of disk storage to be allocated to the NetWare SYS volume. The minimum recommended space is 2 GB, but you should consider using at least 4 GB and then leave some unpartitioned disk space on the drive to allow for expanding the volume. In Chapter 3, you learn how to add partitions and volumes for storing user data and software.

Pattern Selection Phase

With NetWare 6.5, Novell offers new server installation options called "patterned server deployment" to help simplify and speed up the installation of specialized servers. The pattern options, shown in Figure 2-5, enable administrators to select the type of server they want to install.

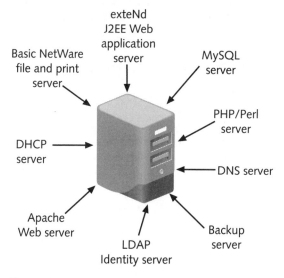

Figure 2-5 NetWare 6.5 pattern options for server installation

For example, if you indicate a DNS/DHCP installation, the patterned installation process asks for the information needed to install DNS and DHCP. After you supply the information, the patterned installation process quickly and automatically installs the necessary software and customizes the server to maximize DNS and DHCP performance.

An important Novell strategy is to support open-source application development fully in NetWare 6.5. Because NetWare 6.5 offers so many open-source development tools, Novell has included the NetWare AMP (which stands for "Apache, MySQL, PHP/Perl") server option to simplify installing and configuring a server specialized for open-source application development.

During the **pattern selection phase**, you select the type of server installation you want to perform and then enter the configuration information required for that type. At the end of this phase, the installation process copies the necessary files into the SYS volume.

Server Configuration Phase

After the necessary files are copied to the server's SYS volume, the **server configuration phase** is used to enter the server's name, protocol, license, and eDirectory information, as described in the following sections.

Server Name

Server names can be from 2 to 47 characters and should help you identify the server and its location or use easily. These names can't start with a period or contain spaces. In addition, the server's name must be unique in the eDirectory tree to which the server belongs. If your server will be accessed from the Internet, you should avoid using underlines or dashes in the server name to maintain compatibility with the Domain Name Service (DNS).

Protocol Information

After you have identified the server's hardware environment, the other major consideration is identifying the network environment in which the server will operate. The network environment consists of network protocols along with the network address and any special frame types to be used for each NIC in the server.

Although TCP/IP is the protocol of choice for most NetWare installations, Novell's earlier Internetwork Packet Exchange (IPX) protocol might also be necessary if you plan to support older software services, such as the print server module (PSERVER.NLM) used with queue-based printing (discussed in Chapter 8). When installing IPX, each network cable system requires a unique network address and frame type. The frame type specifies the format of data packets sent across the network cable. The default frame type used with IPX packets is Ethernet 802.2. The IPX network address works much like a ZIP code, in that it allows packets to be delivered efficiently to the correct recipient network. When installing the first NetWare IPX server on the network cable, you can use any network address consisting of up to eight bytes, expressed with hexadecimal digits. Additional servers attached to the same network cable need to use the same network address of the existing server; IPX protocol servers on other network segments must use different IPX network addresses. For example, Eric has selected a network address of 1EEE8022 for the 10BaseT network card to represent the IEEE 802.2 standard his Ethernet card uses.

In addition to providing the legacy IPX protocol, Novell enables NetWare 6.5 to communicate directly by using TCP/IP. Although more complex to implement, TCP/IP is a more universal protocol and enables you to connect the server to the Internet through an ISP or provide services directly to a company intranet. Because of the existing clients and applications, UAS has decided to install support initially for both IPX and TCP/IP on the server. After converting all computers and applications to TCP/IP, the corporation can remove support for IPX from the NetWare 6.5 servers. If you're using IPX, you should enter frame types and corresponding IPX network address information on your NetWare Server Installation Planning form. The same IPX network address must be assigned to all servers that share the network segment and frame type. In addition, when using IPX, each server is assigned a unique eight-digit hexadecimal number called the server ID, which uniquely identifies the server on the network segment and is assigned automatically during installation, but can also be entered manually.

eDirectory Installation

As described in Chapter 1, eDirectory is Novell's directory service used to organize and manage network objects and configuration. Within the eDirectory database, network objects are stored in containers in much the same way that files are stored in folders. Containers are organized in a hierarchical fashion called the directory tree. In Chapter 4, you learn more about the architecture and operation of eDirectory.

During NetWare installation, you have a choice of placing the new server in an existing tree or creating a new tree. To place the server in an existing tree, you need to be able to log in as the Admin user of the existing tree and enter the context of the container where the server will be created. To create a new tree, you need to determine its name and the path to the container where the new server object and Admin user will be placed. As a result, an important step in preparing for NetWare installation is to identify the name of the eDirectory tree and the path to the container where the server object will be placed. On his NetWare Server Installation Planning form, Eric Kenton, the UAS network administrator, identified the context for the new UASHOST server as the UAS Organization within a new tree named UAS_Tree.

Configuring Novell Modular Authentication Service (NMAS)

You can use the NMAS options shown in Figure 2-6 to select from a variety of industry-standard security options.

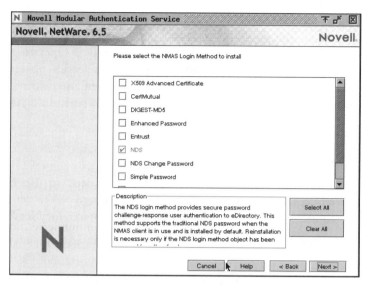

Figure 2-6   Novell Modular Authentication Service options

In addition to the default NDS login method, you should select the Simple Password login method so that Windows client computers can log in without using the Novell client. Selecting all options gives the server the widest range of authentication protocols.

Activity 2-1: Planning a NetWare 6.5 Server Installation

Time Required: 10 minutes

Objective: Identify information needed to prepare for a NetWare 6.5 server installation.

Requirements: If you're using IPX (so that you can load PSERVER.NLM in Chapter 8), document your frame type and IPX network address:

IPX frame type (such as Ethernet 802.2):

_____

Network address (such as 1EEE8022):

_____

Description: Eric Kenton has asked you to install a new NetWare 6.5 server for evaluating the Novell Open Enterprise Server product. In this activity, you work with information your instructor provides to complete the NetWare Server Installation Planning form shown in Figure 2-2.

1. Obtain a copy of the NetWare Server Installation Planning form from your instructor.

2. Use hardware information provided by your instructor to fill in the Initial Installation Information section of your NetWare Server Installation Planning form. (If you're using IPX, enter the frame type and network address your instructor supplies. IPX is necessary only if you're loading PSERVER.NLM in Chapter 8.)

3. Enter the following NetWare components under "Custom components to install" in the Pattern Selection Information section of your form:

   - **Apache2 Web Server and Tomcat 4 Servlet Container (required for iPrint)**
   - **iPrint**
   - **Novell iManager 2.5**
   - **Novell Virtual Office framework**

4. Use information provided by your instructor to fill in the Server Configuration section of the NetWare Server Installation Planning form.

5. Have your instructor check your form before proceeding to the next activity.

PERFORMING A NETWARE 6.5 INSTALLATION

The NetWare 6.5 OS comes on two CDs: Operating System CD 1 and Products CD 2. Operating System CD 1 is bootable and contains the files needed for the initial installation and pattern selection phases. Before starting the installation, you need to make sure your existing network and server are configured correctly. The following sections describe the steps for preparing your existing network and server and performing the actual NetWare 6.5 installation.

Upgrade an Existing eDirectory Network

If you're planning to install NetWare 6.5 into an existing eDirectory tree, you need to use NetWare Deployment Manager (Nwdeploy.exe) to ensure that the existing eDirectory tree is updated to version 8.6. For example, Eric performed the following procedure to prepare the UAS eDirectory tree for NetWare 6.5:

1. First, Eric installed Novell Client on his Windows XP Professional computer, as described in Chapter 4.

2. Next, he inserted the NetWare 6.5 Operating System CD 1 into the CD-ROM drive to start NetWare Deployment Manager automatically. (You can also start this software by running Nwdeploy.exe from the root of the NetWare 6.5 Operating System CD 1.)

3. When NetWare Deployment Manager started, he viewed the tasks required for the upgrade process by double-clicking the Network Preparation folder and reading the Overview section.

4. He then backed up the existing NetWare server and eDirectory data by following the instructions in the Back Up Data section.

5. After the backup was finished, Eric updated eDirectory by selecting the View and Update eDirectory Version option.

6. To complete the upgrade, Eric extended the eDirectory tree structure by selecting the Prepare for eDirectory option. (You learn more about upgrading eDirectory in Chapter 4.)

After Eric completed the upgrade, the existing eDirectory tree was ready to receive the new NetWare 6.5 server installation, as described in the following sections.

Prepare the Server

Preparing the server starts with verifying that the hard drive has no existing partitions. You can do this by booting the computer from a DOS disk and then running the Fdisk program to display any existing partitions. If your system contains existing partitions, use Fdisk to delete these partitions before starting the installation. You can also use a live or runtime version of Windows or Linux to initialize the hard drive.

A live or runtime version of an OS on a CD allows you to boot the OS from the CD and access your system and hard drive in much the same way that earlier DOS versions could be booted from a floppy disk.

After ensuring that your hard drive is empty, the next step is to determine the NetWare 6.5 installation startup method. If your computer will boot from the CD-ROM drive, you should use your CMOS Setup program to ensure that the system is set to boot from the CD-ROM drive first. If your system does not boot from the CD, you can create a DOS bootable disk that contains the CD drivers, and then start the NetWare 6.5 installation by using the DOS boot disk as described in the following steps:

1. Create a DOS bootable disk.

2. Install the DOS CD driver for your CD-ROM drive on the bootable disk.

3. Create a Config.sys file to load the CD drivers.

4. Create an Autoexec.bat file to start the NetWare 6.5 installation. This file should contain the following commands to map the CD to the E: drive and start the installation program:

```
MSCDEX.EXE /D:cdname /L:E
E:
INSTALL
```

Install NetWare 6.5 on the Target Computer

As described in the "Preparing for NetWare 6.5 Installation" section, NetWare 6.5 installation consists of four general phases: installation startup, initial installation, pattern selection, and server configuration. When installing NetWare 6.5 Open Enterprise Server, during the initial installation phase you have the option to perform an Open Enterprise Server installation or a traditional NetWare 6.5 installation. The Open Enterprise Server option includes Support Pack 3, iManager 2.5, Virtual Office 1.5, and the new QuickFinder server. The traditional NetWare 6.5 SP3 option includes iManager 2.0, Virtual Office 1.0, and Web Search Server. For the purposes of this book, you need to select the Open Enterprise Server installation to get the versions of iManager and Virtual Office used in the activities.

The best way to learn about the NetWare installation process is to go through an actual installation of a NetWare 6.5 server. In the following activity, you go through the four phases of installing a NetWare 6.5 server for the UAS network. If you won't be installing NetWare 6.5, your instructor might perform this activity for you as a demonstration.

Activity 2-2: Installing NetWare 6.5 Open Enterprise Server

Time Required: 50 minutes

Objective: Install NetWare 6.5 Open Enterprise Server.

Description: Eric has asked you to install a new NetWare 6.5 server for evaluating the Novell Open Enterprise Server product. Use the NetWare Server Installation Planning form you filled out in Activity 2-1 to supply the required information.

1. If you're using VMware, you should create a NetWare 6.5 virtual computer first as described in Appendix C. If you're using a system with a removable hard drive, insert a blank hard drive.

2. To start the installation process, insert the Open Enterprise NetWare 6.5 Operating System CD 1 into the server's CD-ROM drive and restart the server to display the language selection screen. Verify that the correct installation language is selected, and then press **Enter** to display the Select the regional settings for the server screen.

If your computer does not boot from the CD drive, you need to create a boot disk as described in the "Prepare the Server" section.

If you're installing the traditional NetWare 6.5, you might need to select the following startup options:

- Select **I** to install a new server.
- Select **A** to automatically search for a CD-ROM driver.
- Select **A** for Auto terminate.
- Select **A** for Auto execute.

3. Press **Enter** again to accept the default regional settings for country, code page, and keyboard.

4. Read the Novell Open Enterprise Server Software license agreement, and then press **F10** to accept and continue. If necessary, press **F10** again to accept the JReport Runtime license agreement and display the Welcome to the NetWare 6.5 server installation window shown in Figure 2-7.

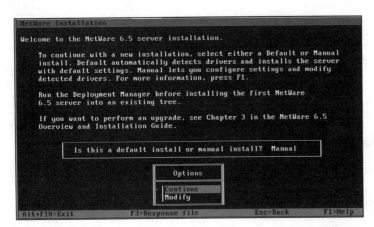

Figure 2-7   The Welcome to the NetWare 6.5 server installation window

5. To customize the installation, press **Enter** to change the default installation type to Manual. Next, press **Tab** to select the Continue option, and press **Enter** to display the Prepare boot partition window.

6. The Prepare boot partition window allows you to create a DOS boot partition within the first 8 GB of the server's hard drive. Although the minimum DOS partition boot size is 500 MB, Novell recommends adding more space to hold a memory dump in case the server undergoes a hardware fault. Select the **Modify** option, highlight **Free Space**, press **Enter**, and then type the size of your system's RAM in megabytes for the DOS partition. Press **Enter** a second time, and the installation program formats the DOS boot partition and returns to the Prepare boot partition window. Press **Tab**, use the arrow keys to select the **Continue** option, and then press **Enter** to display the Server Settings window.

7. Write down the server ID number on the NetWare Server Installation Planning form you completed in Activity 2-1, and then press **Enter** to start the file-copying process, during which files are copied from the Operating System CD 1 to the DOS partition. These files include the server startup software as well as configuration files and drivers.

    The initial installation phase uses text-based menus and screens from the Operating System CD 1 to select the LAN drivers and create the SYS volume. This phase includes a screen called the NSS Main Menu that you can use to create additional partitions, pools, and volumes. (You learn more about creating file system objects in Chapter 3.) To access the NSS Main Menu after installation, enter the command NSSMU at the server console.

8. After the files are copied, the installation program displays the detected platform support module's driver. Press **Enter** to accept and load the detected driver and display the detected HotPlug and Storage adapters.

9. Verify that the detected devices match those on your NetWare Server Installation Planning form, and then press **Enter** to display the detected storage devices. Again, verify that these devices are correct, and then press **Enter** to continue and load them.

10. Next, the installation program displays the drivers that support the detected LAN adapter. Verify that the detected driver identified by your computer hardware configuration is correct, and then press **Enter** to display the Device types and Driver names window. Press **Enter** again to accept the devices and continue loading the drivers. After the drivers are loaded, the installation program displays the Create SYS Volume window shown in Figure 2-8.

11. Press **Enter** to accept the default 4 GB SYS volume size and display the NSS Main Menu shown in Figure 2-9. This installation menu is a new addition to NetWare 6.5 and allows you to customize or change the configuration of devices, storage pools, and volumes without restarting the installation program.

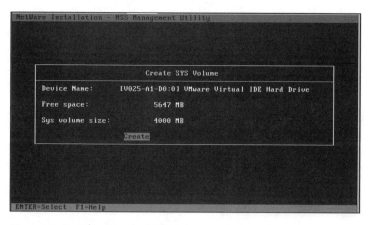

Figure 2-8 The Create SYS Volume window

Figure 2-9 The NSS Main Menu for installation

12. Verify that the Continue Installation option is highlighted, and then press **Enter** to start another file copy. This file-copying process copies all the system files to the SYS volume and then loads the server program. This process takes several minutes.

In the pattern selection phase, you select the type of server installation you want to perform, and then enter the configuration information required for that type. At the end of this phase, the installation process copies the necessary files into the SYS volume.

13. When installing NetWare 6.5 Open Enterprise Server, after the server program loads, the Product Installation Type window is displayed (see Figure 2-10).

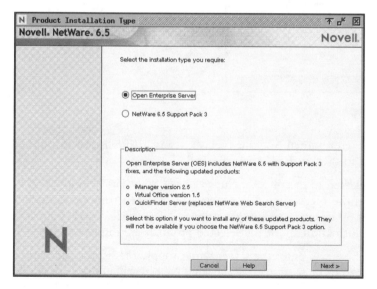

Figure 2-10 The Product Installation Type window

14. Verify that the Open Enterprise Server option button is selected, and then click **Next** to display the Choose a Pattern window shown in Figure 2-11.

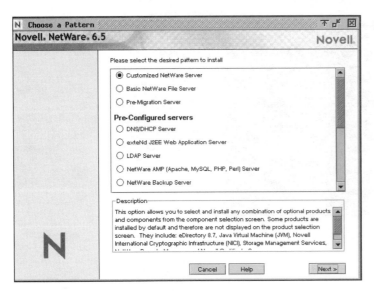

Figure 2-11   Selecting a pattern option for installation

15. Because this server will be a general-purpose one, verify that the default Customized NetWare Server option button is selected, and click **Next** to display the Components window shown in Figure 2-12.

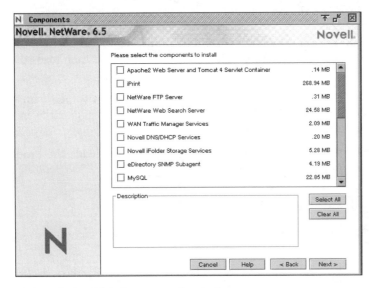

Figure 2-12   The Components window

16. Select the installation options you wrote down on your NetWare Server Installation Planning form in Activity 2-1, and then click **Next** to display the Summary window.

17. Verify that all the products you selected to install are included in the Summary window, and then click the **Copy files** button. Insert the NetWare 6.5 Products CD 2 when prompted, and click **OK**. Because this file copy takes almost 30 minutes, you might want to take a well-deserved break. During the file copying, windows with information about the selected products are displayed.

    During the server configuration phase, you enter the server name, supply the license information, select and configure any network protocols to be used, specify the time zone, install eDirectory, and select any additional login methods for network clients.

18. Next, the installation process displays the Enter the server name window. Enter the name from your NetWare Server Installation Planning form in the Server Name text box, and then click **Next** to display the Protocols window.

19. Click the **IP** check box and enter the IP address and mask for the NetWare 6.5 server that you wrote down earlier on your NetWare Server Installation Planning form. If selected, configure IPX as defined on your NetWare Server Installation Planning form.

20. Click **Next** to display the Domain Name Service window. If there's no DNS server on the local network, leave all fields blank and click **Next**. When you receive a warning message stating that some services have limited functionality without the DNS service, click **OK** to continue.

21. Next, select your time zone and click **Next** to initialize the eDirectory service and display the eDirectory Installation window.

22. Click the **Create a new eDirectory tree** option button, and then click **Next** to display the eDirectory Installation window shown in Figure 2-13.

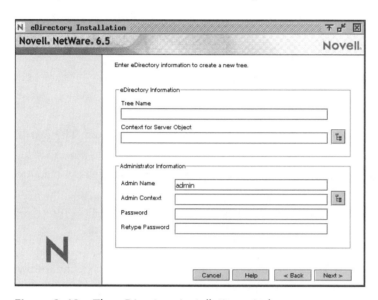

Figure 2-13   The eDirectory Installation window

23. Enter the name of your eDirectory tree (the one you wrote down on your NetWare Server Installation Planning form) in the Tree Name text box and your Organization name in the Context for Server Object text box. Enter a password for your Admin user in the Password and Retype Password text boxes, and then click **Next** to install eDirectory and display the eDirectory Summary window. Record the information from this window on your NetWare Server Installation Planning form, and then click **Next** to display the Licenses window.

24. The Licenses window can be used to install licenses for the NetWare 6.5 server and users during server installation. License files have an .nlf extension and can also be installed after server installation by using iManager as described in Chapter 5. Click the browse button to locate the license certificate on your floppy disk, and then add it to the License(s) to be installed list box (see Figure 2-14).

A sample MLA license certificate for evaluation purposes is included on the NetWare 6.5 Products CD in the License\eval folder.

NOTE

25. Click **Next** to display the MLA License Certificate Context window. You use the Select the NDS context text box to specify the context where licenses are installed. The licenses are then valid for all users in the selected context and below. Verify that the context is set to your UAS Organization, and then click **Next** to install the licenses and display the LDAP Configuration window.

26. Record the default clear text and SSL/TLS port numbers on your NetWare Server Installation Planning form, and then click **Next** to accept the default port settings and display the Novell Modular Authentication Service (NMAS) window shown previously in Figure 2-6.

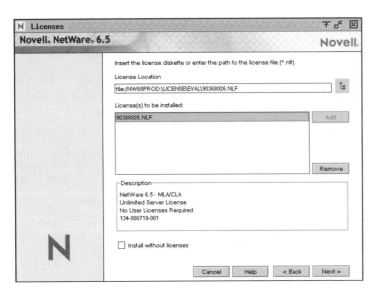

Figure 2-14   The Licenses window

27. To provide for all login methods, click the **Select All** button and then click **Next**. The installation program continues by configuring each selected service.

28. When prompted, restart your server. Congratulations! Your NetWare 6.5 server is now ready for use.

29. To shut down your NetWare server correctly, press **Ctrl+Esc** on the server console to display the console selection menu, and then select the **System console** option to display the console prompt. The following section describes using the NetWare server console and commands.

30. Type the command **DOWN** and press **Enter**. When the DOS prompt is displayed, you can safely power off your server. (You learn more about the DOWN and EXIT commands in the following section.)

WORKING WITH THE SERVER CONSOLE

As described in the "Preparing for NetWare 6.5 Installation" section, a NetWare server contains at least two disk partitions: one for DOS and one for NetWare. A NetWare server starts first from the DOS partition (C: drive). As shown previously in Figure 2-1, the NetWare server consists of the Server.exe kernel software and modules that are loaded to provide services. The Server.exe kernel supplies the core NetWare services, such as file sharing, and provides a software bus for NetWare Loadable Modules and Java applications. Most network services, such as Novell Distributed Print Services (NDPS) and Novell eDirectory, and device drivers are provided by software modules called **NetWare Loadable Modules (NLMs)**, which are loaded during or after the server startup process.

To start the NetWare server, you begin by running the Server.exe program from the DOS partition. During installation, the Server.exe program, its support files, and its disk driver modules are stored on the DOS boot partition in the C:\Nwserver directory. If you selected to start the server automatically during the installation process, the commands needed to start the server are placed in the Autoexec.bat file. When the computer starts, DOS automatically performs the commands placed in the Autoexec.bat file. For example, the following commands were placed in the Autoexec.bat file of the UASHOST server:

```
C:\>cd nwserver
C:\nwserver>server
```

As the Server.exe program is loading, it reads commands from the Startup.ncf file, also located in the C:\Nwserver directory. This file contains the names of the disk drivers and other configuration commands, as shown in Figure 2-15.

```
                     File: STARTUP.NCF

LOAD IDEHD.CDM
LOAD IDECD.CDM
LOAD IDEATA.HAM PORT=1F0 INT=E
LOAD IDEATA.HAM PORT=170 INT=F
```

Figure 2-15   A sample Startup.ncf file

After Server.exe has loaded its disk drivers, it mounts the SYS volume and continues to read commands from the Autoexec.ncf file stored in the System directory of the SYS volume. As shown in Figure 2-16, the Autoexec.ncf file contains commands that identify the server's name, internal address, and any NLMs, such as the network card drivers, that must be loaded for server operation.

```
NetWare Configuration

                        File: AUTOEXEC.NCF

set Bindery Context = O=UAS
SET Daylight Savings Time Offset = 1:00:00
SET Start Of Daylight Savings Time  = (APRIL SUNDAY FIRST  2:00:00 AM)
SET End Of Daylight Savings Time = (OCTOBER SUNDAY LAST  2:00:00 AM)
SET Time Zone = CST6CDT


# Note: The Time zone information mentioned above
# should always precede the SERVER name.
SEARCH ADD SYS:\JAVA\BIN
SEARCH ADD SYS:\JAVA\NWGFX\BIN
SEARCH ADD SYS:\JAVA\NJCLV2\BIN
SEARCH ADD SYS:\NI\UPDATE\BIN

Save file            <F10>         Previous screen     <Esc>
Mark and unmark text <F5>          Delete marked text  <Del>
Save marked text     <F6>          Insert marked text  <Ins>
Help                 <F1>          Abort nwconfig <Alt><F10>
```

Figure 2-16   Reading commands from the Autoexec.ncf file

After startup, the server console displays the Novell Open Enterprise Server screen. You can change the background of the GUI screen by clicking Novell, pointing to Settings, and then clicking Backgrounds. In addition to the GUI console, the NetWare 6.5 server has a text-based console screen and console screens for several modules. You can flip between console screens with the Alt+Esc key combination, or you can select a console screen by pressing Ctrl+Esc to display all consoles and then enter the number of the screen you want to display (see Figure 2-17).

```
Current Screens

   1.  System Console                       ╱ OS
   2.  Logger Screen                         ╱ OS
   3.  *NOVELL SSL Server Handshake Screen   ╱ OS
   4.  Apache 2.0.52 for NetWare             ╱ OS
   5.  *Apache2 Web Manager                  ╱ ADMINSRV
   6.  *PKERNEL                              ╱ OS
   7.  X Server -- Graphical Console         ╱ OS

If a screen name is preceded by *, select it to unhide the screen.

Select screen to view: _
```

Figure 2-17   Selecting a NetWare console

For example, to change to the System Console screen, press Ctrl+Esc to display the list shown in Figure 2-17. Type 1 and press Enter to display the console prompt showing the server name followed by a colon. You can use the System Console screen to enter console commands and load modules as described in the following sections.

Console Commands

To become a CNA and effectively operate a server console, you need to know how to use the basic **console commands** built into the NetWare operating system. Table 2-2 summarizes the purpose of the server console commands, and the following sections describe some of these commands in more depth and provide examples of using them to perform server operations. In Activity 2–3, you practice using console commands.

Table 2-2 Essential console commands

Command Syntax	Description
BIND *protocol* TO *drive/board_name* [*drive_parameters*]	Attaches a protocol to a LAN card. Replace *protocol* with the protocol name (IPX or IP, for example). Replace *drive/board_name* with the name of the NIC or an optional name assigned to the network board. You can optionally replace *drive_parameters* with the hardware settings that identify the NIC (such as I/O port and interrupt).
LOAD [*path*]*module_name* [*parameters*]	Loads an NLM in the file server's RAM. Optionally replace *path* with the DOS or NetWare path leading to the directory containing the module to be loaded. Replace *module_name* with the name of the NLM you want to load. Optional parameters can be entered depending on the module being loaded.
CONFIG	Displays configuration information about each NIC, including hardware settings, network address, protocol, and frame type.
DISPLAY *servers*	Displays all servers in the file server's IPX router table, including the number of routers (hops) to get to each server. This command is not available unless IPX is selected during server installation.
MEMORY	Displays the total amount of memory available to the file server.
SET *time*	Allows you to change the file server's current system date and time.
CLS/OFF	Clears the file server console screen.
DISABLE /ENABLE LOGIN	Prevent or enable new user logins.
BROADCAST	Send the specified message to all currently logged-in users.
DOWN	Closes all files and volumes, disconnects all users, and takes the file server offline.
MOUNT *volume_name* [ALL] DISMOUNT *volume_name*	Places a volume online or offline. Replace *volume_name* with the name of the volume you want mounted, or use ALL to mount all NetWare volumes.
MODULES	Lists all currently loaded modules starting with the last module loaded.
SEARCH [ADD/DEL]	Displays and updates the paths where the server will look for modules. Use this command to add and delete paths for loading modules.
SECURE CONSOLE	Provides additional security to help protect the server from unauthorized access.
SEND "*message*" [TO] *user_name/connection_number*	Sends a message to a specified user. Replace *message* with a message line you want sent and replace *user_name/connection_number* with the name of the currently logged-in user or the connection number assigned to the user. The *connection_number* can be obtained from the Connection option of the MONITOR NLM.

Table 2-2   Essential console commands (continued)

Command Syntax	Description
UNBIND *protocol* [FROM] *LAN_driver\board_name*	Removes a protocol from a LAN card. Replace *protocol* with the name of the protocol stack (such as IPX) you want to remove from the card. Replace *LAN_driver\board_name* with the name of the driver program that has been loaded for the NIC or the name assigned to the network card by the LOAD command.
UNLOAD *module_name*	Removes an NLM from memory and returns the memory space to the OS. Replace *module_name* with the name of the currently loaded module given in the MODULES command.
VOLUMES	Displays a list of all mounted volumes along with the volume type (NSS or traditional) and supported namespaces.
PROTOCOLS	Displays a list of all currently loaded protocols.
HELP *command*	Displays information on the specified command. For example, to obtain information on the syntax and use of the BIND command, enter HELP BIND and press Enter.

CONFIG

The CONFIG command displays information about the server and NIC configuration, as shown in Figure 2-18.

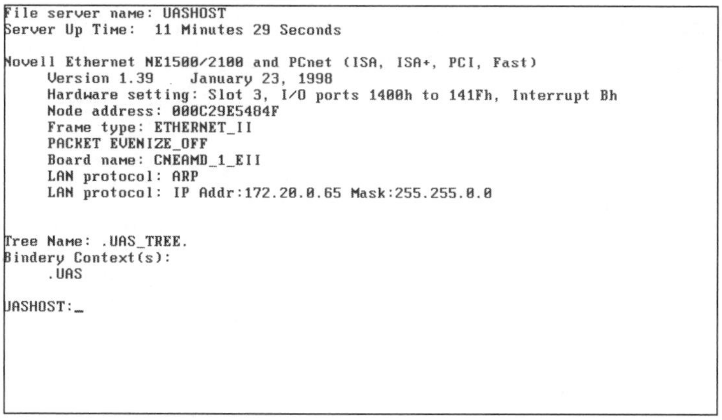

```
File server name: UASHOST
Server Up Time:  11 Minutes 29 Seconds

Novell Ethernet NE1500/2100 and PCnet (ISA, ISA+, PCI, Fast)
     Version 1.39    January 23, 1998
     Hardware setting: Slot 3, I/O ports 1400h to 141Fh, Interrupt Bh
     Node address: 000C29E5404F
     Frame type: ETHERNET_II
     PACKET EVENIZE_OFF
     Board name: CNEAMD_1_EII
     LAN protocol: ARP
     LAN protocol: IP Addr:172.20.0.65 Mask:255.255.0.0


Tree Name: .UAS_TREE.
Bindery Context(s):
     .UAS

UASHOST:_
```

Figure 2-18   The results of a CONFIG command

Notice that in addition to displaying the file server's name and internal network address, the CONFIG command displays the following information about each network adapter in the file server:

- Name of the LAN driver
- Board name assigned when the LAN driver was loaded
- Current hardware settings, including interrupt, I/O port, memory address, and DMA channel
- Node (station) address assigned to the network adapter
- Protocol stack that was bound to the network adapter
- Network address of the cabling scheme for the network adapter
- Frame type assigned to the network adapter
- Tree name
- Bindery context (used for backward compatibility with NetWare 3.0 servers)

You should use the CONFIG command before installing network adapters in the server so that you have a current list of all hardware settings on the existing boards. This helps you select unique interrupt and I/O address settings for the new cards. In addition, the CONFIG command can be used to determine the network address of a cable system before adding another server to the network. If you accidentally bring up another server using a different network address for the same cable system, router configuration errors between the servers interfere with network communications.

DISABLE/ENABLE LOGIN

The DISABLE LOGIN command prevents new users from accessing services on the NetWare server. Before shutting down the server, you should first issue the DISABLE LOGIN command to prevent any additional users from accessing the server and then use the BROADCAST command to send a message to all existing users telling them that the server will be coming down at the specified time and that they should close all files and log out of the server. If the DISABLE LOGIN command is not issued, new users might log in to the server after the message was broadcast and not be aware the server is going down shortly. Another use of the DISABLE LOGIN command is to temporarily prevent users from logging in while you perform certain maintenance work, such as loading new drivers or backing up the system. After the work is finished and the server is ready for use, you can issue the ENABLE LOGIN command to allow users to log in again and use the server.

DOWN

The DOWN command deactivates the NetWare server operating system, removes all computer connections, and returns the server to the DOS prompt. Before issuing the DOWN command, you should disable new logins and broadcast a message to all users, as shown in Figure 2-19. If active sessions exist, the NetWare operating system issues a warning message asking if you want to terminate active sessions.

```
UASHOST:
UASHOST:DISABLE LOGIN

 3-20-2002   8:19:52 am:    CONNMGR-5.60-85  [nmID=90013]
     Login is now disabled

UASHOST:BROADCAST Server going down in 15 minutes. Please save work and logout.
UASHOST:
UASHOST:DOWN
Java: Cleaning up resources, Please Wait.
```

Figure 2-19 Shutting down a server

If you see this message, you should cancel the DOWN command and use the Monitor utility (described later in "Using the Monitor Utility") to determine which connections have open files and then send a message to the user to log out. If no one is at the computer and data files have been left open, you might need to go to the computer to close the files and log out the user. In this case, you should be sure to remind users that their computers should not be left unattended while data files are open.

LOAD

The LOAD command loads an NLM into memory and runs it. By default, the LOAD command searches for the requested module in the SYS:System directory unless a different path is specified. Valid paths can include NetWare volume names as well as DOS local drive letters. When a module is loaded into memory, it remains there until the console operator ends the program or uses the UNLOAD command to remove the software from memory. Optional parameters can be placed after the LOAD command, depending on the needs of the module being loaded.

Beginning with NetWare 5.0 and continuing with NetWare 6.5, it's no longer necessary to use the LOAD command to run an NLM. By simply typing the name of the NLM, the system automatically performs the load process.

SEARCH

When you enter a command, the server first checks to see whether the command is one of the standard internal commands described in this section. If the entry is not a recognized internal command, the server attempts to load an NLM with that name from the SYS:System directory (see Chapter 3). With the SEARCH command, you can specify other paths for the server to find NLMs. For example, you could use this command to add a search path to the DOS boot partition:

```
SEARCH ADD C:\
```

You can also use the SEARCH command to display your server's search paths by simply entering the word SEARCH on the system console. Figure 2-20 shows an example of adding the DOS partition to the search path, displaying all existing search paths, and then removing the DOS partition from the search path.

```
UASHOST:SEARCH ADD C:\
Search 12: C:\
UASHOST:
UASHOST:SEARCH
Search 1: SYS:\SYSTEM\
Search 2: C:\NWSERVER\ (default directory)
Search 3: C:\NWSERVER\DRIVERS\
Search 4: SYS:\JAVA\BIN\
Search 5: SYS:\JAVA\NWGFX\BIN\
Search 6: SYS:\JAVA\NJCLV2\BIN\
Search 7: SYS:\PHP\
Search 8: SYS:\PHP\EXT\
Search 9: SYS:\APACHE2\
Search 10: SYS:\TOMCAT\4\BIN\
Search 11: SYS:\NI\UPDATE\BIN
Search 12: C:\
UASHOST:
UASHOST:SEARCH DEL 12
Removed search 12: C:\
UASHOST:_
```

Figure 2-20   Using the SEARCH command

SECURE CONSOLE

The SECURE CONSOLE command adds the following security features to help protect the server from unauthorized access:

- Prevents loading NLMs from other sources, such as floppy disks, the DOS partition, or CDs. Requiring NLMs to be loaded only from the SYS:System directory helps prevent an intruder from loading a potentially harmful NLM from a floppy disk or a user directory on the server. Using the SECURE CONSOLE command disables any paths entered with the SEARCH command.

- Allows only the console operator to modify the date and time.

- Prevents keyboard entry into the internal debugger software. This feature is important because programmers could use the debugger to change OS parameters.

SEND

The SEND command is used to send a message to a specific client. The most common use of the SEND command is to request a user to log out before shutting down the file server. Messages can be sent to a user's login name or connection number. For example, to send a message to the user at connection number 9, enter this command:

```
SEND "Server going down in 5 minutes" TO 9
```

SET

The SET command enables you to view and configure OS parameters from the command line. Although the default settings for server configuration parameters are set to maximize network performance in most environments, your particular network might require modifying some of the settings. You learn more about how to monitor your server's performance and determine whether any changes are necessary in "Monitoring Server Health and Performance" later in this chapter. You can view a list of SET categories by typing the command SET at the server console, as shown in Figure 2-21.

```
UASHOST:SET
Settable configuration parameter categories
     1. Communications
     2. Memory
     3. Traditional File System
     4. Common File System
     5. Novell Storage Services
     6. Disk
     7. Time
     8. NCP
     9. Miscellaneous
    10. Error Handling
    11. Directory Services
    12. Multiprocessor
    13. Service Location Protocol
    14. Licensing Services
Which category do you want to view: _
```

Figure 2-21   SET command categories

To view the current settings of parameters in any category, you simply enter the number to the left of that category. You can then use any key to display additional parameters. For example, Figure 2-22 shows the SET parameters for the Communications category after scrolling down several screens.

```
Maximum Packet Receive Buffers:  10000
   Limits: 50 to 3303820
   Can be set in the startup ncf file.
   Description: Maximum number of packet receive buffers that can be allocated
               by the server

Minimum Packet Receive Buffers:  2000
   Limits: 10 to 32768
   Can be set in the startup ncf file.
   Description: Minimum number of packet receive buffers allocated by the
               server

Maximum Physical Receive Packet Size:  4224
   Limits: 618 to 65642
   Can only be set in the startup ncf file.
   Description: Size of the largest packet that can be received by an MLID

New Packet Receive Buffer Wait Time:  0.1 seconds
   Limits: 0 seconds to 20 seconds
   Description: Minimum time to wait before allocating a new packet receive
               buffer

<Press ESC to terminate or any other key to continue>_
```

Figure 2-22   SET parameters for the Communications category

Pressing the Esc key exits the SET command and returns you to the console prompt. You can change a parameter's setting by entering the SET command followed by the parameter and its new setting. For example, the Maximum Physical Receive Packet Size by default is set to 4224 bytes. Because there are a minimum of 2000 packet receive buffers, this setting can take up about 8 MB of your server RAM. If you're using an Ethernet network, you can save server memory by using the SET command to change this setting to 1524, as shown here:

```
SET Maximum Physical Receive Packet Size = 1524
```

The SET command can also be used to change the server's current time or date. In a multiple-server network tree consisting of 30 or fewer servers, a single server is designated as a reference server. All other servers on the network synchronize their time to the reference server. As a result, in a multiple-server network, you should change time only at the reference server. Novell recommends checking the time from DOS or CMOS and then making any corrections before starting the SERVER program. The following commands show several ways of using SET TIME to change the file server's current date and time to 3:00 p.m., October 30, 2006.

```
SET TIME 10/30/2006 3:00p [sets date and time]
SET TIME October 30, 2006 3:00p [sets date and time]
SET TIME October 30, 2006 [sets just the date; time left unchanged]
SET TIME 3:00 [sets the time using a 24-hour clock; in this case, 3:00 a.m.]
SET TIME 15:00 [sets the time using a 24-hour clock; in this case 3:00pm]
```

Activity 2-3: Using Console Commands

Time Required: 10 minutes

Objective: Use NetWare server console commands.

Description: To perform this activity, you need to have access to your server console. An important task for every network administrator is to develop and maintain documentation on network and server configurations. Follow these steps to record the requested server and network information.

1. If necessary, press **Ctrl+Esc** on the server console to display the console menu, and then enter **1** to change to the system console prompt.

2. Use the **CONFIG** command to record the following server data here:

   ■ Server name:

   _____

   ■ Internal IPX number (if your server is using IPX):

   _____

   ■ NIC driver:

   _____

   ■ Interrupt:

   _____

   ■ Port:

   _____

   ■ Network address:

   _____

   ■ Node address:

   _____

   ■ Frame type:

   _____

   ■ Bindery context:

   _____

   ■ Currently mounted volumes:

   _____

3. Use the **MEMORY** command to find the amount of RAM on your server. Record your findings here:

_____

4. Use the **VOLUMES** command to record the name of each volume here:

_____

5. Use the **SEARCH** command to enter a search path to the DOS partition and then display the existing search paths. Record the command you used and your existing search paths here:

_____

_____

6. Follow these steps to use the SET command to change your packet receive buffer size:

   a. Enter the **SET** command to display the SET categories.

   b. Type **1** and press **Enter** to display the Communication parameters.

   c. Press the spacebar until you see the Largest Ping Packet Size value.

   d. Use the **SET** command to set the Maximum Physical Receive Packet Size to 1524. Record the command you used here:

   _____

7. Use the command for disabling logins. Record the command and the results here:

_____

8. Use the command for enabling logins. Record the command and the results here:

_____

9. Use the command for securing the console. Record the command and the results here:

_____

10. Use the correct key strokes to return to the graphical console, and record the procedure you used here:

_____

11. Leave the server console window open for the next activity.

NetWare Loadable Modules (NLMs)

One of the strengths of NetWare is its use of NLMs to add functionality to the core OS. Because NLMs play such an important role in tailoring the NetWare network, a CNA should be familiar with the standard NLMs included with the NetWare OS. As shown in Table 2-3, NLMs can be classified into four general categories based on their function, with each category having its own extension.

Table 2-3   NLM categories

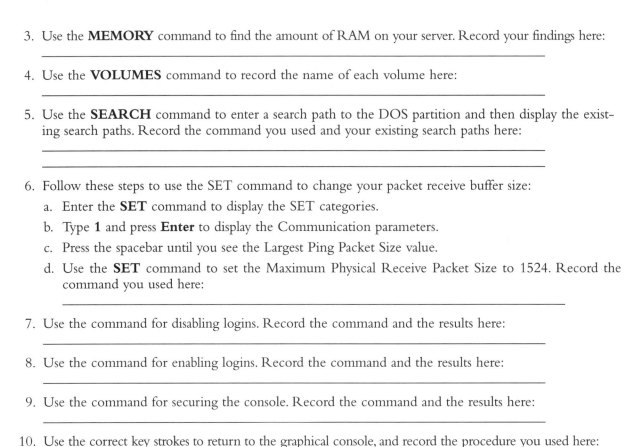

Category	Extension	Description
Disk drivers	.ham and .cdm	Controls access to NetWare disk partitions. Commands to load these modules are usually placed in the Startup.ncf file.
LAN drivers	.lan	Each NIC must be controlled by a compatible LAN driver. Commands to load these modules are placed in the Autoexec.ncf file.
Namespace	.nam	Contains logic to support other computer-naming conventions, such as those for Apple Macintosh computers or OS/2 and UNIX-based computers. Commands to load namespace modules are usually placed in the Startup.ncf file.
General-purpose	.nlm	Adds services and functions to the file server's operating system.

In addition to the special modules for controlling disk drivers and NICs, NetWare comes with a number of general-purpose NLMs in the SYS:System directory that can be used for a wide range of capabilities, as shown in Table 2-4. In the following sections, you learn about several of these modules that CNAs must be able to use to manage their network file servers.

Table 2-4   General-purpose NLMs

NLM	Description
CDROM.NLM	Used to mount a CD when it's first inserted in the server's CD-ROM drive. After this module is loaded, it automatically detects the removal and insertion of CDs.
DSREPAIR	Checks eDirectory tree replicas for any problems and synchronizes all replicas with the master.
NWCONFIG.NLM	Used to work with NetWare partitions, volumes, and system files.
MONITOR.NLM	Used to monitor file server performance, hardware status, and memory usage.
REMOTE.NLM	Used to view and operate the NetWare server console from a remote computer. Requires a password.
RSPX.NLM	Allows the REMOTE module to send and receive console screens and commands over the local network cable.
RS232.NLM	Allows the REMOTE module to send and receive console screens and commands over the asynchronous port.
RCONAG6.NLM	Provides an IP-based remote Java console for use with ConsoleOne, as described in Chapter 5.
SCRSAVER	Provides a method to lock the server console by using a password. To access the server console, the operator must enter the specified password or the Admin user's password.
VREPAIR.NLM	Checks the specified traditional volume for errors and allows you to write corrections to the disk volume. This command works only with traditional volumes. To correct problems with NSS volumes, you need to use the NSS /REBUILD command.

The NLMs shown in Table 2-4 can be classified into three general categories based on their function.

The Disk Repair Modules

The DSREPAIR and VREPAIR NLMs are used to identify and fix problems in the file system. A major difference between these NLMs is that DSREPAIR is used to work with NSS volumes and VREPAIR is used with traditional volumes. You learn more about NSS and traditional volumes in Chapter 3.

The Remote Access Modules

NetWare 6.5 has a number of NLMs that support remote access to the server console. The REMOTE, RSPX, and RS232 NLMs are used for backward compatibility with the older Remote console utility, but with NetWare 6.5, you should use RCONAG6.NLM or Remote Manager to access the server console remotely. Remote Manager is Novell's OneNet utility for managing the server environment from a Web browser running on any network. You learn how to use Remote Manager to view your server's performance in "Monitoring the Server with Remote Manager" later in this chapter.

Server Console Management Modules

The server console management modules include CDROM, MONITOR, NWCONFIG, and SCRSAVER. CDROM mounts a CD onto the file system. MONITOR provides a way of managing your server's performance and is covered in detail in the following section. NWCONFIG provides a number of server configuration options, including modifying the server startup files (see "Modifying Server Startup Files" later in this chapter). SCRSAVER has a line called the "worm" that moves around the server's screen. The length of the worm indicates the server activity. The longer the line, the busier the server. In addition to providing an interesting screen saver, SCRSAVER is also useful in securing the server console. You learn how to use SCRSAVER to lock your server console in Activity 2-4.

MONITORING SERVER HEALTH AND PERFORMANCE

As a network administrator, one of your responsibilities will be ensuring that the server is running smoothly and efficiently. This involves being able to monitor server performance and change configuration parameters, if necessary. Novell has two utilities for managing your server performance. The first is the Monitor utility, which is an NLM loaded at the server console that has many options for viewing server performance and configuring parameters. The second utility is Remote Manager, which you run from a Web browser on any desktop computer. In the following sections, you learn how to use both these utilities to manage your server's health and performance.

Using the Monitor Utility

The Monitor utility is useful for monitoring and configuring system performance. In this section, you learn how to use it to view server performance, connection information, and disk and network statistics. To start the Monitor utility, you need to load the MONITOR NLM into the server's memory by typing the command MONITOR at the server console prompt. Next, the General Information screen shown in Figure 2-23 is displayed.

Figure 2-23   The General Information screen of the Monitor utility

This screen displays the version and date of the NetWare OS and several important system parameters about your server's available memory and performance. The lower half of the screen displays a menu of Monitor options. You can view parameters in the Available Options menu by pressing Tab. Figure 2-24 shows the results of selecting the Disk cache utilization option.

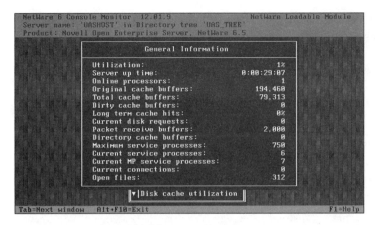

```
NetWare 6 Console Monitor  12.01.9           NetWare Loadable Module
Server name: 'UASHOST' in Directory tree 'UAS_TREE'
Product: Novell Open Enterprise Server, NetWare 6.5

                 ┌─────────────────────────────────────┐
                 │         General Information          │
                 ├─────────────────────────────────────┤
                 │ Utilization:                     1%  │
                 │ Server up time:          0:00:29:07  │
                 │ Online processors:                1  │
                 │ Original cache buffers:     194,460  │
                 │ Total cache buffers:         79,313  │
                 │ Dirty cache buffers:              0  │
                 │ Long term cache hits:            0%  │
                 │ Current disk requests:            0  │
                 │ Packet receive buffers:       2,000  │
                 │ Directory cache buffers:          0  │
                 │ Maximum service processes:      750  │
                 │ Current service processes:        6  │
                 │ Current MP service processes:     7  │
                 │ Current connections:              0  │
                 │ Open files:                     312  │
                 └─────────────────────────────────────┘
                   ┌▼│Disk cache utilization ║
Tab=Next window  Alt+F10=Exit                              F1=Help
```

Figure 2-24 The Available Options menu

Only the first seven available options are shown in the Monitor menu. You can view additional options by pressing the down arrow. To best use the Monitor utility to manage your server's performance, you should be aware of the options and settings listed in Table 2-5.

Table 2-5 Monitor statistics

Statistic	Description	Values
Utilization	Percentage of time the processor is being used.	Generally, this statistic should not be higher than 80%.
Server up time	Length of time the NetWare server has been running since it was last started.	This statistic is used to determine when the server was last started.
Online processors	Number of enabled processors.	This statistic is important if using a multiprocessor system to verify that all CPUs are running.
Original cache buffers	Number of cache buffers available when the server is first started represents the amount of memory in your server after the NetWare kernel is loaded.	Use this statistic along with total cache buffers to determine the amount of memory the server is using.
Total cache buffers	Number of buffers available for file caching.	This value decreases as modules are loaded into memory. Novell recommends that total cache buffers be at least 40% of the original cache buffers.
Dirty cache buffers	Number of buffers containing information that needs to be written to disk.	If this value is consistently 30% or more of the total cache buffers, the speed of the disk system should be checked to see whether it could be improved by installing additional disk controllers or faster drives.
Long term cache hits	Number of times the server found requested data in memory instead of having to read from the disk.	For best performance, long term cache hits should be 80% or higher. Adding more memory can increase this statistic.
Current disk requests	Number of disk requests in a queue waiting to be serviced.	A consistently high value for this statistic along with a large number of dirty cache buffers could indicate a slow disk system.

Table 2-5   Monitor statistics (continued)

Statistic	Description	Values
Packet receive buffers	Number of buffers available to receive requests from computers.	The default value of 2000 should be more than enough. On networks with fewer than 50 computers, this value can be decreased to 1000 to provide more memory for cache buffers.
Directory cache buffers	Number of buffers allocated for directory caching.	Normally, this value does not need to be adjusted.
Maximum service processes	Number of task handlers allocated for user computer requests.	Normally, this value does not need to be adjusted.
Current service processes	Number of task handlers that have been allocated for station requests. If the number of station requests in the packet receive buffers exceeds a certain limit, the server adds extra task handlers to carry out the requests. Of course, this in turn reduces the amount of memory and processing time for other activities.	If the combined number of service processes and MP service processes approaches the default maximum of 570 and you have a high processor utilization, you might need to unload NLMs or add another file server to decrease the load on the current server.
Current MP service processes	Number of multiprocessor-based task handlers.	See the preceding entry for "Current service processes."
Current connections	Number of licensed and unlicensed connections currently in use by the server.	This number should consistently be lower than the number of connections in the license. If the value approaches the maximum available licensed connections, additional connections might need to be purchased.
Open files	Number of files being accessed via the network server in user computers.	Tracking this value can help determine server usage.

Together, the utilization, total cache buffers, packet receive buffers, and dirty cache buffers statistics can give you a quick picture of your server's health by simply verifying that utilization is under 70%, the total cache buffers value is at least 50% of the original cache buffers, and the dirty cache buffers value is less than 30% of the total cache buffers.

In addition to the General Information screen shown in Figure 2-23, the Monitor utility's Available Options menu contains several options for viewing information about your server's performance and operation. Selecting the Connections option displays a window showing all active connections and the name of the user currently logged in. If no user is logged in to a given connection number, the message "NOTLOGGED-IN" appears next to the connection number. You can use this option to check for user activity before shutting down the server. To disconnect a user, highlight the user name and press Delete. To view information about any connection, select the connection number and press Enter. The Volumes option lists all mounted volumes and the percentage of volume space used. The Storage devices option shows the hardware setting used by the current disk drivers. The LAN/WAN drivers option displays information on all LAN drivers loaded, including driver name, frame type, port, and interrupt. The System resources option is a convenient way to view the percentage of cache buffers used. The Cache Utilization Statistics screen shown in Figure 2-25 is a good way to determine whether your server has enough memory.

2

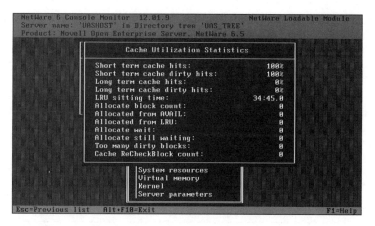

Figure 2-25   The Cache Utilization Statistics screen

TIP

Novell recommends that the long term cache hits should be higher than 90%. If this value is less than 90%, adding more memory or unloading NLMs can increase server performance.

The Server parameters option is used to modify server configuration parameters, such as the maximum number of packet receive buffers or server time type. In the following activity, you use SCRSAVER and the Monitor utility to lock your server console and to document your server configuration and performance settings.

ACTIVITY

Activity 2-4: Using SCRSAVER and the Monitor Utility

Time Required: 10 minutes

Objectives: Secure the server console with the SCRSAVER command and use the Monitor utility to view server performance.

Requirements: Access to the NetWare 6.5 Open Enterprise Server console

Description: Now that your NetWare 6.5 server is installed and running, Eric wants you to use the Monitor utility to create a baseline of network performance. A baseline of normal server activity helps you identify changes that can reduce network performance. In addition, Eric wants to ensure that other users do not access the server console, so you use the SCRSAVER module to lock the server console, and then use the Monitor utility to build a baseline of server performance for your UASHOST server.

1. If necessary, open the server console window by pressing **Ctrl+Esc** to display a list of console screens, and then type **1** and press **Enter** to display the System Console command prompt.

2. Follow these steps to lock the server console:

   a. At the server prompt, type **SCRSAVER** to load the screen saver utility.

   b. At the server prompt, type **SCRSAVER HELP** to view screen saver options. If requested by your instructor, record a sample command here for future reference:

   _____

   c. At the server prompt, type the command to lock the server console with a delay of five seconds. Record the command you used here:

   _____

   d. Press any key to display the Server Console Authentication screen.

   e. Enter **Admin** in the User name field, and then press **Enter**.

   f. Enter the password you used for your Admin user in the Password field, and then press **Enter** twice to open the console.

g. Type the **SCRSAVER ENABLE; DELAY=10; DISABLE LOCK** command, and then press **Enter** to display the screen saver without locking the console.

h. If required by your instructor, document the results of using this command:

_____

i. (Optional) Disable the screen saver by typing **SCRSAVER DISABLE** and pressing **Enter**.

3. Type **MONITOR** and then press **Enter** to start the Monitor utility.

4. Press **Tab** to display all server statistics. Record the following baseline statistics here:

- Server up time:

_____

- Original cache buffers:

_____

- Total cache buffers:

_____

- Dirty cache buffers:

_____

- Long term cache hits:

_____

- Current disk requests:

_____

- Directory cache buffers:

_____

- Current connections:

_____

- Open files:

_____

5. Press **Esc**, select **Yes**, and then press **Enter** to exit the Monitor utility.

Monitoring the Server with Remote Manager

Remote Manager enables you to monitor your server's health, change configuration parameters, and perform diagnostic and debugging tasks. To use Remote Manager, the server and computer must meet the software requirements shown in Table 2-6.

Table 2-6 Remote Manager software requirements

Software	Requirement
NetWare operating system	NetWare 5.1 or later
Browser	Netscape 4.5 or later, Internet Explorer 5 or later, or NetWare server browser

To access the Remote Manager utility, start your Web browser and enter the URL _https://ServerIPaddress:8009_ or _http://ServerIPaddress:8008_ to go directly to the Remote Manager Login window. After you enter your administrator user name and password, the Remote Manager opening window shown in Figure 2-26 is displayed.

NOTE

The contents of the Remote Manager opening window depend on the administrative rights of the user name you used to log in. Users who don't have administrative rights to the server see only the volumes and directories they have rights to. You learn more about assigning administrative rights to user accounts in Chapters 6 and 7.

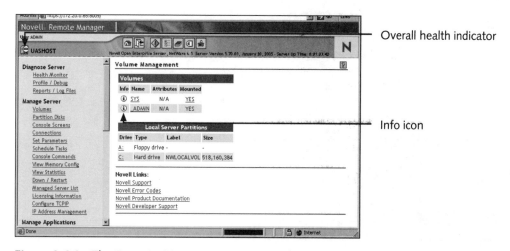

Overall health indicator

Info icon

Figure 2-26   The Remote Manager opening window

The overall health indicator in the upper-left corner (in Figure 2-26, it's the server icon to the left of UASHOST) gives you a quick look at your overall server health. The header pane at the top center contains general information about the server and icons used to exit Remote Manager and to view volumes, the health monitor, and configuration information. The navigation pane at the left side lists general tasks you can perform in Remote Manager and supplies links to specific pages for performing these tasks. You can use the scrollbar to view additional tasks.

The main content pane in the middle changes depending on which link you click in the header or navigation pane. The online help pane displays help information for the content being viewed in the main content pane. In the activities in the following sections, you learn how to use these panes to diagnose your server's health, manage NetWare servers and volumes, check server application usage, view server hardware configurations, access Novell eDirectory information, and monitor license usage.

The overall health indicator in the upper-left corner gives you a quick indication of the overall server status by displaying one of the following colors:

- *Green*—Represents a server in good health.

- *Yellow*—Provides a warning of possible problems with the server's health or performance.

- *Red*—Represents a server in bad health, which requires the administrator's response.

- *Black*—Indicates that communication with the server has been lost (the server might be down).

If the overall health indicator is not green, you can click the Health Monitor link under the Diagnose Server heading to view the status of individual indicators (see Figure 2-27).

If any indicator in the Status column is yellow or red, it needs attention. For example, if the Available Memory indicator is yellow or red, it indicates that the system is running short of memory. You can view more detailed information by clicking the indicator. For example, to see memory usage statistics, scroll down and click the Available Memory indicator, as shown in Figure 2-28.

In Figure 2-28, the memory usage is in good shape, with almost half the memory reserved for caching files. The cache memory dropping below 30% of the total memory might indicate that RAM should be added to the server. If NLM memory usage is more than the cache memory, you might be able to correct the problem by unloading unneeded modules. For example, exiting the X Server graphical console can free up quite a bit of memory.

When viewing Health Monitor, you can click the Threshold Configuration link to view or set suspect and critical values for a variety of indicators. For example, Figure 2-29 shows an example of viewing the Threshold Configuration window.

Figure 2-27 Server health monitor indicators

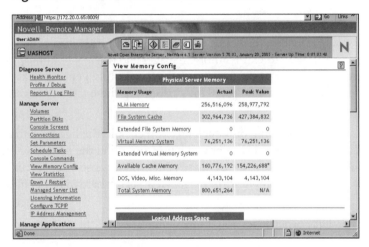

Figure 2-28 The current memory usage statistics

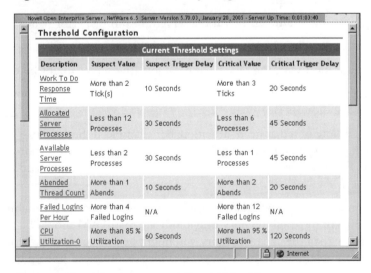

Figure 2-29 Viewing current threshold settings

The Suspect Value column identifies criteria for displaying a yellow indicator, and the Critical Value column identifies criteria for displaying a red indicator. To change the criteria, click the indicator, enter the new suspect or critical value, and then click OK. In the following activity, you use the Health Monitor to view performance indicators on your server.

Activity 2-5: Monitoring Server Health

Time Required: 10 minutes

Objective: Use Remote Manager to check server health and performance.

Requirements: Access to an administrative user with the Supervisor right to your server and a Windows XP or SUSE Linux 10 computer configured with the correct IP address to communicate with your NetWare 6.5 server

Description: Eric noticed that the server was not responding as fast as he thought it should. To help identify any problems, he wants you to use Remote Manager to check individual server indicators. In this activity, you use Remote Manager to document several performance indicators.

1. If necessary, start your computer and log on.

2. Start your Web browser, and enter the URL **https://*ServerIPaddress*:8009** (replacing *ServerIPaddress* with the IP address of your server) to open the Enter Network Password dialog box.

3. Enter the user name and password of the user who has the Supervisor right to your server, and then click **OK** to display the Remote Manager main window.

4. Click the **Health Monitor** icon to display the Health Monitor window, similar to the one shown previously in Figure 2-27.

5. Scroll through your server's health monitors and check their status. Record any yellow or red indicators here:

   _____

6. Click the **Info** icon (an *i* in a circle) next to the Available Memory indicator to display the Available Memory information window.

7. Record the criteria for the green, yellow, and red indicators:

   _____

8. Close the Available Memory information window.

9. Click the **Threshold Configuration** link, and record the entries in the Suspect Value and Critical Value columns:

   _____

10. Stay logged in and leave Remote Manager open for the next activity.

In addition to monitoring performance, server management includes managing volumes and user connections, viewing and setting parameters, viewing system statistics, and accessing current console screens. Being able to access server console screens remotely is a powerful management feature when troubleshooting or repairing NetWare server problems. In the following activity, you use the Manage Server options in Remote Manager to view and record information about your server's SYS volume and memory usage.

Activity 2-6: Performing Server Management Tasks

Time Required: 10 minutes

Objective: Use Remote Manager to view server volumes and memory usage.

Requirements: Same as Activity 2-5

Description: Being able to manage the UASHOST server from remote locations has been convenient for Eric when he's away from the office. In this activity, you use server management options in Remote Manager to see how Eric was able to manage the server on the road.

1. If necessary, follow the steps in Activity 2-5 to start Remote Manager.

2. In the main window, click the **Volumes** link under the Manage Server heading to display the Volume Management window showing the status of all volumes. Record the names and attributes of the first four volumes:

   _____

   _____

   _____

   _____

3. Click the **Console Commands** link to display a list of all console commands.

4. Click the **Info** icon next to these commands: CONFIG, CLEAR STATION, and CLS. Record the description of each command and the sample command shown in the Info window:

   _____

   _____

   _____

5. Click the **View Memory Config** link to display the View Memory Config window. Record the total system memory size and current cache memory:

   _____

6. Stay logged in and leave Remote Manager open for the next activity.

Activity 2-7: Viewing the Server Hardware Environment

Time Required: 10 minutes

Objective: Use Remote Manager to view hardware information.

Requirements: Same as Activity 2-5

Description: Using Remote Manager, you can view your server's current hardware configuration settings, which is useful when diagnosing problems or planning for new equipment. For example, at Comdex Eric found a 1 GB network card that he wanted to install in the UASHOST server. He used Remote Manager to view the server's hardware configuration so that he could check the slots and interrupts to determine the feasibility of installing the new network card. In this activity, you use the options under the Manage Hardware heading to document your server's available ports and interrupts.

1. If necessary, follow the steps in Activity 2-5 to start Remote Manager.

2. Scroll down the navigation pane to the Manage Hardware heading, and record the options under this heading:

   _____

3. Click the **Processors** link to display the Processor Information window. Record the processor information here:

   _____

4. Under the Manage Hardware heading, click the **Disk/LAN Adapters** link.

5. Click the **Info** icon next to Network Adapter. Record the interrupt, slot, and ports used by your network adapter:

   _____

6. Under the Manage Hardware heading, click the **Other Resources** link to display the Hardware Resources window.

7. Click the **Interrupts** option to display the Hardware Resources/Interrupts window. List the interrupts in use and any available or unused interrupts:

   _____

8. Click the **Exit** button, and, if necessary, click **Yes** to close the Remote Manager window.

Using Java on the Server

One of the features of NetWare 6.5 is that the server is a highly efficient environment for running Java applications. The Java language, developed by Sun Microsystems, can be used to develop Internet applications that run on multiple platforms, including Web browsers such as Netscape. Having the capability to run Java applications opens up many possibilities for running client-server applications on the NetWare server in the future. A client-server application is one in which at least part of the application runs on the server, and the user interface component runs on the client computer. The major reason many organizations install servers is their capability to run server-based software. NT/2000-based applications are typically limited to the Microsoft platform, but one of the strengths of Java applications is their capability to run on multiple platforms. As a result, many Internet and client-server applications are developed in Java to take advantage of OS platform independence. As one of the most powerful and fastest Java machines, NetWare 6.5 is in a good position to be a preferred choice for running Java applications over the Internet as well as on company intranets.

Running Java applications on the server console requires extra hardware resources. Novell recommends at least 256 MB of RAM, a PS/2 or serial mouse, and a PCI video card that conforms to the VESA 1.2 or later specification. If your video card does not meet VESA 1.2 standards, NetWare loads a default driver that supports only 640 × 480 resolution with 16 colors. JAVA.NLM is loaded automatically along with the X Server graphical console when your server starts. If you're not using any Java-based applications, after your server starts, you can exit the GUI interface and unload the Java language by entering the UNLOAD JAVA command at the server console screen.

Using the NetWare GUI Interface

With NetWare 6.5, Novell has included a Java GUI console interface. The GUI platform is provided by an implementation of X Window, allowing Java programs that conform to the Abstract Windowing Toolkit (AWT) to be displayed with the X Window interface. To load GUI support, type the STARTX command at the server console. Although the NetWare GUI is not intended to be a full-featured desktop computer, it does provide a graphical way to interact with the NetWare console. For example, Eric used the GUI interface to install the WebAccess product by following these steps:

EXAMPLE

1. After using the STARTX command to display the GUI console, Eric clicked the Novell button to display a menu containing options for Console One, Install, Programs, Utilities, Settings, and Run.

2. Then he clicked the Install option to display a list of products already installed.

3. To install additional products, he clicked the Add button and entered the path to the installation CD.

4. Then he selected the product he wanted to install and clicked Next to display a product summary window. He explained that you can customize any of the selected products by highlighting the product and clicking the Customize button.

5. After completing his customizations, he clicked the Finish button to install the selected product, and then restarted the server as prompted. He noted that if any users are logged in, you should be sure to enter the DISABLE LOGIN command and broadcast a message before shutting down the server.

The GUI interface can also be used to configure video resolution, background, and keyboard configurations and to run the ConsoleOne utility, which gives administrators a way to work with eDirectory objects and the file system from the server console so that they don't have to return to client computers to create a user or copy a file, for example. You learn more about working with ConsoleOne in future chapters. In past versions of NetWare, it was necessary to perform all file and user maintenance from a Windows computer running the Novell client and the NetWare Administrator utility.

Modifying Server Startup Files

When the server first starts, it runs commands from the Startup.ncf and Autoexec.ncf startup files to load drivers, set configuration parameters, and load NLMs. Sometimes a network administrator must modify commands in startup files to perform such functions as modifying the server's IPX network address, preventing the GUI console from loading automatically when the server starts, or adding modules such as NDPS Broker and Manager to the startup process. To view and modify startup files from the server console, you use the Nwconfig utility. In Activity 2-8, you use this utility to view and modify the contents of the Autoexec.ncf file.

Activity 2-8: Viewing the Server Startup Files

Time Required: 10 minutes

Objectives: Use the Nwconfig utility to view file server startup files.

Requirements: Access to the NetWare 6.5 server console

Description: Because the graphical console isn't used often, Eric would like you to modify the server's Autoexec.ncf file to prevent automatic loading of the graphical environment in an effort to improve server performance. In this activity, you use the Nwconfig utility to disable loading the graphical environment.

1. From the server console, press **Ctrl+Esc** to display the Current Screens menu.

2. Type **1** to select the System Console option, and then press **Enter** to display the System Console command prompt.

3. Type the **NWCONFIG** command and then press **Enter** to display the NetWare Configuration menu shown in Figure 2-30.

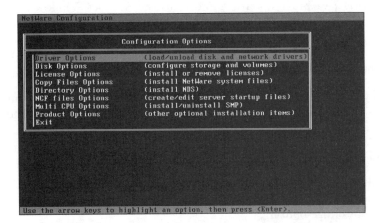

Figure 2-30   The NetWare Configuration menu

4. Press the **down arrow** to highlight NCF files Options, and then press **Enter** to display the Available NCF Files Options menu shown in Figure 2-31.

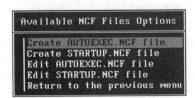

Figure 2-31   The Available NCF Files Options menu

5. Highlight the **Edit AUTOEXEC.NCF file** option, and then press **Enter** to display the contents of the Autoexec.ncf file.

6. Scroll down to the end of the file and type **#** in front of the STARTX command, as shown in Figure 2-32.

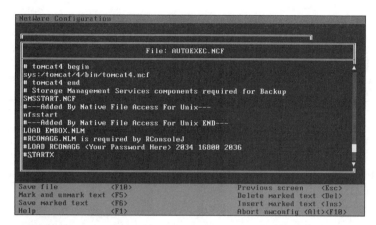

Figure 2-32 Modifying the contents of the Autoexec.ncf file

7. Press **Esc** and then press **Enter** to save the changes and return to the Available NCF Files Options menu.

8. Press **Esc** again to return to the NetWare Configuration menu.

9. Press **Esc** and then press **Enter** to exit the Nwconfig utility.

10. Shut down your server.

In addition to working directly from the server console, you can use the Novell remote management tools, Remote Manager, and OpenSSH to access the server console from a client computer located on the local network or across the Internet. You learn more about using Remote Manager in Chapter 3 and working with OpenSSH in Chapter 11.

CHAPTER SUMMARY

❑ The NetWare 6.5 installation process is divided into four phases: installation startup, initial installation, pattern selection, and server configuration.

❑ In the installation startup phase, you select the server language and accept the license agreements. The initial installation phase is used to establish installation options, select LAN and disk drivers, and create disk partitions. The pattern selection phase is used to select the server type and pattern options for installation. The server configuration phase provides the server name, license, eDirectory, and configuration information.

❑ Preparing for NetWare server installation involves defining the server name and hardware information along with additional products and services.

❑ The server's name can be from 2 to 47 alphanumeric characters, including underscores and dashes. No spaces or periods are allowed.

❑ When using IPX, each server must be assigned a common IPX network address and a unique internal network number consisting of up to eight hexadecimal digits.

❑ The Deployment Manager software is included on the NetWare 6.5 Operating System CD 1. It provides options for viewing and updating the eDirectory version and installing NetWare 6.5 products.

❑ Console commands are built into the NetWare 6.5 kernel and allow an administrator to perform a variety of functions. Commonly used console commands include CONFIG, LOAD and UNLOAD, BROADCAST, DISABLE LOGIN, DISPLAY SERVERS, BIND, and TIME.

❏ Network administrators can add services and features to the NetWare kernel by loading programs called NetWare Loadable Modules (NLMs). The MONITOR and NWCONFIG NLMs can be used to view and change server configuration parameters. The NSS and VREPAIR NLMs are used to check and correct disk volume problems. The DSREPAIR NLM can be used to view and correct problems with eDirectory. The RCONAG6 and REMOTE NLMs can be used to provide access to the server console from a client computer.

❏ Server performance can be monitored and configuration parameters modified by using the Monitor utility or the Remote Manager utility. The Monitor utility is run from the server console, and Remote Manager is run via a Web browser on any client computer.

KEY TERMS

console commands — A command function built into the NetWare kernel Server.exe program, so it's always in memory.

Custom Device Modules (CDMs) — Software drivers used to manage disk drives through the HBA software. *See also* Host Bus Adapters (HBAs).

Host Bus Adapters (HBAs) — Software drivers used to manage disk controller cards.

initial installation phase — The NetWare 6.5 installation phase in which the installation language is selected.

installation startup phase — The NetWare 6.5 installation phase in which the disk and LAN drivers are loaded and the SYS volume is created.

NetWare Loadable Modules (NLMs) — Software modules that can be loaded in the server's memory to provide network services or perform administrative operations.

pattern selection phase — The NetWare 6.5 installation phase in which server installation options are selected.

server configuration phase — The NetWare 6.5 installation phase in which you specify the server name, install eDirectory, and provide network settings.

REVIEW QUESTIONS

1. To meet the minimum NetWare 6.5 server hardware requirements, a computer must have at least _____ RAM.

   a. 256 MB

   b. 1 GB

   c. 512 MB

   d. 768 MB

2. To meet the minimum NetWare 6.5 server hardware requirements, a computer must have at least _____ disk space reserved for the boot partition.

   a. 1 GB

   b. 2 GB

   c. 500 MB

   d. 4 GB

3. To meet the minimum NetWare 6.5 server hardware requirements, a computer must have at least _____ disk space reserved for the SYS volume.

   a. 1 GB

   b. 2 GB

   c. 500 MB

   d. 4 GB

2

4. When installing NetWare 6.5 into an existing eDirectory tree, the eDirectory tree must be _____ or later.

   a. version 7.0

   b. version 8.6

   c. version 6.0

   d. version 2.0

5. Which NetWare volume is created automatically during installation?

   a. System volume

   b. SYS volume

   c. DOS volume

   d. NetWare volume

6. In which installation phase is the server's name entered?

   a. initial installation phase

   b. pattern selection phase

   c. eDirectory installation phase

   d. server configuration phase

7. In which installation phase is the boot partition created?

   a. installation startup

   b. initial installation phase

   c. pattern selection phase

   d. server configuration phase

8. In which installation phase is the eDirectory context selected?

   a. initial installation phase

   b. pattern selection phase

   c. eDirectory installation phase

   d. server configuration phase

9. Which of the following is not an optional NetWare 6.5 installation component?

   a. iPrint

   b. eDirectory

   c. NFAP

   d. iFolder

10. Which of the following commands or modules can be used to correct problems with NSS volumes?

    a. VREPAIR

    b. NSS /REBUILD

    c. REBUILD

    d. DSREPAIR

11. The _____ command assigns a protocol to a LAN driver.

    a. CONFIG

    b. BIND

    c. LOAD

    d. NETBIND

12. The _____ command is used to assign a frame type and an I/O port to a LAN driver.

    a. CONFIG

    b. BIND

    c. LOAD

    d. NETBIND

13. The _____ command shows the total file memory available on the file server.

    a. MEMORY

    b. SYSTEM

    c. MONITOR

    d. CONFIG

14. The _____ command displays the network addresses assigned to each LAN in the file server.

    a. MEMORY

    b. DISPLAY SYSTEM

    c. MONITOR

    d. CONFIG

15. The _____ command allows you to specify other paths to look for NLMs.

    a. SECURE CONSOLE

    b. SEARCH

    c. LOAD

    d. PATH

16. Write a console command that changes the server's clock to 11:59 p.m. on December 31, 2006.

17. Write the sequence of commands a network administrator should enter before shutting down the server in the middle of the day.

18. After starting the file server, you notice that a traditional volume named TEXT did not mount because of errors in the file allocation table (FAT). Identify which NLM could be used to fix the volume and the command for bringing the TEXT volume back online.

19. The _____ console command prevents NetWare from loading NLMs from the SYS: Public\NLM directory.

    a. SEARCH

    b. LOCK CONSOLE

    c. SECURE CONSOLE

    d. CONFIG

20. If the number of total cache buffers shown in the Monitor utility is less than _____ of the original cache buffers, you need to add more memory to your file server.

    a. 80%

    b. 90%

    c. 40%

    d. 25%

CASE PROJECTS

Case Project 2-1: Preparing for NetWare Server Installation

The Engineering Department at Universal AeroSpace has budgeted $5000 to add a NetWare 6.5 server to the existing network for hosting Internet applications. The network administrator, Eric Kenton, has asked you to research some server hardware options and come up with two alternatives in this price range. He would also like you to fill out a NetWare Server Installation Planning form for the server hardware you recommend. The new server will be installed into the existing UAS_Tree eDirectory tree and placed in your assigned UAS container. In this project, you use the Internet to find two server-class computer systems that meet the recommended NetWare 6.5 specifications and then fill in the NetWare Server Installation Planning form for the server you think is the best value. The server should use the NetWare AMP server pattern and allow all NMAS authentication methods.

HANDS-ON PROJECTS

Hands-on Project 2-1: Performing a NetWare 6.5 Open Enterprise Server Installation

To do this project, you should have completed Case Project 2-1 and have access to a computer with a blank hard drive or a computer running VMware 4.1 or later. If you're using VMware, follow the instructions in Appendix C to create a new NetWare 6.5 virtual machine. Next, follow the procedure in this chapter to perform a NetWare 6.5 server installation and document your results.

Hands-on Project 2-2: Building a Server Baseline

Although the UAS network is performing fine at this time, increased demands and equipment failures could cause future performance problems. To help identify performance problems that might occur, you need to determine the server's typical performance by using Monitor to build a baseline that shows server performance during typical work periods. In this project, you use the Monitor utility to determine server baseline statistics on the server you installed in Activity 2-2 or on your assigned server. Document your results.

3

WORKING WITH THE NETWARE FILE SYSTEM

After reading this chapter and completing the activities, you will be able to:

♦ Identify network file service components

♦ Set up a network file system by planning the volume and directory structure and using Remote Manager to create file system components

♦ Access volumes by using NFAP and Web-based network clients

In Chapter 2, you learned how to perform a NetWare 6.5 installation and work with the server console. You were introduced to two essential NetWare file system components: the DOS boot partition and the SYS volume. To manage a NetWare 6.5 server and its data effectively, you need to be familiar with the file system structure and know how to create and maintain partitions and volumes for user applications and data. In this chapter, you learn the components of the NetWare file system and see how to use NetWare remote management tools to set up a network file system for an organization such as Universal AeroSpace. Because providing access to the server's file system from client computers is essential to a network's operation, you also learn how to access NetWare volumes and directories from a standard Windows client. In later chapters, you see how users can access data from the Linux desktop or across the Internet by using a standard Web browser.

NetWare File System Components

The NetWare file system offers many benefits for making information available on a network. These benefits can be classified into the following categories:

- *Centralized management of data and backups*—When data is stored on a server, many users can have access to centralized database files that contain current and accurate information. In addition, centralizing data enables critical files to be backed up regularly and makes it easier to recover from lost data or a file server failure.

- *Improved security*—Prevents users from modifying or accessing data that they aren't responsible for maintaining or aren't authorized to use.

- *Improved reliability and fault tolerance*—NetWare's disk-mirroring and duplexing features can be used to ensure that duplicate copies of data are automatically available for users in the event of hardware failures. NetWare 6.5 includes disk clustering technology that allows multiple servers to share access to the same networked disk system. In this chapter, you learn how disk clustering can be used to increase reliability and fault tolerance.

- *Shared and private storage areas*—Shared storage areas enable users to share files or transfer files to other users without having to carry disks between machines. With private storage areas, users can save their own work in a secure area of the file server.

- *Access to data*—An important part of Novell's Open Enterprise vision is giving users access to the data and documents they need from a computer attached to any interconnected network by using common clients and operating systems (OSs). In this chapter, you learn how Novell's Native File Access Pack (NFAP) allows the NetWare file system to support Apple, Linux, and Windows clients, which reduces hardware costs because there's no need for separate servers to support each OS. As more users and applications are added to the network, it becomes more important for a CNA to know how to give users secure access to the data they need, both inside and outside the corporate network.

Because of the importance of organizing and securing the information stored on the network, a good file system design is necessary to facilitate your network's setup, use, and growth. Starting with NetWare 6.0, Novell improved the network file system by implementing **Novell Storage Services (NSS)** version 3. Earlier versions of NSS included with NetWare 5.0 were more complex to implement and didn't support the SYS volume. As a result, on NetWare 5.0 servers NSS was typically used only with very large data volumes. Because of the advanced features of NSS, Novell has made NSS version 3.2 the primary file system on all NetWare 6.5 volumes, including the SYS volume. As you learned in Chapter 2, an NSS SYS volume of at least 4 GB is required during NetWare 6.5 installation.

As shown in Figure 3-1, the main components of the NetWare 6.5 file system are disk partitions, storage pools, and volumes.

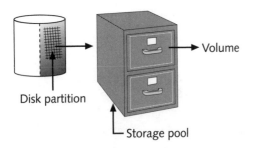

Figure 3-1   NetWare 6.5 NSS file system components

The disk drive is first divided into one or more partitions. The partition space from one or more drives is then combined to form storage pools. A single storage pool can contain space from one or more disk partitions. After a storage pool is created, volumes can be defined within that storage pool. Figure 3-2 shows an example of the partitions, storage pool, and SYS volume created during an initial NetWare 6.5 server installation (on a VMWare virtual computer) as viewed in Novell's Remote Manager utility.

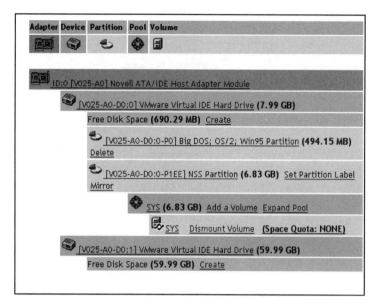

Figure 3-2   Using Remote Manager to view NSS components

Remote Manager displays icons at the top for the disk adapter, disk drive (labeled Device), partition, storage pool, and volume. Notice in Figure 3-2 that there are two virtual disk drives. The first drive is an 8 GB drive with two partitions: the 500 MB DOS boot partition and a partition containing the SYS pool and SYS volume. The second drive contains 60 GB of free space. Later in this chapter, you learn how to use Remote Manager to create disk partitions, storage pools, and volumes from your client computer.

Disk Partitions

To format and manage storage on a physical disk drive, the disk drive needs to be divided into one or more **partitions**. Originally, a disk drive could have a maximum of four disk partitions defined, and only one of these partitions could be a NetWare partition. With Novell Storage Services, you can have an almost unlimited number of NSS partitions. As you learned in Chapter 2, the NetWare 6.5 installation program requires a DOS boot partition of at least 500 MB, with a recommended size of 1 GB. In addition to the DOS partition, during installation a default 4 GB NSS partition is created for the SYS volume, which is used to store OS files. Additional partitions are then created for the organization's shared applications and data. When planning how to allocate the remaining drive space, leaving some unpartitioned space for future expansion is a good idea. The unpartitioned space can be used later to create new partitions for holding new storage pools or extending the space of existing storage pools. For example, when establishing storage space for the Universal AeroSpace disk drive, Eric Kenton divided his 200 GB drive into three partitions, as shown in Figure 3-3. By leaving disk space unpartitioned, Eric has the option of using this space to extend the SYS or CORP storage pools (described in "Storage Pools" later in this chapter).

Partition Fault Tolerance

Having all OS files and user data on one drive creates a potential single point of file service failure if the drive or its controller card fails. **Fault tolerance** is the system's capability to continue functioning despite the failure of a major component. In NetWare, you can ensure increased reliability when you create an NSS partition by enabling the Mirror feature. With this feature, NetWare automatically synchronizes the data on two partitions located on different drives, as shown in Figure 3-4. If one of the drives in the mirror set fails, data is still available from the other mirrored drive.

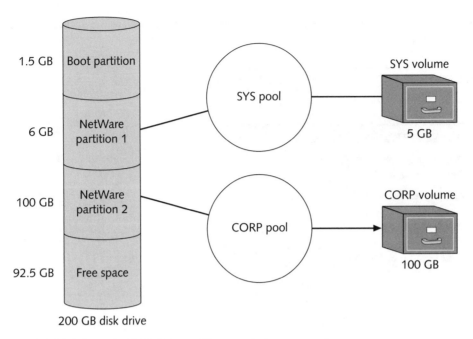

Figure 3-3   Sample UAS disk partitions and storage pools

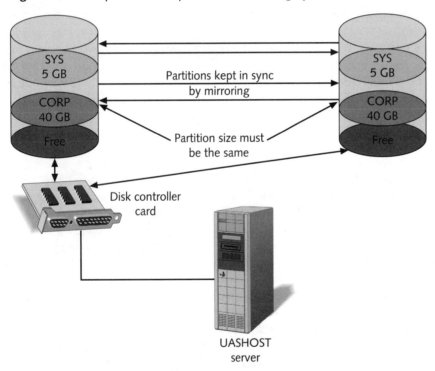

Figure 3-4   Mirroring in NetWare

The process of synchronizing partitions that are attached to the same controller is called **mirroring**. If you have multiple hard drives on your server, you can implement mirroring simply by clicking the Mirror option in Remote Manager (shown previously in Figure 3-2) and then selecting the free space on the drive where you want that partition mirrored (see Figure 3-5). When adding a partition to an existing mirror group, the data area of the new partition is made the same size as the existing partition in the mirror group.

Additional fault tolerance and faster performance can be gained by placing mirrored partitions on separate controller cards. The term **duplexing** describes using the Mirror feature for disk partitions that exist on separate controller cards. Using two controller cards enables duplexing to provide faster speeds and continuous

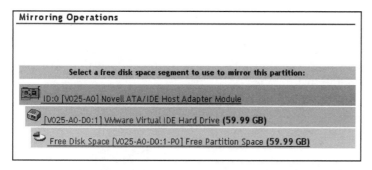

Figure 3-5   Selecting a disk space segment for mirroring

operation in the event of a controller card failure. For example, to provide maximum speed and reliability, Eric used two 60 GB drives attached to separate controller cards on the UASHOST server to duplex the SYS and CORP partitions (see Figure 3-6). If one of the drives or controllers fails, the system continues reading and writing to the other drive. When the problem is fixed, NetWare automatically rebuilds the new drive so that the two drives are the same.

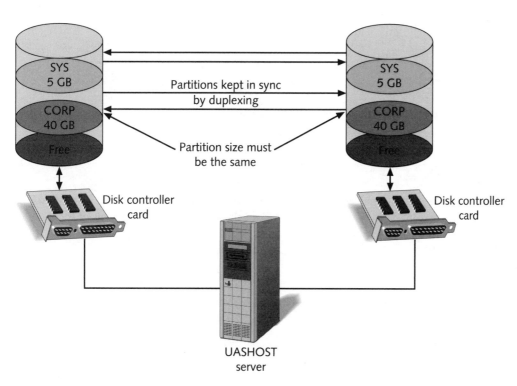

Figure 3-6   Duplexing partitions

 The process of using Remote Manager to enable duplexing is the same as mirroring; the only difference is that the two partitions are located on disks attached to different controller cards.

Storage Pools

After a disk has been partitioned, the next job in setting up an NSS file system is creating one or more storage pools. As shown in Figure 3-7, **storage pools** are created from disk partitions and can be extended by adding disk partitions. When a disk partition is added to a storage pool, the amount of free space in the pool is increased by the size of the disk partition. If you're adding a new disk partition from a second drive to an existing storage pool, you should consider mirroring or duplexing the new partition on another disk to prevent the failure of one drive from bringing down the entire storage pool. As described previously, leaving some unpartitioned space on a new drive gives you the option of extending a storage pool without adding another drive. During installation, a storage pool named SYS is created for the SYS volume. The SYS volume is then used to hold OS files and programs. To separate OS files from the organization's data, a network administrator must create one or more additional storage pools.

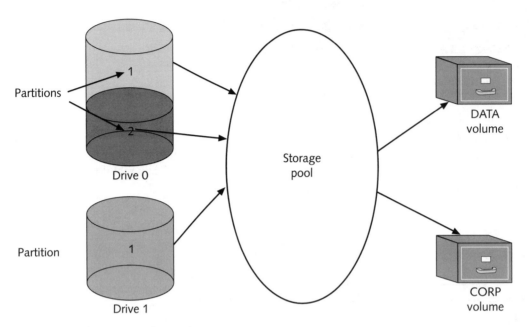

Figure 3-7   Storage pools

Creating Storage Pools

In NetWare 6.5, you create storage pools and their associated partitions by using the File System Creation Operations window (see Figure 3-8), which is accessed from the Partition Disks options of Remote Manager.

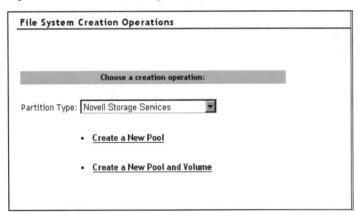

Figure 3-8   Creating a storage pool in Remote Manager

Notice that this window has two options: Create a New Pool and Create a New Pool and Volume. The Create a New Pool option displays the NSS Pool Create window (see Figure 3-9), where Remote Manager automatically creates a new partition of the size specified in the Pool Size text box and then assigns that partition space to a new storage pool with the physical pool name specified in the Pool Name text box. You should use the Create a New Pool option when you want to create a storage pool that holds multiple volumes.

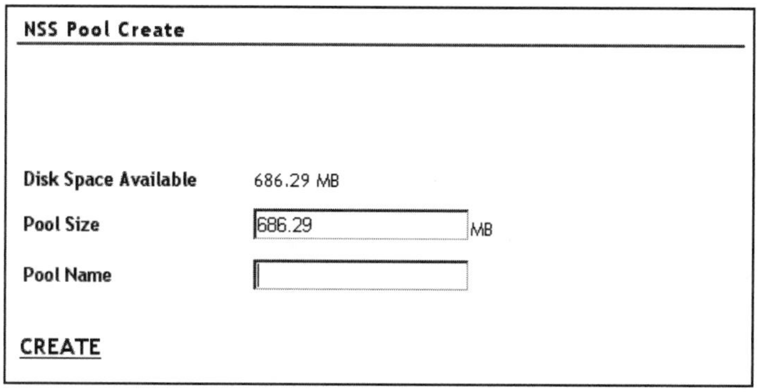

```
NSS Pool Create
────────────────────────────────────────────────────────

Disk Space Available     686.29 MB

Pool Size            [686.29              ] MB

Pool Name            [                    ]

CREATE
```

Figure 3-9   The NSS Pool Create window

The simplest way to create a partition and storage pool for a single volume is to use the Create a New Pool and Volume option to display the NSS Volume Create window (see Figure 3-10).

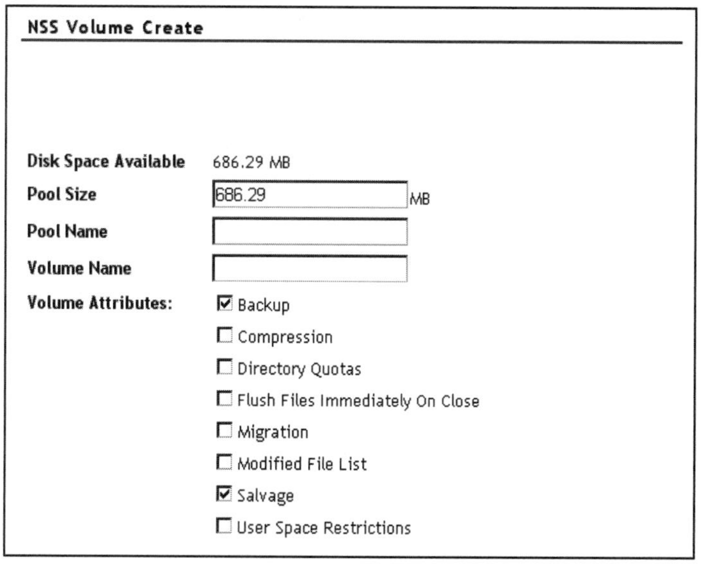

```
NSS Volume Create
────────────────────────────────────────────────────────

Disk Space Available     686.29 MB

Pool Size            [686.29              ] MB

Pool Name            [                    ]

Volume Name          [                    ]

Volume Attributes:      ☑ Backup
                        ☐ Compression
                        ☐ Directory Quotas
                        ☐ Flush Files Immediately On Close
                        ☐ Migration
                        ☐ Modified File List
                        ☑ Salvage
                        ☐ User Space Restrictions
```

Figure 3-10   The NSS Volume Create window

This window includes the Volume Name and Volume Attributes text boxes in addition to the new pool settings. You learn more about volumes and attributes in the "Volumes" section.

Extending the Size of a Storage Pool

When additional disk space is available on the system, storage pools can be expanded by adding partitions to the storage pool as shown in Figure 3-11. For example, because additional free space is available, the size of the SYS storage pool shown previously in Figure 3-2 can be expanded by clicking the Expand Pool option in Remote Manager and then selecting the location for the storage pool (see Figure 3-12). After a storage pool is expanded, the new space can be allocated to existing or new volumes as described in the following section.

NSS Volumes

Volumes are the basic storage unit in the NetWare file system and are necessary to give users access to network directories and files. NetWare 6.5 supports both traditional volumes and NSS volumes. Traditional volumes use the older file allocation table (FAT) technology and are included with NetWare 6.5 to provide backward compatibility with earlier NetWare versions. You learn more about traditional volumes in "Traditional Volumes and Partitions" later in this chapter.

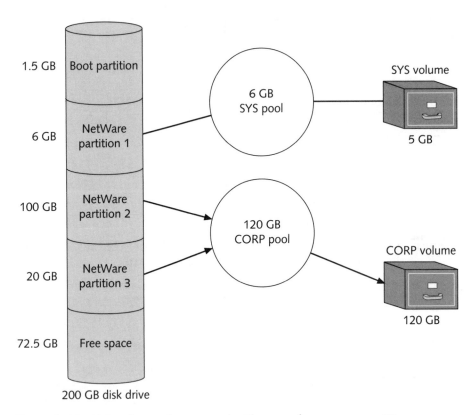

1.5 GB   Boot partition

6 GB   NetWare partition 1

100 GB   NetWare partition 2

20 GB   NetWare partition 3

72.5 GB   Free space

200 GB disk drive

6 GB SYS pool

120 GB CORP pool

SYS volume

5 GB

CORP volume

120 GB

Figure 3-11   Extending a storage pool with space from a new partition

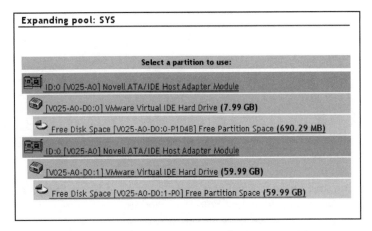

Expanding pool: SYS

Select a partition to use:

ID:0 [V025-A0] Novell ATA/IDE Host Adapter Module

[V025-A0-D0:0] VMware Virtual IDE Hard Drive **(7.99 GB)**

Free Disk Space [V025-A0-D0:0-P1D4B] Free Partition Space **(690.29 MB)**

ID:0 [V025-A0] Novell ATA/IDE Host Adapter Module

[V025-A0-D0:1] VMware Virtual IDE Hard Drive **(59.99 GB)**

Free Disk Space [V025-A0-D0:1-P0] Free Partition Space **(59.99 GB)**

Figure 3-12   Expanding a storage pool in Remote Manager

NSS volumes are logical divisions of an NSS storage pool that contains one or more disk partitions. NSS volumes can be given a specific size up to the storage pool's maximum size, or they can be allotted an initial size and then allowed to grow up to the storage pool's size. By configuring a volume to enable this type of growth, you can extend the volume size in the future by simply adding another partition to the storage pool. For example, assume that your SYS volume is the only volume in a storage pool consisting of one 6 GB disk partition. If the SYS volume is allowed to grow to the size of the storage pool, its maximum size will be 6 GB. If you later add another 5 GB partition to the storage pool, the SYS volume size will be allowed to grow to a maximum of 11 GB.

Like storage pools, when you create a NetWare NSS volume, you assign the volume a physical name. In addition to creating the physical volume, Remote Manager creates a volume object in eDirectory for the new volume and then automatically assigns it a name consisting of the server's name, an underscore, and the physical volume name you assigned. In this way, each volume has two names, as shown in Figure 3-13. You learn more about working with eDirectory objects in Chapter 4.

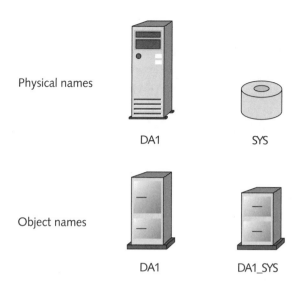

Physical names

DA1   SYS

Object names

DA1   DA1_SYS

Figure 3-13   Volume names

You can change the volume's physical name or eDirectory object name later in Remote Manager or iManager. In Activity 3-4, you learn how to use Remote Manager to create and rename physical volumes. In Chapter 4, you learn how to use iManager to create and rename eDirectory objects.

NSS volumes are usually preferred over traditional volumes because they offer additional capacity and high-speed mounting. Table 3-1 lists some advantages of NSS volumes over traditional volumes. As a CNA, you should understand how the NSS volume features benefit the network file system. These benefits are covered in more detail in the following sections. Later in this chapter, you learn how to use Remote Manager to configure and view NSS volume features and attributes.

Table 3-1   NSS versus traditional volumes

Feature	Traditional Volume	NSS Volume
Maximum number of volumes	64	255
Maximum number of files	16 million	Unlimited
Memory required to mount 20 GB volume	320 MB of RAM	32 MB RAM
Mounting speed	Several minutes for large volumes	Less than one minute even for very large volumes
Support for file compression	Yes	Yes
Support for block suballocation	Yes	No
Support for large block sizes (more than 4 KB)	Yes	No
Support for overbooking	No	Yes
Support for clustering	No	Yes
Support for file snapshots	No	Yes
Support for salvaging	No	Yes
Support for user space restrictions	Yes	Yes
Support for directory space restrictions	Yes	Yes
Support for hot fixes	Yes	No

Table 3-1   NSS versus traditional volumes (continued)

Feature	Traditional Volume	NSS Volume
Support for automatic error correction and data recovery	No	Yes
Modified file list support	No	Yes
Software RAID support	No	Yes

Additional Capacity and Speed

As listed in Table 3-1, before NSS, the traditional file system supported up to 64 volumes per server and 16 million files per volume. By contrast, NSS version 3 now supports up to 255 mounted volumes per server and a virtually unlimited number of files per volume.

The increased speed of mounting NSS volumes on the server is a benefit that network administrators appreciate. In the past, mounting a volume involved loading the FAT into the server's memory. On large volumes, this process could take several minutes and require megabytes of RAM; for example, a 10 GB volume could take 160 MB of RAM to mount. Instead of a large FAT, NSS uses a more memory-efficient file allocation system called **balanced trees (B-trees)**. Using B-trees, large volumes of more than 400 million files can be mounted in just seconds and require a maximum of 32 MB of RAM. In addition, NetWare can retrieve any file blocks not in memory in just four processor cycles, making NSS much faster than previous file system versions.

Overbooking

Assume you have a 40 GB storage pool to be divided into two volumes: one for Accounting data and another for Sales data. After analyzing the storage needs for each department, you conclude that Sales will eventually need 35 GB, but Accounting could get by with 15 GB. Although no one volume can exceed the storage pool size, overbooking allows the sum of all volumes in the storage pool to be larger than the pool size; therefore, with this feature, you could create a Sales volume and set the quota to 35 GB and then create an Accounting volume with a quota of 15 GB. If both volumes grow to their capacity, you could expand the storage pool size by adding more disk partitions, as described previously in the "Storage Pools" section. For example, Figure 3-14 shows two 500 MB volumes within a storage pool that has only 686 MB available. The overbooking feature allows the total size of all volumes in the storage pool to exceed the pool size.

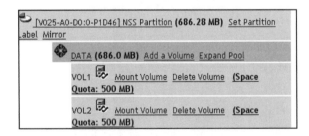

Figure 3-14   Overbooking volume size in a storage pool

Clustering

Although mirroring and duplexing can provide fault tolerance if a drive or controller fails, the server's hardware itself could still cause loss of network services. To provide fault tolerance in the event of a server failure, NSS supports **server clustering**, in which volumes are shared among two or more servers, as shown in Figure 3-15. Shared volumes are usually placed on a networked storage device that's attached to a high-speed storage area network (SAN). If one of the clustered servers has a hardware failure, another server automatically takes the role of making data on the shared volume available to network users. The process of switching from the failed server to an operational server is called **failover** and occurs in just a matter of seconds.

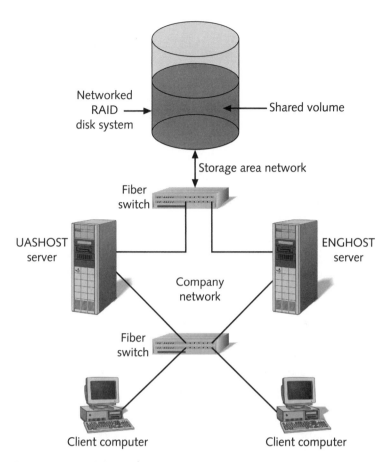

Figure 3-15   Server clustering

Another possible source of downtime is the failure of a disk drive in the network storage device. Typically, networked storage devices use hardware-based RAID 5 technology to provide fault tolerance in case there's a hardware failure on a network storage device's disk drives. When using RAID 5, a network storage device writes data and control information to multiple drives in such a way that if any one drive fails, its information can be recovered by using the control information stored on the other drives.

File Snapshots

In the past, backing up file servers that are accessed around the clock created problems with getting good backups of open files. For example, if a backup program is running while a file is being changed, the backup contains an incomplete copy of the new data. NSS offers a solution to this problem through its File Snapshot capability, which keeps the most recent copy of a closed file for backup purposes. Using this feature ensures that you can restore a valid copy of a previously closed file if your data is lost between backup copies.

Setting NSS Volume Attributes

In addition to faster mounting and lower server memory requirements, NSS volumes incorporate several attributes that make them beneficial for network storage. Most of these attributes can be set when you create the NSS volume, as shown in Figure 3-16.

Backup

The Backup attribute indicates to third-party backup software that the volume contains data you want backed up. You can clear this setting if the volume is empty or doesn't contain data that needs to be copied to a backup device regularly. For example, if a volume contains software that doesn't change often, you should disable the Backup attribute and then manually back up the volume after changes such as software updates or service packs are made.

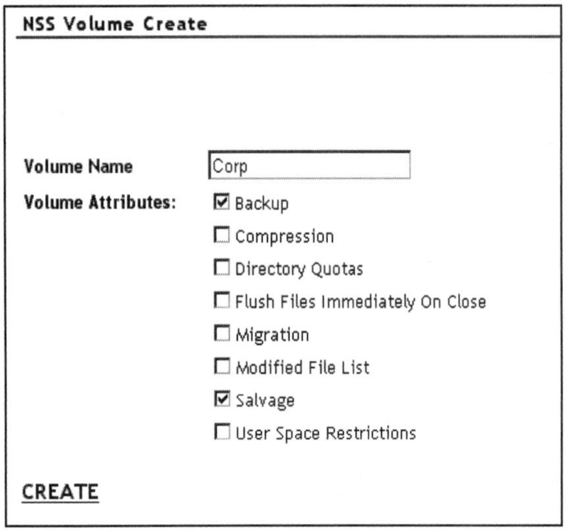

```
┌─────────────────────────────────────────────────┐
│ NSS Volume Create                                │
│                                                  │
│                                                  │
│                                                  │
│  Volume Name        │Corp          │             │
│  Volume Attributes: ☑ Backup                     │
│                     ☐ Compression                │
│                     ☐ Directory Quotas           │
│                     ☐ Flush Files Immediately On Close │
│                     ☐ Migration                  │
│                     ☐ Modified File List         │
│                     ☑ Salvage                    │
│                     ☐ User Space Restrictions    │
│                                                  │
│  CREATE                                          │
│                                                  │
└─────────────────────────────────────────────────┘
```

Figure 3-16   NSS volume attributes

Compression

A feature common to both traditional and NSS volumes is **file compression**. Like other volume attributes, you can enable the Compression attribute during volume creation or later by using Remote Manager. When file compression is enabled on a volume, the server automatically compresses all files that haven't been used for a specified time. By default, the server compresses files that haven't been used for seven days if the compression will result in at least a 5% savings in disk space. In Chapter 6, you learn how to enable or disable compression selectively on files and directories.

Directory Quotas and User Space Restrictions

With traditional volumes, administrators could restrict the space used on the basis of individual users or an entire directory structure. Because managing user restrictions and directory quotas on large volumes requires extra processing time, however, user space restrictions and directory quotas are optional on NSS volumes. When creating NSS volumes, administrators can decide whether they want to restrict volume space by selecting the User Space Restrictions or Directory Quotas attributes when the volume is created or modified.

Flush Files Immediately On Close

You can select the attribute to flush files immediately during or after volume creation. This option causes a file to be saved to disk immediately after it's closed, instead of waiting for the next server disk write cycle. Writing closed files to disk immediately decreases the chance of data loss if the server has a hardware or power failure.

Migration

The Migration attribute enables the volume's data to be copied (or migrated) automatically by third-party software to offline storage media after it's inactive for a specified period. This attribute is useful for applications that require large volumes of data on an infrequent basis. For example, a company keeps an audit trail of all customer transactions made over several years. Using the Migration attribute, the transaction database could be stored on relatively inexpensive offline mass storage (such as tape or DVD) and then brought into the server's file system only when an audit of a customer's account is necessary. After the data is accessed, the files could be migrated back to the offline storage system, saving server disk space for more frequently accessed data.

Modified File List

Previous versions of the NetWare file system determined which files needed to be backed up by setting an attribute flag (described in Chapter 6) whenever a file's data changed. This system required the backup utility to scan all file names for attribute flags to determine which files to back up. When you create NSS volumes, you can select the Modified File List attribute, which causes the volume to track the names of any files that have changed since the last backup. Using this feature can speed up making a backup of large volumes.

Salvage

With NSS volumes, you can also salvage deleted files. When a file is deleted from a volume that supports salvaging files, the file name and data are kept until the space is needed for new files. When new space is needed, the space from the oldest deleted files is used first. On a large volume, it might be months before the OS reuses space from a deleted file. Deleted files can be salvaged, or undeleted, until the space is reused by the OS or the file is purged. With NSS volumes, network administrators have the option of enabling the Salvage attribute on a volume-by-volume basis when a volume is created or modified. Although being able to salvage deleted files can be important on volumes containing shared user data, the additional processing time to maintain deleted files might not be worthwhile for volumes containing system software or highly secure documents. For example, disabling the Salvage attribute on the SYS volume can save processing time when applying a new support pack, which deletes and replaces older program files with newer ones. Because salvaging deleted system files after installing a support pack can cause system errors, you might want to turn off the Salvage attribute to prevent salvaging deleted files and to improve system performance. Security can also be a reason to turn off this attribute if the volume contains confidential information that users don't want to be accessed after the file is deleted.

Traditional Volumes and Partitions

Although NSS volumes offer many advantages over traditional volumes, when you upgrade a NetWare server to NetWare 6.5, any existing volumes remain traditional. **Traditional volumes** can be converted to NSS volumes by creating an NSS volume and then transferring the data from the traditional volume to the new NSS volume. Because traditional volumes are created directly from traditional disk partitions, they don't offer the flexibility and scalability of NSS volumes, which are created from storage pools. Traditional partitions and volumes are created by using the NetWare Traditional File System option in the File System Creation Operations dialog box, as shown in Figure 3-17. With this option, you can create an empty partition or a partition that holds a single volume, as with NSS volumes (see Figure 3-18).

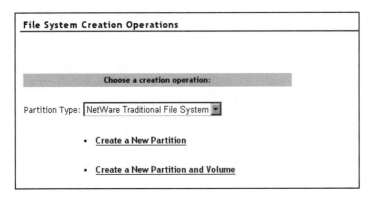

Figure 3-17   Creating a traditional volume in Remote Manager

Traditional partitions contain an additional fault-tolerance feature called a **hot fix**, which increases partition reliability by detecting bad disk blocks and then automatically redirecting the data being written to the bad disk block to another area of the disk called the reserved area. As shown in Figure 3-18, the size of the hot fix area is set automatically to approximately 2% of the partition size. The small amount of space reserved for bad blocks and the very small amount of server processing time needed to maintain hot fix blocks make hot fixes a good feature for traditional volumes.

Block Size

Data is written to disk in units called blocks. A **block** is the amount of data written to or read from disk at one time. The block size is set when a storage pool or traditional volume is created and can range from 4 KB to 64 KB. The block size on storage pools is set automatically to 4 KB when the storage pool is created, but

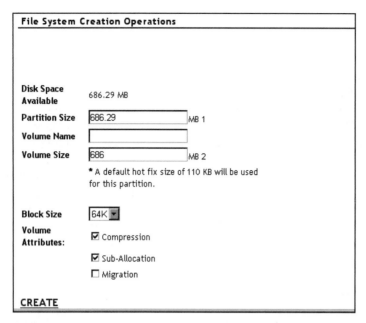

Figure 3-18   Creating a traditional partition containing a volume

you can set the block size on traditional volumes when you create them. Larger block sizes can speed up disk access because it takes fewer disk requests to read or write large files. As a result, network administrators often prefer to use large block sizes for traditional volumes containing large files, such as those in desktop publishing or other graphics applications.

Block Suballocation

In addition to customizing the block size, traditional volumes offer a suballocation feature not available with NSS volumes. Without suballocation, each block in a volume can be assigned to only one file, meaning that small files on volumes with large block sizes waste disk space; for example, if you stored a 1 KB file on a volume with 16 KB blocks, 15 KB of disk space would be wasted. This problem is solved in traditional volumes by **suballocation**, which allows storing data from multiple files in the same block by dividing the block into 512-byte suballocation units. When using suballocation, a file must always start at the beginning of a block; other files can then use the space remaining in the block as necessary. Figure 3-19 illustrates using suballocation to store three files on the CORP volume. File1 requires 2.5 KB and occupies the first five suballocation units in Block 1. File2 is 1.5 KB and occupies the first three suballocation units in Block 2. File3 requires 7 KB and uses all of Block 3, along with three suballocation units in Block 1 and three suballocation units in Block 2.

Viewing NSS Information

In Chapter 2, you learned how to use console commands to manage the server from any location. Before NetWare 6.0, viewing and managing file system information often required administrators to work from the server console with the Nwconfig utility. Starting with NetWare 6.0, administrators can create, manage, and view disk partitions, storage pools, and volumes from a computer with ConsoleOne or from a Web browser running Remote Manager. In this section, you learn how to use Remote Manager to view information on partitions, storage pools, and volumes. In "Implementing the File System" later in this chapter, you use Remote Manager to create storage pools and volumes.

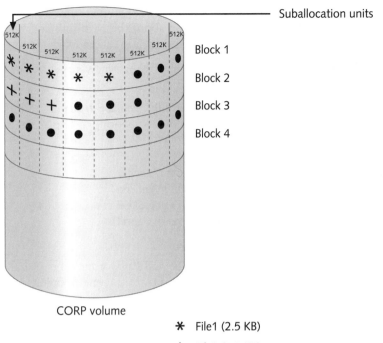

Figure 3-19   Suballocation in traditional volumes

 NOTE   Although the NSS file system can be managed with ConsoleOne or Remote Manager, Remote Manager is the utility required for the NetWare 6.5 CNA test because it runs in most Web browsers and does not require Novell Client.

As a network administrator, you need to know how the storage space of your server's file system has been used so that you can make decisions about the location of new network directories and plan for system expansion. In the following activity, you learn how to use Remote Manager to view information about your NSS partitions, pools, and volumes.

 NOTE   If you're using VMware, you can start your NetWare 6.5 virtual computer and then access it from the desktop system, as described in Appendix C. Depending on your lab environment, your instructor might perform some activities in this chapter as classroom demonstrations.

 ACTIVITY

Activity 3-1: Viewing NSS Information

Time Required: 10 minutes

Objective: Describe NSS components.

Requirements: A Web browser (Internet Explorer or Java-enabled Firefox) and access to a NetWare 6.5 server from a client computer running SUSE Linux or Windows XP as well as the following information, which is also used for subsequent activities:

IP address of the NetWare 6.5 server you're using:

_____

User name and password with administrative rights to the server:

_____

Description: Viewing information on NSS components is useful when documenting your network file system. In this activity, you use Remote Manager to view information about the partitions and storage pools on your NetWare 6.5 server.

1. If necessary, start your desktop system. If you're using VMware, start your NetWare 6.5 virtual computer.

2. Start your Web browser and enter the URL **https://IPaddress:8009** (replace *IPaddress* with the IP address of the NetWare 6.5 server you recorded in the Requirements section) to display the Login window.

> **NOTE**
> Depending on your Web browser settings, before seeing the Remote Manager Login window, some certificate or security message prompts might be displayed. If this occurs, click OK to respond to them. (If you're using SUSE Linux, you might see a prompt from the KDE Wallet System. If so, click Cancel to display the Remote Manager Login window.)

3. Enter your administrative user name and password in the Username and Password text boxes and then click the **Login** button to display the Remote Manager window, similar to the one in Figure 3-20.

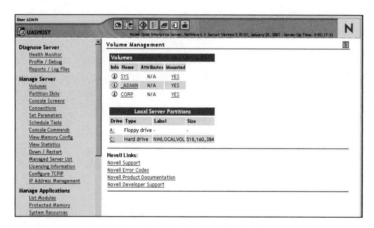

Figure 3-20   The Remote Manager window

4. Click the **Partition Disks** link under the Manage Server heading to display partition information similar to what was shown previously in Figure 3-2. Record the following information:

   Disk adapter:

   _____

   Description and size of each partition:

   _____

   Name and size of each pool:

   _____

5. Click the **SYS** volume link to display volume information and options. Record the available volume options:

   _____

6. Record the following volume information:

   Loaded name spaces:

   _____

   Compression status:

   _____

   Block size:

   _____

3

Total space: _____

Free space: _____

7. Click the **Exit** button to return to the Login window, and leave your Web browser open for the next activity.

On some OSs, clicking the Exit button might automatically close the Web browser. If this happens, you'll need to restart your Web browser.

NOTE

Directories and Subdirectories

Just as file cabinet drawers are organized by using hanging folders, NetWare volumes are divided into multiple directories and subdirectories, which enable you to keep files in a volume separated. You can also place space restrictions on directories and subdirectories to prevent certain applications or users from occupying too much of a volume's disk space. As a CNA, you must know which directories NetWare 6.5 needs and how to create directories for organizing data. In the following sections, you learn about the NetWare required directories along with suggested directory structures that you can use to meet your organization's data and software storage needs.

As shown in Table 3-2, the NetWare OS stores its required system files and utilities on the SYS volume under several directories. The most common directories administrators use include Login, Public, and System. The following sections explain how NetWare uses these three directories and where certain types of files are stored.

Table 3-2   System-created directories

Directory Name	Purpose
Apache	Contains the Apache Web Server files
Audit	Contains files for auditing system activity and Web server access
Etc	Contains configuration files for TCP/IP and the certificate server
iFolder	Contains configuration files for iFolder, covered in Chapter 10
Java	Contains Java language files
Login	Files and software available to clients before logging in to the network
Mail	Contains no files and is used for backward compatibility with earlier versions of NetWare
Ndps	Contains files used with Novell Distributed Print Services, covered in Chapter 8
Netbasic	Contains files needed to run the NETBASIC language used with certain Web applications
NetStorage	Configuration files and software for NetStorage, covered in Chapter 10
Ni	Contains configuration and software used by Certificate Services security
Novonyx	Contains Web server files for the Novonyx Web server

Table 3-2   System-created directories (continued)

Directory Name	Purpose
Nsn	Contains files used by Web Services
Odbc	Contains database and configuration files for Web Services
Perl	Contains programming software used by Web Services
Public	Contains files and software available to all users after logging in
Pvsw	Contains license file information
Queues	Used for backward compatibility with legacy NetWare print queues, described in Chapter 8
System	Contains files and software used by the NetWare operating system
Tmp	Used to store temporary files
Ucs	Contains NetWare modules used by the operating system
Webapps	Contains Web application software for NetStorage, Web Manager, and WebAccess
XTier	Contains NetWare Loadable Modules used by the operating system
Zenworks	Contains applications and configuration files for the Z.E.N.works application management system, described in Chapter 9

Login

The **Login directory** contains files and programs that can be accessed before logging in. In the past, DOS clients used the Login directory to access commands needed to log in to the network. NetWare 6.5 makes use of the Login directory to find commands needed to access or start network services from a Web browser. Three important DOS programs in the Login directory are Cx.exe, Map.exe, and Login.exe. These utilities are mostly used when logging in from or working on DOS-based computers. In addition to storing DOS commands, many network administrators like to use the Login directory to store files and programs that users often use during the startup process. When these programs release a new version, you can update them easily by simply copying the new software into the Login directory, instead of having to copy them to each computer's hard disk drive.

Public

The **Public directory** contains utility programs and files, such as the CX, MAP, and RIGHTS commands, that are available to all users after they have logged in. You use these commands in later chapters. ConsoleOne and NetWare Administrator are also stored in the Public directory.

System

The **System directory** contains NetWare OS files and utilities that are accessible only to the network administrator. Many of these system files are flagged as Hidden and System to protect them from accidental access. Only the Admin user should be given rights to the System directory to avoid the possibility of users erasing or modifying system files and using commands that affect the file server's functioning. Some network administrators move program files they don't want users to run, such as NetWare Administrator, from the Public directory to the System directory. This improves security by preventing users from using that utility to browse the eDirectory database.

Other System Directories

In addition to the three major system directories, you also find the Etc and Deleted.sav directories on the SYS volume. NetWare 6.5 creates the Etc directory to store sample files that help configure the server for the TCP/IP network protocol. To help users recover lost files, the Deleted.sav directory is created automatically on each volume and is part of NetWare's file recovery system that enables you to salvage a file even after the directory containing the file has been deleted. In "Working with Network Files" later in this chapter, you get a chance to salvage and purge deleted files.

Activity 3-2: Viewing Information on SYS Volume Directories

Time Required: 10 minutes

Objective: Identify important NetWare-created directories and describe their purposes.

Requirements: Same as Activity 3-1

Description: In this activity, you use Remote Manager to display information about the SYS volume directories on your NetWare 6.5 server.

1. If necessary, start your desktop system, start your Web browser, and enter the URL **https://IPaddress:8009** (replacing *IPaddress* with the IP address of your NetWare 6.5 server) to display the Login window.

2. Enter your administrative user name and password in the Username and Password text boxes, and then click the **Login** button to display the Remote Manager window.

3. Click the **Volumes** link under the Manage Server heading to display the Volume Management window, similar to the one in Figure 3-21.

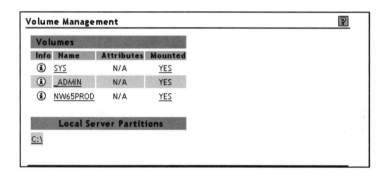

Figure 3-21   The Volume Management window

4. In the Name column, click the **SYS** volume link to display all its directories, as shown in Figure 3-22.

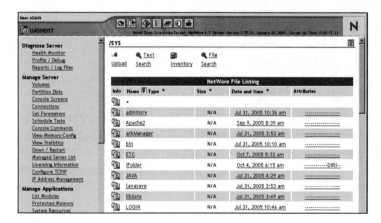

Figure 3-22   Contents of the SYS volume

5. Scroll down to the **PUBLIC** directory.

6. Click the **Info** icon next to the directory name to display information about the Public directory. Record the owner and trustee information here:

_____

7. Click the **Back to directory listing for: /SYS** option to return to the SYS volume contents window.

8. Repeat Steps 6 and 7 to record the owner and trustee information for the Login and System directories and then return to the SYS volume contents window.

_____

9. Use the following steps to record the contents of the Hosts file in the Etc directory:

   a. Click the **ETC** directory to display its contents.

   b. Scroll down and click the **hosts** file to display its contents.

 If you're using SUSE Linux Konqueror, click the **Open** button, expand the **editors** heading, click the **KWrite** application, and then click **OK** to open the Hosts file. If you're using SUSE Linux Mozilla, click **OK** and then click the **Desktop** folder. Click **Open** and then **Save** to save the Hosts file to your desktop. You can then close the Download window and open the Hosts file with the KWrite application.

   c. Record the contents here:

_____

10. Click the **Volumes** link under the Manage Server heading to display all NetWare 6.5 server volumes.

11. Click the **Exit** button to return to the Login window, and leave your Web browser open for the next activity.

As you learned in this section, the required directories are created during installation to give the NetWare OS the storage areas it needs to perform its functions. In addition to these required directories, however, your organization will need more directories to store user applications and data. You learn how to plan and implement volumes and directories for user data in the following section.

IMPLEMENTING THE NETWARE FILE SYSTEM

Now that you know the components of a network file system, the next step is to design and implement a directory structure that meets your organization's file-processing needs. Designing the directory structure involves identifying the directories and subdirectories you need for users' storage requirements and deciding where these directories should be placed in the structure. After you have defined storage requirements, you can design a directory structure in a logical, organized fashion. To set up the directory structure, you use Remote Manager to create NetWare pool and volume objects, and then create and manage the directories and files.

When designing a directory structure, you should be aware that not all network administrators agree on a single best method; instead, network administrators develop their own styles and preferences for how they like to define and arrange directories. In this section, you learn how Eric applied the concepts of file system design to the Universal AeroSpace file system. You then use Remote Manager to create storage pools and volumes on your NetWare 6.5 server.

Defining Processing Needs

In many ways, designing a file system is similar to creating a blueprint for a building. Just as a blueprint helps builders determine construction details and materials, the design of the file system structure helps network administrators allocate storage space and implement the file system on a network.

The first step in designing a file system structure is to determine storage requirements for the file services the network will be providing to users. For example, Eric met with users and administrative assistants in each UAS department to document their processing needs (see Figure 3-23).

All Users

All Universal AeroSpace users will require a home directory to store temporary files, files related to a project with which they are working, and document or spreadsheet files for which only they are responsible. All users will also need access to shared directories that they can use to exchange files with other users in the corporation. The organization has established a standard set of word processing forms for a variety of uses, including purchase orders, outside correspondence, and internal memos. These standard forms and templates need to be easily accessible by all users.

All Universal AeroSpace users will need access to Microsoft Office software. As a result, the installation and program files for Microsoft Office and Windows need to be placed in directories available to all computers. In addition, a temporary directory should also be reserved for storage of temporary files created by certain applications.

Currently, Universal AeroSpace is hiring an Internet service provider to publish the corporation's Web site information. Kellie Thiele is responsible for the Web site and currently has all files on her computer. The Web site files should be moved from Kellie's computer and placed on the CORP volume. In the future, this will facilitate Eric's plans to move the Web site to Universal AeroSpace's own Web server.

Universal AeroSpace is replacing its old inventory system with a Windows-based package that allows shared access by users throughout the company. Terry Blackwell is currently responsible for auditing the inventory database, adding new parts, and making weekly inventory reports for the Marketing and Manufacturing departments. The new inventory package will enable the users in the Shipping and Receiving areas to enter data as well as allow the Marketing Department to enter new orders and track production.

Engineering and Manufacturing

The CAD application software used by the Engineering Department is installed on each computer, but the CAD drawing files for the two NASA projects and the current aircraft design projects for Boeing need to be shared by multiple users and should be stored in separate directories on the network. The Engineering Department also plans to use the network to pass CAD files between computers as well as provide shared access to document and spreadsheet files. In addition, some drawing files need to be made available for the Desktop Publishing Department to use when creating instruction manuals. At this time, the file system for Engineering will be stored on the CORP volume. However, in the near future, Eric wants to install a separate Engineering server and move all Engineering and Manufacturing data from the CORP volume to the Engineering server.

The Manufacturing Department plans to install a network-based Requirements Planning System (RPS) to plan raw material purchases based on projected shipments. Russ Pence will be responsible for maintaining the system, but Kari Means in Engineering, as well as the users in the Marketing Department, will need to be able to update the RPS database with sales projections and new requirements based on product design.

As the network administrator, you will need a work area to store software and other files with which you are working. In addition, you have several software utilities that you would like to place on the network so that you can access them from any client computer.

Figure 3-23 Sample Universal AeroSpace processing needs

The next step is to use the information you have collected to establish capacity needs for your NetWare file system. Figure 3-24 shows a sample of the Storage Requirements Form Eric created from the information he collected.

Storage Requirements Form

Created by: Eric Kenton

Date:

Organization: Universal AeroSpace

Workgroups:

Workgroup Name	Members
Admin	David Heise, Lynn Dai, Maria Frias
Accounting	Terry Blackwell, George Perez, Amy Pan
Marketing	Laura Hiller, Michael Horowitz, Darrell Minick
Desktop Publishing	Diana Brady, Julie Damrau
Engineering	Kari Means, Lianne Jarka, Tony Rucci, Paul Alm, Bradley Dahl
Manufacturing (Mfg)	Russ Pence, Receiving station, Shipping station
Information Technology (IT)	Kellie Thiele, You, Luke McMann, Eric Kenton

Directories:

Directory Description	Type	Users	Capacity	Directory Name
Home directory for each user	Private data	All staff	.5 GB each = 10 GB	(User login name)
General word-processing (WP) forms and templates	Shared WP data	All users	500 MB	Forms
Shared documents	Shared data	All users	1 GB	Shared
Windows applications	Master software for installation	All users	3 GB	Apps
Inventory system	Vertical application package	Business, Marketing, and Engineering	1 GB	Inventory
Engineering	Software and files	Engineering	18 GB	Engineer
Engineering shared data	Shared documents and drawings	Engineering and Mfg	5 GB	Shared
Information Technology	Software and files	IT	2 GB	IT
Utilities	Software utilities	IT	500 MB	Utility
NASA ISS project	Shared CAD drawings	Engineering	5 GB	ISS
NASA Rover project	Shared CAD drawings	Engineering	5 GB	Rover
Aircraft	Shared CAD drawings	Engineering	5 GB	Aircraft
Web	Web site files	Kellie Thiele and Julie Damrau	1 GB	Web
CAD software	Installation files	Engineering	1 GB	Cad
RPS	RPS software	Russ Pence and Kari Means	1 GB	RPS
Temporary	Temporary files needed by certain applications	All users	1 GB	Temp
Desktop themes	Shared Windows data	All users	1 GB	Desktop
Department shared directories	Shared files for each department	All department users	5 GB each	Shared
Management data	User home directories and data for Mgmt department	Mgmt department users	10 GB	Mgmt
Manufacturing data	Directory structure for Mfg shared data	Mfg and Engineering departments	10 GB	MfgData

Figure 3-24   Sample Universal AeroSpace storage needs

Planning and Implementing NetWare Volumes

After identifying storage needs, the next step is to determine what volumes are needed and what their capacities should be. To avoid filling up the SYS volume and causing system problems, generally you should plan to place user data and applications on separate volumes. The SYS volume should be used only for NetWare OS files and possibly third-party software, such as virus detection and backup and recovery utilities. To reserve the SYS volume for OS files, many network administrators prefer to use at least two volumes in their network's file structure. When using multiple volumes, a network administrator creates one or more data volumes to store the organization's data files, print queues, and applications. By placing the organization's data files and applications on separate volumes, the administrator can ensure that free space is always available on the SYS volume for NetWare's use. As a network administrator, you should use the following Novell guidelines for planning NetWare volume usage:

- Reserve the SYS volume for NetWare OS files.

- Create one or more additional volumes for application and data files.

- Consider placing files from computers that support special name formats, such as Macintosh or UNIX, on separate volumes.

Like many other network administrators, Eric decided to separate the SYS volume from the organization's data storage by creating a CORP volume for company data. A separate CORP volume ensures adequate free space on the SYS volume for system functions. This separate volume also makes it possible to perform maintenance and backup tasks on company data without taking the SYS volume offline, which is important because taking the SYS volume offline prevents access to necessary system software and makes the server unavailable for network use.

Creating NSS Pools and Volumes

After the storage needs for the network file system were defined, Eric's next step was to create the NSS CORP volume. Because NSS volumes exist within storage pools, creating the NSS CORP volume also involves creating a new disk partition and storage pool. In the following activity, you learn how to create the necessary NSS file system objects.

Activity 3-3: Creating an NSS Storage Pool and Volume

Time Required: 10 minutes

Objective: Create NSS storage pools and volumes.

Requirements: Same as Activity 3-1; if you're using a shared classroom server, your instructor will supply the following information:

Assigned disk drive:

_____

Pool size:

_____

Pool name:

_____

Volume name:

_____

Description: To help evaluate the NetWare 6.5 server file system, Eric has asked you to create a CORP volume similar to the one he's using on the existing network. In this activity, you use Remote Manager to create an NSS storage pool and associated CORP volume. If you're sharing a server with other students, your pool and volume names should start with your assigned student number.

1. If necessary, start your desktop system, start your Web browser, and enter the URL **https://*IPaddress*:8009** (replacing *IPaddress* with the IP address of your NetWare 6.5 server) to display the Login window.

2. Enter your administrative user name and password, and then click the **Login** button to display the Remote Manager window.

3. Click the **Partition Disks** link under the Manage Server heading to display the Partition Disks window, similar to the one shown previously in Figure 3-2. Record your server's available disk drives:

   _____

4. Click the **Create** option next to the free space on your assigned disk drive to display the Choose a creation operation window (shown previously in Figure 3-8).

5. Click **Create a New Pool and Volume** to display the NSS Volume Create window, similar to the one shown previously in Figure 3-10.

6. Enter a name for your storage pool and volume in the Pool Name and Volume Name text boxes. (Use the names your instructor assigned.)

7. Click to select the **Directory Quotas** and **User Space Restrictions** check boxes. Record all the selected options:

   _____

8. Click **CREATE** and then click **OK** to create the new pool and volume and return to the Partition Disks window.

9. Click the **Exit** button to close Remote Manager and return to the Login window. Leave the Login window open for the next activity.

Creating Traditional Volumes

Traditional partitions and volumes sometimes best meet the storage needs of certain applications. For example, users in the UAS Engineering Department often share large CAD design files. Because of the size of these files, Eric determined that a larger block size would help increase processing speed by reducing the number of disk reads required to load a CAD file. To allow a larger block size, he decided to create a NetWare traditional volume to share these large CAD files. In the following activity, you learn how to use Remote Manager to create a traditional partition and volume.

Activity 3-4: Creating Traditional Partitions and Volumes

Time Required: 10 minutes

Objective: Create traditional partitions and volumes.

Requirements: Same as Activity 3-3. In addition, if you're using a shared classroom server, your instructor will assign a disk drive along with a volume name and size. (If you're using a dedicated server, use the volume name SOURCE with a size of at least 10 MB.) Record this information here:

Assigned disk drive:

_____

Traditional volume name:

_____

Traditional volume size:

_____

Description: To help evaluate the NetWare 6.5 server file system, Eric has asked you to create a sample traditional volume named CAD that will have a block size of 32 KB. In this activity, you learn how to create a traditional pool and volume. If you're working on a shared server, your volume name should be preceded by your assigned student number.

1. If necessary, start Remote Manager.

2. Log in to Remote Manager with your administrative user name and password.

3. Click the **Partition Disks** link under the Manage Server heading to display the Partition Disks window.

4. Click the **Create** option next to the free space on your assigned disk drive to display the Choose a creation operation window.

5. Click the **Partition Type** list arrow, and then click the **NetWare Traditional File System** option (shown previously in Figure 3-17).

6. Click the **Create a New Partition and Volume** option to display the traditional partition and volume information shown previously in Figure 3-18.

7. Enter your assigned volume name and size. Record the default block size and attributes here:

   _____

8. Click the **Block Size** list arrow, and click **32K** in the list of options. Click **CREATE** and then click **OK** to create the traditional volume and return to the Partition Disks window.

9. Scroll down and verify that your new traditional partition and volume are created. Explain how you can identify your new partition as a traditional partition:

   _____

10. Click the **Exit** button, and leave the Login window open for the next activity.

Planning the Directory Structure

After creating the necessary volumes, the next task in setting up the file system is to plan the directory structure for each volume. The network administrator creates a directory structure to organize data and software on the file server. As a CNA, you should be aware of the three basic types of directories that Novell suggests should be part of an organization's file system:

- Application directories
- Shared directories
- User home directories

For example, Figure 3-25 shows the volume structure Eric used for the file system on the Universal AeroSpace CORP volume. This volume structure provides storage areas for application, shared, and user data, as described in the following sections.

Application Directories

Application directories hold installation files needed to install or run software on users' computers. For example, Figure 3-25 shows that Eric included an application directory named Apps in the CORP volume structure to store software files for a number of network applications.

Shared Directories

One of the benefits of using a network is access to shared files. As a CNA, you'll need to establish network directories so that users can work with common files and documents. Files stored in **shared directories** are generally available to only one user at a time, so having a file accessed simultaneously by multiple users requires database software written to prevent one user's changes from overwriting another user's changes. At first, you might think that storing data on the server makes it less secure. Actually, with proper security, data stored on the server is more secure than on a user's local computer, where someone else could gain access to his or her computer. In Chapter 6, you learn how to use file system security to ensure that only authorized users have access to network data.

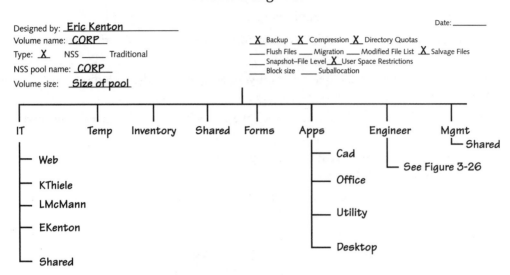

Figure 3-25 A sample Universal AeroSpace directory structure

Notice in Figure 3-25 that Eric identified Shared directories for each department in addition to a Shared directory for the entire company. Although it would be possible to get along with only one shared directory for the entire company, multiple directories help keep the files separate, making it easier for users to find the files they need. Having separate directories also increases security; users in the Engineering Department, for example, don't have access to budget files or other information that doesn't affect them.

User Home Directories

Each user needs his or her own **home directory** for storing files and documents. Home directories, from the earliest versions of NetWare, solved the problem of limited or no local file storage on the client computer. Hard drives were simply too expensive. Today, home directories solve a much bigger problem: backup and fault tolerance. Users seldom have convenient means of backing up their own local work files. Home directories can help if users take advantage of them and administrators perform backups routinely. When planning your disk storage needs, you should allow space for all users to store personal projects and files. Generally, users aren't given access to files in other users' home directories; instead, files needed by multiple users should be stored in separate shared directories. Depending on your directory structure, user home directories can be located within a departmental structure, as shown in Figure 3-25, or all user home directories can be located within a single parent directory, as described in the following section.

Documenting a Directory Structure

When documenting the directory structure for a data volume, drawing all directories and subdirectories on one sheet of paper can be difficult. To help document the UAS directory structure for the CORP volume, Eric used two different design forms. As shown in Figure 3-25, a Volume Design Form was used to document all directories under the root of the volume as well as directories containing only a few subdirectories. In addition to showing the volume's first level of directories, this form contains fields for NSS attributes and maximum capacity. You might also want to show subdirectories for directories that have a simple structure. Eric placed all directories containing files shared by multiple departments, such as Forms and Apps, under the root of the CORP volume. The departmental directories will be used to store user home directories and files and applications unique to each department.

For more complex directory structures, such as the Engineering Department, Eric used a separate Directory Design Form (see Figure 3-26) to show all subdirectories in that directory structure. Using a separate form gives you more room to diagram the directory structure and make changes without affecting other directory structure designs.

Directory Design Form

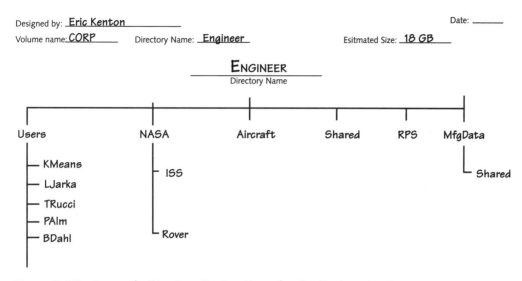

Figure 3-26 A sample Directory Design Form for the Engineering Department

The directory structure Eric used is referred to as a **departmental structure** because the user home directories, shared directories, and applications are located within the departments that control them. Directories containing files available to all users, such as Forms and Inventory, are located at the root of the volume. Shared directories are located within each department's directory to provide separate shared file access for all users in the department. The Shared directory off the root of the CORP volume is available so that users in all departments can exchange files or work on common projects. For example, the Engineering Department can use the CORP:Shared directory to save files the Desktop Publishing and Sales employees need to prepare documentation and presentations.

Another way to organize directories on a volume is by application rather than by department. Figure 3-27 shows an example of how the directories for Universal AeroSpace might be organized in an application-oriented structure.

Notice that in an **application-oriented structure**, all user home directories are placed under a common directory called Users. Shared directories can then be grouped according to their use, and applications can be placed in separate directories under the root of the volume. The advantage of an application-oriented structure is that it's fairly shallow, making it easier to locate files without going through several layers of directories. In larger directory structures, however, this shallow nature can actually be a disadvantage, making it difficult to know which departments use which directories. When using an application-oriented structure, a network administrator needs to make more trustee assignments because a user's rights don't flow automatically into other directories. In Chapter 6, you learn how to make trustee assignments that grant users rights to the directory structure.

The organization method you select for a directory structure depends on personal preference, the organization's size, and the way users access data. Generally, smaller network file systems are easier to organize by using an application-oriented structure because it keeps the design simple and easy to use. With larger file systems that encompass several departments and many data directories, often a departmental structure makes it easier to maintain security and locate data. In some cases, you might find that a combination of both structures works the best. No matter what design method you use, a good rule of thumb is not to exceed three subdirectory layers, with no more than 20 subdirectories in any one directory (which makes it easier to view all directories onscreen at the same time).

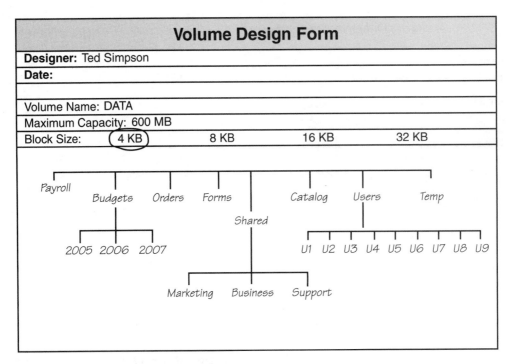

Figure 3-27   An application-oriented directory structure

Implementing the Directory Structure

After creating volumes and designing directory structures, you're ready to start creating the directories shown on your volume and directory design forms. The directory structure can be created by using the local client computer's OS or by using Remote Manager. For example, from a client computer running Windows XP, you can map a drive to the NetWare volume and then create the network directory structure in My Computer or Windows Explorer, just as on a local hard drive. You can also use ConsoleOne or Remote Manager to create and work with the network directory structure. An advantage of Remote Manager is that it conforms to Novell's OneNet vision by allowing you to manage the file system from any client system or from a remote location.

Implementing the directory structure involves two main tasks: creating directories and subdirectories and setting directory space limitations with directory quotas. Because the Novell CNA exam requires you to know how to perform file system functions from Remote Manager, in the following activities you use this utility to create some of the Universal AeroSpace directories shown in Figure 3-25 and then set directory quotas on these directories.

Activity 3-5: Creating a Directory Structure with Remote Manager

Time Required: 10 minutes

Objective: Create directories with Remote Manager.

Requirements: Same as Activity 3-1

Description: Eric wants you to implement a directory structure on the NetWare 6.5 server for evaluation purposes. He would like the directory structure to match the directory structure on the existing system. In this activity, you use Remote Manager to create part of the Universal AeroSpace directory structure shown in Figure 3-25.

1. If necessary, start Remote Manager using the IP address of your assigned NetWare 6.5 server.

2. Log in with your administrative user name and password.

3. Click the **Volumes** link under the Manage Server heading to display the Volume Management window.

4. If your new volume is not mounted, click **NO** in the Mounted column for your volume name. The "NO" should change to "YES" when the volume is mounted.

5. Click your assigned volume to display the NetWare File Listing window, similar to the one in Figure 3-28.

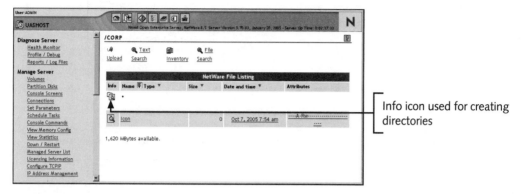

Info icon used for creating directories

Figure 3-28   The NetWare File Listing window

6. Follow these steps to create the Apps directory in the root of the volume:

   a. Click the **Info** icon in the first row of the NetWare File Listing table to display the Directory entry information window, similar to the one in Figure 3-29.

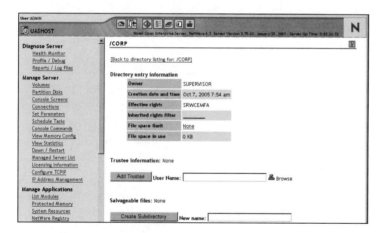

Figure 3-29   The Directory entry information window

   b. Scroll down and enter **Apps** in the New name text box (next to the Create Subdirectory button) to add the Apps directory to the NetWare File Listing window. Click the **Create Subdirectory** button to create the new subdirectory

7. Repeat Step 6 to create the **IT** and **Forms** directories.

8. Click the **Apps** directory to display its contents (see Figure 3-30).

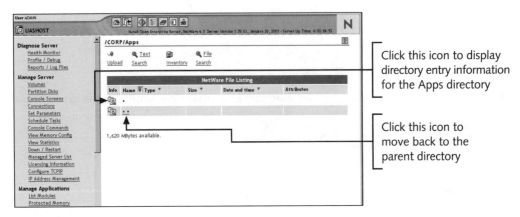

Figure 3-30   The Apps directory content

9. Create the Cad subdirectory within the Apps directory structure by following these steps:

   a. Click the **Info** icon in the first row of the NetWare File Listing table to display the Directory entry information window for the Apps directory (refer to Figure 3-30).

   b. List the options available for the Apps directory:

   _____

   c. Enter the name **Cad** in the New name text box, and click the **Create Subdirectory** button to add this subdirectory to the Apps structure.

10. Repeat Step 9 to create the **Office**, **Utility**, and **Desktop** subdirectories under the Apps directory.

11. Click the **..** link to return to the root of your volume, and stay logged in for the next activity.

Activity 3-6: Implementing Directory Quotas

Time Required: 10 minutes

Objective: Use Remote Manager to set directory quotas.

Requirements: Successful completion of Activity 3-5

Description: Eric wants you to implement a directory quota on the volume to prevent directories from exceeding their planned sizes. In this activity, you use Remote Manager to set directory quotas on the directories you created in Activity 3-5.

1. If necessary, follow Steps 1 to 3 in Activity 3-5 to start Remote Manager and open the Volume Management window.

2. Set a directory quota of 4 GB for the IT directory by following these steps:

   a. If necessary, click your assigned volume to display the NetWare File Listing window.

   b. Click the **Info** icon next to the IT directory to display the Directory entry information window.

   c. Next to the File space limit text box, click **None** to display the Directory Space Quota window.

   d. Enter **4000000** in the Set Space Restriction in KB text box, and then click the **Set Space Restriction** button to set the file space limit.

   e. Click the **Back to directory listing for** link to return to the root of your assigned volume.

3. Use the procedure in Step 2 to set a directory quota of 500 MB (500000 KB) for the Forms directory. Record the value you enter for the space restriction:

   _____

4. Click the **Exit** button to log out of Remote Manager, and close your Web browser.

ACCESSING THE NETWARE FILE SYSTEM

As described in Chapter 1, network services need both client and server software components to operate. The client software component must work closely with the local OS and the server to provide access to network services. The client software formats a request and then uses a network protocol to send that request to a server. A service running on the server processes the request and then sends the results back to the client. As shown in Figure 3-31, each type of network OS requires its own client to be loaded on the computer to communicate with services running on the server. To access services on Windows servers, Microsoft clients use the Common Interface File System (CIFS) to format service requests. Before NetWare 6.0, accessing file services on NetWare servers required the computer to have Novell Client to format requests with NetWare Core Protocol (NCP). UNIX/Linux clients use the Network File System (NFS) protocol to access files, and Macintosh clients use AppleTalk Filing Protocol (AFP) to access file services on other Macintosh computers. Web browsers are clients that use the HTTP and WebDAV protocols to access resources and services running on Web servers.

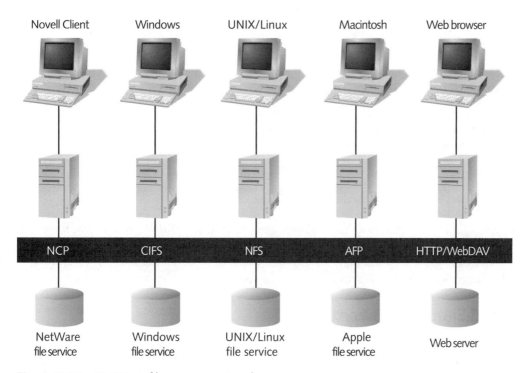

Figure 3-31   NetWare file access protocols

Native File Access Pack

An important part of Novell's OneNet strategy is to provide network services that are compatible with the variety of clients shown in Figure 3-31. Although previous versions of NetWare depended on the Novell client being installed on client computers, NetWare 6.5 provides direct support for Web browser clients and includes Novell's Native File Access Pack (NFAP), which enables NetWare 6.5 servers to process file service requests formatted by non-Novell clients, such as Microsoft, Apple, and Linux. With multiple client alternatives available for accessing NetWare servers, network administrators can select a client that best suits the needs of the user's computer environment and applications. Table 3-3 lists clients that can be used with Windows to access NetWare servers.

Table 3-3   NetWare client options

Client	Advantages	Disadvantages
Web client	Allows access to NetWare services and administrative tasks from any computer attached to the Internet; does not require a Novell client on the computer.	Does not yet provide access to all NetWare services and resources.
Microsoft client	Included with Windows XP and Windows 2000 Professional; users view the NetWare server in the same way as other Windows servers.	Requires NFAP simple passwords to be configured on the NetWare 6.5 server; uses different passwords that aren't as secure as Novell Client passwords. Users might have to maintain multiple passwords. Does not allow access to certain NetWare services and administrative utilities.
Microsoft Net-Ware client	Available as an option on Windows XP and Windows 2000 Professional, making it easy to install and configure. Less administrative overhead required to maintain. Uses the same Novell eDirectory user names and passwords as the Novell client.	Does not allow access to certain NetWare services and administrative utilities. Requires IPX/SPX on the NetWare server.
Novell Client	Provides access to all NetWare services and administrative utilities.	Requires more administrative time to install and maintain; might conflict with some Windows features.

Accessing certain eDirectory applications from a Windows client still requires Novell Client to be installed on the computer. Because eDirectory services are necessary to ensure security and manage certain eDirectory objects and services, Novell Client still plays an important role in a Novell network. In Chapter 4, you learn how to install and configure Novell Client on Windows computers.

User Names and Simple Passwords

As described previously, Open Enterprise Server (OES) includes NFAP to allow Windows, Macintosh, and Linux clients to access the NetWare server without having Novell Client installed. NFAP is an important feature because many organizations want to minimize software complexity on user computers. The downside to using a computer's native client protocol is that certain NetWare features aren't available, such as the additional security built in to Novell Client's eDirectory password encryption. When a client using one of the NFAP protocols attempts to connect to a NetWare 6.5 server, the user is asked to enter a user name and password. The user name entered must be a valid user account in eDirectory, as described in Chapters 4 and 5. NFAP then searches the eDirectory tree for the user account by using the Ctxs.cfg search file in the SYS:Etc directory. In Chapter 4, you learn how to update this search file with the locations of your user accounts. When a client computer uses NFAP to access a NetWare 6.5 OES server, it uses its own password encryption algorithm to secure the password. This requires eDirectory to maintain two passwords: one for Novell Client encryption and another for native client protocols, called a "simple password" to differentiate it from the more secure eDirectory password. NetWare stores the simple password separately from the eDirectory password, using a different encryption system that's compatible with the computer's native client.

Activity 3-7: Changing Simple Passwords

ACTIVITY

Time Required: 10 minutes

Objective: Change simple passwords.

Requirements: The location of your Admin user name (if you're using a dedicated server, it's in your server's UAS Organization; if you're using a shared classroom server, your assigned ##Admin user name and ##UAS container are in the CLASS Organization)

> **NOTE**
> If you're using SUSE Linux with the Mozilla Web browser, you might see a message informing you that the Web browser isn't supported by this version of iManager; however, it won't interfere with performing the activity.

Description: To simplify installation and maintenance, Eric wants computers in the UAS Manufacturing Department to access the NetWare 6.5 server with only the Microsoft client. Eric asks you to test NFAP on the NetWare 6.5 server to help determine the feasibility of using only the Microsoft client on these computers. Before testing NFAP, you need to enable the simple password on your Admin user account. In this activity, you use iManager to enable simple passwords in your UAS container.

1. Start your Web browser, enter the URL **https://IPaddress/nps/iManager.html** (*IPaddress* represents the IP address of your NetWare 6.5 server), and then press **Enter** to open the iManager Login window.

2. Enter your administrative user name and password, and then click the **Login** button to display the iManager main window shown in Figure 3-32. (If you see a "The Secret Store is currently locked" message, enter your administrative password in the Old Password text box and click **Continue**. If this message appears a second time, click **Close**.)

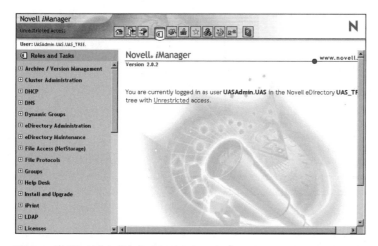

Figure 3-32   The iManager main window

3. Scroll down the Roles and Tasks pane and then click to expand **NMAS**.

4. Click the **NMAS Login Methods** link to open the NMAS Login Methods window shown in Figure 3-33.

5. View the current status of your NMAS login configuration container by following these steps:

   a. In the Select a login method drop-down list, click the **Simple Password** option.

   b. Click the **View Login Method Properties** button to display the Simple Password configuration window. Record the supported platforms on the following lines:

   _____

   _____

   _____

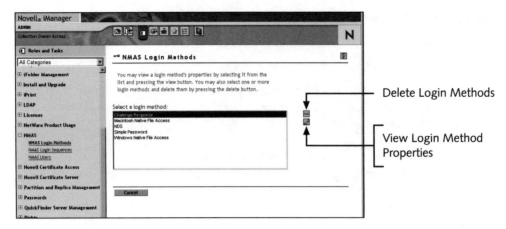

Figure 3-33 The NMAS Login Methods window

6. Follow these steps to enable simple passwords on your Admin account:

   a. Click the **NMAS Users** link to display the Select user window.

   b. Click the **Object Selector** button, click your **Admin** account, and then click **OK** to display the NMAS User window, similar to the one in Figure 3-34.

Figure 3-34 The NMAS User window

   c. Click the **Simple Password** option and then enter a new password in both the Set simple password and Confirm simple password text boxes.

   d. Click **OK** to return to the iManager main window.

7. Click the **Exit** button to end your iManager session. Your Admin user and any new users you create should now be able to log in from the Microsoft or Novell client with the same password.

Using the Common Interface File System (CIFS) Client

The Microsoft client is needed to access shared resources and services from other Windows based computers. The Microsoft client is optional on Windows 9x but is installed automatically with Windows 2000 and XP. Because the Microsoft client is so common on desktop computers, it's a natural choice for accessing NetWare file services on computers that don't need additional Novell services. For example, in the UAS network, the computers in the Shipping and Receiving departments need only file and print services to access inventory files on the NetWare server and to print shipping labels. As a result, Eric decided to simplify these computers' configuration by using only the Microsoft client.

As you learned in Chapter 1, in peer-to-peer networks, Windows servers are organized into workgroups. For Microsoft clients to access the NetWare server, NFAP makes the NetWare 6.5 server appear to the Windows client as another Windows server in a workgroup. During installation, a Microsoft server name and workgroup are assigned automatically to the NetWare 6.5 server along with the volumes to be shared with Microsoft clients. The default method is to share all volumes and place the NetWare server in the WORKGROUP workgroup, using a Microsoft server name that includes the NetWare server name followed by an underscore character and a "W." For example, the Microsoft server name for UASHOST is UASHOST_W. The default CIFS parameters can be changed by using ConsoleOne as described in Chapter 6.

A Windows user can access data volumes on the NetWare server by browsing the network in Windows Explorer or entering the Universal Naming Convention (UNC) path for the data volume. A **path** defines the location of an object, such as a file or directory, by listing the components that lead to the object. For example, a complete path to a file often consists of the server name, volume name, and directory name. A UNC path has two backslashes preceding the server name and a backslash separating the server and shared volume name. For example, the name for the CORP volume on the UASHOST_W server is \\UASHOST_W\CORP. In Activity 3-8, you use a UNC path to map a drive to the UASHOST_W server's CORP volume.

When a computer running a Microsoft client attempts to access a NetWare server running NFAP, the Windows client submits its local user name and password to the NetWare server in the same way it would attempt to log on to a Microsoft server. Access is granted if the user account and password exist on the NetWare server. If the user account and password on the NetWare server don't match the user account and password for logging on to the Microsoft client, an Enter Network Password dialog box opens, prompting the user to enter a user name and password for the UASHOST_W server.

Activity 3-8: Accessing the NetWare File System from Windows

Time Required: 10 minutes

Objective: Map network drives from a Windows XP client computer.

Requirements: A Windows XP computer and a Windows XP local user name and password in addition to the NetWare information obtained for Activity 3-1

Description: Eric wants you to test the network file system by mapping a drive to the CORP volume and then copying files to the Apps directory.

1. If necessary, start your Windows XP computer and log on to the local computer with your assigned local user name and password.

2. Follow these steps to map a network drive to your assigned volume:

   a. Open Windows Explorer.

   b. Right-click **My Computer** and then click **Map Network Drive** to open the Map Network Drive dialog box.

   c. Record the default drive letter:

   _____

   d. Click the **Browse** button next to the Folder text box to open the Browse For Folder dialog box.

   e. If necessary, click to expand **Entire Network** and **Microsoft Windows Network**.

    f. Click to expand the workgroup named **WORKGROUP**.

    g. Right-click your assigned server name, and then click **Explore** to open the Connect to UASHOST-W dialog box.

    h. Enter your assigned user name and password, and then click **OK** to log in to the server.

    i. Right-click your assigned server, and then click **Expand** to display the available volumes.

    j. Click your assigned volume name, and then click **OK** to place the network path in the Folder text box. Record the contents of the Folder text box:

    _____

    k. Click to clear the **Reconnect at login** check box.

    l. Click **Finish** to map the network drive.

3. Copy the **Mspaint.exe** file from the Windows\System32 directory to your **Apps** directory.

4. Create the following text files in your Forms directory (refreshing the screen after creating each file): Expense.doc, Absentee.txt, Junk.txt, and Salvage.txt.

5. Delete the **Salvage.txt** file.

6. Close all windows, and stay logged on for the next activity.

Using the AppleTalk Filing Protocol (AFP) Client

With NFAP installed and passwords configured, your NetWare 6.5 Open Enterprise server is ready to allow Macintosh users to access the NetWare file system. They can use the familiar Chooser application or the Go menu to view network files and even create aliases. With NFAP, Macintosh users can open, copy, move, save, and delete files from the NetWare file system just as they can with any local Macintosh drive. The AFP service is started automatically, but you can use the AFPSTOP and AFPSTART commands from the NetWare server console to stop and start the service as necessary. The same Ctxf.cfg search file used with Windows is also used to find Macintosh user names in eDirectory. You can also rename NetWare volumes so that they appear with a different name for Macintosh users. To rename a NetWare volume, you can follow these steps:

EXAMPLE

1. Create a file named Afpvol.cfg in the SYS:Etc directory of the NetWare server containing the volume you want to have a special Macintosh name.

2. For each volume you want to rename, enter the volume's current name along with the Macintosh name in quotes. For example, to name the CORP volume "Corporation data," enter the following line in the Afpvol.cfg file:

```
Prv-serv1.corp "Corporation data"
```

3. Save the Afpvol.cfg file.

Macintosh users can use the Chooser application to access NetWare files and directories as needed or create an alias with the following steps:

EXAMPLE

1. In Mac OS 8 or 9, click the Apple menu. Click Chooser, AppleTalk, Server IP Address. In Mac OS X, click Go, Connect to Server.

2. Specify the IP address or DNS name of the NetWare server, and then click Connect.

3. When prompted, enter a valid eDirectory user name.

4. Enter the simple password assigned to the eDirectory user name, and then click Connect.

5. Select a volume to be mounted on the desktop.

Files on the NetWare volume can then be accessed as though they were on a Macintosh server. If you want to create a perpetual link to the volume, create an alias.

Using the Network File System (NFS) Client

Although NFS support is installed and started as part of the NetWare 6.5 installation, accessing the NetWare file system from Linux requires a few more steps than Windows or Macintosh. An important component of the NFS file system is the NFS server, which makes directories on the local system available to the network. NFS running on the NetWare server can be stopped and started from the NetWare server console with the NFSSTOP and NFSSTART commands. Before a NetWare directory can be accessed from Linux clients, it needs to be exported to the NFS server software running on your NetWare 6.5 server. You can use iManager to export a NetWare volume to the NFS server by performing the following steps:

EXAMPLE

1. Start iManager and log in with a user name that has administrative rights.
2. Expand the File Protocols heading and click NFS.
3. Click the Export button to open the Export Options window.
4. In the Path text box, enter the path to be exported, using forward slashes to separate directory names. (For example, to export the shared directory in the IT structure, enter /Data/IT/Shared.)
5. In the Access Control text box, specify Independent or NetWare mode. Independent mode means that NetWare and NFS rights are managed separately. NetWare mode means that rights are managed from NetWare and mapped to NFS accordingly. You learn about NetWare file access rights in Chapter 6 and NFS permissions in Chapter 13.
6. Use the Global permissions field to specify what permissions will be granted to all trusted computers by default.
7. In the Trusted Host and Access Permissions table, specify the NFS host you want to make a trusted host for the exported path and the rights to be granted to the export host.

After a directory has been exported, it can be mounted on the Linux computer by following these steps from the Linux system:

EXAMPLE

1. Use the mkdir command to create a directory for storing the NetWare 6.5 NFS export.
2. Use the mount command to link the new directory to the NetWare 6.5 Open Enterprise Server export.
3. Access the NetWare exported directory from Linux with standard Linux commands (described in Chapter 13).

NOTE

In Chapter 13, you export and mount a NetWare directory on a Linux system.

Web Browser Clients

Web browsers are clients that use the HTTP and WebDAV protocols to make requests to Web servers. Today many Internet applications are written to provide access to data and services from Web browsers. As you have learned, an important part of Novell's OneNet strategy is to allow administrators and users to use their Web browsers as clients to manage the network and access file and print services. In addition to Remote Manager, you learn about a number of Web-enabled applications, including iManager, iFolder, NetStorage, and iPrint, that are included with NetWare 6.5. In the following section, you learn how to use iManager to enable Novell NFAP passwords. In Chapters 4 and 5, you use iManager to help set up and manage the eDirectory tree for your version of the UAS network. In Chapter 10, you learn how to configure iFolder so that users can access their files from any location by using Web browsers.

Working with Network Files

Files are used to store data in the network file system in much the same way they're used to store data and software on your local disk drives. Planning the location of files on network volumes is an essential part of organizing the file system. Although files can exist on the root of a volume, placing them in directories and subdirectories results in a more organized file system and increases file system security, as described in Chapter 6.

NetWare stores information about each file in the **directory entry table (DET)** located at the beginning of each volume. In addition to the file's name and storage location, NetWare includes such information as owner, size, creation dates, access dates, trustee assignments, and attributes. By default, the file owner is the user who creates the file. By keeping track of file owner and size information, NetWare enables network administrators to limit disk space usage on a user-by-user basis. Network administrators also need creation and access dates to perform such functions as listing files that haven't been accessed for a specified period.

Salvaging Deleted Files

As discussed previously, one strength of NetWare's file system is that files can be recovered reliably even after they have been deleted for a long time. When a file is deleted, NetWare does not overwrite its space until space from all previously deleted files has been reused. Deleted files are kept track of within the directory they were deleted from and can be salvaged from their parent directory. As a result, a user can often recover deleted files from the parent directory many months after the file has been deleted. Even if the entire directory structure that contained the file is deleted, the deleted files are still kept track of and can be recovered from the Deleted.sav directory by the network administrator.

Standard users do not have rights to salvage files from the Deleted.sav directory. Only the network administrator has this right by default.

For security reasons or for OS efficiency, however, sometimes you want to give deleted file space back to the OS immediately for reuse—a process called purging files. When files are purged, NetWare reclaims their space and they can no longer be recovered. As a result, purging deleted files can be important for security purposes because it prevents the deleted files from being salvaged. If purged files exist on an NSS volume and the Salvage attribute, described earlier in this chapter, is not enabled, purged files are overwritten with random patterns of characters to help make sure the deleted data can't be accessed or viewed. Another advantage of purging files is to make space immediately available to the NetWare server to reuse. Purging not only increases NetWare's efficiency, but also prevents other possibly valuable files from being reused as quickly. For example, say a user recently installed a software package in the Apps directory and then decided to delete the software directory and place it on her local computer. Purging files in the Apps directory makes any disk space used by the application files immediately available for other purposes. In the following activity, you practice using Remote Manager to work with network files.

Activity 3-9: Deleting and Salvaging Network Files in Remote Manager

Time Required: 10 minutes

Objective: Manage network files with Remote Manager.

Requirements: A Windows XP system and successful completion of Activity 3-8

Description: In addition to managing volumes and directories, you can use Remote Manager to work with network files. In this activity, you practice using Remote Manager to upload a file, salvage deleted files, and purge deleted files.

1. If necessary, start Remote Manager using the IP address of your assigned NetWare 6.5 server.

2. Log in with your administrative user name and password.

3. Click the **Volumes** link under the Manage Server heading, and then click your assigned volume to display the directories.

4. Click the **Forms** directory to display all files, as shown in Figure 3-35.

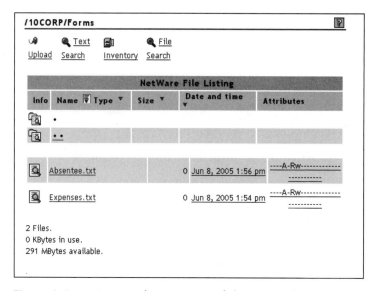

Figure 3-35   Viewing the contents of the Forms directory

5. To salvage the deleted file, follow these steps:

a. Click the **Info** icon in the first row of the NetWare File Listing table to display directory information (see Figure 3-36).

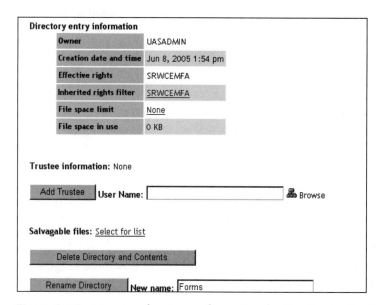

Figure 3-36   Viewing directory information for the Forms directory

b. Click the **Select for list** link next to the Salvagable files text, and record the salvageable files here:

_____

c. Click the **Salvage** option next to the Salvage.txt file to restore this file.

d. Click the **Back to directory page for** link and then the **Back to directory listing** link to return to the NetWare File Listing window.

e. Click your **Forms** directory and verify that the Salvage.txt file has been restored.

6. To delete the **Junk.txt** file, follow these steps.

    a. Click the **Info** icon to the left of the Junk.txt file and record the file name, size, and deletor information for one deleted file:

    _____

    _____

    _____

    b. Scroll down and click the **Delete file** button, and then click **Yes** to delete the Junk.txt file.

7. Follow these steps to purge deleted files from the Forms directory:

    a. Click the **Info** icon next to the Forms directory.

    b. Click the **Select for list** link next to the Salvagable files text.

    c. Click the **Purge all files** button.

    d. Click the **Back** button on your browser to return to the Directory entry information window.

    e. Record the salvageable files:

    _____

8. Click **Exit** to return to the Remote Manager Login window.

9. Close your Web browser and return your computer to the standard lab configuration.

CHAPTER SUMMARY

❏ The basic components of Novell Storage Services (NSS) include partitions, pools, volumes, directories, and files. Storage pools are made up of one or more physical disk partitions. The volume is the logical division of the storage pool and is comparable to a file cabinet drawer in that it holds folders and files. Each server is required to have a minimum of one NSS volume named SYS consisting of at least 4 GB.

❏ During installation, NetWare creates a number of system directories on the SYS volume, including the Login, Public, and System directories. The Login directory contains programs and files needed to log a user into the network. The Public directory contains program commands and utilities that may be run by a user after logging in to the network. The System directory contains OS files and utilities available only to the network administrator. It's important that the SYS volume doesn't run out of available space. Because running out of space on the SYS volume can bring down the server, network administrators usually plan one or more data volumes to contain the organization's files and applications.

❏ Files are used to store network data and software. In addition to file name and size, NetWare stores additional information about each file, including owner, access dates, and attributes in the directory entry table located at the beginning of each volume. Network administrators can use Remote Manager from a Web browser to manage the network file system.

❏ An important job of a network administrator is to plan and implement a structure for the network file system that supports the organization's processing needs. When planning the directory structure, Novell suggests setting aside private home directories for each user, shared directories to store files that multiple users need, and application directories. To provide space for these directories, many network administrators use multiple volumes. The SYS volume is reserved for OS files, and one or more data volumes are usually designated to store print queues, user files, and applications.

❏ After a directory structure has been designed, any necessary volumes are created in ConsoleOne or Remote Manager.

❏ After all volumes are created and mounted, a network administrator can create the necessary directories and subdirectories by using Windows Explorer, Linux Konqueror (file-management utility), ConsoleOne, or Remote Manager.

❑ The NetWare 6.5 file system can be accessed from client computers with any of the following protocols: HTTP, CIFS, NFS, or NCP. Although NCP requires Novell Client to be loaded on a Windows XP or 2000 Professional system, it offers the most options for accessing and managing the NetWare file system.

❑ NetWare 6.5 includes the option to salvage and purge deleted files in Remote Manager. Purging files performs a "paper shredding" process that's important in preventing secure documents from being accessed after they are deleted.

KEY TERMS

application directories — Directories that hold installation files needed to install or run software on users' computers.

application-oriented structure — This directory design provides a simple directory structure in which data and applications are arranged by type of use rather than by department.

balanced trees (B-trees) — An indexing system that enables NSS volumes to be mounted more quickly and with less RAM than traditional volumes require.

block — The smallest unit of disk storage on a NetWare volume. NSS volumes use a block size of 4 KB; blocks in traditional volumes can be set from 4 KB to 64 KB.

departmental structure — A directory design in which user home directories, shared directories, and applications are located within the departments that control them.

directory entry table (DET) — A storage location at the beginning of each volume for storing information on files and directories, including name, size, location, owner, and access dates.

duplexing — A technique of increasing file service reliability by keeping two disks attached to separate controller cards synchronized on the server.

failover — The process of switching from a failed server to an operational server.

fault tolerance — The capability of a server or device to continue operations in spite of a component failure.

file compression — A NetWare technique to save disk space by automatically compressing files that have not been accessed for a specified time period.

home directory — A directory created for each user for storing his or her own files and documents.

hot fix — An area of the hard disk that the NetWare file system uses to store data from damaged disk tracks.

Login directory — The NetWare SYS volume directory that's available before a client logs in to the system.

mirroring — The process of automatically synchronizing the information on two partitions located on different disk drives attached to the same controller.

Novell Storage Services (NSS) — The file system used primarily by NetWare 6.5. In NSS, logical volumes are created from storage pools that consist of one or more disk partitions.

NSS volumes — Logical divisions of the NSS storage pool used to store system and user data.

partitions — Areas of hard disk storage formatted for a specific operating system. NetWare 6.5 uses NSS-formatted disk partitions to form storage pools.

path — The location of a file or directory in the network file system, often consisting of the server name, volume name, and directory name.

Public directory — A required NetWare-created operating system directory that contains NetWare utility programs and commands available to all users.

server clustering — A setup in which two or more servers can share a common disk system, making the data available in case one of the servers has a hardware failure.

shared directories — Directories that are available for multiple users to store and retrieve data files.

storage pools — An NSS file system component used to group one or more partitions into a storage area that can be divided in one or more volumes.

suballocation — A feature of traditional volumes that divides blocks into smaller 512-byte increments so that multiple files can share the same block, thus saving disk space.

System directory — A required NetWare-created operating system directory that contains system software and commands available only to the server and Admin user, not to other users.

traditional volumes — Divisions of traditional NetWare partitions that use the older NetWare file system architecture. Traditional volumes can be used to store user and application data for backward compatibility with previous versions of NetWare.

volumes — The major division of NetWare storage. All files are stored in volumes associated with a specific NetWare server.

REVIEW QUESTIONS

1. What are the logical divisions of NSS storage pools?

2. List the three major components of the NSS file system.

3. The _____ volume is required on all NetWare 6.5 servers.

4. Which of the following is a required NetWare directory that's created when NetWare is installed on a server? (Choose all that apply.)
   a. Login
   b. Public
   c. System
   d. Shared

5. The _____ directory contains files and programs that can be accessed and run before logging in to the network.
   a. Public
   b. System
   c. Login
   d. Etc

6. The _____ directory contains NetWare utility programs that are available to all users.
   a. Public
   b. System
   c. Login
   d. Etc

7. The _____ directory contains operating system files that aren't available to users.
   a. Public
   b. System
   c. Login
   d. Etc

8. List three types of directories that Novell suggests you create in the file system.

9. Larger file systems are easier to manage when using a departmental directory structure. True or False?

10. What is the advantage of leaving some unallocated disk space when creating partitions for a NetWare 6.5 server?

11. The_____ eDirectory object is used to access the file system from eDirectory.
    a. root
    b. storage pool
    c. volume
    d. partition

12. Purged files are placed in the Deleted.sav directory until their space is needed by NetWare. True or False?

13. NSS volumes are created within _____ .

    a. partitions

    b. storage pools

    c. containers

    d. clusters

14. Which of the following attributes is not found on NSS volumes?

    a. block suballocation

    b. clustering

    c. file compression

    d. user space restrictions

15. Mirroring involves synchronizing data on two different _____ .

    a. storage pools

    b. partitions

    c. volumes

16. Which of the following protocols is used to access network servers from a Web browser?

    a. NCP

    b. IPX

    c. HTTP

    d. NSF

17. Which of the following clients requires NFAP to be installed on the NetWare 6.5 server?

    a. Microsoft client

    b. Web browser client

    c. Microsoft NetWare client

    d. Novell Client

18. Which of the following clients provides compatibility with all eDirectory application services?

    a. Microsoft client

    b. Microsoft NetWare client

    c. Novell Client

    d. Web browser

19. List an advantage of using Novell Client.

20. Which of the following is an advantage of the Microsoft CIFS client? (Choose all that apply.)

    a. uses the Novell eDirectory password and context system for logging in to NetWare

    b. makes the NetWare server appear as part of a Windows workgroup

    c. allows use of Novell management utilities, such as ConsoleOne

    d. does not require an additional client to be installed on the local Windows computer

3

CASE PROJECTS

Case Project 3-1: Identifying Storage Requirements

You have seen how Eric Kenton developed processing needs for the Engineering and Manufacturing departments to create a Storage Requirements Form. Using the processing needs he developed for the Business Division and Marketing Department (see Figure 3-37), fill out a Storage Requirements Form that includes the following information for each directory: description, directory type, users (that is, in which department), name, and estimated size. Your instructor will supply blank forms for you to use.

Business Division Processing Needs

The Business Division uses a DOS-based software package that includes general ledger and payroll applications. Currently, Terry Blackwell, George Perez, and Amy Pan in the Accounting Department are using this package. However, to improve performance, security, and reliability, a new Windows accounting package has been purchased and will be installed on the NetWare 6.5 server in a single directory structure named AcctApp within the Business directory. The storage requirements for the accounting packages and data should not exceed 5 GB. In addition to the accounting applications, all business staff use the Excel spreadsheet program to create and update budget data. Because Terry, George, and Amy need access to the budget accounting data, it should be stored in a shared Budget subdirectory within the Business directory. Currently, the projected storage needs for the Budget directory do not exceed 3 GB.

In addition to having access to the new inventory system, the Marketing users use Microsoft Access to keep a database of the customers and vendors they work with on their notebook computers. Because the Marketing staff often work with the same customers and vendors, sometimes they have conflicting information on their notebook computers. To solve this problem, separate directories for the customer and vendor databases will be stored in the Marketing directory structure on the NetWare 6.5 server. These directories should not exceed 3 GB each. The department secretary, Laura Hiller, will maintain the customer and vendor database files by entering new data from the Marketing staff. When in the office, the database files will be accessed directly from the network. Initially, the Marketing staff members need to be able to copy the database files to their notebook computers before going on the road. In the future, they would like to have direct access to the server database from a dial-up connection. In addition, the Marketing staff use word-processing software for correspondence and work on promotional material. The Marketing staff will need a 5 GB shared document directory to exchange promotional material in their department and with the Desktop Publishing users.

The Desktop Publishing Department is responsible for working with the Engineering and Marketing departments to create operation and installation manuals for the NASA and Mars Rover projects. As a result, shared directories of up to 10 GB need to be created for these projects within the Desktop directory structure.

Figure 3-37   Processing needs for the Business Division and Marketing Department

Case Project 3-2: Designing a Directory Structure

Eric also used the Storage Requirements Form to develop a directory design for Universal AeroSpace. For this project, use the Storage Requirements Form you created in Case Project 3-1 to create a directory design for the Business Division and Marketing Department. Using the Directory Design Form your instructor supplies, create a structure for each department.

3

HANDS-ON PROJECTS

Hands-on Project 3-1: Completing the UAS Directory Structure

In Activity 3-5, you learned how to use Remote Manager to create several UAS directories on your assigned NetWare 6.5 volume. In this project, you use Remote Manager to complete the directory structure shown in Figures 3-25 and 3-26. After creating the directory structure, use your Windows computer to map a drive to your assigned volume and then print the directory structure.

Hands-on Project 3-2: Creating the Accounting and Marketing Directory Structure

In this project, use Remote Manager to create the directory structure you designed in Case Project 3-2. Then use your Windows computer to map a drive to your Accounting directory and print the structure. Repeat this process to print your Marketing directory structure.

4

NOVELL eDIRECTORY SERVICES

After reading this chapter and completing the activities, you will be able to:

♦ Explain general directory service terms and describe how a directory system is structured

♦ Identify the role and benefits of eDirectory

♦ Describe eDirectory components and object classes

♦ Plan a basic eDirectory structure and create eDirectory objects

♦ Install and work with Novell Client

In Chapter 1, you learned that a directory service provides a central means of storing, managing, and accessing information about network objects. In this chapter, you learn about Novell's eDirectory service and how it's used to organize information about network objects and services. In addition, you learn how to install Novell Client and use the iManager utility to create eDirectory objects. Throughout this book, you'll continue to work with iManager and eDirectory services to set up, configure, and access network objects, including servers, users, groups, data volumes, and printers.

OVERVIEW OF DIRECTORY SERVICES

Novell defines a **directory service** as a combination of a database and related services that provide the following network capabilities:

- Integrate diverse systems to provide centralized organization and management

- Give users access to data and resources they need to perform their duties

- Help provide connectivity between users, both within the organization and across the Internet

- Coordinate organization and network information and resources

 Although Novell uses "Directory" (uppercase) to refer to the directory service technology and "directory" (lowercase) to refer to the folder structure when discussing file storage, in this book "directory service" refers to the technology, and "directory database" refers to the database of network objects.

In addition to providing a way to organize and store network object information, directory services play an important role in integrating different network OSs into one system that can be centrally administered and accessed. Having resources from many different OSs, such as NetWare, Linux, and Windows, work together as one network makes it convenient for users to access information anytime, from any computer, without needing to interact with a different OS environment.

The **directory database** is made up of **entries** storing information about network objects in containers organized into a hierarchical tree structure. Directory services provide the discovery, security, storage, and relationship-management functions that make information in the database valuable. Directory services are available from several different vendors. A common element of these services is their roots in the X.500 directory standard originally developed by the International Organization for Standardization (ISO) and International Telecommunication Union (ITU) committees in 1988. As a CNA, you'll be required to know the basics of the X.500 standard, Novell's eDirectory, and Lightweight Directory Access Protocol (LDAP), as described in the following sections.

X.500 Directory Standard

The ITU and ISO originally developed the Open Systems Interconnection (OSI) model to standardize the functional layers that make network communications work between different OSs and hardware environments. In the client-server environment of the OSI model's application layer, directory functionality (administration, authentication, and access control) was initially developed to handle management of e-mail addresses and the OSI Message Handling application (X.400). However, this functionality was recognized as having potential use with many applications, so it was defined as a separate module or standard: ITU-T Recommendation X.500 (also known as ISO/IEC 9594: *Information Technology—Open Systems Interconnection—The Directory*).

Early network directory systems were usually developed for a particular OS environment. In these proprietary systems, there was little or no incentive to work with any other environments. To help make network directory systems more compatible, an international standard was needed. Using the OSI model as a foundation, the ITU created specifications for a series of recommendations known as **X.500** that define directory services. The first X.500 specification—the Directory Information Model, released in 1988—was a basic model showing how directory service information should be displayed for users. With the release of the 1993 X.500 specification, the ITU provided a number of additional models to describe directory services, as shown in Table 4-1.

Table 4-1 X.500 directory service models

Model	Description
User Information Model	Describes how data from the directory should be displayed and accessed by users
Directory Functional Model	Describes the overall operation of directory service components
Operational and Administrative Information Model	Describes directory service administration functions
DSA Information Model	Explains how Directory System Agents (DSAs) work together to provide directory access
Directory Distribution Model	Describes how DSAs distribute information between themselves
Directory Administrative Authority Model	Describes how a directory is administered
Security Model	Describes authentication and access control

The X.500 model describes a directory as a collection of systems that work in a client-server relationship representing information about network objects in the real world. In the X.500 directory architecture, the client queries and receives responses from one or more servers in the server's directory service, with Directory Access Protocol controlling communication between the client and the server.

The X.500 model contains many components, but the following are the most vital to the operation of a basic directory:

- Directory Information Base (DIB)
- Directory Information Tree (DIT)
- Directory User Agent (DUA)
- Directory System Agent (DSA)
- Directory Access Protocol (DAP)
- Directory Service Protocol (DSP)
- Directory Information Shadowing Protocol (DISP)

Figure 4-1 shows the interrelationship between these directory components. In the following sections, you learn how these basic components work together to create a complete directory service.

Directory Information Base (DIB)

A directory database is made up of entries containing information about objects in the real world, such as users, printers, computers, and data volumes. These entries are collectively known as the **Directory Information Base (DIB)**. Within the DIB, each entry is made up of a collection of information fields called attributes. As shown in Figure 4-2, an entry is made up of several attributes, each with one or more values defining information about the network object.

Directory Information Tree (DIT)

Entries in the DIB are stored in one or more containers that act like folders in the file system. Just as subfolders are arranged within folders in the file system, the hierarchical relationship between containers in the DIB enable them to be arranged into a tree structure called the **Directory Information Tree (DIT)**, shown in Figure 4-3.

To keep the directory organized, a set of rules known as the **directory schema** is enforced to ensure that information in the DIB is not damaged or lost as modifications are made. The directory schema defines a set of attributes and valid object classes. An object class defines a type of network object, such as a user or printer, and includes all attributes that make up that type of object. The directory schema prevents entries from having incorrect attribute types and forces all entries to be members of a defined object class.

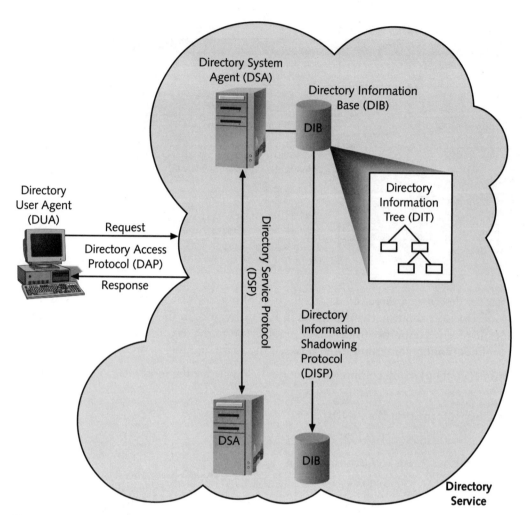

Figure 4-1   X.500 directory service components

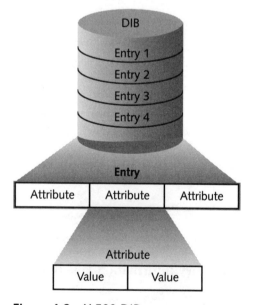

Figure 4-2   X.500 DIB components

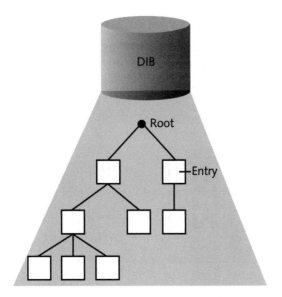

Figure 4-3   Structure of the X.500 DIT

Directory User and Service Agents

The X.500 specification takes a client-server approach in communicating information to the directory. The directory client, called the **Directory User Agent (DUA)**, provides a standardized functionality that supports searching or browsing through directory databases and retrieving directory information. The DUA's functionality can be used in all types of user interfaces through dedicated DUA clients, Web server gateways, or e-mail applications. DUAs are currently available for almost all types of computers (DOS, Windows, Macintosh, OS/2, and UNIX, for example).

Processing a DUA request for information from the directory service consists of four steps, as shown in Figure 4-4:

1. The DUA, usually running on a user computer, acts as the client to send the user's request to the **Directory System Agent (DSA)** running on a server.

2. The DSA uses a collection of services and protocols that manage specific portions of the DIB to search and find the requested information.

3. The information is retrieved from the DIB and sent back to the DSA.

4. The retrieved information is sent from the DSA back to the DUA, where it's presented to the user.

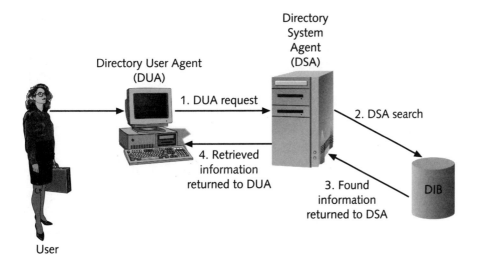

Figure 4-4   Directory agents

Directory Service Protocols

Directory service protocols are rules that handle formatting and communicating requests and responses between DUAs and DSAs. **Directory Service Protocol (DSP)** controls the interaction between two or more DSAs so that users can access information in the directory without knowing the exact location of a piece of information. **Directory Access Protocol (DAP)** is used for controlling communication between a DUA and a DSA. As shown in Figure 4-5, DAP handles formatting and transmitting data between the DUA and the DSA.

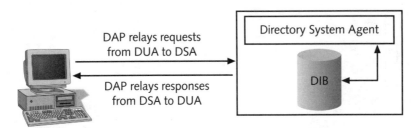

Figure 4-5   Directory Access Protocol

If a DSA can't fulfill a DUA's request, it passes the request to another DSA. The DSP controls communication between DSAs, as shown in Figure 4-6.

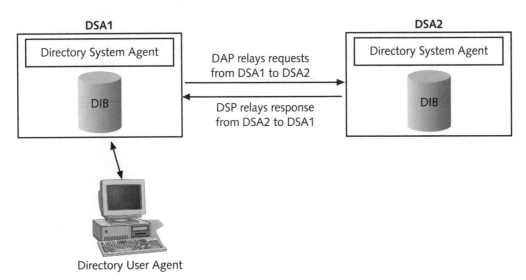

Figure 4-6   Directory Service Protocol

In X.500 terminology, the process of distributing and synchronizing the DIB among multiple locations is called **shadowing**. **Directory Information Shadowing Protocol (DISP)** is a special DSP that's responsible for keeping multiple copies of the DIB synchronized (see Figure 4-7).

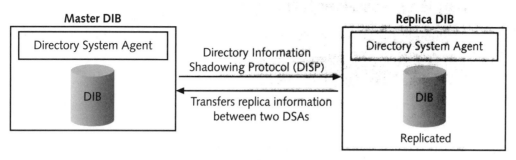

Figure 4-7   Directory Information Shadowing Protocol

The LDAP Directory Standard

Approved in 1988, the X.500 directory standard has matured under the ITU's aegis and was enhanced in the 1993 edition, currently in use. Although the coverage was comprehensive, users have criticized it as being too complex and, therefore, too difficult to implement. Until recently, few "pure" X.500 implementations were in operation.

The University of Michigan addressed the issue of the X.500 DAP being too complex for most directory implementations by developing a simpler TCP/IP-based version of X.500 DAP for use on the Internet: **Lightweight Directory Access Protocol (LDAP)**. LDAP specifies a common set of directory operations and commands that can be implemented on multiple vendor platforms. Novell, Microsoft, and SUSE Linux currently support LDAP functions in their directory services. Using LDAP, a user can log in to a Novell network and access resources on NetWare, Linux, *and* Windows servers. For example, a computer can use an LDAP client running on a Netscape browser to submit a login request to an LDAP service running on a NetWare 6.5 server. After being logged in, the user's computer can send additional LDAP requests to access data from the NetWare server that the user has rights to view. To print the data on a printer attached to a Windows server, the LDAP client running on the user's computer sends a login request to the Windows LDAP service, and after being authenticated, uses the Windows-based network printer. Because of this flexibility, most major suppliers of e-mail and directory services software have expressed interest in LDAP, which is fast becoming a de facto directory protocol for the Internet.

NOTE   Although LDAP started as a simplified component of the X.500 directory, it's being developed into a complete directory service. Using Internet naming services, developers are building layers of security and adding capabilities of X.500 directory components. Some analysts fear that when the missing functionality is added (such as security control, replication of data between multiple sites, and use of character sets more complex than plain ASCII), LDAP will be as complex as the X.500 suite is said to be.

LDAP also has a standard naming convention that separates object types by commas. An LDAP-compatible DUA uses standardized rules and naming conventions when formatting a request independent of the OS and sends the request to an LDAP-compatible DSA running on a server. The DSA then processes the LDAP request based on the standard set of services and returns the result to the DUA. In this way, any vendor's directory can be made LDAP compatible by including the capability to process LDAP requests based on that directory service's structure. Netscape Directory Server, Microsoft Active Directory, and eDirectory comply with LDAP standards to varying degrees, making it possible to transfer and share information between directory services. The Lightweight Directory Interchange Format (LDIF) file is based on the LDAP model. Both Novell and Microsoft use LDIF files, which enable objects to be imported into a directory database from text files. In Chapter 5, you learn how to use an LDIF file to import new user accounts into eDirectory.

Installing a directory service has become an essential part of setting up a network system. Some directory services can run on multiple types of OSs, making it possible to integrate varying platforms into one directory system. Other vendors' directory services, such as Microsoft Active Directory, are specialized to use features of only a particular OS and can't be installed on different platforms. However, other client environments, such as Linux and Macintosh, can access and manage Active Directory information because it offers LDAP compatibility. In the following section, you learn how to plan for installing and implementing eDirectory on a NetWare server.

NOVELL EDIRECTORY SERVICES

As you learned in Chapter 1, **eDirectory** is Novell's directory service that runs on a variety of network OSs, including Novell NetWare, Windows Server 2003, and Linux. Novell eDirectory gives network administrators the capabilities and tools to manage network resources, such as servers, users, and printers, from an organizational perspective. eDirectory is an LDAP-compatible directory service and database that maintains information about all network resources. The database is properly referred to as the "Novell eDirectory database," but it's often shortened to "directory database" or just "eDirectory." All three terms refer to the same part of the eDirectory service. Novell has been perfecting the use of directory services since the early 1990s, when Novell Directory Services (NDS) was introduced in NetWare 4.0.

Novell eDirectory was called Novell Directory Services (NDS) in earlier versions of NetWare. As a result, you might see references to "NDS" in Novell manuals and software.

eDirectory Architecture

Novell's eDirectory service, based on X.500 standards, offers several additional features over NDS, including:

- Client libraries and LDAP tools for Linux, Solaris, and Tru64 UNIX
- An import/conversion export (ICE) engine to import or export LDIF files and perform server-to-server migration
- A merge utility for combining eDirectory trees
- The iManager utility to manage eDirectory objects
- The iMonitor utility to monitor and diagnose servers in the tree from a Web browser
- The Index Manager utility to create and manage eDirectory database indexes
- The capability to run on multiple platforms, including NetWare, Windows NT, Windows 2003/XP, Linux, Solaris, and Tru64 UNIX

Effectively managing and troubleshooting eDirectory is important to understanding how eDirectory works and how it's different from earlier NDS implementations.

eDirectory Operation

Instead of the fixed-length record files used in previous NDS versions, eDirectory uses FLexible and Adaptive Information Manager (FLAIM), a highly scalable, indexed database developed to store information for the GroupWise e-mail system. The structure and purpose of files in the FLAIM database are shown in Figure 4-8.

- The NDS.db file acts as the control file for the database and contains the rollback log used to abort incomplete transactions.
- The 00000001.log file in the SYS\NetWare\NDS.rfl directory tracks completed transactions and the current transaction. By default, the 00000001.log file is installed in No Keep mode, which means transactions are eventually overwritten and no additional log files are created. The log file can be changed to Keep mode if additional backup is required. In Keep mode, additional log files named 00000002.log, 00000003.log, and so on are created when specified log file conditions, such as maximum size, are met.

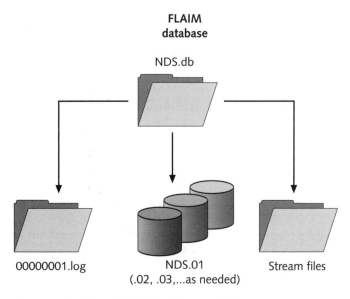

Figure 4-8   The FLAIM database architecture

- The NDS.xx files contain all records and indexes stored on the server. When an NDS.xx file reaches the maximum of 2 GB, additional files named NDS.02, NDS.03, and so on are created for the remaining data. Limiting NDS files to 2 GB allows scalability yet still offers high performance. The following indexes are maintained in NDS.xx files to enhance performance:

  - Attribute substring indexes for the CN and uniqueID fields

  - Attribute indexes for the Object Class field

  - Attribute indexes that include strings beginning with CN, uniqueID, Given Name, and Surname

- The Stream files have an .nds extension and are named with hexadecimal characters (0–9, A–F). Stream files hold information such as print job configurations and login scripts.

In place of the Transaction Tracking System (TTS) used in previous NDS versions, the FLAIM database system uses log files to back out and roll forward transactions in the event of a system failure. Completed transactions, called committed transactions, are placed in the log file. Noncommitted, or incomplete, transactions may or may not be placed in the log file. In a system failure, eDirectory can roll forward to reapply the committed transactions in the log file that might not have been fully written to the disk. Earlier versions of NetWare need to be updated to use eDirectory 8.6 or later to take advantage of its improved performance and scalability. These enhancements, along with eDirectory's capability to run on multiple OSs, make it the most versatile and scalable directory service available today.

Benefits of eDirectory

eDirectory offers several benefits beyond those of earlier domain services or the bindery services in NetWare 3.x:

- *Login*—Using eDirectory, a user logs into the directory service and is given access to whatever resources he or she has rights to. If those resources are files on three different file servers, the user has access to the servers where those resources are located.

- *Administration*—With eDirectory, you can work with all your network resources at the same time using a variety of administrative tools, including the iManager utility for managing eDirectory from a Web browser.

- *Security*—eDirectory uses the RSA encryption algorithm, which enables a secure, encrypted single login to the network.

- *Reliability*—Because the directory database is distributed and replicated, eDirectory provides fault tolerance for the network. For example, because information about users is stored on at least two servers, a single server failure doesn't prevent users from logging in to the network and accessing resources they have rights to.

- *Scalability*—**Scalability** makes it possible to work with systems of different sizes. eDirectory works as well with global networks with hundreds of servers as with small networks with only one server. If your network expands, eDirectory can easily handle the expansion. No matter how large or small the network, eDirectory can still be administered from one location.

IDENTIFYING eDIRECTORY COMPONENTS

To work with Novell eDirectory, you need to know the components that make up its database and how they work together. The eDirectory system uses a tree structure to organize network components in much the same way that files and directories are organized on a hard disk. The **eDirectory tree** is the visual and logical design created to organize network components in the directory database into a hierarchical structure. In computer terminology, the word *tree* refers to a hierarchical structure for organizing data or information. The tree usually is drawn inverted, meaning that unlike a real tree, the root is at the *top* of the diagram, as shown in Figure 4-9.

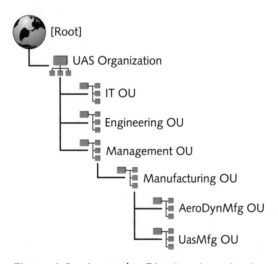

Figure 4-9   A sample eDirectory tree structure

Objects in the eDirectory tree can be classified into these three general categories:

- The Root object
- Container objects
- Leaf objects

In the following sections, you learn about these object types and how they can be used to design and implement an eDirectory tree that meets your organization's needs.

The Root Object

The **Root object** is important because it represents the beginning of the network directory service tree, in much the same way the root of a disk volume represents the beginning of disk storage space on a drive. As shown previously in Figure 4-9, the eDirectory tree starts at a single point (denoted as "[Root]" in eDirectory) and branches out from there. Each eDirectory tree can have only one Root object, which is used to identify the name of the tree and represent all objects within it. For example, if you give the root of the tree rights to access a specific data file, all users defined in your eDirectory database inherit those rights. In this way, the Root object can be used to assign rights to all valid users on your network system.

The root of the tree is usually shown in square brackets—[Root]—to match its on-screen appearance in NetWare utilities.

Container Objects

Container objects are used to group and store other objects. Table 4-2 lists the six common classes of container objects.

Table 4-2   eDirectory container objects

Container Object Name	Description
Country	**Country container objects** must be assigned a valid two-digit country code and can exist only within the root of a directory tree. Because they create an extra level in the directory tree, most network administrators don't use Country container objects unless they work in a multinational organization.
Domain	**Domain container objects** are used to store DNS component objects, such as the DNS Server and DNS Scope objects. Domain container objects can be created at the root of the tree or within any Organization, Organizational Unit, or Country container.
Organization (O)	**Organization container objects** are used to hold all eDirectory objects in an organization's structure. An Organization object must exist within a Country container or directly under the root of the directory tree. Every tree must have at least one Organization container object.
Organizational Unit (OU)	**Organizational Unit (OU) container objects**, which must exist within an Organization container or within another OU container, divide users and other leaf objects into workgroups, such as company divisions or departments.
Role Based Services (RBS)	**Role Based Services (RBS) container objects** are used to store the administrative tasks you authorize users to perform in eDirectory. You learn more about creating RBS roles and specifying tasks for them in Chapter 7.
Security	**Security container objects** are used to hold global policies that relate to security properties, such as login, authentication, and key management.

In the sample UAS tree shown previously in Figure 4-9, notice that the UAS Organization has three OU containers named IT, Engineering, and Management. The Manufacturing OU has a subcontainer named UasMfg.

Leaf Objects

As shown in Figure 4-10, **leaf objects** represent network entities, such as users, groups, volumes, and servers. Although certain leaf objects can exist directly off the root of the eDirectory tree, most leaf objects exist only within Organization or OU containers.

Table 4-3 describes the common leaf objects used in most eDirectory trees and shows the corresponding icons. Each type of object has certain properties or attributes associated with it. A **property**, also called an **attribute**, is a data field containing information about an object. Not all object types have the same properties associated with them. A leaf object, such as a printer, has different properties than a user object does.

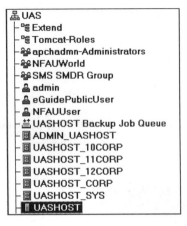

Figure 4-10   Sample leaf objects

The term "attribute" comes from the LDAP standard and has been adopted by Novell for use in NetWare 6.5. In this book, the term "attribute" is used along with "property."

NOTE

Table 4-3   eDirectory leaf objects

Object Name	Abbreviation	Icon	Description
Alias	CN=		A pointer to an object in another container. Alias objects are used to make it easier to access objects that are not in your current context.
Computer	CN=		An object used to represent a client computer (user workstation).
Group	CN=		A group object can be used to represent one or more users. Group objects are often used to grant access rights to several users.
Directory Map	CN=		Contains the path to a directory in the network file system and can be used in MAP commands or directly in Windows Explorer.
NetWare Server	CN=		An object representing a NetWare 6.5 server and its location in the eDirectory structure.
Print Server	CN=		A print server object represents a process that takes jobs from print queues and sends them to the assigned network printer.
Printer	CN=		An object representing a network printer and its configuration.
Print Queue	CN=		An object representing a print queue on the network containing print jobs and configuring information.

Table 4-3   eDirectory leaf objects (continued)

Object Name	Abbreviation	Icon	Description
Profile	CN=		Contains login script commands that can be assigned to user accounts. (You learn how to use Profile objects with login scripts in Chapter 9.)
User	CN=		A user object represents a person who uses the network. This object is used to manage and maintain information about the user, including login restrictions and his or her access rights.
Volume	CN=		A volume object is used to represent a physical file storage area on a NetWare server. Volume objects are created when a server is installed on the network.

You can assign values to each property of an object. Some object properties, such as a user's telephone number or the print queue of a printer object, are multivalued, meaning they can contain more than one entry. Each object has certain property values that are required when the object is created. For example, each user object must be assigned a login and last name value when the user is created. Other property values are optional and can be added later. Throughout this book, you learn how to create and configure many of the leaf objects shown in Table 4-3. In this chapter, you learn about the Admin, volume, and alias leaf objects.

The Admin User Object

The **Admin user object** is created when the first server is installed in the eDirectory tree. Admin is an important user object because it has Supervisor rights to the entire eDirectory tree, allowing the Admin user to create and manage all other objects in the tree structure. As you learned in Chapter 2, a password is given to the Admin user during the initial server installation. If you're the Admin user, make sure you remember this password because without it, you must reinstall the eDirectory tree to regain Supervisor rights. Because of the importance of the Admin user account, many organizations create a backup Admin user and then secure this user name and password in a safe place, such as the company vault or safety deposit box. In Chapter 5, you learn how to secure your Admin user account and create a backup Admin user account.

Volume Objects

As described in Chapter 3, when you create a physical NetWare volume on a server, a **volume object** is created in the eDirectory tree in the same context as the NetWare server it resides on. The volume object acts as a pointer to a physical volume object and contains status and configuration information for the volume (see Figure 4-11).

The volume object name defaults to a combination of the server's name and the volume's physical name separated by an underscore. For example, a server named UASHOST in the UAS Organization has a physical volume named CORP. The default volume object for the CORP physical volume is created in the UAS Organization with the name UASHOST_CORP. Because the eDirectory volume object acts as a pointer to the volume's physical data, often it's convenient to create additional volume objects for a physical volume in other containers. For example, if users in the Engineering and Management containers access data from the CORP volume, volume objects that point to the CORP volume can be created in both the Engineering and Management containers. These volume objects can be given the same or different names. For example, you can name the volume object in the Engineering container EngCorpVol and then point it to the CORP volume on the UASHOST server.

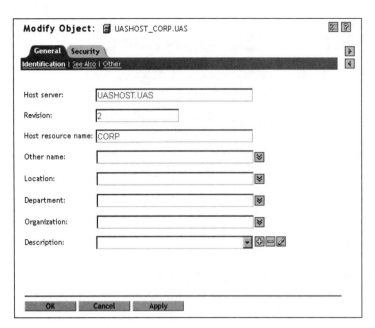

Figure 4-11   Volume object properties

Alias Objects

You can have multiple eDirectory volume objects for a single physical volume, but most other object types, such as servers, printers, and users, can be represented by only one eDirectory object. So if you want to access a printer or server object from another container, you need to select that printer or server object by navigating to the container holding the object or by typing its distinguished name as described in the next section. Alias objects can be used to simplify access to objects in other containers. The **alias object** holds no data about the original object; it acts only as a pointer. For example, users in the IT Department frequently need to access the server object to check configuration data. Instead of requiring users to navigate the eDirectory tree to locate the actual server object, you can create an alias object in the IT container that points to the actual server object in the UAS container. In the next section, you learn how to create an alias object for your UASHOST server.

Directory Map Objects

Moving data directories to other volumes or servers is sometimes done because volumes fill up or new servers are added to the network. Moving a data directory to a new location can require a lot of maintenance on the network administrator's part to find and change drive mappings on many user computers. **Directory Map objects** offer an alternative by storing the physical path to a data directory, as shown in Figure 4-12. When a data directory is moved to a new location, the network administrator needs to change only the path in the Directory Map object.

For example, in Figure 4-12 the Path property of the Directory Map object called Shared can be changed to point to the ENGDATA volume on the ENGHOST server. Because drive L: on the client computer is mapped through the Shared object, when the path is changed to the ENGDATA volume, the user is directed to that directory without making any changes to the client computer's drive settings. In Chapter 7, you learn how to create Directory Map objects.

Object Naming

Each object in the eDirectory tree is given a name known as its **common name (CN)**. An object's common name must be unique within the container that houses the object. In addition to a common name, each eDirectory object has a context. Just as a path is used to specify a file location on a disk drive, the **context** specifies the location of an object in an eDirectory tree. One difference between a path to a file location and an eDirectory context is that the context is indicated with X.500 notation, which starts with the object and works up the tree. In contrast, a disk path is specified from the root of the drive down to the file name. For

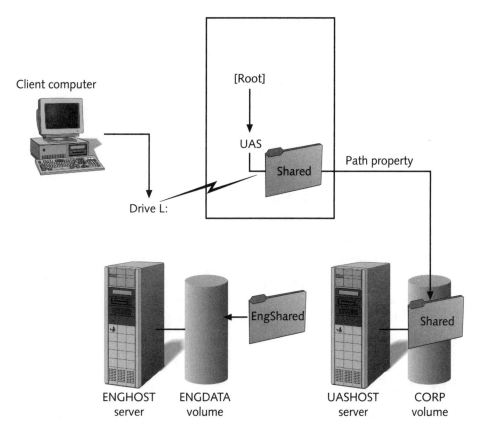

Figure 4-12   A Directory Map object

example, to identify the path to the Memo file in the Document directory of the C: drive, you use C:\Document\Memo, but to identify the context of the user EKenton in the IT container shown previously in Figure 4-9, you use .EKenton.IT.UAS. Another difference between an eDirectory context and a path is that the eDirectory context is formatted with periods to separate each level instead of the slashes or backslashes used in paths. The period at the beginning of the context specifies starting at the root of the eDirectory tree in much the same way that a slash is used at the beginning of a path.

Each object in the eDirectory database can be uniquely identified by its **distinguished name**, which consists of the object's name and its complete context, leading to the root of the eDirectory tree. A context specification that includes object abbreviations is referred to as **typeful**. For example, the user EKenton could be identified by using this typeful distinguished name:

`.CN=EKenton.OU=IT.O=UAS`

The two-letter abbreviation preceding the name of an object identifies the object's type. For example, CN= identifies EKenton as the common name for a leaf object, the OU= identifies IT as an Organizational Unit container object, and the O= identifies UAS as an Organization container object.

Using typeful distinguished names that include the object type abbreviation and the context requires extra time and opens up the possibility of errors. As a result, eDirectory can assume object types as long as the rightmost object is an Organization or Organizational Unit. A distinguished name that doesn't contain object type abbreviations is referred to as **typeless**. For example, this is the typeless distinguished name for the user EKenton:

`EKenton.IT.UAS`

When you log in to eDirectory, your client computer is assigned to a location in the eDirectory tree structure in much the same way that your command prompt is assigned a position in the file system when you open a command prompt window. The default location of your client computer in the eDirectory tree is referred to as its **current context**. By setting the client's current context during the login process, you make it easier for users to log in by simply typing the common name for their user accounts. If users need to log in outside their current context, they can by specifying the distinguished names for their user accounts. For example, Eric wants to log in from another computer that has its current context set to the Engineering OU. To log in, he could type his distinguished name—.EKenton.IT.UAS—in the Username text box, or click the Advanced button to set the current context to the IT container. In "Working with Novell Client" later in this chapter, you learn how to customize Novell Client to set your computer's current context to a specific location in the eDirectory tree.

If your client computer's current context is set to one of the containers specified in the distinguished name, you can save keystrokes by using a relative name. A **relative distinguished name** starts with the client's current context and is specified by omitting the leading period. For example, if the client's current context is set to the UAS container, Eric could log in by entering a relative name or distinguished name in the Username text box:

- EKenton.IT (relative distinguished name—note that the name does *not* start with a period)

- .EKenton.IT.UAS (distinguished name—note that the name starts with a period)

Another way to specify a relative name is by ending the name with a period, which causes the eDirectory system to move the current context up one level before searching for the object. For example, if the current context is .Engineering.UAS, Eric could log in to the IT container by entering EKenton.IT. in the Username text box.

PLANNING THE eDIRECTORY TREE STRUCTURE

One of the first tasks in setting up eDirectory is to design the eDirectory tree structure for the organization. A first step is analyzing the organization's workflow and resource-sharing needs to determine what containers are needed. Although this task can be complex for large corporate networks, it can be quite simple for small single-server networks. Eric did this for the UAS eDirectory tree by grouping the objects into containers based on resource sharing. When grouping objects, you should keep the design as simple as possible to reduce the number of containers that are needed. A basic guideline is to avoid creating containers for fewer than 10 objects. An exception to this guideline is when user objects are located in separate geographical areas with their own server and independent resources. Grouping objects in different geographic areas into separate containers makes it possible to partition the eDirectory database for better efficiency, as described in "Implementing eDirectory Partitions and Replicas" later in this chapter. For example, Universal AeroSpace has a small subsidiary named AeroDyn that needs only five user accounts. Because the AeroDyn facility is in another city, Eric has decided to create a separate OU for it, even though it has fewer than 10 users.

The next step is to design the eDirectory tree structure for the organization by placing the containers in a hierarchical tree structure. Novell recommends that each tree have only one Organization container for objects shared by the entire organization. In a simple tree design, the Organization container might be the only container object needed. Although this design would work for a small company, most organizations need to divide network objects into OU containers for department and workgroups. When designing your eDirectory tree hierarchy, you should strive to keep the number of OU within OUs to a minimum. Placing OUs with other OUs creates long distinguished object names and can make finding objects in the tree more difficult. However, sometimes this method can be useful for mirroring departmental structures, as in the UAS eDirectory tree used throughout this book.

Figure 4-13 shows the tree design Eric developed for UAS. Because the Engineering Department monitors many of the manufacturing processes, Eric decided to place the container for Manufacturing in the Engineering OU. Both the Universal AeroSpace and AeroDyn divisions have manufacturing facilities in different cities, so Eric designed separate containers for AeroDynMfg and UasMfg in the Mfg OU. Eric plans for the Business OU to include leaf objects for the Business Division, including the Desktop Publishing, Accounting, and Marketing departments.

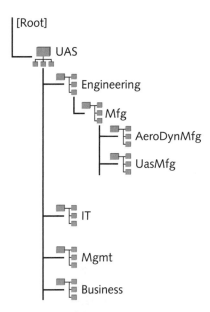

4

Figure 4-13   A sample UAS eDirectory tree design

Because users in each department have different needs in terms of resources and access rights, separating them makes it easier to assign user access rights, partition the database, and manage the network in the future. Although the Sales and Desktop Publishing departments could also be separated from the Business OU, the few objects in those OUs wouldn't justify the complexity of the additional network directory design. In addition, because of their physical proximity, users in these departments often share access to network printers and other resources as compared to the Manufacturing Department, which has network objects spread between the AeroDyn and UAS facilities in two different cities.

Creating eDirectory Objects

To implement and maintain the eDirectory tree, you need to become familiar with Novell's management utilities. In previous NetWare versions, implementing and managing the eDirectory tree required running the ConsoleOne or NetWare Administrator utility on a computer with Novell Client installed. In NetWare 6.0, Novell introduced a new network management tool called iManager. Like Remote Manager, the iManager utility is designed to be run from the Web browser of any desktop OS, enabling the administrator to perform network management tasks from any location. In this chapter, you work with iManager to set up containers and leaf objects for the UAS eDirectory tree. In Chapter 5, you learn how to use ConsoleOne and NetWare Administrator in the Windows environment to manage the eDirectory tree.

Using the iManager Utility

As you learned in Chapter 1, one of Novell's objectives in the OneNet strategy is to make it easier to manage and maintain the organization's network from any computer, regardless of the type of computer you're working on or the network system it's attached to. In Chapters 2 and 3, you learned how to use Remote Manager to manage the NetWare 6.5 server via a Web browser. In addition to Remote Manager, NetWare 6.5 ships with the iManager 2.5 utility, which makes managing and maintaining eDirectory possible from a Web browser. To run iManager, start your Web browser and then enter the iManager URL of /nps/iManager.html. For example, if your server is assigned the IP address 172.20.0.65, you enter "https://172.20.0.65/nps/ iManager.html." The "https" tells the browser to use a secure connection with Secure Sockets Layer (SSL), and "/nps/iManager.html" directs the NetWare Web server to open the Novell iManager Login window shown in Figure 4-14.

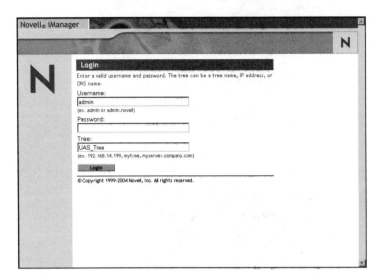

Figure 4-14   The Novell iManager Login window

Before the iManager Login window is displayed, you might see a security alert message informing you that you're about to view pages over a secure connection. Click OK to continue. You might see another security alert message informing you that the security certificate was issued by a company you have not chosen to trust. Security certificates accompany the key sent from the server to the client to encrypt data before sending it over the Internet. Certificates are described in more detail in Chapter 11.

After you log in successfully, iManager displays the main window shown in Figure 4-15.

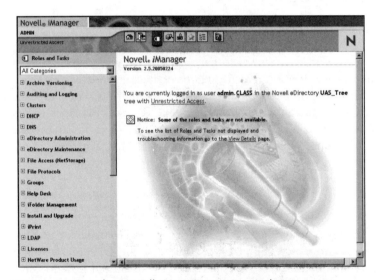

Figure 4-15   The Novell iManager main window

In Activity 4-1, you use iManager to set up the eDirectory structure shown previously in Figure 4-13. After creating the structure, you use iManager to create an alias object in Activity 4-2 and user accounts in Activity 4-3.

Activity 4-1: Creating an eDirectory Structure in iManager

Time Required: 10 minutes

Objectives: Use iManager to create eDirectory components.

Requirements:

- Windows XP or SUSE Linux 10 system using Internet Explorer or Java-enabled Firefox
- Access to a NetWare 6.5 server
- The administrator's distinguished user name and password. If you're using a dedicated server, your distinguished name should be Admin.UAS. If you're using a classroom server with the standard setup, your distinguished name should be ##Admin.CLASS (## represents your assigned student number). Record the distinguished name of your administrator account here:

  _____

- The path to your UAS container. If you're using a classroom server with the standard setup, the path should be ##UAS.CLASS (## represents your assigned student number). Record the path to your UAS container here:

  _____

With some Linux Web browsers, steps in iManager might take a little longer to perform.

NOTE

Description: Eric wants you to create a simplified version of the UAS eDirectory structure to be used in testing the NetWare 6.5 server. In this activity, you use iManager to set up the eDirectory structure shown previously in Figure 4-13.

1. If necessary, start your system and log on to your local computer. If you're using your Windows XP Professional computer with Novell Client, click the **Workstation Only** check box to prevent logging in to the eDirectory tree.

2. Start your Web browser, and enter the URL **https://IPaddress/nps/iManager.html** to display the iManager Login window.

3. Enter your administrative user name, password, and tree information, and then click the **Login** button to display the Novell iManager window shown previously in Figure 4-15.

4. In the Roles and Tasks pane on the left, click to expand the **eDirectory Administration** heading. Record the six eDirectory Administration options here (two per line):

   _____
   _____
   _____

If you're using Linux, you might need to use the drop-down list under the Roles and Tasks heading and select All Categories before doing Step 4. See Appendix B for more information on using iManager with Linux.

NOTE

5. Create the Engineering OU within your assigned container by following these steps:

   a. Click the **Create Object** link to display the Create Object window shown in Figure 4-16.

   b. In the Available object classes list box, scroll down and click **Organizational Unit** and then click **OK** to display the Create Organizational Unit window shown in Figure 4-17.

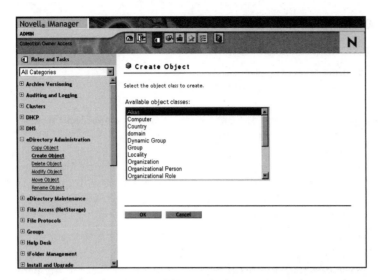

Figure 4-16   The Create Object window

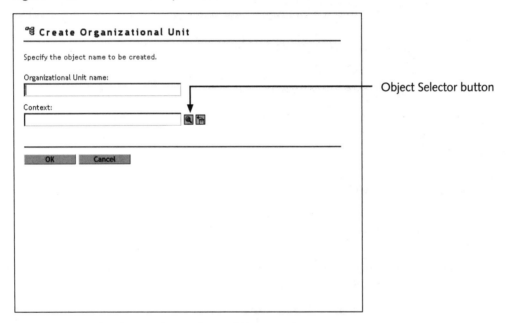

Figure 4-17   The Create Organizational Unit window

   c. Enter **Engineering** in the Organizational Unit name text box.

   d. Click the **Object Selector** button next to the Context text box to enter the path to your assigned container, using one of these two options:

     ■ If you're using a classroom server, navigate to the path you recorded for your UAS container in the Requirements section.

     ■ If you're using your own server, navigate to the UAS Organization container.

   e. Click **OK** to display the completion message, and then click **OK** to return to the Novell iManager main window.

6. Follow the procedure in Step 5 to create the **IT** OU.

7. Follow these steps to create the Mfg OU within the Engineering container:

   a. Click the **Create Object** link to display the Create Object window.

   b. In the Available object classes list box, click **Organizational Unit** and then click **OK** to display the Create Orgnizational Unit window.

c. Enter **Mfg** in the Organizational Unit name text box.

d. Click the **Object Selector** button next to the Context text box to select the path to the Engineering container you created in Step 5.

e. Click **OK** to display the completion message, and then click **OK** to return to the Novell iManager main window.

8. Leave iManager open for the next activity.

Activity 4-2: Creating Leaf Objects in iManager

Time Required: 10 minutes

Objectives: Use iManager to create eDirectory components.

Requirements:

- Windows XP or SUSE Linux 10 system with access to a NetWare 6.5 server

- NetWare 6.5 user name and password with rights to create objects in iManager

- Successful completion of Activity 4-1

- The context of your UASHOST server. If you're using a shared classroom server, the recommended context is ##UAS.CLASS. If you're using a dedicated server, the context should be .UAS. Record the context for your UASHOST server here:

_____

Description: Eric wants you to be able to access the UASHOST server easily from the IT OU. In this activity, you use iManager to create an alias object for your UASHOST server in the IT OU you created in Activity 4-1.

1. To create an alias object for the UASHOST server in the IT OU, follow these steps:

a. If necessary, click to expand the **eDirectory Administration** heading.

b. Click the **Create Object** link.

c. Verify that the Alias object class is selected in the Available object classes list box, and then click **OK** to display the Create Alias window shown in Figure 4-18.

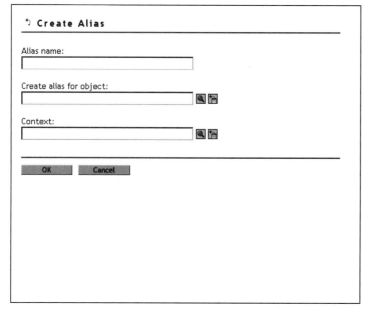

Figure 4-18   The Create Alias window

     d. Enter **UasHost** in the Alias name text box.

     e. Click the **Object Selector** button next to the Create alias for object text box, and then navigate to the container for your UASHOST server (based on the information in the Requirements section).

     f. Click your **UASHOST** server object to place it in the Create alias for object text box.

     g. Click the **Object Selector** button next to the Context text box, and then navigate to the IT OU you created in Activity 4-1 to place its distinguished name in the Context text box.

     h. Click **OK** to create the alias object and display the completion message.

2. Click **OK** to return to the iManager main window, and leave iManager open for the next activity.

Activity 4-3: Creating User Objects in iManager

Time Required: 10 minutes

Objectives: Use iManager to create eDirectory components.

Requirements:

- Windows XP or SUSE Linux 10 system with access to a NetWare 6.5 server
- NetWare 6.5 user name and password with rights to create objects in iManager
- Successful completion of Activity 4-1

Description: Eric wants you to create a user object that he can use to log in to the NetWare 6.5 eDirectory tree. In this activity, you use iManager to create a user account for yourself and Eric in the Engineering and IT OUs you created in Activity 4-1.

1. Scroll down and click to expand the **Users** heading in the Roles and Tasks pane. Record the user options here:

        _____

        _____

2. To create a user name for Eric Kenton in the IT OU, follow these steps:

     a. Click the **Create User** link to display the Create User window shown in Figure 4-19. Record all required fields (indicated by a red star) here:

        _____

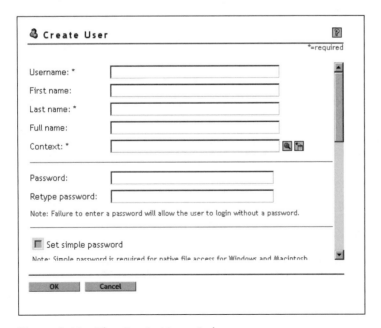

Figure 4-19   The Create User window

b. Enter the following information:

- Username: **EKenton**

- First name: **Eric**

- Last name: **Kenton**

- Context: If you're using your own server, enter **IT.UAS**; if you're using a classroom server, enter **IT.##UAS.CLASS** (## represents your assigned student number)

c. Scroll down and enter **password** in the Password and Retype password text boxes.

d. Click to select the **Set simple password** check box.

e. Scroll down and click **OK** to create the new user account for Eric.

f. Click **OK** to return to the Novell iManager main window.

3. Repeat the process in Step 2 to create a user name for yourself in the Engineering container. Record your user name here:

_____

4. If you're not going on to the next activity at this time, click the **Exit** button to return to the iManager login window. You can then close your Web browser and log out of your local client computer. If you're continuing to the next activity, however, leave iManager open and stay logged in.

Implementing eDirectory Replicas and Partitions

The first NetWare 6.5 server installed in the eDirectory tree stores the global eDirectory database in its SYS volume. The copy of the eDirectory database placed on a new server is called a **replica**. There are five types of replicas: Master, Read/Write, Filtered, Read-Only, and Subordinate. The eDirectory service automatically creates Read-Only and Subordinate replicas, so these two types aren't a concern for small to medium networks. A Master replica is the original main copy of the eDirectory data. As a network administrator, you might want to create additional Read/Write (R/W) replicas for two major reasons: They improve performance by reducing the time required to authenticate or access a network object, and they ensure additional reliability and fault tolerance. For example, future expansion plans for Universal AeroSpace include adding a dedicated NetWare 6.5 server for Engineering and Manufacturing use. When the new server is added, eDirectory automatically places a copy of the entire eDirectory database on the new server, as shown in Figure 4-20.

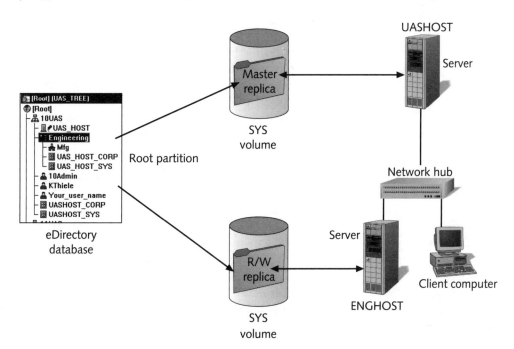

Figure 4-20   Adding a copy of the eDirectory database to a new server

Placing a Read/Write replica on the Engineering Department's server, ENGHOST, would improve performance for those users because the ENGHOST server could authenticate access to network objects immediately, without having to communicate with the primary UASHOST server. Reliability and fault tolerance would also be improved by maintaining separate replicas of the eDirectory database on the Engineering server. For example, if the primary server, UASHOST, is down, users in the Engineering Department could still log in and access resources on the ENGHOST server. In addition, the eDirectory replica stored on the ENGHOST server would enable other UAS users to log in and access certain resources, such as network printers and e-mail, and use information stored on the ENGHOST server. The data files stored on the primary UASHOST server's file system would, of course, not be accessible until that server is brought back online.

Filtered replicas are similar to Read/Write replicas, except that you can use a filter to specify what types of objects are included in the replica. Filtered replicas are useful when remote users in an organization must use a slow WAN connection. For example, placing a Filtered replica that contains only user accounts on the remote server enables users to log in without the overhead of keeping the organization's entire eDirectory database synchronized with the remote server. When users at the remote location log in, the server at their location can check its copy of the eDirectory database to authenticate logins without needing to use the slow WAN connection to access the main server. Without a replica at the remote server, each user's login request would have to be sent across the WAN connection for authentication.

eDirectory Partitions

Although keeping a complete copy of the eDirectory database on each server offers more reliability and improved performance when authenticating objects, it can also create extra communication overhead time, especially when servers are connected over WANs. The extra communication time is caused by the need to synchronize any changes to eDirectory objects across all servers containing replicas of the eDirectory database. Creating Filtered replicas of the database on servers located on other LANS can help reduce synchronization time by synchronizing only certain object types, such as user accounts. However, they can still require a lot of data flow between the server with the Filtered replica and a server with a full replica when users access object types not included in the Filtered replica. To reduce this overhead, Novell has made it possible to partition the eDirectory database. An **eDirectory partition** is a division of the eDirectory database that enables a network administrator to replicate only a part of the entire eDirectory tree. Initially, the eDirectory tree contains only one partition that starts at the root and is referred to as the **root partition**. Additional partitions begin at a container object and include all objects and subcontainers from that point down the tree. A partition is named by the container at the "top" of that partition. The start of an eDirectory partition is referred to as the "partition root."

For example, in addition to the new server in Engineering, Eric is planning to install another server in the Desktop Publishing Department. He's concerned that creating replicas of the entire eDirectory tree on all three servers would create extra communication overhead to maintain partition synchronization. As a result, he's planning to make the Engineering container a separate partition from the root partition. This way, objects in the Engineering partition can be replicated only on the ENGHOST and UASHOST servers. The Desktop Publishing server could then contain only a Read/Write replica of the root partition. Figure 4-21 shows this partitioning scheme.

Notice that the root partition contains all objects in the UAS Organization except the Engineering objects, which are stored in the Engineering partition. The PUBHOST server contains only a Read/Write replica of the root partition objects. UASHOST contains Master replicas of the root partition and the Engineering partition. The ENGHOST server contains only a Read/Write replica of the Engineering partition. When changes such as adding new users to the IT Department are made to the root partition, these changes have to be synchronized only between the UASHOST and PUBHOST servers. Additions or changes made to objects in the Engineering Department are synchronized only between the UASHOST and ENGHOST servers. In addition, notice that Eric arranged the replicas so that if any server goes down, at least one replica of each partition is available to the network. For example, if the UASHOST server goes down, all objects in the root and Engineering partitions are still available from both the PUBHOST and ENGHOST servers.

In NetWare 6.5, both iManager and ConsoleOne can be used to view, create, move, or merge partitions. As shown in Figure 4-22, iManager enables you to identify the partition replicas stored on a server by selecting

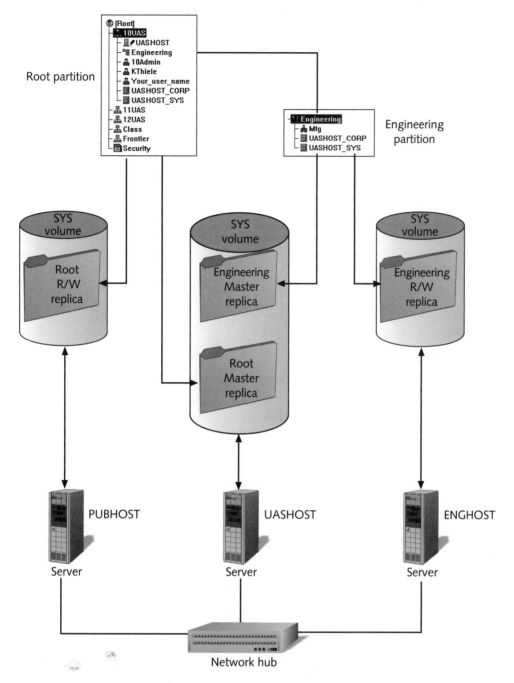

Figure 4-21 Partitioning the eDirectory database

the server name with the Object Selector button. Notice in Figure 4-22 that the only partition stored on the UASHOST server is a Master replica of the root of the eDirectory tree, which is the first and only required partition in the eDirectory tree. When new servers are added to the tree, they receive a Read/Write replica of the root partition. The Add Replica button enables you to add a replica of a different partition to the UASHOST server.

You can also use iManager's Replica View option to find all replicas of a partition, as shown in Figure 4-23, by using the Object Selector button to select a partition. When viewing a partition, the Replica View window displays the servers containing replicas of the selected partition as well as the replica type and state.

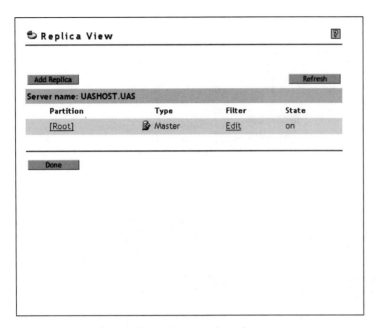

Figure 4-22   The Replica View window for a server

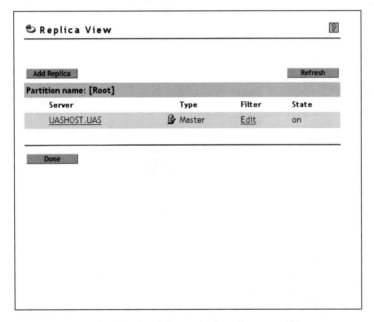

Figure 4-23   The Replica View window for a partition

In Figure 4-23, notice that the eDirectory root partition is stored only on the UASHOST server. If your classroom network contains multiple servers, you might find that the root partition is also stored on other servers. The State column indicates the status of the replica on that server. You should not create or merge partitions if the state is not "on." In the following activities, you learn how to use iManager to view current replicas and create a new partition for the Engineering container.

4

Activity 4-4: Viewing Partitions and Replicas

Time Required: 10 minutes

Objective: Use iManager to view and work with partitions and replicas.

Requirements:

- Successful completion of Activities 4-1 and 4-2
- Windows XP or SUSE Linux 10 system with access to a NetWare 6.5 server

Description: At a UAS meeting, the CEO, Dave Heise, expressed concern about how to scale the network to meet the rapid growth expectations for the company. Eric assured David that NetWare 6.5 is quite scalable and can handle the expected growth. In this activity, you use iManager to identify all partitions and replicas in your eDirectory tree.

1. If necessary, start your client computer and log in to the local computer.

2. If necessary, start your Web browser and then start iManager as described in Activity 4-1.

3. Scroll down and click to expand the **Partition and Replicas** heading.

4. Click the **Replica View** link.

5. Click the **Object Selector** button, and click the **UASHOST** server object to insert it into the Partition or Server object text box.

6. Click **OK** to view all replicas stored on the UASHOST server. Record the replicas and their types here:

_____

7. Leave the Replica View window open for the next activity.

Activity 4-5: Creating a Partition

Time Required: 10 minutes

Objective: Use iManager to view and work with partitions and replicas.

Requirements: Same as Activity 4-4

Description: Because of the recent NASA contract, Dave Heise is expecting rapid expansion in the Engineering Department. To meet these expansion needs, servers dedicated to engineering and desktop publishing applications will be added in the future. To prepare the eDirectory tree for this expansion, Eric wants you to create a separate partition for the Engineering OU. In this activity, you use iManager to create a new partition for the Engineering Department.

1. If necessary, click to expand the **Partition and Replicas** heading.

2. Click the **Create Partition** link to display the Create Partition window.

3. Click the **Object Selector** button next to the Container text box. Navigate down the tree, and then click the **Engineering** OU to place its context in the Container text box (see Figure 4-24).

4. Click **OK** to start the partition creation process. Wait until the "Complete: Create Partition" message is displayed, and then click **OK** to return to the iManager window.

5. Click the **View Partition Information** link to display the Partition selection window.

6. Click the **Object Selector** button, navigate to your **UAS** container, and then click the **Engineering** OU.

7. Click **OK** to view information on your Engineering partition, and record the location of the Master replica and the number of replicas here:

_____

_____

8. Click the **Exit** button to return to the iManager Login window. Close your Web browser and stay logged in to your local computer for the next activity.

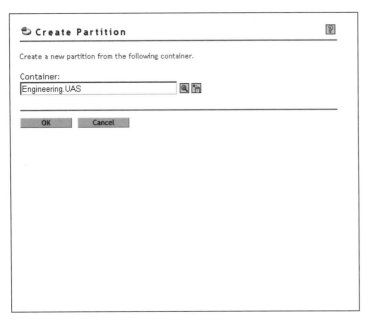

Figure 4-24   The Create Partition window

WORKING WITH NOVELL CLIENT

You have learned how objects in the eDirectory tree can be identified by using distinguished and relative names. In this section, you learn how to install Novell Client and then use it to log in to your eDirectory tree and local Windows computer.

Installing Novell Client on Windows

In Chapter 3, you learned how NFAP can be used to log in and access basic NetWare file and print services. Although the Microsoft NetWare client can also be used to log in and access basic NetWare file and print services, it does not have all the capabilities of the Novell client that ships with NetWare 6.5. For example, Novell Client offers the following advantages over using the Microsoft NetWare client when logging in to the server:

- Easy access to network services through the addition of the Novell menu in the taskbar and extra NetWare options in My Computer, Network Neighborhood, and Windows Explorer menus

- More secure passwords

- Use of NetWare utilities, such as ConsoleOne and NetWare Administrator

- Support for older eDirectory applications

As shown in Table 4-4, there have been several versions of the Novell client for different OSs. Earlier versions required using IPX/SPX to communicate with NetWare servers. As a result, some applications still need IPX/SPX to operate. The Novell client that ships with NetWare 6.5 has backward compatibility with earlier clients and applications because it supports the IPX/SPX application interface over TCP/IP.

Table 4-4   Novell clients

Novell Client Version	Description
NetX	The NetX client, used with DOS and Windows 3.1, provided network access using only IPX/SPX. The NetX client acted as a shell to the DOS environment, enabling it to use network services. It was loaded with the Autoexec.bat file to run the NIC driver, load the protocol, and run the client.

Table 4-4 Novell clients (continued)

Novell Client Version	Description
Client 32	Client 32, an early version of Novell Client, was used with Windows 95. Like the NetX client, Client 32 depended on IPX/SPX to access NetWare servers. Client 32 used the capabilities of a 32-bit OS to enhance the client's features and performance. Because OSs such as Windows 9x, 2000, and XP are more network aware than DOS, Client 32 worked with the OS to provide access to NetWare services instead of acting as a DOS shell.
Novell Client	Novell Client is an improved version of Client 32 that provides access to NetWare services by using IPX/SPX or TCP/IP. Versions of Novell Client are available for Windows-based computers. The latest Novell Client is required if you need to use NetWare 6.5 management tools, such as ConsoleOne, and access application services, such as Z.E.N.works.

Installing Novell Client from a CD on every computer in a network is usually too time consuming. Fortunately, Novell offers multiple installation or upgrade methods to make this job easier. As a network administrator, you can select any of the following methods to install Novell Client, depending on the computer's configuration and your personal preferences:

- *Install from CD-ROM*—This method is best used on new computers that aren't currently connected to the network. If the computer has a CD-ROM drive, Novell Client can be installed quickly from the Client CD.

- *Install from the network*—Another good use of Novell NFAP is installing Novell Client on a new Windows computer. With NFAP, a new computer can log in to the network using only the default Microsoft NetWare client. Novell Client can then be installed from a shared copy of the client installation software on the NetWare server. Installing from the network is faster and more convenient than installing from a CD. For example, when setting up a new computer for the UAS organization, Eric often installs Novell Client from a shared network directory on the NetWare server instead of from the Client CD. With this method, he can install several clients at the same time without having multiple copies of the Client CD. To do this, Eric uses the Microsoft client on the new computer to access the Novell Client folder on the NetWare 6.5 server.

- *Automatic Client Upgrade (ACU)*—You can use the ACU method to automate upgrading older Novell Client versions to the latest Novell Client when a user logs in from the computer. The ACU method involves placing special commands in the container login script file, as described in Chapter 9, that starts the upgrade. This method can be a little tricky to set up, but it's helpful when you're upgrading multiple computers to the latest version of Novell Client.

Activity 4-6: Installing Novell Client

Time Required: 15 minutes

Objective: Install Novell Client.

Requirements:

- A Windows XP computer

- A user name and password that has administrative rights to your Windows system

- A copy of the Novell Client CD version 4.91 or later

Description: In this activity, you learn how to install Novell Client using a CD or a network directory. If you're using a classroom server, your instructor will provide the location of the Novell Client files on the classroom server. If you're using a dedicated server, this activity should be performed using the Novell Client CD. To change your Windows XP network configuration in this activity, you need to log on to your local Windows computer with a user name and password that has administrative privileges.

1. If necessary, start your computer and log on to your local Windows computer with your assigned Windows administrator user name and password.

2. If you're using a classroom server, follow these steps to map a drive to the network directory containing the Novell Client files:

    a. Click **Start**, **Run** and then enter *IPaddress* (substituting the IP address of your classroom server).

    b. In the login window, enter your assigned user name and password.

    c. Navigate to the **SYS** volume and open the **Public** directory.

    d. Navigate to the **NovellClient** folder and click the **SETUPNW.exe** program.

    e. Skip to Step 4.

3. If you're using a dedicated server, insert the Novell Client CD in the CD-ROM drive. If the Novell Client installation doesn't start automatically, use Windows Explorer to open the CD-ROM drive, and then double-click **SETUPNW.exe** to start the Novell Client Installation Wizard.

4. Click the client installation option for your Windows version.

5. Read the license information, and then click the **Yes** button to accept the license agreement.

6. Verify that the Typical Installation option button is selected, and then click the **Install** button.

7. After the installation is finished, click the **Reboot** button to restart your computer.

8. When the computer restarts, the Novell Login window should be displayed. Do not log in at this time. In the next section, you customize Novell Client and use it to practice logging in to your eDirectory tree.

Logging in with Novell Client

Before accessing resources or services on a network, users must first authenticate themselves by providing a valid user name and password to the client software. The client software then uses the user name and password to authenticate the user to the network. Novell refers to the process of using Novell Client to authenticate a user as **logging in** to the network. To access the local Windows computer, Microsoft also requires the user to authenticate by using a valid user name and password. Microsoft refers to this authentication process as **logging on** to the computer. As a result, when you access the Novell network from a Windows system, you need to perform two authentication processes. First, you log in to the eDirectory tree using Novell Client. Novell Client then attempts to log on to the local Windows computer with the local user name specified in the Windows tab and the password you supplied to Novell Client. If your local Windows computer has a user account with the specified local user name and password, you're automatically logged on to the local computer; if not, you see a Windows logon window and must then enter a valid user name and password to authenticate to the local computer before proceeding.

To allow users to access the Novell network, the network administrator needs to create a user account in Novell's eDirectory for each user. To make accessing the local computer easier, the network administrator can also create a user account on the Windows computer with the same user name and password as the Novell user name. Because Novell's eDirectory service stores user accounts in containers arranged in a tree structure, users must supply their context along with their user names and passwords when logging in. Figure 4-25 shows the Novell Login window after clicking the Advanced button. Notice that the window contains text boxes for Username, Password, Tree, Context, and Server.

By default, the Username text box contains the name and context of the last user who logged in from your computer. If no one has logged in since the client was installed, the Username text box is blank. The Password text box is where you enter the password for your user account. This field is kept blank to prevent someone else from logging in as the previous user. Your password is used like a signature, allowing the eDirectory service to verify that you're the actual user of the account.

The Context text box is used to specify the path leading to the container where your user name is stored. You can use the buttons to the right of each text box to browse for a tree, container, or server instead of typing in the object's exact name (see Figure 4-26). The list arrows next to each text box enable you to select from previously used trees and contexts.

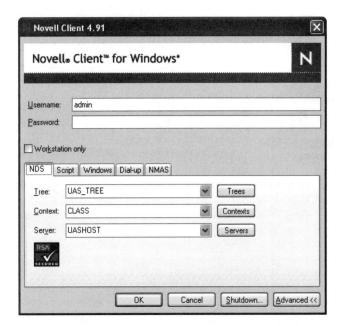

Figure 4-25   Options available after clicking the Advanced button

Figure 4-26   Selecting an eDirectory context in Novell Client

The Advanced options also include a Windows tab where you can specify the user name and computer or domain to be used for logging into the Windows OS (see Figure 4-27). Notice that this window contains two text boxes at the bottom: Local username is used to specify the Windows user name, and From is used to specify the name of your local Windows computer (UAS1 in Figure 4-27) or a Windows domain name. If a computer name is used, Novell Client attempts to log on locally to the Windows system specified in the From text box. If a domain name is used, Novell Client attempts to log on to a Windows Active Directory domain controller for the domain name specified. In both cases, the password you enter for the eDirectory user name in the top window is used along with the local user name for the Windows logon attempt. For example, in Figure 4-27, the system attempts to log in to eDirectory with the Admin user name and then tries to log on to the local Windows system with the EKenton user name. The password entered for the Admin user name is used for both authentication attempts. If a user's eDirectory and Windows passwords are the same, the logon to the Windows system is automatic. If the password is different from the password assigned to the local user name, a Windows Logon dialog box is displayed, where the user enters the user name and password to be used on the Windows system. In Activity 4-7, you learn how to customize Novell Client to set certain properties. In Activities 4-8 and 4-9, you practice logging in to eDirectory and the local Windows computer with both distinguished and relative distinguished user names.

Figure 4-27   Entering a local Windows user name in Novell Client

Activity 4-7: Customizing Novell Client

Time Required: 10 minutes

Objectives: Customize and view settings in Novell Client.

Requirements:

- Windows XP computer with Novell Client installed from Activity 4-6
- Access to the NetWare 6.5 server
- The context of your UAS container; if you're using a classroom server, the suggested context is .##UAS.CLASS (## represents your assigned student number)

Description: To make it easier for users to log in, Eric has customized Novell Client in each department to default to the department's container. In this activity, you explore some of the options available when customizing Novell Client.

1. If necessary, start your computer to display the Novell Login window.

2. Click the **Workstation Only** check box, and then log on to your local Windows computer with your local administrator user name and password.

3. Right-click **My Network Places**, and then click **Properties** to open the Network Connections window.

4. Right-click **Local Area Connection** and then click **Properties** to open the Local Area Connection Properties dialog box.

5. Record the items listed under "This connection uses the following items":

_____

6. Click to highlight **Novell Client for Windows** and then click the **Properties** button to open the Novell Client for Windows Properties dialog box.

7. If necessary, click the **Client** tab to select it, as shown in Figure 4-28. Notice the text boxes for First network drive, Preferred server, and Preferred tree. These text boxes can be used to change the default settings when a user first logs in. In addition, the Client tab contains the version number of the client and the latest service pack. This information is important to ensure that the client is current. The bottom section of the Client tab contains the default context where eDirectory looks to find the user name.

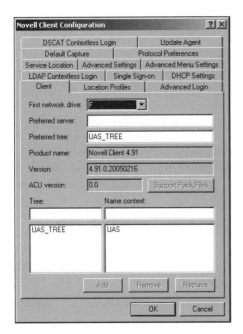

Figure 4-28 Options in the Client tab

8. Verify that the First network drive is set to F and that the Preferred tree text box contains UAS_ TREE. (Your tree name might vary if you're using your own server.)

9. Follow these steps to change the default context so that it points to the Engineering container in the UAS Organization:

  a. In the Tree text box, enter your eDirectory tree name (**UAS_TREE** if you're using a shared classroom server or your eDirectory tree name if you're using a dedicated server).

  b. In the Name context text box, enter **.UAS**. (If you're using a shared classroom server, enter the context of your UAS container, such as .##UAS.CLASS.)

  c. Click the **Add** button to insert the context.

10. Click the **Advanced Login** tab, where you set which options are displayed when you click the Advanced button during login. Record the current settings here:

_____

11. Click the **Advanced Menu Settings** tab, where you can set the options available on various menus. If necessary, click the **Change Password** option, and then record the description here:

_____

12. Click the **Advanced Settings** tab, where you control parameters used to communicate on the network. Click the **File Caching** option, and then record the description here:

_____

13. Click the **LDAP Contextless Login** tab, which is used to specify a global catalog of objects. The global catalog makes it possible to log in or access a resource without specifying which container the user account or resource is located in. Record whether contextless login is enabled on your computer:

_____

14. Click **OK** to close the Novell Client for Windows Properties dialog box.

15. Click **Close** to close the Local Area Connection Properties dialog box.

16. Click **OK** to restart your computer.

Activity 4-8: Logging in with Distinguished Names

Time Required: 10 minutes

Objective: Use distinguished names to access network objects.

Requirements:

- Windows XP computer
- Completion of Activities 4-1 through 4-3, Activity 4-6, and Activity 4-7

Description: Eric typically has to log in from computers in other departments to test and maintain network services. In this activity, you practice logging in as Eric Kenton from a computer in the Engineering Department by using a distinguished name instead of clicking the Advanced button to change your current context.

1. If necessary, start your computer to display the Novell Login window, and click to clear the **Workstation Only** check box.

2. Click the **Advanced** button and verify that the context is set to the eDirectory tree and UAS container you entered in Activity 4-7.

3. To log in using a typeful distinguished name for EKenton in the IT OU of the UAS Organization, follow these steps:

   a. In the Username text box, enter the typeful distinguished name for EKenton:
   .CN=EKenton.OU=IT.O=UAS (if you're using your own server) or
   .CN=EKenton.OU=IT.OU=##UAS.O=CLASS (if you're using the classroom server, substituting your student number for ##).

   b. In the Password text box, enter **password**, and then click **OK**.

4. Use the CX command to record your current context:

   a. Click **Start**, point to **All Programs**, point to **Accessories**, and then click **Command Prompt**.

   b. At the command prompt, type **CX**, and then press **Enter**.

   c. Record the current context here:

   _____

   d. Type **exit**, and then press **Enter** to close the command prompt window.

5. Log out.

6. Use the procedure in Step 3 to log in as Eric Kenton, using a typeless distinguished name. Record the name you enter here:

   _____

7. Log out.

8. Follow the procedure in Step 3 and attempt to log in as Eric Kenton with the typeless relative distinguished name **EKenton.IT.UAS** (which does not contain a leading or ending period). Record your results along with the reason this method does or does not work:

   _____

9. Log out.

10. Follow the procedure in Step 3 to log in with the user name you created for yourself in the Engineering container (see Activity 4-3) by using a typeful distinguished name. Record the name you entered:

_____

11. Log out.

Activity 4-9: Logging in with Relative Distinguished Names

Time Required: 5 minutes

Objective: Use relative distinguished names to access network objects.

Requirements: Same as Activity 4-8

Description: When he knows the current context settings of a computer, Eric often uses a relative distinguished name when logging in to the network to save time and reduce the chance of typos. In this activity, you learn how to use typeless and typeful relative distinguished names to log in as Eric Kenton from computers configured for different default contexts.

1. If necessary, start your computer to display the Novell Login window.

2. Click the **Advanced** button, and change your default context by entering **.UAS** in the Context text box. (If necessary, click the **Trees** button to select your eDirectory tree before setting the context.)

3. Follow these steps to log in with the relative distinguished name **EKenton.IT**:

   a. In the Username text box, enter the relative distinguished name **EKenton.IT**, and enter **password** in the Password text box.

   b. Click **OK** to log in to the Novell network. (If you're using a Windows 2000 client, log on to your local Windows computer with your ##Admin user name and password.)

4. Log out to display a new Novell Login window.

5. Click the **Advanced** button, and verify that the default context is set to UAS.

6. Follow the procedure in Step 3 to use a typeful relative distinguished name to log in to the IT container as EKenton. Record the name you used:

_____

7. Log out to display a new Novell Login window.

8. Click the **Advanced** button, and then enter **.Engineering.UAS** in the Context text box to change your current context to the Engineering container.

9. Follow the procedure in Step 3 to log in as Eric Kenton by entering the typeless relative distinguished name **EKenton.IT.** (note the ending period) in the Username text box and **password** in the Password text box.

10. Log out to display a new Novell Login window.

11. Click the **Advanced** button, and change your current context by entering **.IT.UAS** in the Context text box.

12. Follow the procedure in Step 3 to log in with the user name you created for yourself in the Engineering container in Activity 4-3. Use a typeless relative distinguished name and a password of "password." Record the name you used:

_____

13. Log out.

Good job! Your tasks for this chapter are finished, and you can now log off the network and proceed to the end-of-chapter projects to apply your skills to creating the eDirectory tree structure for the Business Department.

CHAPTER SUMMARY

❏ Directory services play an important role in administrating and managing networks consisting of diverse operating systems and locations. Most directory services today are based on the X.500 standard, which defines protocols for the Directory Information Base, Directory Information Tree, Directory User Agent, and Directory Service Agent.

❏ One of the major capabilities of NetWare is the eDirectory database, which allows NetWare servers to share access to a common set of network objects that can be organized into a hierarchical tree structure. eDirectory objects can be classified as Root, container, or leaf objects. The Root object represents the entire tree. Container objects are used to organize other objects and include the Country, Domain, Organization, Organizational Unit, Role Based Service, and Security objects. Leaf objects represent actual network entities, such as users, printers, groups, servers, and volumes.

❏ Small networks can have a simple tree structure consisting of all leaf objects within a single Organization container. Larger organizations require more complex trees divided into multiple Organizational Units.

❏ The location of an object within the eDirectory tree is called its context. Specifying its name along with its complete context path, called its distinguished name can always uniquely identify an object. A distinguished name can be typeful or typeless. A typeful distinguished name includes the object type, such as OU, along with the name of the object. A typeless name, such as .EKenton.IT.UAS, does not include object type specifications, and although it's not as specific, it's much easier to type.

❏ The location of the client computer within the eDirectory tree is called the current context. The current context can be used to make access to objects easier by simply entering the object's common name.

❏ NetWare 6.5 has three graphical Windows-based utilities for managing eDirectory objects: iManager, ConsoleOne, and NetWare Administrator. Although iManager is the primary utility, ConsoleOne and NetWare Administrator are sometimes more convenient and faster to use on Windows-based computers. These utilities can be used to browse an eDirectory tree structure, view information about specific objects, and create leaf and Organizational Unit objects.

❏ Replicas are copies of the eDirectory database that are placed on NetWare servers. Replicas provide fault tolerance in the event a server is down and allow faster access to network resources by placing replicas on local servers. When an eDirectory database becomes large or is spread over several servers, a network administrator can increase performance by breaking the database into smaller segments called partitions. Replicas of partitions can be kept only on servers that need that data, thereby decreasing the amount of network traffic required to keep all servers synchronized.

❏ To communicate on a NetWare network, a computer must have a card driver program, a protocol stack, and a client. Installing Novell Client enables you to take advantage of certain eDirectory features, such as enhanced security, and allows you to use Windows-based NetWare utilities, such as ConsoleOne and NetWare Administrator.

❏ Novell Client can be installed from a CD, across the network, or automatically via the Automatic Client Upgrade (ACU).

❏ Novell Client can be customized by using the Properties button in Windows My Network Places. The Advanced button in Novell Client is used to specify the context of an eDirectory user name and the user name for the Windows system.

KEY TERMS

Admin user object — An important user object with Supervisor rights to the entire eDirectory tree.

alias object — An object used as a pointer to another object located in a different container of the eDirectory tree.

attribute — *See* property.

common name (CN) — The name given to an object in the eDirectory tree. A common name must be unique within the container that houses the object.

container object — An eDirectory object used to store other objects.

context — The location of an object in the eDirectory tree.

Country container objects — A special type of container object used to group Organization container objects by country. Country containers must be assigned a valid two-digit country code and can exist only at the root of an eDirectory tree.

current context — The default location of a client computer in the eDirectory tree.

Directory Access Protocol (DAP) — A protocol that handles formatting and transmitting data between the DUA and DSA.

directory database — A database used to store information about network objects.

Directory Information Base (DIB) — The name of the X.500 directory database.

Directory Information Shadowing Protocol (DISP) — A special form of the DSP that's responsible for keeping multiple copies of the DIB synchronized.

Directory Information Tree (DIT) — A tree structure for the DIB containers that represents the hierarchical relationship between entries.

Directory Map objects — Objects in the eDirectory tree that contain a path to a volume and directory in the network file system.

directory schema — A set of rules for ensuring that information in the DIB is not damaged or lost.

directory service — Software that provides discovery, security, relational management, storage, and retrieval of directory database information.

Directory Service Protocol (DSP) — A protocol that handles communication between DSAs.

Directory System Agent (DSA) — Software running on a server that consists of a collection of services and protocols that manage specific portions of the DIB.

Directory User Agent (DUA) — Software that runs on the user's computer and acts as a client to send requests from the user to the directory service.

distinguished name — A name that uniquely identifies an object in the eDirectory database.

Domain container objects — eDirectory containers used to store DNS information.

eDirectory — Novell's directory service; provides directory services to a wide range of network operating systems, including NetWare, Windows, and Linux.

eDirectory partition — A division of the eDirectory structure that starts with a single container and includes any subcontainers.

eDirectory tree — A hierarchical structure of eDirectory objects that places leaf objects within containers.

entries — Records in the directory database that store information on network objects.

leaf objects — eDirectory objects used to represent network entities, such as users, groups, printers, and servers. Leaf objects must exist within Organization or Organizational Unit containers.

Lightweight Directory Access Protocol (LDAP) — A simplified version of X.500 that makes it easier for compatible systems to exchange directory information.

logging in — The process of being authorized to the eDirectory tree.

logging on — The process of being authorized to a Microsoft Windows system.

Organization container object — An eDirectory object used to group objects that belong to an organization. Organization objects can exist at the root of an eDirectory tree or within a Country container.

Organizational Unit (OU) container object — An eDirectory object used to group leaf objects that belong to a subdivision of an Organization container. OU containers can exist within an Organization container or within another OU.

property — A field containing information about an object. Not all object types have the same properties.

relative distinguished name — A distinguished name that starts with the current context of the client but omits the leading period.

replica — A copy of the eDirectory database stored on a NetWare server.

Role Based Services (RBS) container objects — eDirectory container objects used to store iManager administrative roles.

Root object — An eDirectory object representing the beginning of the network's directory service tree.

root partition — The initial division of the eDirectory tree that starts at the root of the tree.

scalability — The capability to work with systems of different sizes.

Security container objects — eDirectory container objects used to store security objects, such as the server certificate.

shadowing — The process of distributing and synchronizing the DIB among multiple locations.

typeful — A distinguished name that includes object type abbreviations (O, OU, and CN).

typeless — A distinguished name that assumes object type based on position instead of including the object type abbreviations.

volume object — An eDirectory object used to represent physical NetWare volumes in the eDirectory tree; provides a link between the eDirectory system and the file system.

X.500 — A set of recommendations created by the International Telecommunications Union that define directory services.

Review Questions

1. In the X.500 model, which of the following components is responsible for initiating a request for directory service information?
   a. DIB
   b. DSP
   c. DUA
   d. DUP

2. Which of the following is the X.500 protocol used to communicate between different directory servers?
   a. DIB
   b. DSP
   c. DUA
   d. DUP

3. Which of the following is a collection of entries that contain information about objects in the real world?
   a. DIB
   b. DSP
   c. DUA
   d. DUP

4. A set of rules known as the _____ ensures that the directory remains well formed as modifications are made over time.
   a. protocol
   b. DUP
   c. directory schema
   d. DSP

5. The process of distributing the X.500 Directory Information Base between servers is called _____ .
   a. synchronizing
   b. replicating
   c. shadowing
   d. stabilizing

6. The object-naming system used in eDirectory is based on an industry naming standard called _____ .

   a. DNS

   b. X.500

   c. SDLC

   d. NetBIOS

7. List three types of container objects.

8. A _____ is a field containing information about an object.

   a. leaf

   b. property

   c. value

   d. container

9. Which object types can be placed in the root of an eDirectory tree? (Choose all that apply.)

   a. users

   b. Organization objects

   c. volumes

   d. Country objects

10. In which types of containers can user objects be placed? (Choose all that apply.)

   a. Country objects

   b. the Root object

   c. Organization objects

   d. Organizational Units

11. List two advantages of placing replicas on multiple servers.

12. A(n) _____ is a division of the eDirectory database that starts at a container.

   a. replica

   b. partition

   c. root

   d. Organization

13. The location of an object in the eDirectory tree is referred to as its _____ .

   a. context

   b. path

   c. partition

   d. environment

14. Write a typeful distinguished name for the user JMeek located in the Sales OU of the AstorFurs Organization.

15. Write a typeless distinguished name for the SAL_HP3 laser printer located in the Sales OU of the AstorFurs Organization.

16. Write a typeless relative distinguished name for the SAL_HP3 laser printer described in Question 15, assuming that your current context is the AstorFurs Organization.

17. List the five types of replicas.

18. The _____ utility enables a network administrator to create and manage eDirectory objects from any network or client via a Web browser.

    a. ConsoleOne

    b. Remote Manager

    c. iManager

    d. WebDAV

19. A _____ starts with the client's current context and is specified by omitting the leading period.

    a. typeless name

    b. relative distinguished name

    c. distinguished name

    d. typeless distinguished name

20. A partition can have only one Master replica. True or False?

CASE PROJECTS

Case Project 4-1: Designing the Business Division Structure

The users in the Universal AeroSpace Business Division are responsible for managing the financial and marketing needs of the company. To help make it easier to manage their resources, Eric Kenton would like you to design a structure that provides separate containers for the Accounting and Marketing objects. In this case project, you design and diagram a modified UAS tree structure that includes containers for the Accounting and Marketing resources.

Case Project 4-2: Modifying the eDirectory Tree Structure

AeroDyn Corporation, a manufacturer of aircraft control systems, is a subsidiary of Universal AeroSpace with office and manufacturing facilities in a different city. The office staff includes seven sales people, three design engineers, four programmers, two accountants, and an Information Technology Department. Management consists of a general manager and two administrative assistants. The accountants and management staff share network resources, such as printers, files and applications. The design engineers and programmers often work together on projects and also need to share resources. Eric Kenton would like you to modify the eDirectory structure for UAS to accommodate the AeroDyn objects. Draw a design showing the OUs you need to add and specifying their location in the structure. In addition, write a brief report listing any additional partitions that should be created if a NetWare 6.5 server is added in the AeroDyn location. Turn your design and report in to your instructor when you're finished.

Case Project 4-3: Designing a New eDirectory Tree

Create an eDirectory design for your school. The design should have separate OUs for faculty, students, and administration. In addition, your design should include partitioning for any branch campus locations.

HANDS-ON PROJECTS

Hands-on Project 4-1: Completing the UAS eDirectory Structure

Follow the procedure in Activity 4-1 and use iManager to create the remaining OUs shown in Figure 4-13. If requested by your instructor, document any objects you create by printing your eDirectory structure or using a text editor to list the containers. Have your instructor check your results.

4

Hands-on Project 4-2: Creating the Business Division Structure

Follow the procedure in Activity 4-1 and use iManager to create the OUs you defined for the Business Division in Case Project 4-1. If requested by your instructor, document any objects you create by printing your eDirectory structure or using a text editor to list the containers. Have your instructor check your results.

Hands-on Project 4-3: Creating the AeroDyn Structure

After you have your design from Case Project 4-2 approved, use iManager to implement your design by creating the necessary containers and partitions. In addition, create an alias object for the UASHOST server and volume objects for the SYS and CORP volumes. If requested by your instructor, document any objects you create by printing your eDirectory structure or using a text editor to list the containers. Have your instructor check your results.

CREATING AND SECURING USER AND GROUP OBJECTS

> ### After reading this chapter and completing the activities, you will be able to:
>
> ♦ Install and use NetWare Administrator and ConsoleOne to access the eDirectory tree
> ♦ Establish login security by using password, address, and time restrictions
> ♦ Create and manage group, user, and Organizational Role objects
> ♦ Update multiple user accounts
> ♦ Import user accounts from LDIF-compatible files
> ♦ Delete, rename, and move eDirectory objects

In addition to establishing a network file system and eDirectory structure, a network administrator must secure the network so that users can access only the network resources and services they have been authorized to use. As you learned in Chapter 1, NetWare 6.5 security consists of several systems: login security, file system security, eDirectory security, printer security, and server console security. Login security provides the basis for all security systems by ensuring that only authorized users have access to network resources. In this chapter, you learn how to use NetWare utilities to set up login security that protects user accounts from unauthorized access. Later chapters cover other security systems in NetWare 6.5. The activities in this chapter walk you through using NetWare utilities to set up and secure user accounts for the users in the Information Technology Department of Universal AeroSpace. In the end-of-chapter projects, you apply what you have learned about login security to planning and setting up login security for the remaining UAS departments.

INTRODUCTION TO NETWARE MANAGEMENT UTILITIES

To work with the eDirectory tree, you need to become familiar with Novell's management utilities. In previous releases of NetWare, creating and managing the eDirectory tree have required running the NetWare Administrator utility on a computer with Novell Client installed. In NetWare 5.0, Novell introduced the ConsoleOne utility, which was written with the Java language so that it could run on multiple platforms, including the NetWare server's console. With NetWare 6.0, Novell introduced a new network management tool called iManager. Although iManager version 1 could perform only a limited number of tasks, network administrators could use it to manage their eDirectory trees from a Web browser instead of requiring a computer with Novell Client. Because it doesn't require the Novell client running on a Windows-based computer, iManager is now an integral part of Novell's OneNet vision, making network management possible from any client computer on a connected network. By default, only the Admin user has rights to use iManager. For other users to run iManager, they need to be assigned to an iManager role by using Novell's Role Based Services (RBS). You learn more about using RBS in Chapter 7.

Each utility has its advantages and disadvantages. For example, ConsoleOne is a Java-based utility that can be run from multiple OSs, including the server console. NetWare Administrator has the advantage of providing high performance on older Windows-based computers, and iManager has the advantage of being able to be used from any network through a standard Web browser. Because of these utilities' different capabilities, a CNA should be familiar with all three. Although iManager is the primary utility used in this chapter to work with eDirectory objects, you also learn how to use NetWare Administrator and ConsoleOne for network tasks. In Chapter 4, you learned how to use iManager to access and create objects in the eDirectory tree. In the following sections, you learn how to install ConsoleOne and NetWare Administrator, and then use these utilities to access the eDirectory tree structure you created in Chapter 4.

Using NetWare Administrator

To run NetWare Administrator, you need a Windows system with at least 64 MB of RAM and the Novell Client software. Although you can access NetWare file and print services via the Microsoft client, it doesn't have the necessary components to run ConsoleOne or NetWare Administrator. During server installation, NetWare Administrator is loaded into the Public directory of the server's SYS volume. There are multiple versions of NetWare Administrator for different OS environments. In this book, you use the NetWare Administrator program in the Public\Win32 folder. In the following activities, you learn how to create a shortcut to run NetWare Administrator, and then use this utility to browse the tree structure and view information on network objects.

Activity 5-1: Creating a NetWare Administrator Shortcut

Time Required: 5 minutes

Objective: Install and configure NetWare Administrator.

Requirements: To perform this activity, you need the following:

❑ A Windows XP computer with Novell Client installed from Chapter 4

❑ A dedicated server or a classroom server and eDirectory tree shared with other students. Record the following information for your lab environment:

Server name:

_____

eDirectory tree name:

_____

Your assigned administrative user name:

_____

The name and context of your UAS Organization:

_____

Description: As the network administrator, Eric Kenton has often used NetWare Administrator to set up and maintain the UAS network system when working from older Windows desktops. To make it easier to start NetWare Administrator, Eric creates a Windows desktop shortcut, and then adds NetWare Administrator to the Start menu. In this activity, you learn how to add a NetWare Administrator shortcut to your desktop and your Start menu.

1. If necessary, start your Windows XP computer, and log in to eDirectory with your administrative user name and password.

2. Open the F:\Public\Win32 folder by following these steps:

   a. Double-click **My Computer**.

   b. Double-click the **F:** drive.

   c. Double-click the **Public** folder and then the **Win32** folder.

3. Right-click the **Nwadmn32** program, and then click **Send To Desktop (create shortcut)** to create a shortcut on your desktop.

4. Close the Win32 dialog box. A shortcut to Nwadmn32 should now appear on your desktop.

5. To add Nwadmn32 to your Start menu, right-click **Start**, and then click **Open** to open the Start Menu window.

6. Right-click the **Nwadmn32** shortcut on the desktop, and drag it to the Start Menu window.

7. Release the right mouse button, and then click **Copy Here** on the shortcut menu to place a copy of the shortcut in your Start menu.

8. Close the Start Menu window, and stay logged in for the next activity.

Activity 5-2: Browsing with NetWare Administrator

Time Required: 10 minutes

Objective: Use NetWare Administrator to browse the eDirectory tree, view object properties, and create new objects.

Requirements: Same as Activity 5-1 and completion of Activities 4-1 and 4-2

Description: Because of its good performance and capability of opening multiple browse windows, Eric periodically uses NetWare Administrator to manage his tree structures. In this activity, you learn how to start NetWare Administrator, open multiple browse windows, change the context, and view objects in the eDirectory tree.

1. Start NetWare Administrator by clicking **Start**, **All Programs**, **Shortcut to Nwadmn32**. The NetWare Administrator utility has a number of toolbar buttons for various tasks, as shown in Figure 5-1. If necessary, read the tip in the Welcome to NetWare Administrator window, and then click **Close**.

2. After NetWare Administrator is started, you see a browse window similar to the one in Figure 5-2.

3. Close the browse window by clicking the **Close** button.

4. Open a browse window to the root of the tree by following these steps:

   a. To open a new browse window, click **Tools**, **NDS Browser** from the menu to open the Set Context dialog box. Notice that the Context text box displays your computer's current context in UAS_Tree.

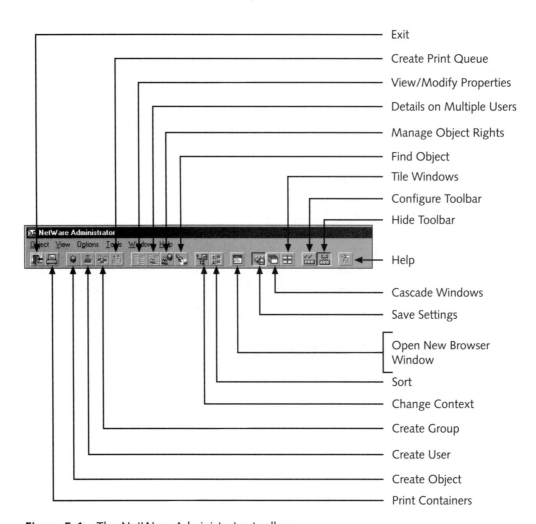

Exit
Create Print Queue
View/Modify Properties
Details on Multiple Users
Manage Object Rights
Find Object
Tile Windows
Configure Toolbar
Hide Toolbar
Help
Cascade Windows
Save Settings
Open New Browser Window
Sort
Change Context
Create Group
Create User
Create Object
Print Containers

Figure 5-1   The NetWare Administrator toolbar

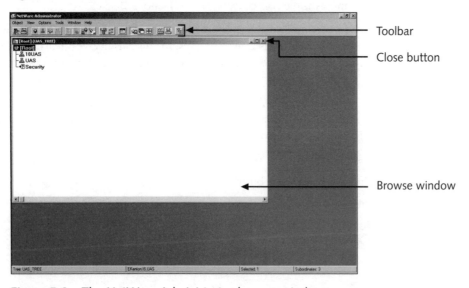

Toolbar
Close button
Browse window

Figure 5-2   The NetWare Administrator browse window

b. Click the **browse** button next to the Context text box to open the Select Object dialog box shown in Figure 5-3. The Browse context section on the right is used to change your current context. The Available objects section on the left lists objects in the selected context.

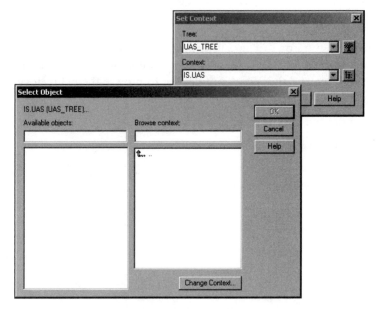

Figure 5-3   The NetWare Administrator Select Object dialog box

c. To move your current context up one level, double-click the **up arrow** in the Browse context section twice. All objects in the [Root] container of the tree are then displayed in the Available objects section.

d. To set the context of the Browse context section to the root of the tree, double-click the **[Root]** object in the Available objects section.

e. Click **OK** to save the new context setting. The browse window should now display all the Organization containers.

f. Record the names and types of all Organization objects displayed in the browse window:

_____

5. View all objects in the UAS container. If you're using a dedicated server, simply double-click **UAS** in the browse window. If you're using a shared classroom server, expand the **CLASS** Organization and then double-click the **##UAS** OU. Record the names of all Organizational Unit objects in the UAS container:

_____

_____

6. Record the names of all group objects in the UAS Organization:

_____

_____

7. Double-click the **UAS** container to collapse it.

8. Close NetWare Administrator by clicking **Object**, **Exit** from the menu, and stay logged in for the next activity.

Using ConsoleOne

ConsoleOne remains the primary Windows-based utility for managing most aspects of the NetWare 6.5 eDirectory tree. In addition to having Novell Client installed, ConsoleOne requires at least 128 MB of RAM and a 300 MHz processor to run effectively. Although the ConsoleOne software can be run directly from the SYS volume of the NetWare 6.5 server, loading ConsoleOne files across the network is slower and uses up network bandwidth. Starting ConsoleOne is much faster if you install it on your local computer. In the following activities, you install ConsoleOne on your Windows desktop, and then practice using it to browse the Universal AeroSpace tree.

Activity 5-3: Working with ConsoleOne

Time Required: 15 minutes

Objective: Use ConsoleOne to browse the eDirectory tree, view object properties, and create new objects.

Requirements: Same as Activity 5-2

Description: In addition to NetWare Administrator, Eric installs ConsoleOne on his local computer to carry out management tasks for setting up and maintaining the UAS network for multiple locations. In this activity, you copy ConsoleOne files to your computer, and then use ConsoleOne to browse the eDirectory tree and create a user account for yourself in the UAS Organization.

1. If necessary, log in with your administrative user name and password.

2. Open the Mgmt folder by following these steps:
    a. Double-click **My Computer**.
    b. Double-click the **Public on Uashost\Sys** drive letter.
    c. Double-click the **Mgmt** folder.

3. Copy the ConsoleOne folder to the root of your C: drive.

4. Create a shortcut to your ConsoleOne executable file:
    a. Click to expand the new **ConsoleOne** folder in your C: drive.
    b. Navigate to the **Bin** directory.
    c. Right-click the **ConsoleOne.exe** file, and then click **Send To Desktop, (create shortcut)**.

5. Start ConsoleOne by double-clicking the link created in Step 4.

6. In the Novell ConsoleOne window, click to expand the **NDS** object, if necessary. Then click to expand **UAS_Tree** and navigate to the **UAS** container.

7. Double-click the **UAS** container. You should see a window similar to the one in Figure 5-4.

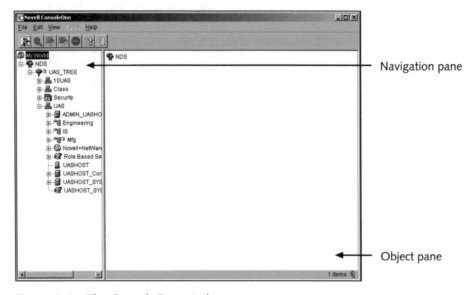

Figure 5-4   The ConsoleOne window

8. On the left is the navigation pane, which displays structure objects, such as containers, servers, and volumes. On the right is the object pane, which displays leaf objects, such as users, groups, and printers. To display leaf objects in the UAS Organization, click the **UAS** Organization and record all user names listed in the object pane:

9. Close the ConsoleOne window by clicking **File**, **Exit** from the menu, and stay logged in for the next activity.

Using Web Manager

In previous chapters, you have learned how to use iManager and Remote Manager for many network administrative tasks. To make accessing and configuring the network easier, NetWare 6.5 includes a OneNet home page called NetWare Web Manager (see Figure 5-5).

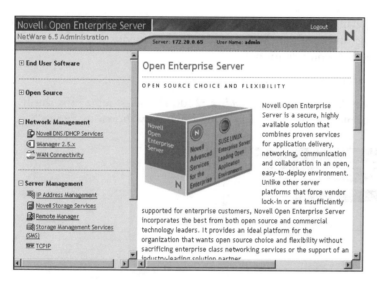

Figure 5-5 The NetWare Web Manager welcome window

NetWare Web Manager is based on the Apache Web Server product installed automatically with NetWare 6.5, which allows you to run two instances of Apache Web Server. One instance is used to support the OneNet services, and the other instance can be used to support e-commerce. By default, Web Manager uses TCP/IP port number 2200 and secures its communications with Secure Socket Layers (SSL).

In Chapter 11, you learn more about SSL as well as installing Apache Web Server for use in e-commerce.

NOTE

Some advantages of using Apache Web Server to host OneNet applications and e-commerce include the following:

- Apache Web Server is open-source software, so it can be adapted for use on multiple platforms, including Linux and Windows.

- A wide range of applications are available for Apache Web Server.

- Apache Web Server has a proven track record of performance and reliability in hosting Web applications.

- Many network administrators are already familiar with Apache Web Server.

To offer additional security, Apache Web Server logs the activity of all its services in Common Log Format (CLF) files that can be viewed from the Web Manager home page. With these files, you can track all user access to the services, see what access has occurred, and detect what errors, if any, have occurred. You can also use Web Manager to install and configure many NetWare 6.5 Web services. As you install additional Web services, their links are automatically added to Web Manager. In the following activity, you access Web Manager, view its default configuration, and view your Apache log files.

Activity 5-4: Using NetWare Web Manager

Time Required: 15 minutes

Objective: Use NetWare Web Manager to access Web services.

Requirements: A Windows XP or SUSE Linux 10 computer and an administrative user name and password for the NetWare 6.5 server

Description: Eric wants you to experiment with Web Manager and then give him a demonstration; he's interested in using it to view access logs and configure Web services. In this activity, you use Web Manager to view your Apache log files and the default configuration.

1. If necessary, start your computer and log on to your local system.

2. Start Web Manager by entering the URL **https://IPaddress:2200** (*IPaddress* represents the IP address of your NetWare 6.5 server) to display the Web Manager Login window shown in Figure 5-6.

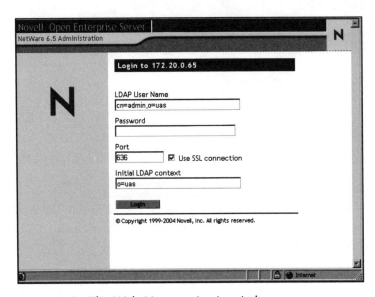

Figure 5-6   The Web Manager Login window

3. Enter your administrative user name and password to display the welcome window.

4. Follow these steps to view the default Apache configuration and log files:

   a. Click to expand the **Open Source** heading on the left.

   b. Click the **Apache 2.0** link.

   c. In the upper-right corner, click the **Administer Single Apache Server** link to display the Server Preferences window shown in Figure 5-7.

   d. Under the Server Status heading, click the **View Configuration** link to display the contents of the Httpd.conf file. Scroll down the file and read through the many configuration parameters.

   e. Under the Server Status heading, click the **Listen Ports** link and record the port numbers:

   _____

   f. Click the **Server Logs** button on the toolbar to display the Server Logs window shown in Figure 5-8.

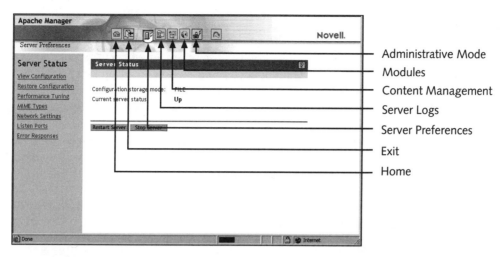

Figure 5-7   The Server Preferences window

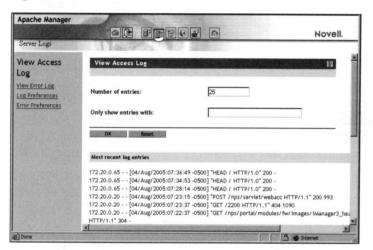

Figure 5-8   The Server Logs window

    g. In the Number of entries text box, enter **10** and click **OK**. Record two IP addresses listed under the Most recent log entries heading:

    _____

    h. Click the **Home** button on the toolbar to return to the Web Manager welcome window.

5. Follow these steps to start iManager:

    a. Click to expand the **Network Management** heading on the left.

    b. Click the **iManager 2.5.x** link. Record the four links listed at the upper right:

    _____
    _____

    c. At the upper right, click the **Open Novell iManager 2.5** link.

    d. Log in to iManager with your administrative user name and password.

    e. Exit iManager.

6. Exit Web Manager, and stay logged in for the next activity.

ESTABLISHING LOGIN SECURITY

Securing access to the network is an important responsibility of network administrators, and NetWare offers many features you can use for this task. As a CNA, you'll need to know how to set up NetWare login security options that meet your users' needs. **Login security** is the process computers and networks use to identify authorized users of the system. As you learned in Chapter 1, login security starts by giving each user a unique user name and password. Although other people might know the user account name, only the owner of the user account should know the password. When a user first logs in, a process called **authorization** verifies the user account name and password by comparing them to values stored in the eDirectory database. During authorization, the client encrypts the password before sending the login request across the network. Encrypting the password prevents attackers who might be scanning network packets from discovering this information. In addition to authorization, NetWare login security relies on NetWare **authentication**, which validates each network request to guarantee the following:

- The authorized user sent the message.

- The message was sent from the client computer where the authorized user logged in.

- The message pertains to the user's current login session.

- The message has not been corrupted or modified.

Because authentication occurs in the background, it's not visible to the user or network administrator. Authentication starts when the user is issued a private key from the Certificate Authority service running on the NetWare server. The Novell client then creates a signature by using the private key along with information identifying the user, computer, and session. The client uses the signature to uniquely code the data in each packet sent from the computer. When the server receives a packet, it uses the packet's signature to verify that the packet came from the authorized user's computer.

Authentication is an ongoing process that prevents intruders from building message packets that appear to the network to have come from authorized users. For example, suppose an intruder captured packets from your client. Without authentication, the intruder could create a message in a packet that seems to come from your client computer, thus giving him or her access to any information or services you have rights to when you're logged in. Authentication prevents packet capturing because each packet has a unique signature created by applying the user's private key to the information in the message. Without the user's password and signature, the intruder can't fool the system into accepting falsified packets.

Creating user objects and assigning passwords are only part of login security, which also consists of user account restrictions and intruder detection. In the following sections, you learn what a CNA needs to know about these security measures and how to apply them to the UAS network.

Setting Up User Account Restrictions

User account restrictions help ensure that the user logging in is actually the authorized person. To do this, network administrators can establish password restrictions, time restrictions, and address restrictions. In this section, you learn how these account restrictions are used to increase network security.

Passwords that are known only to their users and that potential intruders can't guess easily are necessary parts of login security. In NetWare, you have a number of ways to increase password security, such as requiring a minimum password length and requiring that users change passwords within the time period you specify. However, passwords have a way of becoming common knowledge among users and, therefore, lose their effectiveness at authenticating users. To help keep passwords secret, users need to change them periodically. Because users often neglect this task, administrators can set NetWare **password restrictions** to require users to change passwords within a specified time. In addition, NetWare password restrictions include a unique option that prevents users from reusing previous passwords.

To increase security in case someone detects a user's password, NetWare offers the option to set time restrictions and address restrictions on user accounts. With these restrictions, you can keep users who work with confidential data, such as payroll information and customer lists, from logging in except during specified time periods or from certain computers. When **time restrictions** are set on a user account, a potential intruder would have to enter the building during normal business hours to log in as that user, even if he or she knows the user password. Other employees would likely notice an unfamiliar person trying to log in during these hours. Another way to increase user account security is through **address restrictions**, which limit the stations (computers) where a user can log in. By default, a user can be logged in concurrently from multiple stations. This default setting can be a security problem for mobile users if they forget to log out before moving to another station. As a result, normally you should restrict user accounts to logging in from only one station at a time.

As a network administrator, you can use the NetWare management utilities to set password, time, and address restrictions on existing users or use templates to apply standard restrictions for new users. Using account restriction templates saves time by automatically applying these restrictions to all users created with that template. In Activities 5-5 and 5-6, you learn how to establish account restrictions on existing users. In "Creating User Templates" later in this chapter, you use iManager to create templates for user account restrictions.

Activity 5-5: Setting User Account Restrictions

Time Required: 10 minutes

Objective: Use iManager to establish user login restrictions.

Requirements: Same as Activity 5-2

Description: To help secure user accounts, Eric places restrictions on them to require a unique password of at least eight characters that must be changed every 90 days. In addition, for certain high-security user accounts, Eric limits the user account to only one connection at a time from one of two computers. In this activity, you secure the user account you created for Eric Kenton in Chapter 4 by using iManager to set up user account restrictions.

1. If necessary, start your computer, and log in with your administrative user name and password.

2. To restrict a user account to a specific station, first you need to identify the IP address of the desktop computer the user account will be restricted to. In this step, you use the Ipconfig command to determine the IP address of your Windows client:

    a. Click **Start**, **Run**, type **cmd**, and then press **Enter** to open a command prompt window.

    b. Type **IPCONFIG**, and then press **Enter**.

    c. Record your computer's IP address and the IP address of another student's computer:

    _____

    _____

    d. Type **exit**, and then press **Enter** to close the command prompt window.

3. Follow these steps to start iManager:

You can perform these steps from a Windows XP or SUSE Linux computer.

    a. Start your Web browser, enter the URL **https://*IPaddress*/nps/iManager.html**, and then press **Enter** to display the iManager Login window.

    b. Log in to iManager with your administrative user name and password.

4. Follow these steps to create an address restriction that limits the user name you created for Eric Kenton in Activity 4-2 to logging in only from your computer:

   a. Click to expand the **eDirectory Administration** heading, and then click the **Modify Object** link to display the Modify Object window.

   b. Click the **Object Selector** button next to the Object name text box.

   c. If necessary, click the **down arrow** next to UAS Organization to display its contents.

   d. Click the **down arrow** next to the IT OU to display its contents.

   e. Click the **EKenton** user to place EKenton.IT.UAS in the Object name text box, and then click **OK** to display the Modify Object window shown in Figure 5-9.

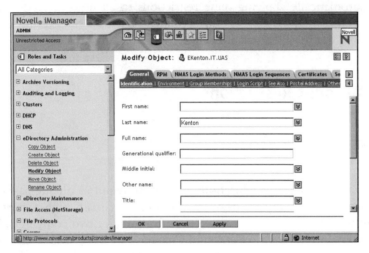

Figure 5-9 The Modify Object window

   f. If necessary, scroll over and click the **Restrictions** tab to display the window shown in Figure 5-10.

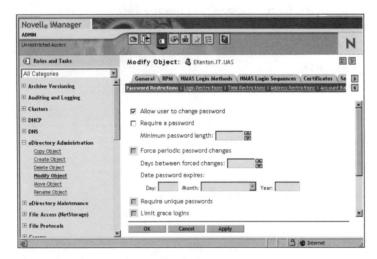

Figure 5-10 The Restrictions tab

   g. Click the **Address Restrictions** link to display the Network address restriction list box shown in Figure 5-11.

   h. Click the **+** button to open the Network Address dialog box shown in Figure 5-12.

   i. Click the **Address type** list arrow, and then click **IP** in the list of options.

   j. Enter the IP address you recorded in Step 2, and then click the **Add** button to place your IP address in the Network address restriction list box.

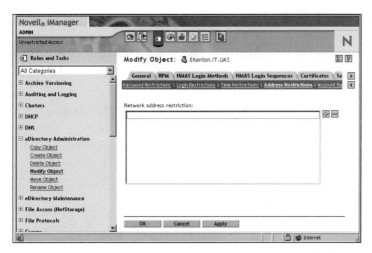

Figure 5-11   The Network address restriction list box

Figure 5-12   The Network Address dialog box

 k. Repeat Steps 4h through 4j to add your partner's IP address to the list.

 l. Click **OK** to save the address restriction and return to the Novell iManager window.

5. Follow these steps to set password restrictions on the EKenton user:

 a. Click to expand the **eDirectory Administration** heading, and then click the **Modify Object** link.

 b. Click the **Object Selector** button next to the Object name text box.

 c. If necessary, click the **down arrow** next to UAS Organization to display its contents.

 d. Click the **down arrow** next to the IT OU to display its contents.

 e. Click the **EKenton** user to place EKenton.IT.UAS in the Object name text box, and then click **OK** to display the Modify Object window shown previously in Figure 5-9.

 f. If necessary, scroll over and click the **Restrictions** tab to display the window shown previously in Figure 5-10.

 g. Click the **Require a password** check box, and then enter **6** in the Minimum password length text box.

h. Click the **Force periodic password changes** check box, and then record the default days between password changes and the date the password will expire:

i. In the Days between forced changes text box, enter **60**, and then click to enable the **Require unique passwords** check box.

j. If necessary, scroll down and record the value in the Limit grace logins text box, and then click **OK** to save your changes and return to the iManager main window.

6. Stay logged in to iManager for the next activity.

Activity 5-6: Establishing Time Restrictions

Time Required: 10 minutes

Objective: Use iManager to establish user login restrictions.

Requirements: Same as Activity 5-5; a Windows XP or SUSE Linux 10 computer

Description: In addition to password and station restrictions, Eric sets time restrictions on high-security accounts so that they can be used only during specified times. In this activity, you use iManager to secure the user account you created for Eric Kenton to restrict its use from 6:00 a.m. to 12:00 a.m. on your assigned computer.

1. Follow these steps to set time restrictions on the EKenton user account:

a. Click to expand the **eDirectory Administration** heading, and then click the **Modify Object** link.

b. Click the **Object Selector** button next to the Object name text box.

c. If necessary, click the **down arrow** next to UAS Organization to display its contents.

d. Click the **down arrow** next to the IT OU to display its contents.

e. Click the **EKenton** user to place EKenton.IT.UAS in the Object name text box, and then click **OK** to display the Modify Object window.

f. If necessary, scroll over and click the **Restrictions** tab.

g. Click the **Time Restrictions** link to display the window shown in Figure 5-13.

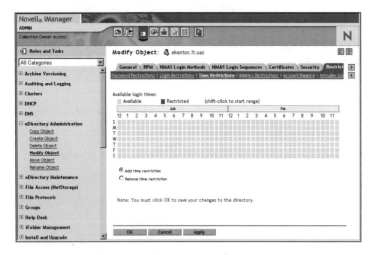

Figure 5-13   The Time Restrictions tab

h. Hold down the **Shift** key and click in the **12** column under the AM heading of the S (for Sunday) row on the top. While holding the Shift key down, drag to the **6** column under the AM heading and then down to the S (for Saturday) row on the bottom. After you have finished, your screen should look similar to Figure 5-14.

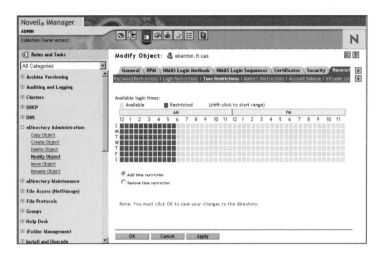

Figure 5-14   Setting a time restriction from 12:00 a.m. until 6:00 a.m.

    i. Click **OK** to save the time restrictions and return to the iManager main window.

2. Stay logged in to iManager for the next activity.

Implementing Intruder Detection Limits

Another potential login security problem is an intruder who is able to guess user passwords successfully. Forcing user passwords to be longer than four characters and training users to create nonobvious passwords that contain numbers as well as characters can go a long way toward preventing password guessing. Having nonobvious passwords is critical because intruders could get lucky with guesses or might have a password-guessing program that can send hundreds of password combinations to a computer in just a few seconds. An effective way to deter password guessing is to set the NetWare Intruder Detection feature in each OU container.

Intruder detection works at the container level by setting a limit on the number of incorrect login attempts that can be made on a user account in that container during a specified time period. When a potential intruder reaches the maximum number of incorrect login attempts in the established time period, the user's account is locked for a specified time period, and the time and station address of the login attempt is recorded on the user's account. The user account becomes available again at the end of the lockout time period, or the Admin user can free the account at any time. In the following activities, you use iManager to set the Intruder Detection option for your UAS network, and then test your security by attempting several invalid passwords to lock out a user account.

Activity 5-7: Enabling Intruder Detection

Time Required: 10 minutes

Objective: Use iManager to configure intruder detection settings.

Requirements: Same as Activity 5-5; a Windows XP or SUSE Linux 10 computer

Description: Because they are working on secure government contracts, some UAS engineers and IT staff have had to sign nondisclosure agreements for the projects they're working on. To help secure user accounts from unauthorized access, Eric has enabled the Intruder Detection option for the UAS, Engineering, and IT containers. In this activity, you use iManager to enable intruder detection to lock out a user's account for five minutes when more than five incorrect login attempts have been made in a 10-minute period.

1. If necessary, start your computer, and log on to your local computer with your assigned user name and password.

2. Start iManager as described in Activity 5-5, and log in with your administrative user name and password.

3. To configure intruder detection settings for the IT OU, follow these steps:

a. Click to expand the **eDirectory Administration** heading, and then click the **Modify Object** link.

b. Click the **Object Selector** button next to the Object name text box. If you're using a shared classroom server, click the **down arrow** next to the CLASS Organization to display the ##UAS container.

c. Click the **down arrow** next to the UAS container to display it contents.

d. Click the **IT** OU to place its distinguished name in the Object name text box, and then click **OK** to display the Modify Object window for the OU.

e. Click the **Intruder Detection** link to display the window shown in Figure 5-15.

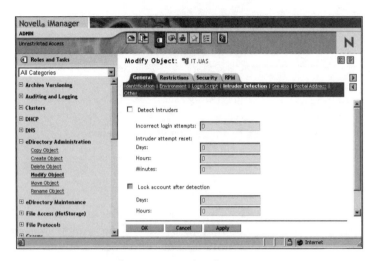

Figure 5-15   Configuring intruder detection settings

f. Click the **Detect intruders** check box and record the default settings for login attempts and reset times:

_____

g. In the Incorrect login attempts text box, enter **5**. In the Minutes text box under Intruder attempt reset, enter **10**.

h. Click the **Lock account after detection** check box and record the default settings for days, hours, and minutes:

_____

i. In the Minutes text box, under Intruder attempt reset, enter **5**. Click **OK** to save your changes and return to the iManager main window.

j. Click the **Exit** button to end your iManager session and return to the Login window.

4. Close your Web browser.

Setting intruder detection on the container storing the Admin user name could result in the user account being locked out for the specified time period, causing a temporary loss of administrative access to the network. To help prevent this problem, you should create a backup Admin account that you can use to manage the network and then rename the Admin user, as described in "Increasing Admin User Security" later in this chapter.

Activity 5-8: Testing Intruder Detection

Time Required: 10 minutes

Objective: Test user login restrictions.

Requirements: Completion of Activity 5-7

Description: The next step in setting up intruder detection is to test the system and practice unlocking a user account. In this activity, you attempt to lock out the EKenton user account, and then wait for the account to clear before logging back in.

1. Attempt to log in with the **EKenton** user name in the IT context, using incorrect passwords and counting each unsuccessful login attempt. After several unsuccessful attempts, you see a NetWare security message box stating that the login is denied because of a possible intruder attack. Record the message you see and the number of login attempts you tried:

   _____

2. Now try logging in with the correct password. Record the error message:

   _____

3. Wait at least 5 minutes to allow NetWare to unlock the EKenton user account.

4. Log in with the **EKenton** user name and correct password.

5. If necessary, log on to your local Windows computer.

6. Log out to display a new Login window.

Increasing Admin User Security

Although all user accounts require good security, the Admin user account is arguably the most critical. There are two major issues in securing the Admin user. The first is to set user account restrictions on the Admin user account to ensure that the Admin user has adequate address, time, and password restrictions. The next is to have a backup Admin account in case the primary Admin account becomes disabled or damaged. For example, as you learned in the previous section, attempting to log in as the network administrator without the correct authentication credentials can lock out the Admin account, making it unavailable for the lockout duration you established. You can also use a backup Admin account if the network administrator leaves the company, taking the Admin user name and password with him or her, or if he or she is incapacitated for any reason.

When creating a backup Admin account, the CEO or office manager should keep the name and password secure. Some network administrators also rename their Admin accounts to make it harder to hack and to help prevent attackers from locking out the Admin account through multiple login attempts. The disadvantage of renaming the Admin account is that certain utilities default to using the Admin user name. However, if your server will be attached to the Internet, the additional security of renaming the Admin account can be worth the inconvenience. For this reason, Eric Kenton renamed the Admin user as UASAdmin before connecting the UAS server to the Internet. In the following activities, you create a backup user account and then rename your existing Admin user account to help prevent hacking and account lockouts.

Activity 5-9: Creating a Backup Admin User Account

Time Required: 10 minutes

Objective: Use ConsoleOne to create and manage user accounts.

Requirements: Completion of Activity 5-3

Description: When planning the network, the IT manager, Luke McMann, asked Eric to create a backup Admin account named Clark Kent. Luke plans to have the company's administrative assistant, Lynn Dai, keep the backup administrator's user name and password locked up in a safe place in case they're needed to recover the main Admin user account and Eric is unavailable. In this activity, you learn how to use ConsoleOne to create a new CKent user account. In Chapter 7, you empower the CKent user to have Supervisor rights for your UAS container.

1. If necessary, start your Windows computer, log in to eDirectory with your administrative user name and password, and log on to your local Windows computer.

2. Start ConsoleOne.

3. In the navigation pane, click to expand your eDirectory tree and the **##UAS** container.

4. Click the **IT** OU to display the objects in the object pane.

5. Create a new user account for Clark Kent by following these steps:

   a. Click the **New User** button on the ConsoleOne toolbar (refer to Figure 5-16 for the location of the New User button).

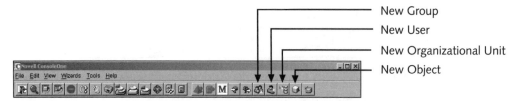

Figure 5-16 ConsoleOne toolbar buttons

   b. In the New User dialog box, type **CKent** in the Name text box.

   c. In the Surname text box, type **Kent**.

   d. Leave all other text boxes and options blank. Click **OK** to open the Set Password dialog box.

   e. Enter **password** in both the New Password and Retype Password text boxes.

   f. Click the **Set Password** button to create the CKent user.

6. Click the **Exit** button on the ConsoleOne toolbar, and stay logged in for the next activity.

 You learn how to give the SysOp Organizational Role object the Supervisor right to the eDirectory tree in Chapter 7. If you're using a dedicated server, you should perform Activity 7-11 at this time so that you can recover if the main Admin user is disabled or deleted.

Activity 5-10: Renaming the Admin User Account

Time Required: 10 minutes

Objective: Use iManager to manage user accounts.

Requirements: Internet Explorer on a Windows XP system or Java-enabled Firefox on a SUSE Linux 10 computer

Description: Before connecting the UASHOST server to the Internet, Eric renamed the Admin user account to help prevent unauthorized access. In this activity, you use iManager to rename the Admin account.

1. Start your Web browser, and then start iManager as described in Activity 5-5.

2. Click to expand the **eDirectory Administration** heading, and then click the **Rename Object** link.

3. Click the **Object Selector** button, and navigate to your administrative account.

4. Click your administrative account to place it in the Object name text box.

5. Enter **##UASAdmin** in the New object name text box. (If you're using a shared classroom server, replace ## with your assigned student number. If you're using a dedicated server, omit the "##" and enter **UASAdmin** in the New object name text box.)

6. Click **OK** to complete the transaction and display the completion message.

7. Click **OK** to return to the iManager main window.

8. Click the iManager **Exit** button, and then close your Web browser.

9. Log off your computer.

NOTE

From now on, you'll need to log in with ##UASAdmin or UASAdmin instead of your previous administrative user name.

CREATING AND MANAGING USERS AND GROUPS

After establishing password restrictions and setting intruder detection for OUs, your next task in setting up an eDirectory system is creating user and group accounts for each department. Group objects play an important role in network management because they make it possible for network administrators to give similar privileges to several users at once, instead of assigning rights separately to each user. In NetWare 6.5, you can use ConsoleOne, NetWare Administrator, or iManager to create and manage user and group objects. Which utility you use depends on your personal preference and needs. If you're working from a LAN using a computer with Novell Client software, you might find that ConsoleOne and NetWare Administrator are faster and easier to use. Because the NetWare 6.5 CNA test requires you to use iManager efficiently, in this chapter you use iManager to create user and group accounts.

Defining and Creating Groups

Often it's convenient to establish groups to give two or more users access to shared resources and services. Instead of assigning rights directly to user accounts, many network administrators would rather assign rights to groups and then make a user a member of the groups that have the necessary rights. For example, in UAS's Engineering Department, only design engineers are given access to certain software and files they need for their work. Instead of repeatedly giving access rights to each design engineer user account, creating a Design group and then adding design engineers as members is more efficient. This group can then be given the rights for accessing restricted resources and services. Groups are also a convenient way to change user job responsibilities. For example, Kellie Thiele and Julie Damrau currently have responsibility for the UAS Web site, so Eric created a group called WebMgrs and made both Julie and Kellie members to give them rights to maintain Web site files. In the future, if Kellie gets too busy with programming, another user could be assigned the responsibility by simply removing Kellie and then adding the new user to the WebMgrs group. Figure 5-17 shows a Group Planning Form that lists the groups and members Eric created in the Engineering and IT departments.

Because user accounts can be assigned group membership when they are first created, Eric simplified the task of assigning users to groups by creating the group objects first, and then assigning each user to his or her groups when creating the user account. If you create group objects after the user accounts have been created, you need to perform another step to assign users to their groups. Activity 5-11 walks you through using iManager to create group accounts for the IT OU in your UAS network. Later in the chapter, you use iManager to create users for the IT Department. In the Hands-on Projects at the end of the chapter, you apply what you have learned to create and secure the remainder of the group objects shown in Figure 5-17.

ACTIVITY

Activity 5-11: Creating Groups with iManager

Time Required: 10 minutes

Objective: Use iManager to create and manage group objects.

Requirements: Completion of Activity 5-10; a Windows XP or SUSE Linux 10 computer

Description: In this activity, you learn how to use iManager to create the ITMgrs and WebMgrs groups shown on the Group Planning Form in Figure 5-17.

1. If necessary, start your local computer and log on. If you're using a Windows XP system, click the **Workstation Only** check box to log on to your local computer.

2. Start your Web browser, and then start iManager as described in Activity 5-5.

3. Log in to iManager with your new administrative user name and password.

Group Planning Form

Organization:		Page	of	
Developed by:		Date:		

Group Name	Members	Context	Description
Design	Lianne Jarka, Tony Rucci, Paul Alm, Kellie Thiele, Kari Means	Engineering.UAS	Design engineers who will be working with CAD software to create and maintain engineering design files (as the programmer in charge of CAD applications, Kellie Thiele needs to be a member to test CAD software)
ITMgrs	Kellie Thiele, Luke McMann, Bernie Muelner Eric Kenton	IT.UAS	IT staff who have rights to install, configure, and manage software and computer environments
Production	Russ Pence, Receiving terminals, Shipping terminals	Mfg.Engineering.UAS	Users who need access to the inventory system to record shipments and receipts and those who need access to read information from the Requirements Planning System
WebMgrs	Kellie Thiele	.UAS	Users who are responsible for the design and maintenance of the UAS home page

Figure 5-17   The UAS Group Planning Form

4. Click to expand the **eDirectory Administration** heading.

5. Follow these steps to create the ITMgrs group in the IT OU:

   a. Click the **Create Object** link to open the window shown in Figure 5-18.

   b. In the Available object classes list box, click **Group** and then click **OK** to display the Create Group window.

   c. Type **ITMgrs** in the Group name text box.

   d. Click the **Object Selector** button next to the Context text box, and then click the **down arrow** to view the contents of the UAS container.

   e. Click the **IT** OU to place it in the Context text box, and then click **OK** to create the ITMgrs group and display the "Complete: The Create Group request succeeded" message.

   f. Click **OK** to return to the iManager main window.

6. Repeat Step 5 to create a group named **WebMgrs** in the IT OU.

Figure 5-18   The Create Object window

7. Stay logged in to iManager for the next activity.

Creating User Templates

After creating groups, the next task is creating accounts for all your users. Although you could create each user individually as you did in previous activities, this method is time consuming, and it's easy to miss a setup task, such as forgetting to add the new user to a group or omitting certain account restrictions. Missing setup steps can result in the user being unable to access data files or having nonstandard login restrictions. Therefore, establishing user templates to simplify and standardize creating user accounts is an efficient method for network administrators to use. A **user template** defines standard settings you want to configure for users, such as account restrictions and the location of home directories. Figure 5-19 shows a worksheet with the template requirements Eric created for the IT and Engineering departments. Using the "T_" prefix before each template name indicates that the object is a template and makes the name different from corresponding group names. In Activity 5-12, you use iManager to create an IT template for your UAS network based on the template Eric defined.

Activity 5-12: Creating a User Template in iManager

Time Required: 10 minutes

Objective: Use templates to help create user accounts.

Requirements: Same as Activity 5-11

Description: Before creating users for the IT and Engineering departments, Eric defined templates for these departments. In this activity, you use iManager to create user templates for users in the IT Department, based on the User Template Planning Form in Figure 5-19.

1. Log in to iManager with your new administrative user name and password.

2. Click to expand the **eDirectory Administration** heading.

3. Follow these steps to create a template for users in the IT Department:

   a. Click the **Create Object** link to open the Create Object window shown previously in Figure 5-18.

   b. In the Available object classes list box, scroll down and click **Template**, and then click **OK** to display the Create Template window.

   c. Type **T_IT** in the Template name text box.

   d. Click the **Object Selector** button next to the Context text box, and then click the **down arrow** to view the contents of your UAS container.

User Template Planning Form	
Organization:	**Page of**
Developed by:	**Date:**
Template name	T_IT
Context	.OU=IT.O=UAS
Home directory path	UASHOST_CORP:IT
Minimum password length	6
Require unique passwords	No
Days between password changes	90
Grace logins	6
Valid login times	5:00 a.m. until 11:59 p.m. Monday through Saturday
Concurrent connections	1
Groups	ITMgrs
Users	Kellie Thiele, Luke McMann
Rights to Login Script property	Read
Rights to home directory	All rights except Supervisor and Access Control
Template name	T_Engineering
Context	OU=Engineering.O=UAS
Home directory path	UASHOST_CORP:Engineer\Users
Minimum password length	6
Require unique passwords	Yes
Days between password changes	90
Grace logins	6
Valid login times	5:00 a.m. until 11:59 p.m. Monday through Saturday
Concurrent connections	1
Groups	ITMgrs
Users	Kari Means, Tony Rucci, Lianne Jarka, Paul Alm, Kellie Thiele, Russ Pence
Rights to Login Script property	Read
Rights to home directory	All rights except Supervisor and Access Control

Figure 5-19   The UAS User Template Planning Form

    e. Click the **IT** OU to place it in the Context text box, and then click **OK** to create the T_IT template and display the completion message.

    f. Click **OK** to return to the iManager main window.

4. Follow these steps to configure the T_IT template as shown in Figure 5-19:

    a. Click the **Modify Object** link. Click the **Object Selector** button to select the T_IT template object and then click **OK**.

    b. Click the **Environment** link on the General tab to display the Home Directory fields. Click the **Object Selector** button to select the path to the IT directory.

    c. Click the **Group Memberships** link, and then select the groups shown for the IT Department in Figure 5-19.

    d. Click the **Restrictions** tab and enter the password restrictions shown in Figure 5-19.

    e. Click the **Login Restrictions** link. In the Maximum connections text box, enter the number shown in the Concurrent connections row of Figure 5-19.

    f. Click **OK** to save your changes.

5. Because the next activity requires using ConsoleOne and Novell Client, you should exit iManager and log off your local computer.

Using Templates to Set Default Security Rights for New Users

Another practical use of templates is changing the default file system and eDirectory rights for new users to enforce your organization's security standards. For example, by default NetWare grants new users rights to their home directories and rights to change their personal login scripts. As you learn in Chapter 9, allowing users to change their login scripts can introduce processing errors and cause standard drive mappings to be overwritten.

In Chapters 6 and 7, you learn about file system and eDirectory security and how users are granted rights to work with and manage files and eDirectory information.

NOTE

New users are also given the default right to grant other users authority in their home directories, but this right can cause security problems when multiple users are given rights to home directories. If you remove Supervisor and Access Control rights from the default rights given to a new user's home directory, users can manage their files without being able to grant rights to others. Unfortunately, iManager version 2.5 doesn't include an option for setting default security rights in user templates, so you need to perform this task in ConsoleOne. In Activity 5-13, you update the IT template to restrict new user rights to their login scripts and home directories.

Activity 5-13: Modifying Templates in ConsoleOne

ACTIVITY

Time Required: 10 minutes

Objective: Use templates to help create user accounts.

Requirements: Completion of Activity 5-12 and a Windows XP computer with Novell Client installed

Description: Kellie Thiele is responsible for maintaining login scripts. Luke McMann doesn't want users to be able to change the login scripts Kellie sets up for them or to change security assignments to their home directories, so Eric wants you to change the template you created to change the corresponding rights. In this activity, you use ConsoleOne to update the IT template you created in Activity 5-12.

1. Log in to eDirectory with your administrative user name and password.

2. Start ConsoleOne, and expand the eDirectory tree and your **UAS** container.

3. Expand the **IT** OU, right-click the **T_IT** template, and then click **Properties**.

4. Follow these steps to give users only the Read right to the Login Script property:

    a. Click the **down arrow** on the New Object NDS Rights tab, and click the **Rights to Other Objects** option to display the NDS Objects window.

    b. Click **<New Object>**, and then click the **Assigned Rights** button to open the Rights assigned to: <New Object> dialog box shown in Figure 5-20.

    c. Click the **Add Property** button.

    d. In the Add Property dialog box, scroll down and click the **Login Script** property to add this property with Read and Compare rights.

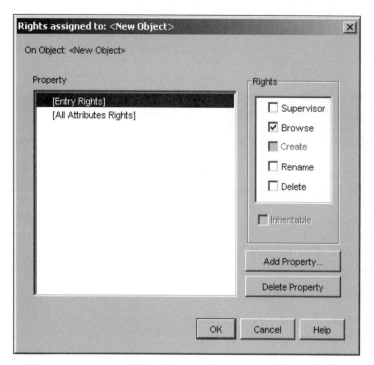

Figure 5-20 The Rights assigned to: <New Object> dialog box

   e. Click **OK** to save your changes.

5. Follow these steps to remove Supervisor and Access Control rights from the default rights to user home directories:

   a. Scroll, if necessary, and click the **New Object FS Rights** tab to display the default rights assignment shown in Figure 5-21.

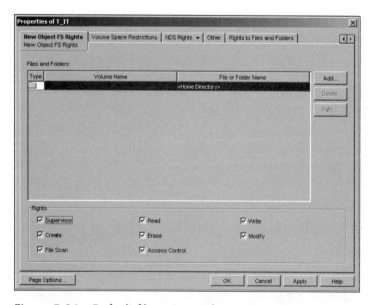

Figure 5-21 Default file system rights assignment

   b. Click to clear the **Supervisor** and **Access Control** check boxes.

c. Click **OK** to save your changes and return to the ConsoleOne main window.

6. Exit ConsoleOne, and stay logged on for the next activity.

Creating User Objects from Templates

In NetWare, network users are given login names by creating a user object in an eDirectory container. You can also use eDirectory to keep track of many other fields of information, called properties, about each user. As you learned in previous activities, at a minimum, user objects must be assigned a login name and a last name; other properties, such as title, address, home directories, passwords, and time restrictions, are optional. Because certain properties, such as the location of the user's home directory or password requirements, are often the same for several users, using templates can make creating user objects easier and more standardized. Before creating users, you should develop a user naming convention and identify which information properties you want to enter on each user account. Popular naming conventions include the following:

- The user's last name followed by the first initial of the first name (for example, Kellie Ann Thiele would have the user login name ThieleK)

- The first letter of the user's first name followed by the last name (for example, Kellie Ann Thiele would have the user login name KThiele)

- The user's first name followed by the first letter of the last name (for example, Kellie Ann Thiele would have the user login name KellieT)

- The first three characters of the first name followed by the first three letters of the last name (for example, Kellie Ann Thiele would have the user login name KelThi)

For the UAS network, Luke McMann decided to have user login names consist of the first letter of the first name followed by the user's last name. Another important consideration is what to do when your network has two users with the same login name. NetWare can support multiple user accounts with the same login name as long as the users' accounts exist in different OUs. For example, if you have the user Kellie Ann Thiele in the IT Department and the user Ken Locke Thiele in the Engineering Department, you could create a user account named KThiele in the IT OU for Kellie and another KThiele account in the Engineering OU for Ken. Novell's eDirectory system can keep each user separate because they exist in different contexts. Although NetWare works with two or more users having the same user login name, this setup can create conflicts when accessing the network from other environments, so you should select a naming convention that creates user login names that are unique throughout the entire tree. For example, Luke and Eric plan to add a number to the end of any duplicate user names to keep them unique. In the preceding example, Ken's login name would be KThiele2.

To define the user accounts, Eric developed the User Planning Form shown in Figure 5-22, which lists users in the IT, Engineering, Management, and Manufacturing departments along with their context and template requirements. In Activity 5-14, you use the template you established in Activity 5-12 to create these user accounts for the IT Department.

Activity 5-14: Creating User Accounts with iManager

Time Required: 10 minutes

Objective: Use iManager to create user and group accounts.

Requirements: Completion of Activities 5-12 and 5-13

Description: In this activity, you use iManager and the IT template you created in Activity 5-12 to create user accounts for the IT Department.

1. If necessary, log in to your local computer. If you're using a Windows computer, click the **Workstation Only** check box to log on to the local computer.

2. If necessary, start your Web browser, open the iManager Login window as described in Activity 5-5, and log in to iManager with your new administrative user name and password.

User Planning Form

Organization: _____   Page _____ of _____

Developed by: _____   Date: _____

User Name	Login Name	Initial eDirectory and Simple Password	Context	Template Name	Home Directory	Groups	Additional Properties
Kari Means	KMeans	password	Engineering.UAS	T_Engineering	Yes	Design	Title: AdmAsst
Lianne Jarka	LJarka	password	Engineering.UAS	T_Engineering	Yes	Design	Title: Engineer
Paul Alm	PAlm	password	Engineering.UAS	T_Engineering	Yes	Design	Title: Engineer
Russ Pence	RPence	password	Engineering.UAS	T_Engineering	Yes	Production	Title: Production Manager Home Dir: CORPEngineer Security same as Engineering
Tony Rucci	TRucci	password	Engineering.UAS	T_Engineering	Yes	Design	Title: Engineer
Bradley Dahl	BDahl	password	Engineering.UAS	T_Engineering	Yes	Design	Title: Engineer
Eric Kenton	EKenton	password	IT.UAS	No template; created separately	Yes	ITMgrs	Title: Network Administrator
Kellie Thiele	KThiele	password	IT.UAS	T_IT	Yes	Design ITMgrs WebMgrs	Password required every 90 days
Luke McMann	LMcMann	password	IT.UAS	T_IT	Yes	ITMgrs	Password required every 90 days
Bernie Muelner	BMuelner	password	IT.UAS	T_IT	Yes	ITMgrs	Title: Network administrator for the AeroDyn division; needs to be able to log in and manage the AeroDyn OU; Password required every 90 days
Receiving 1	Receiving1	password	Mfg. Engineering.UAS	No template; created with LDIF	No	Production	Title: Enter Receipts
Receiving 2	Receiving2	password	Mfg. Engineering.UAS	No template; created with LDIF	No	Production	Title: Enter Receipts
Shipping 1	Shipping1	password	Mfg. Engineering.UAS	No template; created with LDIF	No	Production	Title: Enter Shipments

Figure 5-22   The UAS User Planning Form

5

User Planning Form

Organization: _____   Page ___ of ___

Developed by: _____   Date: _____

User Name	Login Name	Initial eDirectory and Simple Password	Context	Template Name	Home Directory	Groups	Additional Properties
Shipping 2	Shipping2	password	Mfg. Engineering.UAS	No template; created with LDIF	No	Production	Title: Enter Shipments
David Heise	DHeise	password	Mgmt.UAS	No template; created with iManager. Home directory path: CORP:Mgmt	Yes	Mgrs	Password required every 90 days
Lynn Dai	LDai	password	Mgmt.UAS	No template; created with iManager. Home directory path: CORP:Mgmt	Yes	Mgrs	Password required every 90 days
Maria Frias	MFrias	password	Mgmt.UAS	No template; created with iManager. Home directory path: CORP:Mgmt	Yes	Mgrs	Password required every 90 days

Figure 5-22   The UAS User Planning Form (continued)

3. Scroll down and click to expand the **Users** heading.

4. Click the **Create User** link to open the window shown in Figure 5-23.

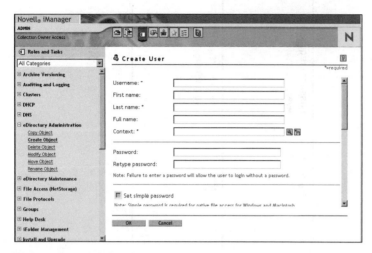

Figure 5-23   The Create User window

5. Follow these steps to create a new user named KThiele in the IT OU:

   a. Type **KThiele** in the Username text box, **Kellie** in the First name text box, and **Thiele** in the Last name text box.

   b. Click the **Object Selector** button next to the Context text box to enter the IT OU.

   c. Scroll down to display the remaining text boxes (see Figure 5-24).

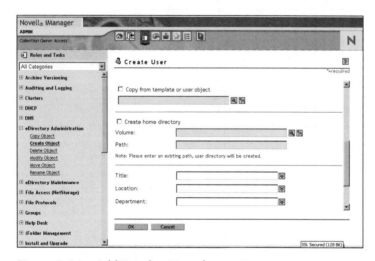

Figure 5-24   Additional settings for creating users

   d. Enter a password for the new user in both the Password and Retype password text boxes. (For the purpose of this book, you might want to use the same password for all your user accounts.)

   e. Click to enable the **Set simple password** check box.

   f. Click to enable the **Copy from template or user object** check box, and then click the **Object Selector** button next to the Template text box to enter the T_IT template.

   g. Click to expand **Title**, and enter the job title **Programmer** for Kellie Thiele.

   h. Click **OK** to create the user account for Kellie Thiele and display the completion message. Notice that this window includes a Repeat Task button.

6. Click the **Repeat Task** button and follow the procedure in Step 5 to create a user account for **Luke McMann**.

7. Click the **Repeat Task** button and follow the procedure in Step 5 to create a user account for **Bernie Muelner**.

8. Click **OK** to return to the iManager main window, and stay logged in for the next activity.

Creating Organizational Role Objects

In addition to reducing the need to assign rights to multiple users, groups are a convenient way to give users the rights they need for certain job responsibilities. However, normally you don't want to create groups that represent positions in the company. For example, David Heise wanted the IT Department to set up a manager for each department's data and user accounts. Currently, Kari Means is assigned to act as the manager for the Engineering Department's data and user accounts, Russ Pence is responsible for the Manufacturing Department's data and users, and the administrative assistant, Lynn Dai, acts as the manager for the Business Division.

In addition, to increase security by limiting use of the network administrator's user name, Eric created separate accounts to perform administrative tasks, such as eDirectory management and printer management. Because the user accounts assigned to these positions will change and could include multiple users, Eric didn't want to assign rights to individual users. Instead of having to create groups for these types of positions, Novell has another object type called an **Organizational Role object**, which enables you to assign rights to an object rather than a specific user. You can then make any user an occupant of the Organizational Role object to gain its associated rights. If the job duties are given to another employee, you simply need to make the new employee an occupant of the Organizational Role object. For example, to give his user account rights to perform eDirectory management functions, Eric made the EKenton user an occupant of the eDirAdm Organizational Role object. Figure 5-25 lists the Organizational Role objects Eric defined for the UAS network.

Organizational Role Planning Form			
Created By:		**Date:**	
Role Name	Context	Purpose	Primary Occupant(s)
SysOp	.IT.UAS	Backup system operator	Clark Kent
eDirAdm	.IT.UAS	Administrative role for maintaining eDirector	EKenton
PrintAdm	.IT.UAS	Administrative role for maintaining Internet printing	EKenton, KThiele
EngMgr	.Engineering.UAS	Engineering Department data manager	Kari Means
ISSEng	.Engineering.UAS	Primary engineer assigned to the International Space Station	Tony Rucci
RoverEng	.Mfg.Engineering.UAS	Primary engineer assigned to the Mars Rover project	Lianne Jarka
MfgMgr	.Mfg.Engineering.UAS	Manufacturing Department data manager	Russ Pence, Bernie Muelner
AdmAsst	.Mgmt.UAS	UAS administrative assistants	Lynn Dai, Kari Means
AeroMgr	.Mfg.Engineering.UAS	Manager of AeroDyn Division network objects	Bernie Muelner

Figure 5-25   The UAS Organizational Role Planning Form

In Chapters 6 and 7, you learn how to assign the rights these Organizational Role objects need for the positions' required functions. In the following activity, you learn how to use iManager to create Organizational Role objects and then assign users as occupants.

Activity 5-15: Creating Organizational Role Objects

Time Required: 10 minutes

Objective: Use iManager to create and manage Organizational Role objects.

Requirements: Completion of Activity 5-14

Description: To meet the directive of having a manager for each department's data, Eric created an Organizational Role object for each department manager and then designated a user account for the occupant. In this activity, you create the Organizational Role objects that Eric defined in Figure 5-25 for the IT Department.

1. If necessary, log on to your local computer, open your Web browser to start iManager, and log in to iManager with your administrative user name and password.

2. If necessary, click to expand the **eDirectory Administration** heading, and then click the **Create Object** link.

3. In the Available object classes list box, click **Organizational Role**, and then click **OK** to display the Create Organizational Role window.

4. Follow these steps to create an Organizational Role object named eDirAdm:

   a. Type **eDirAdm** in the Organizational Role name text box.

   b. Click the **Object Selector** button next to the Context text box, and set the context to the **IT** OU.

   c. Click **OK** to display the "Complete: The Create Organizational Role request succeeded" message.

5. Click the **Repeat Task** button. Follow the procedure in Step 4 to create an Organizational Role object named **PrintAdm** in the IT OU.

6. Click **OK** to return to the iManager main window.

7. Follow these steps to add EKenton as an occupant of the eDirAdm Organizational Role:

   a. If necessary, click to expand the **eDirectory Administration** heading.

   b. Click the **Modify Object** link to display the Modify Object window.

   c. Click the **Object Selector** button next to the Object name text box, and then navigate to the **IT** OU. Click the **eDirAdm** object to place it in the Object name text box.

   d. Click **OK** to open the Modify Object window for the eDirAdm object.

   e. Click the **Role occupant** link to display the Role occupant list box shown in Figure 5-26.

   f. Click the **Object Selector** button, and if necessary, navigate to the **IT** OU (see Figure 5-27).

   g. Click the **EKenton** user account to add it to the Selected Objects list box at the bottom of the Object Selector window.

You can use the Object Selector window to add multiple users to the Selected Objects list box.

   h. Click **OK**. EKenton should then appear in the Role occupant list box.

   i. Click **OK** to save your changes and return to the iManager main window.

8. Repeat Step 7 to add both **EKenton** and **KThiele** as occupants of the **PrintAdm** Organizational Role object.

9. Stay logged in to iManager for the next activity.

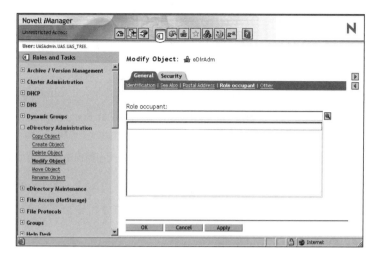

Figure 5-26   The Role occupant list box

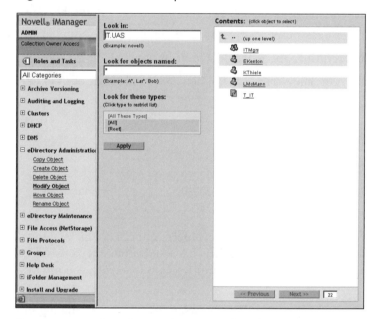

Figure 5-27   The Object Selector window for the Organizational Role occupant

UPDATING MULTIPLE USER ACCOUNTS

As a network administrator, you'll often find that after creating user accounts, you need to make changes that affect several different users, such as preventing users from being logged in to the network between midnight and 4:00 a.m. so that you can perform a network backup. To make this job easier, you can use iManager or ConsoleOne to simultaneously modify multiple user accounts. In ConsoleOne, to change properties common to several users, such as an address or login restriction, you can select multiple users by pressing the Ctrl key to highlight user names, selecting a group, template, or container, and then selecting File, Properties of Multiple Users from the menu. If you select a group or container object, all users in that group or container are modified. If you select a template object, all user accounts created with that template can be modified. You can also use iManager to modify multiple user accounts. In the following activities, you use ConsoleOne and iManager to modify all users in a container and update specific users.

Activity 5-16: Updating All Users in a Container or Template

Time Required: 10 minutes

Objective: Use ConsoleOne to update multiple user accounts.

Requirements: Completion of Activity 5-14 and a Windows XP computer with Novell Client installed

Description: IT Department users share a fax machine, and management wants that fax number set up on all IT user accounts. In this activity, you learn how to update all user accounts in the IT OU.

1. If necessary, start your Windows computer, and log in to eDirectory with your administrative user name and password.
2. Start ConsoleOne, and expand your eDirectory tree and the **UAS** container.
3. Click the **IT** OU.
4. Click **File**, **Properties of Multiple Objects** to display the Available classes dialog box.
5. Click the **User** object class and then click **OK** (if you receive a warning message, click **OK** to continue) to open the Properties of Multiple Objects dialog box showing all users in the IT OU.
6. Click the **General** tab, and then enter a fax number of your choosing in the Fax Number text box.
7. Click **OK** to update the objects and return to the ConsoleOne main window.
8. Double-click a user object in the IT OU, and verify that the new fax number has been entered.
9. Exit ConsoleOne and log out.

Activity 5-17: Updating Selected Users

Time Required: 10 minutes

Objective: Use iManager to create and manage multiple user accounts.

Requirements: Completion of Activity 5-14

Description: Sometimes you need to change settings for only a few users. You can do this by using the Select multiple objects link in the Modify User window. For example, Eric has asked you to set password restrictions for both Luke McMann and Kellie Thiele to restrict access on Sundays. In this activity, you use iManager to set these restrictions for both users.

1. If necessary, log on to your local computer, start your Web browser, start iManager, and log in to iManager with your administrative user name and password.
2. If necessary, click to expand the **Users** heading, and then click the **Modify User** link.
3. Click the **Select multiple objects** link to display the Username window.
4. Click the **Object Selector** button next to the Username text box.
5. If necessary, navigate to the **IT** OU. Click the **KThiele** and **LMcMann** user accounts to add them to the Selected Objects list box.
6. Click **OK** to return to the Modify User window. Both KThiele and LMcMann should then appear in the Username window.
7. Click **OK** to display the Modify User window for multiple objects shown in Figure 5-28.
8. Click the **Restrictions** tab, and then click the **Time Restrictions** link to display the Available login times window.
9. Hold down the **Shift** key and click in the 12 column under the AM heading for the S (for Sunday) row on the top. Drag along the Sunday row to highlight all hours, and then click in the 11:30 column under the PM heading to select all hours in that day.
10. Click the **down arrow** next to the Ignore option, and then click **Replace**.

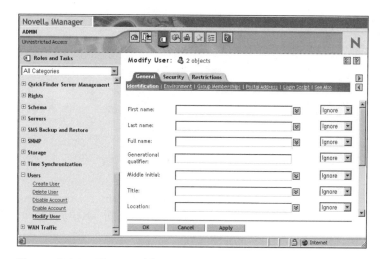

Figure 5-28   The Modify User window for multiple users

11. Click **OK** to save the time restriction, and then click **Close** to return to the iManager main window.

12. Follow these steps to check the time restrictions for the Luke McMann user:

   a. Click the **Modify User** link, and then click the **Object Selector** button next to the Username text box to select the Luke McMann user account.

   b. Click **OK** to display the Modify User window.

   c. Click the **Restrictions** tab, and then click the **Time Restrictions** link to display the current time restrictions. The time restrictions should match those you entered in Step 9.

13. Repeat Step 12 to check time restrictions for the Kellie Thiele user account.

14. If you're continuing to the next activity, stay logged in to iManager. If you have completed your session, click the **Exit** button to return to the iManager Login window, and then close your Web browser and log off your local computer.

IMPORTING LDAP OBJECTS

As described in Chapter 4, eDirectory uses the industry-standard X.500 naming system to store information on network objects. Because eDirectory is based on an industry-standard system, information can be exported or imported from other directory systems, such as Windows 2000 Active Directory, that are also based on X.500. Lightweight Directory Access Protocol (LDAP) is a simplified version of X.500 that makes it easier for compatible systems to exchange directory information. NetWare 6.5 includes an LDAP Import and Export Wizard with ConsoleOne that network administrators can use to transfer information to and from eDirectory with **Lightweight Directory Interchange Format (LDIF)** files. LDIF files are simple ASCII text files that use a standardized syntax to add, change, or delete objects. The basic syntax of an LDIF file consists of a distinguished name, a change type, an object class, and attribute values, as shown in Table 5-1.

Table 5-1   LDIF command syntax

Command Line	Purpose
dn: *distinguished name*	Distinguished name of object to be created, modified, or deleted
changetype: add/modify/delete	Specifies the type of change: add, modify, or delete
ObjectClass: *object class*	Specifies an object class to be used with this entry; an object can have multiple object classes defined for it
uid: *user name*	The user's login name
cn: *common name*	The user's last name

Table 5-1 LDIF command syntax (continued)

Command Line	Purpose
ACL: *access control list (rights to eDirectory)*	Multiple ACL entries are used to assign the new user object rights to certain properties, as described in Chapter 7
groupMembership: *groups*	Distinguished name of group objects the user will be added to
securityEquals	Identifies other objects with the same rights that the new object will have; usually specifies the group the new user account will belong to

Unlike eDirectory distinguished names, LDAP distinguished names use a typeful format with commas instead of periods to separate the components and do not start with a period. For example, Kellie Thiele's LDAP distinguished name is as follows:

```
cn=KThiele,ou=it,o=uas
```

The changetype field specifies the action: add, modify, or delete. The object class specifies the type of object being created or modified, such as a user, container, or printer. The attribute fields specify information properties that are unique to the specified object class. Examples of attributes for a user object include givenName, fullName, and Title. UAS has several computers in the Manufacturing Department used mostly for entering shipping and receiving data. Instead of creating user accounts for each user who can enter data on these computers, Russ Pence has recommended having a generic account for each computer based on its function. Although Eric could use ConsoleOne to create accounts for the computers in these departments, because these accounts will be similar, he decided to use an LDIF file to create the accounts. Using an LDIF file makes it easy to add computer stations in the future because the file can simply be edited to insert the new station name and location. Figure 5-29 shows an example of an LDIF file Eric used to create two computer station accounts named Receiving1 and Shipping1 in the Mfg OU.

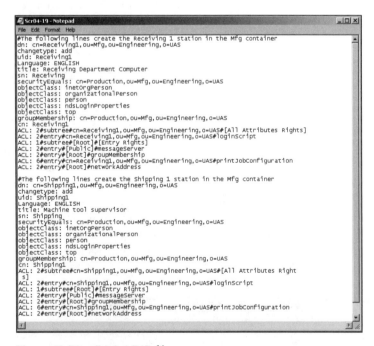

Figure 5-29 Eric's LDIF file

In Activity 5-18, you use Eric's LDIF file as a model to create your own LDIF file containing the station accounts listed earlier in Figure 5-20. You then use iManager to import users from your LDIF file into the UAS container.

Activity 5-18: Importing Users from an LDIF File

Time Required: 20 minutes

Objective: Use iManager to import users from an LDIF file.

Requirements: To complete this activity, you need a copy of the file shown in Figure 5-29. You can use a text editor to create this file or obtain a copy from your instructor. If you're using a shared classroom server, this file should be located in the SYS:Public\Shared directory.

Description: In this activity, you edit the LDIF file Eric used, and then use iManager to create your additional Mfg users by importing the modified LDIF file.

1. If necessary, log on to your computer.

2. Copy the **Stations.ldif** file to your C: drive. If you're using a shared classroom server, copy the file from the SYS:Public\Shared directory by following these steps:

    a. Browse to the **SYS:Public\Shared** directory.

    b. Right-click the **Stations.ldif** file, and then click **Open with**.

    c. Paste the file to the **My Documents** folder.

3. Use Notepad to edit the existing LDIF file to create the Shipping and Receiving stations:

    a. If you're using a shared classroom server, check each line and change the Organization name from UAS to **##UAS.CLASS** (## represents your assigned student number).

    b. To create an account for a second Receiving station, copy the lines for creating the Receiving1 station and paste them at the end of the LDIF file. In the copied lines, replace the name Receiving1 with **Receiving2**.

    c. To create an account for a second Shipping station, copy the lines for creating the Shipping1 station and paste them at the end of the LDIF file. In the copied lines, replace the name Shipping1 with **Shipping2**.

    d. Click **File**, **Exit** from the menu, and then click **Yes** to save your changes and exit Notepad.

4. To use clear text passwords when importing an LDIF file, you need to enable the clear text port 389 on your server by following these steps:

    a. If necessary, start iManager, and log in with your administrative user name and password.

    b. Expand the **eDirectory Administration** heading, and click the **Modify Object** link.

    c. Click the **Object Selector** button next to the Object name text box.

    d. Click the **down arrow** next to your UAS Organization.

    e. Click the **LDAP Group – UAS** object to insert it into the Object name text box.

    f. Click **OK** to display the LDAP Group properties window.

    g. Click to clear the **Require TLS for Simple Binds with Password** check box.

    h. Click the **Apply** button to save your changes.

    i. Click **OK** to return to the iManager main window.

    j. If necessary, expand the **eDirectory Administration** heading, and click the **Modify Object** link.

    k. Click the **Object Selector** button next to the Object name text box.

    l. Click the **down arrow** next to your UAS Organization, and then click the **LDAP Server – UAS** object to insert it into the Object name text box.

    m. Click **OK** to display the LDAP Group properties window.

    n. Click the **Connections** tab, and verify that the Require TLS for all operations check box is cleared.

    o. Click **OK** to return to the iManager main window.

5. Follow these steps to import the LDIF file from iManager:

   a. Click to expand the **eDirectory Maintenance** heading, and then click the **Import Convert Export Wizard** link to display the ICE Wizard window.

   b. Verify that the Import data from file on disk option button is selected, and then click **Next**.

   c. Verify that LDIF is displayed in the File type text box.

   d. Click the **Browse** button next to the File to import text box, and navigate to the folder containing the Stations.ldif file.

   e. Double-click the **Stations.ldif** file, and then click **Next** to display the Select import destination window.

   f. Enter the IP address of your NetWare 6.5 server in the Server DNS name/IP address text box.

   g. Scroll down and click to select the **Authenticated login** option button.

   h. If you're using a dedicated server, enter **cn=uasadmin,o=uas** in the User DN text box. If you're using a shared classroom server, enter **cn=##uasadmin,o=Class** (replacing ## with your assigned student number).

   i. Enter the password for your administrative user in the Password text box.

   j. Scroll down to Advanced settings and click the **Allow forward references** check box. Click **Next** to display the generated command line. Record the command here:

   _____

   k. Click **Finish** to import the LDIF file objects.

   l. Click **Download log file**, click **Open**, and then click **Notepad** to display the LDAP Import messages.

   m. Verify that the import was successful, and record the number of objects imported here:

   _____

   n. Click **Close** to return to the iManager main window.

   o. Click the **Exit** button to return to the Novell iManager Login window.

6. If you have any errors, correct the Stations.ldif file, delete any users created in Step 5, and then repeat Step 5.

7. Use iManager to verify that the new accounts exist.

8. Leave iManager open for the next activity.

DELETING, RENAMING, AND MOVING OBJECTS

When working with the eDirectory tree, you might need to rename, delete, or move an object from one location to another to better organize the structure. As you'll learn in Chapters 6 and 7, users often obtain rights to access files and use eDirectory objects by being a member of an OU. In addition, login scripts are usually associated with OUs to provide drive mappings and computer setups for all users in an OU. When moving objects, keep in mind that moving an object to a different location can change the drive mappings and computer setups users have when they log in and affect users' rights to access files and other network objects, such as printers.

To rename an object in ConsoleOne or NetWare Administrator, you simply right-click the object, select Rename, and then type a new name. To rename an object in iManager, you use the Rename Object link under the eDirectory Administration heading. Deleting leaf objects with ConsoleOne or NetWare Administrator, such as user accounts and groups, is as easy as clicking the object and pressing Delete; when deleting container objects, however, you need to remove all objects from the container before deleting it. To delete an object in iManager, you use the Delete Object link under the eDirectory Administration heading. In the following activity, you practice renaming and deleting eDirectory objects in iManager.

The complex part of renaming, deleting, or moving objects is understanding how the change affects other objects in the tree. For example, deleting a group object that has been given rights to a directory or printer could prevent users from accessing network information or resources. To move a leaf object in ConsoleOne, you simply need to select the object and choose File, Move from the menu. Moving container objects is more difficult because NetWare moves only partitions. To move an OU from one location to another, you must first make the container a separate partition, as described in Chapter 2. You can then move the container's partition to another location and merge it back into the tree. In the following section, you use iManager to move user and container objects.

Activity 5-19: Renaming, Deleting, and Moving Objects in iManager

ACTIVITY

Time Required: 5 minutes

Objective: Use iManager to rename, delete, and move leaf objects.

Requirements: Completion of Activity 5-14 and a Windows XP computer with Novell Client installed

Description: Although Eric originally placed the WebMgrs group in the IT container, because users throughout the company use this group, he moved the object up one level to the UAS Organization. In this activity, you use iManager to delete and rename user objects and then move the WebMgrs group from the IT OU to the UAS Organization.

1. If necessary, start your computer, and log on to your local computer. If you're using Windows XP, click the **Workstation Only** check box.

2. Start your Web browser, and open the iManager Login window as described in Activity 5-5.

3. Log in to iManager with your administrative user name and password.

4. Follow the procedure in Activity 5-14 to use your T_IT template to create a user named **JaredSmith** in the IT OU.

5. Follow these steps to rename the Jared Smith user as **JSmith**:

   a. Click the **Rename Object** link under the eDirectory Administration heading.

   b. Click the **Object Selector** button next to the Object name text box. Click to select your **JaredSmith** user account.

   c. Enter **JSmith** in the New object name text box, and click **OK** to rename the user.

6. Delete the JSmith user account:

   a. Click the **Delete Object** link under the eDirectory Administration heading.

   b. Click the **Object Selector** button next to the Object name text box. Click to select your **JSmith** user account.

   c. Click **OK** to display the warning message. Click **OK** to continue with the object deletion process and display the completion message.

   d. Click **OK** to return to the main iManager window.

7. Follow these steps to move the WebMgrs group from the IT OU to the UAS container:

   a. Click to expand the **eDirectory Administration** heading, and then click the **Move Object** link to display the Move Object window shown in Figure 5-30.

   b. Click the **Object Selector** button next to the Object name text box, navigate to the **IT** OU, and then click the **WebMgrs** group object.

   c. Click the **Object Selector** button next to the Move to text box to move up two levels, and then click the **UAS** container.

   d. Click **OK** to move WebMgrs to the UAS container and display the completion message. Click **OK** to return to the iManager main window.

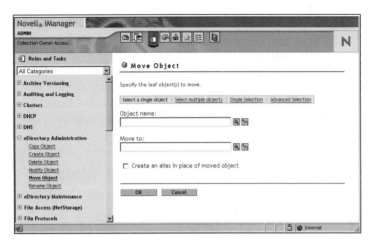

Figure 5-30   The Move Object window

8. Click the **Exit** button to end your iManager session and return to the iManager Login window.

9. Close your Web browser and log off the local computer.

Moving a Container Object

When managing the structure of the eDirectory database, sometimes you need to move a container object from one location to another within the eDirectory hierarchy to make access to resources easier, for example. As discussed in Chapter 7, when a container becomes a subcontainer of another container object, the subcontainer has access rights to objects in the parent container. For example, Mfg is currently a subcontainer of the Engineering container, but Luke McMann has suggested that Mfg be made a separate container to prevent accidental access to Engineering Department resources.

Moving a container object is more complex than moving a leaf object because it changes the hierarchy of the eDirectory tree, thereby reorganizing the eDirectory database. In Chapter 4, you learned that the eDirectory database is divided into one or more partitions, starting with the root partition. Each partition is a separate file or replica located on one or more NetWare servers. The main reason for creating additional partitions is to divide a large eDirectory database into smaller files or replicas for more efficient access. However, partitioning eDirectory also makes it easier to move containers. When a container is made a separate partition, it becomes a separate file that can be moved and synchronized to another location in the hierarchical structure of the eDirectory database. As a result, to move a container object to another location in the eDirectory tree, you need to perform these three steps:

- Create a partition that starts with the container to be moved (the Mfg OU, in this example).

- After a partition has been created for the container, use ConsoleOne or iManager 2.5 to move the container's partition to the new location. (iManager version 2.0 does not include an option to move container objects.)

- Complete the move by merging the Mfg container's partition back into the root partition.

Another consideration when moving container objects is that creating and merging partitions requires changes to the root partition of the eDirectory tree. As a result, to move container objects, NetWare requires that your user name have the Supervisor right to the root of the eDirectory tree, as described in Chapter 7. In Activity 5-20, you perform a three-part procedure to move one of your OUs to a new location.

Activity 5-20: Moving an OU in ConsoleOne

Time Required: 10 minutes

Objectives: Use ConsoleOne to move a container object.

Requirements: A Mfg OU within the Engineering OU (created in Chapter 4)

Description: This activity consists of three parts. In Part I, you make a separate partition for the Mfg container. In Part II, you move the Mfg container to the UAS Organization, and in Part III, you merge the Mfg partition into the UAS root partition.

If you don't have an Engineering or Mfg OU, you have to create these objects before performing the following steps.

Part I: Creating a New Partition

Before you can move a container object, you need to make the container a separate partition. Follow these steps:

1. If necessary, log in to eDirectory with your administrative user name and password.
2. Start ConsoleOne.
3. To display partition information in the ConsoleOne window, click your **UAS** Organization, and then click **View**, **Partition and Replica View** from the menu.
4. If necessary, expand the **Engineering** OU to display the Mfg OU, and then click the **Mfg** OU to select it.
5. Click **Edit**, **Create Partition** from the menu to open the Create Partition dialog box.
6. Click **OK** to create a new partition and return to the ConsoleOne Partition and Replica view. Record the change to the Mfg container icon:

_____

Part II: Moving the Container

After the container is a separate partition, you can use ConsoleOne to move the Mfg container beneath the UAS Organization by following these steps:

1. Right-click the **Mfg** partition, and then click **Move** to open the Move dialog box.
2. Click the **browse** button next to the Destination text box to open the Select Object dialog box.
3. Navigate to and click your **UAS** container, and then click **OK**.
4. Click **OK** to move the Mfg OU.

Part III: Merging the Mfg Partition Back into the Root Partition

Although he could have left Mfg as a separate partition, Eric wanted to keep the number of partitions to a minimum to reduce administrative overhead. In this part of the activity, you merge the Mfg partition back into the root partition by performing these steps:

1. Click the **Mfg** partition to select it.
2. Click **Edit**, **Merge Partition** from the menu to open the Merge Partition dialog box.
3. Click **OK** and wait for the Mfg partition to be merged back into the parent UAS partition. After the merge is finished, the partition icon is removed from the Mfg OU.
4. Change the view back to the Console view by clicking **View**, **Console View** from the menu.
5. Click the **Mfg** OU to confirm that all objects have been moved along with the Mfg container to be placed under the UAS Organization.
6. Exit ConsoleOne, and log out.

Congratulations! You're well on your way to becoming a CNA. Now that you've established login security by creating user, group, and Organizational Role objects for the IT Department, you can apply what you've learned to set up login security for the other UAS departments by performing the end-of-chapter projects. In Chapter 6, you secure the file system by granting users the rights they need to access files and applications.

CHAPTER SUMMARY

- Network administrators must know how to set up the eDirectory system by creating the necessary objects and establishing a login security system. Although ConsoleOne is a powerful and easy-to-use Windows-based utility that Novell CNAs use when setting up and securing the network, NetWare 6.5 relies primarily on the iManager utility to create and maintain user and group objects via a Web browser.

- Login security consists of account restrictions, intruder detection, and authentication. Account restrictions include password, time, and address restrictions and can be set for user and user template objects. Intruder detection, enabled on a container-by-container basis, helps protect against attackers guessing user passwords by locking user accounts after the specified number of incorrect login attempts have been made in a given time period.

- User templates make creating user objects more efficient. You can use them to define the path to users' home directories and set common account and password restrictions.

- LDAP provides a way to exchange directory information between systems that are X.500 compatible, such as eDirectory and Microsoft Active Directory, by using LDIF files. You can use LDIF files as a quick way to create user objects.

- Novell supplies an Organizational Role object that's useful when assigning rights to certain user accounts. Organizational Role objects are similar to groups, except that they usually represent positions in the organization. If another user is assigned the responsibilities, you simply need to change the occupant of the organizational role to give him or her the required privileges.

- When managing an eDirectory system, often you need to move objects from one container to another. Although moving leaf objects is fast and easy, moving a container from one location to another requires creating a partition starting at the container to be moved, moving the partition to the new location, and then merging the new partition with the parent partition of the container it has been moved into.

KEY TERMS

address restrictions — Security restrictions that require a user to log in only from specified client IP addresses.

authentication — The part of NetWare security that helps protect against attackers by validating each network packet to guarantee that it was sent from an authorized user.

authorization — The process of verifying a user's name and password to allow himr or her to access network resources.

intruder detection — A part of login security that works at the container level by setting a limit on the number of incorrect login attempts that can be made on a user account during a specified time period.

Lightweight Directory Interchange Format (LDIF) — An ASCII text file format that uses a standardized syntax to add, change, or delete objects in LDAP-compatible directory systems.

login security — The security system used to perform the authorization process. *See also* authorization.

Organizational Role object — An object type that enables you to assign rights to a job position, for example, rather than a specific user.

password restrictions — Security restrictions that force users to use passwords that exceed or meet a minimum length and must be changed within a specified period.

time restrictions — Security restrictions that allow users to log in to the network only during specified hours.

user template — A property that defines standard settings and configures restrictions for each user in a container.

REVIEW QUESTIONS

1. List five security systems used in setting up a NetWare 6.5 network.

2. Which of the following enables a network administrator to define standard settings, such as the location of home directories and password restrictions for new users?

    a. groups

    b. templates

    c. organizational roles

    d. LDIF files

3. List the three steps for moving the Production container from the Engineering container to the Business container.

4. Which of the following is *not* a component of login security?

    a. password restriction

    b. intruder detection

    c. administrative task

    d. station restriction

5. List three types of account restrictions.

6. Which of the following security measures do you use to set the maximum number of times a user can enter an incorrect password?

    a. password restriction

    b. account restriction

    c. intruder detection

    d. authorization

7. Authentication involves validating a user's login request. True or False?

8. Which of the following involves validating each network packet to make sure it has come from an authorized user?

    a. authorization

    b. authentication

    c. password security

    d. intruder detection

9. Which of the following NetWare 6.5 utilities can be used to move a container to another location in the eDirectory tree? (Choose all that apply.)

    a. ConsoleOne

    b. NDSMgr

    c. NetWare Administrator

    d. iManager 2.5

10. Which of the following objects should be used to provide a backup Admin account?

     a. group

     b. Organizational Role

     c. Organizational Unit

     d. user

11. Using the naming conventions explained in this chapter, write four possible user names for Kari Means.

12. A user template can be used to change the default rights new users have to their home directories. True or False?

13. Which of the following is *not* a password restriction in NetWare?

     a. minimum password length

     b. require unique password

     c. require complex passwords

     d. date password expires

14. Which of the following protocols can be used to transfer objects between X.500-compatible directories?

     a. LDIF

     b. LDAP

     c. TCP

     d. IP

15. Which of the following utilities can be used to import an LDIF file?

     a. LDAP

     b. ConsoleOne

     c. iManager

     d. both b and c

16. Intruder detection works at which of the following levels by setting a limit on the number of incorrect login attempts that can be made on a user account during a specified time period?

     a. user

     b. Root

     c. container

     d. Organization

17. A user is granted rights to use iManager to create eDirectory objects through which of the following?

     a. eDirectory security

     b. Role Based Services

     c. membership in the Admin group

     d. login security

18. Which of the following object types is best suited for giving users the rights needed for a particular position in the company?

     a. Organizational Unit

     b. group

     c. Organizational Role

     d. security equivalent

19. In an LDIF file, which of the following fields specifies information properties that are unique to the specified object class?

   a. attribute

   b. property

   c. name

   d. entry

20. Which of the following utilities can be used to add users via a Web browser?

   a. Remote Manager

   b. ConsoleOne

   c. iManager

   d. both a and c

5

CASE PROJECTS

Case Project 5-1: Identifying Business Division Groups

Using the information in the UAS organizational chart from Chapter 1, fill in a Group Planning Form (supplied by your instructor) for the Business Division of the eDirectory tree you designed in Case Project 4-1.

Case Project 5-2: Planning Users and Templates for the Business Division

Using the information in the UAS organizational chart, fill in a Template Planning Form (supplied by your instructor) that identifies account restrictions and the home directory path for users in the Business Division. Refer to the directory structure you designed for the Business Division in Chapter 3's Case Projects to determine the correct path for user home directories.

After you have designed the new templates, fill in a User Planning Form (supplied by your instructor) that shows all user accounts for the Business Division and the associated templates for creating those users. Include any groups the user accounts will be assigned to.

Case Project 5-3: Planning Organizational Role Objects

Using the information in the UAS organizational chart, fill in an Organizational Role Planning Form (supplied by your instructor) that lists account restrictions and the home directory path for users in the Business Division.

HANDS-ON PROJECTS

Hands-on Project 5-1: Creating Groups and Users

Refer to the procedures in this chapter to perform the following tasks:

1. Use iManager or ConsoleOne to create group accounts for all groups (except ITMgrs) shown in Figure 5-17.

2. Create the Engineering template shown in Figure 5-19.

3. Use iManager to create users in the Engineering Department using the template you created in Step 2 (refer to Figure 5-22).

4. Create the remaining users shown in Figure 5-22.

5. Create the Organizational Role objects shown in Figure 5-25 that you didn't create in the chapter activities.

HANDS-ON PROJECTS

Hands-on Project 5-2: Creating the Business Division Objects

Using the planning forms you developed for the case projects, create the groups, templates, user accounts, and Organizational Role objects for the Business Division of Universal AeroSpace.

6

WORKING WITH NETWARE FILE SYSTEM SECURITY

After reading this chapter and completing the activities, you will be able to:

♦ Describe NetWare file system security components (trustee rights, effective rights, and inheritance), make trustee assignments, and determine a user's effective rights

♦ Explain concepts of file system security

♦ Describe file and directory attributes and use NetWare utilities and commands to view and set attributes

---

In Chapter 4, you learned how to create user accounts with ConsoleOne and iManager. Now that you have created your users, by default they have rights to access and save files only in their home directories. To enable them to use the network file system fully, you need to set up file system security so that they have the rights to access and maintain network files they're responsible for, and you can still protect sensitive network information from unauthorized access. In this chapter, you learn how to plan and implement file system security for your version of the Universal AeroSpace Corporation.

FILE SYSTEM SECURITY COMPONENTS

NetWare file system security consists of two levels: access rights security and attribute security. **Access rights** are like a set of keys given to users to allow them to work in specific rooms in a building; similarly, access rights ensure that users can work with data only in certain files and directories. A user gains access rights through direct assignment or by being a member of a group or container. In the following sections, you learn how to grant NetWare access rights to users so that they can work with the network file system. **Attributes** are flags attached to files and directories to limit the functions that can be performed in those files or directories. For example, setting the Read Only attribute on a file prevents its contents from being modified, even by users with rights to change data in the directory containing the file. Later in the "Attribute Security" section, you learn about NetWare file and directory attributes and using iManager and ConsoleOne to set up attribute security.

NetWare Access Rights

File system security is based on the concept of making an eDirectory object, such as a user, group, or container, a trustee of a file or directory with certain assigned access rights. File system security consists of a single group of eight access rights used to control the operations a trustee can perform in the file system. Each network directory and file has an entry in the **directory entry table (DET)** containing information about it, including the file or directory name and the access control list (ACL). The ACL lists each trustee assignment for the directory or file and the access rights associated with that trustee assignment. Table 6-1 lists the NetWare file system access rights and their effects in files or directories.

Table 6-1   NetWare access rights

Access Right	Effect in Directory	Effect in File
Supervisor [S]	Grants all rights to the directory and all subdirectories; this right can't be blocked or reassigned at a lower subdirectory or file level.	Grants all rights to the specified file.
Read [R]	Allows users to read files or run programs in the directory.	Allows users to read or run the specified file or program when they don't have Read rights at the directory level.
Write [W]	Allows users to change or add data to files in this directory.	Allows users to change or add data to the specified file when they don't have Write rights at the directory level.
Create [C]	Allows users to create files and subdirectories.	Allows users to salvage the specified file if it's deleted.
Erase [E]	Allows users to delete files and remove subdirectories.	Allows users to delete the specified file when they have not been granted Erase rights at the directory level.
Modify [M]	Allows users to change file and subdirectory names and use the FLAG and FLAGDIR commands to change attribute settings on files or subdirectories.	Allows users to change the name or attribute settings of the specified file when they don't have Modify rights at the directory level.
File Scan [F]	Allows users to view a directory of file and subdirectory names.	Allows users to view the specified file name or a directory listing when they don't have File Scan rights at the directory level.
Access Control [A]	Allows users to grant access rights to other users for this directory.	Allows users to grant access rights to the specified file when they don't have Access Control at the directory level.

The **Read [R] right** and **File Scan [F] right** are often used together to allow trustees to call up files or run programs in a certain directory. For example, by default, any container with a server object is given [R] and [F] rights to the SYS:Public directory so that users in that container can run NetWare commands and utilities in the Public directory.

With the **Create [C] right** to a directory, users can create new files and subdirectories in that directory. Having only the Create right to a directory enables users to copy files into the directory as long as no other file in the directory has the same name, and having the Create right to a shared directory allows users to copy or create new files in the directory and create subdirectories. Having the Create right to an existing file might seem redundant, but it means that users can salvage the file if it's deleted.

In addition to erasing files, the **Erase [E] right** to a directory allows users to remove the entire directory and its subdirectories. Notice the difference between the Write and Modify rights: The **Write [W] right** grants the privilege of changing or adding data to an existing file, but the **Modify [M] right** allows users to change only a file's name or attributes, not its contents.

As its name implies, the **Access Control [A] right** allows users to grant access rights to other users to control which users have access to a certain directory or file. However, allowing users to grant rights to other users can make it difficult for a network administrator to keep track of file system security, so the Access Control right shouldn't normally be given to other users.

Having the **Supervisor [S] right** is different from having all rights because it can't be changed or blocked at a lower-level directory or file, and it can be assigned only by another user who has the Supervisor right to the directory. Having the Access Control right doesn't allow users to assign the Supervisor right to themselves or to another user. The Supervisor right is often granted to workgroup managers so that they can control some section of the file system's directory structure. For example, if Kari Means is the workgroup manager for the Engineering Department, she could be granted the Supervisor right to the CORP:Engineer directory structure.

NOTE

If users have the Access Control right, but not the Supervisor right, in a directory, they could restrict themselves from working in the directory by accidentally assigning their user names fewer rights than they need to the directory. For that reason, the Access Control right usually shouldn't be granted to a user unless it's absolutely necessary for the user to assign rights to others.

To help you better understand which access rights are necessary for carrying out functions in the network file system, Table 6-2 lists typical operations users need to perform on files and directories and the access rights required for those operations.

Table 6-2   Rights required for common functions

Task	Rights Required
Read a file	Read
View a directory listing	File Scan
Change the contents of data in a file	Write
Write to a closed file using a text editor that creates a backup file	Write, Create, Erase, Modify (not always required)
Run a program file	Read
Create and write to a new file	Create
Copy a file from a directory	Read, File Scan
Copy a file into a directory	Create
Copy multiple files to a directory with existing files	Create, File Scan
Create a subdirectory	Create
Delete a file	Erase
Salvage deleted files	Read and File Scan on the file; Create in the directory or on file name
Change attributes	Modify
Rename a file or subdirectory	Modify
Change the Inherited Rights Filter	Access Control
Make or change a trustee assignment	Access Control

Trustee Assignments

Trustee assignments give users, groups, or containers rights to access and maintain the file system and can be made to directories or individual files. A **directory trustee** is a user, group, or container object that has been granted access rights to a directory, and directory trustees are kept track of in each volume's DET. A DET entry can hold up to six trustee assignments. If more than six trustees are assigned to a directory, an additional entry is made in the DET for that directory's name. For this reason, you should keep trustee assignments to six or fewer for each directory. This is usually done by making a group a trustee of a directory and then adding users to the group if they need access to that directory. A **file trustee** is a user or group that has been granted access rights to a file. As with directory trustees, file trustees are kept track of in the DET. If more than six trustees are assigned to a file, the file name needs another entry in the DET.

The term **effective rights** is used to define which access rights a user has in a specific directory or file. Effective rights are a combination of the access rights users have from their trustee assignments, plus any access rights from being a member of a group or container. In the UAS network, for example, the Design group was made a trustee of the NASA directory with Read and File Scan rights. Paul Alm, a member of the Design group, is made a trustee of the NASA directory with Create and Write rights. In this case, Paul's effective rights are [R W C F], a combination of Paul's trustee assignment—[W C]—plus his rights from being a member of the Design group—[R F]. Basically, a user's effective rights to a directory or file are the result of one or more of these factors:

- A trustee assignment is made directly to the user name.
- A trustee assignment is made to a group of which the user is a member.
- A trustee assignment is made to a container where the user or user's group resides.
- A file or directory inherits container, group, and user rights from a higher-level directory.
- Inherited rights are blocked by an Inherited Rights Filter applied to a directory or file.

In this chapter, you learn how a user acquires effective rights and how to apply this knowledge to establish file system security for your UAS network.

Making User Trustee Assignments

The simplest and most straightforward way for a user to get effective rights to a directory or file is by being granted a direct trustee assignment consisting of a specific set of access rights to the directory or file. The user's name and assigned access rights are then stored in the ACL property of the DET for that directory or file. This process is called a **trustee assignment** because it makes the user a trustee of the directory or file with certain access privileges. Provided no trustee assignments have been made to any groups or containers of which the user is a member, the user's effective rights are always equal to his or her trustee assignment. Access rights are usually indicated with the first letter of each right enclosed in brackets. For example, [R C F] indicates that a user has Read, Create, and File Scan rights. [All] is often used to represent all access rights, including Supervisor, and is easier than specifying each right individually.

The most common application of user trustee assignments is granting users all rights to their home directories. When you created home directories for users in Chapter 5, each user was given a trustee assignment based on access rights you defined in the user template. By default, a new user gets [R W C E M F A] rights to his or her home directory; however, the UAS network administrator, Eric Kenton, believes that giving users Access Control or Supervisor rights to their home directories creates potential security problems. With the Access Control or Supervisor right, users can make other objects trustees of their directories, which increases the probability of intruders accessing or destroying data and makes managing the file system more difficult. In addition, if users have the Access Control right without the Supervisor right, they could accidentally reassign their own rights to a file or subdirectory, possibly locking themselves out of a portion of their directories and eventually requiring your assistance to bail them out. For those reasons, the templates you used when creating user accounts in Chapter 5 have been modified to remove Supervisor and Access Control rights from each user's home directory trustee assignment.

When Novell Client is installed on a computer, you can use My Computer, My Network Places, or Windows Explorer to make and change trustee assignments. Making trustee assignments in Windows is often convenient, but the NetWare utilities ConsoleOne, NetWare Administrator, and Remote Manager offer additional capabilities for making and maintaining trustee assignments. For example, you need to use one of the NetWare utilities to assign the Supervisor right, make multiple trustee assignments to a user, or view a user's effective rights. In Activities 6-1 and 6-2, you practice using ConsoleOne and Windows Explorer to make and modify trustee assignments for users in your IT Department.

NOTE

The NetWare 6.5 CNA exam requires that you know how to use Windows Explorer in addition to ConsoleOne and Remote Manager to grant trustee assignments. You use ConsoleOne and Windows Explorer in Activities 6-1, 6-2, and 6-3. Some later activities focus on using Remote Manager.

ACTIVITY

Activity 6-1: Modifying User Trustee Assignments

Time Required: 10 minutes

Objective: Use ConsoleOne to assign rights to users, groups, and containers.

Requirements: To perform this activity, you need the following:

- Completion of Activities 3-5 and 5-12
- A Windows XP Professional computer with Novell Client installed from Activity 4-5
- The path to your CORP volume data (for a shared classroom server, the suggested path is *IPaddress*\STUDENTS\##Corp, with *IPaddress* representing the IP address of your classroom server and ## representing your assigned student number; for a dedicated server, the suggested path is UASHOST\CORP):

  _____

- Server name and IP address:

  _____

Description: To manage their files and documents when they are away from the office, Luke McMann wants Eric Kenton and Kellie Thiele to grant him Supervisor rights to their home directories when they're away from the office. To do this, Eric decided to make all users in the IT Department supervisors of their own home directories. In this activity, you use ConsoleOne to carry out this task. In Activity 6-2, you test the system by logging in as Kellie and using Windows to grant Luke rights to Kellie's home directory.

1. If necessary, start your computer, and log in with your administrative user name and password.
2. Start ConsoleOne, and click to expand your eDirectory tree and your **UAS** container.
3. Follow these steps to display subdirectories of the IT directory in the object pane:
   a. Click to expand the **IT** OU and the **CORP** volume object and display all directories in the navigation pane.
   b. Click the **IT** directory to display all subdirectories in the object pane.
4. Give your user name the Supervisor right to your home directory by following these steps:
   a. Right-click your user name's home directory, and then click **Properties** to open the Properties dialog box.
   b. Click the **Trustees** tab and record your default rights here:

   _____

   c. If necessary, click the **Supervisor** check box to enable this access right.
   d. Click **OK** to save your assignment.
5. Repeat Step 4 to give Kellie the Supervisor right to her home directory.
6. Repeat Step 4 to give Luke the Supervisor right to his home directory.
7. Exit ConsoleOne, and log out.

Activity 6-2: Making User Trustee Assignments in Windows

Time Required: 10 minutes

Objective: Use Windows to assign rights to users, groups, and containers.

Requirements: Same as Activity 6-1

Description: Kellie is taking a vacation, and before leaving, she wants to grant Luke the rights to manage files in her home directory. In this activity, you log in with the account you created for Kellie in Chapter 5, and then use Windows Explorer to add Luke as a trustee of Kellie's home directory with Read and File Scan rights.

1. Log in with the user name you created for Kellie in Chapter 5:

   a. Enter **KThiele** in the User name text box and the password you set for Kellie in the Password text box.

   b. Click the **Advanced** button, click the **Context** browse button, navigate to your UAS container, click the **IT** OU, and then click **OK** to place IT.UAS in the Context text box.

   c. Click **OK** to log in.

2. If necessary, log on to your Windows computer with your local user name and password.

3. Follow these steps to map drive letter L: to the IT directory:

   a. Right-click **My Network Places**, and then click **Novell Map Network Drive** to open the Map Drive dialog box.

   b. Click the **Choose the drive letter to map** list arrow, and then click **L:** in the list of options.

   c. Enter **\\\\IPaddress\\volumepath\\IT** (with *IPaddress* representing your server's IP address and *volume-path* representing the path to your CORP volume data) in the Enter the network path to the resource text box, and then click the **Map** button to open a window for the IT directory.

4. Follow these steps to add Luke as a trustee of Kellie's home directory:

   a. Right-click Kellie's home directory, and click **Properties** to open the KThiele Properties dialog box.

   b. Click the **NetWare Rights** tab to display the Trustees list box shown in Figure 6-1.

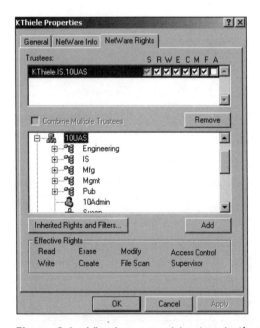

Figure 6-1   Viewing current trustees in the KThiele Properties dialog box

   c. If necessary, expand the **IT** OU in the lower pane.

   d. Click **LMcMann**, and then click the **Add** button to add Luke to the Trustees list box. Record Luke's default rights here:

_____

e. If necessary, change LMcMann's rights to only Read and File Scan access rights.

f. Click **OK** to save the assignment.

5. Close the IT directory window, and stay logged in for the next activity.

Viewing Effective Rights

When working with file system security, often you need to verify a user's effective rights to a directory. Although you can use Windows Explorer or Remote Manager to view your effective rights in any directory or file, you can't view another user's effective rights. To verify effective rights in the file system, you should use ConsoleOne or NetWare Administrator. In Activity 6-3, you learn how to use ConsoleOne to check a user's effective rights in a directory.

Activity 6-3: Viewing Effective Rights with ConsoleOne

Time Required: 5 minutes

Objective: Use ConsoleOne to list rights for users.

Requirements: Same as Activity 6-1

Description: In this activity, you use ConsoleOne to view Luke's effective rights to Kellie's home directory.

1. If necessary, log in to eDirectory with your administrative user name and password, start ConsoleOne, and then click to expand your eDirectory tree and **UAS** container.

2. If necessary, click to expand the **IT** OU.

3. Follow these steps to view the trustees of Kellie's home directory:

   a. Right-click the **KThiele** directory, and then click **Properties** to open the Properties of KThiele dialog box.

   b. Click the **Trustees** tab to display all trustees of Kellie's home directory. Record the trustees here:

   _____

4. Follow these steps to check Luke's effective rights to Kellie's home directory:

   a. Click the **Effective Rights** button to open the Effective Rights dialog box, shown in Figure 6-2.

Figure 6-2   The Effective Rights dialog box

   b. Click the **browse** button next to the Trustee text box to open the Select Object dialog box.

   c. Click the **up arrow** to display all users in the IT OU.

d. Click **LMcMann**, and then click **OK** to display effective rights for Luke. Record the effective rights here:

_____

e. Click **Close** to close the Effective Rights dialog box.

5. Click **Cancel** to close the Properties of KThiele dialog box. Exit ConsoleOne, and log out.

Group Trustee Assignments

As described in Chapter 5, groups are network objects that help organize users with common network requirements and are useful in simplifying trustee assignments. When a group is made a trustee of a directory or file, all members of that group are also considered trustees of the directory or file, with the same rights assigned to the group. When users are members of a group, their effective rights in a directory are a combination of any personal trustee assignments plus any rights they have from being group members. For example, all IT Department users need to have Read and File Scan rights to the Apps\Utility directory to run certain software. To do this, you can make the ITMgrs group created in Chapter 5 a trustee of the Apps\Utility directory with Read and File Scan rights. Because Eric, Kellie, and Luke are members of the ITMgrs group, they have Read and File Scan rights to the Apps\Utility directory. If you want Kellie's user account to be responsible for changing data, you could also make her a trustee of the Utility directory with Create, Write, Erase, and Modify rights, as shown in Figure 6-3.

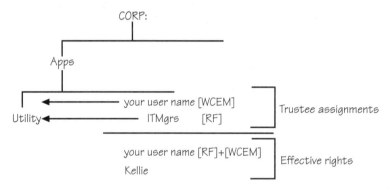

Figure 6-3   A sample group trustee assignment

Kellie's effective rights would then be [R W C E M F]; the [R F] rights come from her membership in the ITMgrs group, and the [W C E M] rights come from the trustee assignment made to the KThiele user account. Luke's effective rights would be [R F] from being a member of the ITMgrs group.

You can also use Remote Manager to make trustee assignments. The advantages of this utility include being able to use the Internet to work from any location and to manage the server from other desktop environments, such as Linux or Macintosh. The main disadvantage is that you can't check effective rights for other users in Remote Manager. Checking a user's effective rights in a directory requires logging in to Remote Manager as that user. In addition to being slower, this method can be difficult if you don't know the user's password. In Activity 6-4, you learn how to use Remote Manager to make the trustee assignments shown previously in Figure 6-3. In Activity 6-5, you use Remote Manager to check effective rights for other users.

Activity 6-4: Making Group Trustee Assignments in Remote Manager

Time Required: 5 minutes

Objective: Use Remote Manager to assign rights to groups.

Requirements: Internet Explorer from a Windows XP computer or Java-enabled Firefox from a SUSE Linux 10 computer

Description: In this activity, you use Remote Manager to make the ITMgrs group a trustee of the Utility directory with Read and File Scan rights. In addition, you give the KThiele user account [W C E M] rights.

1. If necessary, start your computer, and log on to your local system. If you're using Windows with Novell Client, you can log in to eDirectory with your administrative user name and password.

2. Start your Web browser and enter **https://IPaddress:8009** (replacing *IPaddress* with the IP address of your NetWare 6.5 server) to display the Remote Manager Login window.

3. Log in to Remote Manager with your administrative user name and password.

4. Under the Manage Server heading, click the **Volumes** link to display the Volume Management window.

5. Click the **CORP** volume to open it. (If you're working on a shared classroom server, click your **STUDENTS** volume first and then click your **##Corp** directory.)

6. Click your **Apps** directory to display all its subdirectories (see Figure 6-4).

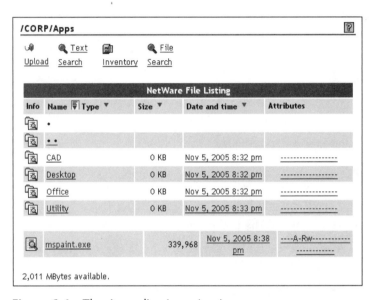

Figure 6-4   The Apps directory structure

7. Click the **Info** icon next to the Utility directory to display the Directory entry information window shown in Figure 6-5.

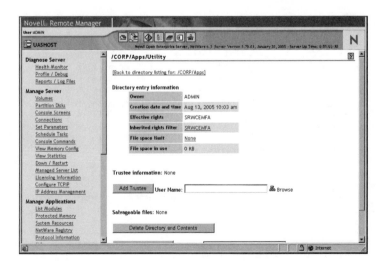

Figure 6-5   The Directory entry information window

8. Follow these steps to add the ITMgrs group as a trustee with Read and File Scan rights:

   a. Click the **Browse** link next to the User Name text box and navigate to the **IT** OU.

   b. Navigate to the **ITMgrs** group, if necessary, and click the link next to the **ITMgrs** group to place the group in the User Name text box.

   c. Click the **Add Trustee** button to display the Trustee rights window shown in Figure 6-6.

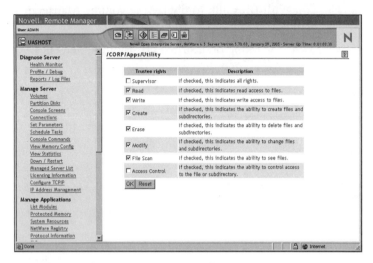

Figure 6-6   The Trustee rights window

   d. Click to clear all check boxes except Read and File Scan.

   e. Click **OK** to save your changes and return to the Directory entry information window.

9. Repeat Step 8 to add KThiele as a trustee of the Utility directory with Write, Create, Erase, and Modify rights.

10. Click the **Exit** button to return to the Remote Manager Login window, and stay logged on to your local computer for the next activity.

Activity 6-5: Checking Effective Rights in Remote Manager

Time Required: 5 minutes

Objective: Use Remote Manager to check effective rights.

Requirements: Same as Activity 6-4

Description: In this activity, you use Remote Manager to check effective rights for Luke and Kellie in the Utility directory.

1. Log in to Remote Manager with the distinguished name and password for Kellie Thiele (such as KThiele.IT.UAS if you're using a dedicated server).

2. Click your volume name under the Volumes heading on the right.

3. Click the **Apps** directory to display its contents.

4. Click the **Info** icon next to the Utility directory to display the Directory entry information window for Kellie. Record Kellie's effective rights:

   _____

5. Click the **Exit** button to return to the Remote Manager Login window.

6. Use the procedure in Steps 1 through 4 to record effective rights for Luke McMann:

   _____

7. Click the **Exit** button to return to the Remote Manager Login window, and stay logged on to your local computer for the next activity.

Container Trustee Assignments

As with a group, when a container object is made a trustee of a file or directory, all users in the container and any subcontainer objects share the rights made in the trustee assignment. When working with container trustee assignments, remember that a child container has the same effective rights as its parent. For example, rights granted to the UAS container also belong to the Mgmt, Engineering, Mfg, and IT subcontainers. In the following activity, you use Remote Manager to make your UAS container a trustee of a directory and then verify effective rights for users in your organization.

Activity 6-6: Making a Container Trustee Assignment

6

Time Required: 5 minutes

Objective: Use Remote Manager to assign rights to containers.

Requirements: Same as Activity 6-5 and completion of Activity 3-5

Description: Eric wanted all users to have rights to access files in the Forms directory located off the root of the CORP volume. To do this efficiently, he made the UAS Organization a trustee of the Forms directory with Read and File Scan rights. In this activity, you use Remote Manager to carry out this task, and then check effective rights for your users.

1. If necessary, start Remote Manager by following Steps 1 and 2 in Activity 6-4.

2. Log in to Remote Manager with your administrative user name and password.

3. Under the Manage Server heading, click the **Volumes** link to display the Volume Management window.

4. Click the **CORP** volume to open it. (If you're working on a shared classroom server, click the **STUDENTS** volume first, and then click your **##Corp** directory.)

5. Click the **Info** icon next to the Forms directory to display the Directory entry information window.

6. Follow these steps to add your UAS container as a trustee with Read and File Scan rights:

   a. Click the **Browse** link next to the User Name text box and navigate to your **UAS** container.

   b. Click the link next to your **UAS** container to place its distinguished name in the User Name text box.

   c. Click the **Add Trustee** button to display the Trustee rights window shown previously in Figure 6-6.

   d. Click to clear all check boxes except Read and File Scan.

   e. Click **OK** to save your changes and return to the Directory entry information window.

7. Click the **Exit** button to return to the Remote Manager Login window.

8. Check effective rights for Luke McMann in the Forms directory by following these steps:

   a. Log in to Remote Manager with the distinguished name and password for Luke McMann (such as LMcMann.IT.UAS if you're using a dedicated server).

   b. Click your volume name under the Volumes heading on the right. (If you're using a shared classroom server, click your **##Corp** directory.)

   c. Click the **Info** icon next to the Forms directory to display the Directory entry information window for Luke McMann. Record Luke's effective rights:

   _____

   d. Click the **Exit** button to return to the Remote Manager Login window.

9. Repeat Step 8 to record effective rights for a user in the Engineering OU. Record that user's name and effective rights:

   _____

10. Close your Web browser and log off your computer.

Because you have to log in as different users to check their effective rights in Remote Manager, the remaining activities focus on using ConsoleOne, Windows, and NetWare Administrator to make it easier to set up trustee assignments and check effective rights. If you prefer to use Remote Manager from a Linux desktop and are using a dedicated server, you might want to run Remote Manager on your desktop and use ConsoleOne from your NetWare 6.5 server console, as described in Chapter 5, to check effective rights.

Inherited Rights

Inherited rights are the NetWare feature that allows a user, group, or container's effective rights to a directory to "flow down" into files and other subdirectories. Inheritance is an essential concept in making file system security efficient by eliminating an excessive number of trustee assignments. For example, Eric wanted all users to have Read and File Scan rights in the Office, Desktop, and Utility subdirectories of Apps to install and run the software stored in these directories. Eric could have assigned rights to all users by making the UAS container a trustee of each subdirectory with Read and File Scan rights. However, by using inherited rights, he was able to simply assign the UAS container Read and File Scan rights to the CORP:Apps directory and then let the effective rights flow down to subdirectories, as shown in Figure 6-7. In Activity 6-7, you use Eric's method to give all your users rights to the software directories in the Apps directory structure.

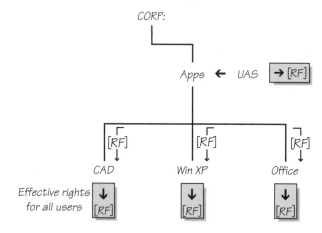

→ Indicates trustee assignment
↓ Indicates inherited rights

Figure 6-7   Using inherited rights

In Figure 6-7, a box for each user and group is included under each directory to indicate the user or group's trustee assignment and effective rights. A vertical arrow above a trustee assignment indicates that the rights are inherited from a higher directory. When calculating inherited rights for a specific object, be sure to remove any rights that will be blocked by an Inherited Rights Filter on that subdirectory or file. A horizontal arrow indicates that a direct trustee assignment has been made to that directory. A user's effective rights consist of the sum of the rights in the user's box combined with the rights in any group or container box to which he or she belongs.

 ## Activity 6-7: Applying Inherited Rights

Time Required: 10 minutes

Objective: Use ConsoleOne to assign rights to containers and check effective rights.

Requirements: Completion of Activities 6-1 through 6-6 and an Apps directory structure containing a Utility subdirectory with at least one user in the Engineering OU created in Chapter 4

Description: The simplest way to give all users in your network rights to run software from application directories is to give your UAS container Read and File Scan rights to the Apps directory. Through inheritance, all users in your UAS Organization then acquire Read and File Scan rights to each application subdirectory. In this activity, you use ConsoleOne to carry out this task and then check users' effective rights in the application subdirectories.

1. If necessary, log in with your administrative user name and password, start ConsoleOne, and click to expand the **CORP** volume.

2. Follow these steps to make your UAS container a trustee of the Apps directory with Read and File Scan rights:

   a. Right-click your **Apps** directory, and then click **Properties**.

   b. Click the **Trustees** tab to display all trustees of Apps.

   c. Click the **Add Trustee** button to open the Select Objects dialog box.

   d. Click the **up arrow** until you see your UAS Organization.

   e. Click your **UAS** container, and then click **OK** to add it to the Trustees list box.

   f. Click **OK** to save your trustee assignment and return to the ConsoleOne window.

3. Follow these steps to view trustees of the Utility directory:

   a. Expand the **Apps** directory.

   b. Right-click the **Utility** subdirectory, and then click **Properties** to open the Properties of Utility dialog box.

   c. Click the **Trustees** tab to display existing trustees. Record any existing trustees here:

   _____

   d. Click the **Effective Rights** button to open the Effective Rights dialog box.

4. Follow these steps to check effective rights for a user from the Engineering OU in the Utility directory:

   a. Click the **browse** button to open the Select Object dialog box.

   b. Click the **up arrow** until the Engineering OU is displayed.

   c. Double-click the **Engineering** OU, and then click a user name.

   d. Click **OK** to display effective rights for the user. Record the user name and his or her effective rights:

   _____

5. Click **Close** to return to the Properties of Utility dialog box, and then close the Properties of Utility dialog box.

6. Click **Cancel** to return to the ConsoleOne window, and leave ConsoleOne open for the next activity.

The Inherited Rights Filter

In some cases, you might not want a lower-level directory to inherit user, group, or container rights. For example, Eric placed the CAD subdirectory in the Apps directory and gave all users Read and File Scan rights to the Apps directory. Through inheritance, all users have Read and File Scan rights to all subdirectories of Apps, including the CAD subdirectory. Because only the engineers should be able to run CAD software, however, Eric wants to prevent other users from inheriting rights to run it. In NetWare 6.5, you can prevent a subdirectory from inheriting rights by adding an **Inherited Rights Filter (IRF)**. An IRF acts as a block to keep selected rights from passing into a subdirectory structure or files. Each directory or file has an IRF field stored in the DET and can inherit any rights specified in the IRF. By default, when you create a directory or file, all rights are included in its IRF. To block a directory or file from inheriting rights, you simply remove those rights from the IRF.

The exception to using an IRF to block rights is the Supervisor right. In file system security, the Supervisor access right can't be removed from an IRF, and an IRF can't be used to block the Supervisor right. Because an IRF filters only inherited rights from the parent directory, it has no effect on trustee assignments made to the directory or file. For example, Kari Means has enough CAD software licenses for just the design engineers. However, because the CAD software is stored in the Apps directory, currently all users could run the CAD software, thereby violating the license agreement. To fix this problem, Eric used an IRF on the CAD subdirectory to block it from inheriting rights granted to the UAS Organization. In the following activity, you set up an IRF on your Utility directory and then check users' effective rights.

Activity 6-8: Using an Inherited Rights Filter

Time Required: 5 minutes

Objective: Use Remote Manager to set an IRF and ConsoleOne to check effective rights.

Requirements: Completion of Activities 6-1 through 6-7

Description: Only users in the IT Department should be able to run programs from the Utility directory. However, through inheritance, all users get Read and File Scan rights to each application subdirectory, including the Utility directory. In this activity, you use Remote Manager to set up an IRF on the Utility directory and then use ConsoleOne to verify that Read and File Scan rights have been removed for all users except members of the ITMgrs group.

1. If necessary, start your computer, and log in with your administrative user name and password.

2. If necessary, start ConsoleOne, and click to expand your eDirectory tree and your **UAS** container. (If you're using a shared classroom server, expand the **CLASS** Organization and then your **##UAS** container.)

3. Minimize the ConsoleOne window.

4. Start your Web browser, and enter **https://IPaddress:8009** (replacing *IPaddress* with the IP address of your NetWare 6.5 server) to display the Remote Manager Login window. Log in with your administrative user name and password.

5. Follow these steps to remove all rights except Supervisor from the Utility directory's IRF:

   a. Under the Manage Server heading, click the **Volumes** link to display the Volume Management window.

   b. Click your **CORP** volume to open it. (If you're working on a shared classroom server, click your **##Corp** directory to open it.)

   c. Click your **Apps** directory to display all its subdirectories.

   d. Click the **Info** icon next to the Utility directory to display the Directory entry information window shown previously in Figure 6-5.

   e. Click the **SRWCEMFA** link next to the Inherited rights filter entry to display the Inherited rights filter window shown in Figure 6-8.

The Supervisor right is not listed in the IRF because it can't be filtered out through an IRF.

   f. Click to clear all check boxes in the IRF.

   g. Click **OK** to save your changes and return to the Directory entry information window. Only the "S" right should be listed next to the Inherited rights filter entry.

   h. Click the **Exit** button to return to the Remote Manager Login window, and minimize your Web browser.

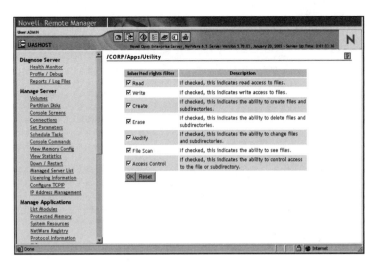

Figure 6-8 The Inherited rights filter window

6. Follow these steps in ConsoleOne to check effective rights for Kellie in the Utility directory:

   a. Click to expand the **CORP** volume. (If you're using a shared classroom server, expand your **##Corp** directory.)

   b. Click to expand the **Apps** directory. Right-click the **Utility** directory, and then click **Properties**.

   c. Click the **Trustees** tab and then click the **Effective Rights** button.

   d. Click the **browse** button next to the Trustee text box, click the **up arrow**, and then double-click the **IT** OU.

   e. Click **KThiele**, and then click **OK**. Record Kellie's effective rights:

   _____

7. Repeat Step 6 to record the effective rights for Luke McMann in the Utility directory:

   _____

8. Repeat Step 6 to record the effective rights for a user in the Engineering OU:

   _____

9. Click **Close** to return to the Properties of Utility dialog box.

10. Close the Properties of Utility dialog box and return to the ConsoleOne window. Leave ConsoleOne and your Web browser open for the next activity.

Combining Trustee Assignments and Inherited Rights

As explained earlier, a user's effective rights in a directory are a combination of the user's trustee assignment or inherited rights (minus rights blocked by an IRF) plus the user's effective rights from any container or group memberships. As a network administrator, you can reduce the number of rights granted to a user by taking group or container rights into consideration. For example, Kellie has recently written a software package for tracking server usage. To install this package, Eric created a subdirectory structure named SUsage in the Apps\Utility directory (see Figure 6-9).

To install and test the package, Kellie needed all rights except Supervisor to the SUsage subdirectory. Through inheritance, Kellie has [R F W C E M] rights to the SUsage subdirectory automatically as follows:

- The ITMgrs group inherits [R F] rights from the assignment made to the Apps directory. Kellie gets [R F] rights from being part of the ITMgrs group.

- Kellie inherits [W C E M] rights from the assignment made to her user name in the SUsage subdirectory.

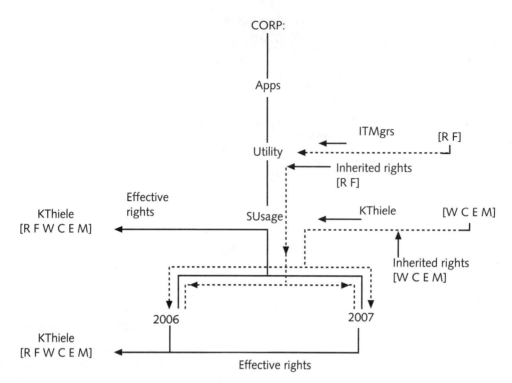

Figure 6-9 Combining inherited rights with a trustee assignment

In the following activity, you practice combining inherited and user rights in your UAS network.

Activity 6-9: Combining Inherited Rights with Trustee Assignments

Time Required: 5 minutes

Objective: Use ConsoleOne to assign rights to users, groups, and containers.

Requirements: Same as Activity 6-1 and completion of Activity 6-7

Description: In this activity, you use ConsoleOne to create a SUsage subdirectory structure, and then check Kellie's effective rights in the new subdirectories.

1. If necessary, start your computer, log in with your administrative user name and password, and start ConsoleOne.

2. If necessary, click to expand the eDirectory tree and your **UAS** container.

3. If necessary, click to expand your **CORP** volume and the **Apps** directory.

4. Follow these steps to create a SUsage subdirectory:

   a. Click to expand the **Apps** directory.

   b. Right-click the **Utility** directory, point to **New**, and then click **Object** to open the New Object dialog box.

   c. Click **Directory**, and then click **OK** to open the New Directory dialog box.

   d. Enter the name **SUsage**, and then click **OK**.

5. Follow these steps to create a 2006 subdirectory under SUsage:

   a. Right-click the **SUsage** subdirectory, point to **New**, and then click **Object** to open the New Object dialog box.

   b. Click **Directory**, and then click **OK** to open the New Directory dialog box.

   c. Enter the name **2006**, and then click **OK** to create the 2006 subdirectory.

6. Repeat Step 5 to create another subdirectory named **2007**.

7. Follow these steps to check Kellie's effective rights in the SUsage subdirectory:

   a. Right-click the **SUsage** subdirectory, and then click **Properties**.

   b. Click the **Trustees** tab, and then click the **Effective Rights** button to open the Effective Rights dialog box.

   c. Click the **browse** button to open the Select Object dialog box, and navigate to the **IT** OU, if necessary.

   d. Double-click **KThiele**, record Kellie's effective rights on the following line, and then click **Close** twice to return to the main ConsoleOne window.

   _____

8. Make Kellie a trustee of the SUsage subdirectory with [W C E M] rights:

   a. Right-click the **SUsage** subdirectory, and then click **Properties**.

   b. Click the **Add Trustee** button and navigate to the **IT** OU.

   c. Click the **KThiele** name, click **OK**, and then click to clear the **Read** and **File Scan** check boxes.

   d. Click to select the **Write**, **Create**, **Erase**, and **Modify** check boxes, and then click **OK**.

9. Repeat Step 7 to record Kellie's effective rights in the SUsage subdirectory:

   _____

10. Follow these steps to check Kellie's effective rights in the 2006 subdirectory:

    a. If necessary, click to expand the **SUsage** subdirectory.

    b. Right-click the **2006** subdirectory, and then click **Properties** to open the Properties of 2006 dialog box.

    c. Click the **Trustees** tab, and record any trustees here:

    _____

    d. Click the **Effective Rights** button to open the Effective Rights dialog box.

    e. Click the **browse** button to open the Select Object dialog box.

    f. Click the **up arrow**, and then double-click the **IT** OU to display all users.

    g. Click **KThiele**, and then click **OK**. Record Kellie's effective rights here:

    _____

11. Close the Effective Rights dialog box, and then click **Cancel** to return to the ConsoleOne window. Leave ConsoleOne open for the next activity.

Calculating Effective Rights

When you're calculating effective rights for a user, NetWare tracks inherited rights separately for each type of object. That means a user object's inherited rights in a directory are kept separate from inherited rights for containers or groups. At the directory or subdirectory level, users' effective rights are calculated by combining their effective rights with the effective rights of any groups or containers to which they belong. As shown previously in Figure 6-9, Kellie Thiele is inheriting [W C E M] rights to the 2006 subdirectory, and the ITMgrs group is inheriting [R F] rights. You can calculate Kellie's effective rights by simply combining inherited rights of the ITMgrs group with the rights the KThiele user account inherits. In addition to using ConsoleOne to calculate effective rights, you can use Windows Explorer to view inherited and effective rights for objects in a directory, as you see in Activity 6-10.

Making a new trustee assignment to a user, group, or container overrides the inherited rights for that object. For example, as shown previously in Figure 6-9, Kellie's effective rights in the Apps\Utility\SUsage\2006 directory are [R F W C E M]. These rights come from a combination of inherited rights for her user account with inherited rights from the containers and groups she belongs to. In Figure 6-9, Kellie gets [R F] rights from membership in the ITMgrs group and inherits [W C E M] rights from her trustee assignment to the SUsage subdirectory. If Kellie's user name is given a new trustee assignment of [M] in the 2006 directory, it overrides inherited rights for her user name, resulting in her effective rights changing to [R M F]. The [R F] rights come from the ITMgrs group and the [M] right comes from her new trustee assignment. In the following activity, you change Kellie's effective rights in the 2006 directory by giving her a new trustee assignment and then use Windows Explorer to check inherited and effective rights.

Activity 6-10: Reassigning Inherited Rights

Time Required: 15 minutes

Objective: Use ConsoleOne and Windows to view inherited and effective rights.

Requirements: Same as Activity 6-1 and completion of Activity 6-9

Description: In this activity, you see how Kellie's effective rights can be modified through a new rights assignment to her user account in the SUsage\2006 subdirectory. You then use Windows Explorer and ConsoleOne to view inherited and effective rights for all objects in the SUsage\2006 subdirectory.

1. If necessary, start your computer, log in with your administrative user name and password, and start ConsoleOne.

2. If necessary, click to expand the eDirectory tree and your **UAS** container.

3. If necessary, click to expand the **CORP** volume, the **Apps** directory, and the **Utility** and **SUsage** subdirectories.

4. Follow these steps to assign Kellie the Modify right to the SUsage\2006 subdirectory:

   a. Right-click the **2006** directory, and then click **Properties** to open the Properties of 2006 dialog box.

   b. Click the **Trustees** tab to display the Trustees list box.

   c. Click the **Add Trustee** button to open the Select Object dialog box.

   d. If necessary, double-click the **IT** OU to view all IT Department users.

   e. Click **KThiele**, and then click **OK** to add Kellie to the Trustees list box.

   f. Click to clear the **Read** and **File Scan** check boxes to remove Read and File Scan rights. (*Note:* Kellie will inherit these rights from the UAS container.)

   g. Click to select the **Modify** check box to grant Kellie the Modify right.

   h. Click **OK** to save your changes and return to the main ConsoleOne window.

   i. Minimize the ConsoleOne window.

5. Follow these steps to map a drive letter to the Apps directory:

   a. Right-click **My Network Places**, and then click **Novell Map Network Drive** to open the Map Drive dialog box.

   b. Click the **Choose the drive letter to map** list arrow, and then click an available drive letter in the list of options.

   c. Enter *servername\volumepath***Apps** in the Enter the network path to the resource text box (replacing *servername* with the name of your NetWare 6.5 server and *volumepath* with the path to your CORP volume).

   d. Click the **Map** button to map the drive and open a window for the Apps directory.

6. Use Windows Explorer to check inherited rights for all objects in the 2006 subdirectory:

   a. Double-click the **Utility** and **SUsage** subdirectories.

   b. Right-click the **2006** subdirectory, and then click **Properties** to open the 2006 Properties dialog box.

   c. Click the **NetWare Rights** tab to display the Trustees list box.

   d. Click the **Inherited Rights and Filters** button to open the Inherited Rights and Filters dialog box shown in Figure 6-10.

   e. To display effective rights for the UAS container, right-click the UAS trustee assignment, and then click **Current Effective Rights**. Record effective rights for the UAS container here, and then click **Close:**

   _____

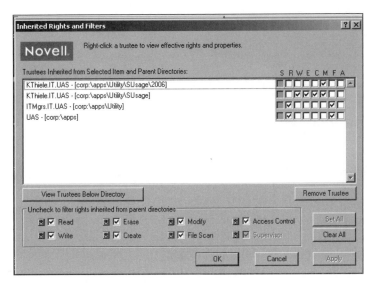

Figure 6-10   The Inherited Rights and Filters dialog box

    f. Click **Cancel** to close the Inherited Rights and Filters dialog box.

    g. Click **OK** to close the 2006 Properties dialog box.

7. Close the window for the SUsage subdirectory.

8. Close any open windows, and leave ConsoleOne open for the next activity.

Working with Supervisor Rights

When combining inherited rights and trustee assignments, you must remember that a new trustee assignment for a user, group, or container object overrides the object's inherited rights and becomes the object's effective rights with one exception: When a user, group, or container has been granted the Supervisor right to a directory, new trustee assignments made to subdirectories or files don't override the inherited Supervisor right. For example, to help limit use of the Admin account, an administrator might want to give a special user account rights to manage certain directory structures. You can do this in one of two ways: Grant a user name or Organizational Role object all rights [R W C E M F A] to the directory structures, or grant the Supervisor right to the directory structures. If you grant all rights, the rights can be redefined in a subdirectory. However, if you grant the Supervisor right to a directory structure, the rights can't be reduced by another trustee assignment or IRF, as shown in Figure 6-11.

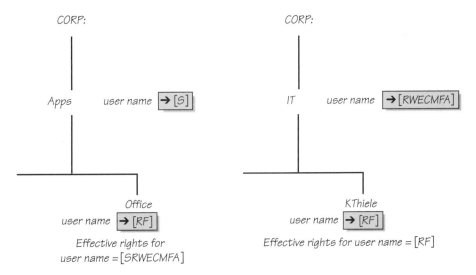

Figure 6-11   Granting the Supervisor right

When the Supervisor right is assigned to a directory, it can't be changed or blocked in one of the subdirectories; it can be changed only at the point of origin. Therefore, the user with the Supervisor right can manage an entire directory structure without being blocked by another user or an incorrect trustee assignment. In the following activities, you practice assigning the Supervisor right to the EKenton user account and then attempt to change your effective rights in the directory structure.

Activity 6-11: Granting Supervisor Rights

Time Required: 10 minutes

Objective: Use ConsoleOne to assign rights to users.

Requirements: Same as Activity 6-1

Description: To manage information in the IT and Apps directory structures without having to log in as the Admin user, Eric made his user account a trustee of the IT directory with the Supervisor right. In this activity, you use ConsoleOne to grant the EKenton user account Supervisor rights to the Apps and IT directories, and then verify effective rights in each location.

1. If necessary, start your Windows computer, log in to eDirectory with your administrative user name and password, and start ConsoleOne.

2. If necessary, click to expand your eDirectory tree and **UAS** container.

3. If necessary, click to expand your **CORP** volume. (If you're using a classroom server, expand your **##Corp** directory.)

4. Follow these steps to add the EKenton user as a trustee of the IT directory with Supervisor rights:

   a. Right-click the **IT** directory, and then click **Properties** to open the Properties of IT dialog box.

   b. Click the **Trustees** tab to display the existing trustees of the IT directory.

   c. Click the **Add Trustee** button to open the Select Object dialog box.

   d. If necessary, click the **up arrow** to navigate to your **IT** OU.

   e. Click the **EKenton** user name and then click **OK** to add it to the Trustees list box.

   f. Click the **Supervisor** right, and then click **OK** to save the assignment.

5. Follow these steps to check Eric's effective rights in the KThiele subdirectory:

   a. If necessary, expand the **IT** directory.

   b. Right-click the **KThiele** subdirectory, and then click **Properties** to open the Properties of KThiele dialog box.

   c. Click the **Trustees** tab, and then click the **Effective Rights** button to open the Effective Rights dialog box.

   d. Click the **browse** button to open the Select Object dialog box.

   e. Click the **up arrow** to navigate to the **IT** OU, click the **EKenton** user name, and then click **OK** to display his effective rights in Kellie's subdirectory. Record the effective rights here:

   _____

6. Close the dialog box, and then click **Cancel** to return to the ConsoleOne window. Leave ConsoleOne open and stay logged in for the next activity.

Activity 6-12: Changing Supervisor Rights

Time Required: 10 minutes

Objective: Use ConsoleOne to assign rights to users.

Requirements: Completion of Activity 6-11

6

Description: Kellie was not happy about Eric having Supervisor rights to her home directory. She would prefer he had only Read and File Scan rights. In this activity, you learn how Eric used ConsoleOne to reduce his Supervisor right in Kellie's home directory by experimenting with different trustee assignments and checking his effective rights.

1. If necessary, start your Windows computer, log in to eDirectory with your administrative user name and password, and start ConsoleOne.

2. If necessary, click to expand your eDirectory tree and **UAS** container.

3. If necessary, click to expand your **CORP** volume (or **##Corp** directory, if you're using a shared classroom server) and the **IT** directory.

4. Follow these steps to add the EKenton user name as a trustee of Kellie's home directory with only Read and File Scan rights:

    a. Right-click the **KThiele** subdirectory, and then click **Properties** to open the Properties of KThiele dialog box.

    b. Click the **Trustees** tab, and then click the **Add Trustee** button to open the Select Objects dialog box.

    c. If necessary, click the **up arrow** to navigate to the **IT** OU.

    d. Double-click the **IT** OU, click the **EKenton** user name, and then click **OK** to add it to the Trustees list box with the default Read and File Scan rights.

    e. Click the **Apply** button to save the assignment.

5. Follow these steps to check Eric's effective rights in Kellie's home directory:

    a. Click the **Effective Rights** button to open the Effective Rights dialog box.

    b. Click the **browse** button to open the Select Object dialog box.

    c. Click the **up arrow** to navigate to the **IT** OU.

    d. Double-click the **IT** OU, click the **EKenton** user name, and then click **OK** to display his effective rights. Record Eric's effective rights and explain how he obtained them:

    _____

    _____

6. Click **Close** twice to return to the ConsoleOne window.

7. For Eric's trustee assignment to work in Kellie's directory, you need to remove the Supervisor right from his trustee assignment in the IT directory at the point of origin and replace it with all rights by following these steps:

    a. Right-click the **IT** directory, and then click **Properties** to open the Properties of IT dialog box.

    b. Click the **Trustees** tab to display the trustee assignments.

    c. Click the **EKenton** user name's trustee assignment, change the access rights to remove the Supervisor right, and then select all other rights.

    d. Click the **Apply** button to save the trustee assignment changes, and then close the dialog box.

8. Right-click the **KThiele** subdirectory, and then click **Properties**. Click the **Trustees** tab, repeat Step 5, and record Eric's effective rights in Kellie's home directory:

    _____

9. Click **Close** and then click **Cancel** to return to the ConsoleOne window.

10. Exit ConsoleOne, and log out.

Using the RIGHTS Command

Documenting user trustee assignments is an important task in managing a network file system. Using ConsoleOne or Remote Manager to view trustee assignments and determine user effective rights in each directory and subdirectory of a large file system can be time consuming. The RIGHTS command is another method of displaying and printing trustee assignments in a directory structure. In addition, the RIGHTS command is convenient for making trustee assignments from the command prompt or creating a batch file or script to assign rights automatically. Because the RIGHTS command has several options, Novell includes a Help function so that you can review the syntax for a specific function. Activity 6-13 gives you a chance to practice using the RIGHTS command to get help information and to view and print trustee assignments and directory IRFs.

Activity 6-13: Using the RIGHTS Command

Time Required: 10 minutes

Objective: Use the RIGHTS command to view trustee assignments.

Requirements: Completion of Activity 6-12

Description: In this activity, you use the RIGHTS command to view help information and print a report showing the current directory trustee assignments and IRFs.

1. If necessary, start your Windows computer and log in to eDirectory with your administrative user name and password. If necessary, enter the user name and password for logging on to your Windows system.

2. Open a command prompt window (click **Start**, **Run**, type **command**, and click **OK**), and change to your **F:** drive.

3. To view help information, type **RIGHTS /?**, and then press **Enter**. If you see the "Bad command or file name" message, enter the command **CD SYS:PUBLIC**, and then repeat this step.

4. To view the trustees of all directories in your ##Corp directory, enter the **RIGHTS CORP:*.* /T** command, and then press **Enter**. After each screen, the system halts and waits for you to press Enter.

5. To view trustee assignments for all directories and subdirectories, you need to include the /S option. Enter the **RIGHTS *.* /S /T** command, and then press **Enter**.

6. You can print this information by including >PRN at the end of the command to redirect output to the printer assigned to your LPT1 printer port. You can also use the > redirector to send your output to a text file that you can open in a word processor. To send the trustee assignment information to a text file on your C: drive, enter the **RIGHTS *.* /S /T > C:\TrusteeLog.txt** command, and then press **Enter**.

7. Close the command prompt window.

8. Use Windows Notepad to open the **C:\TrusteeLog.txt** file and print its contents to the classroom printer.

9. Close all windows and log off your computer.

PLANNING FILE SYSTEM SECURITY

NetWare file system security is a sophisticated, complex system with many options for ensuring access to network data. Giving users the effective rights they need to perform their work while protecting data from unauthorized access requires careful thought and planning by the network administrator. To make file system security simpler and easier to maintain with multiple group and user trustee assignments, you should plan the security system to keep trustee assignments and IRFs to a minimum. The following sections offer several guidelines and suggestions for designing a secure network file system. You also learn how these guidelines can be applied to defining trustee assignments for the Engineering Department. In the end-of-chapter projects, you have an opportunity to apply what you have learned to make the trustee assignments described in this section.

File System Security Guidelines

To help keep file system security as simple and effective as possible, Novell suggests that CNAs follow certain guidelines. In this section, you learn how the Novell-recommended guidelines can be used to improve your file system security plan.

Identify Rights Needed for Each User

The first guideline in establishing file system security successfully is to analyze each user's processing needs and then determine and document the access rights each directory needs to meet processing requirements. An advantage of this analysis is that you can identify processing needs that are common to multiple users, which reduces and simplifies the number of trustee assignments you need to make. When several users need the same rights to a set of files, it's much easier to keep track of and maintain a single trustee assignment to a group or container than to make the same trustee assignments repeatedly for several users.

Proper Directory Structure Design

A proper directory design takes advantage of the principle that lower-level directories and files inherit rights from higher-level directories—a top-down inherited rights strategy. Planning a directory structure is the key to taking advantage of this top-down strategy and preventing users from inheriting rights to directories in which they don't belong. The following list of suggestions can help you set up a top-down strategy:

- Design a directory structure with directories requiring the most security near the top of the structure, separated from the directories that allow general user access. A well-designed directory structure can help reduce the number of trustee assignments by using the inherited rights principle so that a common set of rights flows down to subdirectories. A good example of this strategy is the UAS Apps directory structure, which has subdirectories for all software packages available to users.

- Directories that limit access to specific users or access rights shouldn't be included in a directory structure that has a trustee assignment for other users. For example, a document directory shouldn't be included in an application directory unless you want all application users to be able to read the documents.

- Use IRFs to protect high-security directories against inheriting unwanted trustees accidentally. An IRF is a good way to prevent effective rights from flowing into the directory from a parent directory accidentally.

Reduce Use of IRFs

The need for an IRF as part of your security plan might indicate that you have placed a directory needing more security within a general-purpose directory, and you need to rethink your directory structure design. For example, the file system on a server in your company has a directory structure like the one in Figure 6-12. The budget files are stored in a subdirectory of the Apps\SP directory, and the root of the tree has been made a trustee of Apps with Read and File Scan rights. Because [Root] is a trustee of Apps with [R F] rights, all users inherit [R F] rights to the Budgets subdirectory, creating a potential security problem in which all users have rights to read the budget data.

To prevent this security problem, you could block inherited rights by removing all rights from the Budgets subdirectory's IRF, giving rights to only the Accting group, which is a trustee of the Budgets subdirectory. Although this solution works, it doesn't address the real problem of placing a subdirectory with higher security needs within a general-purpose directory. A better solution is to move the Budgets subdirectory to a secure location in the file system and then make the appropriate trustee assignments, as shown in Figure 6-13.

Another method many network administrators use is reducing the number of IRFs whenever possible to use an explicit trustee assignment for reducing a user or group's effective rights. In addition, troubleshooting explicit trustee assignments is usually easier than tracing IRFs.

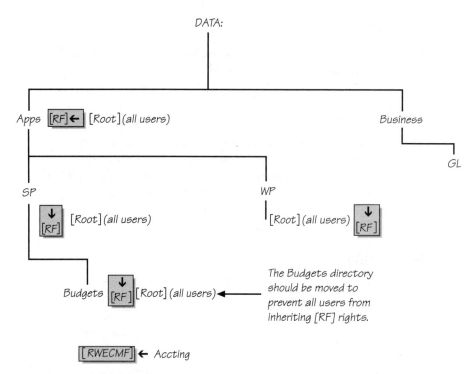

Figure 6-12   Poor directory design

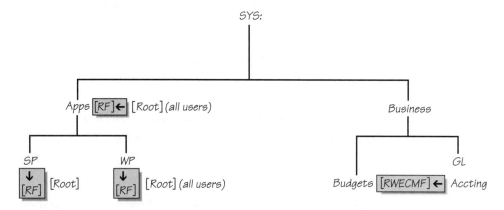

Figure 6-13   Proper directory design

Minimize Trustee Assignments

When planning trustee assignments, often you can keep user trustee assignments to a minimum by assigning rights to the containers or groups with the most users, and then proceeding to user trustee assignments. Some network administrators go to the extreme of never making trustee assignments to users; instead, they make the trustee assignment to a group name and then make the users who need access rights members of the group. Although it might mean having to create and maintain additional group names, this approach makes it easier for network administrators to deal with several users changing job functions, which can happen during a company reorganization, for example.

A similar technique you can use in NetWare 6.5 is to create an Organizational Role object (covered in Chapter 5), and then make it the trustee of a directory or file instead of making a user the trustee. The Organizational Role object can then be assigned to users who need access to the directory or file. If your company does a lot of reorganizing, you might consider using groups or Organizational Role objects instead of assigning rights to users. An effective way to minimize trustee assignments is to make these assignments in the following order:

1. Assign rights to containers.
2. Assign rights to departmental groups.
3. Assign rights to Organizational Role objects.
4. Assign rights to individual users.

Avoid Complex Combinations

The last guideline in planning file system security is to avoid combinations of assignments to groups, containers, and individual users within the same directory structure. To keep things as simple as possible, don't rely on users inheriting certain rights because of membership in certain groups and containers; instead, make users explicit trustees of a directory or file with just the rights needed for access.

Universal AeroSpace File System Security

As described previously, the first step in planning file system security is to define the processing functions each user needs to perform. Table 6-3 shows file system use information Eric documented for each user in the Management, Engineering, and Manufacturing departments.

Table 6-3   UAS file system use

User	File System Use
All Users	Read files from the Forms directory Run all applications except utility and CAD software Read files in the Web directory Rights to create and update files in the CORP:Shared and Temp directories
Management Lynn Dai	Updates and maintains files in the CORP:Forms directory Maintains the Management directory structure
Engineering Department	Creates and updates files in the Engineer\Shared directory Reads files in the NASA and Aircraft directories Runs CAD software
Kari Means (EngMgr Organizational Role)	Maintains the Engineer directory structure but should have only Read access to user home directory files Also needs to be able to update engineering files in the Web directory
Lianne Jarka	Currently the lead engineer responsible for the Rover project (ISS), but this could change as additional engineers are moved on or off the project
Tony Rucci	Currently the lead engineer assigned to the ISS project, but as the needs for this project change, additional engineers might be moved on or off the project
Paul Alm	Senior engineer who works on all projects, so needs rights to Aircraft and NASA directories
Bradley Dahl	Responsible for the Aircraft project
Manufacturing Department	Works with files in the Engineer\Shared directory Needs Read, File Scan, and Write rights to the Inventory directory
Russ Pence (MfgMgr Organizational Role)	As head of the Manufacturing Department, needs rights to maintain Requirements Planning System (RPS) and Manufacturing data

The next step is to review the directory structure to determine whether it meets the directory guidelines described previously. In the UAS directory structure, the CAD software is currently in a subdirectory of the Apps directory. Because the UAS container is a trustee of Apps with [R F] rights, all users inherit [R F] rights to the CAD subdirectory, creating a potential licensing problem because the company has software licenses only for Engineering Department users. You could prevent other users from accessing CAD software by removing all rights from the CAD subdirectory's IRF, and then grant [R F] rights only to the Design group by making the group a trustee of the CAD directory. However, this solution doesn't address the problem of placing a subdirectory with higher security needs in a general-purpose directory. A better solution is moving the CAD subdirectory to the Engineer directory and then making trustee assignments. To improve file system security, you should also create a subdirectory in the Web directory for engineering files. This structure would allow Kari Means to update engineering Web-based files without affecting other Web documents that Julie Damrau and Kellie Thiele maintain. In the end-of-chapter projects, you have an opportunity to change your UAS directory structure.

The next step is to plan trustee assignments. You should strive to minimize the number of trustee assignments by following the guidelines described previously. To help with this task, Eric created a Directory Trustee Worksheet, shown in Figures 6-14 and 6-15.

Using the Novell guidelines, Eric filled in the worksheet to show trustee assignments for each directory and any changes to the directory's IRF. Each row on the worksheet represents trustee assignments for the directory path designated in the first column. The second column indicates the rights allowed by the IRF. The remaining columns designate trustee assignments. Eric placed each object that needs a trustee assignment in a Trustee column. On the first page, he listed container objects followed by groups. On the second page, he listed Organizational Role objects and any user names. He indicated each directory's trustee assignment by placing the directory path in the leftmost column and listing access rights in the corresponding container, group, or Organizational Role column. Because some directories have trustee assignments from container, group, and Organizational Role objects, the second page repeats certain directory paths with additional trustee assignments. Notice that Eric used Organizational Role objects to reduce trustee assignments made to users.

On each page of the worksheet, Eric organized the Directory Path column starting with the highest-level directories and working down to the lower levels. Making trustee assignments in the higher-level directories first helps reduce the number of trustee assignments through inheritance. Eric arranged the columns with containers and groups on the left, followed by Organizational Role objects and user assignments. Making assignments to containers and groups first helps reduce the number of trustee assignments and simplifies maintaining file system security. The IRF for the directory is listed in the second column. Access rights to be granted to each directory are then listed in the remaining columns of the corresponding row under the Trustee headings. In this example, the top-level container, UAS, is listed in the first Trustee column and given a trustee assignment to the Apps, Forms, Shared, Inventory, and IT\Web directory structures. Next, the Engineering OU is listed in the second Trustee column and given a trustee assignment to the Engineer\Shared, Engineer\Aircraft, and Engineer\NASA directories.

After rights have been assigned to containers and groups, Organizational Role objects and users who need special rights are made trustees of the necessary directories. As the occupant of the EngMgr Organizational Role object, for example, Kari Means has rights to maintain the Engineer directory structure and work with files in the Web\Engineer directory. Also, the IRF of the Engineer\Users directory has been modified to allow only [R F] rights to pass to users' home directories. Although Eric set most of the rights for the Engineering Department, in the end-of-chapter projects, you fill out the Directory Trustee Worksheet to include Business Division users and grant access to their directories.

Directory Trustee Worksheet

DIRECTORY TRUSTEE WORKSHEET for:

Page ___ of ___

Directory Path	IRF	Trustee: UAS container	Trustee: Engineering container	Trustee: Mfg container	Trustee: Mgmt container	Trustee: Design group	Trustee: ITMgrs group	Trustee: WebMgrs group	Trustee: Production group
Apps	All	RF							
Apps\Utility	None						RF		
Forms	All	RF							
Shared	All	RWECMF							
Inventory	All	RF		RWF					
Mgmt\Shared					RWECMF				
IT\Web	All	RF						RWECMF	
IT\Shared	All						RWECMF		
Engineer	All								
Engineer\CAD	All					RF			
Engineer\RPS	All			RF					
Engineer\Shared	All		RWECMF	RWECMF					
Engineer\Aircraft	All		RF						
Engineer\NASA	All		RF						
MfgData\Shared	All								RWECMF
Apps\SUsage	All			RWF					

Figure 6-14   The UAS Directory Trustee Worksheet, page 1

6

Directory Trustee Worksheet

DIRECTORY TRUSTEE WORKSHEET for:

Page ____ of ____

Directory Path	IRF	Trustee: AdmAsst role	Trustee: ISSEng role	Trustee: RoverEng role	Trustee: EngMgr role	Trustee: AeroMgr role	Trustee: MfgMgr role	Trustee: PAlm user
CORP volume	All							
Mgmt	All	SRF						
IT\Web\Engineer	All	RWECMF			RWECMF			
Engineer	All				RWECMFA			
Engineer\Aircraft	RF					RWECMF		RWECMF
Engineer\NASA	All							RWECMF
Engineer\NASA\ISS	All		RWECMF					
Engineer\NASA\Rover	All			RWECMF				
Engineer\user name	RF							
MfgData	All					RWECMF	RECMF	

Figure 6-15　The UAS Directory Trustee Worksheet, page 2

ATTRIBUTE SECURITY

Attributes are flags or codes that you can associate with files and directories so that the network operating system can determine what type of processing can be carried out on the file or directory. Network administrators often set attributes on directories and files as additional protection against accidental change or deletion or to specify special processing, such as controlling file compression, making a file sharable, or purging files immediately after they're deleted. As a CNA, you'll need to know the file and directory attributes, what they are used for, and how to use NetWare utilities to work with attributes.

File and Directory Attributes

Attributes set on files and directories override a user's effective rights in that file or directory. If a file is flagged with the Read Only attribute, for instance, no matter what the effective rights are, the only operations you can perform on the file are Read and File Scan. For example, Kari Means has all rights to the Engineer directory and, therefore, would inherit all rights to files and subdirectories in the Engineer directory structure. If a file named Partlist.dat in the NASA directory is flagged with the Read Only attribute, even though Kari has all effective rights as a result of the trustee assignment, she still has only Read and File Scan access to the Partlist.dat file. However, because Kari has inherited the Modify right to the directory as a result of her trustee assignment to the Engineer directory, she can remove the Read Only attribute and then change or even delete the Partlist.dat file.

File Attributes

Table 6-4 lists the NetWare file attributes with their abbreviations. In the following sections, these attributes are described briefly.

Table 6-4   File attributes

Attribute	Abbreviation	Attribute	Abbreviation
Archive Needed	A	Immediate Compress	Ic
Copy Inhibit	Ci	Migrated	M
Delete Inhibit	Di	Purge	P
Don't Compress	Dc	Read Only	Ro
Don't Suballocate	Ds	Rename Inhibit	Ri
Don't Migrate	Dm	Sharable	Sh
Execute Only	X	System	Sy
Hidden	H	Transactional	T

The **Archive Needed (A)** attribute is assigned to files automatically when the file contents are modified. Copy or backup utilities can remove this attribute after copying the file to another storage location. This attribute controls which files are copied to a backup disk, making it possible to back up only the files that have changed since the last backup.

The **Copy Inhibit (Ci)** attribute is used only to prevent Macintosh users from copying specified files, such as programs that won't work on Macintosh computers. Setting this attribute prevents Macintosh computers running AppleTalk Filing Protocol 2.0 and later from copying the file.

The **Delete Inhibit (Di)** attribute prevents a file from being deleted but still allows the file to be renamed or changed. To delete the file, a user must first be granted the Modify right to remove the Delete Inhibit attribute. The Delete Inhibit attribute is often useful for protecting an important data file from being deleted accidentally yet still allowing its contents to be changed. You should consider setting the Delete Inhibit attribute on many of your organization's permanent files, such as customer, payroll, inventory, and accounting data.

Users or network administrators can set the **Don't Compress (Dc)** attribute to prevent a file from being compressed automatically. Preventing file compression can produce a minor improvement in performance when that file is accessed because the file doesn't need to be decompressed.

Users or network administrators can set the **Don't Suballocate (Ds)** attribute to prevent a file from being suballocated to other files. With this attribute, you can run certain applications and use a database system that doesn't work with files that have been suballocated.

The **Don't Migrate (Dm)** attribute prevents the file from being moved offline by third-party software when the volume has the Migrated attribute set.

The major use of the **Execute Only (X)** attribute is to protect software files from being copied illegally. Execute Only can be set only on .exe and .com files by a Supervisor-equivalent user; once set, it can't be removed, even by the network administrator. Do *not* assign Execute Only to files unless you have backup copies of them. Certain program files don't run when they are flagged Execute Only because these programs need to copy information into the computer's memory, and the Execute Only attribute prevents them from applying the copy functions. Because the Execute Only attribute can't be removed, to get rid of it, you need to delete the file and reinstall it from another disk.

The **Hidden (H)** attribute is used to hide files from DOS utilities and certain application software. NetWare utilities display hidden files when the Hidden attribute is enabled. A simple way to help protect software from illegal copying is to use the Hidden attribute to hide software directories and files from normal DOS utilities, and then move the NCOPY and NDIR commands from the SYS:Public directory to the SYS:System directory or some other location where typical users don't have access to them.

The **Immediate Compress (Ic)** attribute is usually assigned to large files that you want compressed immediately after they're closed to save disk space. As described in Chapter 3, by default, files are compressed after seven days of no activity.

The system sets the **Migrated (M)** attribute on files that have been migrated to a high-capacity storage medium, such as an optical disk drive or a tape backup system. Although migrated files are accessible to users, there might be a long delay to restore them before they can be accessed.

Deleted files can be salvaged by using the Salvage utility until the deleted file's space is reused by the file server or the directory is purged with the Purge command. After files have been purged, that space is no longer available to the OS, so those files can't be recovered with the Salvage utility. The **Purge (P)** attribute can be assigned to a file if you want the NetWare server to reuse the space from that file immediately after it's deleted. The Purge attribute can also be assigned for security reasons to files containing confidential data, thereby preventing an intruder from salvaging and then accessing information from these files after they have been deleted.

In some utilities, such as Remote Manager and ConsoleOne, the Purge attribute is called "Immediate Purge."

NOTE

The **Read Only (Ro)** attribute applies only to files and can be used to protect file contents from being modified. Its function is similar to opening the write-protect tab on a disk. Files whose contents aren't normally changed, such as a zip code file or a program file, are usually flagged Read Only. When you first set the Read Only attribute, the Delete Inhibit and Rename Inhibit attributes are also set by default. If you want to allow the file to be renamed or deleted but don't want its contents changed, you can remove the Rename Inhibit and Delete Inhibit attributes.

When assigned to a file, the **Rename Inhibit (Ri)** attribute protects the file name from being changed. During installation, many software packages create data and configuration files that might need to be updated or changed, but those file names must remain constant for the software to operate correctly. After installing a software package that requests certain file names, it's a good idea to set the Rename Inhibit attribute on these files to prevent future changing of the file or directory name, which could cause the program to crash or signal an error.

Files are available to only one user at a time. For example, suppose you create the Budget06.wk1 file on the file server and a co-worker opens it with a spreadsheet program. If you or another user attempt to access this file, an error message would state that the file is in use or is not accessible. With spreadsheet files and word processing documents, you don't want more than one user to have a copy of the file at one time because any changes made could be overwritten by another user. Program files and certain database files, however, should be made available to multiple users simultaneously. For example, you want all licensed users to be able to run word processing software or access a common database of customers. To allow a file to be opened by more than one user at a time, the **Sharable (Sh)** attribute for that file must be set. If you want multiple users to be able to copy or run a program simultaneously, you need to flag all program files as Sharable after software installation.

The **System (Sy)** attribute is often assigned to files that are part of the NetWare OS. Like the Hidden attribute, the System attribute hides files from DOS utilities and software packages but also marks the file as being for OS use only.

The **Transactional (T)** attribute can be assigned only to files and indicates that the file is protected by the **Transaction Tracking System (TTS)**. TTS ensures that when changes or transactions are applied to a file, either all transactions are completed or the file is left in its original state. This system is particularly important when working with database files, when a computer might start updating a record and then crash before the update is finished. For example, you're using a NetWare file server to maintain an online order entry system containing customer and inventory files. When entering an order, at least two transactions are necessary: one to update the customer's account balance and the other to record the inventory item to be shipped. Suppose that while entering the order, your computer crashes after it updates the customer balance and fails to record the item on the shipping list. In this case, the TTS cancels the transaction and restores the customer's balance to its original amount so that you can enter the complete order again. Because TTS is a feature used by application software, using the Transactional attribute does not ensure TTS protection. You also need to have the correct system design and application software.

Directory Attributes

With the exception of the Don't Migrate attribute, the directory attributes shown in Table 6-5 are actually a subset of the file attributes and have similar functions. Some directory attributes affect only the directory, and others apply to all files in the directory. As a network administrator, you should know the differences between directory attributes and file attributes and how directory attributes affect the files stored in a directory.

Table 6-5   Directory attributes

Attribute	Abbreviation
Delete Inhibit	Di
Don't Compress	Dc
Don't Migrate	Dm
Normal	N
Hidden	H
Immediate Compress	Ic
Purge	P
Rename Inhibit	Ri
System	Sy

NOTE   As with file attributes, you might see the Purge directory attribute called "Immediate Purge" in some utilities.

Setting the Delete Inhibit (Di) attribute on a directory prevents the directory's name from being removed but doesn't prevent the directory's contents from being deleted. You might want to protect the fixed parts of your organization's directory structure from being modified by flagging all main directories with the Delete Inhibit attribute.

Setting the Don't Compress (Dc) attribute on a directory prevents all files in the directory from being compressed. If disk space isn't a problem, preventing file compression in a directory can result in slightly faster performance because NetWare doesn't have to decompress the file when a user opens it.

If you have data migration enabled on a volume, you can set the Don't Migrate (Dm) attribute on a directory to prevent its files from being migrated to a high-capacity storage device. Preventing migration can be helpful if users need quick access to these archive files and don't want to wait for the data migration system to load them from the high-capacity storage medium.

The **Normal (N)** directory attribute removes all directory attributes.

As with the file attribute, the Hidden (H) directory attribute is used to hide directories from DOS utilities and certain application software. Although hidden directories can still be viewed in NetWare utilities, DOS commands and Windows applications can't see the directory structure. The Hidden directory attribute can be useful when you have Windows computers because it's easy for users to explore the directory structure in Windows Explorer. By hiding directories, you can make the file structure much less accessible.

The Immediate Compress (Ic) attribute is usually assigned to directories containing several large files that you want compressed immediately after they're closed to save disk space.

The Purge (P) attribute can be assigned to a directory so that the NetWare file server immediately reuses the space from any files deleted in that directory. When the Purge attribute is assigned to a directory, any file deleted from the directory is purged automatically and its space reused. The Purge attribute is often assigned to directories containing temporary files so that the temporary file space can be reused as soon as the file is deleted.

Using the Rename Inhibit (Ri) attribute on a directory prevents that directory's name from being changed but still allows files and subdirectories in that directory to be renamed. Directories that are part of system drive mappings and application software paths should be protected by the Rename Inhibit attribute because changing the directory's name affects the running of software and drive mappings made to data in that directory structure.

The System (Sy) attribute is often assigned to directories that are part of the NOS or certain client software. Print queues, described in Chapter 8, are actually subdirectories and are flagged with the System attribute. Like the Hidden attribute, the System attribute hides directories from DOS utilities and application software packages but also marks directories as being for OS use only.

Planning Directory Attribute Use at Universal AeroSpace

Users who have been granted Erase and Modify access rights to a directory can remove or rename the directory and its files. Without adequate planning, renaming directories in a structure could cause problems with directory map commands and could prevent some applications from finding data in a predefined path. An important use of directory attributes is protecting the directory structure from name changes and accidental deletion. In addition to the Delete Inhibit and Rename Inhibit attributes, some directories can be further protected by hiding them from DOS or Windows with the Hidden attribute. The Purge attribute is useful on directories containing temporary files that are deleted frequently. Using the Purge attribute on these directories allows deleted files from other directories to be salvageable for a longer time. Figure 6-16 shows directory attributes Eric planned for directories in the UAS file system.

Eric has recommended setting the Delete Inhibit and Rename Inhibit attributes on all major directories to prevent deletion or name changes. By setting the Purge attribute on the IT\Web, Apps, and Apps\Office directories, the system can immediately reuse space from old deleted files when a new version of the software is copied to these directories.

Planning File Attribute Use at Universal AeroSpace

The most commonly used file attributes are Read Only and Shared. As shown in Figure 6-17, the software programs in the Apps\Office directory are used by multiple users and need to be flagged with the Shared attribute so that more than one user can run or copy a program simultaneously.

The Read Only attribute is often used on program files to prevent the software from being changed or deleted accidentally and to protect against virus infection. If users are granted only Read and File Scan rights to a software directory, protecting the program files with the Read Only attribute isn't necessary. However, with some software packages, such as the UAS CAD software, users need to maintain configuration or temporary files in the same software directory as the program files. As a result, Eric needed to grant the Design users Write, Create, and Erase rights in addition to Read and File Scan rights. When users have more than Read and File Scan rights in a software directory, placing the Read Only attribute on program files is essential to protect them from deletion or changes by users or computer viruses. In addition to the Shared and Read Only

Directory Attribute Form	
Created by:	
Date:	
Directory	**Attributes**
Shared	Di, Ri
Inventory	Di, Ri
Forms	Di, Ri
IT\Web	Di, Ri, P
Engineer	Di, Ri
Apps	Ri, P
Apps\Office	Di, Ri, P, Ic, H
Apps\Utility	Di, Ri, H

Figure 6-16   The UAS Directory Attribute Form

File Attribute Form	
Created by:	
Date:	
File	**Attributes**
Apps\Office*.exe	Sh
Engineer\CAD*.*	Ro
Apps\Utility*.exe	X

Figure 6-17   The UAS File Attribute Form

attributes, the Execute Only attribute is important when software is used in an environment where there's a possibility of illegal copying.

Implementing Directory and File Attributes

As a network administrator, you need to be able to use NetWare utilities and Windows to set directory and file attributes in the network file system. Knowing how to use Remote Manager is required for the CNA test, but as a network administrator, you'll also find it convenient to know how to use Windows utilities. In the following activities, you learn how to use Remote Manager and ConsoleOne to set and view file and directory attributes.

Activity 6-14: Setting Directory Attributes in Remote Manager

Time Required: 5 minutes

Objective: Use Remote Manager to assign attributes to directories.

Requirements: A Windows XP or SUSE Linux 10 computer and completion of Activity 3-5

Description: In this activity, you use Remote Manager to set directory attributes on the Apps directory structure. You'll set attributes for the remaining directories shown in Figure 6-16 in the end-of-chapter projects.

1. If necessary, start your computer, and log on to your local system. If you're using Windows with Novell Client, log in to eDirectory with your administrative user name and password.

2. Start your Web browser and enter **https://IPaddress:8009** (replacing *IPaddress* with the IP address of your NetWare 6.5 server) to display the Remote Manager Login window.

3. Log in with your administrative user name and password to display the Remote Manager Volume Management window.

4. Navigate to your **CORP** volume (or **##Corp** directory, if you're using a shared classroom server).

5. Click in the **Attributes** column of the Apps directory to display the Folder Attributes window shown in Figure 6-18.

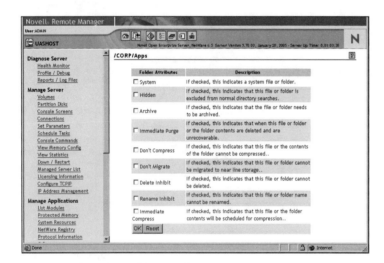

Figure 6-18   The Folder Attributes window

6. Click to enable the **Rename Inhibit** and **Immediate Purge** check boxes.

7. Click **OK** to save your settings and return to the NetWare File Listing window.

8. Click the **Apps** directory to display its contents.

9. Click in the **Attributes** column of the Office directory to display the Folder Attributes window.

10. Click to enable the **Delete Inhibit**, **Rename Inhibit**, **Immediate Purge**, **Immediate Compress**, and **Hidden** check boxes.

Many systems and utilities display hidden files and directories. By default, however, Windows XP doesn't display hidden files or directories unless you select Tools, Folder Options from the Windows Explorer menu and click the Show hidden files and folders option button in the View tab.

11. Click **OK** to save your attribute settings and return to the NetWare File Listing window.

12. Click the **Exit** button to return to the Remote Manager Login window.

13. Close your Web browser, and stay logged in for the following activity.

Activity 6-15: Setting Attributes in ConsoleOne

Time Required: 5 minutes

Objective: Use ConsoleOne to set directory attributes.

Requirements: Completion of Activity 6-14 and a Windows XP computer with Novell Client installed

Description: In this activity, you use ConsoleOne to set the remaining attributes Eric defined in Figure 6-16 for the Apps directories.

1. If necessary, start your computer, and log in to eDirectory with your administrative user name and password.

2. Start ConsoleOne.

3. Expand your **UAS** container and navigate to your **CORP** volume (or **##Corp** directory, if you're using a shared classroom server).

4. Click to expand the **Apps** directory.

5. Follow these steps to set attributes for the Utility subdirectory:

   a. Right-click the **Utility** directory and click **Properties** to open the Properties of Utility dialog box shown in Figure 6-19.

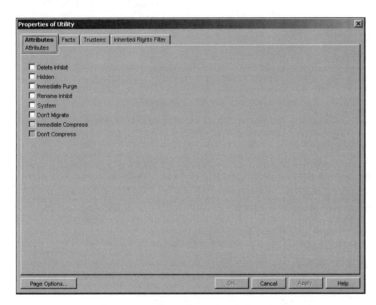

Figure 6-19   The Properties of Utility dialog box

   b. If necessary, click the **Attributes** tab.
   c. Click to enable the **Delete Inhibit**, **Rename Inhibit**, and **Hidden** check boxes.
   d. Click **OK** to save the attribute changes and return to the ConsoleOne window.

6. Close ConsoleOne, and stay logged on for the next activity. You set the remaining directory attributes in the end of chapter hands-on projects.

The FLAG Command

Just as the RIGHTS command is useful for documenting or setting access rights from the DOS prompt, the NetWare FLAG command is useful for documenting and setting directory and file attributes. The FLAG command has two different options for working with file or directory attributes. As a network administrator, you should know how to use the FLAG command's directory and file options to work with attributes.

Setting and Documenting Directory Attributes

The FLAG command uses the /DO parameter to set and view directory attributes:

```
FLAG path [+/-] attribute_list /DO
```

You can replace *attribute_list* with one or more of the directory attributes shown previously in Table 6-5. Use the + operator if you want to add the attribute to the directory or the – operator to remove the attribute from the directory. The *path* parameter is optional, and if you enter only the FLAG /DO command, you see a list of attribute settings for all subdirectories of the current directory. In the following activity, you practice using the FLAG command to view attribute settings.

Activity 6-16: Documenting Attribute Settings with the FLAG Command

Time Required: 5 minutes

Objective: Use the FLAG command to document attribute settings.

Requirements: Completion of Activity 6-15

Description: In this activity, you use the FLAG command to document your directory attributes and then set attributes for the Forms directory.

1. If necessary, start your computer, and log in with your administrative user name and password.

2. Open a command prompt window (click **Start**, **Run**, type **command**, and click **OK**), and change to drive **F:**.

3. View help information on the FLAG command by entering **FLAG /?** and pressing **Enter**. If you see the "Bad command or file name" message, enter **CD SYS:\PUBLIC**, press **Enter**, and repeat the FLAG command.

4. To view help information on setting directory attributes, enter the **FLAG /? DO** command, and then press **Enter**.

5. To view all your directory attribute settings, enter the **FLAG** *volumename***:*.* /DO** command (substituting the path to your ##Corp directory for *volumename*), and then press **Enter**. (For example, if you're using a shared classroom server, enter the command **FLAG STUDENTS:##Corp*.*** **/DO**, replacing ## with your assigned student number. If you're using a dedicated server, enter the command **FLAG CORP:*.* /DO**.)

6. To view attribute settings for all subdirectories, enter the **FLAG** *volumename***:*.* /DO /S** command, and then press **Enter**.

7. To set the Delete Inhibit and Rename Inhibit attributes on your Forms directory, enter the **FLAG** *volumename***:Forms +Di +Ri /DO** command, and then press **Enter**.

8. Exit the command prompt window, and log out.

In a recent department meeting with David Heise and other department managers, Eric reported that he had planned the NetWare 6.5 file system security in the Engineering and Manufacturing departments, which will enable users to take advantage of the network's file system. Of course, managers were anxious to know when their departments would be ready to go online with the new NetWare 6.5 server. Eric explained that he had documented their processing needs and that you would be working with him to set up their file system access rights (see the projects at the end of this chapter).

CHAPTER SUMMARY

◻ Just as a building needs to be secured by using locks and keys, the NetWare file system must be secured by using trustee assignments to grant rights that allow users to access the storage areas they need. NetWare has eight access rights: Read, File Scan, Write, Create, Erase, Modify, Access Control, and Supervisor.

◻ The Access Control right allows users to assign other rights, except Supervisor, to other users. The Supervisor right can be assigned only by a Supervisor-equivalent user and gives users all rights to a directory and its subdirectories, including the right to assign the Supervisor right to other users. In addition, because the Supervisor right can't be revoked or blocked at lower levels, assigning the Supervisor right is a good way to make a user act as a supervisor of a portion of the directory structure.

◻ Trustee assignments are used to grant rights to users or groups for a directory. Effective rights for a user are a combination of the user object's rights and the rights given to any groups of which the user is a member. A user or group's trustee assignments for a directory are then inherited by all the subdirectories and files in the directory where the trustee assignment was made. A user's effective rights often include inherited rights from a trustee assignment made to a group or user in a higher-level directory.

◻ Each directory and file has an Inherited Rights Filter (IRF) to control which rights it inherits from higher-level directories. When a file or directory is first created, the IRF allows all rights to flow down to that directory or file. You can use an IRF to block the directory or file from inheriting those rights.

◻ You can use ConsoleOne, Remote Manager, Windows Explorer, or the RIGHTS command to set and view trustee assignments.

◻ Attributes play a vital role in file system security because they enable you to protect files and directories from certain operations, such as deleting, renaming, and copying.

◻ You can use Remote Manager, ConsoleOne, and the FLAG command to set attributes on files and directories.

KEY TERMS

Access Control [A] right — An access right that allows a user to grant access rights for a directory to other users.

access right — A file system permission that can be granted to users, groups, or containers. Access rights include Supervisor, Read, Write, Create, Erase, Modify, File Scan, and Access Control.

Archive Needed (A) — A file attribute that indicates the file has been changed since it was last backed up.

attribute — A flag or code associated with files and directories to control what type of processing can be performed on them.

Copy Inhibit (Ci) — A file attribute that prevents Macintosh computers from copying the file.

Create [C] right — An access right that allows users to create files and subdirectories.

Delete Inhibit (Di) — An attribute that protects a file or directory from being deleted.

directory entry table (DET) — An area of the hard drive containing information about files and directories, including name, location, and trustee assignments.

directory trustee — A user, group, or container object that has been granted access rights to a directory.

Don't Compress (Dc) — A file attribute that tells the operating system not to compress the file. When applied to a directory, none of the files in the directory will be compressed.

Don't Migrate (Dm) — A file or directory attribute that prevents files or directories from being migrated to a high-capacity storage device.

Don't Suballocate (Ds) — A file attribute that tells the operating system not to use block suballocation on the file.

effective rights — A subset of access rights that controls which functions a user can perform in a directory or file.

Erase [E] right — An access right that allows the user to delete files and remove subdirectories.

Execute Only (X) — A file attribute that can be applied to .com and .exe files to prevent them from being copied. Once applied, the Execute Only attribute can't be removed.

File Scan [F] right — An access right that allows the user to view a directory of file and subdirectory names.

file trustee — A user, group, or container object that has been granted access rights to a file.

Hidden (H) — A file or directory attribute that prevents standard DOS and Windows applications from seeing the associated file or directory.

Immediate Compress (Ic) — A file or directory attribute that tells the system to compress a large file immediately after it has been used.

Inherited Rights Filter (IRF) — A method of reducing inherited rights in a subdirectory or file by allowing only the access rights specified in the filter to be inherited.

Migrated (M) — A file attribute set by the system indicating that a file has been moved to an archive data medium.

Modify [M] right — An access right that allows the user to change file and directory names—without changing the file contents—and use the FLAG command to change attribute settings on files or subdirectories.

Normal (N) — A directory attribute that removes all other directory attributes.

Purge (P) — A file or directory attribute that prevents files in a directory from being salvaged after deletion.

Read [R] right — An access right that allows the user to read files or run programs in a directory.

Read Only (Ro) — A file attribute that prevents the contents of a file from being modified.

Read Write (Rw) — A default file attribute that allows the contents of a file to be changed.

Rename Inhibit (Ri) — A file or directory attribute that prevents the name of a file or directory from being changed.

Sharable (Sh) — A file attribute that allows multiple users to use a file at the same time.

Supervisor [S] right — An access right that grants all rights to a directory and its subdirectories; this right cannot be blocked or reassigned at a lower subdirectory or file level.

System (Sy) — A file or directory attribute that flags a file or directory for operating system use.

Transaction Tracking System (TTS) — A system that protects the Transactional attribute, ensuring that all transactions are completed or left in the original state.

Transactional (T) — A file attribute used on database files to enable the system to restore the file to its previous state if a transaction is not completed.

trustee assignment — An entry in the ACL for a file or directory that makes the user a trustee of a directory or file.

Write [W] right — An access right that allows the user to change or add data to files in a directory.

REVIEW QUESTIONS

1. Which of the following defines file system functions that users can perform in the NetWare file system?

    a. attributes

    b. access rights

    c. eDirectory

    d. NSS

2. Which of the following rights allows a user to change data in an existing file?

     a. Modify

    b. Write

    c. Create

    d. Access Control

3. Which of the following rights allows a user to assign rights to other users?

    a. Modify

    b. Write

    c. Create

    d. Access Control

4. Which of the following rights can't be revoked or blocked in the directory structure it defines?

    a. Modify

    b. Supervisor

    c. Create

    d. Access Control

5. Which of the following are flags that control directory and file characteristics?

    a. attributes

    b. properties

    c. rights

    d. permissions

6. You are a member of the Admin group that has been granted [R W F] rights to the Business directory, and you have a trustee assignment of [R C F] to that directory. What are your effective rights in the Business directory?

7. You have been given a trustee assignment of [R C F] to the Business directory and a trustee assignment of [W E] to the Business\Spdata\Budgets subdirectory. What are your effective rights in the Business\Spdata subdirectory?

    For Questions 8 through 11, use the following file system information:

    You have a trustee assignment of [W E C] to the Business directory and a trustee assignment of [W E] to the Business\Spdata\Budgets subdirectory. In addition, you belong to a group that was granted [R F] rights to the Business directory.

8. What are your effective rights in the Business\Spdata\Budgets subdirectory?

9. Assume that all rights except [R] and [F] are removed from the IRF of the Business\Spdata subdirectory. What are your rights in the Business\Spdata subdirectory?

10. What are your rights in the Business\Spdata\Budgets subdirectory?

11. Write the command to list all trustee assignments in the Business directory structure.

12. The user Joeman was given a trustee assignment of [R W E C M F] to the Business\Spdata directory and a trustee assignment of [R W F] to the Business\Spdata\Budgets subdirectory. What are Joeman's effective rights in the Business\Spdata\Budgets subdirectory after deleting his trustee assignment to the Budgets directory?

13. Did Joeman gain or lose rights in the Budgets directory? Why?

14. If you're using Windows, which of the following utilities could you use to make the user Billsim a trustee of the Business\AR directory? (Choose all that apply.)

    a. Windows Explorer

    b. iManager

    c. ConsoleOne

    d. Remote Manager

15. Which of the following attributes are used with directories? (Choose all that apply.)

   a. Purge

   b. Shared

   c. Read Only

   d. Delete Inhibit

   e. Copy Inhibit

   f. Hidden

   g. System

   h. Don't Migrate

16. Which of the following attributes prevents deleted files in the SYS:Software\Temp directory from being salvaged?

   a. Purge

   b. Shared

   c. Read Only

   d. Delete Inhibit

17. Which of the following DOS-based commands can be used to set NetWare file attributes?

   a. RIGHTS

   b. FLAG

   c. NDIR

   d. ATTRIB

18. Which of the following is the minimum right you need in a directory to change trustee assignments?

   a. Supervisor

   b. Modify

   c. Access Control

   d. Full Control

19. Which of the following is the minimum right you need in a directory to flag all files as Delete Inhibit?

   a. Supervisor

   b. Modify

   c. Access Control

   d. Full Control

20. When a user is first added as a trustee of a directory, which of the following rights is he or she given by default?

   a. Supervisor

   b. Read Only

   c. Read and File Scan

   d. File Scan

CASE PROJECTS

Case Project 6-1: Planning Access Rights

Now that you understand the steps Eric used in setting up file system security for the Engineering, Manufacturing, Management, and IT departments, your next step is to apply what you've learned to planning file system security for the Business Division based on the processing needs in Table 6-6.

Table 6-6 Business Division file system use

User	File System Use
Marketing Department	Creates and updates files in the Mktg\Shared directory Reads information from the Inventory directory and enters new orders by writing to the database
Michael Horowitz	Reads the customer and vendor database files
Darrell Minick	Reads the customer and vendor database files
Laura Hiller	Updates the customer and vendor database files
Desktop Publishing Department	Creates and updates files in the Publish\Shared directory Reads files from the Engineering Department's Shared directory
Diana Brady	Responsible for working on promotional materials in the Publish directory Reads information from the Publish\Manuals directory maintained by Bradley Dahl
Julie Damrau	Works with Diana to maintain the Publish\Promote directory files Responsible for Web site design and development and belongs to the WebMgrs group
Accounting Department	Creates and updates files in the Accounting Department's Shared directory Needs all rights to run the accounting software package and update files
Terry Blackwell	Maintains files in the Inventory directory Maintains the Accounting\Budget files
Amy Pan	Performs weekly payroll and updates files in the accounting software directory (Accounting\Apps) Works with Terry Blackwell to maintain the Accounting\Budget files
George Perez	Performs monthly general ledger processing and maintains files in the accounting software directory (Accounting\Apps)

Before completing the trustee assignments for UAS, you need to apply the guidelines described in this chapter to finish planning access rights for users or groups to perform the processing functions Eric defined. To do this, you need a copy of the Directory Trustee Worksheet, which your instructor will supply. Then plan trustee assignments for the Business Division, using the requirements shown in Table 6-6. Before continuing to Case Project 6-2, have your instructor check the trustee assignments against the recommendations you have made.

Case Project 6-2: Planning Directory and File Attributes

To set up attribute security, you need a copy of the Directory Attribute Form, which your instructor will supply. Then use it to identify the attributes you think are needed for the Accounting, Publish, and Mktg directory structures. At a minimum, you should define attributes that protect the directory structures from being renamed or deleted as well as attributes you think are important to the file system's security and operation.

HANDS-ON PROJECTS

Hands-on Project 6-1: Modifying Your Directory Structure

In this project, use Remote Manager to make the following modifications to your UAS directory structure as described in the "Planning File System Security" section:

❑ Move the CAD directory from the Apps directory structure and place it in the Engineer directory structure.

❑ Move the MfgData structure from the Engineer directory and place it in the root of your CORP volume.

❑ Create an Engineer subdirectory in the IT\Web directory structure.

Hands-on Project 6-2: Completing Trustee Assignments

In this project, you use Remote Manager, ConsoleOne, and Windows to complete the trustee assignments Eric defined in Figures 6-14 and 6-15:

❑ Use Remote Manager to make trustee assignments and set IRFs in the Engineer directory structure.

❑ Use Windows Explorer to make trustee assignments for the IT directory structure.

❑ Use ConsoleOne to make trustee assignments for the Shared, Inventory, and MfgData directories.

Hands-on Project 6-3: Documenting Trustee Assignments

In this project, use the correct option of the RIGHTS command to create a file containing trustee assignments and IRFs for the following directories:

❑ IT

❑ Engineer

❑ Forms

❑ Apps

❑ Mgmt

If required by your instructor, print the trustee assignments and IRFs for these directory structures.

Hands-on Project 6-4: Setting and Documenting Attributes for Universal AeroSpace

In this project, use Remote Manager and ConsoleOne to set the directory attributes shown in Figure 6-16. Use Remote Manager to set attributes for the Shared, Inventory, and Forms directories. Use ConsoleOne to set attributes for the Engineer and IT directories. Use the FLAG command to create a file that shows your attribute settings. If required by your instructor, print your attribute settings.

Hands-on Project 6-5: Making Business Division Trustee Assignments

Before doing this project, you need to have your instructor check the Directory Trustee Worksheet you created in Case Project 6-1. Log in to the network with your administrative user name and password, and then use Remote Manager or ConsoleOne to create the trustee assignments on your finalized Directory Trustee Worksheet. Next, use the RIGHTS command to create one or more files documenting your trustee assignments. If required by your instructor, print the trustee assignments and IRFs for these directory structures.

Hands-on Project 6-6: Setting Business Division Attributes

Use Windows, ConsoleOne, or Remote Manager to set the attributes you defined in Case Project 6-2. Use the FLAG command to assign all files in the Forms directory the Delete Inhibit and Rename Inhibit attributes. Write down the command you used. Next, use the FLAG command with the > PRN option to create one or more files documenting your results.

6

7

MANAGING eDIRECTORY SECURITY AND OPERATIONS

After reading this chapter and completing the activities, you will be able to:

♦ Describe eDirectory security rights, including trustee assignments, effective rights, and inherited rights

♦ Explain how to delegate administrative rights

♦ Plan eDirectory security needs following Novell security guidelines

♦ Set up Role Based Services and assign administrative roles

♦ Use iMonitor to check the eDirectory system

♦ Describe NetWare time synchronization options

In Chapter 6 on file system security, you learned that users, groups, and containers are made trustees of directories or files and then granted certain access rights. In a similar way, to access or manage network objects, you can use eDirectory security to make users, groups, or containers trustees of other objects in the eDirectory tree. In this chapter, you learn how to set up eDirectory security so that users can access and maintain network objects and how to delegate administrative tasks to other users.

WORKING WITH eDIRECTORY SECURITY

Just as file system security gives users rights to access and manage files in the NetWare file system, eDirectory security gives users rights to access and manage objects in the eDirectory tree. NetWare, by default, provides most of the eDirectory security rights users need to work with objects. However, sometimes a network administrator needs to modify these default assignments to grant users the rights to read data from certain objects, such as the Directory Map and Profile objects described in Chapter 4. In addition, an administrator might want to reduce default assignments to prevent users from performing certain tasks, such as modifying personal login scripts, as described in Chapter 9.

Another use of eDirectory security is to delegate work by giving users rights to manage other users and objects in certain containers. In addition, eDirectory security can be used to create a backup administrator account or establish an exclusive administrator for a container; an exclusive administrator is a user account with the Supervisor right to manage all objects in a container and its subcontainers. Establishing an exclusive container administrator blocks the main network administrator's rights to that container. Having exclusive container administrators can be beneficial for large organizations and government agencies that don't want to put the entire network under the control of one all-powerful network administrator with Supervisor rights to all data and objects in the eDirectory tree. In the following sections, you learn what a CNA needs to know about eDirectory security rights and inheritance and how to use iManager and ConsoleOne to view, assign, or modify these rights.

eDirectory Rights

As you learned in Chapter 2, each object in the eDirectory database contains fields of information called properties. All eDirectory objects have the **access control list (ACL)** property, which contains the names of users, groups, or containers granted rights to the object. NetWare also includes two special objects named [Root] trustee and [Public] trustee that can be made trustees of another object. The **[Public] trustee object** represents all client computers attached to the network and running Novell Client. An example of [Public] rights is being able to use the Contexts browse button in the Novell Login window to locate a context. If the [Public] trustee isn't given rights to browse the eDirectory tree, you must enter the distinguished context of the OU where the user account is located instead of browsing to it. The **[Root] trustee object** represents all users in the eDirectory tree. To gain the access rights granted to the [Root] trustee, a user must first be authenticated by logging in to the eDirectory tree.

For the CNA test, remember that when you're assigning rights, any rights granted to the [Root] trustee object are effective for all users in the eDirectory tree. As a result, you should be careful when making [Root] a trustee of another object.

Any object placed in another object's ACL property becomes a trustee of the other object with certain rights. In Chapter 5, you learned that file system security consists of a group of eight access rights that control which operations users can perform in a directory or file. In eDirectory security, rights are divided into two categories: entry (or object) rights and attribute (or property) rights, as described in the following sections.

Although NetWare Administrator uses the terms "object rights" and "property rights," ConsoleOne uses "entry rights" to describe a trustee's object rights and "attribute rights" to describe a trustee's rights to an object's properties. In this chapter, the terms "entry rights" and "attribute rights" are used.

Entry Rights

Entry rights control what a trustee can do to an object, such as renaming, creating, or deleting it. As shown in Table 7-1, entry rights consist of Supervisor, Browse, Create, Delete, Rename, and Inheritable rights.

Table 7-1   eDirectory entry rights

Right	Description	Comparable File System Right
Supervisor	Grants all access privileges, including Supervisor right to All Attributes.	Comparable to the Supervisor right in the file system, except that the eDirectory Supervisor right can be blocked or reassigned at a lower level; the Supervisor right in the file system security cannot be blocked or reassigned.
Browse	Grants the right to view network objects in the eDirectory tree.	Comparable to the File Scan right in the file system, which allows users to see file and directory names.
Create	Grants the right to create objects in a container.	Performs the same function as in file system security.
Delete	Grants the right to delete the object or leaf objects from a container.	Performs the same function as in file system security.
Rename	Grants the right to change the name of the object.	Performs the same function as in file system security.
Inheritable	Allows leaf objects and subcontainers to inherit trustee assignments.	No comparable right in the file system security.

As in the file system, the **Supervisor entry right** includes all other rights. When you assign this right, the trustee is automatically given Supervisor rights to all the object's attributes or properties. Unlike file system security, however, the eDirectory Supervisor right can be reassigned or blocked in a subcontainer or leaf object, as you see later in this chapter. The **Browse entry right** is similar to the file system's File Scan right in that it allows users to find the object, and most users need only this right to access objects in a container. If one user is supposed to control other users or manage a container, the network administrator needs to make him or her a trustee of other users or the container by assigning additional rights. The **Create entry right** applies only to container objects and allows the trustee to create new subcontainer or leaf objects. Having the **Rename entry right** and the **Delete entry right** enables trustees to change an object name, delete an object, or move an object to another location. The **Inheritable entry right** allows leaf objects and other subcontainers to inherit the trustee's assignment. Figure 7-1 shows an example of the default entry rights that [Public] is given to the root of the eDirectory tree. In this example, having Browse rights enables users to find the context for their user names when logging in from Novell Client.

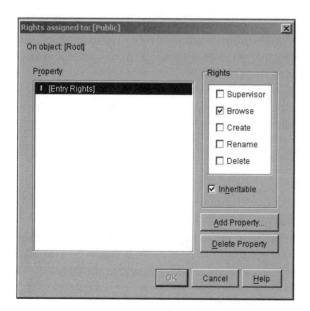

Figure 7-1   A sample entry rights assignment

Attribute Rights

Attribute rights control access to an object's attributes (properties) and include the six rights in Table 7-2.

Table 7-2   eDirectory attribute rights

Right	Description	Comparable File System Right
Supervisor	Grants all rights to the property unless blocked by an object's Inherited Rights Filter.	Comparable to the Supervisor right in the file system in that it grants all other rights; however, unlike the Supervisor right in file system security, it can be blocked or reassigned at a lower level.
Read	Grants the right to view the values stored in the object's property fields. Includes the Compare right.	Comparable to the Read right in the file system, which allows a trustee to view or copy the contents of a file.
Compare	A special case of the Read right that allows the trustee to compare the value of a property field to a fixed value returning true or false, without being able to view a property's contents.	No comparable right in the file system.
Write	Grants the right to add, change, or remove any value of a property field. Includes the Add Self right.	Comparable to the Write right in the file system, which allows a trustee to change the contents of a file. Having the Write right to the ACL attribute enables the trustee to change an object's trustee assignments in much the same way as having the Access Control right allows a trustee in the file system to add, change, or remove trustee assignments to a file or directory. In addition, having the Write right to the server object's ACL attribute gives the trustee Supervisor file system rights to all the server's volumes.
Add Self	A special case of the Write right that allows trustees to add or remove themselves as a value of the property field. This right is applicable for properties that contain object lists, such as group membership and mailing lists.	No comparable right in the file system.
Inheritable	Allows leaf objects and subcontainers to inherit trustee assignments.	No comparable right in the file system.

The two major attribute rights are Read and Write. The **Read attribute right** includes the Compare right and allows the trustee to view and compare values in attribute fields. The **Compare attribute right**, a limited version of the Read right, enables trustees to find an object based on information in the property without allowing them to actually view the attribute information. For example, the Universal AeroSpace administrative assistant, Lynn Dai, needs to be able to find users by their social security numbers. If Lynn has the Compare right to the Social Security attribute, she can find users by entering their social security numbers as a search parameter, but she can't browse the eDirectory tree to view users' social security numbers directly.

The **Write attribute right** includes the Add Self right and allows trustees to change information in attribute fields. The **Add Self attribute right** enables trustees to make themselves members of a group or remove their user names from a group. The **Supervisor attribute right** assigns all attribute rights and is normally assigned only to administrator accounts. Like the Inheritable entry right, the **Inheritable attribute right** enables leaf objects and subcontainers to inherit attribute rights in a container trustee assignment.

Figure 7-2 shows the attribute rights assigned to the Students group for the UAS Organization container. In this example, having Read and Compare rights means that all users in the Students group can view information about objects in the UAS Organization but can't make any changes.

Attribute rights can be assigned to all an object's attributes or just to specific attributes. Notice in Figure 7-2 that the All Attributes Rights option is selected, a blanket way of granting rights to all the object's attributes. This option means that the Students group has been given the Compare right to view all information

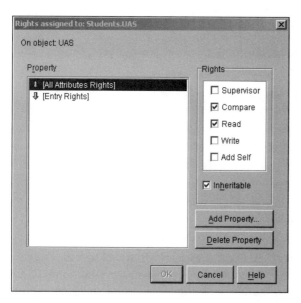

Figure 7-2   A sample attribute rights assignment

attributes in the UAS Organization. In addition, because the Inheritable right is selected, the Students group can read attribute information for objects in all subcontainers of the UAS Organization.

You can also add selected attribute rights to give a trustee special rights to a property. Selected attribute rights override the rights assigned through the All Attributes Rights option. For example, in Figure 7-3, the Students group has been assigned no rights to the Account Balance property. This assignment overrides the Read and Compare rights granted through the All Attributes Rights option and prevents group members from viewing the account balance information of other objects in the UAS Organization.

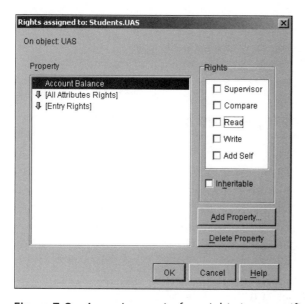

Figure 7-3   An assignment of no rights to a specific attribute

eDirectory Trustee Assignments and Effective Rights

As you learned in Chapter 6, effective rights are the actual rights a user has to an object, and they dictate what actions a user can perform on that object. As in file system security, a user's effective rights in the eDirectory tree can be the result of one or more of these factors:

- A trustee assignment made directly to the user object

- A trustee assignment made to a group (that the user is a member of) or an Organizational Role object (that the user is an occupant of)

- A trustee assignment made to the user's parent container

- Container, group, and user rights inherited from a trustee assignment made to a parent container

- Inherited rights blocked by a container or leaf object

Because effective rights are determined by a combination of factors, sometimes it's difficult to know what effective rights a user has in a container or leaf object. To make it easier, Novell includes an Effective Rights option similar to the one in file system security. In the following sections, you learn how to use ConsoleOne and iManager to make trustee assignments and check effective rights. In the end-of-chapter projects, you apply what you have learned about eDirectory security to set up the remaining trustee assignments for your UAS directory tree.

Trustee Assignment to a User

The most direct way to give a user effective rights to an object is by making the user a trustee of the object and then granting the necessary entry and attribute rights. For example, when Kellie Thiele temporarily needed rights to manage objects in the Mfg OU to test and implement a new software package, Eric Kenton assigned her all entry and attribute rights (except Supervisor) to the Mfg OU, which allows her to create new objects and manage user accounts in that container. In the following activity, you practice using ConsoleOne to make a trustee assignment and check effective rights.

 The activities in this chapter assume that you have created the eDirectory tree structure shown in Figure 4-12. In addition, you need to have created the objects in the IT OU described in Chapter 5.

NOTE

 ACTIVITY

Activity 7-1: Making User Trustee Assignments in ConsoleOne

Time Required: 10 minutes

Objective: Use ConsoleOne to make an eDirectory trustee assignment and check effective rights.

Requirements:

- A Windows XP desktop system with Novell Client installed and administrative access to your assigned UAS container

- Successful completion of activities in Chapters 4 and 5 so that you have IT and Mfg OUs and associated user and group accounts

Description: In this activity, you make Kellie Thiele a trustee of the Mfg OU with all entry and attribute rights except Supervisor. You then use ConsoleOne to check her effective rights in the Mfg OU.

1. If necessary, start your computer, and log in to eDirectory with your administrative user name and password.

2. Start ConsoleOne, and then expand the eDirectory tree and your **UAS** container.

3. Right-click the **Mfg** OU, and then click **Properties** to open the Properties of Mfg dialog box.

4. Click the **NDS Rights** tab to display the trustees of the Mfg OU.

5. Follow these steps to make Kellie Thiele a trustee of the Mfg OU and assign rights:

   a. Click the **Add Trustee** button to open the Select Objects dialog box.

   b. If necessary, click the **up arrow** to navigate to the IT OU.

   c. Expand the **IT** OU, click **KThiele**, and then click **OK** to open the Rights assigned to selected objects dialog box, shown in Figure 7-4.

Figure 7-4   The Rights assigned to selected objects dialog box

   d. Verify that the Browse and Inheritable check boxes are selected in the Rights section, and then click to select all rights except Supervisor.

   e. Click the **All Attributes Rights** option in the Property section and verify that the Compare and Read check boxes are selected, as shown in Figure 7-5.

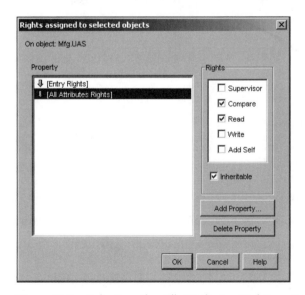

Figure 7-5   Selecting the All Attributes Rights option

   f. Click to select all rights except Supervisor, and then click **OK** to save the trustee assignment and return to the Properties of Mfg dialog box.

   g. Click the **Apply** button to apply your trustee assignment.

6. Follow these steps to check Kellie's effective rights in the Mfg OU:

    a. Click the **down arrow** on the NDS Rights tab to display the NDS Rights menu.

    b. Click the **Effective Rights** option to display the Effective Rights to Mfg window. Notice that by default, effective rights for the logged-in user are displayed.

    c. Click the **browse** button next to the For Trustee text box, and then browse to and click the **KThiele** user name.

    d. If necessary, click the **All Attributes Rights** option and record Kellie's effective rights:

    _____

    _____

    e. Click the **Entry Rights** option and record Kellie's effective rights:

    _____

    _____

    _____

7. Repeat Step 6 to record effective rights for Luke McMann:

    Effective All Attribute Rights:

    _____

    Effective Entry Rights:

    _____

8. Click **Close** to return to the ConsoleOne main window.

9. Exit ConsoleOne, and stay logged in for the next activity.

Trustee Assignment to a Group

As in file system security, a better way for users to gain effective rights is through assignments to groups or Organizational Role objects. Granting rights to Organizational Role objects makes it easier to maintain security when users change job responsibilities. When multiple users need effective rights to an object, you can use a group trustee assignment to reduce the number of trustee assignments and thereby simplify eDirectory security. In Activity 7-2, you make a group a trustee of an object and then check the group members' effective rights.

ACTIVITY

Activity 7-2: Making Group Trustee Assignments in iManager

Time Required: 10 minutes

Objective: Use iManager to make trustee assignments and check effective rights.

Requirements: Same as Activity 7-1, except that you can use a Windows XP or SUSE Linux 10 computer

Description: Luke McMann wants Eric to set up eDirectory security so that IT users can create and modify objects in the IT OU. To do this, Eric made the ITMgrs group a trustee of the IT OU with Create and Rename entry rights and the Write attribute right to all attributes. In this activity, you give ITMgrs a trustee assignment to the IT OU and then check effective rights for IT users.

1. If necessary, start your computer, and log on with your local computer user name and password.

2. Start your Web browser and enter the URL **https://IPaddress/nps/iManager.html** (substituting the IP address of your NetWare 6.5 Open Enterprise server for *IPaddress*) to display the iManager Login window. Enter your administrative user name and password to display the iManager main window.

3. Scroll down the Roles and Tasks pane and click to expand the **Rights** heading.

4. Click the **Modify Trustees** link to display the Modify Trustees window.

5. Click the **Object Selector** button next to the Object name text box, navigate to your UAS container and click the **IT** OU, and then click **OK** to display the Modify Trustees window shown in Figure 7-6.

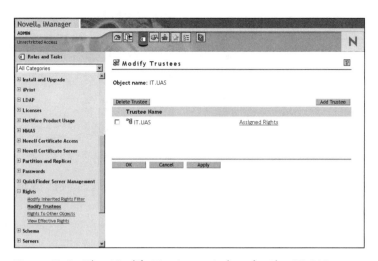

Figure 7-6   The Modify Trustees window for the IT OU

6. Follow these steps to add the ITMgrs group as a trustee of the IT OU:

   a. Click the **Add Trustee** button to display the Object Selector window.

   b. Navigate to the IT OU, and click the **ITMgrs** group to insert its distinguished name in the Selected Objects list box at the bottom.

   c. Click **OK** to return to the Modify Trustees window with ITMgrs added to the Trustee Name list.

   d. Click the **Assigned Rights** link next to the ITMgrs group to display a trustee assignment window, similar to the one in Figure 7-7.

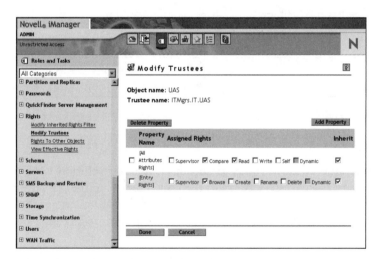

Figure 7-7   The trustee assignment window

   e. Click to select the **Rename** check box in the Entry Rights assignment, and verify that the Read, Compare, and Inherit check boxes are selected in the All Attributes Rights assignment.

   f. Click **Done** to save the new assignment and return to the Trustee Name list.

   g. Click the **Apply** button to save your changes.

7. Follow these steps to check effective rights for EKenton in the IT OU:

   a. In the Roles and Tasks pane, click the **View Effective Rights** link under the Rights heading to display the View Effective Rights window.

   b. Click the **Object Selector** button next to the Trustee name text box, and then click the **EKenton** object to insert his distinguished name.

   c. Click **OK** to display the View Effective Rights window shown in Figure 7-8.

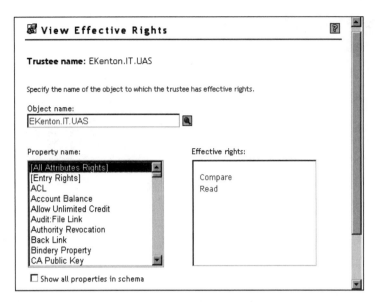

Figure 7-8 The View Effective Rights window

    d. Record the effective All Attributes Rights for the EKenton user:

    e. Click the **Entry Rights** option and record the entry rights for the EKenton user:

    f. Click **Done** to return to the iManager main window.

8. Repeat Step 7 to record effective rights for KThiele:

    Effective All Attribute Rights:

    Effective Entry Rights:

9. Leave iManager open for the next activity.

Trustee Assignment to a Container

When all users in a container need the same effective rights to an object, the best solution is to make the container a trustee of that object and assign the necessary rights to the container. As in the file system, when a container is made a trustee of an object, all users in that container have the entry and attribute rights granted to the container added to their effective rights. In addition, when a container is made a trustee of another object, all subcontainers inherit the same entry and attribute rights.

A good example of using a container trustee assignment is granting rights to a Directory Map object. As you learned in Chapter 4, a Directory Map object contains a Path property that points to a directory in the file system. By reading the directory path from the Path property, client computers can use a Directory Map object to map a drive letter to a directory in the file system. (You learn how to map drive letters with Directory Map objects in Chapter 9.) As a result, to use a Directory Map object, users must have the Read right to the Directory Map object's Path property.

Eric Kenton wants to create a Directory Map object so that all users can access a shared directory in the CORP volume. To do this, he plans to create a Directory Map object in the UAS Organization and then give the UAS container rights to read the Path property, as shown in Figure 7-9. Because the entire UAS structure is treated as a single unit, rights granted to the UAS Organization also belong to users in all subcontainers. In this way, all users in the IT, Engineering, Mgmt, and Mfg OUs have rights to use the Directory Map object to access the SharedData directory on the CORP volume. In the following activity, you use ConsoleOne to make trustee assignments to a Directory Map object and then check effective rights for users in the IT OU.

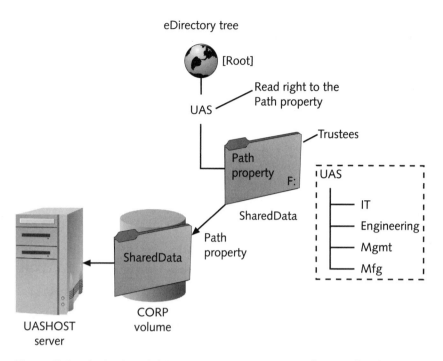

Figure 7-9   Assigning rights to a container grants rights to all subcontainers

NOTE

You can't create Directory Map objects in iManager 2.5, so ConsoleOne is used for Activity 7-3. This is a good example of why knowing how to use more than one utility is important.

ACTIVITY

Activity 7-3: Creating a Directory Map Object and Assigning Rights

Time Required: 10 minutes

Objective: Use ConsoleOne to assign eDirectory rights to a Directory Map object.

Requirements: Completion of Activity 7-1 and a Shared directory in your CORP volume (refer back to Figure 3-25). If you don't have a Shared directory in your CORP volume structure, you need to create one before performing this activity.

Description: To make it easier for all users in the organization to access the Shared directory, Eric wants you to create a Directory Map object named SharedData in the UAS Organization and then make this container a trustee with the Read attribute right to the Path property. In this activity, you use ConsoleOne to carry out this task and then check effective rights for a sample user.

1. If necessary, start your computer, and log in to eDirectory with your administrative user name and password.

2. If necessary, start ConsoleOne and expand the eDirectory tree.

3. Follow these steps to create a Directory Map object named SharedData in your UAS container:

   a. If necessary, navigate to and click your **UAS** container.

   b. Click the **New Object** button, click the **Directory Map** object type, and then click **OK** to open the New Directory Map dialog box shown in Figure 7-10.

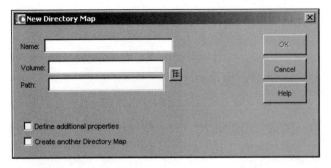

Figure 7-10   The New Directory Map dialog box

    c. Enter **SharedData** in the Name text box.

    d. Click the **browse** button next to the Volume text box and navigate to your **CORP** volume structure. (If you're using a shared classroom server, navigate to your **##Corp** directory in the STUDENTS volume.)

    e. Click to select the **Shared** directory, and then click **OK** to place the directory path in the Volume and Path text boxes.

    f. Click **OK** to create the Directory Map object and return to the main ConsoleOne window.

4. Follow these steps to assign rights for the SharedData Directory Map object:

    a. Right-click the **SharedData** object and click **Properties** to open the Properties of SharedData dialog box.

    b. Click the **NDS Rights** tab and then click the **Add Trustee** button to open the Select Objects dialog box.

    c. If necessary, click the **up arrow** to display your UAS container.

    d. Click your **UAS** container and click **OK** to open the Rights assigned to selected objects dialog box.

    e. Click the **All Attributes Rights** option, and verify that the Read and Compare rights are selected.

    f. Click **OK** to save your changes and return to the Properties of SharedData dialog box.

5. Follow these steps to record effective rights to the Path property of the SharedData Directory Map object for selected users:

    a. Click the **Effective Rights** button to open the Effective Rights dialog box shown in Figure 7-11.

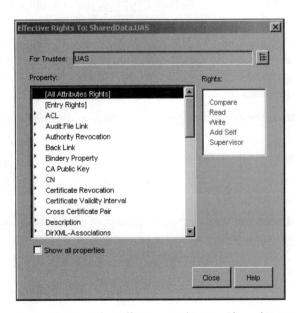

Figure 7-11   The Effective eRights To: SharedData.UAS dialog box

b. Click the **browse** button next to the For Trustee text box, navigate to the **IT** OU, and click the **LMcMann** user.

c. Scroll down and click the **Path** property. Record Luke's effective rights here:

_____

6. Repeat Step 5 to check effective rights for a user in the Engineering OU. Record the user name and effective rights to the Path property here:

User name:

_____

Effective rights:

_____

7. Close ConsoleOne, and stay logged in for the next activity.

Inherited Rights

To reduce the number of trustee assignments you need to make, NetWare allows trustee rights granted in a container to flow down to any subcontainers or leaf objects. As you learned for file system security, the process of rights flowing down the tree structure is called **inherited rights**. For example, in Chapter 5 you created the eDirAdm Organizational Role object. The occupant of this role needs rights to create, change, and modify objects in the eDirectory tree, so the eDirAdm Organizational Role object must have all rights except Supervisor to the UAS Organization and all its OUs. To do this, you can simply make the eDirAdm object a trustee of the UAS Organization. Through inheritance, the eDirAdm object receives all assigned rights to OUs in the UAS Organization, as shown in Figure 7-12.

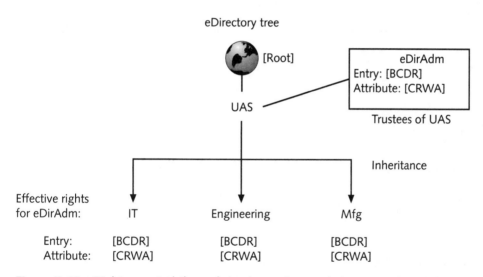

Figure 7-12 Rights granted through trustee assignments to a parent container are inherited by subcontainers and leaf objects

Without inheritance, you would have to make several trustee assignments granting eDirAdm rights to each OU in the UAS structure. In Activity 7-4, you use iManager to make a trustee assignment and then check inherited rights.

Activity 7-4: Viewing Inherited Rights

Time Required: 10 minutes

Objective: Use iManager to check inherited rights.

Requirements: Same as Activity 7-1, except that you can use a Windows XP or SUSE Linux 10 computer. In addition, you need the eDirAdm Organizational Role object created in Activity 5-15.

Description: Eric wants you to grant the eDirAdm object rights to manage the UAS Organization. In this activity, you observe inherited rights in action by using iManager to make eDirAdm a trustee of the UAS Organization and then check effective rights for this object.

1. If necessary, start your computer, and log on with your local computer user name and password.

2. If necessary, start iManager and log in as described in Activity 7-2.

3. Use iManager to make the eDirAdm object a trustee of the UAS container with all rights except Supervisor.

4. Follow these steps to check effective rights for eDirAdm in the IT OU:

   a. Click the **View Effective Rights** link under the Rights heading of the Roles and Tasks pane to display the View Effective Rights window.

   b. Click the **Object Selector** button next to the Trustee name text box and then click **eDirAdm** to insert its distinguished name in the Trustee name text box.

   c. Click **OK** to display the View Effective Rights window.

   d. Record the effective attribute rights for the eDirAdm object:

   _____

   e. Click the **Entry Rights** option and record the entry rights for the eDirAdm object:

   _____

   f. Click **Done** to return to the iManager main window.

5. In Chapter 5, you made Eric Kenton the occupant of the eDirAdm object. Repeat Step 4 to record effective rights for EKenton in the Engineering OU:

   Effective All Attributes Rights:

   _____

   Effective Entry Rights:

   _____

6. Leave iManager open for the next activity.

Using the Inheritable Entry Right

A powerful feature of NetWare 6.5 eDirectory security is that you can use the Inheritable right to specify whether subcontainers or leaf objects can inherit the entry and attribute rights you give a trustee. You might want a trustee to have Supervisor rights in a container but not in subcontainers, for instance. To do this, you can use an IRF to block the Supervisor right in subcontainers, but a simpler method in NetWare 6.5 is to remove the trustee's Inheritable right. The trustee is then limited to having Supervisor rights in just the container where the right is assigned. For example, to reduce the number of times he needed to log in with the Admin user name when maintaining objects in the UAS container, Eric wanted to assign his user name the Supervisor right in only the UAS Organization, not in OUs. Eric solved this problem by removing the Inheritable entry right from his trustee assignment to the UAS Organization. In Activity 7-5, you practice using the Inheritable entry right in iManager.

Activity 7-5: Using the Inheritable Entry Right

Time Required: 10 minutes

Objective: Use iManager to assign eDirectory rights.

Requirements: Completion of Activity 7-1, except that you can use a Windows XP or SUSE Linux 10 computer

Description: In this activity, you grant Eric the Supervisor entry right to the UAS Organization and then remove the Inheritable entry right to prevent him from inheriting the Supervisor right to any OUs. You then check Eric's effective rights in the UAS and IT containers.

1. If necessary, start your computer, and log on with your local computer user name and password.

2. If necessary, start iManager and log in as described in Activity 7-2.

3. If necessary, scroll down the Roles and Tasks pane and click to expand the **Rights** heading.

4. Click the **Modify Trustees** link to display the Modify Trustees window.

5. Click the **Object Selector** button next to the Object name text box, navigate to and click the **UAS** container, and then click **OK** to display Modify Trustees window.

6. Follow these steps to give EKenton the Supervisor right to the UAS container:
   a. Click the **Assigned Rights** link next to the EKenton user object to display the trustee assignment window.
   b. Click to select the **Supervisor** check box in the Entry Rights assignment.
   c. Click to clear the **Inherit** check box in the Entry Rights assignment.
   d. Click **Done** to save the new assignment and return to the Trustee Name list.
   e. Click the **Apply** button to save your changes.

7. Follow these steps to check effective rights for EKenton in the UAS container:
   a. In the Roles and Tasks pane, click the **View Effective Rights** link under the Rights heading to display the View Effective Rights window.
   b. Click the **Object Selector** button next to the Trustee name text box, and then click **EKenton** to insert his distinguished name in the Trustee name text box.
   c. Click **OK** to display the View Effective Rights window.
   d. Click the **Object Selector** button next to the Object name text box, and navigate to and click the **UAS** container to display Eric's effective rights. Record the effective attribute rights for EKenton:

   _____

   e. Click the **Entry Rights** option and record the entry rights for EKenton:

   _____

   f. Click **Done** to return to the iManager main window.

8. Repeat Step 7 to record effective rights for EKenton in the IT OU:

   Effective All Attributes Rights:

   _____

   Effective Entry Rights:

   _____

9. Leave iManager open for the next activity.

Using the Inheritable Attribute Right

Before eDirectory, NDS subcontainers could inherit only assignments to the All Properties rights. This created a lot of work if you wanted to give a user rights to administer only certain properties, such as addresses or phone numbers. In NetWare 6.5, you can set the Inheritable right to allow OUs and leaf objects to inherit selected attribute rights from their parent containers. For example, Lynn is in charge of changing address and phone number information for the entire company, so Eric gave her only the attribute rights she needed to maintain this information. In Activity 7-6, you practice using the Inheritable right, and in Activity 7-7, you work with IRFs.

Activity 7-6: Setting the Inheritable Option on Selected Attribute Rights

Time Required: 15 minutes

Objective: Use iManager to assign eDirectory rights.

Requirements: Same as Activity 7-5

Description: In this activity, you work with the Inheritable attribute right for selected properties to make Kellie Thiele a trustee of the UAS container with only the rights needed to change login scripts for users in all OUs.

1. If necessary, start your computer, and log on with your local computer user name and password.

2. If necessary, start iManager and log in as described in Activity 7-2.

3. If necessary, scroll down the Roles and Tasks pane and click to expand the **Rights** heading.

4. Click the **Modify Trustees** link to display the Modify Trustees window.

5. Click the **Object Selector** button next to the Object name text box, navigate to and click the **UAS** container, and then click **OK** to display the Modify Trustees window.

6. Follow these steps to give Kellie rights to change only the Login Script property in the UAS container:

   a. Click the **Add Trustee** button to display the Object Selector window.

   b. Navigate to the **IT** OU and then click the **KThiele** user to insert her distinguished name in the Selected Objects list box at the bottom.

   c. Click **OK** to return to the Modify Trustees window.

   d. Click the **Assigned Rights** link next to the KThiele object to display the trustee assignment window.

   e. Click the **Add Property** button to display the Add Property window shown in Figure 7-13.

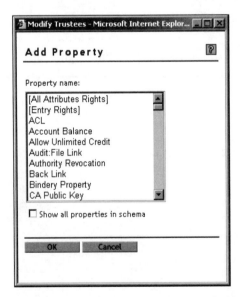

Figure 7-13   The Add Property window

   f. Scroll down and click the **Login Script** property, and then click **OK** to add this property to the Modify Trustees window, as shown in Figure 7-14.

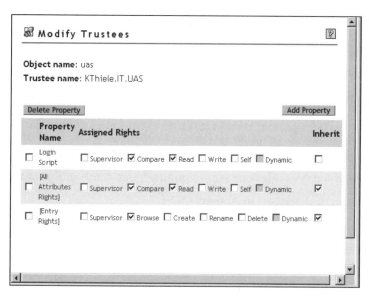

Figure 7-14 Viewing assigned rights for the Login Script property

    g. Click to select the **Write** and **Inherit** check boxes.

    h. Scroll down and click **Done** to save the new assignment.

    i. Click the **Apply** button to save your changes.

7. Follow these steps to check effective rights for KThiele in the IT OU:

    a. In the Roles and Tasks pane, click the **View Effective Rights** link under the Rights heading to display the View Effective Rights window.

    b. Click the **Object Selector** button next to the Trustee name text box, and then click the **KThiele** user to insert her distinguished name in the Trustee name text box.

    c. Click **OK** to display the View Effective Rights window.

    d. Click the **Object Selector** button next to the Object name text box, and navigate to and click the **IT** OU to display KThiele's effective rights. Record the effective rights to the Login Script property for KThiele:

    _____

    e. Click the **All Attributes Rights** option and click the **Login Script** property. Record attribute rights for KThiele:

    _____

    f. Click **Done** to return to the iManager main window.

8. Leave iManager open for the next activity.

Using the Inherited Rights Filter

As in the file system, inherited rights can be blocked by using an Inherited Rights Filter (IRF). A difference between eDirectory security and file system security is that with eDirectory security, you can block a container or leaf object from inheriting Supervisor rights. You use this feature later in the "Planning eDirectory Security" section. In the following activity, you use iManager to work with IRFs.

Activity 7-7: Working with Inherited Rights Filters

Time Required: 10 minutes

Objective: Use iManager to set an Inherited Rights Filter.

Requirements: In addition to requirements for previous activities, a Mgmt OU in your assigned UAS container

Description: In this activity, you use iManager to create an IRF to block the Mgmt OU from inheriting all rights except Supervisor. You then use iManager to check effective rights for Eric Kenton in the Mgmt OU.

1. If necessary, start your computer, and log on with your local computer user name and password.

2. If necessary, start iManager and log in as described in Activity 7-2.

3. Click to expand the **Rights** heading, and click the **Modify Inherited Rights Filter** link.

4. Click the **Object Selector** button next to the Object name text box, navigate to your **UAS** container, and click the **Mgmt** OU.

5. Click **OK** to display the Modify Inherited Rights Filter window shown in Figure 7-15.

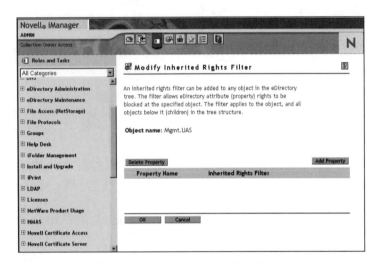

Figure 7-15   The Modify Inherited Rights Filter window

6. Click the **Add Property** button to display the Add Property window shown previously in Figure 7-13.

7. Verify that the All Attributes Rights option is selected, and click **OK**.

8. In the All Attributes Rights assignment, click to clear the **Write** and **Self** check boxes.

9. Click the **Add Property** button, click the **Entry Rights** option, and then click **OK**.

10. In the Entry Rights assignments, click to clear all check boxes except Supervisor and Browse, as shown in Figure 7-16.

11. Click **OK** to save your changes and then click **OK** to return to the main iManager window.

12. Exit iManager, close your Web browser, and stay logged in for the next activity.

In addition to being able to set an IRF for the All Attributes option, each property has its own IRF that can be used to block rights to just that property. For example, Kellie Thiele has been given rights to change login scripts for all users in the UAS Organization, and Luke wants users in the IT Department to manage their own login scripts. Figure 7-17 shows an example of using iManager to block all rights except Read and Compare to the Login Script property of the IT OU.

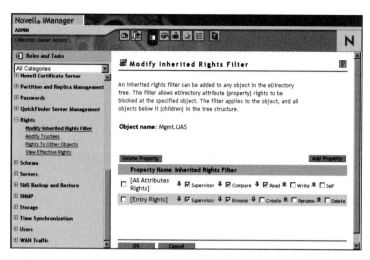

Figure 7-16   Completing the IRF assignments

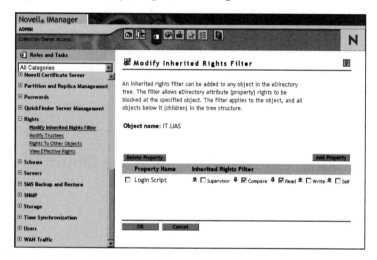

Figure 7-17   Setting an IRF on the Login Script property of the IT OU

eDirectory Default Rights

The eDirectory security system is powerful and flexible, so network administrators can tailor their systems to meet special needs. Knowing what rights are available by default and where they come from is important in planning and troubleshooting eDirectory security. When eDirectory is installed on the first server, the [Public], [Root], and Admin objects are created. The Admin object is assigned the Supervisor entry right to the root of the new eDirectory tree, thereby making Admin a supervisor of the entire network, including all servers. Giving the Supervisor entry right to a Server object automatically gives that user Supervisor file system rights to the server's volumes and file system, as described in Chapter 6.

In addition to the Admin user assignment, during installation the [Public] trustee is given the Browse entry right all the way to the root of the tree, so users can view all objects in the tree by using the CX /T /A /R command before logging in. If this creates a security problem in your organization, you need to remove [Public] as a trustee of the root of the tree, and then assign the Browse entry right to individual users, groups, or containers. You can give all users who have logged in to the network rights to browse the entire tree by making the [Root] object a trustee of the tree with Browse entry rights. In the following activities, you learn more about eDirectory default assignments by using NetWare Administrator to view default trustees for the root of the eDirectory tree, a new container, and a new user.

Activity 7-8: Viewing Default Trustees of the eDirectory Tree

Time Required: 5 minutes

Objective: Identify default entry and attribute rights for the eDirectory system.

Requirements: A Windows XP computer with Novell Client installed

Description: In this activity, you use NetWare Administrator to record the trustees of the root of the tree and their entry and attribute rights.

1. If necessary, start your computer, and log in to eDirectory with your administrative user name and password.
2. Double-click the **Shortcut to nwadmn32** desktop icon.
3. Follow these steps to open a browse window showing the root of the tree:
   a. Click **View**, **Set Context** from the menu.
   b. If necessary, enter **[Root]** in the Context text box, and then click **OK**.
4. Right-click the **[Root]** object, and then click **Trustees of this Object**.
5. Record the trustees of the [Root] object and their assigned entry and attribute rights:

   _____

   _____

6. Click **Cancel** to return to the NetWare Administrator browse window.
7. If you're continuing to the next activity, leave NetWare Administrator open and stay logged in. If not, exit NetWare Administrator, and log out.

Activity 7-9: Viewing Default Rights Assigned to the Server Object

Time Required: 5 minutes

Objective: Identify default entry and attribute rights for the Server object.

Requirements: Same as Activity 7-8

Description: When a Server object is installed in the eDirectory tree, default rights are given to the Server object and the [Public] trustee object. In this activity, you use NetWare Administrator to record the default trustees and rights assigned to the server.

1. If necessary, start your computer, log in to eDirectory with your administrative user name and password, and start NetWare Administrator.
2. Open a browse window to the UAS container.
3. Right-click the **UASHOST** server, and then click **Trustees of this Object**.
4. Record the trustees of the Server object and their assigned entry and attribute rights:

   _____

   _____

5. Click the **[Public]** trustee object, and then click the **Selected properties** option button.
6. Scroll down the Selected properties list box, and click to clear any property right assignments. Record the rights assignment for each property you select:

   _____

   _____

7. Click **Cancel** to return to the NetWare Administrator browse window.
8. If you're continuing to the next activity, leave NetWare Administrator open and stay logged in. If not, exit NetWare Administrator, and log out.

Activity 7-10: Documenting the Default Trustees of a New User

Time Required: 5 minutes

Objective: Identify the default trustees of a new user.

Requirements: Same as Activity 7-8

Description: When a new user object is created in eDirectory, certain attribute rights are granted automatically to give the user access to basic network resources. Knowing the default rights assignment for a new user can help you plan and set up an eDirectory security system that meets the needs of the organization and users. In this activity, you use NetWare Administrator to document the default trustees of a new user.

1. If necessary, start your computer, log in to eDirectory with your administrative user name and password, and start NetWare Administrator.

2. If necessary, open a browse window for your UAS container:
   a. Click **View**, **Set Context** from the menu.
   b. Click the **Browse** button next to the Context text box.
   c. Double-click the **UAS** container in the Available objects section, and click **OK**. (If you're using a shared classroom server, expand the **CLASS** Organization, and then double-click your **UAS** container.)

3. Follow these steps to create a user name for yourself in the UAS container:
   a. With the UAS container selected, click the **Create User** button on the toolbar.
   b. Enter your information in the Login name and Last name text boxes, and then click **Create**.

4. Right-click your new user name, and then click **Trustees of this Object**.

5. Record the trustees of your user name and your assigned entry and attribute rights on the following lines. Click the **Selected properties** option button to include any selected attribute rights.

   _____

   _____

6. Click **Cancel** to return to the NetWare Administrator browse window.

7. Exit NetWare Administrator, and log out.

DELEGATING ADMINISTRATIVE RIGHTS

As explained in Chapter 5, the occupant of the SysOp Organizational Role object is a backup administrative user whose account can be used if the main NetWare Admin user account is disabled or its password becomes compromised. One way to give the SysOp occupant the capability to act as a network administrator is to make the object a trustee of the [Root] object with Supervisor rights. In the following activity, you make the SysOp object a backup administrator for your system.

Be careful when assigning the Write attribute right to the All Attributes Rights option. If users have the Write attribute right to the ACL property, for example, they can modify their trustee assignments, even to the point of making themselves a Supervisor of an object. In addition, having the Write attribute right to the Server object's ACL property gives the trustee Supervisor rights to all volumes on that server—the one exception when assigning eDirectory rights affects file system security. Making users a Supervisor of the Server object grants them all rights to the file system, which can't be blocked or overridden in any subdirectories or files.

Activity 7-11: Empowering a Backup Administrator Account

Time Required: 10 minutes

Objective: Use iManager to assign eDirectory Supervisor rights.

Requirements: Same as Activity 7-1 and the SysOp Organizational Role object created in Chapter 5; a Windows XP or SUSE Linux 10 computer

Description: In this activity, you use iManager to give the SysOp Organizational Role object Supervisor rights to your eDirectory tree. If you're using a dedicated server, you grant the Supervisor right to the [Root] object; if you're using a shared classroom server, you grant the Supervisor right to your UAS container.

If you didn't create the SysOp object (assigned to the CKent user account) in Chapter 5, create it in the IT OU before starting this activity.

1. If necessary, start your computer, and log on with your local computer user name and password.

2. If necessary, start iManager and log in as described in Activity 7-2.

3. Scroll down the Roles and Tasks pane and click to expand the **Rights** heading. Click the **Modify Trustees** link to display the Modify Trustees window.

4. Click the **Object Selector** button next to the Object name text box. Then click the **[Root]** object, if you're using a dedicated server, or the **UAS** container, if you're using a shared classroom server.

5. Click **OK** to display the Modify Trustees window.

6. Follow these steps to give the SysOp Organizational Role object the Supervisor right to your eDirectory tree:

   a. Click the **Add Trustee** button to display the Object Selector window.

   b. Navigate to the **IT** OU, and click the **SysOp** object to insert its distinguished name in the Selected Objects list box at the bottom.

   c. Click **OK** to return to the Modify Trustees window with the SysOp object added to the Trustee Name window.

   d. Click the **Assigned Rights** link next to the SysOp object to display the trustee assignment window.

   e. Click to select all check boxes in the Entry Rights assignment and all check boxes in the All Attributes Rights assignment. Verify that the Inherit check box is selected for both assignments.

   f. Click **Done** to save the new assignment and return to the Trustee Name list.

   g. Click the **Apply** button to save your changes.

7. Follow these steps to check the SysOp object's effective rights to the UAS container:

   a. In the Roles and Tasks pane, click the **View Effective Rights** link under the Rights heading to display the View Effective Rights window.

   b. Click the **Object Selector** button next to the Trustee name text box, and then click the **SysOp** object to insert its distinguished name in the Trustee name text box.

   c. Click **OK** to display the View Effective Rights window.

   d. Record the effective attribute rights for the SysOp object:

   _____

   e. Click the **Entry Rights** option and record entry rights for the SysOp object:

   _____

   f. Click **Done** to return to the iManager main window.

8. Leave iManager open for the next activity.

Setting Up an Independent Container Administrator

Because you can use an IRF to block the Supervisor right, you can set up a container that's administered by a user other than Admin. Of course, misuse of this feature can cause some major problems, such as locking a container out from administrative access. To help prevent blocking your Admin user accidentally, NetWare requires you to establish a user with Supervisor rights in a container before removing the Supervisor right from the IRF. Without this safety check, carelessly removing the Supervisor right from a container or leaf object's IRF would mean that no one, including the network administrator, has rights to manage that container or leaf object. As a result, before you can use an IRF to block the Supervisor right from a container, you need to make an explicit trustee assignment to grant another object or the main Admin user the Supervisor right to that container. A disadvantage of having a separate container administrator is that certain eDirectory operations, such as merging two eDirectory trees, require the Admin user to have Supervisor rights to the entire tree. To address this possibility, the independent container administrator can grant the main Admin user the Supervisor right to the container for the duration of the operation.

For example, Luke asked Eric to establish the AeroDyn OU as an independent container in the UAS_Tree that's managed by the occupant of the AeroMgr organizational role, not the Admin user account. As a backup in case the occupant of AeroMgr is disabled, Luke also wants the SysOp occupant, Clark Kent, to have the Supervisor right to the AeroDyn OU. To do this, Eric made AeroMgr and SysOp trustees of the AeroDyn OU with Supervisor rights, and then modified the AeroDyn OU's IRF to block the Admin user from inheriting the Supervisor right, as shown in Figure 7-18.

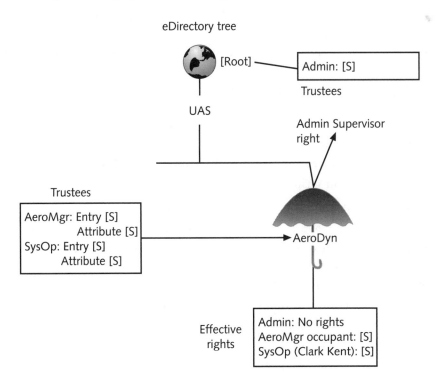

Figure 7-18   Setting up an independent container administrator

According to Luke's plan, major tree changes would be handled by having the occupant of AeroMgr grant the Supervisor right to the Admin user for the time needed to make the changes. In the following activity, you establish an independent container administrator in your eDirectory structure.

ACTIVITY

Activity 7-12: Creating a Container Administrator

Time Required: 10 minutes

Objective: Establish an independent container administrator.

Requirements: Same as Activity 7-1 using a Windows XP or SUSE Linux 10 computer

Description: Eric wants you to check into creating an independent container administrator by setting up a test OU and then making his user name the only administrator. In this activity, you use iManager to make the EKenton user an exclusive administrator of a test OU and then check his effective rights.

1. If necessary, start your computer, and log on with your local computer user name and password.

2. If necessary, start iManager and log in as described in Activity 7-2.

3. Create a new OU named **Test** in the UAS container.

4. Scroll down the Roles and Tasks pane and click to expand the **Rights** heading. Click the **Modify Trustees** link to display the Modify Trustees window.

5. Click the **Object Selector** button next to the Object name text box, and navigate to the UAS container. Click the **Test** OU, and then click **OK** to display the Modify Trustees window.

6. Follow these steps to add the EKenton user as a trustee of the Test container:

   a. Click the **Add Trustee** button to display the Object Selector window.

   b. Navigate to the **IT** OU and click **EKenton** to insert his distinguished name in the Selected Objects list box.

   c. Click **OK** to return to the Modify Trustees window with the EKenton object added to the Trustee Name list.

   d. Click the **Assigned Rights** link next to the EKenton object to display the trustee assignment window.

   e. Click to select the **Supervisor** check box in the Entry Rights assignment and the **Supervisor** check box in the All Attributes Rights assignment.

   f. Click **Done** to save the new assignment and return to the Trustee Name list.

   g. Click the **Apply** button to save your changes.

7. Follow these steps to remove all rights from the IRF of the Test OU:

   a. Click to expand the **Rights** heading and click the **Modify Inherited Rights Filter** link.

   b. Click the **Object Selector** button next to the Object name text box, click the **Test** OU, and then click **OK** to display the Modify Inherited Rights Filter window.

   c. Click the **Add Property** button, verify that All Attributes Rights is selected, and click **OK**.

   d. Click to clear all check boxes in the All Attributes Rights assignment.

   e. Click the **Add Property** button, click **Entry Rights**, and then click **OK**.

   f. Click to clear all check boxes in the Entry Rights assignment.

   g. Scroll down and click **OK** to save your changes and return to the iManager main window.

8. Exit iManager, and then log in to iManager again as **EKenton**.

NOTE
Because your Admin user has been blocked from the Test OU, you need to log in as EKenton to view effective rights to that OU.

9. Follow these steps to check effective rights for EKenton in the Test OU:

   a. In the Roles and Tasks pane, click the **View Effective Rights** link under the Rights heading to display the View Effective Rights window.

   b. Click the **Object Selector** button next to the Trustee name text box, and then click the **EKenton** object.

   c. Click **OK** to display the View Effective Rights window.

   d. Click the **Object Selector** button next to the Object name text box, and navigate to and click the **Test** OU to display Eric's effective rights. Record the effective attribute rights for EKenton:

   _____

   e. Click the **Entry Rights** option and record entry rights for EKenton:

   _____

   f. Click **Done** to return to the iManager main window.

10. Repeat Step 9 to check effective rights for your administrative user in the Test OU. Record the rights here:

    _____

    _____

11. Leave iManager open for the next activity.

Using Security Equivalence

Another way users are given rights is through **security equivalence**. By default, all new users are security equivalents to the [Root] and [Public] objects, giving all users the right to browse the eDirectory tree and submit login requests. By default, all users are also made security equivalent to the groups they belong to, so a security assignment made to a group is effective for all users in that group. In addition to the default security equivalents, you can use an explicit security equivalence assignment to make one user account security equivalent to another. For example, when Eric takes a vacation, Kellie fills in for him. A simple way to allow Kellie to perform Eric's duties is to make Kellie security equivalent to Eric's user account. When he returns, the security equivalence assignment can be removed.

Using security equivalence has some disadvantages, too. First, explicit security equivalent assignments aren't recorded in an object's access control list, making these assignments difficult to track. Second, if the object to which a user is security equivalent is deleted, the user loses all rights associated with the deleted object. For this reason, it's *not* a good idea to make a backup administrator account security equivalent to the Admin user. Should the main Admin account become deleted or corrupted, the backup administrator would lose rights to manage the eDirectory tree. In the following activity, you learn how to use iManager to make a user security equivalent to another user's account.

Activity 7-13: Assigning a Security Equivalent

Time Required: 10 minutes

Objective: Use iManager to make a user security equivalent to another object.

Requirements: Same as Activity 7-12

Description: Eric is on a 10-day tour of Iceland and wants you to make Luke's user account a security equivalent to his so that Luke can perform administrative tasks during Eric's absence. In this activity, you use iManager to create and test the security equivalent.

1. If necessary, start your computer, and log on with your local computer user name and password.

2. If necessary, start iManager and log in as described in Activity 7-2.

3. Follow these steps to make Luke McMann a security equivalent to Eric Kenton:

   a. If necessary, expand the **eDirectory Administration** heading and click the **Modify Object** link to display the Modify Object window.

   b. Click the **Object Selector** button and click the **EKenton** user.

   c. Click **OK** and then click the **Security** tab to display the window shown in Figure 7-19.

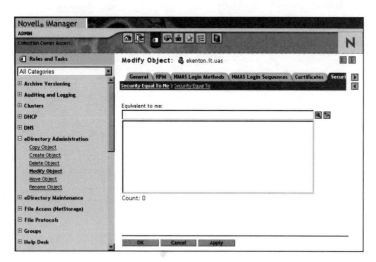

Figure 7-19 Assigning a security equivalent in iManager

   d. Click the **Object Selector** button next to the Equivalent to me text box and navigate to the **IT** OU.

   e. Click the **LMcMann** user to add Luke to the Selected Objects list box, and then click **OK** to insert his distinguished name in the Equivalent to me text box.

   f. Click **OK** to return to the iManager main window.

4. Apply the process in Step 9 of Activity 7-12 to checking Luke McMann's effective rights to the UAS Organization. Record the results here:

   _____

5. Remove Luke from EKenton's security equivalent list.

6. Exit iManager, and log off.

PLANNING EDIRECTORY SECURITY

As with file system security, when setting up eDirectory security, you should identify and document the effective rights users need for accessing their resources or performing their management responsibilities. After meeting with department managers, Luke sent a memo to Eric, shown in Figure 7-20, that documents the UAS eDirectory security requirements.

MEMO

To: Eric Kenton

From: Luke McMann

Date: 5/15/06

Subject: eDirectory security meeting notes

1. Kellie Thiele will be responsible for maintaining user login scripts for all users except those in the AeroDyn OU. Users should not be able to change their own login scripts.
2. To reduce the number of times Eric has to log in as Admin, his user name should be given Supervisor rights to objects in only the UAS Organization.
3. All users in the ITMgrs group should have rights to create and rename objects in all containers except the AeroDyn.Mfg OU.
4. Lynn Dai will be responsible for maintaining user postal address information for all users except those in the AeroDyn OU.
5. All users in the Engineering OU need rights to use the EngData Directory Map object.
6. All users in the IT OU need rights to use the ISData Directory Map object.
7. All users in the Mgmt OU need rights to use the MgmtData Directory Map object.
8. The MfgMgr Organizational Role object should have Supervisor rights to all objects in the Mfg OU structure except the AeroDyn.Mfg OU. The occupant of the MfgMgr Organizational Role should be able to create objects only in the AeroDyn.Mfg OU.
9. The occupant of the AeroMgr Organizational Role object, the network administrator, and the backup administrator should be the only users with Supervisor rights to the AeroDyn.Mfg OU.
10. The occupant of the SysOp Organizational Role object should have Supervisor rights to the entire UAS Organization.

Figure 7-20   UAS eDirectory security requirements

In the following sections, you learn how Eric applied eDirectory security to meet the security needs listed in the memo.

Defining Trustee Assignments

After identifying an organization's security needs, the next step is to define trustee assignments for carrying out the security plan. To help you plan eDirectory trustee assignments, the following list describes six Novell security guidelines. You should become familiar with these security guidelines before taking the Novell CNA exam.

- *Start with the default trustee assignments*—With the exception of certain objects, such as the Directory Map and Profile objects (described in Chapter 4), eDirectory's defaults enable users to access basic network resources and services in their assigned containers. To keep eDirectory security assignments to a minimum, attempt to place objects that users need to access, such as volumes and printers, in users' default contexts.

- *Minimize trustee assignments*—As with file system security, you can often keep user trustee assignments to a minimum by assigning rights to containers first. Assign rights to groups when you don't want to include all users in a container, or if you want to include selected users from multiple containers. Instead of assigning rights to individual users, consider using Organizational Role objects.

- *Use caution when assigning a trustee the Write attribute right to the ACL property of another object*—If users have the Write attribute right to another object's ACL property, they can create and remove trustees of the object and change their own trustee assignments. This includes making themselves or another user a Supervisor of the object and modifying the object's IRF. In a worst-case scenario, trustees with the Write attribute right to a container's ACL property could make their user names the Supervisor of the container and lock out the Admin user by removing the Supervisor right from the container's IRF.

- *Avoid using the All Attributes option when assigning the Write attribute right*—Use caution when assigning a trustee the Write attribute right for all attributes because with this right, the trustee can change any property values, including the ACL property. Through inheritance, the All Attributes rights assigned to a container flow down to all subcontainer and leaf objects. As a general rule, it's better to assign only the Read attribute right in All Attributes and use the Selected Properties option when assigning the Write attribute right.

- *Use caution when granting a trustee the Supervisor entry right to a container with a Server object*—When a user has the Supervisor entry right to a Server object, he or she also becomes a Supervisor of the server's file system by gaining the Supervisor access right to the root of all volumes. Usually, this problem happens when another user is made the manager of a container by being assigned the Supervisor entry right to that container. If the container happens to contain a Server object, the new trustee has all rights to the file system on the server. To prevent a user from accidentally inheriting Supervisor rights to the Server object, you can make the Admin user a Supervisor of the Server object by adding an explicit trustee assignment for Admin, and then removing the Supervisor rights from the Server object's IRF.

- *Use caution when filtering Supervisor rights with an IRF*—In NetWare, you can't remove the Supervisor right from an object's IRF until you add an explicit trustee assignment that has been granted the Supervisor entry right for that object. However, it's still possible to lose administrative control of part of the tree by adding a user as a trustee with Supervisor rights, removing the Supervisor rights from the IRF, and then accidentally deleting the user who has the Supervisor trustee assignment. If this happens, essentially you lose control of the container or leaf object because it would have no supervisor.

Using these guidelines, Eric created the worksheet shown in Figure 7-21 to make trustee assignments for the UAS network. Each row in the eDirectory Security Worksheet lists the name and object type of an object that needs a special trustee assignment. The Trustee columns lists the trustee name and the rights to be assigned. The Inherit Right columns show the settings for the inherited rights associated with that object or property.

Notice in Row 8 of the eDirectory Security Worksheet that the SysOp Organizational Role object is granted the Supervisor entry and attribute rights to the UAS Organization along with all the remaining entry and attribute rights. Although the Supervisor right would grant all the other rights, often it's a good idea to add the other rights so that if the Supervisor right is blocked, the administrative user can still manage the eDirectory tree.

Another administrative task that Eric wanted to delegate was maintaining login scripts. Because Kellie is a programmer, Luke wants her to be in charge of writing and maintaining login scripts for all users, so in Row 7 Eric indicated that Kellie needs the Read, Write, and Inheritable rights to the Login Script property of the UAS Organization. This assignment allows her to maintain login scripts for all users through inheritance. By default, users are given rights to create and modify their own login script files. However, Kellie doesn't want users to modify the login script commands she sets up for them. To address that need, Eric plans to remove the Write right from each user's Login Script property, as shown in Row 10. (In Chapter 4, you learned how to remove the Login Script's Write right from the template for creating new users.)

eDirectory Security Worksheet							
Developed by: Eric Kenton				**Tree Name: UAS Tree**			
		Trustee					
Object Name	Type	Name/Type	Entry Rights	Inherit Right*	Property Name	Attribute Rights	Inherit Right*
UAS	Organization container	ITMgrs.IT.UAS	BCR	I	All ACL	CRW CR	I
UAS	Organization container	Lynn Dai	B	I	Postal Code, Postal Address, Postal Office Box	W	I
EngData. Engineering.UAS	Directory Map object	.Engineering.UAS/ container	B	I	Path	R	I
ITData.UAS	Directory Map object	.IT.UAS/contianer	B	I	Path	R	I
MfgData	Directory Map object	Mfg.UAS/container	B	I	Path	R	I
MgmtData	Directory Map object	Mgmt.UAS/container	B	I	Path	R	I
UAS	Organization container	.KThiele.UAS	B	I	Login Script	RW	I
UAS	Organization container	SysOp.IT.UAS	S	I	All	S	I
All users	User object	The user's name		I	Login Script	R	I
Mfg.UAS	OU container	.MfgMgr.Mfg. UAS/org role	SBCR D	I	All	S	I
AeroDyn.Mfg.UAS	OU container	AeroMgr.Mfg. UAS/org role	SBCR D		All	S	I
AeroDyn.Mfg.UAS	OU container	MfgMgr.Mfg. UAS/org role	BC	I	All	R	I

* The Inherit Right column indicates whether subcontainers will inherit the assigned right.

Figure 7-21 The eDirectory Security Worksheet

Planning for Inherited Rights Filters

Using the information in the memo shown previously in Figure 7-11, Eric also developed the eDirectory IRF Worksheet, which lists the names and contexts of containers or leaf objects with IRF settings that will change (see Figure 7-22).

eDirectory IRF Worksheet					
Object Name	Type	Entry Rights IRF	All Attributes IRF	Property Name	Property IRF
Mfg	OU	S	All		
AeroDyn.Mfg	OU	S	S	Postal Code	R
				Postal Address	R
				Postal Office Box	R
				Login Script	R

Figure 7-22   The eDirectory IRF Worksheet

Notice that in the Mfg OU, all rights except Supervisor are removed from the Entry Rights IRF, and in the AeroDyn OU, all rights except Supervisor are removed from the Entry Rights and All Attributes IRFs. In addition, in the AeroDyn OU, all rights except Read are removed from the IRF of the postal properties. After creating the eDirectory security assignment plan, Eric's next step was to implement the trustee assignments and check users' effective rights. You can practice what you have learned in the end-of-chapter projects by using iManager and ConsoleOne to set up the trustee assignments and IRFs Eric defined in Figures 7-21 and 7-22.

IMPLEMENTING iMANAGER ROLE BASED SERVICES

As you learned in Chapter 4, to use iManager to manage the eDirectory tree, a user needs to be assigned to an administrative role. With **Role Based Services (RBS)**, Novell has created a standardized system of assigning administrative roles to users that allows them to use iManager on both Linux and NetWare servers. RBS consists of administrative tasks grouped into roles that can be assigned to users in a specific eDirectory context. Table 7-3 lists the RBS objects for these roles.

Table 7-3   RBS eDirectory objects

RBS Icon	Name	Description
	rbsCollection	A container object that holds all rbsRole and rbsModule objects. A tree can have multiple rbsCollection objects located in any of the following containers: Country Domain Locality Organization Organizational Unit The main rbsCollection is normally located in the same container as the server holding the master copy of the eDirectory partition.
	rbsRole	Specifies the tasks that users who are members of the role are allowed to perform. rbsRole is a container object that holds rbsTasks and can be located only within an rbsCollection container. Role members can be users, groups, or Organizational Units and are associated with a specific context in the tree called a scope. rbsRole objects are automatically created and deleted as necessary by Role Based Services.
	rbsTask	Represents a leaf object that holds a specific function, such as creating printers or resetting passwords.

Table 7-3   RBS eDirectory objects (continued)

RBS Icon	Name	Description
	rbsBook	Represents a leaf object located in an rbsModule that consists of pages containing roles and tasks for members.
	rbsScope	Represents a leaf object used for access control list (ACL) assignments instead of assigning rights for each user object. rbsScope objects define the context in the tree where a role will be performed and are associated with rbsRole objects.
	rbsModule	Used to organize available rbsTask objects into functional groups. With this object, administrators can assign a user a specific function within a product or service.

In iManager, administrators can delegate administrative tasks to users and give them only the options they need to perform their assigned tasks. RBS requires a set of extensions to the eDirectory schema to allow creating RBS objects. The RBS objects are placed in the eDirectory tree as shown in Figure 7-23.

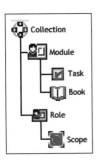

Figure 7-23   RBS tree objects

In the following sections, you learn how to set up Role Based Services and assign administrative roles to user accounts.

Installing and Configuring RBS

Before delegating tasks with administrative roles, you need to set up Role Based Services on your server by extending the eDirectory schema. By default, RBS is set up during the NetWare 6.5 Open Enterprise server installation. If RBS is not set up on your server, you can perform the following steps to install RBS with the iManager Configuration Wizard:

EXAMPLE

1. Start iManager and log in with your administrative user name and password.

2. Click the Configure button on the toolbar (fourth button from the right, which looks like the Organizational Role object icon).

3. Click to expand the Role Based Services heading, and then click the RBS Configuration link.

4. Click the Configure iManager link in the Notice window to display the Collection Information window shown in Figure 7-24. (If you don't see a Notice window, RBS is already installed on your server.)

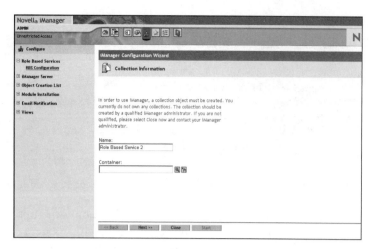

Figure 7-24 The Collection Information window

5. Click the Object Selector button, click your UAS Organization, and then click Next to display the window shown in Figure 7-25.

6. This window lists all modules to be included in iManager for this collection. The Scope text box identifies the area of the eDirectory tree to be managed by this collection and is specified by selecting an Organization or OU. All containers and objects in the selected container then become part of the collection's scope. If necessary, click the Select All button to install all modules, and then click the Object Selector button to select the scope to be included in the collection. Figure 7-25 shows an example of selecting all modules with a scope that includes the entire eDirectory tree.

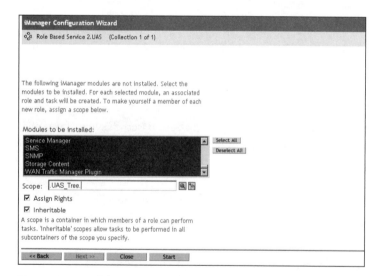

Figure 7-25 Selecting modules to be installed

7. Click the Start button to install the selected modules.

8. When the completion message is displayed, click the Close button to return to the iManager main window.

Assigning Users to an Administrative Role

By default, when RBS is installed on an Open Enterprise server, only the network administrator is configured as a user of iManager. To give other users rights to administer eDirectory objects in a Linux or NetWare environment, you need to assign them to a role. Standard administrative roles include DHCP Management, DNS Management, eDirectory Administration, iPrint Management, and License Management. Roles are stored in RBS Collection objects and can be viewed in iManager by following these steps:

1. Start iManager and log in with your administrative user name and password.
2. Click the Configure button and expand the Role Based Services heading.
3. Click the RBS Configuration link to display the RBS collections (see Figure 7-26).

7

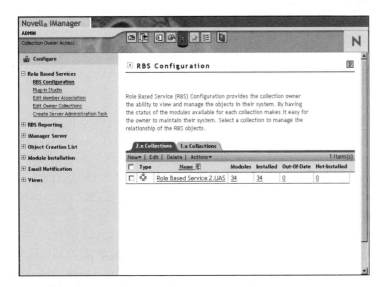

Figure 7-26 The RBS Configuration window

4. In the 2.x Collections tab, click the RBS collection you want (Role Based Service 2.UAS in Figure 7-26) to display the roles for that collection (see Figure 7-27).

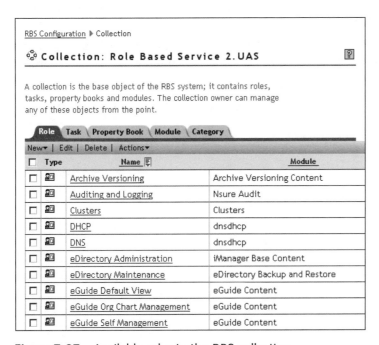

Figure 7-27 Available roles in the RBS collection

5. To see the tasks in a role, you can click the corresponding role. For example, clicking the eDirectory Administration role displays the tasks shown in Figure 7-28. You can then use the Add and Remove links to add or remove tasks.

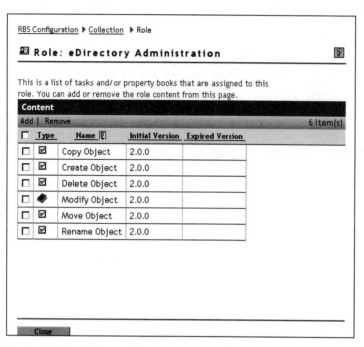

Figure 7-28   Tasks in the eDirectory Administration role

Users can be made members of existing administrative roles. In the following steps, you see how to grant Kellie Thiele the rights to use iManager for eDirectory management. To perform these steps, you need access to a user name and password with the Supervisor right to the eDirectory tree of your NetWare server.

EXAMPLE

1. Start iManager and log in with your administrative user name and password.

2. If necessary, click the Configure button to open the Configure window.

3. To add a user to the eDirectory Administration role, expand the Role Based Services heading and then click the Edit Member Association link.

4. Click the Object Selector button next to the Member name text box, click the User option under the Search for these types heading, and then click the Search button to display all users.

5. Click the KThiele user name to insert her distinguished user name.

6. Click OK to display the Edit Member Association window shown in Figure 7-29.

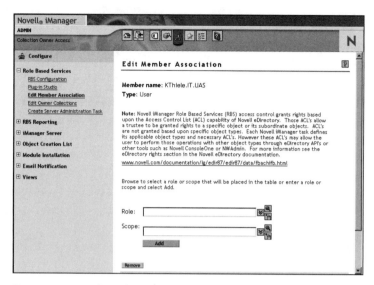

Figure 7-29   The Edit Member Association window

7. Click the Object Selector button next to the Role text box, and click the eDirectory Administration role from the Role Based Service 2 collection (see Figure 7-30). (*Note:* You might have to click Next to page down to the eDirectory Administration role.)

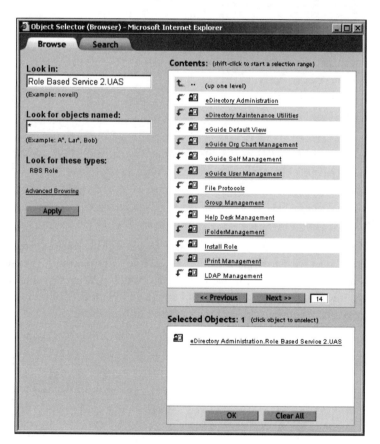

Figure 7-30   Selecting a role from the Role Based Service 2 collection

8. Click Add to add the role to the Edit Member Association window.

9. Next, you need to select the scope where the user will be able to perform administrative tasks in the selected role. For example, to allow Kellie to use eDirectory Administration tasks in the IT OU, click the Object Selector button next to the Scope text box, and then click the IT OU.

10. Click the Add button to add the association to the role list at the bottom of the window (see Figure 7-31).

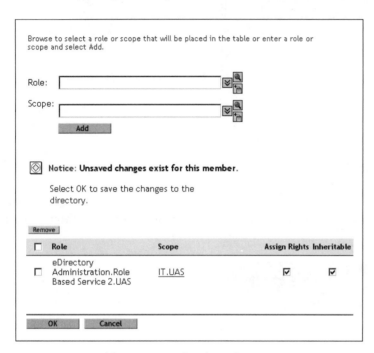

Figure 7-31   Adding a scope for the role

11. Click OK and then click OK again to return to the iManager main window. Kellie can now use iManager to perform eDirectory administration tasks in the IT OU.

MONITORING eDIRECTORY OPERATION

Monitoring and diagnosing the eDirectory tree requires administrators to be able to view partitions and replicas on a server basis. The iMonitor utility used for this purpose can run on any platform that supports eDirectory 8.6, including NetWare, Windows NT/2000, Linux, and Solaris. On NetWare servers, iMonitor listens on the default HTTP port 8008. At login, the user's port is redirected to 8009. In the following activity, you learn how to use iMonitor to access and monitor your eDirectory tree information.

Activity 7-14: Using iMonitor

Time Required: 10 minutes

Objective: Use iMonitor to perform eDirectory management tasks.

Requirements: Same as Activity 7-13

Description: Although eDirectory is an extremely stable and reliable platform, occasionally problems can occur as a result of replication errors caused by communication media failure or server hardware problems. In this activity, you use iMonitor to check the status of your eDirectory tree.

1. If necessary, start your computer, and log on to your computer with your local user name and password.

2. Start your Web browser, and enter the URL **https://IPaddress:8009/nds** (replacing *IPaddress* with the IP address of your server) to display the Login window.

3. Enter your administrative user name and password and click the **Login** button.

4. Scroll down to the Manage eDirectory heading, and click the **NDS iMonitor** link to display the Agent Summary window (see Figure 7-32).

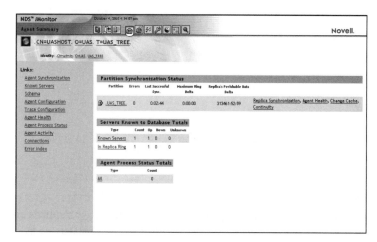

Figure 7-32   The Agent Summary window in iMonitor

5. A useful eDirectory troubleshooting technique is performing a DSTRACE on eDirectory tree transactions to look for error conditions or messages to identify and correct a problem. In this step, you perform a DSTRACE and record your observations:

   a. Click the **Trace Configuration** link to display the Trace Configuration window shown in Figure 7-33.

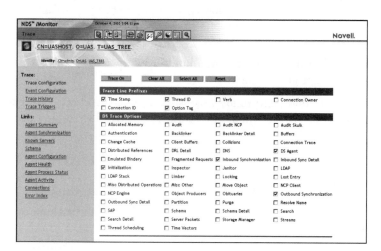

Figure 7-33   The Trace Configuration window

   b. In the DS Trace Options section, verify that the following options are selected: Inbound Synchronization, Initialization, Outbound Synchronization, and DS Agent. Click to select the **NCP Client** and **Streams** check boxes.

   c. At the top of the Trace Configuration window, click the **Trace On** button and then click the **Update** button to start the trace.

   d. Wait three minutes and then click the **Trace Off** button.

   e. Click the **Trace History** link at the left to display a list of traces that have been made (see Figure 7-34).

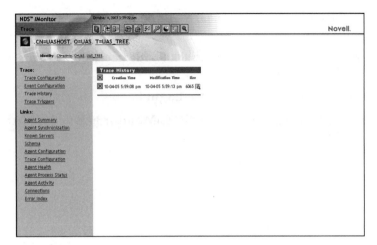

Figure 7-34   The Trace History window

    f. In the Trace History section, click the **View** icon (magnifying glass).

    g. Scan the output, and record two trace messages here:

         _____

         _____

6. Another eDirectory troubleshooting technique is checking to make sure eDirectory replicas are synchronized on the servers. Follow these steps to view your replica synchronization status in iMonitor:

    a. Click the **Agent Synchronization** link under the Links heading to display the Partition Synchronization Status window.

    b. The Partition Synchronization Status window contains information on each partition. If necessary, scroll down the list and locate your UAS partition information. Record the Error Count and Last Successful Sync information for your partition:

         _____

         _____

    c. Click the **UAS** partition and scroll down to view the information. Record the date and time your UAS partition was created:

         _____

    d. Click the **Home Server Manager** button (a server with a bull's-eye target next to it) at the top of the iMonitor window to return to Remote Manager.

7. The DSREPAIR utility is useful for identifying and fixing inconsistencies in the eDirectory partition replicas. Follow these steps to run DSREPAIR and then view the DSREPAIR log for any possible problems:

    a. Scroll down and click the **NDS iMonitor** link under the Manage eDirectory heading to return to the iMonitor window.

    b. Click the **Repair** button (a wrench icon) to display the NDS Repair Switches window.

    c. Record the repair option settings on the following lines. (You can write more than one option per line, if needed.) Do not start the repair at this time unless your instructor tells you to do so.

         _____

         _____

8. Exit iMonitor by clicking the **Logout** button, and log out.

NETWARE TIME SYNCHRONIZATION

Keeping eDirectory partitions located on multiple servers synchronized with each other requires using a reliable time source that can be shared among the NetWare servers. With a common time source, each eDirectory transaction can be stamped with the time it occurred. Using time stamps allows eDirectory servers to apply transactions to their database in the correct sequence. To provide a common network time that all servers and computers can share, Novell has added time servers that support an industry-standard time synchronization protocol called **Network Time Protocol (NTP)**. NetWare servers that get their time from a central time server are referred to as **secondary time servers**. If you have a multiple-server network, most of your servers will be secondary time servers that get their time from one of the types of time servers discussed in the following paragraphs.

The first server installed in an eDirectory tree by default becomes a **single reference time server** for all servers in the tree. As shown in Figure 7-35, this server can use an external Internet clock or the internal clock on the server's system board to provide time to network clients and other secondary time servers. The secondary time servers provide network time to clients and use the network time to post transactions to the eDirectory database.

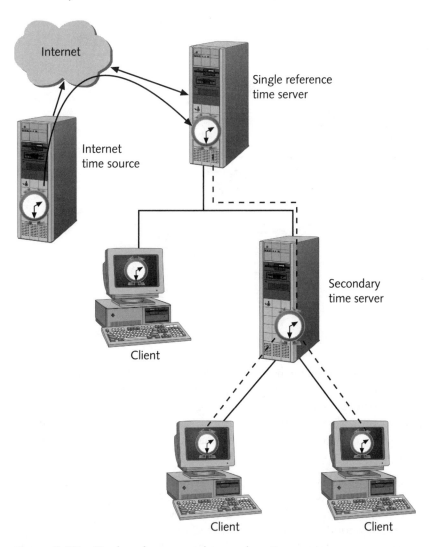

Figure 7-35   Single reference and secondary time servers

A **reference time server** is similar to a single reference time server except that it's used in large network environments where it maintains network time by participating in a time provider group that includes other servers called primary time servers (see Figure 7-36).

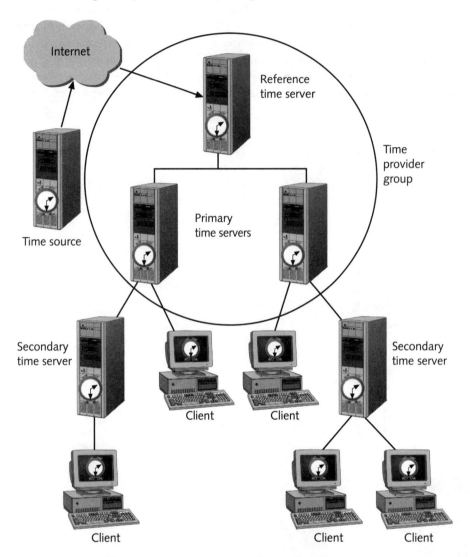

Figure 7-36   A time provider group with reference and primary time servers

Despite their name, **primary time servers** don't generate network time; instead, they get their time from the reference time server. If the reference time server is down or unavailable, primary time servers participate in a polling process to determine the correct network time. During the polling process, each primary time server in the time provider group votes on a correct time. The time with the most votes becomes the official network time. Each primary time server then synchronizes its internal clock to the consensus network time and helps distribute that time to secondary time servers and clients in its geographical area.

The choice of time synchronization strategy depends on the network's size and geographical distribution. The default single reference time server strategy works fine for networks that have fewer than 30 servers and are mostly contained in a single geographical region. When a network grows beyond 30 servers, the amount of time synchronization traffic between secondary time servers and the single reference time server can create a bottleneck, especially when servers are separated by WANs. When this happens, you should set up a time provider group, which must have a minimum of one reference time server and two primary time servers.

To configure time servers, you use the Timesync.cfg file in the SYS:System directory. You can modify this file directly with a text editor, in a utility such as iMonitor running on the server console, or through a Web browser using Remote Manager. Figure 7-37 shows time server parameters for a single reference time server in Remote Manager.

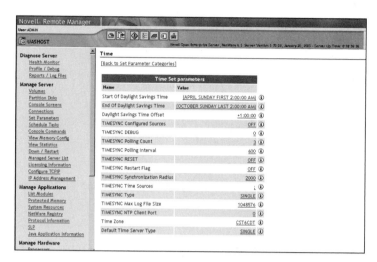

Figure 7-37　The Time Set parameters window

Notice that the default TIMESYNC (time server) Type setting is SINGLE, the TIMESYNC Configured Sources setting is OFF, and the TIMESYNC Time Sources setting is blank (indicated by a semicolon). These settings tell you that the server is using its own internal clock to obtain the network time. If you want the single reference time server to get its time from an Internet time source, you could modify these parameters and enter the IP address of the Internet time server, as described in the following activity.

Activity 7-15: Configuring NetWare Time Services

Time Required: 10 minutes

Objective: Use Remote Manager to view and configure NetWare time synchronization settings.

Requirements: Same as Activity 7-13. Access to the Internet is required to configure the server to use an external time source.

Description: To ensure that network time is more accurate, Eric wants you to experiment with using an external time source on the NetWare 6.5 Open Enterprise server. In this activity, you use Remote Manager to view your server's time synchronization parameters and then configure it to use an external time source.

1. If necessary, start your computer, and log on with your local user name and password.

2. If you have access to the Internet, start your Web browser and search for Internet time sources. Record the IP address of an Internet time source. (Your instructor might provide the IP address of an Internet time source.):

   _____

3. Start Remote Manager by entering the URL **https://IPaddress:8009** (replacing *IPaddress* with the IP address of your NetWare 6.5 Open Enterprise server).

4. Log in to Remote Manager with your administrative user name and password.

5. Click the **Set Parameters** link under the Manage Server heading to display the Set Parameters window shown in Figure 7-38.

6. Click the **Time** link to display the Time Set parameters window, similar to the one shown previously in Figure 7-37.

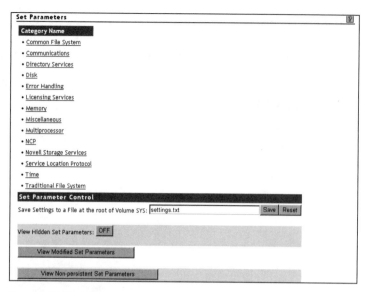

Figure 7-38   The Set Parameters window

7. Record the values for these settings: TIMESYNC Configured Sources, TIMESYNC Time Sources, and TIMESYNC Type.

_____

_____

_____

8. Change the TIMESYNC Configured Sources setting to **ON**.

9. Change the TIMESYNC Time Sources setting to the IP address of the Internet time source you recorded in Step 2.

10. Change the TIMESYNC Restart Flag setting to **ON** to apply your changes.

11. Exit Remote Manager, close your Web browser, and log out.

Congratulations! Luke is pleased with your progress as a student intern, but the work of a network administrator is never over. In the end-of-chapter projects, you finish setting up eDirectory security for your UAS eDirectory system and then begin setting up printing in Chapter 8.

CHAPTER SUMMARY

❑ eDirectory is the backbone of the NetWare network, providing access to all network objects. As a result, a network administrator must know how to set up the eDirectory security system to give users rights to access and manage the objects they are responsible for. eDirectory security consists of entry and attribute rights assigned to trustees. Each object in the eDirectory database has an access control list (ACL) property. An object is made a trustee of another object by placing the name of the object to be the trustee in the ACL property of the other object.

❑ Entry rights allow users to view and manage objects in the eDirectory tree and consist of Supervisor, Browse, Create, Delete, Rename, and Inheritable rights.

❑ Attribute rights allow users to access and maintain information stored in an object and consist of Supervisor, Read, Compare, Write, Add Self, and Inheritable rights.

❑ A trustee granted the Supervisor entry right is automatically granted the Supervisor right to all attributes.

❑ Special trustee objects include [Public] and [Root]. The [Public] object represents all clients that have Novell Client loaded and are attached to the network, but have not yet logged in. The [Root] object represents all network objects, including clients, that have logged in using authorized user names.

❑ Entry and attribute rights assigned to a trustee of a container can flow down from the container to leaf and subcontainer objects, unless reassigned or blocked by an Inherited Rights Filter (IRF). Effective rights consist of the actual rights a user has to an object as a result of a combination of explicit trustee assignments, inherited rights, group memberships, or rights assigned to the user's container object.

❑ Default rights play an important role in managing eDirectory security because they give the Admin user Supervisor rights to the eDirectory tree and give users rights to browse the network and access objects.

❑ Although the default eDirectory rights work in most cases, certain network objects, such as the Directory Map object, require the administrator to assign rights for users to access the object.

❑ With eDirectory security, you can set up an independent container administrator by granting a user object Supervisor rights to an OU and then using an IRF to block the OU from inheriting Supervisor rights from the system administrator.

❑ Role Based Services can be used to delegate the authority to perform administrative tasks in iManager, such as eDirectory administration, printer management, and licensing.

❑ You must use iManager to set up Role Based Services before using it to delegate administrative tasks.

❑ The iMonitor utility can be used to check the operation and status of the eDirectory system.

❑ eDirectory require all servers to use a common time so that update transactions are applied correctly. Novell uses a system of time servers to distribute a common time throughout the network. Time server types include single reference, reference, primary, and secondary.

❑ Secondary time servers get their network time from primary or reference time servers and then distribute the time to network clients. In the default configuration, a single reference time server distributes time to all secondary time servers. In a customized time synchronization configuration, a time provider group consisting of a reference time server working with two or more primary time servers distributes time throughout the network. Customized time server configurations are best used on networks of more than 30 servers.

KEY TERMS

access control list (ACL) — A property of an object that lists other objects, such as users, groups, or containers, that have been made a trustee of the object along with the assigned entry and attribute rights.

Add Self attribute right — A special case of the Write attribute right that allows trustees to add or remove their membership in a group.

attribute rights — A group of eDirectory security rights used to define the rights granted to read and modify data in the properties of an object. Attribute rights include Read, Compare, Write, Add Self, Inheritable, and Supervisor.

Browse entry right — An eDirectory security right that grants the right to view an object.

Compare attribute right — A special case of the Read right that allows trustees to find an object without viewing property information.

Create entry right — An eDirectory security right that grants the right to create objects in a container.

Delete entry right — An eDirectory security right that grants the right to delete an object in a container.

entry rights — A group of eDirectory security rights used to control what a user can do with an object. Consists of Browse, Create, Delete, Inheritable, Rename, and Supervisor rights.

Inheritable attribute right — An eDirectory security right that enables leaf objects and subcontainers to inherit attribute rights in a container trustee assignment.

Inheritable entry right — An eDirectory security right that allows leaf objects and other subcontainers to inherit the trustee's assignments.

inherited rights — A group of entry or attribute rights that flow down to other containers or leaf objects.

Network Time Protocol (NTP) — An industry-standard time synchronization protocol.

primary time servers — Time servers that work in a time provider group with at least one other primary time server and a reference time server to distribute the correct time throughout the network.

[Public] trustee object — A special trustee object created during the NetWare installation that consists of all client computers attached to the network.

Read attribute right — An eDirectory security right that includes the Compare right and allows the trustee to view values stored in an object's property fields.

reference time server — Similar to a single reference time server, except it's used in large network environments and participates in a time provider group that includes primary time servers.

Rename entry right — An eDirectory security right that grants the right to change the name of an object.

Role Based Services (RBS) — The NetWare service used to assign users the rights needed to perform tasks in iManager.

[Root] trustee object — A special trustee object that represents all users defined in the eDirectory tree. All users who have logged in to the eDirectory tree are part of the [Root] trustee object.

secondary time servers — Time servers that get their time from a central time source and then distribute it to network clients.

security equivalence — A security assignment that grants an object rights equal to that of another object.

single reference time server — In the Novell default time server configuration, it's the first server installed in the eDirectory tree, and it distributes the time to secondary time servers and clients.

Supervisor attribute right — An eDirectory security right that grants all rights to a property unless blocked by an object's IRF.

Supervisor entry right — An eDirectory security right that grants all access privileges, including the Supervisor right to all the object's attributes or properties.

Write attribute right — An eDirectory security right that includes the Add Self right and allows the trustee to change information in property fields.

REVIEW QUESTIONS

1. When creating a Directory Map object, which of the following security assignments allows users to use the Directory Map object?

   a. Read right to All Attributes

   b. Read entry right

   c. Browse entry right

   d. Write right to the Path property

2. Which of the following security services enables users to use iManager to view, access, create, and modify objects in the eDirectory tree?

   a. eDirectory security

   b. file system security

   c. login security

   d. Role Based Services

3. Having the _____ right to the _____ property of the Server object is the one exception to eDirectory security affecting file system security.

4. In the exception in Question 3, what rights does the trustee of the Server object have in the SYS volume?

5. Any object placed in the ACL property of another object becomes a _____ of that object with certain entry and attribute rights.

   a. supervisor

   b. trustee

   c. manager

   d. user

6. Which of the following objects represents all users whose computers are attached to the network?

    a. [Root]

    b. [Public]

    c. Organization

    d. network

7. Which of the following objects represents all authorized users in the eDirectory tree?

    a. [Root]

    b. [Public]

    c. Organization

    d. network

8. List the six entry rights.

9. List the two major attribute rights.

10. Which of the following is a special case of the Write attribute right?

    a. Browse

    b. Create

    c. Add Self

    d. Compare

11. Which of the following is another name for entry rights?

    a. attribute rights

    b. property rights

    c. object rights

    d. trustee rights

12. Describe one advantage of granting the Supervisor entry right compared to other entry rights.

13. Which of the following describes rights flowing down the eDirectory structure?

    a. effective rights

    b. inherited rights

    c. trustee rights

    d. access rights

14. Only rights assigned with the All Attributes option flow down from a container object to all leaf objects. True or False?

15. Which of the following is the actual eDirectory rights a user has to an object?

    a. trustee rights

    b. effective rights

    c. inherited rights

    d. attribute rights

16. Which of the following is a property of every object and contains a list of users and groups who have rights to that object?

    a. owner

    b. trustee list

    c. membership list

    d. access control list

17. Which of the following is a default right that a user has to his or her own object? (Choose all that apply.)

   a. Supervisor right to All Attributes

   b. Write right to All Attributes

   c. Read right to All Attributes

   d. Write right to the ACL property

   e. Write right to the Login Script property

18. Which of the following is a task that can be performed by a member of the eDirectory Administration role? (Choose all that apply.)

   a. create objects

   b. delete objects

   c. assign rights

   d. rename objects

19. By default, all clients have which of the following rights to the eDirectory tree?

   a. Read

   b. Browse

   c. Compare

   d. List

20. Assigning a user the Supervisor entry right to which of the following objects gives a user all rights to the file system? (Choose all that apply.)

   a. The Volume object

   b. The Server object

   c. The container that holds the Server object

   d. The container that holds the Volume object

   e. The [Root] object

21. The Novell default time server configuration uses which types of time servers? (Choose all that apply.)

   a. primary

   b. secondary

   c. reference

   d. single reference

22. A customized time server configuration is recommended if your network has more than _____ servers.

23. A time provider group must consist of at least _____ primary time servers.

CASE PROJECTS

In the following case projects, you plan eDirectory trustee assignments to give Business Division users the rights they need to access and manage resources.

CASE
PROJECTS

Case Project 7-1: Defining Trustee Assignments

Figure 7-39 shows a memo Eric received from Lynn Dai summarizing results of the eDirectory security meetings he had with Business Division managers. Use this information to fill out an eDirectory Security Worksheet similar to the one in Figure 7-21. (Ask your instructor for a blank form.) Your worksheet should show the trustee assignments you make to meet the requirements shown in Figure 7-39.

MEMO

To: Eric Kenton

From: Lynn Dai

Date: 5/15/06

Subject: Notes from the Business and Marketing security meeting

- A new container needs to be established for AeroDyn office staff.
- Add a user account for a new user named Bernie Muelner in the AeroDyn OU.
- Only Bernie and your Admin user should have rights to create, rename, or delete objects in the AeroDyn office staff container.
- Lynn Dai should have rights to maintain address information on all users in the AeroDyn containers.
- Kellie Thiele has rights to maintain login scripts for all UAS users, but only Bernie Muelner should have rights to maintain login scripts in the AeroDyn staff container.
- All users in the Accounting, Desktop Publishing, and Marketing departments need rights to use their corresponding Directory Map objects.
- Both the design engineers and the desktop publishing staff need to be able to use the PubData Directory Map object.

Figure 7-39   eDirectory security requirements for the Business Division

Case Project 7-2: Defining Inherited Rights

Fill out an eDirectory IRF Worksheet, similar to the one Eric created in Figure 7-22. (Ask your instructor for a blank form.) Your worksheet should show any IRFs you need to meet the requirements shown previously in Figure 7-22. When you have finished your worksheets, have your instructor check them before continuing to the Hands-on Projects.

HANDS-ON PROJECTS

Hands-on Project 7-1: Setting up UAS Trustee Assignments

Use ConsoleOne to create the following Directory Map objects:

- *ITData*—Set the path to your IT directory.
- *EngData*—Set the path to your Engineer directory.
- *MfgData*—Set the path to your Mfg directory.
- *MgmtData*—Set the path to your Mgmt directory.

Use iManager to set up Eric's trustee assignments shown in Figure 7-21.

Hands-on Project 7-2: Setting up UAS IRFs

Use iManager or ConsoleOne to set up the IRFs Eric identified in Figure 7-22.

Hands-on Project 7-3: Managing Role Based Services

Use the procedure described in this chapter to add your KThiele user to the eDirectory Administration role with a scope of managing objects in the IT OU.

Hands-on Project 7-4: Setting up the Business Division Trustee Assignments

After you have verified your eDirectory trustee and IRF plans with your instructor, use iManager to make the trustee assignments you defined in Case Project 7-1.

Hands-on Project 7-5: Setting up the Business Division IRFs

Use ConsoleOne and iManager to set up the IRFs you defined in Case Project 7-2.

IMPLEMENTING AND MAINTAINING NETWORK PRINTING

After reading this chapter and completing the activities, you will be able to:

♦ Describe the basic process and components of network printing

♦ Explain how Novell Distributed Print Services supports iPrint

♦ Configure printer clients

♦ Define a network printing environment

♦ Troubleshoot network printing

As described in Chapter 1, sharing printers is an important benefit of a network system. Network printing offers cost savings, increased workspace for users, and multiple printer selection options. To become a NetWare CNA, Novell requires you to know how to use iPrint technology and Novell Distributed Printing Services to set up, customize, and maintain a network's printing environment. Novell's iPrint, which is included with Open Enterprise Server, enhances network printing by enabling administrators and users to install, access, and configure network printers through a Web browser. This chapter covers the printing concepts and skills needed to plan, implement, and troubleshoot a network printing environment using NDPS and iPrint technology.

INTRODUCTION TO NETWORK PRINTING

As shown in Figure 8-1, the basic function of network printing is to send output formatted by an application running on the user's computer to a shared printer attached to the network.

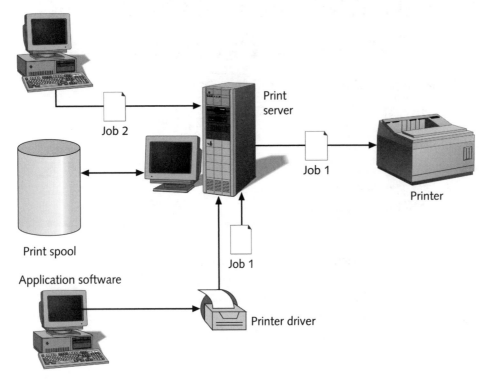

Figure 8-1 Network printing overview

Because a printer can print output from only one application at a time, network printing needs to control the flow of output from multiple user applications to a single network printer. In previous versions of NetWare, network printing has been accomplished by sending output from a printer driver on a user's computer to a print job on a server, where it's held in a print queue until the network printer it needs is available. Print server software running on the NetWare server then transfers the print job to the physical printer attached to the server's printer port or attached remotely to a client computer. This network printing system, known as **queue-based printing**, is still supported by NetWare 6.5. To format and print information with this system, the application running on a client computer must be configured with the correct printer driver for the network printer's make and model. In the queue-based system, you have to select this driver manually and make sure it's up to date. In the following section, you learn how to set up a queue-based printing system in NetWare Administrator.

Overview of the NetWare Queue-Based Printing System

Queue-based printing, available since NetWare 3, was designed to support simple printers and DOS-based applications. Because many older NetWare networks still use queue-based printing, as a CNA, you should be familiar with its basic components and operation. Before setting up a queue-based printing environment, you need to understand how its basic components work together. As shown in Figure 8-2, the queue-based system consists of three major components, discussed in more detail in the following sections:

- Print queue
- Print server
- Printer

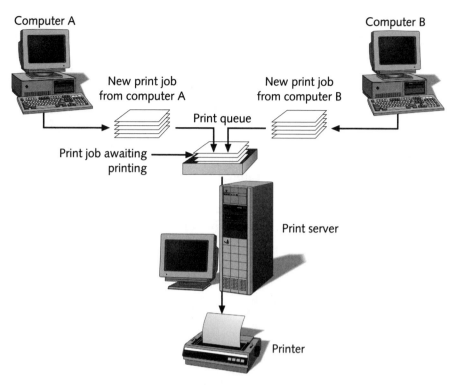

Figure 8-2   The NetWare queue-based printing system

Print Queues

A **print queue** is a network object that represents a holding area for storing output from computers in a form ready to send directly to a printer. As shown in Figure 8-3, multiple computers on a network can use the same printer by storing printer output from each client computer as a separate print job in a print queue. After being stored in the print queue, print jobs are then printed one at a time as the printer becomes available.

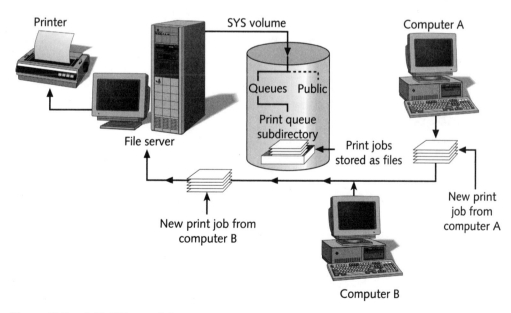

Figure 8-3   A NetWare print queue

In queue-based printing, print jobs are actually files containing output formatted for a printer. In many ways, having a client computer send output to a print queue is similar to storing files on a volume. For example, when saving a file on a server, data is transferred from the client computer to the server and then stored in a file in the specified directory. Because an application's printer output is actually data being transmitted to a printer, placing a job in a print queue is a similar process, in which printer data from the application is stored in a file called a print job.

Just as data files are stored in directories, print job files are stored in print queue directories, which are actually subdirectories of the Queues directory and can be placed on any volume. Because print queues can use a lot of disk space, Novell recommends placing print queues on data volumes, not on the SYS volume. Remember: If the SYS volume fills up, it could bring down the NetWare server. As described later in "Setting Up a Queue-Based Printing System," print queues are created in NetWare Administrator, and at least one print queue is created for each network printer. For client computers that need to print to a specific printer, you use the Add Printer Wizard to configure sending their output to a print queue. DOS-based applications can be directed to send output to a print queue with the NetWare CAPTURE command-line utility. After print jobs have been stored in the print queue, the printer assigned to the print queue prints the jobs in the order they were received. After a job has been printed, it's deleted from the print queue automatically.

One administrative task in network printing is managing jobs in print queues. By default, the network administrator who created the print queue becomes the print queue operator, authorized to rearrange the sequence of print jobs, remove a print job, or place a print job on hold. However, other users besides network administrators can be assigned the role of print queue operator.

Print Servers

A **print server** actually makes queue-based printing happen by sending print jobs from print queues to the assigned printer, as shown in Figure 8-4.

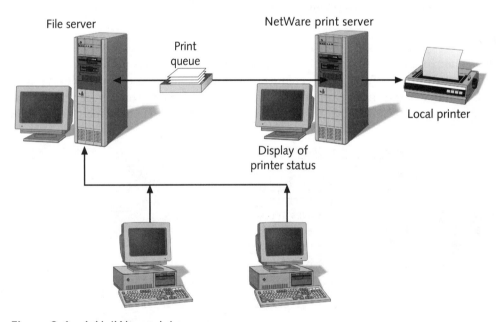

File server   NetWare print server

Print queue

Local printer

Display of printer status

Figure 8-4 A NetWare print server

Printers can be attached directly to the print server or attached remotely through a client or device, such as the HP JetDirect. In addition to printing, print servers are responsible for sending control commands to printers and reporting printer status to the print server operator. By default, the print server operator is the Admin user; however, this role can be delegated to other users in NetWare Administrator. In queue-based printing, each print server is defined by an eDirectory print server object containing the print server name and the names of up to 255 printer objects. After the print server object has been created and configured, NetWare print server software can be loaded and run on the file server by loading the PSERVER.NLM program. (PSERVER.NLM is one of the NetWare Loadable Modules, which were discussed in Chapter 2.)

Printers

Printers come in a wide variety of makes, models, and capabilities. To format and print information, the application running on the client computer must be configured with the correct printer driver for the printer's make and model. Because of the variety of makes and models available, you should have this driver information for configuring network printers so that you can make sure formatted output goes to the correct printer. For example, a client computer might be configured to support both a Lexmark Optra Plus laser printer and a Hewlett-Packard (HP) Deskjet inkjet printer. When a user selects the Lexmark laser printer and prints a document, the network printing configuration must be set up to ensure that the output is sent to the laser printer for which it was formatted.

As shown in Figure 8-5, in queue-based printing, printers can be attached to the network in one of the following ways:

- Locally to the print server
- Remotely through Novell Client
- Directly to the network cable

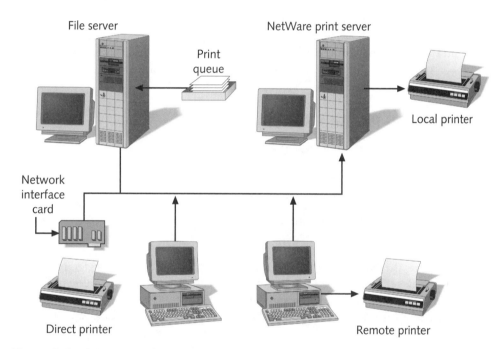

Figure 8-5   Printer attachment options

When configuring the network printing environment, consider the advantages of each attachment method to determine how it affects the way printers are distributed on the network. Many network administrators use a combination of printer attachments, based on the type of printer and its use.

Remotely attached printers are attached to other clients on the network and are also called **manual load printers** because you must load software manually on the client computer to connect the printer to the print server. After the software has been loaded, print jobs can be sent to the remote printer by using the network cable to transmit packets of printed data from the print server to the client with the remotely attached printer. NetWare includes the NPTWIN95 utility, which can be loaded on a Windows 95/98 client computer that has an attached printer. NPTWIN95 receives packets of printer output directed to it from the print server, and then prints the output on the attached printer without interfering with the Windows 95/98 client being used for other processing.

The advantage of using remote or manual load printers attached to client computers is that you can select a convenient location for the printer, making it easier for users to retrieve printed output. The disadvantages of these printers include the lack of support for attaching remote printers to Windows 2000 and XP computers, the additional setup time to load NPTWIN95 on Windows 95/98 computers, the need to leave the client computer on to access network printers, and the possible decrease in printing performance for large graphical print jobs. This performance decrease is caused by applications running on the client computer and the extra load on the network cable when sending printer output from the print queue to the network printer.

Locally attached printers are attached directly to a printer port on the NetWare server running the print server. In NetWare, these printers are also referred to as **automatic load printers** because there's no need to load additional software, as with remote or manual load printers. When using local or automatic load printers, the output is sent directly from the print server to the printer through ports on the NetWare server. Local printers can be attached to the **parallel port (LPTn)** or **serial port (COMn)** of the server running the print management software. Compared to remote or manual load printers, the advantages of local or automatic load printers include better printing performance and reduced network traffic. The improved performance is a result of less software overhead because the print server doesn't have to communicate with a client computer. Network traffic is reduced because print jobs don't need to be sent from the print server running on a NetWare server to a printer attached to a client on the network.

Network attached printers have their own built-in network card, which allows them to communicate directly with computers on the network. Today, network attached printers are rapidly becoming the most common type of network printer. However, the NetWare queue-based printing system was designed before the age of network attached printers, and the print server software isn't designed to communicate directly with network attached printers. To use a network attached printer with the NetWare print server, the printer must be configured to appear as a remote or manual load printer. You learn more about using network attached printers in "Using the Open Enterprise iPrint System" later in this chapter.

Setting Up a Queue-Based Printing System

Setting up a queue-based printing system involves these basic steps:

1. Create a print queue for each printer.

2. Create an eDirectory printer object to represent each printer.

3. Create a print server object to send output from print queues to the corresponding printer.

4. Load the print server and any remote printer software.

Although Novell still supports the queue-based printing system, it hasn't included management components for it in ConsoleOne or iManager, so you need to use NetWare Administrator. In the following activities, you use NetWare Administrator to perform these setup steps so that you can create print queue, print server, and printer objects. To load the print server software (PSERVER.NLM) on a NetWare 6.5 Open Enterprise server, IPX must be installed on the NetWare server (see Chapter 2). In addition, only one iteration of the print server can be loaded at one time.

If you're using a shared classroom server, you need to coordinate the final activity of loading and testing your print server with other students in the class. If you're using a dedicated NetWare server, you can perform all these activities on your server. If you don't have a printer attached, you can still perform the activities and view the output in your print queue.

NOTE

Activity 8-1: Creating a Print Queue

ACTIVITY

Time Required: 10 minutes

Objective: Set up a queue-based printing system.

Requirements: A Windows XP computer with Novell Client installed

Description: Before setting up a queue-based printer, you need to define the names of the print queue, printer, and print server and determine in what context to place these objects. After determining this information, Eric Kenton used NetWare Administrator to create queue-based printing objects. In this activity, you use NetWare Administrator to create a print queue object in your UAS tree.

1. Start your Windows computer, and log in to eDirectory with your administrative user name and password.

2. Start NetWare Administrator and, if necessary, open a browse window to the UAS container.

3. Follow these steps to create a print queue object in the IT OU:

   a. If necessary, double-click the **UAS** container to display the OUs.

   b. Click the **IT** OU, and then press **Insert** to open the New Object dialog box.

   c. Scroll down and double-click the **Print Queue** object to open the Create Print Queue dialog box, shown in Figure 8-6.

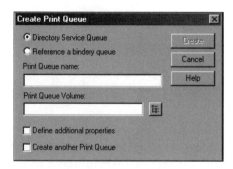

Figure 8-6   The Create Print Queue dialog box

   d. Type **IT_Q** in the Print Queue name text box. (If you're using a shared classroom server, add your assigned student number to the beginning of the queue name.)

   e. Click the **browse** button next to the Print Queue Volume text box.

   f. Double-click your **CORP** volume object in the Available objects section.

   g. Click the **Create** button to create the print queue and return to the NetWare Administrator browse window.

4. Follow these steps to add the ITMgrs group as the print queue operator:

   a. Navigate to and then double-click the **IT_Q** print queue object to open the Print Queue dialog box.

   b. Click the **Operator** button (see Figure 8-7), and record any existing print queue operators here (write multiple names on the line if necessary):

   _____

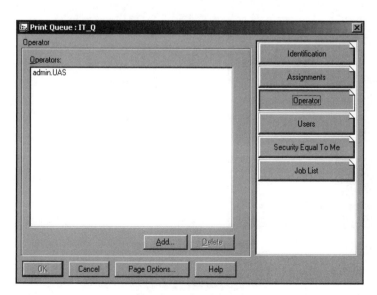

Figure 8-7   The Print Queue dialog box

    c. Click the **Add** button to open the Select Object dialog box.

    d. Double-click the **ITMgrs** group to add it as a print queue operator.

5. Click the **Users** button, and record the existing print queue users here:

_____

6. Notice that by default the container where the print queue is located is made a user of the print queue. Because your IT.UAS container is a user, all users in the IT OU can send output to this print queue. Click **OK** to save your changes and return to the NetWare Administrator browse window.

7. If you're continuing to the next activity, leave NetWare Administrator open and stay logged in. If not, exit NetWare Administrator, and log out.

Activity 8-2: Creating a Printer Object

Time Required: 10 minutes

Objective: Set up a queue-based printing system.

Requirements: Same as Activity 8-1

Description: Now that you've created a print queue and defined users and operators, the next step is to create and define the printer object, the printer attachment method, the port and interrupt, and the print queue from which the printer gets its output. In this activity, you use NetWare Administrator to create and configure a printer object.

1. If necessary, log in to eDirectory with your administrative user name and password, start NetWare Administrator, and open a browse window to the UAS container.

2. Follow these steps to create a printer object in the IT.UAS container:

    a. Click the **IT** OU, and then press **Insert** to open the New Object dialog box.

    b. Scroll down and double-click the **Printer (Non NDPS)** object to open the Create Printer dialog box.

    c. Enter **IT_P** in the Printer name text box, and click the **Define additional properties** check box.

    d. Click the **Create** button to create the printer object and open the Printer (Non NDPS) dialog box shown in Figure 8-8.

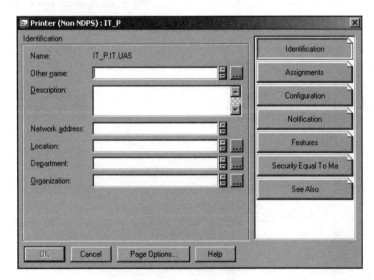

Figure 8-8   Configuring the printer object in the Printer (Non NDPS) dialog box

3. For your newly created printer object to receive output, follow these steps to identify which print queue the printer will use:

    a. Click the **Assignments** button, and record any print queue assignments here:

    _____

    b. Click the **Add** button to open the Select Object dialog box.

    c. Double-click the **IT_Q** print queue in the Available objects section to add it to the print queue assignment.

4. Follow these steps to define the attachment method and the printer port and interrupt:

    a. Click the **Configuration** button to display configuration information (see Figure 8-9). By default, the printer is defined as a parallel printer with a text banner type. The service interval of 5 means that the print server checks the print queue every five seconds for any jobs to be printed. The "Minimize form changes within print queues" setting tells the printer to print jobs starting with forms number 0 before checking for jobs with forms number 1, and so on.

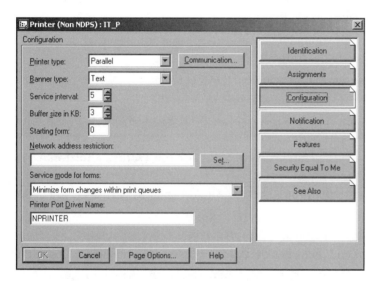

Figure 8-9   Viewing printer configuration information

    b. To set the port and interrupt information, click the **Communication** button to open the Parallel Communication dialog box shown in Figure 8-10. The default port is LPT1 with the Polled interrupt setting. With the polled method, the computer checks the printer frequently to see whether it's ready. This method prevents the printer from interrupting the computer processor every time it's ready to print and can improve server performance.

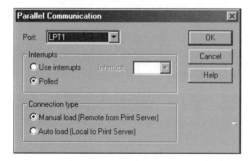

Figure 8-10   The Parallel Communication dialog box

    c. The connection type (attachment method) is also defined by default. Because your classroom printer will be attached directly to the server, click the **Auto load (Local to Print Server)** option button.

d. Click **OK** to save your changes and return to the Printer (Non NDPS) dialog box.

e. Click **OK** to return to the NetWare Administrator browse window.

5. If you're continuing to the next activity, leave NetWare Administrator open and stay logged in. If not, exit NetWare Administrator, and log out.

Activity 8-3: Creating a Print Server Object

Time Required: 10 minutes

Objective: Set up a queue-based printing system.

Requirements: Same as Activity 8-1

Description: For queue-based printing to work, the print server software needs to know what printers it controls and who the print server operators and users are. This information is supplied when you create and configure an eDirectory print server object. In this activity, you create a print server object for the UAS container and then configure it to manage the IT_P printer.

1. If necessary, log in to eDirectory with your administrative user name and password, start NetWare Administrator, and open a browse window to the UAS container.

2. Follow these steps to create a print server object in your UAS container:

   a. Click the **UAS** container, if necessary, and press **Insert** to open the New Object dialog box.

   b. Scroll down and double-click the **Print Server (Non NDPS)** object to open the Create Print Server dialog box.

   c. Enter **UAS_PS** in the Print Server name text box, and click the **Define additional properties** check box.

   d. Click the **Create** button to create the print server object and open the Printer (Non NDPS) dialog box.

3. Follow these steps to assign your printer to the new print server:

   a. Click the **Assignments** button, and then click the **Add** button to open the Select Object dialog box.

   b. Double-click the **IT** OU in the Browse context section to display the printer in the Available objects section.

   c. Double-click the **IT_P** printer in the Available objects section.

4. Follow these steps to document the default users and operators of the print server and make the ITMgrs group a print server operator:

   a. Click the **Users** button, and record the users of the print server here:

   _____

   b. Click the **Operator** button, and record the name of the print queue operator here:

   _____

   c. Click the **Add** button to open the Select Object dialog box, and then double-click the **IT** OU in the Browse context section.

   d. Double-click the **ITMgrs** group in the Available objects section.

5. Click **OK** to save your print server configuration and return to NetWare Administrator.

6. Exit NetWare Administrator. If you're continuing to the next activity, stay logged in. If not, log out.

Activity 8-4: Setting Up a Network Printer on a User Computer

Time Required: 10 minutes

Objective: Set up a queue-based printing system.

Requirements: Same as Activity 8-1

Description: There are two methods for sending output from a Windows client computer to the print queue. You can create a network printer by using the Add Printer function, or you can redirect a local printer port to the NetWare print queue. The disadvantage of the second method is that you have to be sure the network printer uses the same printer driver as the local printer. If you send output to a network printer that's formatted for another type of printer, you might generate a lot of garbage output. It's usually better to create a network printer that uses the correct printer driver for the queue you have selected. In this activity, you create a printer that sends output to the IT_Q print queue.

1. Click **Start**, **Control Panel**, and if necessary, click **Switch to Classic View**.

2. Double-click **Printers and Faxes**, and under Printer Tasks at the left, click **Add a printer** to start the Add Printer Wizard. Click **Next** to continue.

3. Click the **Network printer** option button, and then click **Next**.

4. Click **Next** to display the Browse for Printer window. Double-click the **NetWare Network** option, and then double-click the **Novell Directory Services** option.

5. Double-click your **UAS** container to display the OUs, and then double-click the **IT** OU to display the printer and print queue objects. Click the **IT_Q** print queue object, and then click **Next** to display a message informing you that the server doesn't have the correct printer drivers installed. Click **OK** to return to the Add Printer Wizard.

6. Select the manufacturer and printer for your classroom printer, and click **OK** to continue. If you see a message that the driver is already installed, click the **Keep existing driver (recommended)** option.

7. If necessary, click **Yes** to use this printer as the default, and then click **Next** to display the summary window. Click **Finish** to return to the Printers and Faxes window with the new printer displayed.

8. Start WordPad, and create a simple document. Print the document to the IT_P printer, and exit WordPad. (This step places your output in the print queue, but no output is printed until you load the print server in Activity 8-5.)

9. Follow these steps to verify that the output is in the print queue:

   a. Start NetWare Administrator, and open a browse window to the UAS container.

   b. Navigate to and then double-click the **IT_Q** print queue object to open the Print Queue dialog box.

   c. Click the **Job List** button to display all jobs in the print queue. Your new entry should be listed. Record the job name here:

   _____

   d. Click **Cancel** to return to the NetWare Administrator browse window.

10. Exit NetWare Administrator, and log out.

Activity 8-5: Loading and Testing Your Print Server

Time Required: 10 minutes

Objective: Set up a queue-based printing system.

Requirements: Access to the NetWare server console containing your print server object and IPX running on the NetWare server to load the print server software

Description: Before network printing can start, you need to run the PSERVER.NLM print server software on the NetWare server. Because only one print server can run on a NetWare server at one time, you need to coordinate this activity with other students in your class. In this activity, you load the print server on the UASHOST NetWare server and retrieve the output.

To perform this activity and test the print server, you need to have the printer model you selected in Step 6 of Activity 8-4 attached to the NetWare server's LPT port.

1. If necessary, install IPX on your server by performing the following steps from the server console.

2. Load PSERVER.NLM with one of these options:

    a. If you're using a shared classroom server, wait for your turn to access the server console. Type **PSERVER .CN=##UAS_PS.OU=UAS.O=CLASS** at the system prompt (replacing ## with your assigned student number), and press **Enter**.

    b. If you're using a dedicated server, type **PSERVER .CN=UAS_PS.O=UAS** at the system prompt, and press **Enter**.

3. Click the **Printer Status** option, and press **Enter** to display a printer list.

4. Press **Enter** to display a printer status window. Your document should now be printing on the classroom printer.

5. Press the **left arrow** key to highlight the Printer control option, and press **Enter** to display a printer control menu.

6. Highlight the **Form feed** option, and press **Enter** to eject a page.

7. Press **Esc** twice to return to the Available Options menu.

8. Follow these steps to unload the print server:

    a. Click the **Print Server Information** option, and press **Enter** to display the Printer Server Information and Status window.

    b. Press **Enter** to display the Print Server Status Options menu.

    c. Click the **Unload after active print jobs** option, and press **Enter** to unload the print server and return to the console screen.

9. Retrieve your printed output.

Troubleshooting Queue-Based Printing

Despite your best efforts, with so many components having to work together, things can go wrong and result in network printing problems. As with any form of problem solving, approaching the problem in a systematic, logical way usually produces the best results. Typically, when you begin troubleshooting a network printing problem, you should gather information about the problem and how it occurs. Part of this process is determining whether the particular printing process worked in the past. If so, you need to look for anything that has changed, such as printer drivers, printer or print queue configurations, or physical moving of equipment. If the printing process hasn't been used previously, look for problems in the initial setup and configuration. For example, one of the most common problems in setting up queue-based printing is forgetting to assign the printer to a print queue. In this case, print jobs are sent to the print queue but aren't printed. The most obvious sign of this problem is a lot of print jobs in the print queue. If printing has been working in the past, before spending a lot of time digging into the details, you should try these Novell-recommended quick-fix techniques:

1. If the printer status is offline or out of paper:

   ■ Turn the printer off and on, and then retry the output.

   ■ Check the printer self-test to make sure the printer functions properly.

   ■ Check the printer cover and paper feed.

   ■ Check the cable type and connections.

   ■ Test the cable with a working printer.

2. If printer output is garbled:

   ■ Check the printer software setting and language.

   ■ Check that the correct printer driver is installed on the computer.

   ■ Turn the printer off and on, and then retry the output.

3. If print jobs aren't going to the print queue:

   ■ Check the print queue setting for the printer on the user's computer.

   ■ Check the language setting on the printer.

If the printing problems can't be corrected with these quick fixes, try these steps to determine whether the problem occurs before or after the print job reaches the print queue:

EXAMPLE

1. Stop print jobs from leaving the print queue by following these steps:

   ■ If necessary, log in as the network administrator or print queue operator, start NetWare Administrator, and expand the container where the print queue is located.

   ■ Right-click the print queue, and click Details to open the Print Queue dialog box, similar to the one shown previously in Figure 8-7.

   ■ Click to clear the Allow service by current print servers check box.

   ■ Click OK to save the setting and minimize NetWare Administrator.

   ■ Use an application such as Notepad to send a job to the printer.

   ■ Maximize NetWare Administrator, right-click the printer, and click Details.

   ■ Click the Job List button to display print jobs.

2. If the print job never arrives at the print queue or if the print job status indicates "Adding" and doesn't change to "Ready," the problem is probably in the computer. Check printer redirection for the computer by following these steps:

   ■ Open Control Panel and open the Printers and Faxes window.

   ■ Right-click the printer being checked, and then click Properties.

   ■ Click the Ports tab, and verify that the print queue is correctly identified in the Port and Printer columns.

3. If the print job is in the print queue and in Ready status, follow these steps to enable service by the print server and monitor the printer status:

   ■ Maximize NetWare Administrator, expand the container where the print queue is located, and click to select the Allow service by current print servers check box.

- Open the Print Queue dialog box (as described in Step 1), click the Assignments button, and verify that the print queue is assigned to a printer and print server.

- Verify that the print server is loaded on the NetWare server by going to the server console and pressing Ctrl+Esc to display all modules. If necessary, load the print server as described in Activity 8-5.

4. If the print job is printed but there's no output from the printer, check the following:

- Turn the printer off and on.

- Check the printer cable.

- Check the printer language settings.

- Check the print server configuration, and then unload and reload the print server. Reloading the print server can sometimes correct printing problems.

Printing problems can be tricky to find and require a lot of checking and experimenting. The more experience you have, the more quickly you can recognize common problems and figure out solutions. If the problem persists, try re-creating printer objects and then adding the new printer to the computer. For a number of reasons, printer objects have been known to become corrupted, and the only solution is to re-create them. As with all troubleshooting, change only one item at a time, and then test the system. Making several changes at once can further complicate the problem, making it harder to solve.

USING THE OPEN ENTERPRISE iPRINT SYSTEM

Although network printing still performs the same basic functions, printer technology and software have advanced to give users more capability and flexibility in their printing options. Novell's Open Enterprise Server (OES) **iPrint** takes advantage of the latest network printing technology so that users can print to any network printer they have rights to, regardless of the printer's location or the client computer's OS. As shown in Figure 8-11, the iPrint system combines Novell Distributed Printing Service (NDPS) components and the **Internet Printing Protocol (IPP)** standard to make it possible to use printers across the Internet as easily as printers attached to the local network.

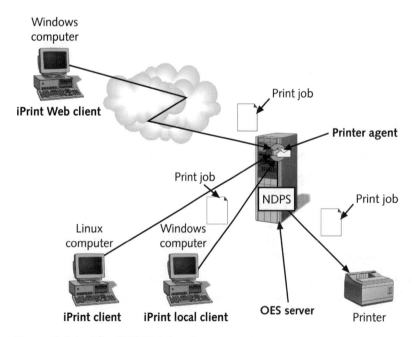

Figure 8-11   The OES iPrint system

Additional iPrint benefits include the following:

- Broad vendor support; iPrint works with equipment from most printer vendors
- Capability to access printers across the Internet as well as within the LAN
- Encrypted print services to protect sensitive data with SSL and TLS (described in Chapter 11)
- Capability to print from any client platform, including Windows, Linux, and Macintosh
- Global control of printing with eDirectory security
- Web-based printer management and user controls
- Automatic downloading of the most current printer driver software for client computers

Practically, these benefits mean that after the iPrint system is up and running, users have access to office printers across the Internet, so mobile employees can print from a hotel room or their homes as easily as they can print from the local network.

Before implementing iPrint, you need to install the iPrint software on at least one NetWare 6.5 OES server. If you didn't select iPrint during the initial installation, you can install it later in iManager by following these steps:

EXAMPLE

1. Start iManager and log in with your administrative user name and password.
2. Click the Install and Upgrade link, and then click the Install NetWare 6.5 Products option.
3. Click the Remote Product Install option on the right.
4. Browse to the location of the Operating System CD 1, and click OK.
5. Browse to and select the OES where you want to install iPrint, and click Next.
6. Authenticate as the Admin user with the Supervisor right to that server.
7. In the Components window, click only iPrint, and then click Next.
8. In the Summary window, click Copy files to install the iPrint software, and then insert the Products CD 2 when prompted.
9. When the iPrint installation is finished, exit iManager.

In the following sections, you learn about the NDPS components used in iPrint and how to set them up on your NetWare 6.5 OES server.

Setting Up iPrint Components

Before setting up a Novell Open Enterprise Server network printing environment, you need to understand the basic iPrint components and how they work together. The OES iPrint system is based on **Novell Distributed Print Services (NDPS)**. NDPS is the result of a joint effort by Novell, Hewlett-Packard, and Xerox to develop a distributed network printing system based on the International Standards Organization (ISO) 10175 Document Printing Application (DPA) standard. Because this standard is supported by most printer manufacturers, NDPS supports existing and future printer products. NDPS is an improvement over earlier NetWare printing solutions because it makes network printing easier to configure, use, and manage. In addition, as part of Novell's OneNet strategy, NDPS is the foundation of iPrint, which is based on the Internet Printing Protocol (IPP) standard. Because iPrint uses the IPP standard, NDPS printers can be accessed and managed across the Internet and within the corporate intranet.

NDPS is designed to simplify setting up and maintaining network printing by taking advantage of new client software and more sophisticated printers. As shown in Figure 8-12, NDPS consists of the following components:

- NDPS Brokers
- Print Manager (also called NDPS Manager)

- NDPS printer agents
- Printer gateways

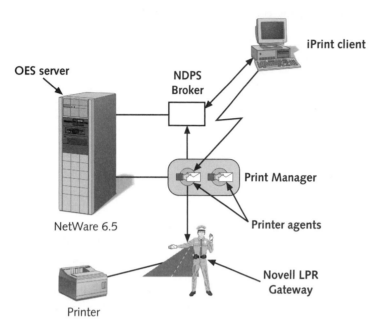

Figure 8-12 NDPS printing components used in iPrint

Each printer in NDPS is represented by a printer agent on the network. A **printer agent** is software that acts as a print server for its associated physical printer. The printer agent queues print jobs from client computers and then prints the jobs when their associated physical printers become available. Printer agents can run on the NetWare 6.5 server or be embedded in the physical printer. When printer agents are embedded in the physical printer, you simply connect the printer to the network to make it available to all users. After it's connected to the network, the NDPS printer agent running on the printer communicates directly with client computers so that users can send output to the printer.

Because most printers currently on the market don't have embedded printer agents, however, Open Enterprise Server includes NDPS Manager. **Print Manager** (previously called the NDPS Manager) is the software for running printer agents on the NetWare 6.5 server, which enables printers without embedded printer agents to be attached to the network with the local, remote, or direct (network) attachment methods. Printer agent software running on the Print Manager transfers data from the user's computer to the printer through a **printer gateway**. NetWare includes NDPS printer gateways for a variety of printer models and attachment methods.

The **NDPS Broker** makes installing printers on computers easier by downloading the necessary printer driver automatically to the user's computer during printer installation. In addition, with the NDPS Broker, users can search the network for printers that have certain capabilities, such as color printing, and view printer status quickly so that they can send jobs to printers that aren't busy. In the following sections, you learn how to set up and configure a NetWare NDPS printing system to meet the needs of UAS users. In subsequent activities, you apply these NDPS components to setting up iPrint for the IT Department. In the end-of-chapter projects, you apply the techniques you have learned to plan and set up iPrint printing for your version of the UAS network.

Creating and Working with NDPS Brokers

Printer agents need to register their printing services on the network and be able to send messages to users and operators. In addition, clients need to be able to locate printers and download the correct printer driver software. The NDPS Broker provides these functions to all printer agents by including the following services:

- *Resource Management Service (RMS)*—This service stores network resources, such as software drivers, fonts, and forms, in a central location and then provides these resources to clients that request them. NDPS uses RMS to download printer drivers and configuration data to clients.

- *Event Notification Service (ENS)*—Printer agents use this service to send printer status messages to users via popup windows, e-mail, or log files.

- *Service Registry Services (SRS)*—This service allows NDPS printers to advertise their presence so that NDPS clients can access them. SRS also maintains printer information, such as the device type, device name, and network address. SRS reduces network traffic because printers don't need to broadcast their presence on the network by sending out Service Advertising Packets (SAPs) at frequent intervals.

Before creating and running printer agents, an NDPS Broker must be running on the local network. If it's not or if the nearest NDPS Broker requires network traffic to go across more than three routers, you need to create and load another NDPS Broker on the NetWare server. An NDPS Broker consists of an eDirectory object and software loaded on the server. You can use iManager to create an NDPS Broker object and then load the Broker software on the server from the server console or in Remote Manager. When creating an NDPS Broker object, you must use a user name that has Supervisor rights to the SYS volume to be able to create the RMS database.

Activity 8-6: (Optional) Creating an NDPS Broker

Time Required: 10 minutes

Objective: Create and configure an NDPS Broker.

Requirements: A Windows XP or SUSE Linux 10 computer with Supervisor rights to the UAS container

If you're using a shared classroom server, your instructor will supply an administrative user name or might perform this activity as a demonstration.

Description: In this activity, you use iManager to create an NDPS Broker object for the UAS container. This activity is optional because to create a Broker object, you must be able to log in to the Novell network with the Supervisor right to the SYS volume.

1. If necessary, start your computer and log on with your local user name and password. If you're using a Windows XP system, click to enable the **Workstation Only** check box, and enter your user name and password for logging on to the local Windows system.

2. Start your Web browser, and start iManager. Log in to iManager with your administrative user name and password.

3. Click to expand the **iPrint** heading, and then click the **Create Broker** link to open the Create Broker window.

4. Type **UAS_Broker** in the Broker name text box.

5. If the UAS container isn't displayed in the Container name text box, click the **Object Selector** button, and then click the **UAS** container.

6. Click the **Object Selector** button next to the RMS volume text box, and then click the **UASHOST_SYS** volume. (You might have problems if you select other volumes.)

7. Click **OK** to create the Broker object, and then click **OK** to close the "The Create Broker request succeeded" message and return to the iManager window.

8. Click the **Exit** button on the toolbar to return to the iManager Login window. You can stay logged in for the next activity.

Loading the NDPS Broker

For an NDPS Broker to perform its functions, the Broker software needs to be loaded on the server using the eDirectory configuration specified in the Broker object. Loading the Broker software before creating and loading other iPrint/NDPS components, such as the Print Manager, is important. The Broker can be loaded directly from the NetWare server console or from a computer using Remote Manager. In the following activity, you use Remote Manager to load the Broker software on the NetWare 6.5 server. If you're using a shared classroom server, your instructor might perform this activity as a demonstration.

Activity 8-7: (Optional) Loading the NDPS Broker

Time Required: 10 minutes

Objective: Load an NDPS Broker in Remote Manager.

Requirements: Same as Activity 8-6

Description: In this activity, you use Remote Manager to load the NDPS Broker on your NetWare 6.5 OES server. To perform this activity, you need access to the NetWare 6.5 server console. If you're using a shared classroom server, this activity is optional because your instructor might have already loaded the Broker on your classroom server.

1. If necessary, start your computer and log on with your local user name and password. If you're using a Windows XP system, click the **Workstation Only** check box, and enter your user name and password for logging on to the local Windows system.

2. Start Remote Manager, and log on with your administrative user name and password.

3. Click the **Console Screens** link under the Manage Server heading to display the Console Screens window shown in Figure 8-13.

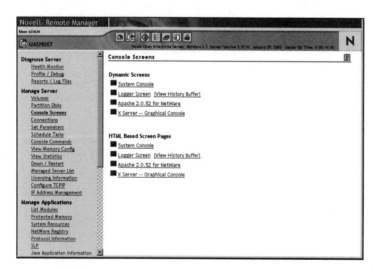

Figure 8-13   The Console Screens window

4. Click the **System Console** link under the HTML Based Screen Pages heading to display the System Console window shown in Figure 8-14.

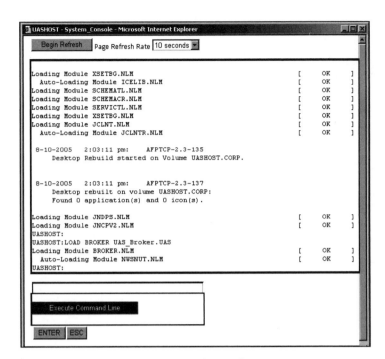

Figure 8-14 The System Console window

5. Click in the text box above the Execute Command Line button and enter the **LOAD BROKER UAS_Broker.UAS** command.

6. Click the **Execute Command Line** button.

7. Click the **Begin Refresh** button at the top left to refresh the console screen.

8. Close the System Console window, and click the **Exit** button to end your Remote Manager session. You can stay logged on for the next activity.

Configuring the NDPS Broker

One of the major tasks of the NDPS Broker is to download driver software for printer agents. To do this, the NDPS Broker maintains a database of printer driver software. Although Open Enterprise Server ships with printer drivers for most printers, as new printers appear on the market or new versions of printer drivers are released, you might need to update the Broker's driver database. You can use the following steps in iManager to view your Broker's printer driver database and update it with new drivers:

EXAMPLE

1. Expand the iPrint heading and click the Manage Broker link.

2. Select your broker, and then click the correct driver link in the Resource Management Service tab to display the default drivers, as shown in Figure 8-15.

3. Click the Add From File button to add a new driver file from a CD or disk or the Add From System button to add a printer driver from your desktop OS. The latter option is convenient for adding a Windows XP printer driver to the Broker's database.

To use iManager to configure an NDPS Broker, you need to have the iPrint client installed on your computer. In the following activities, you install the iPrint client on your computer, and then use iManager to view your Broker's printer drivers and add drivers.

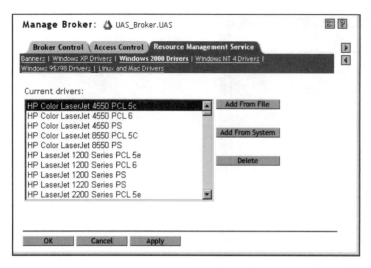

Figure 8-15 Printer drivers for the NDPS Broker

Activity 8-8: Installing the iPrint Client

Time Required: 10 minutes

Objective: Install the iPrint client.

Requirements: A Windows XP computer and completion of Activity 8-7

This activity is required to perform subsequent activities.

Description: In this activity, you install the iPrint client on your Windows XP computer.

1. If necessary, start your computer, and log on with your local user name and password. If you're using a Windows XP system, click to enable the **Workstation Only** check box, and enter your user name and password for logging on to the local Windows system.

2. Start your Web browser, and enter the URL **https://IPaddress/ipp** (substituting the IP address of your NetWare 6.5 server for *IPaddress*) to open the iPrint client window shown in Figure 8-16.

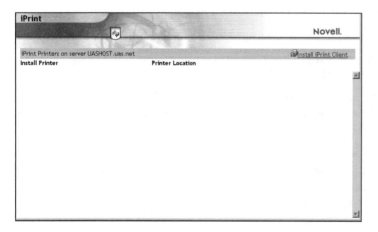

Figure 8-16 The iPrint client window

3. Click the **Install iPrint Client** link at the top right to open the File Download dialog box, and follow the on-screen prompts to download the file.

4. Click the **Open** button to display the Install iPrint client startup window.

5. Click **Next** to install the client. When the Install Complete message is displayed, click **Finish** to complete the iPrint installation.

6. If necessary, close the iPrint client window, and stay logged on for the next activity.

Activity 8-9: (Optional) Configuring the NDPS Broker

Time Required: 10 minutes

Objective: Configure an NDPS Broker.

Requirements: Completion of Activity 8-7

Description: In this activity, you use iManager to configure the Broker object, created in Activity 8-7, to add a new printer driver.

8

1. If necessary, start your computer, and log on with your local user name and password. If you're using a Windows XP system, click to enable the **Workstation Only** check box, and enter your user name and password for logging on to the local Windows system.

2. Start iManager, and log in with your administrative user name and password.

3. Click to expand the **iPrint** heading, and then click the **Manage Broker** link.

4. Click the **Object Selector** button next to the NDPS Broker name text box, click the **UAS_Broker** object, and then click **OK** to display the Manage Broker window shown in Figure 8-17.

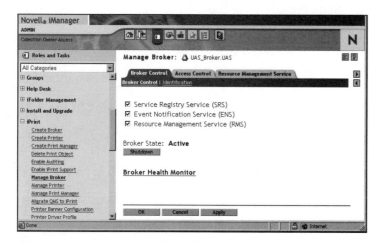

Figure 8-17 The Manage Broker window

5. Click the **Resource Management Service** tab to display the Banners window.

6. Click the **Windows XP Drivers** link to display the currently available drivers. If you have any existing XP drivers, record them here:

_____

7. Follow these steps to add a Windows XP driver for your printer to the Current drivers window:

   a. Click the **Add From System** button to display a list of drivers in the XP system.

   b. Scroll down and click the driver that best matches your network printer. (If you aren't using an actual network printer, click to select the Lexmark Optra R Plus Series driver.)

   c. Click **OK** to add the selected driver to the Current drivers window.

8. Repeat Step 7 to add any drivers needed for your printer configuration.

9. Click **OK** to save your changes. Leave iManager open and stay logged in for the next activity.

Creating the Print Manager

NDPS-enabled printers have printer agent software embedded in the physical printer, but non-NDPS printers don't, so their printer agent software must run on a NetWare server. Print Manager consists of software and an eDirectory object used to create, manage, and run printer agents for printers without embedded printer agents. The eDirectory object contains configuration information that tells Print Manager software where to store print jobs and which users have rights to perform management tasks. After the Print Manager object is created, Print Manager software needs to be loaded on the server to create and run printer agents. Print Manager also enables administrators to manage and configure printer agents from the NetWare server console. Figure 8-18 shows the relationship between Print Manager, printer agents, and physical printers.

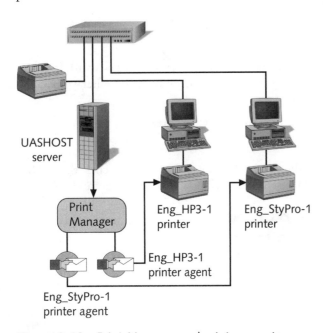

Figure 8-18   Print Manager and printer agents

 Only one Print Manager at a time can be loaded on a NetWare server.

NOTE

There's no limit on the number of printer agents that can be controlled from one Print Manager, but a large network can have multiple Print Managers running on separate NetWare servers to delegate administrative tasks or reduce network traffic across routers and WANs, as shown in Figure 8-19.

When printers don't have embedded printer agent software, you need to create and load a Print Manager object in the eDirectory tree before creating printer agents. For the UAS network, the UAS_NDPSM object contains configuration and security information needed to load Print Manager software. When configuring this object, Eric selected the CORP rather than the SYS volume as the location for the print job database. Using a volume other than SYS for storing print jobs protects the SYS volume from filling up with print jobs waiting to be printed. If the SYS volume becomes full, the NetWare server will go down, with the possible loss of data and productivity.

Because of Novell's OneNet strategy, NDPS printer management tasks have been included in iManager rather than ConsoleOne; NetWare Administrator still retains NDPS management functions from earlier NetWare versions. Although NetWare Administrator or iManager can be used to create NDPS objects, Eric elected to use iManager to get more experience with Novell's OneNet strategy. After creating the Print Manager object,

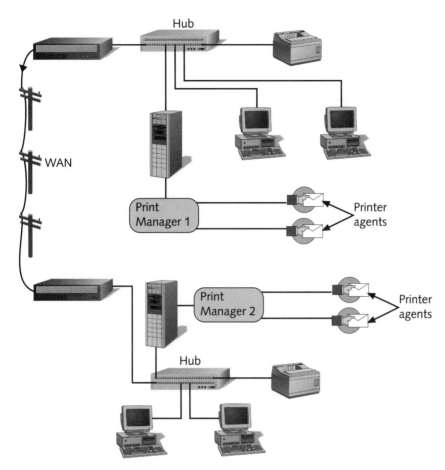

Figure 8-19   Multiple Print Managers

Eric activated it by loading the Print Manager software on the UASHOST server and updating the startup files. In the following activity, you use iManager to create a Print Manager for your version of the UAS network.

Activity 8-10: Creating a Print Manager

Time Required: 10 minutes

Objective: Create and configure a Print Manager.

Requirements: A Windows XP or SUSE Linux 10 computer and your assigned administrative user name. If you're using a dedicated NetWare 6.5 server, you need to have loaded your NDPS Broker by completing Activity 8-7. If you're using a shared classroom server, your instructor should have already loaded the NDPS Broker.

Description: In this activity, you use iManager to create a Print Manager for your UAS container.

Because the classroom server can have only one Print Manager loaded at a time, you must use the UAS_NDPS object set up by your instructor, rather than your own Print Manager object, to create printer agents.

NOTE

1. If necessary, start your computer, and log on with your local user name and password. If you're using a Windows XP system, click to enable the **Workstation Only** check box, and enter your user name and password for logging on to the local Windows system.

2. If necessary, start iManager, and log on with your administrative user name and password.

3. Click to expand the **iPrint** heading, and then click the **Create Print Manager** link to open the Create Print Manager window shown in Figure 8-20.

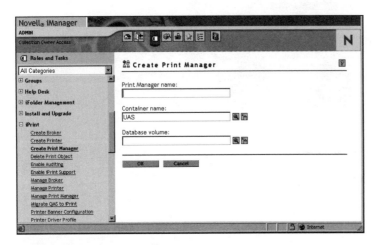

Figure 8-20   The Create Print Manager window

4. Enter **UAS_PrtMgr##** (replacing ## with your assigned student number) in the Print Manager name text box.

5. If your UAS container isn't displayed in the Container name text box, click the **Object Selector** button, and then click your **UAS** container.

6. Click the **Object Selector** button next to the Database volume text box, and click the **UASHOST_CORP** volume.

7. Click **OK** to create the Print Manager object, and then click **OK** to return to the iManager main window.

8. Click the **Exit** button on the toolbar to return to the iManager Login window.

9. Close your Web browser, and stay logged in for the next activity.

Loading Print Manager Software

Before creating the other NDPS objects, both the NDPS Broker and Print Manager components need to be loaded on the NetWare server. In Activity 8-7, you learned how to use Remote Manager to load the UAS_BROKER software on the NetWare 6.5 server. In the following activity, you perform a similar process to load Print Manager software.

Activity 8-11: (Optional) Loading Print Manager Software

Time Required: 10 minutes

Objective: Load Print Manager software in Remote Manager.

Requirements: Completion of Activity 8-7 and the Supervisor right to the NetWare 6.5 server; this activity is intended for a dedicated NetWare 6.5 server

Description: In this activity, you use Remote Manager to load the Print Manager you created in Activity 8-10 on the NetWare 6.5 OES server.

If you're using a shared classroom server, your instructor might demonstrate this process, as only one Print Manager can be loaded on a NetWare server.

1. If necessary, start your computer, and log on with your local user name and password. If you're using a Windows XP system, click to enable the **Workstation Only** check box, and enter your user name and password for logging on to the local Windows system.

2. Start Remote Manager, and log on with your administrative user name and password.

3. Click the **Console Screens** link under the Manage Server heading to display the Console Screens window shown previously in Figure 8-13.

4. Click the **System Console** link under the HTML Based Screen Pages heading to display the System Console window.

5. Click in the text box above the Execute Command Line button and enter the **LOAD NDPSM .UAS_PrtMgr.UAS** command.

6. Click the **Execute Command Line** button.

7. Click the **Begin Refresh** button at the top left to refresh the console screen.

8. Close the System Console window, and click the **Exit** button to end your Remote Manager session. You can stay logged on for the next activity.

Creating Printer Agents

As described previously, printer agents are software components that represent network printers, forming the core of the NDPS architecture; each physical printer on the network must be represented by a printer agent. Printer agents perform the following basic functions for a networked printer:

- Receive spooled output from applications running on client computers and store the output as a print job in a database on the NetWare server

- Act as a print server by sending print jobs from the server database to the printer

- Provide printer status and control information to network clients through the Broker

For non-NDPS printers, such as the UAS printers, the printer agent is contained in the Print Manager software running on the NetWare 6.5 server. This software acts as a liaison between the physical network printer it represents and the client computer (see Figure 8-21).

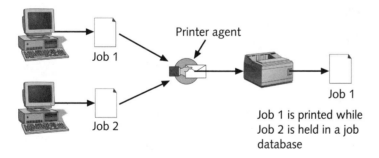

Printer agent

Job 1

Job 2

Job 1

Job 1 is printed while Job 2 is held in a job database

Figure 8-21   Printer agent operation

When a user prints to a network printer, the output first goes to the printer agent representing that printer, which spools the output to a database file on the NetWare server until the printer is ready. When the printer is available, the printer agent takes a print job from the database file and then uses its assigned gateway to transmit the print job, along with any special configuration commands, to the network printer.

To spool printer output and work with other network services, a printer agent needs to be configured with basic printer information, including the physical printer's name, make, and model and the gateway used by the printer attachment method. In addition, to access printers with IPP, printer agents need to be IPP enabled (which they are by default). When the first printer agent on a Print Manager is IPP enabled, NetWare automatically loads the IPPSRVR.NLM module to handle IPP-based printing functions. You can disable IPP printing by using the printer's Client Support option in iManager. Printer agents that aren't IPP enabled are accessible only to users who have Novell Client loaded.

Printer agents can be classified as public access or controlled access. As the name implies, **public access printers** are available to anyone with an attachment to the network. These printers are the easiest to set up because they don't require a corresponding eDirectory object. The disadvantage of public access printers is that they can't be managed from iManager and are limited to being accessed only from computers using the Novell NDPS client. **Controlled access printers** offer more security and administrative control, but for each controlled access printer, you need to create and configure an eDirectory object and then grant access to that object for users or groups. By default, the container in which a controlled access printer is located is made a user of the printer agent. For example, to allow only the IT Department to use a certain printer, Eric created a controlled access printer agent named IT_Optr_1 in the IT OU.

Setting Up Gateways

Before creating the printer agent, you need to define a gateway for connecting the printer agent to the physical printer. As you can see in Figure 8-22, gateways are used to connect physical printers to their associated printer agents running on Print Manager.

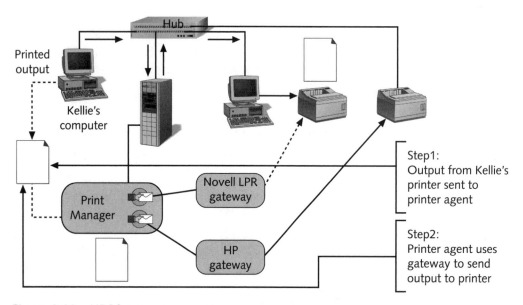

Figure 8-22 NDPS gateway operation

Gateways ensure that printer agents can communicate with physical printers regardless of the attachment method or port. When you create a printer agent, in addition to selecting the Print Manager that hosts the agent, you need to identify the gateway and the physical printer's make, model, and connection information (port and address).

In addition to the local and remote attachment methods, the Novell LPR gateway supports direct (network) printer attachment. Today, most network printers are attached directly to the network cable with a special network card for the printer or a dedicated print server device, such as Hewlett-Packard's JetDirect products. Dedicated print server devices have a network port, one or more printer ports, and built-in software that enables them to receive print jobs from the network and print them on attached printers. Many high-speed laser printers have an option that includes a network card for attaching printers directly to the network cable. With the direct/network attachment method, the printer can become its own client and print jobs directly from a printer agent. Currently, only the Novell LPR gateway ships with Open Enterprise Server. This gateway handles most printers using IP. Third-party gateways are also available but must be installed from the server console before a printer agent can use them.

To send output from the printer agent to the correct printer, you configure a gateway with the connection information that identifies the physical printer. The method for identifying the physical printer depends on the gateway type. For example, printers attached to the network through dedicated print server interfaces, such as the HP JetDirect printers at UAS, can use the Novell LPR gateway supplied with Open Enterprise Server. The Novell LPR gateway requires identifying the printer by the IP address assigned to the dedicated print server interface. In the following activities, you learn how to create controlled access and public access printer agents using the Novell LPR gateway.

Activity 8-12: Creating a Controlled Access Printer Agent with the Novell LPR Gateway

Time Required: 10 minutes

8

Objective: Create and configure a printer agent using the Novell LPR gateway.

Requirements: Same as Activity 8-10. In addition, you need the printer's IP address and a loaded Print Manager. If you're using a shared classroom server, you need to use the Print Manager loaded on the classroom server. If you're using a dedicated server, you need to have loaded a Print Manger by completing Activity 8-11. In addition, this activity assumes the existence of a network attached printer. If you don't have a network-attached printer, you can still complete this activity by using an IP address that's not assigned to another device. Record the IP address you're using for the network printer:

Description: In this activity, you use iManager to create a controlled access printer agent named IT_Optr_1 using the Novell LPR gateway. This activity is written so that you can create the printer agent even if you don't have a network attached printer.

1. If necessary, start your computer, and log in to eDirectory with your administrative user name and password.

2. Start iManager, and log on with your administrative user name and password.

3. Click to expand the **iPrint** heading and click the **Create Printer** link to display the Create Printer window shown in Figure 8-23.

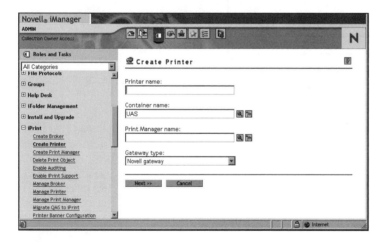

Figure 8-23   The Create Printer window

4. Enter **IT_Optr_1** in the Printer name text box.

5. Click the **Object Selector** button next to the Container name text box, and click the **IT** OU.

6. Click the **Object Selector** button next to the Print Manager name text box, and click the Print Manager loaded on your server. (If you're using a shared classroom server, enter the name of the Print Manager running on your classroom server.)

If the Print Manager isn't loaded, you can load it at this time by clicking the Manage Print Manager link under the iPrint heading.

7. Verify that the Novell gateway is selected, and click **Next** to display the Configure Novell gateway for printer window shown in Figure 8-24.

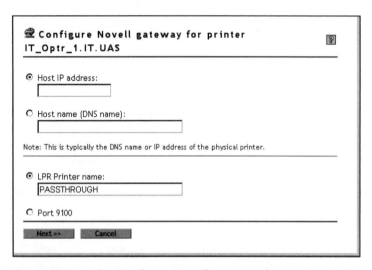

Figure 8-24   The Configure Novell gateway for printer window

8. Enter the IP address or host name for your printer, and click **Next** to display the Select default drivers for printer window shown in Figure 8-25.

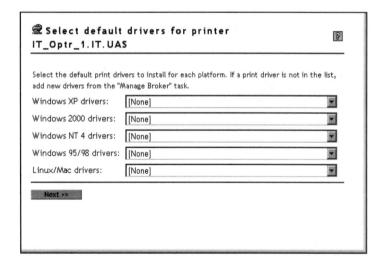

Figure 8-25   Selecting a default driver for your printer

9. Select the appropriate drivers, and click **Next** to display the completion message.

10. Click **OK** to return to the iManager main window, and stay logged in for the next activity.

Activity 8-13: Creating a Public Access Printer Agent with the Novell LPR Gateway

Time Required: 10 minutes

Objective: Use NetWare Administrator to create a public access printer agent.

Requirements: Same as Activity 8-12. If you're using a shared classroom server, you need a user account with the Supervisor right to the classroom Print Manager.

Description: In this activity, you use NetWare Administrator to create a public access printer agent named IT_Optr_2 using the Novell LPR gateway. To perform this activity, you need to have a printer attached to your classroom network using the HP JetDirect or an equivalent interface.

1. If necessary, log in to eDirectory with your administrative user name and password.

2. Start NetWare Administrator.

3. Expand your **UAS** container, and double-click **UAS_PrtMgr##** (## represents your assigned student number) to open the NDPS Manager: UASPrtMgr window. (*Note:* If you're using a shared classroom server, select the classroom Print Manager.)

4. Click the **Printer Agent List** button to display all existing printer agents.

5. Click the **New** button to open the Create Printer Agent dialog box.

6. Enter **##UAS_Public** (replacing ## with your assigned student number) in the Printer Agent (PA) Name text box, and then click **OK** to open the Configure Novell PDS for Printer Agent dialog box.

7. Scroll down and select the printer type (Lexmark Optr R) in the Printer Type list box, and then click **OK** to open the Printer Port Handler dialog box.

8. Click **Next** to accept the default Novell LPR printer gateway (SNMP) and display the Host Address text box.

9. Enter the IP address you identified for your network printer, and then click **Finish**. If you see a warning message informing you that the printer agent needs attention, click **OK** to continue and display the Select Printer Drivers dialog box.

10. Click to select the **Lexmark Optra R** printer driver in the Windows 2000 tab, and then click **Continue** to display the driver summary.

11. Click **OK** to accept the selected drivers and return to the Printer Agent List.

12. Verify that your new public access printer has been added to the Printer Agent List, and then click **Cancel** to return to the main NetWare Administrator window.

13. Exit NetWare Administrator, and log off.

Printer Pooling

When a number of users share printers of the same type in a department, knowing what printer will be available can be difficult, much like picking a checkout line at the grocery store. You might pick a short line only to find that the person in front of you wants to cash a check with no ID. On the other hand, when checking in at an airport, there's one long line but several people who can check you in. You don't have to select a particular person; you just stand in the waiting area until your turn comes up. This analogy applies to printers, too. If you have several printers of the same type, instead of having users choose which printer to use, you can place all printer agents in a printer pool. Users submit jobs to the pool, and the printer agents then print the jobs when a printer becomes available. Of course, all agents in the printer pool must use the same print driver to format output for the printer correctly. To create a printer pool, you use the following steps:

1. In iManager, expand the iPrint heading and click the Printer Pool configuration link.

2. Specify the Print Manager for which you're creating the printer pool.

3. Select the Create Printer Pool option in the drop-down list.

4. Enter a name for the printer pool, and then select the printer agents to be included in the pool.

5. Save your settings.

After creating the printer pool, the printers in the pool automatically share print jobs sent to any printer. For example, if both IT Department printers are placed in a pool and a user sends a job to the IT_Optr_1 printer while it's busy, the job is transferred automatically to the IT_Optr_2 printer if it's available.

CONFIGURING PRINTER CLIENTS

As you have learned, for users to access network printers, they need client software and the necessary printer drivers installed on their computers. With Open Enterprise Server, network administrators have these basic methods, explained in the following sections, for installing printers on user computers:

- Manual printer installation performed by a user
- Automatic printer installation
- Printer installation from a facility map

Installing Printers Manually

After the iPrint client is installed on a computer, users can install printers manually by conducting a search based on printer name and specifications or selecting the printer from a list. In the following activity, you learn how to manually install an iPrint printer.

The following activity assumes you have a Print Manager running on your server and you have completed Activities 8-11 and 8-12.

NOTE

ACTIVITY

Activity 8-14: Installing a Printer Manually with iPrint

Time Required: 15 minutes

Objective: Use iPrint to install a printer on a computer.

Requirements: Completion of Activities 8-11 and 8-12

Description: In this activity, you use the iPrint client to install and send output to your IT Department printer.

1. If necessary, start your computer, and log on with your local user name and password. If you're using a Windows XP computer, click to enable the **Workstation Only** check box, and enter your user name and password for logging on to the local Windows system.

2. If necessary, start your Web browser, and enter the URL **https://*IPaddress*/ipp** to display the iPrint client window. The IT_Optr_1 printer should be displayed.

3. Click the **IT_Optr_1** printer object, and then click **OK** to install that printer.

4. When you see the message informing you that the printer is installed, click **OK** to continue and return to the iPrint client window.

5. Close the iPrint client window.

6. Open the Printers and Faxes window by clicking **Start**, **Control Panel** and double-clicking **Printers and Faxes**. Verify that the IT_Optr_1 printer is installed on your computer, and stay logged in for the next activity.

Installing Printers Automatically

In Activity 8-14, you learned how to use iPrint to select and install a printer to which you have access rights. However, installing printers in this manner can be time consuming, and training users to install their own printers might require extra time and effort. To speed up and simplify this task, Novell has included an automatic installation option in iPrint. With iPrint, network administrators can use **Remote Printer Management (RPM)** to specify which printers should be installed on client computers based on the user's context. When a user logs in, Novell Client checks the user's context and group to automatically download and install any printers specified for that user's configuration. You can access Remote Printer Management from iManager with the following steps:

EXAMPLE

1. In iManager, expand the iPrint heading and click the RPM Configuration link.

2. In the RPM Configuration window, specify the object for which you want to configure RPM. Valid objects include Organizations, Organizational Units, Groups, or Users.

3. Next, specify the RPM settings. You can enable or disable RPM, select printers to install automatically, select a default printer, and even specify printers that should be removed.

4. Save your settings.

After it's configured, RPM automatically applies the printer specifications when a user logs in from the scope specified in the RPM configuration. For example, to save the time it takes to select each printer manually for Engineering and Mgmt users, Eric configured the printers to be installed automatically when users log in. In the following activity, you use iManager to configure RPM for the IT OU.

ACTIVITY

Activity 8-15: Configuring Automatic Installation of Printers

Time Required: 10 minutes

Objective: Use iManager to configure automatic installation of printers.

Requirements: Completion of Activity 8-12

Description: Installing and configuring printers manually on users' computers can be time consuming, even when using iPrint. As a result, Eric configured RPM to install department printers automatically on user computers. In this activity, you configure RPM to install the IT_Optr_1 printer automatically for users in the IT OU.

1. If necessary, start your computer, and log on with your local user name and password. If you're using a Windows XP system, click to enable the **Workstation Only** check box, and enter your user name and password for logging on to the local Windows system.

2. Follow these steps to remove the existing IT_Optr_1 printer:

    a. Click **Start**, **Control Panel** and double-click **Printers and Faxes** to display the Printers and Faxes window.

    b. Right-click the **IT_Optr_1** printer and click **Delete**. Click **Yes** to confirm the deletion.

    c. Close the Printers and Faxes window.

3. Start iManager, and log in with your administrative user name and password, if necessary.

4. Click to expand the **iPrint** heading, and click the **RPM Configuration** link to display the RPM Configuration window shown in Figure 8-26.

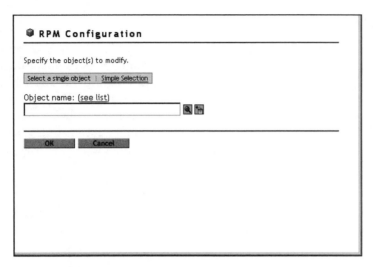

Figure 8-26   The RPM Configuration window

5. Click the **Object Selector** button next to the Object name text box, click the **IT** OU, and then click **OK** to display the RPM Configuration window for the IT OU (see Figure 8-27).

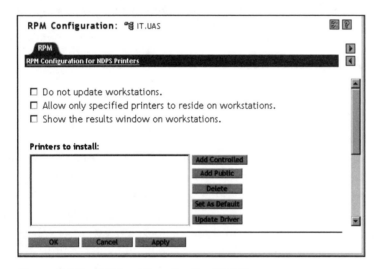

Figure 8-27   RPM settings for the IT OU

6. Click to select the **Show the results window on workstations** check box.

7. Click the **Add Controlled** button under Printers to install to display an Object Selector window similar to the one in Figure 8-28.

8. Navigate to the **IT** OU, and click the **IT_Optr_1** printer object.

9. Click **OK** to add the selected printer to the Printers to install list box in the RPM Configuration window.

10. Click **OK** to save your changes and return to the iManager main window. Log off your computer.

11. Log in to eDirectory with the **EKenton** user name and password, and verify that the IT_Optr_1 printer has been installed automatically. When you're finished, log out, and leave your system running for the next activity.

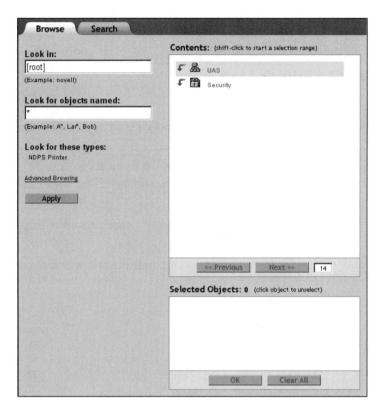

Figure 8-28 The Object Selector window for printers

Using the iPrint Map Utility

For users to access network printers, they need to have iPrint or Novell Client installed along with the necessary printer drivers. However, occasionally users need to send output to printers in other locations that aren't included in the automatic printer setup. Although Eric plans to train users on how to use iPrint to select and install printers, they might not know the name of the printer they want to use. To make selecting a printer easier, Novell has included the Map utility with iPrint, which enables network administrators to place printer icons on a map of the facility. The map can be displayed in a Web browser, and users can select and install a printer by simply clicking the location of the printer they want to use. In this section, you learn how to use the iPrint Map utility to construct a map of your UAS printers, and then use it to install printers on user computers. Using this utility involves the following steps:

EXAMPLE

1. *Create a Web directory for the IPP map documents.* Eric created a Web directory for the printer map by copying the Ippdocs directory structure from the SYS:Apache2\Htdocs directory to the CORP: IT\Web directory.

2. *Scan in a map of the facility and save it as a JPG file.* Eric scanned in a copy of the UAS floor plan and saved it as a JPG file in the CORP:IT\Web\Ippdocs\Images\Maps directory. Storing the image in this directory is important so that the default iPrint Web server configuration can access it.

3. *Use the iPrint Map utility to add existing printers to the facility map.* After saving the scanned image, Eric used Internet Explorer 5.5 (the required version for the Map utility) to run the Maptool.htm file on the NetWare 6.5 server. This file is used to place icons representing printers on a scanned image. Each icon shows the printer's IP address, description, and name. Eric used the iPrint Map utility to place each printer on the UAS floor plan.

4. *Save the facility map in a directory accessible to users.* After adding all printers, Eric saved the floor plan map in the CORP:IT\Web\Ippdocs subdirectory as an HTML file. Because the printer map is in the Login directory, all users can access it to select and install printers on their computers, even if they're using a computer in another part of the country.

In the following activity, you use the iPrint Map utility to create a printer map showing the IT Department printer.

Activity 8-16: Creating a Facility Printer Map

Time Required: 15 minutes

Objective: Use the iPrint Map utility to create a map of printers in a facility.

Requirements: A Windows XP computer and completion of Activities 8-12 and 8-13; if you're using Windows XP, Internet Explorer version 5.5 or later. You also need a Web subdirectory in your IT directory structure. In addition, if you're using a classroom server, you need a user account with the Read right to the SYS:Apache2 directory.

Description: In this activity, you use a floor plan map Eric saved previously to create a facility map for users to find and install printers.

1. If necessary, start your computer, and log into eDirectory with your administrative user name and password.

2. Map a drive letter to the SYS:Apache2\Htdocs directory.

3. Copy the **Ippdocs** directory structure to your IT\Web directory.

4. Follow these steps to use the Map utility to open a facility map:

   a. Start Internet Explorer (version 5.5 or later).

   b. Click **File**, **Open** from the menu, and then click the **Browse** button. Double-click to select the **Maptool.htm** file in the Ippdocs directory you copied in Step 3.

   c. Click **OK** to open the iPrint Map Designer window shown in Figure 8-29.

 If you see a message about blocking ActiveX when opening Maptool.htm, select the option to continue.

NOTE

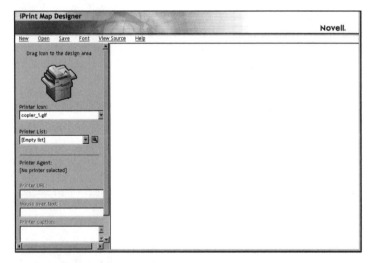

Figure 8-29   The iPrint Map Designer window

5. Click the **Printer icon** list arrow, and then click **laser_4c.gif** in the list to display a laser printer icon. Notice the icons you can use to represent different types of printers. (The number after the name indicates the icon size; smaller numbers are larger icons.)

6. To select printers, follow these steps to identify the IP address of your Print Manager:

a. Click the **Locate printers** button next to the Printer List text box to open the Change printer list – Web Page Dialog window.

b. Enter the IP address of the UASHOST classroom server in the Print Manager Address text box, and then click **OK**.

c. If asked to log in, enter your administrative user name and password.

7. The next step in building a printer map is to select a graphics file for the floor plan. When the Map utility loads, it scans the Login\Ippdocs\Images\Maps directory automatically for any graphics files. Scroll down and click the **Background** list arrow to display all graphics files in the Maps directory, and then click the **Office.gif** file to display a sample office layout in the main window.

8. Follow these steps to place the IT_Optr_1 printer on the floor plan:

a. Click the **Printer List** list arrow to display all printers managed by the Print Manager you selected in Step 6.

b. Click the **IT_Optr_1** printer.

c. Drag the printer icon to the Engineering Department in the UAS layout, next to Kari Means.

d. In the Printer URL text box, enter **http://*IPaddress*/ipps/IT_Optr_1**. (Replace *IPaddress* with the IP address of your NetWare server.)

9. Follow these steps to save the facility printer map:

a. Click the **Save** link at the top to open the Save dialog box.

b. Navigate to the **IT\Web\Ippdocs** directory, enter **UASPrinters** in the File name text box, and click the **Save** button.

10. Close your Web browser.

 You learn how to link to the UASPrinters Web page from the Apache Web server in Chapter 11.

11. Close all open windows, and log out.

ESTABLISHING A PRINTING ENVIRONMENT

Now that you have had a chance to become familiar with setting up NDPS/iPrint components, it's time to apply this new knowledge to setting up network printers for your version of the UAS network. Eric's first task in establishing the printing environment was to define the printing needs to be supported on the network, which involved these steps:

1. Determine the number and types of printers, and define printing requirements for each user's applications.

2. Determine printer locations and attachment methods.

3. Define names for all printers and identify any required print queues.

4. Plan the eDirectory context for each printer object.

In the following sections, you apply these steps to defining a network printing environment for your UAS organization using the NDPS Definition Form that Eric developed.

Step 1: Defining Printing Requirements

The first step is to identify the number and types of network printers the organization needs. To do this, you need to analyze the requirements of all users' applications and their printing needs. Table 8-1 summarizes the printing needs for Engineering, Mgmt, and Mfg users in the UAS network.

Table 8-1   UAS printing requirements

All Users	All users should have access to a color inkjet printer.
Engineering	The department's Lexmark Optra laser printer will be connected directly to the network and be available to all Engineering users to print correspondence and instruction manuals.
Mgmt	The department's Lexmark Optra laser printer will be connected directly to the network and available to the Mgmt users.
Mfg	Until they are attached directly to the network by using a JetDirect print server, the two Lexmark Optra laser printers in the Mfg department will be attached to the Receiving1 and Shipping1 computers. Russ Pence will manage the printers.

After determining printing needs, the next step is to identify each network printer agent and the gateway for attaching it to the Print Manager. In a multiserver environment, you should also consider how many Print Managers are needed to reduce network traffic across routers. Eric used the NDPS Definition Form, shown in Figure 8-30, to list the printer agents, gateways, and Print Managers in the UAS network.

NDPS Definition Form

Print Manager: _UAS_NDPSM_   eDirectory Context: _UAS_
Server: _UASHOST_   Database Volume: _CORP_
Managers: _UasADMIN_

Printer Name	Make/Model	NDPS Printer Classification	eDirectory Context	Attachment Method	Gateway Type	Port Interrupt	Associated Print Queue	Users	Operators
IT_Optr_1	Lexmark Optra R	Controlled access	.IT.UAS	File server	Novell	LPT1 Polled	IT_Optr1_Q	IT OU	ITMgrs group
IT_Optr_2	Lexmark Optra R	Controlled access	.IT.UAS	Direct using JetDirect box	HP			IT and Engineering OUs	ITMgrs group
UAS_Color	HP Color LaserJet 5	Public access		Direct using JetDirect box	HP			All users	ITMgrs group
Eng_Optr_1	Lexmark Optra R	Controlled access	.Engineering.UAS	Direct using JetDirect box	HP			Engineering and Mgmt OUs	EngMgr org role
Mgmt_Optr_1	Lexmark Optra R	Controlled access	.Mgmt.UAS	Direct using JetDirect box	HP			Mgmt OU	AdmAsst org role
Rec_Optr_1	Lexmark Optra R	Controlled access	.Mfg.UAS	Remote to Receiving computer	Novell	LPT1 Polled	Rec_Optr1_Q	Production group	MfgMgr org role
Shp_Optr_1	Lexmark Optra R	Controlled access	.Mfg.UAS	Remote to Shipping computer	Novell	LPT1 Polled	Shp_Optr1_Q	Production group	MfgMgr org role

Figure 8-30   The NDPS Definition Form

The top part of the NDPS Definition Form lists the Print Manager object and the NetWare server running Print Manager software. Because a Print Manager can support an unlimited number of printer agents, one server running Print Manager software is usually enough for most organizations, except when the organization's network is connected over a WAN. For example, because the AeroDyn division is connected across a T1 line, Eric plans to use a separate NDPS Definition Form for the AeroDyn division. The NDPS Definition Form also includes columns for identifying the printer mode and users for each network printer attached to a print server. To keep the printing system as simple as possible, Eric standardized the make and model of printers to be used on the network.

After analyzing UAS users' needs, Eric installed one laser printer for generating word processing documents and reports in each department. In addition, he installed a color laser printer available to all users for printing graphs and presentation materials; to simplify setup and maintenance, he defined this printer as a public access printer. Because output to the Shipping and Receiving printers initially comes only from computers in those departments, Eric decided to attach these printers to the LPT ports of the Shipping and Receiving computers so that they can print directly to the local printer, thus reducing network traffic. Because he created NDPS printer agents for these printers, they will also be available on the network.

Step 2: Determining Printer Location and Attachment Method

After identifying the printers to meet users' projected printing requirements, the next consideration is the physical location and attachment method for printers. Eric used the following guidelines for determining this information:

- Attempt to place the printer close to the user who is most responsible for it.

- Determine whether the printer will be attached locally to the server, remotely to a client computer, or directly to the network.

- Identify the printer port and interrupt each printer is going to use.

- Avoid attaching remote printers to clients that aren't running 32-bit OSs, such as Windows 95 or later.

- Use direct (network) attachment for printers that multiple users access.

The NDPS Definition Form shows that Eric has listed the attachment method and location for each printer in the UAS network. The form also shows the gateway and the printer port/interrupt used with Novell gateways to connect the printer to the network.

Step 3: Defining Printer and Print Queue Names

To keep your printing system as simple as possible, select printer and print queue names that enable you to find these objects quickly. One method is using one- to six-character codes that specify the printer's location, model, and number separated by hyphens or underscores. For example, Eric used Eng_Optr_1 to identify the first Lexmark Optra R laser printer installed in the Engineering Department. If additional Optra laser printers are installed in the Engineering Department, their names would be Eng_Optr_2 and Eng_Optr_3.

NOTE

If you're using a shared classroom server, you need to precede the printer name with your assigned student number for all students to share the same Print Manager.

Notice that the NDPS Definition Form contains a column for print queue names. If a printer agent is required to support non-NDPS clients, a print queue must be created. In this case, the print queue name should be the same as the printer agent name, followed by an underscore and the letter Q. As described earlier, each print queue consists of a subdirectory in the Queues directory. Because any NetWare volume can be used to store print queues, you need to assign each print queue to the NetWare volume where its Queues directory is located.

TIP

To prevent print queues containing many large print jobs from filling up the SYS volume, Novell recommends placing large print queues on a volume other than SYS.

In addition to using printer names when creating printer agents and queues, it's a good idea to use a permanent marker to label each printer in the office with its assigned name. This makes it easier for the network administrator and users to identify printers when working with the printing system.

Step 4: Planning the eDirectory Context

As with all network objects, you need to define printers, print queues, and print servers in the eDirectory tree. Placing printers and print queues in the same container as users gives you convenient access because you can select the printer by its name instead of specifying its context. For example, if the Eng_Optr_1 laser printer object is placed in the Engineering OU, all users in the Engineering Department could send output to the printer easily. Users with eDirectory contexts in another container would have to browse to the printer or use its distinguished name.

Another reason for placing printer agents in the container where they're accessed most often is that by default, the container storing the printer agent becomes a user of that printer agent. Notice that in the NDPS Definition Form, Eric has given the Mgmt OU rights to the Engineering laser printer so that Mgmt users can access this printer if their printer is down. In addition, Eric has granted Engineering users rights to use the IT printer in case their printer is out of action.

By default, only users in the container where the printer agent is created are users of the printer. To allow users from other containers to use a printer agent, their user names or groups they belong to need to be added to the printer agent's access control list.

The Print Manager object is accessed from the NetWare server and can service printers and users in any container. As shown in the top line of the NDPS Definition Form, Eric has placed the Print Manager object in the UAS Organization along with the NetWare server. In the end-of-chapter projects, you apply what you have learned to setting up the printing system Eric defined.

TROUBLESHOOTING NETWORK PRINTING

Many of the basics you learned about troubleshooting queue-based printing problems also apply to iPrint printing. Following are some "quick" fixes Novell recommends for solving problems that occur when setting up network printing with iPrint:

1. Attempt to resolve any error messages received for the server, printer agent, or client computer by trying these methods:

   - If the error message says that the client computer couldn't connect to the printer agent, verify that the Print Manager and Broker are both loaded and running. If they are both loaded, unload and then load the Print Manager again.

   - Verify that the Autoexec.ncf file contains a LOAD NDPSM command and includes the correct distinguished name of the Print Manager.

   - If the error message says that a print job was rejected, check to see that the spooling volume for the printer agent has enough free space. If possible, use a volume other than SYS and set a limit on the spooling space.

2. If a network printing problem is limited to a single computer, check the following:

   - Check the printer's job list to ensure that the job is getting to the spooling volume.

   - Review any changes made since the printer agent was working correctly.

   - Check the printer configuration.

3. If a network printing problem affects several computers, check the following:

   - In iManager, check the Printer Information dialog box for any NDPS error messages.

   - Check for printer error conditions (printer beeps or LCD panel lights) and error messages.

   - Turn the printer off and on. If the job is still in the printer agent's job list, delete it.

The following tables include tips for troubleshooting NDPS printing based on the scope of the printing problem. Table 8-2 has suggestions for isolating printing problems for a single computer that's unable to print to an iPrint printer that other user computers are using successfully. Table 8-3 has suggestions for troubleshooting problems that could prevent an NDPS printer from printing jobs for all computers.

Table 8-2   Isolating single-computer printer problems

Condition	Possible Problem	Action
The user workstation is printing to a print queue, but the printer receives no output. This could happen for non-NDPS clients, such as DOS or Macintosh computers.	The print queue is not being serviced by a printer agent or queue-based print server.	Use NetWare Administrator to verify that the print job is in the print queue. Verify that the print queue is being serviced by a print server or printer agent. If necessary, associate the print queue with the appropriate NDPS printer agent and verify that the printer agent is printing jobs for other workstations.
	The print job is being sent to the wrong print queue.	Check the printer configuration on the workstation to be sure it's associated with the correct print queue.
	The printer is using an incorrect print driver, causing the print device to disregard the print job.	Check the printer configuration on the workstation to make sure the printer is using the correct driver for the printer agent that services the corresponding print queue.
Print jobs do not appear in the printer agent's job list.	The Windows printer configuration is not correct.	Click Start, Settings, Printers, and check the printer status to see if any problems are evident. Check the driver and printer port configuration. The port should be configured to print to the correct printer agent or print queue.

Table 8-3   Isolating NDPS printer problems

Condition	Possible Problem	Action
Printer agent problem	Printer agent is unable to connect to the print device.	Check the printer status on the server console or through NetWare Administrator.
Printer not connected	The printer agent is configured as a local printer on the Novell gateway, and the printer is not attached to the server or is turned off.	Attach or turn on the printer and retry printing.
	The printer agent is configured as a remote printer on the Novell gateway, and the NPTWIN95 remote printer software is not loaded, or the computer hosting the printer has been shut down.	Load the NPTWIN95 software on the workstation hosting the print device and connect it to the correct printer agent. Start the computer hosting the print device and retry.
I/O error	The printer agent is configured as a local printer on the Novell gateway, using the same port as a printer agent that's already loaded.	Determine which printer agent should be using that printer port on the server and then delete the incorrectly configured printer agent and re-create it, using a different gateway or printer port.
	The printer agent is configured as a directly attached printer using a printer interface, and the printer interface is not connected to the network or is turned off.	Reconnect or turn on the printer interface and try again. If necessary, wait until there's no printer activity, and then unload and load the Print Manager on the server.
	The printer agent is configured as a printer attached directly to the network, using a gateway such as HP JetDirect, and the printer interface is disconnected from the network or turned off.	Reconnect the printer interface and then turn it off and on. If the status does not change after a few minutes, wait until there's no printing activity and then unload and reload the Print Manager on the server.
Printer not bound	The printer gateway is not available, or the print device is disconnected from the gateway.	Reconnect the printer to the printer interface and retry.

Table 8-3   Isolating NDPS printer problems (continued)

Condition	Possible Problem	Action
Printer offline	The printer is out of paper or turned off.	Make sure the print device is on, and check for any error messages on the print device panel.
	The printer cable is defective or disconnected.	Check the printer cable to make sure it's securely attached to the print device and interface. If the printer still shows offline status, test and replace the printer cable.
Printer status is grayed out	Print Manager is not loaded.	Load the Print Manager on the server console.
	The wrong Print Manager is loaded.	If you have multiple Print Managers in your tree, verify that the correct Print Manager for the printer is loaded. If necessary, unload the incorrect Print Manager and load the correct one.
	The new printer agent encountered an error when first loading.	If a print device or interface is not attached to the network, the printer is turned off, or the remote printer software has not yet been loaded on a Windows 95/98 computer, you'll see an error message when creating the printer agent and the status will be grayed out in the Printer Control dialog box. Close the Printer Control dialog box, and then reopen it to view the printer status.
Jobs print but remain in the job list	User or operator hold is on.	Click the Configuration button in the Printer Control dialog box, and then modify the Job Hold settings of any job configurations listed in the Printer Configurations dialog box.
Jobs removed from the job list but not printed	Incorrect driver language	Verify that the correct printer driver is configured for the printer agent. Incorrect drivers can cause the printer to disregard print jobs.
	Cable problem	Faulty printer cables or broken wires can prevent data from reaching the print device. Test and replace the printer cable.
Jobs not displayed in the job list	Computer printer configuration problem	Check the printer configuration on the computer to make sure it's using the correct driver and is printing to the correct printer agent or print queue.
	Users do not have rights to print to the printer.	Verify that the printer agent is in the same container as the users who are printing. Verify that users who are not in the same container as the printer agent have been added to the access control list.

CHAPTER SUMMARY

❑ The NetWare queue-based printing system uses print queues to store output from client computers until the network printer becomes available. Print server software monitors the print queue and controls output to the printer.

❑ Common queue-based printing troubleshooting techniques including checking to see whether the queue is assigned to a printer, reloading the print server object, and verifying that the print queue is being serviced by the correct printer type.

❑ Printers can be attached to the network with the local, remote, or network attachment method. The local attachment method uses a shared port on the print server. Remote attachments use a shared printer on another client computer. The network attachment method uses a network port on the printer to enable it to receive print jobs from the server.

❑ iPrint is the latest Novell network printing technology that takes advantage of the capabilities of modern printers and client software to allow users to print from any computer to printers located in the LAN or across the Internet.

❑ In cooperation with Hewlett-Packard and Xerox, Novell developed a network printing environment called Novell Distributed Printing Services (NDPS). As a CNA, you'll need to know the printing components and utilities that make up NDPS and be able to set up and maintain a NetWare printing environment consisting of a Print Manager, printer agents, gateways, NDPS Brokers, print queues, and client computers.

❑ Printer agents are software that make up the core of iPrint/NDPS. Client computers send formatted printer output to printer agents, which then control the physical printer. When setting up iPrint/NDPS, you need to create and configure one printer agent for each physical printer.

❑ As part of the Novell OneNet strategy, iPrint uses Internet Printing Protocol (IPP) to enable printers to be installed, accessed, and managed anywhere via a Web browser. iPrint consists of three components: the IPPSRVR.NLM module on the NetWare server, a Web browser client, and NDPS printers enabled for IPP access.

❑ The component used to create and run printer agents is called Print Manager. By using specialized gateways, printers can be attached remotely to client computers, attached locally to the server, or attached directly to the network.

❑ Because not all clients are immediately compatible with NDPS, Novell offers backward compatibility through the use of print queues, which consist of a directory on the file system for holding print jobs until the printer is ready to use them. Installation methods for clients include installing directly from Windows, enabling automatic printer installation in Remote Printer Management (RPM), and using the Map utility via a Web browser.

❑ To establish the printing environment, you need to determine the number and types of printers needed and define the printing requirements for users' applications, determine printers' locations and attachment methods, define printer and print queue names, and plan the eDirectory context for all printing objects.

❑ Common iPrint troubleshooting techniques include verifying that the Broker and Print Manager are loaded on the server, verifying that the print job is listed in the print agent job list, and using iManager to check the Printer Information dialog box for any error messages.

KEY TERMS

automatic load printers — *See* locally attached printers.

controlled access printers — NDPS printers that exist as an object in the eDirectory tree. By default, only users in the same container as a controlled access printer can send output to it.

Internet Printing Protocol (IPP) — An industry-standard system for installing and accessing network printers by using HTTP across the Internet.

iPrint — Novell's IP-based printing system that uses Internet Printing Protocol (IPP) through a Web browser to install and communicate with network printers from a local network or across the Internet.

locally attached printers — Printers attached directly to a server's printer port or to a port on the client computer.

manual load printers — *See* remotely attached printers.

network attached printers — Printers that have their own network port, which allows them to be connected to the network cable without needing additional hardware.

NDPS Broker — An NDPS component responsible for sending printer messages and notifications, using the Event Notification System (ENS), Resource Management Service (RMS), and Service Registry Services (SRS).

Novell Distributed Print Services (NDPS) — A printing system developed by Hewlett-Packard and Novell to make network printer configuration and access more convenient.

parallel port (LPTn) — A common printer port used on personal computers. Parallel ports require thicker cables to transmit several bits of information at one time.

Print Manager — The NDPS component that manages the printer agent for printers that don't have one embedded.

print queue — A network object representing a holding area where print jobs are kept until the printer is available. In NetWare, a print queue is a subdirectory of the Queues directory, located in the volume specified during print queue creation.

print server — A component of queue-based printing that manages network printers by taking jobs from print queues and sending them to the appropriate network printer.

printer agent — The software component of NDPS that transfers output from the client and controls the physical printer.

printer gateway — The NDPS component that works with the printer agent to send output from the printer agent to the network print device.

public access printers — NDPS printers that are attached to the network but don't have an eDirectory object in the tree. Any user attached to the network can send output to a public access printer without having to log in to the network.

queue-based printing — A printing system originated in NetWare 3 that's designed to support simple printers and DOS-based applications.

remotely attached printers — Printers attached to the port of a networked computer and controlled by the print server.

Remote Printer Management (RPM) — Novell's system for using a Web browser to manage network printers.

serial port (COMn) — A printer port often used to connect communication devices, such as modems and printers, to send signals over long cables. Serial ports send only one bit of data at a time, so serial cables can consist of only a few wires.

REVIEW QUESTIONS

1. Which of the following is the network printing component that provides backward compatibility by storing printed output until the printer is ready to print?

    a. print server

    b. print queue

    c. gateway

    d. printer agent

2. Which of the following is the queue-based printing component that controls print jobs on the physical printer?

    a. print server

    b. print queue

    c. gateway

    d. printer agent

3. Which of the following utilities can be used to create print queues?

    a. NetWare Administrator

    b. ConsoleOne

    c. iManager

    d. Remote Manager

4. In the queue-based printing system, user computers send their output to which of the following?

    a. print server

    b. print queue

    c. gateway

    d. printer agent

5. Which of the following is the NDPS component that manages each physical printer?

    a. print server

    b. print queue

    c. gateway

    d. printer agent

6. Which of the following must be running before you can create printer agents? (Choose all that apply.)

    a. Print Manager

    b. IPPSRVR

    c. NDPS Broker

    d. print server

7. A network printer attached to a client computer is called a _____ printer.

    a. locally attached

    b. network attached

    c. system

    d. remotely attached

8. Which of the following is the first step in setting up a network printing environment?

    a. Create printer agents.

    b. Create and load the NDPS Broker.

    c. Create and load the Print Manager.

    d. Install IPP on your administrative computer.

9. Which of the following utilities can be used to create printer agents?

    a. iManager

    b. Remote Manager

    c. ConsoleOne

    d. NetWare Administrator

10. A printer attached to a server is referred to as which of the following?

    a. manual load printer

    b. locally attached printer

    c. network attached printer

    d. system printer

11. "Automatic load printers" is the term Novell uses for _____ attached printers.

    a. locally

    b. remotely

    c. directly

    d. IPP

12. Printer agents that can be accessed without logging in are referred to as which of the following?

    a. automatic load printers

    b. controlled access printers

    c. public access printers

    d. global printers

13. Which of the following NDPS components helps clients find network printer agents?

    a. Print Manager

    b. printer agent

    c. NDPS Broker

    d. print queue

14. Novell's iPrint is based on which of the following industry standards?

    a. IPP

    b. 802.3

    c. IEEE

    d. X.500

15. Most printers today have embedded printer agents. True or False?

16. What is the URL for accessing the iPrint utility?

17. Remotely attached printers are also called which of the following?

    a. automatic load printers

    b. controlled access printers

    c. manual load printers

    d. global printers

18. Write the command for loading the Print Manager named .UAS_PM.UAS on the NetWare server.

19. Which of the following is not a step in establishing a network printing environment?

    a. defining printer names

    b. defining the context for printing objects

    c. creating a Printers container

    d. defining printer attachment methods

20. If a network printing problem is linked to a single computer, which of the following should you do? (Choose all that apply.)

   a. Check the printer for error conditions, such as being out of paper or blinking panel lights.

   b. Check the printer job list to ensure that output is getting from the application to the printer.

   c. Turn the printer off and back on to reset it.

   d. Review any recent changes made to the printer agent.

CASE PROJECTS

Case Project 8-1: Defining Business Division Printing Needs

Use the NDPS Definition Form your instructor supplies to define printers, print queues, operators, and users to meet the printing needs for the Business Division and the Marketing Department, as defined in Table 8-4. If your lab has a laser printer attached to the network, use it instead of the Lexmark Optra R mentioned in the table for the Business Division.

After completing your NDPS Definition Form, have your instructor check it. Make any necessary changes to include all the printer information in the master NDPS Definition Form so that you can do the projects in later chapters.

Table 8-4　Business Division and Marketing Department network printing needs

Department	Network Printing Needs
Accounting	All Accounting users should have access to the Lexmark Optra R printer attached to Amy Pan's computer.
Marketing	The Marketing Department will share a Lexmark Optra R printer attached to the network by using the HP JetDirect dedicated print server.
Desktop Publishing	A high-resolution PostScript laser printer will be attached directly to the network and shared by Desktop Publishing users to print manuals and sales fliers. Kari Means and Lynn Dai also need to be able to send output to this printer.

HANDS-ON PROJECTS

Hands-on Project 8-1: Creating Printer Agents

Use iManager to create the printer agents Eric defined in Figure 8-30. When you have created all printer agents, have your instructor check your printer setup.

Hands-on Project 8-2: Creating a Printer Facility Map

Add the printer agents you created in Hands-on Project 8-1 to the printer facility map you started in Activity 8-16.

Hands-on Project 8-3: Setting Up Network Printing for the Business Division

Use iManager to create the printer objects you defined for the Business Division in Case Project 8-1.

Hands-on Project 8-4: Testing Your Printing Setup

Test your Business Division printers by sending output to the printer and then using iManager to verify that the results have been sent to the correct printer agent.

Hands-on Project 8-5: Performing a Print Services Quick Setup for the Business Division

Follow these steps to perform a quick setup for the Business Division's print services:

1. If necessary, start your computer, and log in with your administrative user name and password.

2. Start NetWare Administrator, and open a browse window to your **UAS** container.

3. Click the **Business** OU.

4. Click **Tools**, **Print Services Quick Setup (Non-NDPS)** from the menu.

5. Record the following information:

   - Print server name

     _____

   - Printer name

     _____

   - Printer type

     _____

   - Print queue name and volume

     _____

6. Change the printer name to **Bus_P1**.

7. Change the name of the print queue to **BUS_Q1**.

8. Click the **Create** button to create these printing objects.

9. Exit NetWare Administrator, and have your instructor check your results.

Hands-on Project 8-6: Troubleshooting Network Printing

In this project, your instructor will create one of the "bugs" described in the "Troubleshooting Network Printing" section. Use the techniques and fixes described in this chapter to find, document, and correct the problem. Write a brief report on your findings, and submit it to your instructor.

MANAGING DESKTOP ENVIRONMENTS WITH NOVELL CLIENT

After reading this chapter and completing the activities, you will be able to:

♦ Explain drive mapping in Windows and use the MAP command to establish drive mappings

♦ Describe the Distributed File System and set up DFS junctions to data directories

♦ Identify the types of login scripts and use them to map network drives, display messages, and run programs

♦ Install and use ZENworks for Desktops to help manage the user environment

---

As you learned in Chapter 1, supporting client environments is an important network administration task. Part of supporting client environments is making network resources and services easy to access from the user's desktop environment. Novell provides a variety of ways to help manage user desktop environments. In this chapter, you learn how to use the MAP command with login scripts in Windows to map a standard set of drive pointers for users. Novell Open Enterprise Server (OES) also includes the NetWare Distributed File System, which allows changing volume paths without affecting user access paths. You also learn about Novell ZENworks for Desktops, an optional product not included with Open Enterprise Server. It's designed to help network administrators manage desktop environments through centralized control of desktop policies and applications.

NETWORK DRIVE MAPPINGS

Drive pointers play an important role in accessing files on network volumes and directories from a Windows desktop system. A **drive pointer** is a letter used to reference storage areas in the file system. By default, Windows reserves the first five drive pointers (A: through E:) to reference storage devices on a local computer, so these letters are often referred to as the **local drive pointers**. For example, A: and B: are reserved for floppy disk drives, C: and D: are used for hard disks, and E: is often reserved for a CD-ROM drive or other external storage device.

Drive Mapping Concepts

Network drive pointers are letters (usually F: through Z:) representing directory paths and volumes in the network file system. Establishing network drive pointers is important for these reasons:

- They make it easier to access data files without needing to specify a complete path. For example, if the G: drive pointer is assigned to the UAS directory on the CORP volume, you can specify a path to the Apps directory by typing G:Apps instead of UASHOST_CORP:UAS\Apps.

- They allow applications and DOS commands that don't recognize volume names to access data and programs on multiple volumes and servers.

Network drive pointers can be one of two types: regular or search. Regular drive pointers are usually assigned to directories containing data files, whereas search drive pointers are assigned to network software directories. A **regular drive pointer** is assigned to a directory path and shows all directories and subdirectories leading to the storage area. A regular drive pointer should also be assigned to each volume so that applications that can't use NetWare complete paths are able to access data on any volume. Figure 9-1 shows how drive pointers are divided into local, regular, and search drive pointers.

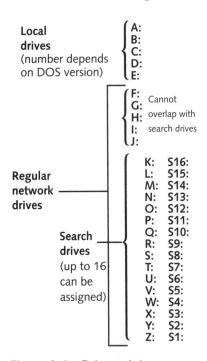

Figure 9-1 Drive pointers

A **root drive pointer** can be used to make drive pointers appear to users or applications as though the directory path is at the beginning of a drive or volume. Figure 9-2 shows an example of using two drive pointers, I: and J:, to access the same directory area. The J: drive pointer is a regular pointer because it shows the entire path leading to the directory, but I: is a root drive pointer that appears as though it were the first level in the directory structure.

```
                      ┌────── On the root drive, the path does not
                      │       appear on the DOS path
                      │
   I:\>dir
    │ Volume in drive I is CTS
    │ Directory of I:\
   INV       DAT              6    12-03-05   6:14p
   INVAPP          <DIR>           12-03-05   6:20p
            1 file(s)                  6 bytes
            1 dir(s)          14,417,920 bytes free

   I:\>j:

   J:\INVENTORY>dir
  ─┐
   │  Volume in drive J is CTS
   │  Directory of J:\INVENTORY
   │
   │ INV      DAT              6    12-03-05   6:14p
   │ INVAPP         <DIR>           12-03-05   6:20p
   │         1 file(s)                  6 bytes
   │         1 dir(s)          14,417,920 bytes free
   │ J:\INVENTORY>
  ─┘
        In regular drive mapping, the path is displayed
        and can be changed from the application
```

Figure 9-2   Regular and root drive pointers

Drive pointers I: and J: are assigned (or mapped) to the Inventory directory and have access to the same file. The advantage of using root drive pointers is that they help prevent an application or a DOS command from changing the drive pointer's mapping to another location in the directory structure. Normally, root drive pointers are used to access user home directories and the starting path to shared data directories.

A **search drive pointer** is a drive pointer added to the DOS path, which specifies a sequence of locations in which DOS and the NetWare shell look for program files not in the current directory. Search drive pointers play an important role in accessing the file system from DOS because they enable network administrators to place data files in separate directories from application software. Search drive pointers act like a Windows shortcut, so a user or an application in one directory path can access software and data elsewhere in the directory structure.

As shown in Figure 9-3, when you enter a command, Windows first determines that it's not an internal command and then looks in the current directory for a program or batch file with the name you specified. If it's not in the current directory, each search drive specified in the path is searched, starting with S1:, until the program is found or the "Bad command or filename" message is displayed. By assigning a search drive to the SYS:Public directory automatically, Novell Client enables you to run command-line utilities, such as MAP and RIGHTS, from any directory in the file system.

Search drives are assigned a sequence number consisting of the letter "S" followed by a sequential number from 1 to 16, and each search drive can point to only one directory location. Subdirectories aren't searched unless they are assigned to separate search drives. Search drives are also given a drive pointer, which starts with Z assigned to S1:, Y assigned to S2:, X to S3:, and so on. Drive pointers are kept in a table stored in each computer's RAM, and any changes are effective as long as the user is logged in. Because each computer keeps track of its own drive pointers in memory, users can assign the same drive pointer to different directory locations. For example, your computer can have the F: drive pointer mapped to the SYS:Public directory and the S3: search drive mapped to SYS:Software\WP; another user might have the F: drive pointer mapped to the CORP volume and the S3: search drive mapped to CORP:Engineer\CAD.

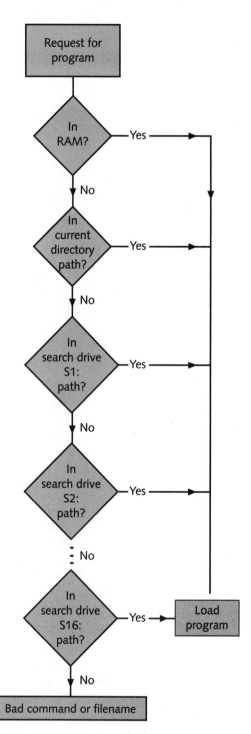

Figure 9-3   Using search drive pointers

Planning Drive Mappings

In a NetWare environment, the network administrator is responsible for establishing drive pointers to reference software and data locations in the directory structure. These drive pointers need to be assigned correctly so that Windows and DOS applications can access network files and directories as though they were on a local hard disk. As you learn in the following sections, planning a good set of drive pointers makes it easier to establish login scripts, install software, work with applications, and provide a standard user environment that's easy to troubleshoot and maintain.

If each computer had an unlimited number of drive pointers available, you could assign a regular or root drive pointer to each data directory and a search drive for each software package. However, having that many drive pointers is confusing to track, and too many search drives slow computer performance because of the number of directories to search through when loading software. Therefore, you need to plan a minimum set of standard drive pointers that enable computers to run the necessary software and give users convenient access to data. First, determine which regular and root drive pointers are needed for easy access to shared and private files with a drive letter instead of a lengthy NetWare path. Typical drive pointers for each user should include the following:

- *A drive pointer to the root of each volume*—These drive pointers give users easy access to data and software stored on volumes. They also serve as a standard path for running applications. Some software requires assigning a drive letter and path to reference file locations, and the same drive letter must be mapped to each volume for all users to run this software. With a two-volume structure, many network administrators map F: to the SYS volume and use another drive letter, such as G:, for the CORP volume. Another use for a volume drive pointer is accessing shared work directories for all users. For example, if a shared work directory named Forms is created on the root of the CORP volume, any user could access files in this directory with the volume drive pointer G:\Forms.

- *A root drive pointer mapped to the user's home directory*—This drive letter is the starting point for users' personal data storage. Making this drive letter a root drive is important because it prevents users from accidentally changing their home directory drive pointers to a different location. Users can create subdirectories within their home directories, and then move around in those subdirectories by using the CD command to return to the beginning of their home directory instead of changing to the root of the volume.

- *A root drive pointer mapped to the user's workgroup directory*—With this drive pointer, users can access shared files within their workgroups. For example, the Engineering Department has its L: drive mapped to CORP:Engineer, and the IT Department has its L: drive mapped to the CORP:IT directory. If a Shared directory is created for each department, any user can get to his or her workgroup's Shared directory with the root drive pointer L:\Shared.

- *Application drive pointers*—Additional drive pointers might be needed to install and access some software packages. When planning these drive pointers, all users running the application must use the same drive letter because the software is installed using this drive letter to access its data and work files. For example, if a program is installed with the L: drive mapped to the Apps directory of the CORP volume, a user with drive letter M: mapped to this directory couldn't install and run the program.

You should also plan search drive pointers so that users can access utilities or applications that run from the command prompt. Keep the total number of search drives to fewer than eight for better performance and less chance of conflicts with regular drive pointers. Windows applications don't need search drives mapped to their software directories because the path is stored in the properties of Windows icons and shortcuts. Most network administrators set up at least these search drive mappings:

- Search drive S1: to the SYS:Public directory
- Search drives S2: through S6: to DOS applications and utilities

A well-planned set of drive pointers should include a standard set of drive pointers that give users easy access to data volumes containing the files and applications they need. Table 9-1 shows the drive pointers Eric Kenton planned for accessing the Universal AeroSpace file system.

Table 9-1   Drive pointers for Universal AeroSpace

Drive Letter	Path
F:	Root of the SYS volume
G:	Root of the CORP volume
H:	Root drive to users' home directories
L:	Root drive to users' department directories, as follows: IT users: CORP:IT Engineering users: CORP:Engineer

Table 9-1   Drive pointers for Universal AeroSpace (continued)

Drive Letter	Path
S1:	SYS:Public
S2:	CORP:Apps\Utility

Eric used the F: drive pointer to the SYS volume to give administrative users access to applications or utilities stored on the SYS volume. Standard users don't need a regular drive letter mapped to SYS because their applications and data should be stored on separate data volumes, such as the CORP volume. A drive letter mapped to SYS should be reserved for administrative users, however.

Establishing Drive Pointers

Drive pointers can be assigned through Windows, with the NetWare MAP command, or from a login script. In the following sections, you learn how to use Windows and the NetWare MAP command; later in "Login Script Processing," you learn how to apply the MAP command to login scripts. An advantage of assigning drive mappings through login scripts is that users see the same drive mappings regardless of the physical computer they're logging in from. You learn how to assign drive mappings from login scripts in "Using Login Scripts" later in this chapter.

Mapping Drives from Windows

When a user logs out, all network drive pointers are disconnected from their assigned paths, requiring a way to reconnect the standard set of drive pointers. When you're using Windows Explorer to create drive mappings, you can select the "Check to always map this drive letter when you start Windows" option (see Figure 9-4) to connect a drive letter to a network path automatically the next time you log on from that computer.

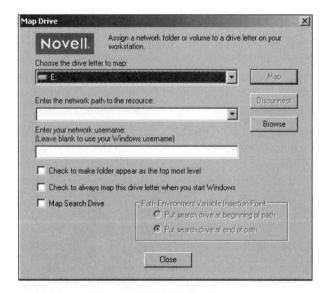

Figure 9-4   The Map Drive dialog box

Windows keeps track of the drive mapping in the local user's profile. When a user logs on to the local computer, Windows checks the profile and then attempts to map any drive letters to the specified network directories. If another eDirectory user logs on from the same computer with the same local Windows user name, the drive letter mappings might fail because the user's eDirectory name doesn't have rights to the NetWare directories in the Windows profile.

Activity 9-1: Mapping Network Drives in Windows

Time Required: 10 minutes

Objective: Use Windows Explorer to create network drive pointers.

Requirements: A Windows XP computer with Novell Client installed and the directory structure created in Chapter 3

Description: You have just logged in to another user's computer and need to revise the drive mappings to access your own directories. In this activity, you use Windows Explorer to create and view drive mappings.

1. If necessary, start your computer, and log in to eDirectory with your administrative user name and password.

2. Open Windows Explorer.

3. Right-click **My Network Places** and click **Novell Map Network Drive** to open the Map Drive dialog box (shown previously in Figure 9-4).

4. In the Choose the drive letter to map drop-down list box, click a free drive letter, and then record the drive letter you selected:

   _____

5. Enter the path to your IT directory structure, and click the **Map** button.

6. Open My Computer and verify that the drive mapping has been created.

7. Leave your system running and stay logged in for the next activity.

Using the MAP Command-Line Utility

The MAP command can be used in login scripts or from the command prompt for creating, modifying, and deleting regular and search drive pointers. A CNA must be familiar with using this command for several tasks, such as assigning a NetWare path to a drive letter. This is the syntax for the MAP command to create a new drive letter:

```
MAP option drive:=path
```

You can replace *option* with one of the parameters in Table 9-2.

Table 9-2 MAP command options

Option	Description
ROOT	Used to make a drive appear as the root of a volume. Using the ROOT option for Windows Explorer to point to the subdirectory is important. Including the ROOT option for all drive mappings is a good practice.
INS	Used to insert a new search drive at the sequence number you specify and then renumber any existing search drives.
DEL	Used to remove the specified regular or search drive mapping.

You use the ROOT option to make the drive pointer a root mapping. The *drive:* parameter can be any letter of the alphabet, and the *path* parameter can be a complete or relative NetWare path leading to the directory. A complete path includes the volume name followed by a colon and all directories leading up to the directory. For example, the following command maps root drive letter R: to the Engineering Department's Rover directory:

```
MAP ROOT R:=UASHOST_CORP:Engineer\NASA\Rover
```

Relative paths use an existing drive letter as a starting point, eliminating the need to specify the volume name and any directories in the path to the existing drive letter. For example, if drive letter G: is mapped to the UASHOST_CORP:Engineer directory, you could use drive letter G: to map the root drive letter R: to the Rover directory, as shown:

```
MAP ROOT R:=G:NASA\Rover
```

If you don't include a path, the MAP command assigns the specified drive pointer to the current path. In the following activities, you learn how to use the MAP command to map regular and search drive letters to paths in the directory structure created in Chapter 3.

Activity 9-2: Using the MAP Command

Time Required: 10 minutes

Objective: Use the MAP command to create network drive pointers.

Requirements: Same as Activity 9-1; also must have Apps and IT directories in your CORP volume structure

Description: You have just logged in to another user's computer and need to revise the drive mappings to access your own directories. In this activity, you use the MAP command to create, view, and remove regular and root drive pointers.

1. If necessary, start your computer, and log in to eDirectory with your administrative user name and password.

2. Click **Start**, **Run**, type **command** in the Open text box, and click **OK** to open a DOS command prompt window. (Typing "cmd" opens a Windows 2000 command prompt window that doesn't support mapping search drives.)

3. Change to the F: drive by typing **F:** and pressing **Enter**.

4. Enter the **MAP** command to display your current drive mappings. Record the regular drive mappings here, and then press **Enter**.

   _____

5. Enter the **MAP ROOT G:=UASHOST_CORP:** command, and then press **Enter** to create a drive pointer to the CORP volume. (If you're using a shared classroom server, enter the **MAP ROOT G:=UASHOST_STUDENTS:##Corp** command, replacing **##** with your assigned student number.)

6. After you have mapped the G: drive to your CORP volume, you can use relative paths that include G: to access other directories in your UAS structure. Use the following commands (pressing **Enter** after each line) to map drive letters to department directories:

```
MAP ROOT I:=G:\Apps
MAP ROOT L:=G:\IT
```

7. The MAP NEXT _path_ command assigns the specified path to the first available drive letter, proceeding from F: through Z:. This command is useful when you want to map an unused drive letter to a directory path and you don't care what letter is used. To map the next available drive letter to the WIN32 directory on the SYS: volume, enter the **MAP NEXT SYS:Public\WIN32** command, and then press **Enter**.

8. Record the drive letter used for the Public directory:

   _____

9. To delete drive mappings, you use the MAP DEL _drive:_ command. To delete the drive letters created in Step 6, enter the following commands (pressing **Enter** after each line):

```
MAP DEL I:
MAP DEL L:
```

10. Enter the **MAP** command and press **Enter**. Record your regular drive pointers:

    _____

11. Enter the **EXIT** command and press **Enter** to return to Windows. You can stay logged in for the next activity.

ACTIVITY

Activity 9-3: Mapping Search Drives

Time Required: 10 minutes

Objective: Plan and create network drive pointers.

Requirements: Same as Activity 9-1

Description: In this activity, you remove all existing search drives on your computer, and then use MAP commands to establish a set of search drive pointers to software directories on your network.

1. If necessary, start your computer, and log in to eDirectory with your administrative user name and password.

2. In this step, you use Notepad to create a simple batch file for testing search drive mappings. Start Notepad and then create a batch file containing the following commands:

```
@echo off
cls
echo CONGRATULATIONS! You have accessed the database software.
echo The contents of your current directory is:
dir
echo If you did this with a search drive, the DB.BAT program echo should
NOT be listed.
echo ..
echo This screen means your search drive worked.
pause
```

3. Save the batch file in your Apps\Office directory with the name **db.bat**, and then close Notepad.

4. Open a DOS command prompt window, as you did in Activity 9-2, and change to your F: drive.

5. Enter the **MAP** command, and press **Enter**. Record your search drives here:

_____

6. Try running the DB program (the db.bat file) without a search drive by typing **DB** at the command prompt, and then pressing **Enter**. Record the message you see:

_____

7. To use the DB program, enter **MAP ROOT S16:=CORP:Apps\Office** (if you're using a dedicated server) or **MAP ROOT S16:=STUDENTS:##Corp\Apps\Office** (substituting your assigned student number for ## if you're using a shared classroom server) to map the last available search drive to your Office directory, and then press **Enter**.

8. Mapping a search drive to S16: adds the search drive mapping to the end of the existing search drives and prevents overwriting an existing path. Test your search drive by typing the **DB** command, and then pressing **Enter**. Record the results. If your new search drive works, the database test screen is displayed. When you're finished, press any key to continue.

_____

9. When inserting a search drive between two existing drives, include the INS option and replace the search drive number with the number of the existing search drive that you want to be placed after the new search drive. When setting up search drives, the most commonly used paths should be given lower search drive numbers to reduce the number of directories NetWare has to search through when looking for a program or file. To insert a search drive mapping between the existing S1: and S2: search drives and view your drive mappings, enter the following commands, pressing **Enter** after each line:

```
MAP INS S2:=SYS:
MAP
```

10. Sometimes it's convenient to add a new search drive to the beginning of the list, and then delete it when it's no longer needed. For example, if you want to run some DOS-based utilities from a CD, you can add a search drive to the beginning of the search list that points to the CD, and then delete that drive mapping

after you finish your work. To add a search drive to the SYS:Public\WIN95 directory before the existing S1: search drive, enter the following commands, pressing **Enter** after each line:

```
MAP INS S1:=SYS:Public\WIN95
MAP
```

NOTE

Drive letter W: was assigned to S1:, and although the other search drives were renumbered, they retained their drive letter assignments. NetWare keeps track of search drive numbers by their sequence in the DOS path; because drive W: is now the first drive in the path, it becomes the S1: search drive.

11. To verify the sequence of search drive letters in your DOS path, enter the **PATH** command, and then press **Enter**.

12. To remove the search drive to the Public\Win95 directory and resequence the search drives, enter the following commands, pressing **Enter** after each line. Notice that the search drive letters (X:, Y:, Z:) appear in the path sequence based on their search number.

```
MAP DEL S1:
PATH
```

13. Because search drives are really the sequence of the drive letter in the DOS path, NetWare doesn't skip search drive numbers. As a result, you can use the command MAP S16:=*path* if you want to add a search drive to the end of the search list but don't know the number of the last search drive. (If you already have 16 search drives, you are given the opportunity to overwrite the existing search drive.) To add a search drive to the end of your list and verify your results, enter the following commands, pressing **Enter** after each line:

```
MAP S16:=SYS:Public\Win95
MAP
```

14. Enter **EXIT** and press **Enter** to return to Windows. You can stay logged in for the next activity.

Using Directory Map Objects

To set up drive pointers, you must know the physical location of the directory being mapped to the drive letter. Maintaining drive pointers for many users can become a problem if files or directories are moved from one volume to another. The Directory Map object simplifies accessing network data and maintaining drive pointers. As described in Chapter 4, it's an eDirectory object containing the path to a volume and directory in the network file system. MAP commands can then establish drive pointers by specifying the Directory Map object instead of entering the complete path. Because drive pointers can be relative to the value in the Directory Map object's Path property, when a directory's location is moved, only the path in the Directory Map object needs to be changed. In addition, MAP commands in login scripts and batch files that use Directory Map objects don't need to be modified. Eric established the Directory Map objects shown in Table 9-3 for each department's directory.

Table 9-3   Directory Map objects for Universal AeroSpace

Name	Context	Path
ITData	IT.UAS	UASHOST_CORP:IT
EngData	Engineering.UAS	UASHOST_CORP:Engineer
MfgData	Mfg.UAS	UASHOST_CORP:Mfg
MgmtData	Mgmt.UAS	UASHOST_CORP:Mgmt

Drive L: points to each department's work directory (refer back to Table 9-1). Currently, the Engineer directory is planned for storage on the CORP volume. However, UAS is planning to add a server for the Engineering Department's use. Using a Directory Map object when mapping drive letters for the Engineer directory means the system can be expanded by simply changing the path to include the new server in the Directory Map object. In the following activity, you create Directory Map objects in your UAS container.

Activity 9-4: Creating and Testing Directory Map Objects

Time Required: 10 minutes

Objective: Create Directory Map objects.

Requirements: An IT directory within your UAS directory structure

Description: In this activity, you use ConsoleOne to create a Directory Map object for the IT Department (as shown in Table 9-3), give the IT Department rights to use the object, and then test the object by using the MAP command to map a drive letter.

1. If necessary, start your computer, and log in to eDirectory with your administrative user name and password.

2. Start ConsoleOne, and expand the eDirectory tree and your **UAS** container.

3. Follow these steps to create a Directory Map object named ITData in the IT OU:

   a. Click the **IT OU**, and press **Insert** to open the New Object dialog box.

   b. Double-click the **Directory Map** object to open the New Directory Map dialog box.

   c. Enter **ITData** in the Name text box, and press **Tab**.

   d. Click the **browse** button next to the Volume text box to open the Select Object dialog box. Click the **UASHOST_CORP** volume, and then click **OK**.

   e. Click the **browse** button next to the **Path** text box, and then double-click the **UASHOST_CORP** volume.

   f. Click the **IT** directory, and then click **OK** to place IT in the Path text box.

   g. Click **OK** to create the Directory Map object in the IT OU.

4. Make the IT OU a trustee of ITData with the Read right to the Path property, as described in Chapter 7.

5. Log out, and then log in to eDirectory with your **Luke McMann** user name and password.

6. Follow these steps to test the newly created Directory Map object:

   a. Open a DOS command prompt window, and change to your F: drive, if necessary.

   b. Map drive letter L: to the IT directory by typing **MAP ROOT L:=ITData** and pressing **Enter**.

   c. Type **MAP**, and then press **Enter** to confirm that the drive letter points to your IT directory.

   d. Type **EXIT**, and then press **Enter** to return to your Windows desktop.

7. Double-click the **My Computer** icon, and record your network drive mappings here:

   _____

8. Close all windows, and log out. Leave your system running for the next activity.

Using the NetWare Distributed File System

Even with Directory Map objects, in large directory structures spread over several servers and volumes, network drive mappings can be difficult to manage and use. The purpose of the NetWare **Distributed File System (DFS)** is to isolate the logical structure of network data from the physical volumes where it's stored. With DFS, it's possible to make a user's data seem as though it's located on a single drive, even when it's stored on several servers scattered throughout the eDirectory tree. In addition to simplifying a user's interface to network-stored data, DFS can reduce the complexity of drive mappings that network administrators must manage.

Setting Up DFS

The NetWare Distributed File System uses **DFS junctions** to represent network volumes. They store the physical path to the NetWare server and volume where a data directory is located. Before using DFS junctions, you must create at least one DFS management context in your eDirectory tree. The DFS management context stores the location of the **Volume Location Database (VLDB)** in eDirectory. The purpose of the VLDB is to store the actual network path to the volume specified in DFS junctions. When a user requests access to a network volume through a DFS junction, Novell Client uses the junction's unique ID to search the VLDB for a physical path to the data (see Figure 9-5). The DFS management context for the server in Figure 9-5 is specified as CN=UASHOST.O=UAS.

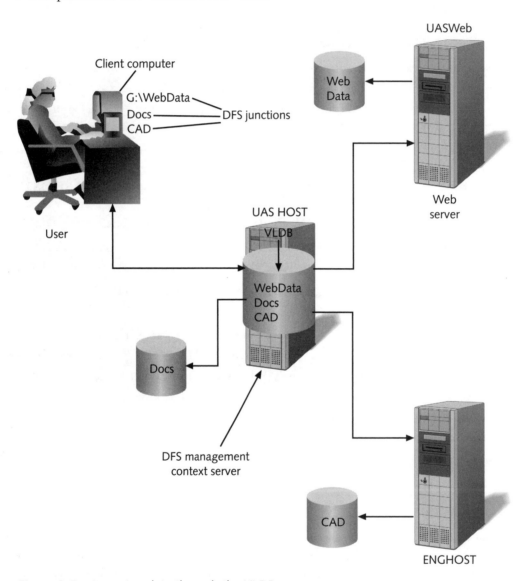

Figure 9-5   Accessing data through the VLDB

Using the VLDB, Novell Client can retrieve data or display volume contents without users having to know where data is actually stored. Because Open Enterprise Server doesn't include a Web-based DFS management console, NetWare DFS must be managed in ConsoleOne. You can create a management context by using ConsoleOne to complete the following steps. Although these steps aren't a required activity, if you have a dedicated server, you need to follow them to create a DFS management context in your eDirectory tree:

EXAMPLE

1. Log in to eDirectory with your administrative user name and password. Start ConsoleOne and browse to the container object to be used as the DFS management context. To make it easier to manage, setting the DFS management context to the same container as the server is usually a good idea. (For example, if you're using a dedicated server, you should navigate to your UAS Organization.)

2. Right-click the container, and then click New, DFS Management Context from the menu to open the Select the Servers window shown in Figure 9-6, where you choose the server where the VLDB will be stored.

9

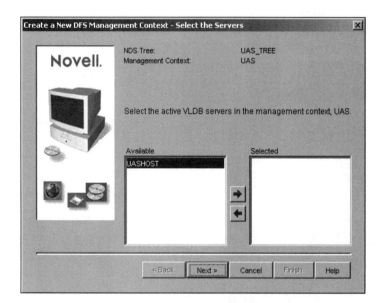

Figure 9-6   Selecting a server to store the VLDB

3. Click the right arrow button to select the server, and then click Next to display the Specify Database Location window shown in Figure 9-7.

4. By default, the VLDB is located in the Etc directory of the SYS volume. Because the VLDB's location must remain fixed to be accessed through the management context, the SYS:Etc path is a good choice because the SYS volume can't be moved or split in the DFS. If you want to place the VLDB in a different directory, you can change the path shown in Figure 9-7. For DFS to work, certain NLMs must be loaded on the server hosting the VLDB. To avoid loading these NLMs manually, make sure the Load NLMs automatically when the server restarts check box is selected.

5. Click Finish to create the management context and VLDB and load the necessary NLMs on the selected server.

You can use ConsoleOne to view VLDB information and perform basic configuration by right-clicking the server object, selecting Properties, and then clicking NSS VLDB on the Supported Services tab (see Figure 9-8). After creating the DFS management context, you can begin creating DFS junctions. In Activity 9-5, you create a DFS junction in the IT directory that points to the SYS volume. You then see how a user in the IT Department could map a drive to the IT directory and use the DFS junction to access files on the SYS volume.

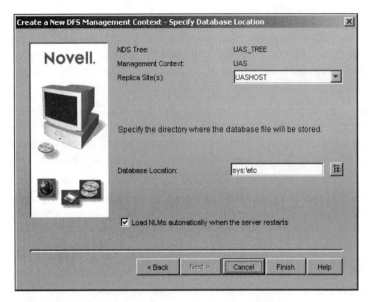

Figure 9-7   Selecting a location for the VLDB

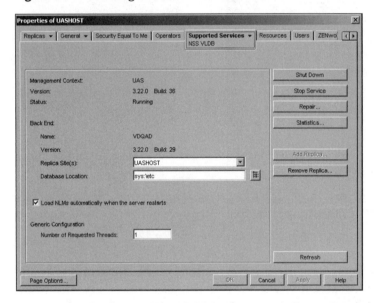

Figure 9-8   Configuring the VLDB in the server's Properties dialog box

Activity 9-5: Creating and Testing DFS Junctions

Time Required: 10 minutes

Objective: Create a DFS junction and use it to access data on another volume.

Requirements: If you're working with a dedicated server, complete the Example steps shown previously in this section to create a DFS management context. If you're using a shared classroom server, your instructor will need to create the DFS management context on the classroom server.

Description: In this activity, you use ConsoleOne to create a DFS junction for the IT Department and then use it to view data on the SYS volume.

1. If necessary, start your computer, and log in to eDirectory with your administrative user name and password.

2. Start ConsoleOne, and expand your eDirectory tree and **CORP** volume.

3. Follow these steps to create a subdirectory within the IT directory:

   a. Click to select the **IT** directory.

   b. Click the **New Object** button to open the New Object dialog box.

   c. Verify that Directory is selected, and then click **OK** to display the New Directory dialog box.

   d. Enter **Shared** in the Name text box, and the click **OK** to create the Shared subdirectory.

4. Follow these steps to give all users in the IT Department rights to the Shared subdirectory:

   a. Right-click the **Shared** directory and click **Properties** to open the Properties of Shared dialog box.

   b. Click the **Trustees** tab and then click the **Add Trustee** button to open the Select Objects dialog box.

   c. Click the **IT** OU and then click **OK**.

   d. Click to select all check boxes except Supervisor and Access Control and then click **OK** to save your changes and return to the ConsoleOne main window.

5. Follow these steps to create a DFS junction that points to the SYS volume:

   a. Click to expand the **IT** directory. Right-click the **Shared** directory, point to **New**, point to **Shortcut**, and then click **Junction** to display the window shown in Figure 9-9.

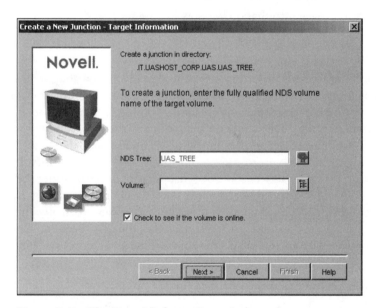

Figure 9-9   The Target Information window

   b. Click the **browse** button next to the Volume text box, navigate to your UAS container, click the **UASHOST_SYS** volume, and then click **OK**.

   c. Click **Next** to display the window shown in Figure 9-10. Enter **SYSPublic** in the Junction Name text box, and then click **Finish**. Note that although the SYSPublic DFS junction appears as a file in the Shared directory in ConsoleOne, it appears as a folder in Windows Explorer.

6. Give all users in the IT OU rights to the SYSPublic junction.

7. Exit ConsoleOne and log out.

8. Follow these steps to test the DFS junction:

   a. Log in to eDirectory with your **Luke McMann** user name. (Click the **Advanced** button in the Novell Login window to set the context to the IT OU.)

   b. Follow the instructions in Activity 9-1 to create a new drive pointer mapped to your IT\Shared directory.

   c. Double-click the **SYSPublic** folder to see the directories on the SYS volume.

9. Log out, and leave your system running for the next activity.

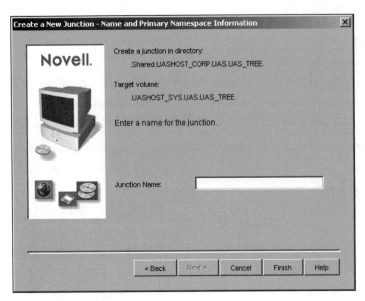

Figure 9-10 The Name and Primary Namespace Information window

Moving and Splitting Volumes

Often it's necessary to make changes in the network directory structure that involve creating new volumes, moving volumes to other servers, or splitting data volumes to provide more space and improve performance. DFS facilitates the process of moving a volume by automatically creating a volume on the new server, moving all data and trustee assignments, and then creating a DFS junction that points to the new volume location. A DFS junction enables users and drive mappings to access data in the new volume with the same path used before the volume move. Splitting a volume allows you to move a portion of an existing NSS volume to a different location, leaving a DFS junction that allows users and drive mappings to find data using the original directory structure. For example, if the UAS network's CORP volume starts to fill up, one solution is splitting the volume by moving the Engineer directory to a new volume on another server. Normally, this process involves changing drive mappings and informing users how to access data from the new location. This process can be simplified, however, because NetWare DFS moves the data to a new volume and creates a DFS junction pointing to the new location.

When moving or splitting volumes, you need to be aware of the following points:

- Although the source volume for a move can be NSS or traditional, only NSS volumes can be split.

- The destination volume for a move or split must be an NSS volume.

- The source volume must be specified with its distinguished name, which includes both leading and trailing periods. (For example, the distinguished name of the UASHOST_CORP volume in the UAS Organization is .UASHOST_CORP.UAS.)

- If a server crashes or some other event interrupts the move or split, DFS supports the capability to resume the operation.

- Perform DFS operations during off hours to prevent files from being open during a move or split. Files in use during a move or split aren't transferred to the new location.

Moving a Volume

The DFS management context and DFS junctions are managed from ConsoleOne, but volume moves and splits are performed in iManager. To move a volume in iManager, you would use these steps:

EXAMPLE

1. Start iManager and log in with your administrative user name and password.

2. Click to expand the Storage heading, and then click the Volumes link.

3. Select the server storing the volume to be moved, and then select the volume name from the list (see Figure 9-11).

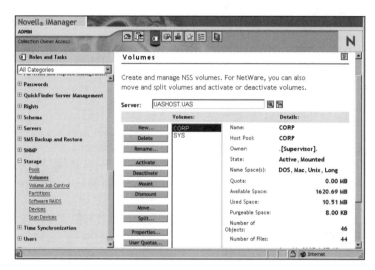

Figure 9-11   Selecting a volume to move

4. Click the Move button to the left of the Volumes list to display the Move Volume window shown in Figure 9-12. You can start the move now or specify a time to move the volume later, such as during off hours.

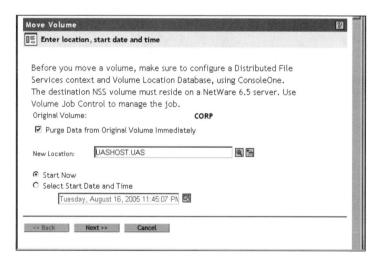

Figure 9-12   The Move Volume window

5. Click Next to display the Create a new volume window. Enter the name of the new volume, remembering that the volume name must be unique on the selected server.

6. Then click Next to display another Create a new volume window, shown in Figure 9-13, where you specify the storage pool to create the volume in and an optional volume quota size. You can also click the New Pool button to create a new storage pool or partition, as discussed in Chapter 3.

Figure 9-13   Entering pool information for the new volume

7. Click Next to display another Create a new volume window, where you select attributes for the volume (see Figure 9-14).

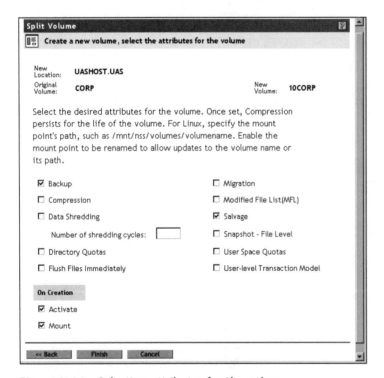

Figure 9-14   Selecting attributes for the volume

8. Select the attributes you want for the volume, and then click Finish to create the volume and move the data. All volume data, attributes, and trustee assignments are moved to the new volume, and a DFS junction is created in the original volume that points to the new location.

Splitting a Volume

To split a volume in iManager, you use these steps:

EXAMPLE

1. Start iManager and log in with your administrative user name and password.

2. Click to expand the Storage heading, and then click the Volumes link.

3. Select the server storing the volume to be moved, and then select the volume name from the list, as shown previously in Figure 9-11.

4. Click the Split button to the left of the Volumes list to display the Split Volume window (see Figure 9-15).

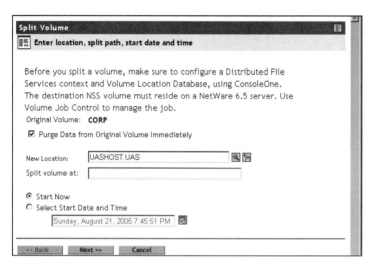

Figure 9-15   The Split Volume window

5. In the Split volume at text box, enter the directory path where you want the split to start. As with moving a volume, you can start the split now or specify a time to move the volume later, such as during off hours.

6. Click Next to display the Create a new volume window. Enter the name of the volume where you want the split data to reside, and click Next to display another Create a new volume window (shown previously in Figure 9-13).

7. Select an existing pool or click the New Pool button to create a new partition and pool. Click Next to display another Create a new volume window for selecting volume attributes (shown previously in Figure 9-14).

8. Click Finish to create the new volume and split the source volume by moving data to the new volume and creating a DFS junction on the source volume.

After splitting the volume, the DFS junction created on the source volume enables users to access the directory structure that was moved as though it were still on the original volume.

USING LOGIN SCRIPTS

Unless you select the option to reconnect drive mappings when you log in, any drive mappings established during a network session are effective only until you log out. The next time you log in, you must reconnect each drive pointer you want to use. This method is time consuming and requires keeping track of all drive pointer names, which could lead to user errors. To solve these problems, Novell provides login scripts for establishing users' network environments each time they log in. A NetWare **login script** consists of a set of

NetWare login commands that Novell Client processes when a user logs in with a valid user name and password. As shown in Figure 9-16, login script commands are stored in eDirectory and then sent to the user's computer from the server.

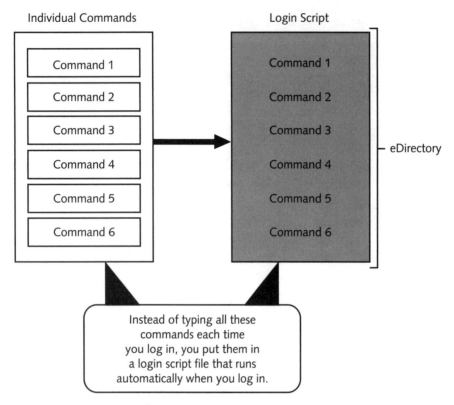

Figure 9-16   NetWare login script processing

The computer processes each command statement, starting with the first command. As shown in Figure 9-17, the Script tab in the Novell Login window has options for controlling how login script commands are processed.

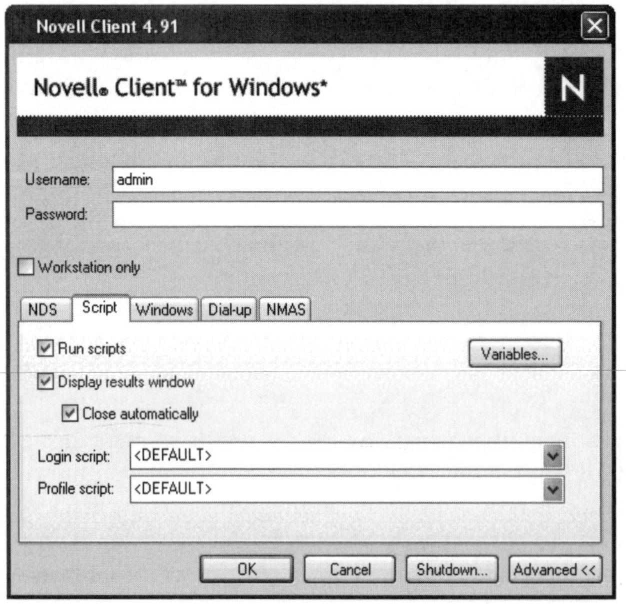

Figure 9-17   Login script options in the Script tab

You use the Run scripts check box to control whether a user's computer processes login script commands. If you want to display a message to users when login scripts run, select the Display results window check box. To close the results window after all login script commands have been processed, select the Close automatically check box.

When testing new login scripts, you should select the Display results window option and disable the Close automatically option so that you can verify the results and check for any error messages. Two problems are common with login scripts. The first is drive mapping commands that don't work because of insufficient rights to the directory in the MAP command. When writing login scripts, you might need to review users' file system rights. The second is users not getting any network drive mappings. Check to make sure the Run scripts option is enabled on their computers. If they are getting some drive mappings but not others, make sure they have at least Read and File Scan rights in the directories being mapped in the login script.

Types of Login Scripts

To understand how NetWare stores and processes login scripts, you need to know the types of login scripts and their purposes. For maximum flexibility, NetWare has four types of login scripts that enable network administrators to give all users a standard environment yet meet individual user needs. A **container login script** is a property of a container used to provide standard setups for all users in that container. **Profile login scripts** are eDirectory objects containing login commands common to multiple users, regardless of the container in which their user object is stored. To address specific user requirements, each user object has its own **user login script** property containing additional statements that run after the container and profile login scripts. The **default login script** is a set of commands in Novell Client that establish a default working environment for users who don't have a user login script. To become a CNA, you need to know how these login scripts work together and the sequence in which they run to set up a reliable, efficient login script system for your network. The flowchart in Figure 9-18 shows the relationship between types of NetWare login scripts.

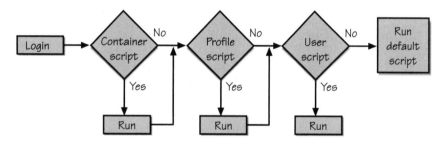

Figure 9-18   The order for processing login script types

When a login script is created for a container, the commands are carried out when users in that container log in to the network. After all commands in the container login script run, NetWare then determines whether the user is assigned to a profile object. If so, NetWare runs any login script commands included in the profile object's Login Script property. The last step is to run commands in the user login script or default login script. If a user doesn't have a user login script defined, Novell Client runs the commands in the default login script.

A good way to remember the order for login script processing is the acronym CPU: *container, profile, user.*

Remember that login script commands processed last take precedence, which means drive mappings made in the user or default login script file can overwrite or replace drive mappings in the container login script. As a result, many network administrators disable processing of the default script and remove the rights of users to change their personal login scripts, as discussed in Chapter 7. In the following sections, you learn more about processing container, profile, user, and default login scripts.

Container Login Scripts

The purpose of container login scripts is to map a search drive to the Public directory and set up drive pointers that all users in a container access. When a user logs in, only login script commands in the user's home container are carried out; login script commands in parent containers aren't run. Each container login script should include all the commands needed to set up a standard working environment for users in that container.

Profile Login Scripts

A profile login script enables you to create a standard set of login commands for selected users. To set one up, you create a Profile eDirectory object in a container, enter login script commands in the object's Login Script property, and then grant users Read attribute rights to the Profile object's Login Script property. Profile login scripts are independent of the container, so they have the advantage of being available to users in any container. A limitation is that users can have only one Profile object associated with their user names.

User Login Scripts

The user login script is located in a user object's Login Script property. Unless the EXIT command is issued in the container or profile login script, Novell Client runs any login script commands in the user's Login Script property. If there are no commands in the user's Login Script property and the NO_DEFAULT command hasn't been issued, Novell Client runs the default login script.

By default, you can access and maintain user login scripts in iManager, ConsoleOne, or NetWare Administrator by selecting the Login Script property in the user's Properties dialog box. If you don't want users to be able to modify their own login scripts, you can use the Selected properties option in ConsoleOne to remove the Write attribute right from the user's Login Script property, as explained in Chapter 7.

Maintaining the login script environment is more difficult with user login scripts because making changes could require modifying many separate user login script files. Therefore, many network administrators try to reduce the need for user login scripts by placing most commands in container or profile login scripts.

Default Login Scripts

The default login script provides basic drive mappings for users until container and profile scripts have been established or if there are no user login scripts. The default login script includes the following statements:

- MAP *1:=SYS: (maps the first network drive, usually the F: drive, to the SYS volume)
- MAP INS S1:=SYS:Public (maps the first search drive to the Public directory)

After a container login script has been established, preventing the default login script from running is important so that drive mappings in the container login script aren't overwritten or duplicated. NetWare has three basic ways to stop the default login script from running:

- Place the NO_DEFAULT command in the container or profile login script.
- Provide a user login script for each user on the network, even if the user login script contains only the EXIT command.
- Include an EXIT command in the container or profile login script, which ends the login script process and, therefore, prevents all subsequent login scripts from running. Placing the EXIT command in the container login script isn't a good option, however, because it also prevents profile login scripts from running.

Although some network administrators avoid large or complex login scripts, most actually prefer having one large container login script for each OU to manage a user's network environment, instead of having several user and profile login scripts that require looking in many different places when problems occur. Based on your network environment and personal preference, you need to decide which method is best.

Entering Login Scripts

NOTE Login scripts can be entered and maintained in ConsoleOne, iManager, or NetWare Administrator. All these utilities work in much the same way: You select an object to modify and then use the Login Script tab to enter login script commands. An advantage of ConsoleOne is that you can use the server console, so you can enter and modify login scripts on the server while using your computer to test scripts. A login script is actually a program or batch file, so making sure all necessary punctuation and symbols are entered correctly is critical. In the following sections, you learn how to use iManager and ConsoleOne to enter login scripts.

Creating a Container Login Script

In Activity 9-6, you enter a container login script that works with the default login script to map drives to the SYS and CORP volumes when you log in as an administrator from the UAS container.

NOTE If you're using a dedicated server, you can use your server console to enter and modify login scripts. You then test scripts from your computer by logging in as a regular user. You don't have to log back in as an administrator to fix a login script error.

Activity 9-6: Creating a Container Login Script

Time Required: 10 minutes

Objective: Create and enter login script commands and variables.

Requirements: A Windows XP computer with Novell Client installed

Description: Currently, when you log in as administrator, you have only the default login script commands. In this activity, you create a login script for your UAS container that maps drive G: to your UASHOST_CORP volume. The default login script then continues to map drive F: to SYS and the search drive to SYS:Public. You also log in with your user name in the IT.UAS container to test your login script.

1. If necessary, start your computer, and log on to your local computer.

2. Start your Web browser and start iManager by entering the URL **https://*IPaddress*/nps/iManager.html** and pressing **Enter**. Log in to iManager with your administrative user name and password.

3. Click to expand the **eDirectory Administration** heading, and then click the **Modify Object** link.

4. Click the **Object Selector** button, click your **UAS** container, and then click **OK** to display the Modify Object window.

5. Click the **Login Script** link. Click in the Login script text box, enter the **MAP G:=UASHOST_CORP:** command, and press **Enter**.

6. Click **OK** to save the login script and return to the main iManager window.

7. Exit iManager, close your Web browser, and log out to display a new Novell Login window.

   In the following steps, you test your container login script to make sure the login script entered in the parent UAS container doesn't run for users logging in from UAS subcontainers.

8. Log in with your administrative user name and password.

9. Double-click the **My Computer** icon, and record the regular network drive mappings:

   _____

   _____

   _____

10. Close the My Computer window, and log out to display a new login window.

11. Change the default context to the **IT.UAS** container, and log in as **LMcMann**.

12. Double-click the **My Computer** icon, and record the network drives. Does Luke have a drive mapped to the UASHOST_CORP volume?

---

13. Close the My Computer window, and log out. Leave your system running for the next activity.

Creating a Profile Login Script

Luke McMann has asked Kellie Thiele to be responsible for the company's login scripts because of her programming background. Kellie decided that using profile scripts to store MAP commands common to users in multiple containers would be easier to manage than repeating them in the IT, Engineering, Mfg, and Mgmt container login scripts. For example, all users in the WebMgrs group have access to the IT\Web directory. Kellie decided to assign drive pointer W: (for Web site) to the directory for WebMgrs group members. To give these group members the same drive mappings, she created a Profile object named WebProfile in the UAS container. Kellie then granted the WebMgrs group the Read attribute right to the Profile object's Login Script property. Next, she assigned the Profile object to the Login Script property of her user account in the IT OU and a WebMgrs user account in the Business OU. In the future, other users can be assigned to help manage the Web site by adding their user names to the WebMgrs group and the WebProfile object. In the following activity, you use ConsoleOne to enter and test a profile login script by creating a WebProfile object for your UAS network.

Activity 9-7: Creating a Profile Login Script

Time Required: 10 minutes

Objective: Create and enter login script commands and variables.

Requirements: A Windows XP computer with Novell Client installed as well as the following items:

- A WebMgrs group (created in Chapter 5)
- A Web subdirectory within the IT directory
- A Kari Means user in the Engineering OU

Description: To give the WebMgrs group members a drive mapping to the IT\Web directory, Kellie decided to create a Profile object and a profile login script. In this activity, you use the same process Kellie did, and then test the profile script by logging in as different users and checking your drive mappings.

1. If necessary, start your computer, and log in to eDirectory with your administrative user name and password.

2. Start ConsoleOne. *Optional:* If you're using ConsoleOne from a dedicated server, click the **Novell** button on the graphical server console, and then click **ConsoleOne**. After starting ConsoleOne on the server, authenticate by performing the following steps:

   a. Click to highlight the **NDS** object.

   b. Click **File**, **Authenticate** from the ConsoleOne menu to display the Novell Login window. Enter your administrative user name and password.

   c. Click the **browse** button to select your eDirectory tree. Enter the context of your administrative user name and click **Login** to authenticate.

3. Expand your eDirectory tree, and if you're using a shared classroom server, expand the **CLASS** Organization to view your UAS container.

4. Click the **New Object** button on the ConsoleOne toolbar to open the New Object dialog box.

5. Scroll down and click the **Profile** object type, and then click **OK** to open the New Profile dialog box. Enter **WebProfile** in the Name text box, and click the **Define additional properties** check box.

6. Click **OK** to create the profile object and open the Properties of WebProfile dialog box.

7. Click the **Login Script** tab, and enter the **MAP ROOT W:=UASHOST_CORP:IT\Web** command in the Login Script text box.

8. Click **Apply**, and then click **Close** to save the login script and return to the main ConsoleOne window.

9. Follow these steps to grant the WebMgrs group the Read right to the profile login script:

   a. In the ConsoleOne window, right-click the **WebProfile** object, and then click **Properties** to open the Properties of WebProfile dialog box.

   b. Click the **NDS Rights** tab to display the trustees of the WebProfile object. Click the **Add Trustee** button to open the Select Object dialog box.

   c. Click the **WebMgrs** group, and then click **OK** to open the Rights assigned to selected objects dialog box. Click **[All Attributes Rights]**, and verify that the Read and Compare rights are selected.

   d. Click **OK** to place your new trustee assignment in the Trustees list box. Click **OK** to save your changes and return to the main ConsoleOne window.

10. Follow these steps to attach the WebProfile object to the KThiele user account:

    a. Click the **IT** OU to display all user objects. Right-click **KThiele** in the object pane, and then click **Properties** to open the Properties of KThiele dialog box.

    b. Scroll to the right, if necessary, and click the **Login Script** tab to display the Login Script text box.

    c. Click the **browse** button next to the Profile text box to open the Select Object dialog box.

    d. Click the **up arrow** to move up one level. Click the **WebProfile** object, and then click **OK** to place it in the Profile text box.

    e. Click **OK** to save the changes to the user login script and return to the main ConsoleOne window.

11. Exit ConsoleOne, and log out to display a new login window.

12. Log in as **KThiele** in the IT OU.

13. Double-click the **My Computer** icon, and record the network drive mappings. Verify that the W: drive is mapped to the IT\Web directory.

    _____

14. If your drive mapping fails, make sure you have made Kellie a member of the WebMgrs group and the WebMgrs group has the necessary rights to the IT\Web directory.

15. Log out to display a new login window. Change the default context to **Engineering.UAS**, and then log in as **KMeans**.

16. Double-click the **My Computer** icon, and record Kari's drive mappings:

    _____

17. Close the My Computer window, and log out. Leave your system running for the next activity.

Login Script Programming

Creating login scripts is much like writing programs; you need to learn the valid commands and the syntax, or rules, for formatting commands. Like any programming language, login script commands can use variables so that one command can have multiple values.

Figure 9-19 shows a sample container login script to map drive letters for all users in an OU. Notice the statements to display a greeting message and establish a network environment by mapping the drive pointers identified earlier. In the following sections, you learn how to use login script commands and variables to set up drive mappings and display messages to users.

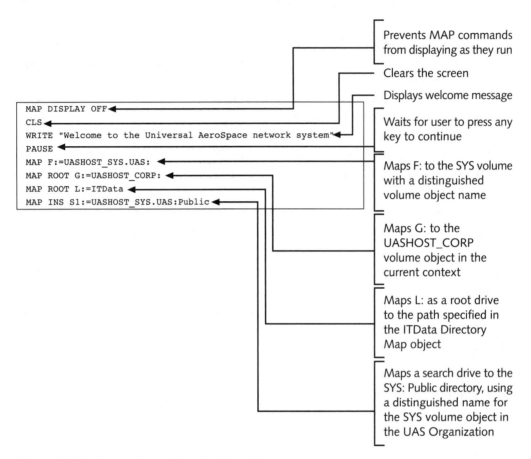

Figure 9-19   A sample container login script

In Activity 9-8, you enter and test the login script commands in Figure 9-19 in your IT OU. In Activity 9-9, you add login commands to your IT container script to create the script Kellie developed as a model for all OUs.

Activity 9-8: Entering the IT OU Login Script

Time Required: 10 minutes

Objective: Use ConsoleOne to create and enter login script commands and variables.

Requirements: A Windows XP computer with Novell Client installed

Description: In this activity, you enter the login script from Figure 9-19 for your IT OU and then practice using Novell Client login script options.

1. If necessary, start your computer, and log in to eDirectory with your administrative user name and password.
2. Start ConsoleOne, and expand your eDirectory tree and your **UAS** container.
3. Right-click the **IT** OU, and then click **Properties** to open the Properties of IT dialog box.
4. Follow these steps to enter your login script:
    a. Click the **Login Script** tab to display the Login Script text box.

b. Enter the login script commands shown in Figure 9-19.

c. Click **OK** to save the login script and return to the main ConsoleOne window.

5. Exit ConsoleOne, and log out.

6. In the Novell Login window, change the context to the **IT** OU and enter Eric Kenton's user name and password.

7. Follow these steps to set login script options in Novell Client:

a. Click the **Advanced** button, and then click the **Script** tab to display the options shown previously in Figure 9-17.

b. If necessary, click to clear the **Close automatically** check box and click to select the **Display results window** check box.

8. Click **OK** to log in. A results window should be displayed with the welcome message you entered in your login script.

9. Press the **spacebar** to continue. The drive mappings are then added to the results window. Record the drive mappings and list any drive letters that are repeated:

_____

_____

_____

NOTE Repeated drive letters could mean that the default login script is running or that the user has a user login script that's changing drive mappings. You learn how to disable the default login script in Activity 9-9.

10. Close the results window, and log out.

11. Change the Novell Client login options and repeat the login process:

a. In the Novell Login window, click the **Advanced** button, and then click the **Script** tab.

b. Click to select the **Close automatically** check box.

c. Click **OK** to log in.

12. Record the contents of the results window**:**

_____

13. Close any open windows, and log out. Leave your system running for the next activity.

Login Script Variables

As with other programming languages, the NetWare login script language allows using variables in many commands. A **login script variable** is a reserved word in the login script language, and its value can change for each user logging in. With login script variables, you can write one login script that works for many different users and computers. Login script variables can be divided into types based on their use: date variables, time variables, user variables, and workstation variables, explained in the following sections.

NOTE Remember to use all uppercase letters for a variable and precede it with a percent sign (%), as explained in "Using Login Script Variables" later in this chapter. For more information on login script commands and variables, check Novell's Web site (*http://novell.com*).

Date Variables

Date variables contain information about the current day of the week, the month, and the year in a variety of formats, as shown in Table 9-4. Date variables can be useful for displaying current date information or to check for a specific day to perform tasks. For example, the Engineering Department needs to meet at 10:00

a.m. each Monday to review weekly work projects. Using the DAY_OF_WEEK variable, you could display a message on Monday morning reminding them of the meeting. The values for date variables are stored as fixed-length ASCII strings.

Table 9-4 Date variables

Variable	Description
DAY	Day of the current month in number format, with possible values from "01" to "31"
DAY_OF_WEEK	Name of the current day of the week, with possible values of "Monday," "Tuesday," and so on
MONTH	The current month in number format, with possible values from "01" for January to "12" for December
MONTH_NAME	The name of the current month, with possible values from "January" to "December"
NDAY_OF_WEEK	The current weekday in number format, ranging from "1" for Sunday to "7" for Saturday
SHORT_YEAR	The last two digits of the current year, such as "05" or "06"
YEAR	The full four-digit year, such as "2005" or "2006"

Time Variables

The **time variables**, shown in Table 9-5, offer a variety of ways to view or check the login time.

Table 9-5 Time variables

Variable	Description
AM_PM	Used to specify day or night (possible values of "am" or "pm")
GREETING_TIME	Used for displaying welcome messages, with possible values of "Morning," "Afternoon," or "Evening"
HOUR	The current hour of the day or night in the range of "01" through "12"
HOUR24	The current hour in 24-hour mode, ranging from "01" for 1 a.m. to "24" for 12 a.m.
MINUTE	The current minute, ranging from "00" to "59"
SECOND	The current second, ranging from "00" to "59"

The GREETING_TIME variable is most often used in WRITE statements to display welcome messages. The HOUR variable requires using the AM_PM variable to determine whether the time is before or after noon, so the HOUR24 variable is often easier to use.

User Variables

The **user variables**, shown in Table 9-6, allow you to view the user's login name, full name, or hexadecimal user ID specified in eDirectory.

Table 9-6 User variables

Variable	Description
FULL_NAME	The user's full name, as defined in the user properties
LOGIN_NAME	The user's unique login name
USER_ID	The hexadecimal number NetWare assigns to the user login name
HOME_DIRECTORY	The path to the user's home directory

LOGIN_NAME and FULL_NAME can be used to personalize greeting messages. You use the HOME_DIRECTORY variable in Activity 9-9 to automate mapping drive H: to a user's home directory.

Workstation Variables

Workstation variables, shown in Table 9-7, are most often used to establish drive mappings for software directories according to the client computer's hardware or OS.

Table 9-7   Workstation variables

Variable	Description
OS	The computer's operating system; the default value is "MSDOS"
OS_VERSION	The version of DOS used on the computer processing the login script
MACHINE	The long machine name that can be assigned in the Shell.cfg or Net.cfg file; the default value is "IBM_PC"
P_STATION	The node address of the computer's network card, expressed as a 12-digit hexadecimal value
SMACHINE	The short machine name that can be assigned in the Shell.cfg or Net.cfg file; the default value is "IBM"
STATION	The connection number assigned to the user's computer; sometimes used by software packages to separate the user's temporary files when multiple users are working in the same shared directory
SHELL_TYPE	The computer's shell version number
NETWORK_ADDRESS	The IPX address of the cable the user's computer is attached to, expressed as an 8-digit hexadecimal number
FILE_SERVER	The name of the current file server

Using Login Script Variables

To see how login script variables work, in this section you use them to display the current date in the greeting message and assign a drive pointer to each user's home directory in the IT OU. Without login script variables, you would have to create a separate script for each user containing a MAP command to his or her home directory, as shown in Figure 9-20. As you can see, creating a separate login script for each user involves a lot of extra work and redundancy.

An alternative is creating a single container login script that works for all users in the OU. As you learned in Chapter 5, each user's home directory is given the same name as the user's login name by default, which you can see in Figure 9-20. The path to the user's home directory is then stored as a property of the user account in eDirectory. When users' home directory paths are included with their user account information, you can reduce the number of statements in the login script by using the HOME_DIRECTORY variable in the MAP command:

```
MAP ROOT H:=%HOME_DIRECTORY
```

The percent sign in front of the variable name is necessary to tell Novell Client to substitute the path to the user's home directory for the HOME_DIRECTORY variable during login. Notice, too, that the variable name is in all uppercase letters.

TIP

Because many login script commands require capitalizing variable names, it's a good practice to capitalize *all* login script variable names.

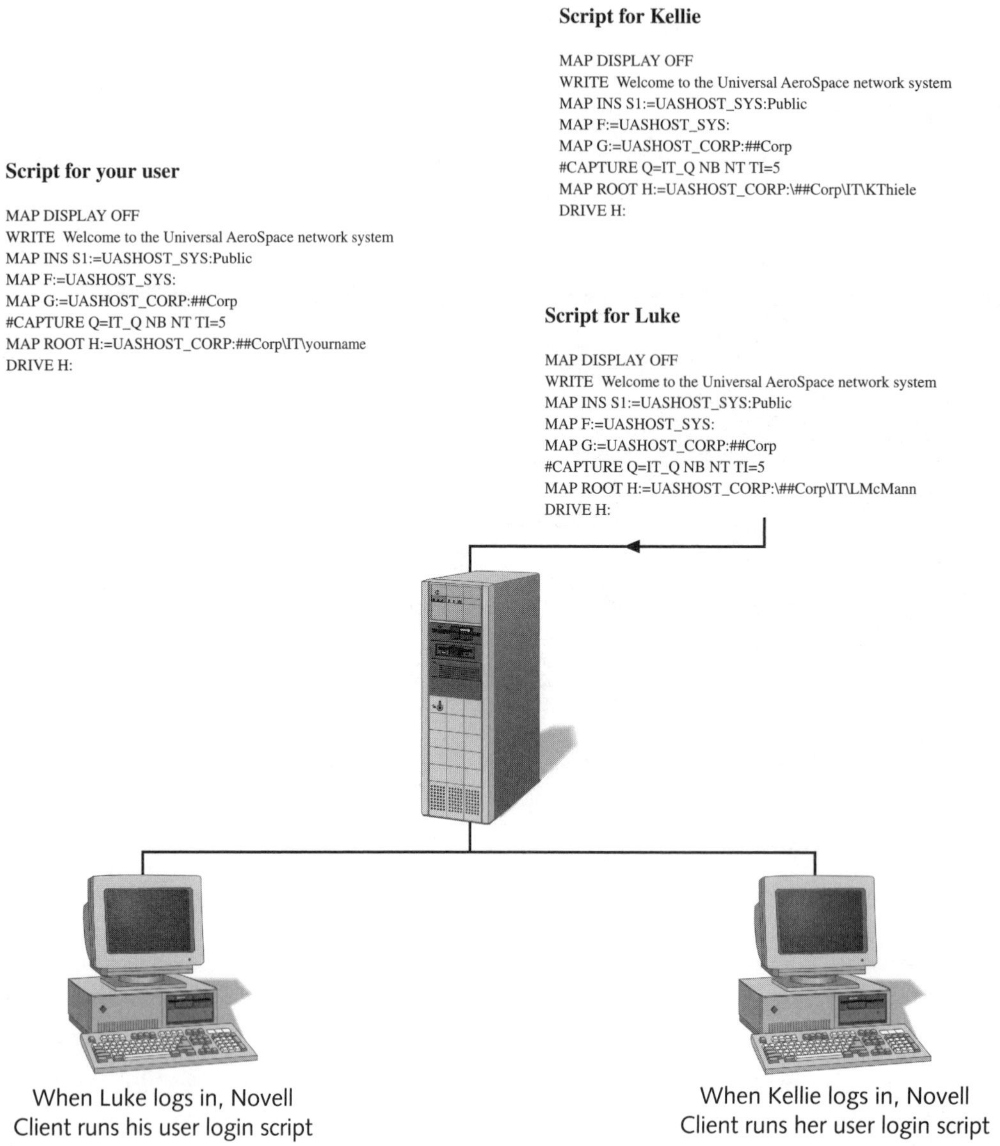

Script for Kellie

MAP DISPLAY OFF
WRITE Welcome to the Universal AeroSpace network system
MAP INS S1:=UASHOST_SYS:Public
MAP F:=UASHOST_SYS:
MAP G:=UASHOST_CORP:##Corp
#CAPTURE Q=IT_Q NB NT TI=5
MAP ROOT H:=UASHOST_CORP:\##Corp\IT\KThiele
DRIVE H:

Script for your user

MAP DISPLAY OFF
WRITE Welcome to the Universal AeroSpace network system
MAP INS S1:=UASHOST_SYS:Public
MAP F:=UASHOST_SYS:
MAP G:=UASHOST_CORP:##Corp
#CAPTURE Q=IT_Q NB NT TI=5
MAP ROOT H:=UASHOST_CORP:##Corp\IT\yourname
DRIVE H:

Script for Luke

MAP DISPLAY OFF
WRITE Welcome to the Universal AeroSpace network system
MAP INS S1:=UASHOST_SYS:Public
MAP F:=UASHOST_SYS:
MAP G:=UASHOST_CORP:##Corp
#CAPTURE Q=IT_Q NB NT TI=5
MAP ROOT H:=UASHOST_CORP:\##Corp\IT\LMcMann
DRIVE H:

When Luke logs in, Novell
Client runs his user login script

When Kellie logs in, Novell
Client runs her user login script

Figure 9-20   Using individual user login scripts to map drives to user home directories

When Kellie logs in, for example, Novell Client replaces %HOME_DIRECTORY with the path to her home directory, and the H: drive is mapped to the IT\KThiele home directory. If a user in the container doesn't have a home directory, an error message is displayed. For example, if you log in with the CKent user name, because no home directory is specified in eDirectory for CKent, the system displays an error message. You learn how to correct this problem in "IF... THEN... ELSE Statements" later in this chapter.

Writing Login Scripts

The rules for processing commands are commonly referred to as the **syntax**. In the following sections, you learn the valid syntax for common NetWare login script commands. Before studying these commands, you should be aware of these general rules for their use:

- Only valid login script command statements and comments can be placed in a login script.
- Login script command lines can be a maximum of 150 characters.
- Long commands can "wrap" to the next line if there's not enough room on one line.

- Novell Client reads login script commands one line at a time, and only one command is allowed on a line.

- Commands can be entered in uppercase or lowercase letters, except for variable values enclosed in quotation marks, which must be preceded by a percent sign (%) and typed in uppercase letters.

- Comments are entered by preceding the text with the REM command, an asterisk (*), or a semicolon (;).

The CLS Command

The CLS command is used simply to clear the screen. Normally, you display messages to users by clearing the screen, displaying the message, and pausing the login script. After the user reads the message and presses a key to continue, you might want to include another CLS command to remove the message from the screen.

The MAP Command

The MAP command you learned to use earlier in "Network Drive Mappings" is perhaps the most important login script command because it can be used to set up both regular and search drive mappings for accessing files and software in the NetWare environment. The syntax of the MAP login script command is similar to the MAP command-line utility described previously except that you can use **identifier variables** (user login name, date, and time, for example) and relative drive numbers and place multiple mappings on the same MAP command. The syntax of the MAP login script command is as follows:

```
MAP option drive:=path variable
```

The *drive*: parameter must be replaced with a valid network, local, or search drive. You can also use a relative drive number, such as *1: to indicate the first network drive, *2: for the second network drive, and so on. If the computer's first network drive letter is F:, *1: is replaced with F:, *2: is replaced with G:, and so forth. Replace *path* with a full directory path, beginning with a DOS drive letter or NetWare volume name.

Additional drive mappings can be placed on the same line by separating them with semicolons. For example, if you want to map the F: drive to the SYS volume and the G: drive to the DATA volume, you could do so with this MAP command:

```
MAP F:=SYS:;G:=DATA:
```

Other special MAP commands include MAP DISPLAY OFF and MAP ERRORS OFF. The MAP DISPLAY OFF command prevents MAP commands from being displayed on user computers and is often included at the beginning of a login script to reduce the amount of information displayed. The MAP ERRORS OFF command prevents displaying error messages generated by MAP commands that specify invalid paths. This command is useful if you include drive mapping commands in a login script that you know won't be valid for all users. Instead of confusing users with error messages that don't affect them, you can include MAP ERRORS OFF before the MAP commands containing drive paths that might not be valid. When testing login scripts, however, you need to see error messages, so don't use these commands until after login scripts have been tested and debugged.

The NO_DEFAULT Command

NO_DEFAULT prevents default login scripts from running when users don't have their own user login scripts. As mentioned, the default login script can overwrite your drive mappings and cause multiple drive mappings and error messages, so including NO_DEFAULT at the beginning of each container login script is important. In Activity 9-9, you use this command in your IT container login script.

The CONTEXT Command

As you learned in Chapter 2, accessing network resources is easier when your current context is set to the container storing the objects you need to use, which is usually done in the Novell Login window. However, if a user logs in with his or her distinguished user name, the client computer's current context isn't changed. With the CONTEXT command, however, you can change the current context to another container when a user logs in. The syntax of the CONTEXT command includes the typeful distinguished name of the container that will become the default context. To set the default container to the IT OU, for example, enter this command:

```
CONTEXT .OU=IT.O=UAS
```

Being able to change the context is important when using Directory Map objects and volume names in login script MAP commands. If the context isn't changed to the correct container, the Directory Map object might not be found or the wrong volume could be used. For example, Kellie often needs to log in from other users' computers to test software. To use her distinguished name instead of selecting the context in the Novell Login window each time she logs in, she included the CONTEXT .OU=IT.O=UAS command in the IT container login script.

The WRITE Command

The WRITE command is used to display simple messages on users' computers. Messages can also contain identifier variables and special control strings, as shown:

```
WRITE "text control string %VARIABLE"
```

Common login script variables used with WRITE include %GREETING_TIME and %LOGIN_NAME (described in Tables 9-5 and 9-6). For example, the following WRITE statement displays a greeting message with the login time and user's full name:

```
WRITE "Good %GREETING_TIME, %LOGIN_NAME"
```

Follow important messages with the PAUSE command to make sure users have time to read the message. In Activity 9-9, you learn how to modify your existing login script to use the WRITE command.

The DISPLAY and FDISPLAY Commands

The DISPLAY and FDISPLAY (for "filtered display") commands are used to show the contents of an ASCII text file on-screen when the login script runs. This is the syntax for both commands:

```
DISPLAY (or FDISPLAY) directory path filename
```

If *filename* is in the current directory, or if a search drive has been established to the directory containing *filename*, the directory path isn't needed. However, in the following example, even though a search drive has been created for SYS:Public, the Welcome.msg file is in the Message subdirectory. You need to use the *directory path* parameter to make sure the message file is found:

```
MAP INS S1:=SYS:Public
FDISPLAY SYS:Public\Message\Welcome.msg
PAUSE
```

An error message is displayed if the file specified in the DISPLAY command doesn't exist.

You should follow DISPLAY or FDISPLAY with a PAUSE command to give users time to read the message. The difference between DISPLAY and FDISPLAY is that FDISPLAY "filters" and formats the specified file's contents so that only ASCII text is displayed. For example, FDISPLAY doesn't display tab characters, but converts them into spaces to make the output more readable. The DISPLAY command displays the exact characters in the file, including "garbage" characters such as printer or word-processing edit codes. Using FDISPLAY is usually preferable; however, if you use a word processing file, be sure to save it in ASCII text format, or not even FDISPLAY can read it.

The # and @ Commands (Execute a DOS Program)

The external program execution commands (# and @) are used to load and run an .exe or .com program without exiting Novell Client. The # command stops the login script from processing until the specified program has finished running, but the @ command starts an executable program and then continues processing login script commands while the executable program runs in the background. The @ command is useful if you want to load continuously running programs, such as virus detection software, into the computer's memory. Using the # command causes the login script to "hang" because the background program runs continuously in memory and doesn't exit back to the login script processor.

IF... THEN... ELSE Statements

You can use the IF statement to customize a login script for users or groups and to perform special processing when a certain condition exists (such as a specific day or time). Here's the syntax for an IF statement:

```
IF condition THEN command
```

The *condition* parameter is replaced with a conditional statement that has a value of true or false. Conditional statements usually consist of an identifier variable and a value enclosed in quotation marks. Table 9-8 shows some common conditional statements.

Table 9-8 Common conditional statements

Condition	Description
MEMBER OF "group"	This statement is true if the user is a member of the specified group.
DAY_OF_WEEK="Monday"	This statement is true if the day is Monday. Possible values range from Sunday through Saturday. Uppercase or lowercase letters can be used.
DAY="05"	This statement is true on the fifth day of the month; valid values range from 01 to 31. Include the leading zero for day numbers lower than 9.
MONTH="June"	This statement is true for the month of June. You can replace "June" with any valid month name from January to December. Uppercase or lowercase letters are accepted.
NDAY_OF_WEEK="1"	This statement is true on Sunday, which is the first day of the week. Valid weekday numbers range from 1 to 7.

The *command* parameter can be replaced with any valid login script command. For example, a simple IF statement with a single condition can be written as follows:

```
IF DAY_OF_WEEK="FRIDAY" THEN WRITE "Hurrah it's Friday!"
```

More complex IF statements consist of multiple commands followed by the END statement. For these statements, use the BEGIN command after THEN, and then place commands after the IF statement, as shown:

```
IF condition THEN BEGIN
    command 1
    command 2
    command n
END
```

All commands between IF and END are performed when the condition is true. For example, to set up drive mappings for members of the Design group, you can use this IF statement in the Engineering container login script:

```
IF MEMBER OF "Design" THEN BEGIN
    MAP ROOT P:=UASHOST_CORP:\Engineer\CAD
```

```
        CLS
        DISPLAY "Daily meeting has been changed to 11:30 today"
        PAUSE
END
```

Sometimes it's best to combine multiple conditions with AND or OR. When using OR, login commands are performed if *either* condition is true. For example, to inform all members of *either* WebMgrs or ITMgrs of a weekly meeting, you could use this statement:

```
IF MEMBER OF "ITMgrs" OR MEMBER OF "WebMgrs" THEN BEGIN
        CLS
        WRITE "Weekly Web meeting in conference rm 100 at 10:00 a.m."
        PAUSE
END
```

Use AND when you want *both* statements to be true. For example, you want to remind all members of the ITMgrs group of a meeting on Friday morning. Before displaying the reminder, you want to make sure the user is a member of the ITMgrs group, the day is Friday, and the login time is before noon. To do this, you use AND to connect these three conditions with the following statement:

```
IF MEMBER OF "ITMgrs" AND DAY_OF_WEEK="Friday" AND HOUR24 < "12" THEN
```

ELSE is a helpful option because it allows you to choose between sets of commands based on a certain condition. For example, the following IF...THEN...ELSE statement maps the I: drive pointer to the IT\Web directory for the WebMgrs group and to the IT\Shared directory for all other IT OU users:

```
IF MEMBER OF "WebMgrs" THEN
        MAP I:=UASHOST_CORP:IT\Web
ELSE
        MAP I:=UASHOST_CORP:IT\Shared
END
```

The EXIT Command

The EXIT command stops the login script from running and returns control to the client computer, so no further login script commands are processed after issuing this command.

The REM Command

REM is used to place a comment line in a login script. You can also use REMARK, an asterisk, or a semicolon to denote the start of a comment line. The login process skips any line beginning with REM, REMARK, *, or ;. Comments can make a login script easier to read and understand, but placing a comment on the same line as other commands causes errors. To make your work easier to maintain, you should use REM statements to include your name (in case of questions about how the login script works), last modified date, and a brief description of commands in each section to help other programmers understand the function of the login script. In Activity 9-9, you document your IT container login script with REM commands, and then modify it to check for group membership.

Activity 9-9: Modifying the IT Container Login Script

Time Required: 10 minutes

Objective: Create and enter login script commands and variables.

Requirements: Completion of Activity 9-8

Description: Kellie wants to use the IT container login script as a model for container login scripts throughout UAS. In this activity, you follow Kellie's model container login script by including many of the commands you have learned in this section.

1. If necessary, start your computer, and log in to eDirectory with your administrative user name and password. If you're using ConsoleOne from your server console, skip to Step 3.

2. Start ConsoleOne.

3. If necessary, expand the eDirectory tree and your **UAS** container.

4. Right-click the **IT** OU, and then click **Properties** to open the Properties of IT dialog box. Click the **Login Script** tab to display the current login script.

5. Add the following REM commands to the beginning of your login script, pressing **Enter** after each command:

```
REM IT Organizational Unit login script
REM Developed by: (insert your name here)
REM Date last modified: (insert date here)
```

6. To prevent the default login script from running, add the **NO_DEFAULT** command to the login script immediately after the last REM statement, and then press **Enter**.

7. To display a greeting message, add the following commands before the PAUSE statement, and then press **Enter**:

```
WRITE "Good %GREETING_TIME, %LOGIN_NAME"
WRITE "It's %HOUR:%MINUTE %AM_PM on %DAY_OF_WEEK, %MONTH/%DAY/%YEAR"
```

8. Add the following IF statement before the PAUSE command, pressing **Enter** after each line (substituting the current weekday for "current day name here" and substituting the next hour for "next hour here"):

NOTE

In the first code line, remember not to press Enter until you have typed THEN. The IF statement should appear on one line.

```
IF DAY_OF_WEEK="current day name here" AND HOUR24 < "next hour here" THEN
    WRITE "Department meeting at 11:30 a.m."
    FIRE PHASERS 2 TIMES
END
```

9. To prevent an error message when logging in as CKent, who has no home directory, enter the following commands at the end of the login script, pressing **Enter** after each line:

```
IF MEMBER OF "ITMgrs" THEN
    MAP ROOT H:=%HOME_DIRECTORY
END
```

10. Click **Apply**, and then click **Close** to save the changes and return to the main ConsoleOne window.

11. Exit ConsoleOne, and log out to display a new login window.

12. Log in as **KThiele**, and record the contents of your results window:

_____

_____

_____

13. Close the results window, and log out. Leave your system running for the next activity.

Documenting Login Scripts

The best way to document login scripts for troubleshooting and planning is to print hard copies. Unfortunately, iManager, ConsoleOne, and NetWare Administrator don't have options for printing login scripts. However, you can use the NLIST command to print login scripts to an attached printer, or highlight the login script commands and use Ctrl+C and Ctrl+V to copy and paste the commands to a text editor. The format of the NLIST command is as follows:

```
NLIST "object type" = context SHOW "Login Script" > PRN
```

Replace *object type* with "Organization" or "Organizational Unit" and replace *context* with the path to the container. For example, to print the contents of the IT OU login script to her attached printer, Kellie used the following command:

```
NLIST "Organizational Unit" = .IT.UAS SHOW "Login Script" > PRN
```

In Activity 9-10, you learn the copy-and-paste method of saving your IT container login script as a text file and then printing the script on your classroom printer.

Activity 9-10: Documenting a Login Script

Time Required: 10 minutes

Objective: Create and enter login script commands and variables.

Requirements: Completion of Activity 9-9

Description: In this activity, you use Ctrl+C and Ctrl+V to paste your IT container login script into Notepad, and then print it on the classroom printer (if one is available).

1. If necessary, start your computer, and log in to eDirectory with your administrative user name and password.

2. Start ConsoleOne, and expand the eDirectory tree and your **UAS** container.

3. Right-click the **IT** OU, and then click **Properties** to open the Properties of IT dialog box. Click the **Login Script** tab to display your login script.

4. Highlight all commands in the Login Script text box, and press **Ctrl+C** to copy the selected commands to the Clipboard.

5. Exit ConsoleOne.

6. Start Notepad. Click in the Notepad window, and then press **Ctrl+V** to paste the commands.

7. Click **File**, **Save as** from the Notepad menu to save the login script in your My Documents folder with the name **ITScript.txt**. *Optional*: Print your login script on the classroom printer.

8. Exit Notepad and log out. Leave your system running for the next activity.

Planning Login Scripts

After you understand the syntax and function of login script commands and variables and how to store and run login scripts, the next task is to apply login scripts to setting up a network login environment for users' computers. Setting up a login script system requires three basic steps:

1. Identify login script requirements for each container and user.

2. Write and enter the script commands.

3. Test login scripts by logging in as different users.

In the following sections, you apply these steps to creating login scripts for users in the UAS Engineering Department.

Identifying Login Script Requirements

To design a login script system for Universal AeroSpace, Eric started by listing user drive mappings and messages on the Login Script Requirements Worksheet (see Figure 9-21).

The first section identifies standard drive mappings and the login script where the mapping is done. Drive letters are assigned to the same path for all users, so they are included in all container scripts. Eric has also included a profile login script named EngProfile with common commands for users in the Mfg and Engineering containers and one named WebProfile for users in the WebMgrs groups. In addition to a common drive letter for each volume, each container login script maps an H: drive to the user's home directory. Directory Map objects are used to map the L: drive to each department's shared work directory. The Messages section lists message needs for users and the login script where the message is placed.

Organization: _Universal AeroSpace_   Page 1 of 2

Developed by: _Eric Kenton_   Date: _____

Drive Mappings			
Users	Drive	Path	Script
ITMgrs	F:	UASHOST_SYS:	All containers
All	G:	UASHOST_CORP:	All containers
All	S1:	UASHOST_SYS:Public	All containers
All	H:	%HOME_DIRECTORY	All containers
Engineering Department	L:	EngData Directory Map object	Engineering container
IT Department	L:	ITData Directory Map object	IT container
Manufacturing Department	L:	MfgData Directory Map object	Mfg container
Engineering and Mfg users	S:	UASHOST_CORP:\Engineer\Shared	EngProfile profile
Design group	P:	UASHOST_CORP:\Engineer\CAD	Engineering container
Mgmt users	H:	%HOME_DIRECTORY	Mgmt container
Mgmt users	L:	MgmtData Directory Map object	Mgmt container
WebMgrs group	W:	UASHOST_CORP:IT\Web	WebProfile profile

Figure 9-21   The UAS Login Script Requirements Worksheet

Organization: _Universal AeroSpace_   Page __2__ of __2__

Developed by: _Eric Kenton_   Date: _____

Messages		
Users	**Description**	**Login Script**
All	Login greeting message	All containers
All	Daily message file for Monday through Friday	All containers
Engineering	Weekly design meeting on Monday morning at 9:00 a.m.	Engineering container
Engineering and Mfg users	Monthly meeting held at 9:00 a.m. on the first Wednesday of each month to discuss documentation and promotional needs	EngProfile
WebMgrs	Monthly Web site meeting at 8:00 a.m. on the first Monday of each month	WebProfile

Figure 9-21 The UAS Login Script Requirements Worksheet (continued)

Writing Login Scripts

The next step is to plan and write login script commands. For the Engineering, Mfg, and Mgmt containers, Eric developed the Container Login Script Worksheet, shown in Figures 9-22 through 9-24. To map the drives, Eric used relative names of the volume objects, which required creating volume objects named UASHOST_SYS and UASHOST_CORP in the Engineering, Mfg, and Mgmt OUs.

REM statements define the start of each section in these worksheets. The REM General Commands section contains initializing commands, such as NO_DEFAULT, MAP DISPLAY OFF, and MAP S1:=UASHOST_SYS:UAS. In addition, this section can be used to clear the screen with the CLS command and display a greeting message. This section also contains drive mappings and messages for all users in the container. In Figure 9-22, for example, the EngData Directory Map object is used to map the L: drive to the Engineer directory.

The REM Commands for Workgroup section contains login script commands for users who are members of the specified groups. In Figure 9-22, if a user is a member of the Design workgroup, he or she gets a P: drive mapping to the L:CAD directory. The REM End of Login Script Commands section contains commands that run for all users before exiting the login script.

Organization: _Universal AeroSpace_   Page __1__ of __3__

Developed by: _Eric Kenton_   Date: _____

Container Context: _Engineering.UAS_

REM General Commands
```
REM Created by: Eric Kenton
REM Last modified: 12/15/2005
NO_DEFAULT
MAP DISPLAY OFF
CONTEXT    .Engineering.UAS
MAP ROOT G:=UASHOST_CORP:
MAP ROOT H:=%HOME_DIRECTORY
MAP L:=EngData
MAP INS S1:=UASHOST_SYS:PUBLIC
CLS
WRITE "Good %GREETING_TIME,   %LOGIN_NAME"
WRITE "Welcome to the Universal AeroSpace network system"
DISPLAY UASHOST_CORP:\Shared\Messages\%DAY_OF_WEEK.MSG
IF DAY_OF_WEEK="Monday" and HOUR24 < "09" THEN BEGIN
    WRITE "Weekly design meeting at 9:00 a.m. in conference
room"
END
PAUSE
```

REM Commands for Design Workgroup
```
IF MEMBER OF "Design" THEN
    MAP ROOT P:=L:CAD
END
```

REM Commands for ITMgrs Workgroup
```
IF MEMBER OF "ITMgrs" THEN BEGIN
    MAP F:=UASHOST_SYS:
END
```

REM End of Login Script Commands

Figure 9-22 The Engineering container login script

Organization: *Universal AeroSpace*   Page 2 of 3

Developed by: *Eric Kenton*   Date: _____

Container Context: *.Mfg.UAS*

REM General Commands
```
REM Created by:Eric Kenton
REM Last modified: 12/15/2005
NO_DEFAULT
MAP DISPLAY OFF
CONTEXT .Mfg.UAS
MAP ROOT G:=UASHOST_CORP:
MAP ROOT H:=%HOME_DIRECTORY
MAP L:=MfgData
MAP INS S1:=UASHOST_SYS:PUBLIC
CLS
WRITE "Good %GREETING_TIME, %LOGIN_NAME"
WRITE "Welcome to the Universal AeroSpace network system"
DISPLAY UASHOST_CORP:\Shared\Messages\%DAY_OF_WEEK.MSG
PAUSE
```

REM Commands for Design Workgroup
```
IF MEMBER OF "Design" THEN
    MAP ROOT P:=L:CAD
END
```

REM Commands for ITMgrs Workgroup
```
IF MEMBER OF "ITMgrs" THEN BEGIN
    MAP F:=UASHOST_SYS:
END
```

REM End of Login Script Commands

Figure 9-23   The Mfg container login script

Organization: *Universal AeroSpace*   Page <u>3</u> of <u>3</u>

Developed by: *Eric Kenton*   Date: _____

Container Context: *.Mgmt.UAS*

```
REM General Commands
REM Created by:Eric Kenton
REM Last modified: 12/15/2005
NO_DEFAULT
MAP DISPLAY OFF
CONTEXT .Mgmt.UAS
MAP ROOT G:=UASHOST_CORP:
MAP ROOT H:=%HOME_DIRECTORY
MAP L:=MgmtData
MAP INS S1:=UASHOST_SYS:PUBLIC
CLS
WRITE "Good %GREETING_TIME, %LOGIN_NAME"
WRITE "Welcome to the Universal AeroSpace network system"
DISPLAY UASHOST_CORP:\Shared\Messages\%DAY_OF_WEEK.MSG
PAUSE
```

```
REM Commands for ITMgrs Workgroup
IF MEMBER OF "ITMgrs" THEN BEGIN
    MAP F:=UASHOST_SYS:
END
```

```
REM End of Login Script Commands
```

Figure 9-24 The Mgmt container login script

Figure 9-25 shows the Profile Login Script Worksheet Eric developed to create a profile login script for Engineering users. In the Hands-on Projects at the end of the chapter, you have the opportunity to enter, test, and debug the container and profile login scripts shown in this section.

```
Organization: Universal AeroSpace     Page   1   of   2

Developed by: Eric Kenton            Date: _____

Profile Script Name: EngProfile       Container Context: Engineering.UAS


  Login script for: EngProfile _____ profile object

  Users:    LJarka _____    TRucci _____

            RPence _____    PAlm _____


  REM Created by: Eric Kenton
  REM Last modified: 12/15/2005
  MAP S:=UASHOST_CORP:\Engineer\Shared
  IF DAY_OF_WEEK="Monday" AND HOUR24 < "09" THEN
      WRITE "Remember meeting at 9:00 a.m. in conference
  room 100"
      PAUSE
  END
```

Figure 9-25   The EngProfile profile login script

MANAGING THE WINDOWS ENVIRONMENT WITH ZENWORKS FOR DESKTOPS

You have learned how to use login scripts to help create standardized drive pointers for users when they log in. However, login scripts are only part of the solution to making a network easy to use and maintain; users also need a consistent desktop environment and access to required applications from any computer they work on. In the past, network administrators had to install applications and modify configurations on many different computers to accommodate varying computing needs. Installing applications manually and setting up or restoring user desktops can be labor-intensive tasks that take time away from other administration priorities. With Novell's ZENworks for Desktops (ZfD) package, network administrators can centrally monitor and manage software and computer configurations so that users have more mobility. In the following sections, you learn what a CNA needs to know about using ZENworks to set up and manage user desktop environments.

ZENworks for Desktops 6.5 Overview

The cost of hardware and software is only a small part of the total cost of owning a computer. The cost of ownership, which is becoming a major concern for many organizations, includes ongoing costs for maintaining and upgrading computer hardware, software installation and configuration, troubleshooting, and user support and training. Although the Windows environment makes it easy for users to interact with their desktop computers, its complexity can actually increase the total cost of ownership; network administrators must spend more time configuring, managing, and supporting Windows environments. In addition, configuration time can increase when users move to different computers, yet want to access their same desktop environments. Another concern is help desk support for users when they have problems or questions.

Novell's **Zero Effort Networking (ZENworks) for Desktops (ZfD)** can make it easier for users to work with the network and reduce the time you spend configuring user computers. In addition, ZfD offers a remote-control capability that gives you a secure way to take control of a client computer's display, keyboard, and mouse; in this way, you can help a user fix a problem or change a computer's configuration without having to physically go to that computer. ZfD consists of client and server components that allow using eDirectory to centralize settings for applications, users, and computers, thus reducing time spent on repetitive tasks for computer configuration and management.

Benefits and Features

ZENworks for Desktops 6.5 has the following features for network management:

- *Application management*—The Application Launcher enables you to centrally distribute, upgrade, and manage applications on any Windows-based computer attached to your network.

- *Workstation management*—The Workstation Manager component allows you to store user and desktop configurations for Windows computers in eDirectory. Because ZENworks uses eDirectory to extend Windows features, such as policies, printers, and user profiles, these features can be managed in ConsoleOne from a centralized location.

- *Remote control*—You can securely manage and interact with computers from a remote location, which makes troubleshooting problems and changing configurations more convenient on large networks.

Hardware and Software Requirements

To use ZENworks for Desktops 6.5, your server must be running NetWare 6.0 or later with the most recent support packs installed. Computers should be running Novell Client version 4.9 or later. Following are the minimum hardware requirements for computers; keep in mind that these minimum requirements might not provide adequate performance:

- Processor: Pentium 200 MHz or higher

- Memory: 128 MB for Windows NT/2000

- Hard disk space: 4 MB (computer) or 24 MB (full installation)

- Windows XP Service Pack 1 or later

In addition, you need to use ConsoleOne because NetWare Administrator and iManager don't currently have ZENworks management capabilities.

Installing ZENworks for Desktops 6.5

Before taking advantage of ZENworks features, you need to install ZENworks for Desktops on your server and, if necessary, update the client on computers. Eric installed it on the UASHOST server using the following process. If you're using a dedicated NetWare 6.5 server, you need to perform these steps on your server before doing the activities in this section. If you're using a shared classroom server, your instructor will perform these steps on your classroom server.

NOTE

You can download a copy of the ZENworks for Desktops 6.5 evaluation software for the activities in this section at *http://download.novell.com*.

EXAMPLE

1. Because installing ZENworks involves shutting down the Java software and could affect server operations, Eric selected a time on the weekend when no users would be logged in.

2. Because the ZENworks installation needs to replace certain Java utilities on the server, Eric entered the UNLOAD JAVA command at the server console to stop Java applications on the server. If this isn't done before starting the installation, the ZENworks installation program issues an error message.

3. Next, Eric logged in with the Admin user name and password to have Supervisor rights to the network.

4. He inserted the ZENworks for Desktops 6.5 CD into the computer's CD-ROM drive. The ZENworks for Desktops installation wizard automatically started and displayed the window shown in Figure 9-26. (If you're using an evaluation copy, you might need to navigate to the ZENworks6.5 folder and run the Winsetup.exe program.)

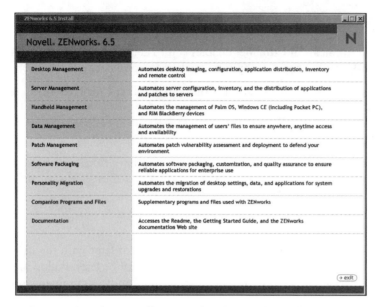

Figure 9-26   The Novell ZENworks 6.5 Install window

5. Eric clicked the Desktop Management option and then selected the English language option to display the options shown in Figure 9-27.

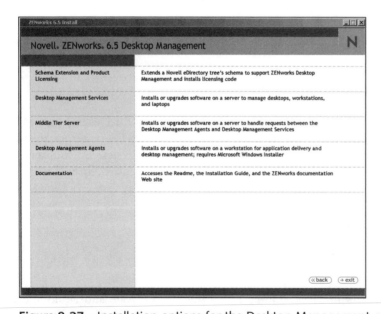

Figure 9-27   Installation options for the Desktop Management option

6. He clicked the Desktop Management Services option to display an installation instructions window, which instructed him to close all programs and unload Java from the server console. Eric had already taken those steps, so he clicked Next to display the License agreement window.

7. He read the agreement, clicked the Accept option button, and clicked Next to continue and display the Installation Prerequisites window. He noted that ZENworks can also be used with Windows Server 2003, and then clicked Next to display the Tree Selection window shown in Figure 9-28.

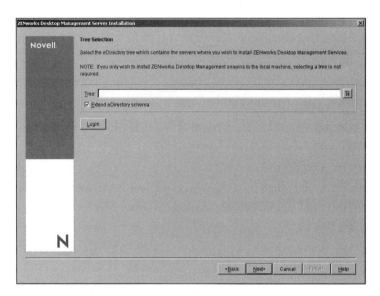

Figure 9-28 The Tree Selection window

8. He verified that the Extend eDirectory schema check box was selected, and then clicked the browse button to select the UAS eDirectory tree. He clicked Next to display the licensing window.

9. He entered his license code number and clicked Next to display the Server Selection window. (If you're using the evaluation version, you can leave the license code blank and have 90 days to use ZENworks 6.5. You can obtain and enter a license code later.)

10. He clicked the Add Servers button to add the UASHOST server. Next, to prevent installing ZENworks on the XP computer, Eric clicked to clear the XP Local Workstation check box. He expanded the Workstation Management folder under UASHOST.UAS and clicked to clear the Remote Management check box. He then expanded the Additional Options folder and clicked to select the Desktop Management Database and Desktop Management Services Snap-ins check boxes (see Figure 9-29).

Figure 9-29 The Server Selection window

11. He clicked Next to accept the default SYS volume location and display the Database Location window.

12. Because the database can take a lot of disk space on large networks, Novell recommends placing the database outside the SYS volume to prevent the SYS volume from filling up. Eric entered the CORP volume name, and then clicked Next to display the Installation Summary window.

13. After reviewing the selected installation options, Eric clicked Finish to start the installation.

14. After the installation was finished, Eric logged off his computer. He went to the server console and used the Monitor utility, described in Chapter 2, to ensure that no users were logged in. He then used the RESTART SERVER command to restart the NetWare OES server so that he could reload Java and make sure the system was working correctly.

15. To update ConsoleOne to use ZENworks, after the server was restarted, Eric logged in from his local Windows XP computer, and then copied the ConsoleOne folder from the SYS:Public\Mgmt directory to the local hard drive of his XP computer. He then created a new shortcut to point to the updated ConsoleOne.exe program.

Managing Computers

In addition to installing and configuring applications, network administrators need to be able to maintain a consistent desktop environment and keep track of hardware and software configurations. The key to managing Windows desktop environments is using policies, which are Windows desktop management tools used to customize user computers. However, in a network with many Windows computers, managing computer and user policies with the Windows 2000 Professional local policy-editing program can be time consuming. With Policy Package eDirectory objects, ZENworks makes Windows policies easier to manage and more powerful.

Policy Package objects enable you to manage the way users access their computers and connect to the network. There are two types of policy packages: Workstation policies and User policies. With Workstation policies, you can configure settings such as the path to Windows setup files, file and printer sharing, computer passwords, and run options (to determine which applications run automatically regardless of the user who logs in). User policies affect users' access to computers and their desktop restrictions, regardless of where they log in to the network. You can define restrictions, such as hiding the Run or Find commands, and define a desktop environment, including wallpaper, screen saver, sounds, and colors.

When a policy package is applied to a Windows computer, the restrictions made in the Registry are applied to the next user, unless he or she has a policy that changes Registry settings. As a result, if the Admin user logs in to a 95/98 computer previously used by a restricted user, the restriction is applied to the Windows environment for the Admin user. When setting up restricted User policies, you should create an open policy package that enables all Windows functions and then associate the open policy with your Admin user. In this way, Admin users will still have access to all Windows features when logging in from a restricted computer. In the following activities, you learn how to set up open and restricted desktop environments.

Activity 9-11: Creating a Standard User Desktop

Time Required: 15 minutes

Objective: Use ZENworks for Desktops to configure a user environment.

Requirements: ZENworks installed on the classroom computer or your dedicated server. (If you're using a dedicated server, you need to complete the Example steps listed previously to install ZENworks on your system.) You also need to have an Apps directory in your UAS directory structure. All users should have Read and File Scan rights to the Apps directory.

Description: The management at UAS wants to create a common desktop for all employees. Eric wants you to experiment with using ZENworks to establish a desktop environment for users in the IT Department. In this activity, you create a User policy package for your IT users.

1. If necessary, log in with your administrative user name and password, and start ConsoleOne.

2. Expand the eDirectory tree and your **UAS** container.

3. Follow these steps to create a Policies directory within the Apps directory on your CORP volume.

   a. Expand your **CORP** volume. (If you're using a shared classroom server, expand the STUDENTS volume and then your ##Corp directory.)

   b. Right-click the **Apps** directory, click **New**, and then click **Object**.

   c. Verify that Directory is highlighted, and then click **OK**.

   d. Enter **Policies** in the Name text box, and then click **OK** to create the directory and return to the ConsoleOne window.

4. Use Windows Explorer to copy the **C:\Windows\Coffee Bean.bmp** file to the Policies folder.

5. If necessary, map a drive letter to the Apps directory (as described earlier in "Network Drive Mappings").

6. Follow these steps to create a Windows 2000 User policy package for the IT OU:

   a. Click the **IT** OU.

   b. Click the **Create Policy Package** icon on the ConsoleOne toolbar to start the Policy Package Wizard.

   c. In the Policy packages list box, click **User Package** (see Figure 9-30), and then click **Windows Group Policy** in the Policies list box.

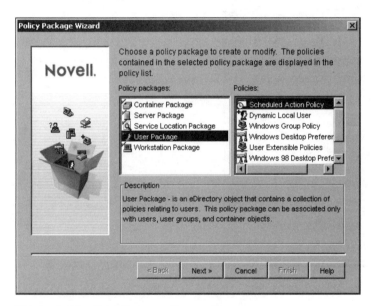

Figure 9-30   Selecting a policy package

   d. Click **Next**, and enter **IT Policy** in the Policy Package Name text box.

   e. Verify that IT.UAS is displayed in the Container text box, and then click **Next** to display the Summary window.

   f. Click the **Define Additional Properties** check box, and then click **Finish** to create the policy package and open the Policies tab of the Properties of IT Policy dialog box.

7. Follow these steps to configure the IT Policy package to use the Coffee Bean wall paper:

   a. Click the **down arrow** on the Policies tab and then click **Windows XP** to display the Windows XP options shown in Figure 9-31.

   b. Click to select the **Windows Desktop Preferences** check box, and then click the **Properties** button to open the Windows Desktop Preferences dialog box.

   c. Click the down arrow on the **Desktop Preferences** tab, and then click **Settings** to display the Settings tab shown in Figure 9-32.

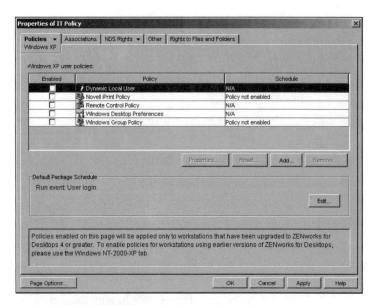

Figure 9-31   The Properties of IT Policy dialog box

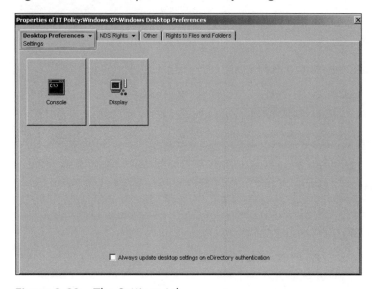

Figure 9-32   The Settings tab

    d. Scroll down and click the **browse** button next to the Network location of existing Group Policies text box, navigate to the Apps\Policies directory, and then click **Open**.

    e. Click the **Display** button to open the Display Properties dialog box to the Background tab (see Figure 9-33).

    f. Click to select the **Wallpaper** option button, and then click the **browse** button to navigate to the Coffee Bean.bmp file in your Apps\Policies directory.

    g. Click **OK** to save your policy and return to the Windows Desktop Preferences dialog box.

    h. Click **OK** to save your changes and return to the Properties of IT Policy dialog box.

8. Follow these steps to associate the IT Policy with all users in the IT OU:

    a. Click the **Associations** tab.

    b. Click the **Add** button and navigate to your **UAS** container.

    c. Click the **IT** OU to add it to the Associations list box.

9. Click **OK** to save your IT Policy and return to the ConsoleOne window.

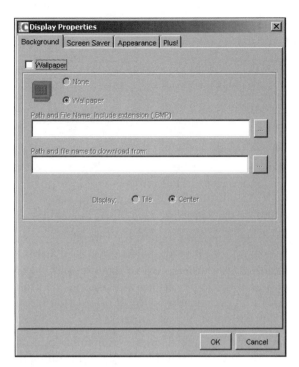

Figure 9-33 The Background tab

10. Exit ConsoleOne, and log out.

11. Test the settings by logging in as **EKenton**. Is the Coffee Bean wallpaper displayed? Record your results here:

_____

12. Log out.

Now that the login scripts and policy packages are operational, all your hard work is starting to pay off; your network users can log in with a consistent desktop and use a standard set of drive pointers to access the network file system.

NOTE

Novell Client for Linux is currently an add-on feature to Novell Linux Desktop. This feature makes it possible to use drive mappings, login scripts, DFS junctions, and ZENworks in the Linux desktop environment. In Appendix B, you learn how to install and use Novell Client for Linux so that you can apply what you have learned in this chapter to the Linux environment.

CHAPTER SUMMARY

❏ Establishing a desktop environment and providing access to network files are important responsibilities of a network administrator. NetWare offers a powerful way to automate computer setups through the use of drive mappings, the Distributed File System, login scripts, and ZENworks for Desktops.

❏ To work with the directory structure efficiently, you need to establish drive pointers to strategic locations in it. Drive pointers are letters assigned to local drives and network directories that make it easier to work with the file system and to access software stored in other directories.

❏ Regular drive pointers are assigned to directories containing data files, and search drive pointers are assigned to application directories to run command-line utilities not located in the Windows directory. Root drive pointers appear to applications as though the directory path were the beginning of a drive or volume, enabling the network administrator to make it more difficult for users or applications to move out of the assigned directory path.

◻ Because drive pointers play a major role in how users and applications access the NetWare file system, network administrators should establish standards for drive pointer use to prevent conflicts and software configuration problems.

◻ NetWare login scripts contain commands to provide drive mappings and other computer setup functions needed during login. Novell supplies a set of commands for mapping drive letters, setting a computer's DOS environment, displaying messages and files, running programs, and issuing certain commands based on specified conditions.

◻ By using login script variables with commands, you can create general-purpose login scripts that work for multiple users. Login script variables are divided into date variables, time variables, user variables, and workstation variables. A common example of using a login script variable is mapping a drive pointer to users' home directories by including MAP ROOT H:=%HOME_DIRECTORY in the login script. The percent sign preceding a variable name tells NetWare to substitute the variable's value when the login script runs.

◻ Novell Client can run four types of NetWare login scripts: container login scripts, profile login scripts, user login scripts, and default login scripts. The container login script is a property of the container object, and its commands run first when users in that container log in. After the container login script has ended, if the login script processor identifies a profile object for a user, the login script commands in the profile object run. Last, the system checks for commands in the user's Login Script property. If no user login script exists, the login script processor runs the default login script stored in Novell Client.

◻ Whenever possible, most login script commands should be stored in the container login script. By including the NO_DEFAULT command in this script, you can prevent NetWare from running the default login script statements. If you place the EXIT command at the end of the container login script, the login script processing ends, and no profile, user, or default login scripts run. Creating a login script for each user prevents the default login script from running and provides extra security.

◻ Both ConsoleOne and iManager are used to maintain container, profile, and user login scripts. ConsoleOne has the advantage of being able to run from the server console; iManager runs from most Web browsers.

◻ The container login script is created and maintained by selecting a container's Login Script property. A profile login script requires creating a profile object and then granting users the Read right to the Login Script property. The user login script is created and maintained by selecting the user object and then clicking the Login Script tab in the Properties dialog box.

◻ When testing login scripts, make sure the user has access rights to directory paths in the MAP statements.

◻ With ZENworks for Desktops, network administrators can manage user desktop configuration and applications centrally through the use of User and Workstation policies.

◻ Policy Package objects are created in the eDirectory tree and then associated with the appropriate users. You should create an open policy package for the Admin user that enables all computer functions so that user workstation restrictions aren't applied.

Key Terms

container login script — A property of a container object that's run by all users in that container when they log in to the network.

date variables — Login script variables that contain date information, such as weekday, month, and year.

default login script — Commands stored in Novell Client that run when a user doesn't have a user login script.

DFS junctions — eDirectory objects that contain a path to a NetWare volume.

Distributed File System (DFS) — The NetWare 6.5 service that allows volumes to be moved to other servers without affecting user access.

drive pointer — A letter used to reference storage areas in the file system.

identifier variable — A login script variable that represents information such as user login name, date, time, and DOS version.

local drive pointer — Drive letters that point to physical devices on the local computer, such as the floppy disk drive, hard drive, or CD-ROM drive.

login script — A list of commands that run when users first log in to the network. An important use of a login script is establishing initial drive pointer mappings.

login script variable — A reserved word in the login script language with a value that's unique to the user logging in. For example, the HOME_DIRECTORY variable contains the path to the user's home directory.

network drive pointer — A letter, usually F: through Z:, used to represent directory paths and volumes in the network file system.

Policy Package objects — eDirectory objects used in ZENworks for managing the way users access their computers and connect to the network.

profile login script — An eDirectory object containing login commands common to multiple users.

regular drive pointer — A drive pointer assigned to a data directory on each volume.

root drive pointer — A regular drive pointer that acts as though it were the root of the volume.

search drive pointer — A drive pointer used to reference executable files and application directories via a DOS path.

syntax — Rules to be followed when writing login script commands.

time variables — Login script variables containing system time information, such as hour, minute, and a.m. or p.m.

user variables — Login script variables that allow users to enter parameters for their own login scripts.

user login script — Personalized login script commands for a single user that are stored in the Login Script property of a user's eDirectory account. A user login script runs after any container or profile script commands are finished.

Volume Location Database (VLDB) — A DFS setting that identifies the server and volume containing the database that stores paths used in DFS junctions.

workstation variables — Login script variables containing information about the computer's environment, such as machine type, operating system and version, and station node address.

Zero Effort Networking (ZENworks) for Desktops (ZfD) — A Novell product that enables network administrators to centrally manage users' desktop environments.

REVIEW QUESTIONS

1. Which of the following drive pointers appears as though the default path is at the beginning of the volume?

    a. search

    b. root

    c. regular

    d. system

2. Which of the following drive pointers is added to the DOS path?

    a. search

    b. root

    c. regular

    d. system

3. Write a MAP command to create an N: drive pointer to the CORP:Engineer\NASA directory that appears at the beginning of the drive.

4. Write a MAP command that adds a search drive to the beginning of the search list for the CORP: Apps\CAD directory.

5. Write a MAP command that maps a search drive to the SYS:Public directory and adds that search drive to the end of existing search drives on the computer.

6. When a client accesses data through the Distributed File System, the user gets the path to physical data from which of the following objects?

   a. eDirectory

   b. the VLDB

   c. a DFS junction

   d. the Master context

7. What is the first step in setting up the NetWare Distributed File System?

   a. Install DFS on the NetWare server.

   b. Create the management context.

   c. Create DFS junctions.

   d. Load VLDB.NLM on the NetWare server.

8. In the Distributed File System, which of the following is used to store location paths for all volumes?

   a. the VLDB

   b. a DFS junction

   c. the management context

   d. the storage pool

9. Which of the following DFS tasks are done in ConsoleOne? (Choose all that apply.)

   a. creating the management context

   b. splitting a volume

   c. creating and managing DFS junctions

   d. configuring the VLDB

10. Which of the following is the main purpose of login scripts?

    a. setting a user's desktop environment

    b. mapping drive letters

    c. providing informational messages

    d. running applications

11. Which of the following login scripts most likely contains the NO_DEFAULT command?

    a. default

    b. user

    c. container

    d. profile

12. Which of the following commands displays the contents of an ASCII text file on-screen? (Choose all that apply.)

    a. DISPLAY

    b. WRITE

    c. MESSAGE

    d. FDISPLAY

13. Which of the following commands displays a brief message on-screen?

    a. DISPLAY

    b. WRITE

    c. MESSAGE

    d. FILE

14. Which of the following login scripts runs first to standardize the environment for all users in an OU?

    a. default

    b. user

    c. container

    d. profile

15. Which of the following login scripts provides drive mappings and other setup commands that are common to users in multiple containers?

    a. default

    b. user

    c. container

    d. profile

16. The default login script runs if there is no _____ login script.

    a. server

    b. user

    c. container

    d. profile

17. Which of the following commands can be used in a container login script to stop the default login script from running but allow profile or user scripts to run? (Choose all that apply.)

    a. NO_DEFAULT

    b. EXIT

    c. SKIP_DEFAULT

    d. EXIT /NO_DEFAULT

18. The first network drive on your computer is the L: drive. Which drive letter does the MAP *3:=DATA: command use to access the DATA volume?

19. Write a MAP command that uses a variable to map H: as a root drive pointer to a user's home directory.

20. Which of the following commands prevents the output of MAP commands from being displayed?

    a. MAP OFF

    b. DISPLAY OFF

    c. MAP DISPLAY OFF

    d. NO_OUTPUT

21. Write a command that maps drive letter W: to the UASHOST_CORP:Inventory directory for all members of AcctGrp.

22. If you need to map a standard set of drives for all administrative assistants in several OUs, what type of login script should you use?

CASE PROJECTS

Case Project 9-1: Planning Drive Mappings

Using the directory structure you created for the Business Division in Chapter 3, plan drive mappings for users in the Business OU. Create a table outlining drive pointer use (refer to Table 9-1 for an example) to document your drive mappings for users in the Business Division.

Case Project 9-2: Writing the Business Container Login Script

Your next task is to create login scripts for users in the Business Division. To do this, use the Container Login Script Worksheet your instructor provides, and refer to the login script requirements in Figure 9-34 to fill out this worksheet.

Login Script Requirements

Organization: _Universal AeroSpace Business Division_   Page __1__ of __1__

Developed by: _Eric Kenton_   Date:_____

Drive Mappings			
Users	**Drive**	**Path**	**Script**
All	G:	UASHOST_CORP:	All containers
All	S1:	UASHOST_SYS:PUBLIC	All containers
All	H:	%HOME_DIRECTORY	All containers
Accounting	L:	Publishing Directory Map object	Business container
Desktop Publishing	L:	Marketing Directory Map object	Business container
Marketing	L:	Accounting Directory Map object	Business container
Accounting and Marketing users	I:	UASHOST_CORP:\Inventory	InvApp profile
Accounting and Marketing users	Search drive	UASHOST_CORP:\Inventory	InvApp profile
Julie Damrau	W:	UASHOST_CORP:\IT\Web	WebProfile profile

Messages		
Users	**Description**	**Script**
All	Login greeting message	Business container
All	Daily message file for Monday though Friday	Business container
Accounting	Weekly budget meeting at 9:00 a.m. Monday	Business container
Accounting	Monthly meeting on the first Monday of each month from 8:00 to 9:00 a.m.	InvApp profile
Marketing	Monthly meeting at 9:00 a.m. on the first Wednesday of each month to discuss documentation and promotional needs	Business container

Figure 9-34   Business Division login script requirements

Be sure to include a command that displays the daily message file. Notice that the Business container login script maps the L: drive to the department's directory. You might want to use IF statements that check which group a user belongs to, and then use a Directory Map object to map a drive letter to the corresponding department's directory.

Case Project 9-3: Writing a Profile Login Script

In Figure 9-34, Eric listed an InvApp profile object. Use the Profile Login Script Worksheet your instructor provides to write the login script for the InvApp Profile object. Before entering and testing your login scripts, have your instructor review them. Although your commands can vary slightly, your instructor will check to be sure your script includes the commands needed to perform the activities in the remainder of this book.

HANDS-ON PROJECTS

9

Hands-on Project 9-1: Creating Directory Map Objects

Each department should have a Directory Map object pointing to that department's directory. Identify a Directory Map object for the Engineering and Management departments, and write down the object names with their path and location in the eDirectory tree. Use ConsoleOne or iManager to create the Directory Map objects you defined. Create a printout of the objects for your instructor to check.

Hands-on Project 9-2: Entering and Testing Container Login Scripts

Use ConsoleOne or iManager to enter and test container login scripts for the Engineering, Mfg, and Mgmt containers, as shown in Figures 9-22 through 9-24. Make sure you have created UASHOST_CORP and UASHOST_SYS volume objects in these containers. If you're using a shared server, you need to modify the paths in the MAP commands to point to your corresponding directories. After all login scripts are working, use the procedure in Activity 9-10 to print your login scripts and submit them to your instructor.

Hands-on Project 9-3: Entering and Testing a Profile Login Script

Use ConsoleOne or iManager to enter and test the EngProfile login script shown previously in Figure 9-25. After the profile login script is working, use the procedure in Activity 9-10 to print the login script and submit it to your instructor.

Hands-on Project 9-4: Entering and Testing Business Division Login Scripts

Use ConsoleOne or iManager to enter and test the login scripts you created in Case Projects 9-2 and 9-3. After all login scripts are working, use the procedure in Activity 9-10 to print the login scripts and submit them to your instructor.

Hands-on Project 9-5: Splitting a Volume

This project requires access to a dedicated NetWare 6.5 OES server running a VMware virtual machine or its own physical system. If you're using a physical system for your server, you need at least 100 MB of free space on the hard drive. If you're using VMware, you can create a new hard drive as described in Appendix C.

Use the NetWare Distributed File System to split your CORP volume by moving the Engineer directory structure to a new volume that you create on your server by performing the following steps:

1. If you haven't already done so, use ConsoleOne to create a DFS management context on your server.

2. Use iManager to split your CORP volume at the Engineer directory.

3. Test your system by attempting to log in as an Engineering user and verify that the drive mappings you specified in the login script are still working.

Hands-on Project 9-6: Creating a Profile for the Engineering Department

Create a desktop policy package for the Engineering Department that uses a unique desktop wallpaper and color scheme; the policy package must also prevent users from using the Run command and My Network Places. After creating the new policy package, log in as Kari Means and record your results. Be able to demonstrate the policy for your instructor.

10

IMPLEMENTING NOVELL ONENET USER SERVICES

> **After reading this chapter and completing the activities, you will be able to:**
>
> ◆ Identify iFolder components and use iFolder to enable users to access files from multiple locations
>
> ◆ Describe the NetStorage service and use NetStorage to access network files
>
> ◆ Use NetDrive to access drive mappings by using HTTP
>
> ◆ Use Virtual Office to set up Virtual Teams that enable users to share data and communicate

In Chapter 9, you learned how to configure Windows desktop environments by using Novell Client. An important consideration for many users is being able to access their documents and data files when they're away from the office. For example, David Heise, the president of Universal AeroSpace, spends time away from the office visiting other facilities and customer sites. In addition, Marketing Department users sometimes need to access the customer database and other documents from laptop computers that aren't always attached to the network. As part of its OneNet strategy, Novell has solved many of these access problems by including the iFolder, NetStorage, and NetDrive utilities with Open Enterprise Server (OES). These utilities, along with the iPrint utility you learned about in Chapter 8, enable users to access network data remotely via Web browsers. To make it easier to use these utilities and communicate with users in a workgroup, Novell has included the Virtual Office system with Open Enterprise Server. In this chapter, you learn how to use these utilities to give users access to their documents and data files from any location.

WORKING WITH NOVELL iFOLDER

Login scripts provide drive mappings for users to access network data, but they aren't effective unless the user's computer is attached to the network and Novell Client is installed. Users with laptop computers often need to access data and files when they're away from the office or not attached to the network. In addition, traveling users might want to access files from computers outside the organization. One goal of Novell's OneNet strategy is to ensure that users have access to their network data and resources independent of the network connection. As shown in Figure 10-1, **iFolder** is an important part of the OneNet strategy because it enables files to be kept on a local computer or laptop and synchronized with the network—either across the Internet or when the user's computer is reattached to the local network.

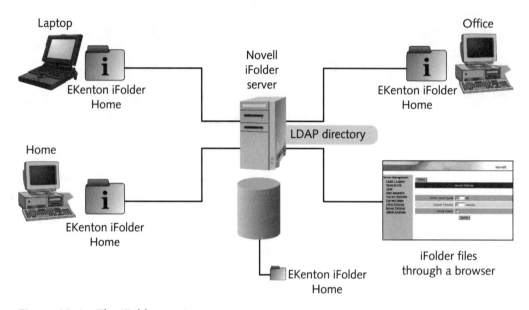

Figure 10-1   The iFolder service

With iFolder, users can have automatic and secure synchronization of files between their hard drives and the iFolder server. Before Eric installed iFolder, Universal AeroSpace users copied the files they needed to their laptops or attached the files to e-mail messages so that they could access the files from remote locations. After iFolder is installed and configured, users can access the latest version of their data from the computers they regularly use or, by using a Java-enabled browser, any computer attached to the Internet. Being able to access their files from any computer at any location has helped eliminate the file-overwriting errors and time-consuming tasks associated with copying files manually between local computers and the network. Novell lists the following benefits of using iFolder:

- A simple and secure way to access, organize, and manage files from any computer
- Automatic synchronization of data across multiple computers, enabling users to access their files from any computer by using the iFolder client or a Web browser
- Secure access to files via a Web browser, allowing users to access their files from computers at other locations
- Encryption of sensitive files stored on the server, protecting them from unauthorized access
- The capability to work on files offline and have them synchronized to the server automatically the next time the computer is attached to the local network

In the following sections, you learn about iFolder's components and how to set up and configure iFolder so that you can access and synchronize files between computers.

iFolder Components and Installation

The iFolder software consists of a server component, a Novell Client component, and a Java applet component. These three components work together to give users access to their iFolder files from anywhere in the world, even if their computers are temporarily offline from the network. In addition to making it possible for mobile users to access their files while offline, iFolder is helpful when users need to access their files but the server is unavailable because of network connection problems or other hardware failures. Because changes are made to local files and then synchronized to the server, users can continue to work on their documents until the server is back online. In the following sections, you learn about iFolder's components and how Eric used them on the UAS network.

The iFolder Server Component

The iFolder server component, the central piece of the iFolder system, is required to synchronize files between computers and allow access to files over the Internet. The server component also includes the iFolder Management console and an iFolder Web site. Network administrators can use the Server Management console to perform administrative tasks for all iFolder user accounts. The iFolder Web site, where the iFolder client software can be downloaded, makes it possible for users to view and download iFolder files through the Java applet running on their Web browsers. Novell has designed the iFolder server component so that in the future it can be installed and run from other server platforms, such as Windows Server 2003 and Linux. The iFolder server component can be installed on the NetWare 6.5 OES server during server installation or later by using iManager. To install iFolder, the server must meet the following minimum requirements:

- There must be 10 MB of free space on the SYS volume.
- The iFolder server must have the Root Certificate to issue public keys for securely encrypting data transmissions through public key cryptography (described in Chapter 11). If necessary, copy the Root Certificate from the certification authority to the server hosting the iFolder service.
- If you're using DNS names for the iFolder server, verify that the DNS name and corresponding IP address of the iFolder server are in the SYS:Etc\Hosts file of the server hosting iFolder.

The iFolder Client Component

The two iFolder client components are the iFolder client and the iFolder Java applet. The iFolder client must be installed on a computer running Novell Client, but the Java applet can be installed on any computer with a Java-enabled Web browser. The requirements to install the iFolder client include the following:

- Windows OS (Windows 95 or later)
- Internet Explorer 5.0 or later
- 2 MB of free disk space

The iFolder client is installed from the iFolder Web site as described in "Using iFolder" later in this chapter. After the iFolder client is installed, you can use it for the following tasks:

- Update data across multiple computers
- Allow access to synchronized files through the computer's My Documents\iFolder directory
- Minimize bandwidth by synchronizing with the server only the data blocks that change in a file
- Use a restore bin to contain files that have been deleted from other computers
- Allow access to files from a computer that's disconnected from the network
- Allow encryption of files stored on the server
- Encrypt files on the client so that confidential files can be transmitted to a server securely and stored in an encrypted state

10

After installing the iFolder client, an icon is placed on the desktop that points to the iFolder home directory, located in My Documents\iFolder*userid*\Home (*userid* is the system ID number assigned to each iFolder user). The iFolder directory acts like any other directory on a user's hard drive, so users can place data in the iFolder directory simply by dragging and dropping files or folders or by saving files directly to My Documents\iFolder*userid*\Home. Users can open and edit files in the iFolder directory just as they would with any other files.

Applications associated with a file in the iFolder directory must be installed on the local computer. For example, if you have a Word document in your iFolder directory, you need to have Microsoft Word installed on your local computer to access the document. When a user places a new file or folder in the iFolder directory, it's synchronized to the iFolder server automatically, and the user can view and access it from any computer with the iFolder or Web browser client. Any changes made to files in the iFolder directory from any computer are automatically synchronized to the iFolder server, ensuring that users are always working with the latest copy of a file or folder. The user or network administrator can determine the frequency of synchronizing iFolder directories by right-clicking the iFolder icon and selecting iFolder Preferences.

The iFolder Java Applet Component

With the iFolder Java applet component, users can access files and perform normal file operations—such as copy, delete, rename, download, and upload—from any Java-enabled browser. An advantage of the iFolder Java applet is that users can access their iFolder files from a computer that doesn't have the iFolder client installed. Users no longer have to bring a laptop with them when traveling because they can use any computer with Internet access to download and work on their files. For this reason, the iFolder Java applet works well in organizations where users often travel to different facilities.

Installing the iFolder Server Component

As described in Chapter 2, to keep the initial installation of the NetWare 6.5 OES server simple, you might choose to install iFolder later. When you're ready to install iFolder on the server, you can use iManager or the NetWare GUI console. During installation, you're prompted to enter the information shown in Figure 10-2.

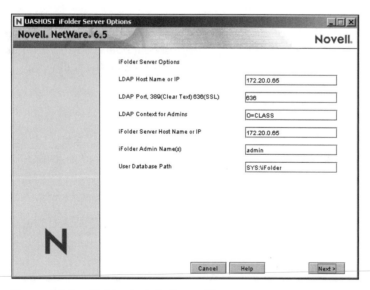

Figure 10-2 iFolder installation settings

The following list explains these settings in more detail:

- *LDAP Host Name or IP*—Enter the host name or IP address of the eDirectory server that authenticates iFolder users. This server must have a replica of the eDirectory root partition.

- *LDAP Port*—Specify the LDAP port to be used for unencrypted and Secure Sockets Layer (SSL) encrypted communications. By default, the unencrypted port is set to 389, and port 636 is used for encrypted communications. When using port 636, make sure the LDAP server is configured to support SSL. Unencrypted LDAP communications (port 389) work well when iFolder and LDAP are running on the same server. If LDAP communications have to cross the network, you should use port 636 to enable SSL encryption.

- *LDAP Context for Admins*—Enter the context of the container storing the names of administrators who need rights to modify iFolder user information. For example, to allow all users in the IT Department to manage iFolder user accounts, Eric entered the context of the IT OU.

- *iFolder Server Host Name or IP*—Specify the domain name or IP address of the server running the iFolder service. This server may or may not be the same as the server entered in the LDAP Host Name or IP text box. On large networks, performance and security can be improved by using a dedicated iFolder server that doesn't have a replica of the eDirectory root partition. Although having a replica of the eDirectory root partition on the iFolder server can improve performance, not having an eDirectory replica on the iFolder server increases security by preventing attackers from gaining access to eDirectory data stored on the iFolder computer's hard disk.

- *iFolder Admin Name(s)*—Enter the user names of iFolder administrators who have rights to configure the iFolder service. Multiple user names are separated with semicolons.

- *User Database Path*—Specify the path to the directory where iFolder user data is stored on the iFolder server. When using a NetWare server, you should specify a data volume instead of placing iFolder data on the SYS volume. If the SYS volume fills up, it could bring down the iFolder server.

After iFolder is installed, you need to enable iFolder user accounts as described in "Configuring iFolder" later in this chapter. In the following activity, you install iFolder via iManager. If you don't have access to a dedicated NetWare 6.5 OES server, your instructor might perform this activity as a demonstration.

Activity 10-1: Installing iFolder

Time Required: 30 minutes

Objective: Install the iFolder service.

Requirements: Access to a dedicated NetWare 6.5 OES server, Operating System CD 1, and Products CD 2

Description: Eric wants to use iFolder so that users can access their data from outside the company's internal network and has asked you to set up an experimental iFolder service on the new server. In this activity, you begin by installing iFolder on your NetWare 6.5 OES server.

1. If necessary, from your server console, change to the X Server - Graphical Console screen.

2. Insert the Products CD 2 into your server's CD-ROM drive.

3. Click the **Novell** button and then click **Install** to display the currently Installed Products window.

4. Click the **Add** button, click the **browse** button, navigate to the NW65PROD CD, click the **Postinst.ni** file, as shown in Figure 10-3, and then click **OK** to copy installation files to the server.

5. Click **OK** again to display the components window shown in Figure 10-4.

6. Click the **Clear All** button, and then scroll down and click the **Novell iFolder Storage Services** check box.

7. Click **Next** to display the Summary window and verify that the Novell iFolder Storage Services component is listed in the Products to be installed window.

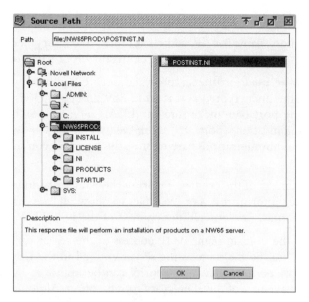

Figure 10-3 Selecting the Postinst.ni file

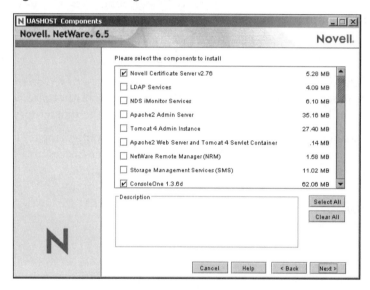

Figure 10-4 Selecting components to install

8. Click the **Copy files** button to copy the iFolder files to your server's SYS volume and display the login window.

9. Enter your administrative user name, password, and context, and then click **OK** to log in to the server and display the iFolder installation settings window shown previously in Figure 10-2.

10. Enter the IP address of your NetWare OES server in the LDAP Host Name or IP and iFolder Server Host Name or IP text boxes.

11. Enter **389** in the LDAP Port, 389 (Clear Text) 636 (SSL) text box, and then click **Next** to finish the iFolder server configuration and display the Installation complete message shown in Figure 10-5.

12. Click the **Reboot Server** button to restart your NetWare 6.5 OES server.

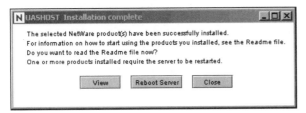

Figure 10-5   The completion message for iFolder installation

Configuring iFolder

After installing the iFolder software on the NetWare 6.5 OES server, you need to use the iFolder Management utility to configure the iFolder server and enable user accounts. The iFolder management utility is accessed from the URL https://*IPaddress*/iFolderServer/Admin (substituting the iFolder server's IP address or DNS name for *IPaddress*). The iFolder Management utility divides iFolder administrative tasks into four major categories, as shown in Figure 10-6.

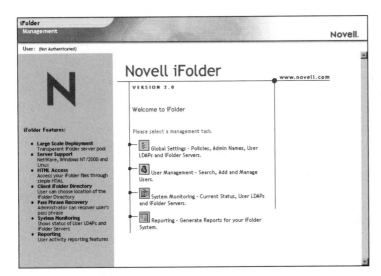

Figure 10-6   iFolder management options window

Before performing these administrative tasks, you need to log in to the iFolder server with the Admin user name and password you specified during iFolder installation. In the following sections, you learn how to use the iFolder management tasks to configure the iFolder environment.

Configure Global Settings

Under the Global Settings heading are the five links shown in Figure 10-7. The General Information window displays basic information about the iFolder server, including the DNS name or IP address, the port being used, the default context, and the vendor version. This information is for reference only and can't be changed.

Clicking the Global Policies link displays options for Client Policies and Server Policies. Administrators can use the Client Policies window shown in Figure 10-8 to set parameters that affect new and existing users. Certain parameters, such as Encryption, Recover Pass Phrase, and iFolder Location, affect only new iFolder user accounts. Automatic synchronization settings enable administrators to set how often the iFolder client synchronizes its data with the server. The iFolder location, set only on new user accounts, identifies the path where iFolder data is stored on the client computer. For most purposes, these default settings don't need to be modified.

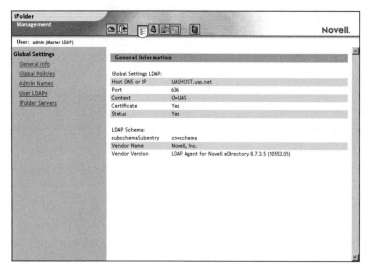

Figure 10-7   Global Settings: General Information window

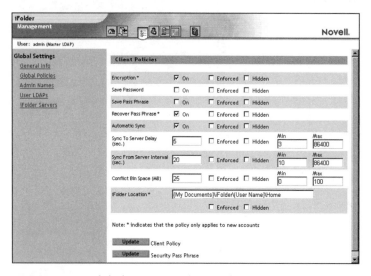

Figure 10-8   Global Settings: Client Policies window

Administrators can use the Server Policies window shown in Figure 10-9 to limit space for each user and to change the default session timeout value.

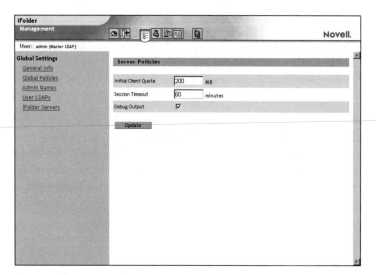

Figure 10-9   Global Settings: Server Policies window

Clicking the Admin Names link displays the window shown in Figure 10-10, where you specify iFolder administrative user names. The users listed in the Admin Names text box can use the iFolder Management utility to configure iFolder settings. Multiple user names are separated by semicolons. All user names entered must exist in the context shown in the General Information window. In the example in Figure 10-10, all user names must exist in the UAS Organization. To add a user, place a semicolon at the end of the last admin user name followed by the new user's login name. Click the Update button to apply your change.

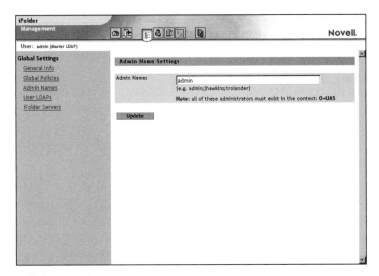

Figure 10-10 Global Settings: Admin Name Settings window

Clicking the User LDAPs link displays a window where you tell the LDAP server which contexts to use when searching for iFolder user names. Before enabling iFolder user accounts, you need to use these steps to set the LDAP context for users:

1. Click the User LDAPs link to display the LDAP iFolder servers (see Figure 10-11).

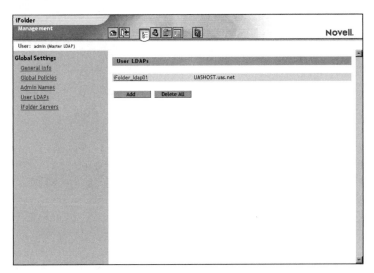

Figure 10-11 Global Settings: User LDAPs window

2. Click the iFolder_ldap01 link to display the configuration window in Figure 10-12.

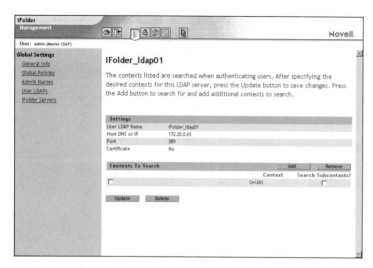

Figure 10-12   The iFolder_ldap01 settings window

3. To search the default context, click the check box in the Contexts To Search column. To find users in any subcontainers, click to select the Search Subcontexts check box. To add a new context, click the Add button and then click Search to display a list of contexts (see Figure 10-13). Click a context and then click Add to include it in the contexts to search. In Activity 10-2, you use iFolder Global Settings to add the IT OU to iFolder contexts.

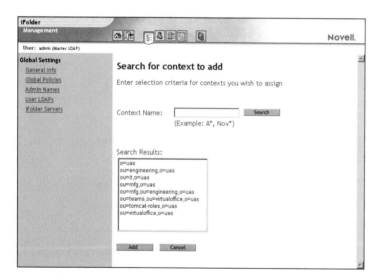

Figure 10-13   The Search for context to add window

4. After modifying the User LDAP contexts, click the Update button to apply your changes.

You can click the iFolder Servers link to add iFolder servers to your eDirectory tree. If your iFolder server is overloaded, you might want to install iFolder on another server and then use this option to add the new iFolder server to your eDirectory tree. With this option, administrators can add and configure iFolder servers and assign users to different iFolder servers for better performance.

Activity 10-2: Viewing and Modifying iFolder Global Settings

Time Required: 10 minutes

Objective: Use the iFolder Management utility to access configuration information.

Requirements: Completion of Activity 10-1 or iFolder installed on the classroom server and Internet Explorer on a Windows XP computer or Java-enabled Firefox on a SUSE Linux 10 computer

If you're using iFolder from the classroom server, you need access to an iFolder administrative user account and password. If you don't have access to an administrative user account, your instructor might perform this activity as a class demonstration.

Description: In this activity, you use the iFolder Management console to document your iFolder configuration settings and add the IT OU to the iFolder search contexts.

1. If necessary, start your computer, and log on to your local computer.

2. Start your Web browser, and then start iFolder Management by entering the URL **https://IPaddress/iFolderServer/Admin** (replacing *IPaddress* with the IP address of your NetWare 6.5 OES server) to display the Novell iFolder menu options.

3. Click the **Global Settings** icon, and then enter your assigned iFolder user name and password to display the General Information window. (If you're using a dedicated server, enter your administrative user name and password.)

4. Record your default port and context:

_____

_____

5. Click the **Global Policies** link, and then click the **Client Policies Display** button. Record the default setting for Sync To Server Delay (sec):

_____

6. Click your browser's **Back** button, click the **Server Policies Display** button, and enter **30** in the Session Timeout text box.

7. Click the **Update** button to apply your changes.

8. Click the **Admin Names** link, and record the iFolder administrators:

_____

9. Click the **User LDAPs** link, and follow these steps to add the IT OU to the Contexts To Search list:

   a. Click the **iFolder_ldap01** link to display the contexts to search (shown previously in Figure 10-12).

   b. Click the **Add** button in the Contexts To Search row to display the Search for context to add window.

   c. Enter **IT*** in the Context Name text box, and then click the **Search** button to display a search results window showing your IT context.

   d. Click the **IT.UAS** container, and then click the **Add** button to add the IT OU to the Contexts To Search list. (If you're using a classroom server, click **IT.##UAS** in the search results window, replacing ## with your assigned student number.)

   e. Click to select the check box next to the IT.UAS context, and then click the **Update** button to apply your changes.

   f. Click the **Home** button to return to the Novell iFolder main window.

10. You can leave the iFolder Management window open for the next activity. If you have finished your session, click the **Exit** button and then close your Web browser.

10

Enable User Accounts with User Management

Before users can start using iFolder, their user accounts must be enabled to create a storage area for them in the iFolder directory structure. You can enable users individually or through search options available under the User Management heading in iFolder Management. Clicking the Search link displays a window where you enter a user name and click the Search button (see Figure 10-14). This option is useful when you're adding a single user and already know the user name.

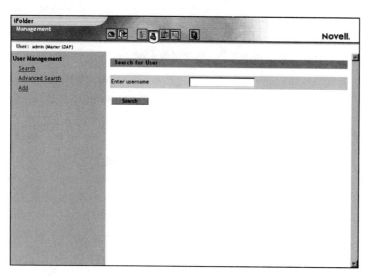

Figure 10-14   Searching for a user

Clicking the Advanced Search link displays a window (see Figure 10-15) where you can enter search criteria, such as a portion of a user name, the context, or even the entire server.

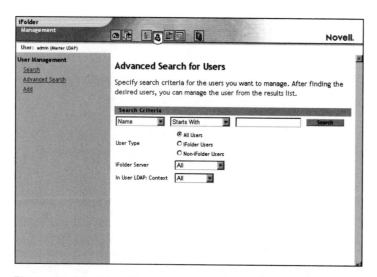

Figure 10-15   User Management: Advanced Search window

Clicking the Search button starts the search process and displays all user accounts matching the search criteria, as shown in Figure 10-16. After the users are listed, you can use the Enable and Disable buttons to enable or disable just the user names you have selected or to enable or disable all users in the search field. In the following activity, you enable all users in your IT Department to use iFolder.

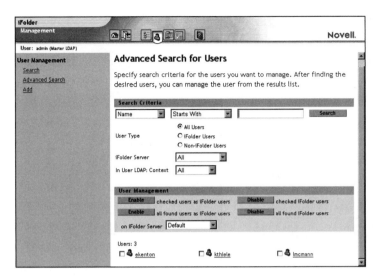

Figure 10-16   Viewing search results

Activity 10-3: Enabling iFolder User Accounts

Time Required: 10 minutes

Objective: Enable iFolder user accounts.

Requirements: Same as Activity 10-2

Description: Eric wants you to test the system by enabling iFolder user accounts for all users in the IT Department.

1. If necessary, start your computer, and log on with your local user name and password.

2. If necessary, start iFolder Management as described in Step 2 of Activity 10-2.

3. Click the **User Management** option and, if necessary, log in as your administrative user to open the window shown previously in Figure 10-14.

4. Click the **Advanced Search** link. In the In User LDAP: Context list box, click the **IT** OU.

5. Click the **Search** button to display the IT user accounts.

6. Click the **Enable all found users as iFolder users** button, and then click **OK** to enable all IT user accounts and return to the Advanced Search for Users window.

7. Exit iFolder Management, and close your Web browser.

System Monitoring

Clicking the System Monitoring option provides a real-time view of the status of your iFolder environment (see Figure 10-17). You can see a list of all iFolder and LDAP servers in your network, including status, number of users, and available disk space.

Notice that this window contains a button for stopping the synchronization process, which might be necessary if the iFolder server needs to be shut down for repair or upgrades. After stopping synchronization, you must restart the iFolder server to resume automatic synchronization with the iFolder clients.

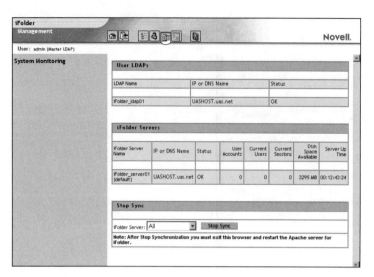

Figure 10-17   The System Monitoring window

Reporting

Clicking the Reporting option for management tasks displays four links that you can use to capture system information in report form. You use this option in Activity 10-5 to check the status of your iFolder users. The General Information window shown in Figure 10-18 displays the number of current users attached to the iFolder server, their total disk quotas, and actual disk space used.

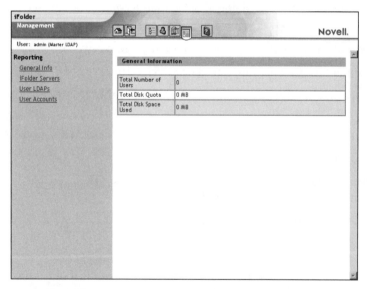

Figure 10-18   Reporting: General Information window

Clicking the iFolder Servers link displays technical information about the iFolder server, similar to the information shown previously in Figure 10-17. Clicking the User LDAPs link displays the status of the LDAP server, the number of enabled iFolder users, and the number of LDAP users available for iFolder access. Clicking the User Accounts link displays detailed information about each current iFolder user, including the user name, the iFolder server the user is attached to, disk space used, last sync time, and file and directory information (see Figure 10-19).

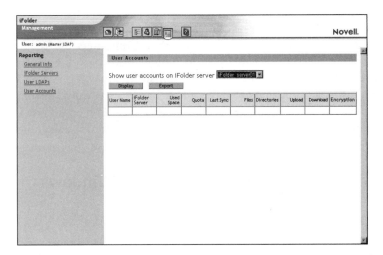

Figure 10-19 Reporting: User Accounts window

Optimizing the iFolder Server

Eric didn't have any problems with the iFolder server's default performance because the UAS network has a limited number of iFolder users. However, as the number of users and the amount of storage space iFolder manages increase, network administrators need to consider improving the iFolder server's performance in the following ways:

- Add more RAM to the server to provide more memory for caching iFolder data. Because memory cache is much faster than disk access, increasing RAM can improve speed significantly when synchronizing data to iFolder clients.

- Add another server to split the processing load. Although the iFolder service could be moved to another server, moving other files and applications from the iFolder server to a new server might be easier. UAS, for example, is planning to install a new server in the Engineering Department to handle processing for CAD applications and data.

- Increase the number of threads available to the NetWare Apache Web server. **Threads** are processes that the CPU is working on, and a multi-CPU server can work on many threads at the same time. Because the Apache Web server runs the iFolder service, increasing the number of threads for the Apache Web server makes more CPU processing available for iFolder requests instead of other Web server work. Although Novell recommends that one thread should be allocated for each iFolder client, iFolder has been tested with up to 25 clients per thread.

- Set quotas limiting the amount of disk space allocated to each user. Allocating large amounts of disk space to users can decrease the iFolder server's performance.

- Increase the default synchronization delay parameters when you have many users and need to improve iFolder performance. Increasing the delay parameters decreases the number of synchronization operations per hour, which allows more time for processing user requests.

Using iFolder

After iFolder has been installed on the NetWare server, users can begin accessing their files from any computer. Except for installing the iFolder server and perhaps changing default settings, the administrator doesn't need to perform any further setup for users. Users can install and use the iFolder client, or they can access iFolder via their Web browsers by using the iFolder Java applet. In the following sections, you learn how to access iFolder using both the iFolder client and the Java applet.

Installing and Using the iFolder Client

With minimum training, users can easily install the iFolder client on their computers by using the Web Manager utility. After installing the iFolder client, users can log in to iFolder from Novell Client or a Web browser. The iFolder service creates accounts for users automatically the first time they log in after installing the iFolder client. When users log in to iFolder, they need to enter a user name, a password, and an optional passphrase. The user name and password authenticate a user as a valid iFolder user. The passphrase is used to encrypt data stored on the local computer. In the following activities, you learn how to install and configure the iFolder client and then access iFolder files from your computer.

Activity 10-4: Installing the iFolder Client Component on Windows

Time Required: 10 minutes

Objective: Install the iFolder client on a computer.

Requirements: A Windows XP computer with Novell Client installed

Description: After hearing about the capabilities of iFolder, Kellie Thiele and Luke McMann were anxious to begin using it so that they could access their files when traveling to other facilities. Eric wants you to test iFolder with his user account as soon as possible. In this activity, you prepare to test iFolder by installing the iFolder client on your Windows computer.

1. If necessary, start your computer, and log in to eDirectory with your administrative user name and password.

2. Start your Web browser, and start Web Manager by entering the URL **https://IPaddress:2200** (replacing *IPaddress* with the IP address of your NetWare 6.5 OES server) to display the Web Manager Login window, shown in Figure 10-20. (Notice that commas are used to separate object types in the distinguished user name.)

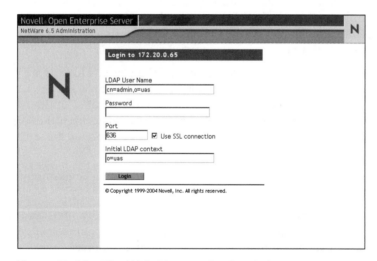

Figure 10-20   The Web Manager Login window

3. In the LDAP User Name text box, enter the distinguished name and password of your administrative user. (*Note*: If you're using a dedicated server, your user name is cn=Admin,o=uas. If you're using a shared classroom server, your user name is CN=##Admin,OU=UAS,O=CLASS.)

4. Click the **Login** button to display the Web Manager welcome window shown in Figure 10-21.

5. Click the **iFolder** link under the End User Software heading to display the Novell iFolder window shown in Figure 10-22.

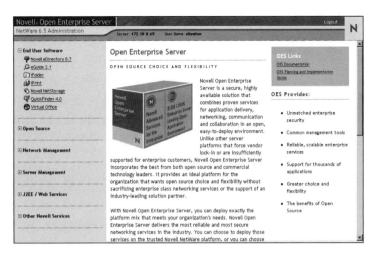

Figure 10-21   The Web Manager welcome window

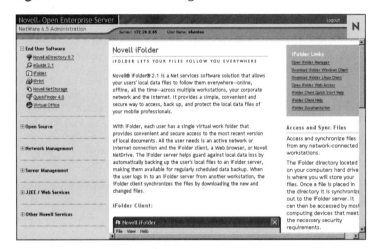

Figure 10-22   The Novell iFolder window

6. Click the **Download iFolder Windows Client** link at the upper right to open the File Download dialog box.

7. Depending on your browser, the files might be extracted automatically. If not, click **Open** or **Run** in the dialog box that opens to extract the files.

8. If you see a Security Warning message, click **Run** to run the iFolderClient.exe program and display the Novell iFolder Setup window.

9. Click **Next** to display the Language selection window.

10. Click **Next** to accept the default English language and display the license agreement window. Read the license agreement, and then click **File**, **Close** from the menu.

11. Click **Yes** to accept the license agreement and display the destination location window. Click **Next** to copy files to the default C:\ProgramFiles\Novell\iFolder location and display the completion window.

12. Click **Finish** to end the installation and display the Readme text file. Record the operating system options:

_____

_____

13. Close the Readme file, and then click **Finish** to restart your Windows system.

Activity 10-5: Using the iFolder Client in Windows

Time Required: 10 minutes

Objective: Configure the iFolder client.

Requirements: Completion of Activity 10-4

Description: Eric wants you to test the iFolder service by configuring his iFolder client and then putting data in his iFolder. In this activity, you configure the iFolder client on your computer, record default configuration settings, and then create files in EKenton's iFolder.

1. If necessary, start your computer, and log in to the Novell network with the EKenton user name and password.

2. Log in to iFolder with the EKenton user name and password.

3. Right-click the **iFolder** icon in the taskbar, and list the available options:

   _____

   _____

   _____

4. Click each option, and be able to describe its contents briefly, if asked.

5. Follow these steps to create a file and save it in EKenton's iFolder directory:

   a. Start WordPad.

   b. Enter your name on the first line, leave a blank line, and type the words **Expense Report** on the third line.

   c. Click **File**, **Save as** from the menu to open the Save As dialog box.

   d. Double-click **iFolder** in the My Documents window, double-click the EKenton user name, and then double-click **Home**.

   e. Enter **Expense** in the File name text box, verify that Rich Text Format (RTF) is selected in the Save as type list box, and then click the **Save** button.

   f. Exit WordPad.

6. Verify that the Expense.rtf file is in the iFolder window by double-clicking the **EKenton Home** icon on the desktop. Double-click the **Expense.rtf** file to open it. Close the file and then close the Home window.

7. To force synchronization with the iFolder server, right-click the **iFolder** icon in the taskbar, and then click **Sync Now**.

8. Start your Web browser, and start the iFolder Management utility.

9. Click the **Reporting** icon in the list of management tasks, and then log in with your administrative user name and password.

10. Click the **User Accounts** link, click the **Display** button, and record the disk space used, the last sync time, and the file and directory information for the EKenton user:

    _____

    _____

    _____

11. Exit iFolder Management, and close your Web browser. Close all windows, and log out. Leave your system running for the next activity.

Installing and Using NetStorage

Although iFolder can give users access to their data from any computer, even one not attached to the network, it requires installing the iFolder client on users' computers as well as placing files in the iFolder directory. Because some users need to access files in shared directories on the server, placing these files in the iFolder directory isn't practical. In addition, when visiting other locations, installing the iFolder client on other people's computers isn't always feasible.

Novell NetStorage solves some of these problems by giving users secure access to files on the NetWare server from any Internet location; it does this by using an existing Web browser or Microsoft Web Folder, with no additional client or applet to download or install on the user's computer. With NetStorage, users can securely copy, move, rename, delete, read, and write files between any Internet-connected machine and the Novell network. NetStorage supports Internet standards such as HTTP, HTTPS, HTML, XML, and WebDAV, making it compatible with most client computer systems, including Windows, Macintosh, and Linux. In addition, NetStorage includes access to NetWare WebAccess so that users can access network files and folders (including files in their iFolder directories) through the NetWare WebAccess page. In the following sections, you learn how to set up and use Novell NetStorage so that users at UAS can access and manage network files.

10

Installing NetStorage

Like iFolder, Novell NetStorage can be installed during the NetWare 6.5 installation or after. Eric chose to install NetStorage later to keep the initial NetWare 6.5 installation as simple as possible. To install and use NetStorage, there must be at least one NetWare 6.5 server in the eDirectory tree where NetStorage is installed, and computers must have a minimum of Netscape 4.7 or Internet Explorer 5.0 installed. During NetStorage installation, you see the window shown in Figure 10-23.

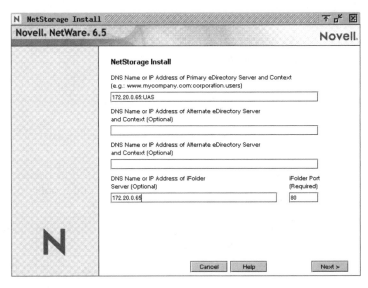

Figure 10-23   Installation information for NetStorage

To install NetStorage correctly, you should make sure the following information is available before beginning:

- Typically, you need to install NetStorage on only one NetWare 6.5 OES server in the eDirectory tree. Before installing NetStorage, you should identify the IP address or DNS name of the primary NetWare 6.5 server, which must have a Master or Read/Write replica of the eDirectory tree. NetStorage doesn't need to be installed on the primary server, but you need to identify this server during NetStorage installation. The primary server comes into play when a user attempts to log in to NetStorage. During login, NetStorage searches eDirectory on the primary server to locate the user name and password. When NetStorage finds the user in the eDirectory database, it authenticates the user to eDirectory.

- Identify the eDirectory context of users who will use NetStorage. NetStorage searches for user accounts in the contexts you specify during NetStorage installation. The context is indicated by inserting a colon after the primary server's IP address or DNS name and then entering the container's distinguished name. For example, to search for users in the UAS Organization, Eric entered "172.20.0.65:UAS."

- In addition to the primary context, the NetStorage Install window contains two more fields where you can specify the primary servers and eDirectory contexts from additional eDirectory trees that the NetStorage service will support.

- The final field in the NetStorage Install window is where you specify the IP address or DNS name of your iFolder server. For users to access their iFolder files through NetStorage, you must specify the iFolder server.

In the following activity, you learn how to install NetStorage on a NetWare 6.5 OES server by using the server's graphical console. This activity requires access to a dedicated NetWare 6.5 server. If you're using a shared classroom server, your instructor might perform this activity as a classroom demonstration.

Activity 10-6: Installing NetStorage

Time Required: 15 minutes

Objective: Install NetStorage on a NetWare 6.5 OES server.

Requirements: Access to a dedicated NetWare 6.5 OES server and the Products CD 2

Description: iFolder is working well for many UAS users, but some want easier access to their files when on the road. To allow UAS users to access their drive mappings and iFolder files remotely via a Web browser, Luke McMann wants to evaluate the use of NetStorage. After identifying the UASHOST server as the primary NetStorage server and obtaining its IP address and DNS name, Eric wants you to install NetStorage by using the NetWare 6.5 server's graphical console. In this activity, you install NetStorage so that you can evaluate its use.

Because installing NetStorage requires shutting down the server and restarting, pick a time for the installation when the server isn't needed.

1. At the Novell X Server - Graphical Console, click the **Novell** button and then click **Install** to display the Installed Products window.

2. Click the **Add** button to display the Source Path window, click the **browse** button to navigate to the Products CD 2 (NW65PROD), click the **Postinst.ni** file, and then click **OK**. The installation files are copied to the server.

3. Click **OK** again to display the Components window, which lists the default installed components. Click the **Clear All** button to prevent reinstalling existing components.

4. Click the **Novell NetStorage** check box, click **Next**, and then click **Copy files**.

5. Log in to the network with your administrative user name and password to display the NetStorage Install window, and then click **OK**.

6. If necessary, enter the UASHOST server's IP address and UAS context in the DNS Name or IP Address of Primary eDirectory Server and Context text box and in the DNS Name or IP Address of iFolder Server text box. (Refer back to Figure 10-23 to see an example.) Verify that port 80 is entered in the iFolder Port text box, and then click **Next** to display the installation summary window.

7. When the Installation complete message box is displayed, click the **RESTART SERVER** button.

Configuring NetStorage

Although the information required to use NetStorage is supplied during installation, sometimes you need to modify the configuration or view the status of your NetStorage service. You can use iManager to configure and monitor NetStorage operation by clicking the File Access (NetStorage) heading and then clicking one of the options shown in Figure 10-24. Table 10-1 describes these options in more detail.

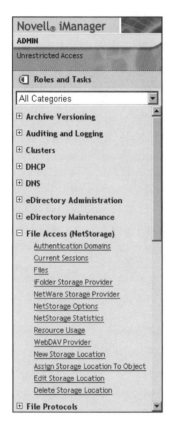

Figure 10-24   NetStorage configuration options

Table 10-1   NetStorage configuration options

NetStorage Configuration Option	Description
Authentication Domains	View or modify authentication domains and contexts. An authentication domain is hosted by an eDirectory server and contains one or more contexts that NetStorage uses to look for users in the eDirectory tree. You can use this option to add servers to NetStorage or to add, prioritize, or remove search contexts within a domain server.
Current Sessions	View the current NetStorage users.
Files	Access iFolder files.
iFolder Storage Provider	Review and change basic iFolder parameters, such as the iFolder server and secure port.
NetWare Storage Provider	View and change parameters for using NetWare mapped drives with NetStorage.
NetStorage Options	View NetStorage options, such as session timeout, LDAP port, and certificate name. In most cases, you shouldn't change these parameters.
NetStorage Statistics	View NetStorage use statistics, such as server uptime, maximum sessions, login failures, and total requests processed.
Resource Usage	View resources used by the system, including memory, locks, and threads.
WebDAV Provider	View Registry information about the WebDAV provider on your computer.

10

Table 10-1   NetStorage configuration options (continued)

NetStorage Configuration Option	Description
New Storage Location, Edit Storage Location, and Delete Storage Location	Use these options to create, edit, and remove a storage location from the eDirectory tree. Storage location objects can be used as pointers to NetWare directories, which makes it easier for users to find and access directories from NetStorage.
Assign Storage Location To Object	Assign a storage location to a user, group, or profile.

Figure 10-25 shows an example of using the Authentication Domains option to view and configure user authentication. Notice that the primary domain is the eDirectory server selected during NetStorage installation, and two contexts are specified in the domain: one for the entire UAS Organization and one for the IT OU. Each context is given a priority. With the IT OU having a priority of 6, NetStorage looks for users in the IT OU first; if the user account isn't found there, NetStorage searches the entire UAS Organization for the user name. In this example, because the IT OU is the most frequent user of NetStorage, Eric placed it as a separate context with a higher priority so that NetStorage could find IT user accounts more quickly. In Activity 10-7, you view your server's authentication domains and then explore other NetStorage configuration options.

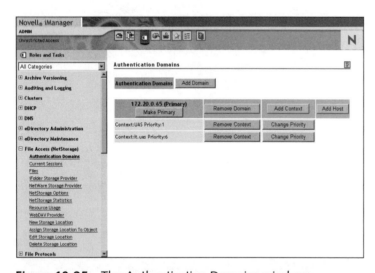

Figure 10-25   The Authentication Domains window

Activity 10-7: Viewing and Modifying NetStorage Configuration Options

Time Required: 10 minutes

Objective: Configure NetStorage on a NetWare 6.5 Open Enterprise server.

Requirements: Access to a user name and password with administrative rights to NetStorage and a Windows XP or SUSE Linux 10 computer

Description: Now that NetStorage has been installed, Eric wants you to document the configuration options and add the IT OU as a separate authentication domain with a priority of 6. In this activity, you use iManager to view your NetStorage configuration options. If you're using a dedicated server, you can add the IT OU as a separate authentication domain.

1. If necessary, log on to your local computer.

2. Start iManager and log in with your administrative user name and password.

3. Click to expand the **File Access (NetStorage)** heading.

4. Click the **Authentication Domains** link to display the Authentication Domains window. Record your primary authentication domain and context(s):

_____

_____

5. If you're using a dedicated server, follow these steps to add the IT OU as a context and set its priority:

   a. Click the **Add Context** button.

   b. In the Enter Context text box, type **IT.UAS** and then click the **Add Context** button to add the context under your primary authentication domain. (If you're using a shared classroom server, enter the IT.##UAS.CLASS context.)

   c. Click the **Change Priority** button next to your IT context.

   d. In the Enter Priority text box, type **6**, and then click the **Change Priority** button to set the priority.

6. Click the **Current Sessions** link and record the names of the six fields:

_____

7. Click the **iFolder Storage Provider** link and record the iFolder server and port number information:

_____

_____

8. Click the **NetStorage Statistics** link and record the server uptime and total requests:

_____

_____

9. Click the other options and record one piece of information for each:

   NetWare Storage Provider _____

   Resource Usage   _____

   WebDAV Provider   _____

10. Exit iManager, and leave your system running for the next activity.

Using NetStorage

Starting NetStorage on the server side happens automatically when the server restarts. To use NetStorage from the client side, the date and time on the server *must* match the date and time on user computers closely. If the time on user computers differs too much from that on the server, file updates might not be synchronized correctly with changes made from the local network. If computers are logging in with Novell Client, the client software sets the computer date and time to match the server automatically. If users are logging in to local computers that don't have Novell Client installed, the computer time must be set to match the server's time for NetStorage to synchronize changes correctly.

After the date and time conditions are met, users can use Microsoft Web Folder or a Web browser to access NetStorage services. To access NetStorage services from a Web browser, enter the URL http://*IPaddress*/ NetStorage (replacing *IPaddress* with the IP address or DNS name of the NetWare server running NetStorage). The NetStorage service then prompts users to enter their eDirectory user names and passwords. After logging in, NetStorage reads drive mappings from the user's login script and then checks the user object's properties to determine the location of his or her home directory. The NetStorage Web page then displays the network files and folders currently accessible to the user. After users log in to NetStorage, they see folders and files that can be modified in much the same way as in Windows Explorer (see Figure 10-26).

The same conventions are used to expand and close directories and to open, move, delete, copy, and rename files. Unlike Windows Explorer, however, local files and folders aren't accessible from the NetStorage window. In addition, users can't map drives or change login scripts from the NetStorage window. In the following activity, you use NetStorage to access files available to your user account.

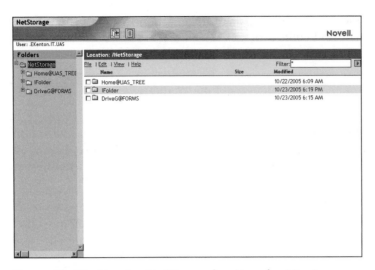

Figure 10-26   Viewing NetStorage locations for EKenton

Activity 10-8: Using NetStorage to Access Files

Time Required: 10 minutes

Objective: Access files by using NetStorage.

Requirements: If you're using a dedicated server, you need to complete Activity 10-6 to install NetStorage on your NetWare server. If you're using a shared classroom server, NetStorage must be installed by your instructor. You also need a Forms directory in your CORP data area and Read and File Scan rights to all users. This activity can be performed on a Windows XP or SUSE Linux 10 computer.

Description: After installing NetStorage on the UASHOST server, Eric tested the system by logging in to the NetStorage server with his EKenton user name and then verified access to his files and folders. In this activity, you log in to the NetStorage server and practice accessing your files and folders.

1. If necessary, log on to your local computer. (If the Novell iFolder Login window is displayed, click **Cancel** to bypass the iFolder login.)

2. Follow these steps to add a drive mapping to EKenton's login script:

    a. Start iManager and log in with your administrative user name and password.

    b. Click to expand the **Users** heading and then click the **Modify User** link.

    c. Click the **Object Selector** button, navigate to your **IT** OU, and then click the **EKenton** user name.

    d. Click **OK** to display information for the EKenton user.

    e. Click the **Login Script** link on the General tab options to display the Login script window.

    f. Enter **MAP M:=UASHOST\CORP:\Forms** if you're using a dedicated server or **MAP M:=UASHOST\STUDENTS:\##CORP\Forms** if you're using a classroom server (substituting your assigned student number for ##).

    g. Click **OK** to save the login script command.

    h. Exit iManager.

3. Start your Web browser, enter the URL **http://IPaddress/NetStorage**, and press **Enter**. (Replace *IPaddress* with the IP address assigned to your NetWare 6.5 server.) Be careful when you enter the URL because it's case sensitive.

4. When the Login window is displayed, log in with EKenton's user name and password to display the NetStorage home page for EKenton. Record the folders in the navigation pane:

_____

_____

_____

5. Click the **M:** drive to display all files in the Forms directory.

6. Open one of the files and view the contents. Record the results:

_____

7. Follow these steps to copy a file from the Forms directory to EKenton's iFolder directory:

   a. Click to select the check box for one of the files.

   b. Click the **Edit** link and then click **Copy**.

   c. Click the **iFolder** option to display all files in EKenton's iFolder directory.

   d. Click the **Edit** link and then click **Paste** to copy the file to Eric's iFolder directory.

8. Click Eric's home directory, and record the files it contains:

_____

9. Follow these steps to create a subdirectory in Eric's home directory:

   a. Click the **Home** folder option.

   b. Click the **File** link and then click **New Folder**.

   c. Enter a name for the new folder and click **OK** to add it to Eric's home directory.

10. Log out of NetStorage and close your Web browser. You can stay logged in for the next activity.

Using iFolder via NetStorage

The iFolder client can be useful when users need access to files on multiple computers or want to access their files from a laptop that's offline. However, the iFolder client requires Novell Client, which might not be available on some computers or in Linux environments. In addition, it's not practical to install the iFolder client and place the iFolder directory on remote computers that users don't access often. For example, David Heise needs to access certain documents when visiting customer locations and doesn't want to install the iFolder client and home directory icon on computers at these locations because he might not use the same computer next time he visits. To solve this problem, Eric trained UAS users on accessing iFolder files via NetStorage. In the following activity, you learn how to use a Web browser to access a file you stored in iFolder.

Activity 10-9: Accessing iFolder via a Web Browser

Time Required: 10 minutes

Objective: Access iFolder files via a Web browser.

Requirements: Completion of Activity 10-5 and Internet Explorer on a Windows XP computer or Java-enabled Firefox on a SUSE Linux 10 computer

Description: Before training UAS users, Eric wants you to test access to his iFolder files by using a Web browser. In this activity, you download and upload your iFolder files using only the iFolder applet.

1. If necessary, start your computer, and log on to your local system. To simulate accessing iFolder files from a computer that doesn't have Novell Client installed, log on to your local computer system. If you're using Windows XP, click to select the **Workstation Only** check box, and then enter your local user name and password.

2. If necessary, click **Cancel** to close the iFolder Login window.

3. Start your Web browser, enter the URL **https://*IPaddress*/iFolder** (replacing *IPaddress* with the IP address assigned to your iFolder server), and then press **Enter**. (Using "https" encrypts data transmissions by using a secure port, thus increasing security.)

4. Click the **Login** option under the Access your Files heading and, if necessary, click **Yes** to proceed with the security certificate. If requested, enter Eric's passphrase used for encryption.

5. Enter Eric's user name and password, and then click **OK** to log in and display the NetStorage window.

6. Click the **iFolder** directory to expand it, and record the file names:

_____

7. Click to select the check box for the file you copied in Activity 10-8.

8. Click the **File** link and then click **Download**, and download the file to your desktop.

9. Minimize your Web browser.

10. Start a text editor such as WordPad, and open the file you copied to your desktop in Step 8. Add the following line of text:

mm/dd/yy   Room   129.00

11. Save the file with a new name, and exit the text editor.

12. Follow these steps to upload the updated file:
    a. Maximize your Web browser.
    b. Click the **iFolder** directory, click the **File** link, and then click the **Upload** button to open the Novell Upload File dialog box.
    c. Click the browse button to select the file you saved in Step 11, and then click **Upload** to start the upload process. The new file should then appear in your iFolder directory.

13. Click the **Logout** option to exit your session, and close your Web browser.

14. Follow these steps to use your Windows system to access your iFolder data:
    a. If necessary, start Windows and log in to eDirectory with the EKenton user name and password.
    b. Log in to iFolder as **EKenton**. Double-click his iFolder home directory, and open the file you uploaded in Step 12.

15. Close any open windows, and log out. Leave your system running for the next activity.

 NOTE

See Appendix B to learn how to install and use the iFolder client on a SUSE Linux 10 computer.

Installing and Using NetDrive

Although NetStorage enables users to view, upload, and download their iFolder and network data from any client, it doesn't provide direct access to data from applications by using standard drive mappings. Novell has made provisions for creating network drive mappings by using HTTP via NetDrive. With **NetDrive**, you can map a network drive to any NetWare 6.5 OES server without using Novell Client. In addition, because NetDrive uses HTTP, you can map the drive from any Internet-connected system. The main disadvantage of using NetDrive compared to NetStorage is that NetDrive requires installing a small client on the local computer. If you're working from a computer where you don't have rights to install the NetDrive client, such as at an airport kiosk or in a hotel room, you can still use NetStorage to access your files online. In the following sections, you learn how to install and use NetDrive to create drive mappings from a Web browser.

NetDrive Prerequisites

NetDrive works on any Windows system, including Windows 9x versions. In addition, you need only 2 MB of hard drive space to install and run the NetDrive client. NetDrive supports the following methods for accessing network files:

- *WebDAV*—NetDrive integrates with NetStorage to provide a comprehensive file-access solution with minimum client requirements. NetStorage must be installed and configured before using NetDrive with WebDAV.

- *FTP*—NetDrive can access network files by using standard FTP. FTP must be installed and configured on the NetWare server to use this option. (See Chapter 11 for information on setting up an FTP server.)

- *iFolder*—After iFolder is installed and configured on the network, NetDrive can access files from a user's iFolder directory.

Before using NetDrive, you need to install the NetDrive client and then add one or more NetDrive sites that use WebDAV, FTP, or iFolder to map network drives. In the following sections, you learn how to install the NetDrive client and then use it to create new sites and map network drives.

NOTE

The NetDrive client is located in SYS:Apache2\iFolder\Server\Netdrive. You might want to copy this file to the SYS:Public folder to make it available to all users.

Installing the NetDrive Client

You can install the NetDrive client from the NetWare 6.5 server by following these steps:

EXAMPLE

1. Log in to eDirectory with your administrative user name and password, and change to the Apache2\iFolder\Server\Netdrive directory.

2. Start the NetDrive client installation by double-clicking the Netdrive.exe file.

3. Select the language, and click OK.

4. Click Next in the Welcome window and accept the license agreements.

5. In the Destination Location window, you can specify the directory where the client will be installed, and then click Next to install the client and finish the installation.

6. Restart the Windows system.

Adding a Site to NetDrive

After the NetDrive client is installed and your system restarts, you see a NetDrive icon in the Windows taskbar. You can use this icon to open the NetDrive configuration dialog box (see Figure 10-27). To add a new site, you can use the following steps:

EXAMPLE

1. Click the New Site button and enter a name for the new site.

2. Type https://*IPaddress* in the Site Address/URL text box (replacing *IPaddress* with the NetStorage server's IP address).

3. Change the Server Type setting to WebDAV, and select a drive letter.

4. Click to clear the Anonymous/Public Logon check box and enter a valid user name and password in the Username and Password text boxes, as shown in Figure 10-27.

5. Click the Connect button to map the selected drive to the NetStorage server.

10

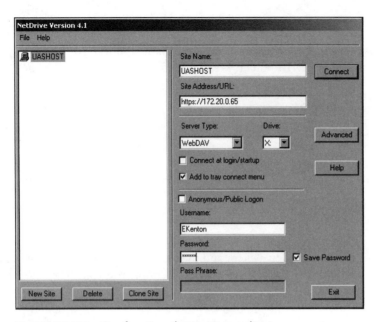

Figure 10-27   Configuring the NetDrive client

USING VIRTUAL OFFICE

The Internet is used often for collaborative tasks, such as sharing data in development and design teams, analytical research, product design, and mergers or acquisitions. Needs for these collaborative tasks include messaging, data sharing, printing, and access to common task-specific applications, such as word processing and data management software. Users can be more productive when these tasks don't depend on their location or having to coordinate times with the other team members. As shown in Figure 10-28, **Virtual Office** is an environment that offers easy access to Novell's OneNet applications, including iFolder, iPrint, Virtual Teams, and eGuide.

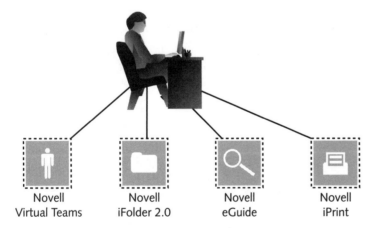

Figure 10-28   The Novell Virtual Office environment

From the Virtual Office window, users can easily access their iFolder data, install and send output to their printers, interact with other users in their teams, and organize and manage their contacts.

Virtual Teams

Users can use NetWare 6.5 Virtual Teams as a way to exchange and share information. You can think of a **Virtual Team** as a group of workers who have shared purposes and work activities. With globalization becoming more common, organizations need to conduct work across geographical and cultural boundaries. Users can take advantage of Virtual Team technology to increase productivity with collaborative communication applications. In Activities 10-10 and 10-11, you see how to create Virtual Teams and use them to share information.

Activity 10-10: Creating Virtual Teams

Time Required: 20 minutes

Objective: Use Novell Virtual Office to create Virtual Teams.

Requirements: Virtual Office installed on the NetWare 6.5 OES server during the NetWare installation in Chapter 2 and a Windows XP computer

Description: UAS is working on a Web-based marketing project that involves three employees. To help them communicate and share data, Luke McMann wants to create a Virtual Team. In this activity, you use Virtual Office to create a Web marketing team and add employees from the IT OU.

1. Start your Web browser, and enter the URL for NetWare 6.5 Web Manager (**https://IPaddress:2200**). Log in to Web Manager with your administrative user name and password to display the Web Manager welcome window.

2. Click the **Virtual Office** link under the End User Software heading.

3. To log in, click the **User Login** link at the upper right to open the Login window.

4. Enter your administrative user name and password, and click the **Login** button.

5. Follow these steps to create a Virtual Team named UASWEBDEV:

    a. Under the Virtual Team Tasks heading on the left, click the **Create Virtual Team** link.

    b. In the Name text box, enter **UASWEBDEV**, and then click **Create**. Click **OK** to respond to the success message.

6. Members can be added to your new Virtual Team by selection or by invitation. Follow these steps to send an invitation:

    a. Under the My Virtual Teams heading on the left, click **UASWEBDEV** to display the Virtual Team window, similar to the one in Figure 10-29.

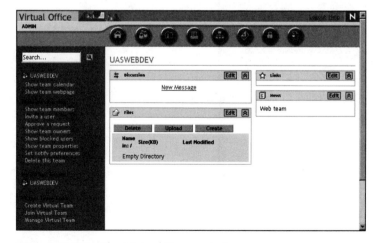

Figure 10-29   The Virtual Team window

    b. Under the Team Membership heading on the left, click the **Invite a user** link.

c. Click the **Add** button to display a search window.

d. Enter **Kenton** in the Last name text box and click **Search**.

e. Click the **Eric Kenton** user, and click **Add** to place his name in the Virtual Team Invitations window.

7. Repeat Step 6 to send invitations to Kellie Thiele and Luke McMann.

8. Click the **Logout** link at the upper right.

9. Follow these steps to log in as Eric Kenton and join the UASWEBDEV team:

a. Log in with your **EKenton** user name and password and start Virtual Office as described in Steps 1 and 2.

b. Click the **Join Virtual Team** link under the Virtual Team Tasks heading.

c. Click **UASWEBDEV** in the Virtual Team inbox, and then click the **Join** button to add the UASWEBDEV team to Eric's My Virtual Teams list.

d. Click the **UASWEBDEV** team under the My Virtual Teams heading, and read the available team information.

e. Click the **Logout** link at the upper right, and leave your Web browser open for the next activity.

10. Log out.

Activity 10-11: Working with Virtual Teams

Time Required: 20 minutes

Objective: Use Virtual Teams to share information

Requirements: Completion of Activity 10-10

Description: In this activity, you upload a file to the UASWEBDEV Virtual Team and then log in as another team member and download the file.

1. Follow the procedure in Activity 10-10 to log in to Virtual Office with your administrative user name and password.

2. Follow these steps to create a team calendar:

a. Click the **UASWEBDEV** team under the My Virtual Teams heading.

b. Click the **Show team calendar** link to display a calendar window, similar to the one in Figure 10-30.

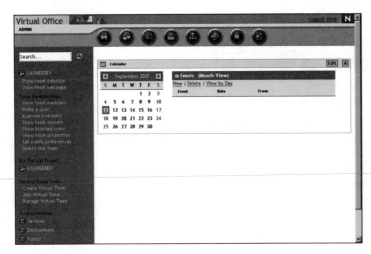

Figure 10-30   The Virtual Team Calendar window

c. Click the **New** link to add an event for today's date.

    d. Click **Save** to save the entry, and then click **Close** to return to the UASWEBDEV Calendar window.

3. Follow these steps to establish a favorite URL for all team members:

    a. Click the **Show team webpage** link at the left to display the Team Page window, similar to the one in Figure 10-31, and then click the **Edit** button.

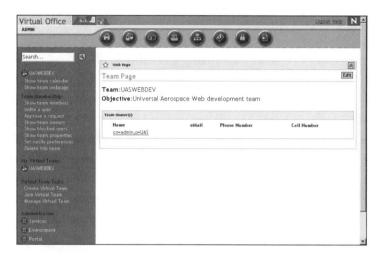

Figure 10-31   The Team Page window

    b. Click the **Published Favorites** check box, and then click the **Edit** button to open the Current Bookmarks window.

    c. Click **Add** to open the Add Bookmark dialog box.

    d. Enter **Novell** in the Name text box, and enter **www.novell.com** in the URL text box.

    e. Click **OK** to place the bookmark in the Current Bookmarks window.

    f. Click **Save** to save the new bookmark and open a Links window. Close the Links window to return to the Team Page window.

4. Follow these steps to upload a file:

    a. Click the **Published Files Edit** button to open the Files window.

    b. Click the **Upload** button, and click the **Browse** button to navigate to your C:\Windows\System32 folder.

    c. Click the **Ping.exe** program, and click **Open** to insert it in the File name text box.

    d. Click the **Upload** button to upload the file and notify all team members.

    e. After the file is uploaded, click **Close** and then close the Files window.

5. Log out.

6. Log in to Virtual Office as **Eric Kenton** and verify that the calendar, Novell URL, and Ping.exe file are available.

7. Log out and close your Web browser.

CHAPTER SUMMARY

❑ By storing files on the local computer and synchronizing them with the network, the iFolder service enables users to access their files from multiple computers without having to be logged in to the network.

❑ To use iFolder, you must first install the iFolder service on a server and then install the iFolder client or a Java applet on a client computer.

❑ You can use the iFolder Management utility to configure global settings, enable user accounts, and view status information on your iFolder server and users.

❑ The iFolder Java applet enables users to access their files from a Web browser without having to install the iFolder client.

❑ The NetStorage service provides access to user files and folders from a Web browser without the need to install any client software on local computers.

❑ NetStorage data is available directly from WebDAV-compatible applications, such as Microsoft Office, but must be downloaded to the local computer to be accessible to all applications.

❑ With NetDrive, users can map drives to network locations by using HTTP. Because NetDrive requires installing a small client on the local computer, using it from computers in libraries or hotels, for example, might not be feasible.

❑ Virtual Office provides an environment for accessing network resources and working in a collaborative environment. Using Virtual Office, users can create Virtual Teams to facilitate communications and file sharing.

KEY TERMS

iFolder — A NetWare service that enables files to be kept on a local computer (or one that's not attached to the network) and synchronized with the network.

NetDrive — A Novell client service that uses NetStorage to map drive letters on the local Windows system to network drives by using HTTP.

Novell NetStorage — A WebDAV-compatible service that makes network files available by using HTTP via a Web browser.

threads — Web server processes that allow multiple CPUs to work on a Web application simultaneously to improve performance.

Virtual Office — A Novell system that enables users to work in Virtual Teams and communicate and access data by using a Web browser interface.

Virtual Team — A group of Virtual Office users who share common files and scheduling.

REVIEW QUESTIONS

1. Which of the following OneNet utilities allows access to network data from a Web browser without adding a client to the user computer?

    a. iFolder

    b. Virtual Office

    c. NetStorage

    d. iManager

2. Which of the following OneNet utilities provides secure and automatic synchronization of files between the local hard disk and the server?

    a. iFolder

    b. NetStorage

    c. WebDAV

    d. Web Manager

3. Which of the following is *not* a benefit of iFolder?

    a. secure access to network files from any computer using only a Web browser or Microsoft Web Folder

    b. automatic synchronizing of data across multiple computers

    c. encryption of sensitive files to protect them from unauthorized access

    d. the capability to work on files offline

4. The iFolder server component can't be installed during NetWare 6.5 installation. True or False?

5. The iFolder client can be installed on which of the following platforms? (Choose all that apply.)

   a. Linux

   b. Windows NT

   c. Windows 2000/XP

   d. Windows 9x

   e. Windows 3.1

   f. Windows Me

6. Accessing iFolder files from a Web browser requires which of the following?

   a. the iFolder client on the computer

   b. a Java applet installed on the Web browser

   c. no additional software

   d. Internet Explorer 5.5 or later installed on the computer

7. In iFolder, you can use the Client Policies link to do which of the following? (Choose all that apply.)

   a. enforce encryption

   b. set user quota limits

   c. save passwords and pass phrases

   d. force password changes after the specified number of days

   e. set session timeout values

8. In iFolder, you can use the Server Policies link to do which of the following? (Choose all that apply.)

   a. set initial disk quotas

   b. set session timeout values

   c. enforce encryption

   d. save passwords and pass phrases

   e. force password changes after the specified number of days

9. If you have multiple CPUs on the server and many iFolder user accounts, you can help improve iFolder server performance by doing which of the following?

   a. increasing the disk quota limits

   b. adding iFolder servers

   c. increasing the number of threads

   d. reducing the default synchronization interval

10. Which of the following actions can be performed by right-clicking the iFolder icon on the taskbar? (Choose all that apply.)

    a. logging in or out

    b. changing passwords

    c. viewing disk quotas

    d. setting synchronization intervals

11. To access iFolder files with a Web browser, you need to download the files to your local disk first. True or False?

12. To access NetStorage files with a Web browser, you need to download the files to your local disk first. True or False?

10

13. Which of the following requirements must be met to use NetStorage on a client computer? (Choose all that apply.)

    a. The NetStorage client software must be downloaded and installed on the client.

    b. The date and time settings must be close to the server's date and time.

    c. NetStorage must be installed on the server.

    d. The context for user accounts must be specified during NetStorage installation.

14. To change the configuration of NetStorage, you need to reinstall it. True or False?

15. Which of the following provides a collaborative computing environment for users to exchange and share information?

    a. iFolder

    b. NetStorage

    c. Virtual Office

    d. Web Manager

16. Novell Virtual Office can provide access to which of the following functions? (Choose all that apply.)

    a. Calendar

    b. iFolder

    c. iPrint

    d. NetStorage

    e. eGuide

17. Novell Virtual Office requires Novell Client to be installed on user computers. True or False?

18. Which of the following iFolder Management options do you use to set the context for LDAP to search for user accounts?

    a. Global Settings: General window

    b. Global Settings: User LDAPs window

    c. User Management window

    d. System Monitoring window

19. What is the default disk quota for iFolder user files?

    a. 1 GB

    b. 200 MB

    c. 500 MB

    d. 100 MB

20. Which of the following drive mappings appears in a user's NetStorage view? (Choose all that apply.)

    a. user home directory

    b. container login script drive mappings

    c. user login script drive mappings

    d. iFolder

CASE PROJECTS

Case Project 10-1: Planning OneNet Use, Scenario 1

Universal AeroSpace recently acquired a small machining company named ACER Tools that makes high-tensile parts for use on the Mars Rover. This company has five computers that need access to the Engineering NASA directory over a WAN. The employees will be on the road and need access to files as they travel. Which Novell OneNet technology described in this chapter best meets the needs of users in the ACER Tools company, and why?

Case Project 10-2: Planning OneNet Use, Scenario 2

Some Engineering users are traveling to ACER Tools and need access to their personal files from computers at both the UAS home office and the ACER Tools facility. Which Novell OneNet technology described in this chapter best meets the needs of these users, and why?

10

HANDS-ON PROJECTS

Hands-on Project 10-1: Using NetStorage

A real test of the NetStorage service came when Eric went on a trip to a NASA space station contractor and wanted to download some CAD drawings for engineers to analyze. In this project, you simulate this situation by performing the following steps:

1. Log in with your administrative user name and password.

2. If necessary, create a user named **DHeise** in your Mgmt OU.

3. If necessary, create a user login script for your DHeise user that maps a drive to the Engineer directory.

4. Give your DHeise user the Read right to the Engineer directory.

5. Use the Paint program to create a simple drawing of a spaceship, and save it in your NASA directory as **SupplyVessel.bmp**.

6. Log out.

7. Log on to your local Windows system, clicking to select the **Workstation Only** check box.

8. Start your Web browser and access the NetStorage page.

9. Log in as the **DHeise** user.

10. Access the drive mapping to the Engineer directory, and then open the **SupplyVessel.bmp** file.

11. Demonstrate your results to your instructor.

Hands-on Project 10-2: Using Virtual Office

The Engineering Department needs to collaborate on a new project to send a robot to the moon as research into a possible lunar base. In this project, create a Virtual Team consisting of all users in the Engineering OU. Test the Virtual Team by logging in as one of the members and placing an entry in the team calendar.

11

IMPLEMENTING AND SECURING INTERNET SERVICES

After reading this chapter and completing the activities, you will be able to:

♦ Describe Novell's Web Services and Net Services

♦ Install and configure Web Services components

♦ Describe technologies for securing Web services, including firewalls and virus protection

♦ Explain encryption security techniques, Novell Certificate Services, and OpenSSH

♦ Describe Novell's backup services

As you have learned, Novell's OneNet strategy uses the Internet to make network services and information available from anywhere at any time. To secure and support the OneNet features of Open Enterprise Server (OES), network administrators need to understand the components that make Internet services available on a NetWare 6.5 server; they also need to know how to implement these services and secure them from unauthorized access and attacks. In addition to Internet services, OES includes Web and FTP services that can be installed and configured to deliver information to the Internet. In this chapter, you learn about the Internet service components in NetWare 6.5 and how to use them to provide Web services and secure a network against unauthorized access.

INTRODUCTION TO NOVELL INTERNET SERVICES

Novell Internet and intranet services simplify setting up business networks by providing a common set of services for accessing data and resources with a variety of computer and server OSs. The NetWare 6.5 Internet service components can be divided into Net Services and Web Services components, as shown in Figure 11-1.

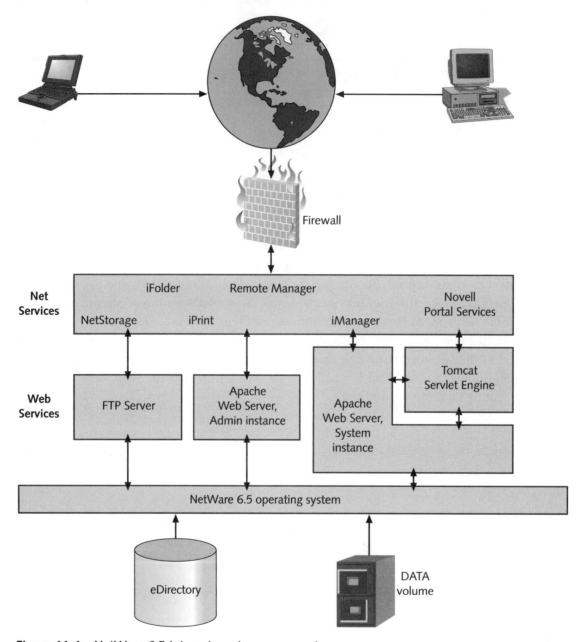

Figure 11-1   NetWare 6.5 Internet service components

Web Services are TCP/IP-based applications that make network data and services, such as Web sites and FTP servers, available to users. To access a Web service, users need the correct client software running on their computers. For example, a Web browser, such as Internet Explorer or Netscape, is needed to access a Web site.

Net Services components extend the capabilities of standard Web services and include many of the services you have worked with already, such as iFolder, NetStorage, iPrint, iManager, and Remote Manager. As shown in Figure 11-1, a network can be configured so that requests for Net Services originating at users' computers are sent via the Internet through a firewall running on a server or router. After being checked through the firewall, the request is routed to a service based on its IP address and port number. IP addresses are used to direct a packet to the correct computer; port numbers are used to transfer the packet's information to the correct application. When an application starts, it provides TCP/IP with its port number. When a packet is received at a computer, the TCP/IP protocol stack uses the port number to determine which application running on the computer should get the packet's information. Table 11-1 lists commonly used applications and their default port numbers.

Table 11-1 Commonly used port numbers

Port Number	Application
21 and 22	FTP
23	Telnet
25	SMTP (e-mail protocol)
80	Web server
100	Post Office Protocol (POP)

To gain access to NetWare files and resources, Net Services run as applications on Web Services components, such as Apache Web Server. Novell chose Apache Web Server to host Net Services components because it's open-source Web server software, meaning it's freely available and can be modified to run on other OS platforms. By running through Apache Web Server, Novell Net Services can be set up on any network operating system (NOS) that supports Apache Web Server, including UNIX, Linux, Windows 2000 Server, and Windows Server 2003. In addition to processing requests for Net Services, Web Services components can make data available through Novell Portal Services. In the following sections, you learn about Web Services components and how Novell Portal Services can be used to customize Web access.

Apache Web Server for NetWare

Apache Web Server is open-source Web server software originally developed by the Apache Group, a nonprofit organization. Currently, more than 60% of all Web-hosting organizations use Apache Web Server; because it's such a common platform for Web-based services, Novell made Apache Web Server an integral part of Open Enterprise Server Internet services. Apache Web Server is used in two ways on Open Enterprise Server. One instance of Apache is used to support Novell Net Services, such as iFolder, and is installed by default during NetWare 6.5 server installation. All configuration files for this Admin instance of Apache Web Server are in the SYS:Adminsrv directory. Because of Apache Web Server's tight integration with Novell Net Services, it requires no special configuration by the network administrator. Apache Web Server is used by these NetWare 6.5 Web-based services:

- NetWare Web Manager
- NetWare Web Search Server
- NetWare WebAccess
- iPrint
- iFolder
- iManager

A second instance of Apache can be installed as a dedicated Web server for hosting an organization's Web site or corporate intranet. You learn how to install and configure Apache Web Server to create a corporate Web site in "Installing and Configuring Web Services" later in this chapter.

Tomcat Servlet Engine for NetWare

The Tomcat Servlet Engine, also developed by the Apache Group, is used to run Java-based Web applications (called **Java servlets**). It's used by several Net Services components, including Novell Portal Services (NPS) and NetWare Web Search Server. Although network administrators rarely need to configure or manage the Tomcat Servlet Engine, programmers developing Web-based applications often work with Tomcat because it runs on a wide variety of OSs.

Novell Portal Services (NPS)

Novell Portal Services (NPS) is a portal strategy for delivering the right information to the people who are authorized to use it. Using NPS, personalized Web pages can be delivered to users regardless of OS platform or network structure, and network administrators can protect and control access to network resources and manage the delivery of personalized data based on users' company roles, locations, and group associations. NPS consists of a number of Java servlets that run on Apache Web Server, as shown in Figure 11-2. NPS enables users to access Web sites and applications they are authorized to use by building customized Web pages based on users' needs and access rights.

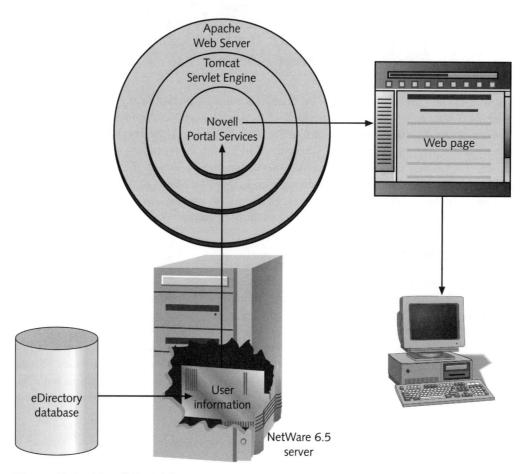

Figure 11-2   Novell Portal Services components

As mentioned, Tomcat Servlet Engine runs Java servlets. To be used in NPS, it must support the Sun Microsystems Java 2.2 Servlet specification so that a variety of Web server platforms can be used. NetWare 6.5 ships with the Java 2.2–compliant Tomcat Servlet Engine. When users access the NPS URL on the NetWare 6.5 server, Apache Web Server, which is hosting the portal service, sends users an authentication page consisting of an HTML form for logging in. Users then submit their user names and passwords to the Apache Web server, which passes the information to the NPS Java servlet running on the Tomcat Servlet Engine. The NPS Java servlet then accesses eDirectory to authenticate users and build a Web page of data that's customized in its content and display. The data's display is based on the user's access rights and the layout format, which can be defined with Extensible Stylesheet Language (XSL).

During installation, NetWare 6.5 automatically creates eDirectory objects to support NPS's additional capabilities. NPS configuration is managed through the Portal Admin browser-based utility, so you can use Netscape Navigator 6.0 or later or Internet Explorer 5.0 or later to access this utility.

NetWare Web Search Server

NetWare Web Search Server makes data on your network or the Internet searchable in minutes. It bridges all types of networks—from file servers to intranets and the Internet—to deliver requested information in a minimum amount of time. Installed by default during the NetWare 6.5 installation, NetWare Web Search Server is ready to run simply by pointing it at the Web or file servers you want included in the search index. It then generates keyword indexes from the information found in the selected locations and returns time-saving keyword searches for users to find data quickly. Using a powerful yet simple template-based architecture, network administrators can customize search forms and search result pages to get the information users need. Administrators can use the parameters, variables, and basic HTML included in Web Search Server to build their own templates for creating customized searches that users can access easily.

NetWare Web Manager

As you learned in Chapter 5, NetWare Web Manager is the portal service used as a home page to access the utilities for configuring, accessing, and managing other Web-based management tools based on the user's access rights. When you access NetWare Web Manager from a browser with the URL *https://IPaddress:2200* (*IPaddress* is the IP address of your NetWare 6.5 server), you get a customized Web page containing the management utilities available on your server. After you select a utility, NPS displays a login window for authenticating your user name and password and customizes the options available in the management utility's main window based on your access rights. Because NetWare Web Manager is a Java-based browser utility, you can use it to access Web Services from any location on the Internet. In the following section, you learn how to use the NetWare Web Manager welcome page to access the utilities for managing the Apache and FTP services.

11

INSTALLING AND CONFIGURING WEB SERVICES

Web Services are generally classified into Web servers and file transfer servers. Web servers operate in a client-server relationship, in which the Web service running on the NetWare server processes requests from clients running on user computers. A Web browser acts as a client requesting information from the Web server. A Web server uses a specified directory in the file system, referred to as the "content directory," to store all files it makes available to clients. Files in the content directory and its subdirectories are available to browser clients.

File transfer services allow users and administrators to download and upload files efficiently and securely between server and client computers. Before the advent of HTTP and World Wide Web servers, File Transfer Protocol (FTP) servers provided a means of transferring files from one Internet host to another. FTP servers are designed as a highly efficient method of transferring files to and from Internet sites. Web servers can transfer files by using HTTP, but FTP servers generally offer more efficient and reliable delivery through their specialized transfer protocol. They are also commonly used to upload content to Web sites. Open Enterprise Server includes an FTP server for transferring files to and from NetWare volumes, posting new content to Web sites, and downloading large documents and software.

Working with Apache Web Server

Open Enterprise Server has continued to enhance Novell's commitment to open-source software by including a number of additional features, such as a second copy of Apache Web Server for hosting corporate Web sites and several developer tools, including MySQL, PHP, and Perl scripting languages. Although these open-source tools and utilities are available to the public, Novell has made them more usable by integrating them with OES and offering support services. In the following sections, you learn how to install, configure, and access Apache Web Server running on the NetWare 6.5 Open Enterprise server.

Installing Apache Web Server

The Admin instance of Apache Web Server is installed automatically during NetWare 6.5 installation and is dedicated to supporting Novell Net Services, such as iFolder, iPrint, NetStorage, and iManager. To set up a

Web server for your organization, you need to install a second instance of Apache Web Server during the initial installation of NetWare 6.5 by using iManager or the server console. To use iManager to install the System instance of Apache Web Server, you can follow these steps:

EXAMPLE

1. Insert the NetWare 6.5 Operating System CD 1 in your client computer.

2. Start iManager and log in with your administrative user name and password.

3. Expand the Install and Upgrade heading, and then click the Install NetWare 6.5 Products link.

4. Click the Remote Product Install link on the right to display the Target Server text box. Select the server you want to install Apache on, and then click Next.

5. In the Components window, click the Clear All button, and then select only Apache2 Web Server and Tomcat 4 Servlet Container.

6. Click Next to display the Summary window. Click Copy files, and then insert the NetWare 6.5 Products CD 2 when prompted to do so.

7. After the files are copied, click Close to finish the installation.

If you have access to the server console, you might find it faster to install Apache that way. In the following activity, you learn how to use the server console's GUI to install Apache Web Server.

NOTE

If you don't have access to a dedicated server, your instructor might perform this activity as a demonstration.

ACTIVITY

Activity 11-1: Installing Apache Web Server

Time Required: 20 minutes

Objective: Install Apache Web Server on your NetWare 6.5 server.

Requirements: Access to a dedicated NetWare 6.5 server console with the Admin user name and password and the Products CD 2

Description: In this activity, you use the server console's GUI on the NetWare 6.5 server to install Apache Web Server.

1. At the NetWare 6.5 server console, verify that the Novell Open Enterprise Server graphical console is displayed. If not, press **Ctrl+Esc** to display the Current Screens list. Enter the number of the X Server – Graphical Console option and press **Enter**.

2. Insert the Products CD 2 in the CD-ROM drive.

3. Click the **Novell** button, and then click the **Install** option to display all currently installed products, including the Apache2 Admin Server and container.

4. Click the **Add** button to display the Source Path window.

5. Verify that the path to install from contains the NW65PROD: name, and then click **OK** to copy the installation files. (If the Path and Response entries aren't set, click the **browse** button, and then click the **NW65PROD** volume and the **Postinst.ni** files.)

NOTE

Novell configuration files on the server CD have an extension of "ni" for "NetWare initialization."

6. After the installation files are copied, the Components window listing installed components is displayed (see Figure 11-3).

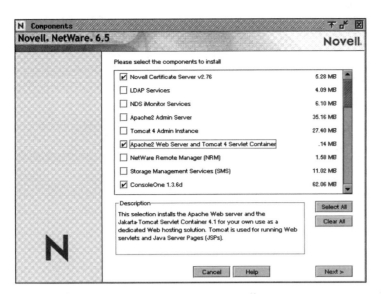

Figure 11-3   Viewing installed components

7. Click the **Clear All** button to clear the default check marks.

8. Click to select the **Apache2 Web Server and Tomcat 4 Servlet Container** check box, and then click **Next** to display the Summary window.

9. Verify that the Apache2 Web Server and Tomcat 4 Servlet Container option is selected, and then click the **Copy files** button to display the login authentication window. Log in with your administrative user name and password.

10. After the installation is finished, an Installation complete message is displayed with options to view the Readme file, reset Apache, or close. Click **Close** to end the installation process and return to the server console.

Configuring Apache Web Server

Apache Web Server is configured by using directives stored in Httpd.conf, a simple text file containing all the information needed to configure the Web server and any other modules that might be loaded. Figure 11-4 shows these directives displayed in Apache Manager. Apache Web Server reads the Httpd.conf file at startup and periodically during operation to maintain the Web server's configuration. The directives and modules included in Httpd.conf are well documented on the Apache Web site, making it easy to configure and manage your server.

However, changing the configuration requires knowledge of the Httpd.conf file's directives and their syntax. When editing the Httpd.conf file manually, it's easy to introduce errors by typing a directive name incorrectly or omitting necessary components of the syntax, which can cause interruptions in Web services that require extra troubleshooting and configuration time. In addition, if you're managing several installations of Apache, keeping all their Httpd.conf files synchronized can waste time and cause additional problems.

NetWare 6.5 solves many of the problems of administering Apache Web Server running on Linux or NetWare servers with a new Web-based administration tool: Apache Manager. Apache Manager is more than a simple GUI interface for editing the Httpd.conf file. With the multiple-server administration mode, you can manage several installations of Apache running on multiple servers (sometimes referred to as a "server farm"). In the multiple-server mode, the Httpd.conf file parameters are stored in eDirectory rather than on the local Apache server. Storing these parameters in eDirectory allows all Apache servers to share access to configuration data. Because Apache Manager is a Java application, it runs on both Linux and NetWare 6.5. This tool offers the following advantages over manually configuring the Httpd.conf configuration file:

- Changes to directives are made electronically, reducing the risk of errors.

- You don't have to know all the directives or modules to configure Apache Web Server.

Configuration view: sys:/apache2/conf/http

ServerRoot	"SYS:/APACHE2"
Timeout	300
KeepAlive	On
MaxKeepAliveRequests	100
KeepAliveTimeout	15
ThreadStackSize	65536
StartThreads	25
MinSpareThreads	10
MaxSpareThreads	50
MaxThreads	1024
MaxRequestsPerChild	0
Listen	80
SecureListen	443 "SSL CertificateDNS"
ServerAdmin	you@your.address
ServerName	172.20.0.65
UseCanonicalName	Off
DocumentRoot	"SYS:/APACHE2/htdocs"
DirectoryIndex	index.html index.html.var
AccessFileName	.htaccess
TypesConfig	conf/mime.types
DefaultType	text/plain
HostnameLookups	Off

Figure 11-4   Viewing the Httpd.conf file in Apache Manager

- You can manage multiple installations of Apache Web Server from a single interface.

- You don't need to edit and maintain several configuration files because many of the same directives are used on all Apache Web servers.

In the following sections, you learn how to use Apache Manager to perform common management functions on the Apache Web server. If you have access to an administrative user name and password, you can make these configuration changes on your Apache Web server.

Starting and Stopping Apache Web Server

Occasionally, you need to stop the Apache Web server to install updates or change features and then restart the server. To do so, simply follow these steps:

1. Start Web Manager by clicking Start, Run, and entering the URL https://*IPaddress*:2200 (replacing *IPaddress* with the address of the NetWare 6.5 server) to open the Login window.

EXAMPLE 2. Log in with your administrative user name and password to display the Welcome window.

3. Click to expand the Open Source heading on the left, and then click the Apache 2.0 link (see Figure 11-5).

4. Click the Administer Single Apache Server link under the Apache 2.0 Links heading on the right to open the Server Status window shown in Figure 11-6.

This window indicates that the server configuration is coming from the Httpd.conf file and the server is currently down. You can use the toolbar buttons to view server logs, modify Web site content locations, view loaded modules, and change administration mode. To stop or restart the Apache Web server, use the Start Server or Stop Server buttons at the bottom. If Web server configuration changes don't seem to be working, restarting the Apache Web server to reload the Httpd.conf directives is a good idea.

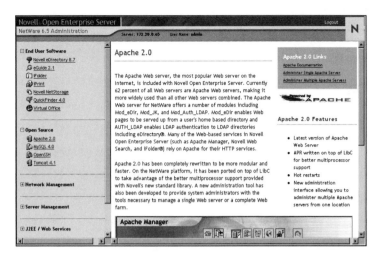

Figure 11-5   Accessing the Apache Web server

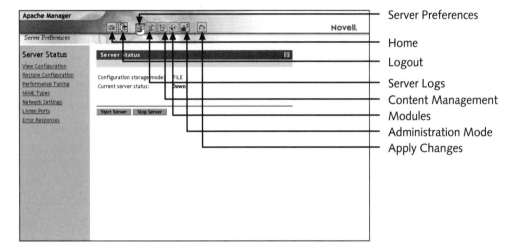

Figure 11-6   The Server Status window in Apache Manager

Changing Administration Mode

Novell Apache 2.0 Web Server can be configured via directives in the Httpd.conf file or through an eDirectory object. When you're administering only a single Apache Web server, using the default Httpd.conf file to store configuration directives is often simpler. However, if you're administering a server farm of several Apache Web servers running on different platforms, working with multiple Httpd.conf files can be time consuming and increase the chance of errors and inconsistencies. Changing the administration mode from File to eDirectory simplifies management by storing configuration directives as an eDirectory object, which can be accessed by all Apache Web servers. To change the Apache Web server's administration mode to eDirectory, you can use the following steps:

EXAMPLE

1. Click the Administration Mode button on the Apache Manager toolbar to display the Administration Mode window shown in Figure 11-7.

2. Click the eDirectory Import Wizard option button, and then click Save to start the Administration Mode Wizard.

3. Click Next to display the Change from File to Directory Mode window, click the Create a new server object option button, and then click Next to display the window shown in Figure 11-8.

4. Select a server group and enter the NetWare 6.5 server's name and IP address.

5. Click Next to display a window that asks whether to use the Httpd.conf file or the inherited eDirectory configuration. Verify that the Import configuration from httpd.conf option button is selected, and then click Next to display a summary window.

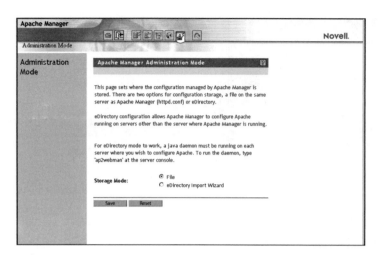

Figure 11-7   The Administration Mode window

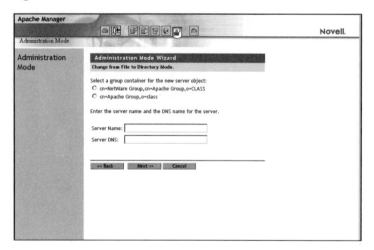

Figure 11-8   Changing from File mode to eDirectory mode

6. Click Finish to complete the conversion from File to eDirectory administration mode.

7. Enter the ap2webman command at the server console so that the Apache server gets its configuration information from eDirectory.

8. You should also use the NWCONFIG utility from the server console (as described in Chapter 2) to place the ap2webman command at the end of your Autoexec.ncf startup file.

Changing the Path of Default Web Content

To prevent the SYS volume from filling up, placing Web site content on another volume is recommended. For example, Eric plans to move the UAS Web site content to the CORP volume. To do this, Eric created an Apache2 directory with a UASWeb subdirectory on the CORP volume and copied all Web content files to the new directory. To configure Apache Web Server to use the new directory, Eric started Apache Manager and clicked the Content Management button to display the Primary Document Directory window shown in Figure 11-9.

He then entered the path CORP:Apache2\UASWeb in the Document root text box and clicked the Save button. Next, he clicked the Logout button on the toolbar to close Apache Manager and return to the Login window. Apache Web Server then looks to the new directory for all incoming Web server requests.

Creating Additional Document Sites

In organizations with several departments, giving each department a separate content directory can simplify management. For example, assume that the UAS Engineering Department will be running its own Web site. To allow the Engineering Department to manage its specialized Web site content, Eric created an additional

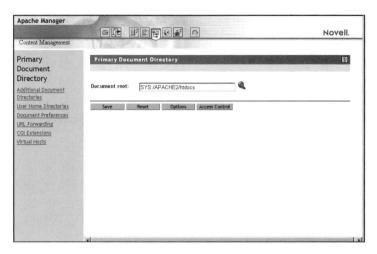

Figure 11-9   The Primary Document Directory window

document site and directory for Engineering as a separate subdirectory of the main IT\Web content directory. Internet users could then access the Engineering Web site with the URL *www.uas.com/engineering*. In the following activity, you use Apache Manager to create an additional document site for the Engineering Department's Web content.

Activity 11-2: Creating an Additional Document Site for Printing

Time Required: 15 minutes

Objective: Use Apache Manager to create an additional document site to display your printer facility map.

Requirements: An administrative account for the Apache Web server running on your dedicated server or a shared classroom server and the path to your assigned directory. In addition, you need to have completed Activity 8-16, in which you created a printer facility map and added an Ippdocs directory. If you're using a shared classroom server, the path should be UASHOST\STUDENTS\##Corp\IT\Web\Ippdocs; for a dedicated server, use ##UASHOST\CORP\IT\Web\Ippdocs, replacing ## with your assigned student number. This activity should be performed on a Windows XP computer.

Description: In this activity, you use Apache Manager to set up an additional document site that points to the Ippdocs directory containing your printer facility map.

1. Follow these steps to start Apache Manager via the Run command:

Using the Run command to enter the URL of the Apache Manager Web page is quicker than starting a Web browser and then entering the Apache Manager URL.

TIP

    a. Click **Start, Run**, enter **https://IPaddress:2200** (replacing *IPaddress* with the IP address of your server), and then press **Enter**. If necessary, click **Yes** to close the security alert message box and open the Login window.

    b. Enter your administrative user name and password and then click **Login**.

    c. Click to expand the **Open Source** heading on the left, and then click the **Apache 2.0** link.

    d. Click **Administer Single Apache Server** under the Apache 2.0 Links heading on the right to display the Server Status window shown previously in Figure 11-6.

2. View the status of your Apache Web server and, if necessary, click the **Start Server** button to start the server. Click **OK** to the confirmation message.

3. Follow these steps to create an additional document site:

    a. Click the **Content Management** button on the toolbar.

11

b. Click the **Additional Document Directories** link on the left to display the Additional Document Directories window (see Figure 11-10).

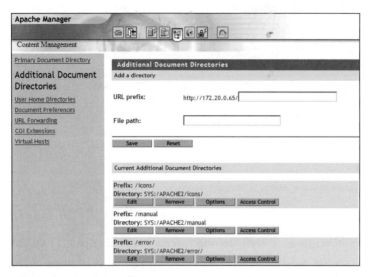

Figure 11-10 The Additional Document Directories window

c. Enter **Printers** in the URL prefix text box. (If you're using a shared classroom server, precede "Printers" with your assigned student number.)

d. Enter the path to your Ippdocs directory (see the Requirements section for this activity) in the File path text box.

e. Click **Save** to open the Save and Apply Changes dialog box.

f. Click **Save and Apply** to apply your changes to the Httpd.conf file and display the Success! message box.

g. Click **OK** to return to Apache Manager.

4. Click the **Logout** button to close Apache Manager and return to the Login window.

5. Close the Login window, and exit your Web browser.

6. Use My Computer to navigate to your IT\Web\Ippdocs directory.

7. Rename the file from UASPrinters.htm to **Index.html**.

8. Close the My Computer window.

9. Follow these steps to test your Printers document site:

a. Start your Web browser and enter the URL **http://*IPaddress*/printers** (replacing *IPaddress* with the IP address of your NetWare 6.5 server). The system should display your printer facility map.

b. Click a printer and follow the prompts to install the printer on your Windows XP system.

c. Close all open windows.

10. You can leave your system running for the next activity.

Working with FTP Server

FTP Server is a Web Services application that enables users to transfer files to and from NetWare volumes that have been configured as part of the FTP content. After logging in to FTP Server, users can navigate to other NetWare servers and volumes where they have access rights, even though the other servers aren't running the FTP Server software. As with other Web-based services, FTP services require server and client components. FTP clients send requests for services to an FTP server on port 21, which then processes the request and returns results to the client. Clients connect to an FTP server with an anonymous user name or by logging in with an authorized user name and password. Typically, anonymous users are limited to downloading files and software from specific directories, whereas authorized users can upload files and access restricted directories and resources not available to anonymous users.

One of the disadvantages of using FTP to transfer files is that FTP doesn't encrypt data packets. Having unencrypted data packets transferred across a network can expose the data to being picked up by unauthorized people using special software that listens to network traffic, in much the same way that people can use radio scanners to listen in on cell phone calls. Novell includes the OpenSSH protocol with Open Enterprise Server, which provides an encrypted file transfer system for secure data transmission. You learn how to use the OpenSSH protocol in "Using the Novell OpenSSH Service" later in this chapter.

To access files on an FTP site, computers must have FTP client software. Most Web browsers have a built-in FTP client for accessing FTP servers with the URL *ftp://IPaddress/DNSname*. In addition to built-in FTP clients, a number of dedicated FTP clients are designed to work directly with FTP servers from various OS and application environments. Many dedicated FTP clients enable users to enter commands directly from the FTP command prompt; other clients, such as FTP Explorer and CuteFTP, use a graphical environment to access the FTP server's files and directories.

Setting up FTP Server requires installing the software on the NetWare 6.5 server and then configuring it to provide access to content directories. In the following sections, you learn how Eric installed FTP Server on the UASHOST server and then configured it for user access. You then use FTP Server to access files and upload content to the FTP document site.

Installing FTP Server

Installing FTP Server consists of copying files from the Products CD 2 and then using iManager to set the IP address and start the FTP service. Although these files can be copied from the Products CD 2 using the graphical server console or iManager, if you have access to the server console, you'll find it faster than iManager. Eric performed the following steps to install FTP Server on the UASHOST server:

1. First, Eric inserted the NetWare 6.5 Products CD 2 in the UASHOST server.

2. At the graphical console, Eric clicked Novell and then Install to display the Installed Products window.

3. He clicked Next and then clicked Add to display the Source Path window, clicked the browse button to select the NetWare 6.5 volume, and then clicked OK. He clicked OK again in the Source Path window to copy installation files to the server, and then the Components window was displayed showing the default installed components.

4. Eric clicked Clear All to prevent reinstalling existing components, clicked the NetWare FTP Server check box, and then clicked Copy files.

5. After the file copying was finished, the Installation complete window displayed the option to view the Readme file. Eric clicked Close to exit the FTP Server installation and return to the X Server – Graphical Console.

Before FTP Server can be used, you need to use iManager to set the IP address and start the FTP service. Eric used the following steps to perform these tasks:

1. After installing the FTP Server software from the UASHOST server console, Eric returned to his Windows XP computer to configure and start the FTP service.

2. Eric started iManager and logged in with his administrative user name and password.

3. He expanded the File Protocols heading and clicked the FTP link to display the FTP Server Administration window.

4. Next, he clicked the Object Selector button next to the Server text box and selected the UASHOST server (see Figure 11-11).

5. He then clicked the sys/etc/ftpserv.cfg link in the Instance path column to display the General tab shown in Figure 11-12.

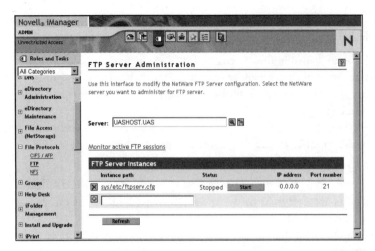

Figure 11-11   The FTP Server Administration window

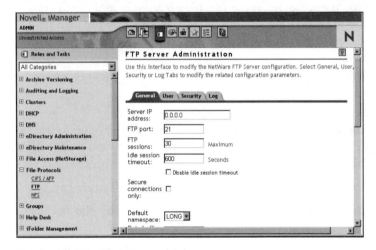

Figure 11-12   The General tab

6. He entered the IP address of the UASHOST server in the Server IP address text box, and then scrolled down and clicked Save to save the settings.

7. To start the FTP service, Eric clicked the Start button under the Status column.

When the FTP service started, the status changed from Stopped to Running. Eric was then ready to configure the FTP server. In the following activity, you learn how to install and start the FTP service on your NetWare 6.5 server.

NOTE

If you're using a shared classroom server, your instructor might perform this activity as a demonstration.

ACTIVITY

Activity 11-3: Installing and Starting the FTP Service

Time Required: 20 minutes

Objective: Install and start the FTP service.

Requirements: Access to a dedicated NetWare 6.5 OES server, a Windows XP computer, and a copy of the Products CD 2

Description: Eric wants you to set up an FTP server on the NetWare 6.5 OES server to permit testing. In this activity, you follow the example given earlier in this section to install FTP Server and then use iManager to configure the IP address and start the FTP service.

1. Insert the Products CD 2 in your server's CD-ROM drive, and then perform the following steps from the server console.

2. If necessary, verify that the Novell Open Enterprise Server graphical console is displayed. If not, press **Ctrl+Esc** to display the Current Screens list. Enter the number of the X Server - Graphical Console option and press **Enter**. Then click the **Novell** button and click **Install** to display the Installed Products window.

3. Click **Add** to display the Source Path window. Click the **browse** button, click the **NW65PROD** volume, click the **PostInst.ni** file, and then click **OK**. Click **OK** again to copy installation files to the server.

4. In the Components window, click **Clear All** to prevent reinstalling existing components, click the **NetWare FTP Server** check box, click **Next**, and then click **Copy files**.

5. After the file copying is finished, the Installation complete window is displayed with the option to view the Readme file. Click **Close** to exit the FTP Server installation and return to the X Server - Graphical Console.

6. Follow these steps on your Windows XP computer:

   a. Start iManager and log in with your administrative user name and password.

   b. Click to expand the **File Protocols** heading, and then click the **FTP** link to display the FTP Server Administration window.

   c. Click the **Object Selector** button next to the Server text box, and then click your UASHOST server.

   d. Click the **sys/etc/ftpserv.cfg** link in the Instance path column to display the General tab shown previously in Figure 11-12.

   e. Enter the IP address of your NetWare server in the Server IP address text box. Scroll down and click **Save** to save your settings.

   f. To start the FTP service, click the **Start** button under the Status column. When the FTP service is started, the status changes from Stopped to Running.

7. Leave iManager running for the next activity.

Configuring FTP Server

FTP Server is managed and configured by using the FTP option under the File Protocols heading in iManager. You can use this option to turn the FTP server on and off, set the default home directory path, and configure user access. As shown in Figure 11-12, the FTP Server Administration window consists of four tabs: General, User, Security, and Log. In addition to setting the IP address and port number of the FTP service, you use the General tab to configure the following:

- Allow only secure connections
- Select long or DOS-based file names
- Set the data buffer size (default 64 KB)
- Set the keep alive time (the time FTP service waits before terminating a session; default is 10 minutes)
- Change the path and name of the welcome banner file
- Set firewall port limits for passive connections
- Set parameters for simulating UNIX FTP replies

You use the User tab shown in Figure 11-13 to enable the FTP service for Web publishing, set the default home server and directory, and enable anonymous users. By default, the home directory is set to the SYS:Public directory of the server hosting FTP services. As a result, most organizations configure the FTP server to point to a different home directory. You can also set the FTP server to use the default home directory rather than the user's home directory. By default, when users log in to the FTP server, their FTP directory path is set to the home directory path stored in their eDirectory accounts. If you want all users to access a common default directory path, enable the check box Always use 'Default home directory' instead of the user's home directory from eDirectory.

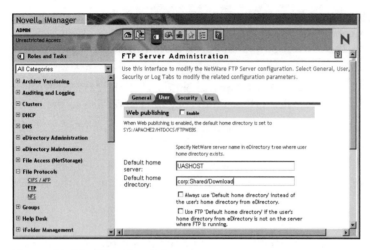

Figure 11-13   The User tab

FTP Server supports an anonymous user account to give users without accounts on the system access to files intended for public use. When enabling anonymous user access, the network administrator needs to specify the path to the anonymous user home directory and indicate whether an e-mail address is required for the password. The e-mail address doesn't cause any access restriction but gives network administrators a way to track access to the FTP site and send messages to users.

You can use the Security tab shown in Figure 11-14 to disable accounts after a specified number of invalid login attempts. Notice that intruder detection settings are divided into Host Intruder Detection and User Intruder Detection sections. Host intruder detection is used to prevent other computers from logging in; user intruder detection process is similar to the intruder detection you learned about for local user accounts in Chapter 5. In both cases, you can block logins for a specified number of minutes after the number of invalid login attempts exceeds the specified setting.

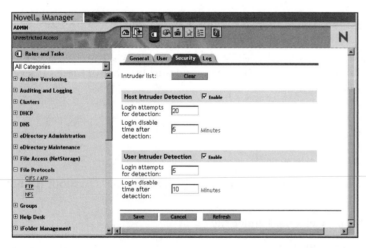

Figure 11-14   The Security tab

Finally, the Log tab shown in Figure 11-15 can be used to set log file location and parameters and to view the contents of log files. If you click the Log file drop-down list, you can change the view to the following settings:

- *FTP daemon Log*—View messages from the FTP service, such as warnings and errors.
- *Audit Log*—View access attempts.
- *Intruder Log*—View invalid login attempts and locked user accounts.
- *Statistics log*—View performance statistics.

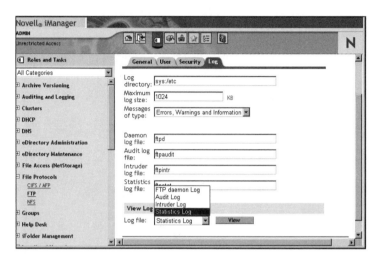

Figure 11-15   The Log tab

 You should view FTP log files periodically to notice any error conditions or invalid access attempts before they become problems.

In addition to settings in iManager, FTP Server uses the Ftprest.txt configuration file stored in the SYS: Etc directory. Administrators can use this file to set access restrictions for containers and users. Restriction lines in the Ftprest.txt file contain the object name (user or container) and one of the following access restrictions:

- *DENY*—Denies access to the FTP server for the specified user or container
- *READONLY*—Gives the Read access right to the specified client
- *NOREMOTE*—Restricts access to allow only local access to the client
- *GUEST*—Allows the specified client to have only the permissions given to the Guest user account
- *ALLOW*—Gives the specified client read and write access to the FTP server directory

When modifying this restrictions file, Novell recommends the following:

- Each line can have only one object and its corresponding access rights. For example, the following line gives all users in the UAS container Read Only rights to the FTP server:

    ```
    *.UAS READONLY
    ```

- Objects are assigned rights in the order they appear in the restrictions file. If different rights apply to the same object, those listed last in the restrictions file apply.
- If the restrictions file is empty or doesn't exist, access is given to all users.

For example, Universal AeroSpace wants to grant all users access to read files from the FTP server but allow only users in the IT OU to upload files. To restrict users other than those in the IT OU to Read Only access, you can use Notepad to edit the Ftprest.txt file, as shown in Figure 11-16. In the following activities, you use iManager to configure the FTP service on your NetWare 6.5 OES server and then set access restrictions in the Ftprest.txt file.

```
# This file contains the restrict ftile format for FTPserver.
# All comment lines should start with a '#'
# If a line continues in the next line, a '\' should be given
# in the end of the first line to indicated the continuation.
# The access rights permitted are
#   DENY - Deny access to FTPserver for that client.
#   READONLY - Gives Readonly Access to the Client.
#   NOREMOTE - Restricts access to remote server navigation.
#   GUEST - Gives only guest access to the user.
#   ALLOW - Gives the user access to ftpserver.
#
#File Format:
# Each line should have one of the Restriction level keywords
#        and access keyword
# For container and User level restrictions, fully distinguished name
#        should be give.
# Container/User name can be Canonical or a Full DN name.
# It should start with a period(.) for user Restriction.
# For Container level Restrictions the line should start with a '*'.
# If container/user name contains spaces, enclose it in double quotes.
# For giving access restrictions to all domain,
#        DOMAIN= ALL should be given.

*.O=UAS              ACCESS= READONLY
*.OU=IT.O=UAS        ACCSSS= ALLOW
```

Figure 11-16 Editing the FTP restrictions file

If you're using a shared classroom server, your instructor might perform this activity as a demonstration.

NOTE

ACTIVITY

Activity 11-4: Configuring the FTP Service

Time Required: 10 minutes

Objective: Configuring the FTP service.

Requirements: Access to a dedicated NetWare 6.5 OES server and a Windows XP computer; completion of Activity 11-3

Description: Universal AeroSpace wants all users to be able to use the FTP server to get software updates from the AeroDyn directory structure but wants only IT users to upload files to the Update directory. In this activity, you create a directory for software updates and then change the default path from SYS:Public to CORP:Shared\Download.

1. From your Windows XP computer, log in to eDirectory with your administrative user name and password.

2. Start ConsoleOne and create a subdirectory named **Download** in the CORP:Shared directory.

3. Use ConsoleOne to add [Public] as a trustee of the Download subdirectory with Read and File Scan rights.

4. To allow the IT Department to manage the Download directory, add the IT OU as a trustee of the Shared\Download directory with all rights except Supervisor and Access Control.

5. To give all users access to the FTP site without having unique user names, use ConsoleOne to create a user named **Anonymous** with no password in your UAS Organization.

6. If necessary, start iManager and log in with your administrative user name and password.

7. Click to expand the **File Protocols** heading, and then click the **FTP** link. In the FTP Server Administration window, click the **Object Selector** button next to the Server text box, and click your NetWare 6.5 OES server.

8. Click the **sys/etc/ftpserv.cfg** link in the Instance path column.

9. To change the default path of the FTP home directory, click the **User** tab and enter **CORP:Shared/Download** in the Default home directory text box.

10. To have all users access the default home directory rather than their home directories, click to select the **Always use 'Default home directory' instead of the user's home directory from eDirectory** check box.

11. To allow the public to download files from the Shared\Download directory, you need to enable anonymous access to the FTP server. To do this, scroll down to the Anonymous Users section, shown in Figure 11-17.

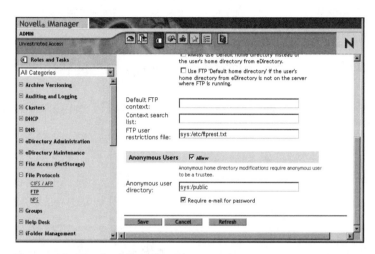

Figure 11-17   Enabling the Anonymous user account

12. Click the **Allow** check box, and then enter the path to the CORP:Shared\Download directory in the Anonymous user directory text box.

13. Click the **Save** button and then click **OK** in the success message box to return to the User tab.

14. Follow these steps to stop and then restart the FTP service:

   a. If necessary, click the **FTP** link under the File Protocols heading to display the main FTP Server Administration window.

   b. Click the **Stop** button to stop the service.

   c. Click the **Start** button to restart the FTP service.

15. After the FTP server status changes to Running, click the **Exit** button to end your iManager session.

16. Follow these steps on your Windows XP computer to modify the Ftprest.txt file in the SYS:ETC directory:

   a. Map drive letter F: to the SYS volume by clicking **Start, Run**, typing **MAP F:=SYS:**, and pressing **Enter**.

   b. Start Notepad. Click **File, Open** from the menu, and open the **F:\Etc\Ftprest.txt** file.

   c. Make the modifications shown previously in Figure 11-16.

   d. Save the file and exit Notepad.

17. Close all open windows, and stay logged in for the next activity.

Accessing FTP Folders and Files

After FTP Server is up and running, you can use any FTP client to log in to the FTP server and transfer files. In the following activity, you use an FTP client to access the classroom FTP server and issue several commands.

Activity 11-5: Working with FTP Services

Time Required: 10 minutes

Objective: Use Web Manager to configure FTP Server.

Requirements: Installation of FTP Server on a dedicated or classroom server. If you're using a dedicated server, you need to have completed Activities 11-3 and 11-4. This activity should be performed on a Windows XP computer.

Description: After configuring the Web server, Eric informed Kellie Thiele that the site was ready to use. Kellie logged in to the FTP server and transferred some files to the Download directory. In this activity, you use an FTP client to log in to your FTP server with the KThiele account and carry out some FTP activities, including creating a directory and transferring files. You then log in as an anonymous user and download a file.

1. If necessary, start your computer, and log in to the Novell network with your administrative user name and password.

2. Use Notepad to create the following text file named ##Readme.txt (replace ## with your assigned student number) in the root of your C: drive:

   ```
   Date: today's date
   Created by: your name
   This file contains instructions on installing the latest
   updates to the station thruster control software.
   ```

3. Exit Notepad and save your file.

4. To open an FTP client window, click **Start**, **Run** and enter **FTP** *IPaddress* (replacing *IPaddress* with the IP address of your server). Then press **Enter** to display the "User *IPaddress*:(none)" login prompt.

5. Enter the distinguished name for KThiele and press **Enter** to display the Password prompt.

6. Enter **password** and press **Enter** to display a message stating that KThiele logged in successfully.

7. Enter **?** and press **Enter** to display a list of FTP commands.

8. Enter the **Put C:\##readme.txt** command and press **Enter** to send your file to the FTP server.

9. Enter **Bye** and press **Enter** to exit the FTP client and return to your Windows desktop.

10. Start your Web browser and enter the URL **ftp://IPaddress** (replacing *IPaddress* with the IP address of your server) to display the Login As window.

11. Click the **Log on anonymously** check box, and then click the **Log on** button to display a window showing all files in the FTP site. (If you can't log in anonymously, log in with your eDirectory administrative user name and password.)

12. Open another student's file by double-clicking it. Read the file and then close the window.

13. If necessary, use My Computer to create a **Downloads** folder at the root of your C: drive.

14. Download a file to your computer. Right-click the file name, and then click **Copy to folder** to open the Browse for Folder dialog box.

15. Navigate to your C: drive, and click the **Downloads** folder. Click **OK** to download the file.

16. Log out by exiting the Web browser.

17. Verify that the file has been downloaded by using My Computer to navigate to your **Downloads** folder, and double-click the new file.

18. Close all windows, and log out. Leave your system running for the next activity.

SECURING WEB SERVICES

Making Net Services and information available on the Internet exposes the NetWare server and user computers to potential attacks. Although public key cryptography secures data through encryption and identifies entities with digital signatures, it doesn't prevent attackers from gaining unauthorized access to network services and data. As network communication becomes more complex, so has the level of attacks against their operations. The most common attacks on information systems fall into these five general categories:

- *Intrusion*—The most common type of attack, **intrusion** involves an unauthorized person gaining access to the system through the illegal use of another user's account, usually accomplished by learning or guessing user names and passwords. Often, intrusion involves knowledge gained from insiders, through guesswork, or with password-cracking software. If potential intruders can gain access to the server console, they might be able to change the administrator's password or download a file containing user names and encrypted passwords. This file can later be entered into a program that attempts to decrypt passwords with a variety of techniques. Intrusion can best be prevented by physically securing servers and ensuring that users have complex passwords (at least eight characters combining both letters and numbers) that are required to be changed regularly.

- *Spoofing*—This attack consists of using underhanded or illegal means to gain access to a computer or network by masquerading as an authorized user or entity. **Spoofing** often involves sending packets to a server that have been modified to make it seem as though they originated from an authorized entity. Public key cryptography helps prevent spoofed packets by requiring a digital signature that can be authenticated only by using the public key the actual entity supplies. Because the intruder doesn't have the actual entity's private key, digital signatures can't be spoofed.

- *Virus attacks*—**Viruses** are programs or macros embedded in other software or e-mail attachments in such a way that when the program or e-mail is opened, the virus code runs. Viruses can spread to other computers on the network by embedding themselves in network software or sending e-mail messages to users in the infected computer's address list. Viruses can simply be nuisances that slow down a computer, or they can be more serious, attacking a local computer's software and causing data loss and system crashes. In this section, you learn more about types of computer viruses and measures for preventing their spread on a network.

- *Denial-of-service attacks*—Although less common than intrusion or virus attacks, **denial-of-service attacks** can prevent users from accessing network services. These attacks are usually caused by a bombardment of packets sent to a server from someone without authorized access. The packet bombardment overloads memory or CPU time, causing legitimate users' connection requests to be denied. In this section, you learn about some common denial-of-service attack methods and how Eric helped secure the UAS network against them.

- *Information theft*—This type of attack involves illegally intercepting and reading information transmitted between computers through the use of wire taps and sniffer software. The best defenses against **information theft** are using public key cryptography and keeping sensitive data on isolated or private networks.

David Heise asked the IT Department to develop an Internet security plan for protecting the UAS network against known security threats and to include a proposal for any additional software needed. After meeting with the other members of the IT Department, Luke McMann decided that the proposal should cover internal security against hacking, firewall security to control access from untrusted networks, a virus protection plan, and defense against common denial-of-service attacks. Figure 11-18 is the diagram he created to show the multiple-level security system he's proposing to management.

The security plan consists of two major layers. The outer perimeter, also referred to as the demilitarized zone (DMZ), is where packets from the outside first enter the UAS network. The inner layer consists of the LAN, which is secured with file system and eDirectory security, as described in previous chapters. The DMZ, the area most vulnerable to attacks, is where the Internet router and firewall software are located. If the firewall server finds no anomalies in a packet, it's passed to the internal router and then relayed to the appropriate service. Rather than expose the UASHOST server to attacks in the DMZ, Luke recommended installing

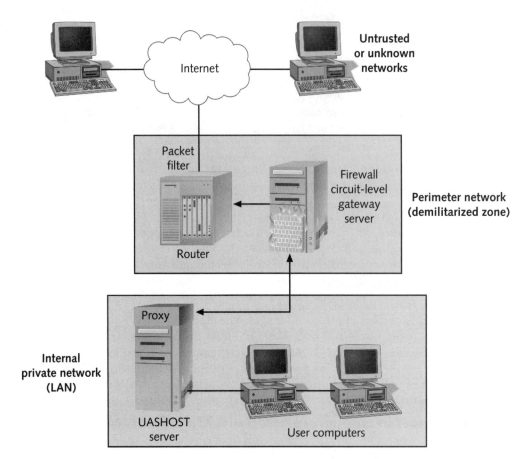

Figure 11-18 The UAS Internet security proposal

another NetWare server for running firewall software. Luke suggested Novell's Border Manager because it includes firewall, packet filter, and proxy server components. In the following sections, you learn about these security measures, and see how Luke and Eric plan to use them in their security plan for the UAS network.

Firewall Security

Outside the network environment, firewalls are often used to separate people and equipment from possible dangers, such as a firewall that separates a car's potentially explosive engine from the driver. In computing environments, firewalls are used in a similar way to protect computers and data from the potential hazards of the Internet environment. Computer firewalls control access between the company's private network and an untrusted external entity on the Internet. **Firewalls** consist of software that runs on a server or specialized hardware, such as a network router, and can be configured to protect against external threats in the following ways:

- Enforce corporate security and access control policies by controlling the type of traffic permitted between the internal private network and the Internet.

- Keep log files of information about external traffic to monitor the source and frequency of unauthorized access attempts.

- Serve as a central point that all network traffic must pass through before reaching the internal private network. Having a single point of access eliminates the possibility of a network being open to external Internet users and makes it possible to redefine access policies in the event of any security breaches.

- Act as a traffic cop by permitting only selected services, such as FTP or World Wide Web (WWW), to access the network.

- Create firewall partitions that limit security breaches or prevent intruder attacks from spreading across the company intranet.

A firewall's primary objective is to prevent entities on untrusted or unknown networks from accessing services and computers on the trusted or internal network. When configuring Internet security, the UAS IT Department needed to identify the network address of each trusted and untrusted network. A **trusted network** consists of your organization's private network along with the firewall server and networks it covers; it can exist within the company intranet and include the network addresses of other computers and networks on the Internet that you communicate with regularly. To avoid having to specify trusted network addresses for users who need to get through the firewall to access services and resources on your internal network, you can set up a **virtual private network (VPN)**, which is a trusted network that sends packets over an untrusted network.

An **untrusted network**, such as the Internet, is an external network with administration and security policies that are either unknown or out of your control. When you configure a firewall server, you can identify any untrusted networks that will interface with the firewall. An **unknown network** is neither trusted nor untrusted and, by default, is treated the same as an untrusted network. You can use firewall software to enable the following security measures on all untrusted and unknown networks:

- *Packet filtering*—A screening router often performs this process before allowing packets into the firewall server. **Packet filtering** examines the destination and source IP addresses to determine whether the packet is from a trusted, an untrusted, or an unknown network. Packets from trusted networks are allowed into the internal network, but packets from other network addresses are routed through the firewall server. Packet-filtering routers also record the interface from which the packet arrives or leaves. Although packet filtering can permit or deny a service, it can't protect unsecured services from unauthorized access.

- *Virtual private networks*—VPNs enable hosts to communicate over a public network via a secure channel. To maintain a secure channel, VPNs encrypt data packets sent between hosts and provide access controls. There are two basic types of VPNs: client and site. Client VPNs connect to the firewall by using dial-in connections or through an ISP over the Internet. Site VPNs, which are usually for departments or external organizations, typically use dedicated network connections. Departments might use a VPN to create a secure connection across the company's private network or the Internet. For example, a college might want a VPN connection between departments across the campus network to prevent students who share the campus network from accessing confidential information, such as grades. Both intranet and Internet site VPNs can be set up with the VPN server in the DMZ zone between the Internet and the private network *or* with the VPN server located on the private network behind the DMZ. VPN servers operating in the DMZ are easier to configure and require less overhead than setting up a VPN server behind the firewall. However, VPN servers in the DMZ are more difficult to secure and are at higher risk from attacks than VPN servers on the private network.

- *Network Address Translation (NAT)*—This firewall technique translates private IP addresses on the internal network to one or more registered IP addresses. NAT enables clients on the private internal network to access the Internet without having a "live" (registered) IP address. Not having an assigned IP address hides the client from outside entities, essentially hiding ports and services on the client from packets that originate on the Internet. NAT doesn't require any special software on users' computers. The computers are simply configured to use the NAT server as their default gateway, causing all packets sent to Internet sites to be routed through the NAT server.

- *IPX/IP gateways*—These gateways perform the same basic function as NAT, with the addition of converting IPX packets to IP. Using an IPX/IP gateway requires client software to place TCP/IP service requests within IPX packets. The IPX packet is then sent to the gateway software, where the IP request is removed from the IPX packet and sent to the Internet. When a response is received, the IPX/IP gateway places the TCP/IP information in an IPX packet and returns it to the client.

11

IPX/IP gateways allow the private internal network to use only IPX, thus isolating the internal network from the Internet.

- *Circuit-level gateways*—**Circuit-level gateways** usually run on a firewall server and inspect additional packet header information, including type of service, port number, user name, and DNS name. Using service packet types enables gateways to permit or deny connections to services based on the destination port number. For example, UAS wants to allow entities from untrusted networks to send requests to the Web server running on port 80 and the FTP service running on port 21. Because other port numbers are used by secured services, such as iPrint, any packets from an untrusted or unknown network to these ports are rejected. Many attacks are based on sending packets to open ports running on servers and computers. Using a circuit-level gateway provides a means of stopping these packets from entering the private network. Because they operate at the session layer of the OSI model, circuit-level gateways have access to user information, so they can accept or reject packets based on a user name or group membership. Circuit-level gateways offer increased firewall security, but they might need special client software and are often slower than other firewall systems, such as NAT.

- *Proxy services*—By receiving and monitoring all network traffic, **proxy services** help prevent denial-of-service attacks and information theft and enable administrators to control most network traffic flowing through the firewall. Because proxy services are applications that operate by inspecting network packets at the application level, they are also referred to as "application-level gateways." A proxy service requires two components: the proxy server and a proxy client. The proxy server acts as the end server for service requests from the private network. The proxy clients run on user computers and communicate with the proxy service rather than with untrusted or unknown networks. Clients from unknown or untrusted networks communicate through the proxy server to request access to FTP or Web services. The proxy server checks incoming packets and allows or disallows them based on the organization's security policy and procedures. Outgoing traffic is also routed through the proxy server. The proxy service determines the validity of the client's request based on established security rules. If the security policy permits the client to contact the outside server, the proxy contacts the outside host on behalf of the client. If the policy prohibits contact, the proxy rejects the request and informs the client of the policy violation. UAS is planning to use Border Manager's proxy service to help control access to outside sites and prevent denial-of-service and information theft attacks.

Protection Against Virus Attacks

After a virus is activated by running a program or opening an e-mail attachment, it can copy itself to other programs or disk storage areas. Each virus has a different signature, which is a bit pattern created when it's embedded in a program or an e-mail attachment. Although viruses don't attack the NetWare OS and services directly, they can use the server and network services, such as e-mail, to spread rapidly to other computers on the network. Firewalls offer security measures to help protect a network from information theft and attacks, but they aren't designed to detect and prevent viruses from entering the network. For virus attacks, the best defense is knowing the types of virus software and how viruses enter a computer network. Viruses are classified based on how they infect computer systems:

- Boot sector viruses attack the boot record, master boot record, or file allocation table (FAT) of a disk drive. When a computer is booted from the infected disk, the virus is loaded into memory where it copies itself to other programs, including those stored in shared directories on the server, or damages information on the local computer. Joshi and Michelangelo are examples of boot sector viruses.

- File viruses, also called Trojan programs, attack executable program files—files ending with .exe, .com, .sys, .drv, .dll, and .bin—by attaching themselves to code in the program. The virus code waits in memory for the user to run another application and uses that event as a trigger to perform an action such as replicating itself or attacking the local computer. A Trojan program is often concealed as part of other software, such as a game or graphics application. Trojan programs can also contain software used for destructive or criminal purposes, such as embezzlement, and self-destruct after they have finished running.

- Macro viruses attack programs that run macros, such as spreadsheet and word-processing applications. These malicious macros start when an infected document or template is opened. The macro can erase or damage data and copy itself to other documents. A well-known example is the Melissa macro virus.

- Stealth viruses (the Tequila virus, for example) can disguise themselves to make it difficult for antivirus software to detect them. Passive stealth viruses can increase file size yet evade detection by displaying the file's original size. Certain types of stealth viruses called encrypted viruses—Cascade, for instance—mask their code or virus signatures to avoid detection by antivirus software.

- Polymorphic viruses are a rapidly growing type of stealth virus with built-in code that creates random changes or mutations to their virus signatures, making reliable detection difficult. SMEG is an example of a polymorphic virus.

- Viruses attach themselves to other programs, becoming in a sense a part of the other program. Worms, however, are independent programs that spread themselves to other computers over a network. Worms can infiltrate legitimate programs to alter or destroy data and degrade system performance. For example, a worm could infect a bank's computer and initiate fund transfers to another account. Viruses can embed themselves in many programs, but worm attacks are usually easier to identify and recover from than other types of viruses because there's only one copy of the program to search for and remove.

11

Virus Prevention Techniques

Virus prevention involves installing a virus protection system, making regular backups, and training users on how to reduce the risk of virus attacks. Virus protection systems scan programs on servers and user computers and monitor program files as they are loaded to detect known virus signatures. In addition to scanning, most antivirus software warns users of any activity that could be caused by a computer virus, such as modifying the disk boot sector or system settings.

Network administrators must also make sure that users know how their computers might be affected by virus infections. By recognizing virus symptoms, users can help identify and remove new viruses before they're propagated to other computers or cause more data loss. After installing and configuring antivirus software on the UASHOST server, Eric trained UAS users to be aware of the following common virus infection symptoms:

- A computer that fails to start normally

- Programs that don't start or fail when using common commands

- Changes in file names or files that become inaccessible

- Unusual words or graphics appearing on-screen

- Disk drives being formatted unexpectedly

- Slow computer performance when loading or running software

David asked Luke to submit a virus protection plan as part of the UAS Internet security plan. Luke's plan includes the following recommendations for configuring antivirus software and policies on the UAS network:

1. Install NetWare-compatible antivirus software from one of the following vendors:

    - NetShield from Network Associates (*www.mcafeeb2b.com*)

    - Server Protect from Trend Micro (*www.antivirus.com*)

    - Norton AntiVirus Corporate Edition from Symantec (*www.symantec.com*)

    - Command Antivirus from Command Software Systems (*www.authentium.com/products*)

2. Check the software vendor's Web site to keep virus signature files up to date on servers and computers.

3. Configure antivirus software to send virus notifications immediately to Eric and the computer user.

4. Enable the virus expiration warning to alert Eric when signature files are out of date.

5. Configure the server's virus-scanning software to scan both incoming and outgoing files of all types, including .exe, .dll, and .zip files.

6. Install an antivirus software package that quarantines files to protect users from accessing a potentially infected file and spreading the virus.

7. Train users on the importance of virus scans and, if possible, disable the option of canceling a virus check.

8. Train users on common types of viruses and explain how they usually spread by running infected programs, opening e-mail attachments, booting from infected disks, or downloading infected files from the Internet.

9. Use Novell's ZENworks for Desktops to distribute the latest virus signature updates to all computers.

10. Create write-protected emergency boot disks to be used if a computer becomes infected or damaged by a virus. Keep emergency boot disks updated with the most recent virus signatures.

11. Scan all incoming and outgoing e-mail messages and attachments.

12. Develop a company policy prohibiting the download of e-mail attachments and software that aren't work related.

13. Train users on antivirus software operation and encourage them to install an antivirus software package on their home computers.

Virus Removal Planning

Despite security measures and antivirus software, with all the new viruses popping up almost daily, there's always the possibility that one could slip by antivirus software and infect a network's computers. After a virus was detected recently on the UAS network, Eric used the following procedure to isolate and remove the virus from all networked computers:

EXAMPLE

1. First, Eric isolated all systems and disks that were known to be, or suspected of being, infected with the virus.

2. He then checked the antivirus software's support site to help determine the type of virus and find any suggested clean-up procedures.

3. Eric located a clean floppy disk formatted with a boot system that he had created earlier with antivirus software. The boot disk also contained a copy of the virus-scanning software.

4. He used the boot disk to start all infected or suspect computers. Starting from a boot disk ensures that no virus code is loaded into computer memory.

5. He used the virus-scanning software on the boot disk to scan all physical and logical hard disks on each infected or suspect computer. He also scanned any floppy disks used with the suspect computers. During the scanning process, he removed any viruses from the files and programs of infected computers.

6. After scanning and removing any virus code, Eric restarted the user's computer and created a system backup that excluded any infected files on the computers or server.

7. Viruses that infect program files can create problems if they replace program instructions; often the program doesn't run correctly or "hangs" when it's loaded. To handle this problem, Eric deleted all infected programs and reloaded the software from the original CD. In one case, system files were damaged, and Eric needed to reformat the hard drive, reinstall the entire computer, and restore the backups.

8. Finally, Eric scanned all network drives and reloaded copies of executable programs from backup tapes.

A server's boot sector and OS files can't be infected unless the server is started from an infected disk. As a result, Eric has developed the habit of scanning all disks before inserting them in the server and has modified the server's CMOS to prevent it from starting from a disk that might have been left in the drive inadvertently.

Defense Against Denial-of-Service Attacks

Although denial-of-service attacks don't usually damage or steal a company's data directly, they can result in high costs by bogging down the organization's Web services, causing lost customer sales and reducing user productivity. Denial-of-service attacks are usually caused by flooding a server with packets or sending oversized packets to a service, causing it to crash. A correctly configured firewall and software designed for Net Services security are the best defenses against denial-of-service attacks. Table 11-2 describes common denial-of-service attacks that Luke listed in his UAS Internet security proposal.

Table 11-2   Common denial-of-service attacks

Type of Attack	Description
Ping of death	The PING command is modified to send Internet Control Message Protocol (ICMP) Echo packets longer than the 64 KB maximum defined in the TCP/IP RFC 791 standard. The extra bytes in the packet can cause unprotected TCP/IP software to overflow the buffer space, resulting in computer hang-ups or crashes.
Teardrop attack	The teardrop attack intentionally overlaps packet fragments, causing errors in fragment reassembly that can result in packets being resent repeatedly and flooding the server.
Land attack	The land attack sends packets with the same source and destination IP addresses, thereby flooding the service with an endless loop of packets being sent to the server.
SYN packet flooding	TCP connections require the following three-way handshake between the server and the client: 1. The client sends a packet in which the SYN flag is set in the TCP header. 2. The server sends a SYN/ACK (acknowledgment) packet back to the client. 3. The client sends an ACK packet so that data transmission can begin. A TCP SYN denial-of-service condition is caused when the client fails to send the last ACK packet and intentionally sends successive TCP connection requests to the server, filling up the server's buffer. After the server's buffer is full, other client requests are rejected, resulting in a denial-of-service condition.
Oversized UPD packets	Like the ping of death, sending oversized UDP packets can result in buffer overflows that cause the server to hang or crash.
Smurf	Smurf attacks use the ICMP Echo in response to PING broadcasts to flood the server.

The ping of death is perhaps one of the best-known denial-of-service attacks. Normally, the Packet Internet Groper (PING) application is used as a diagnostic utility on TCP/IP networks to send Echo packets to selected hosts and receive responses if the network and host are operational. By default, Echo packets contain only 64 bytes of data, but the RFC standard allows up to 64 KB. The ping of death occurs when a PING command is sent to an IP host with more than 64 KB of data. Some older software can't handle these large Echo packets, which can cause the TCP/IP stack to overflow, thereby slowing down or crashing the server. It's the OS software vendor's responsibility to ensure that its TCP/IP implementation can handle oversized Echo packets.

By going to Novell's Technical Information Web site at *http://support.novell.com*, Luke verified that Novell's current TCP/IP products since NetWare 3.11 are designed to discard oversized packets without hanging or crashing. In addition, Luke learned that earlier 16-bit versions of the Novell client might pause for up to 15 seconds when receiving oversized PING packets. Luke also discovered that although the Novell TCP/IP stack isn't affected by the teardrop attack, it might be affected by the land attack when the transport protocol is using UDP. In this case, the land attack could cause the server to hit 100% utilization. Novell has a TCP/IP stack fix that corrects this problem by dropping packets if the software determines that the source and destination IP addresses are the same and the IP address isn't the loopback address (127.0.0.1). The problem can be fixed by downloading the Ftcpsv01.exe file from the Novell site. Although this fix isn't necessary for the NetWare 6.5 server, Luke plans to make sure it's installed on older servers at the AeroDyn facility.

After ensuring that the system software has been updated to fix any known problems, the next part of the UAS Internet security plan to prevent denial-of-service attacks is to configure the Border Manager firewall to send security alerts for the following conditions:

- Security-sensitive NLMs being loaded or unloaded
- Oversized PING packets
- SYN packet flooding
- Oversized UDP packets

Border Manager alerts can detect many other types of denial-of-service attacks (smurf, teardrop, or land) because these attacks share common techniques, such as using ICMP Echo packets, overlapping fragments, and packets with the same source and destination IP addresses to create server overloads.

WORKING WITH ENCRYPTION SECURITY

In addition to the measures described in the "Securing Web Services" section, security systems need to protect information from being captured and read as it's transmitted across the network. Keeping passwords and data secret is especially important when using the Internet because intruders might have access to login and data packets as they travel across network routers and cables. Keeping passwords and data unreadable by anyone except the intended receiver is accomplished through some type of encryption. Basically, encryption is the process of converting plaintext into a secret message (called "ciphertext"), which can be read only after it's decrypted by reversing the encryption process. The algorithm used to encrypt and decrypt a message is called a "cipher." The science of encrypting data, called cryptography, involves using algorithms with a special value called a key (often the user's password) to hide information from all but intended recipients by "scrambling" data packets (see Figure 11-19). The only way to read the scrambled data packet is to decrypt the data packet by reversing the process and using the corresponding key value.

Cryptography Techniques

The two major types of cryptography techniques are symmetric and asymmetric. In symmetric cryptography, the same key, usually the user's password, is used to encrypt and decrypt the message. The advantage of symmetric cryptography is that it's simple and efficient; however, both the sender and receiver must have the same key. Exchanging the same key securely between server and client can be a problem when communicating over public networks, such as the Internet.

 Symmetric encryption can be up to 1000 times faster than asymmetric, which is often used to exchange synchronous passwords.

NOTE

Asymmetric cryptography, also called **public key cryptography**, is a security system that authenticates users and organizations to ensure that they are who they claim to be and encrypts data transmissions to prevent information from being intercepted by unauthorized people. Public key cryptography gets around the

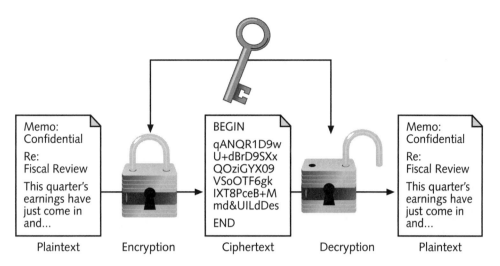

Figure 11-19 The cryptography process

problem of exchanging a common key between the sender and receiver by using a set of two keys: a public key and a private key. This key pair is unique to an individual, application, or organization. The **private key** is kept solely by the key pair's owner and used to create encrypt and decrypt data. The **public key** is made available to all network users and used by outside entities to encrypt data sent to the key pair owner. This process is shown in Figure 11-20.

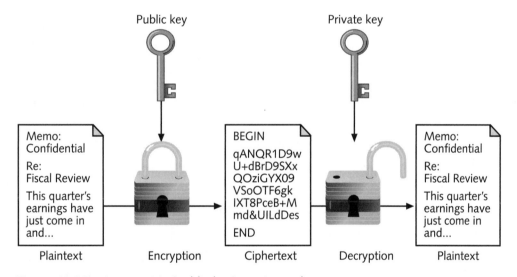

Figure 11-20 Asymmetric (public key) cryptography

Public key cryptography can also be used to create digital signatures, which authenticate an electronic document as being from a specific user or organization. To create a digital signature, the cryptography software that creates the signature mathematically links the data being signed with the sender's private key. The receiver of the data then uses the sender's public key to verify the digital signature. This process is shown in Figure 11-21 using a banking transfer as an example.

An important part of public key cryptography is verifying that the public key used to encrypt data and check digital signatures is actually from the person or organization it claims to be. One method of providing reliable public keys is to meet with the person or the organization's representative and exchange public keys by using a physical medium, such as a disk. Exchanging public keys on disks isn't always feasible, however, so a more efficient, practical method of distributing reliable public keys was developed. Public key cryptography uses a certification authority (CA) service to mediate the exchange of public keys. To get a public key authorized, an entity needs to send its public key with other identification information to a recognized CA, such as the

1. You authorize the transfer using your banking application.

2. Your application creates a digital signature for the transfer request using your *private* key (which only your application can access).

3. The application then sends the request and your digital signature to your bank.

4. Your bank's computer receives the request and your digital signature.

5. A system operator then validates your signature against the request using your *public* key.

   If the results compute correctly, the signature is authenticated.

   If not, the signature, the message, or both are assumed to be fraudulent, and the transaction is denied.

Figure 11-21   Digital signature authentication

VeriSign organization. The CA validates an owner's key pair by creating a certificate containing the owner's public key along with the CA's digital signature. As shown in Figure 11-22, the CA is responsible for verifying that the requesting entity's identity is established before validating the requester's public key certificate.

Public key certificates contain, at a minimum, the entity's public key, a subject name, and a CA-generated digital signature. Public key certificates generated by most commercial CAs use the X.509v3 format and contain the following information:

- The name of the user or organization (subject name)
- The public key of the user or organization
- The length of time the public key certificate is valid
- The name of the CA that signed the public key certificate (issuer)
- The digital signature created by the CA

Before using an entity's public key to encrypt data or verify a digital signature, the cryptography service running on the user's computer checks the digital signature on the public key certificate against a list of known CAs. If the digital signature isn't recognized as coming from a known CA, the cryptography service discards the data or asks the user if he or she wants to trust the entity issuing the public key.

NOTE   Having a public key is analogous to having a passport, a driver's license, or other certified picture ID instead of, say, a student ID. A student ID can get you into campus activities, but it isn't recognized as a valid form of ID at the airport.

When planning cryptography services, you need to determine the type of CA service your applications and users require. There are two basic types of CA services: external and internal. When using an external CA service, you need to submit requests for public key certificates to recognized organizations, which verify your identity and supply a public key certificate that can be imported into applications and clients. Using recognized external CAs is important for Web servers and other Internet services that deliver information and services to the public sector. By using public key certificates signed by recognized external CAs, such as

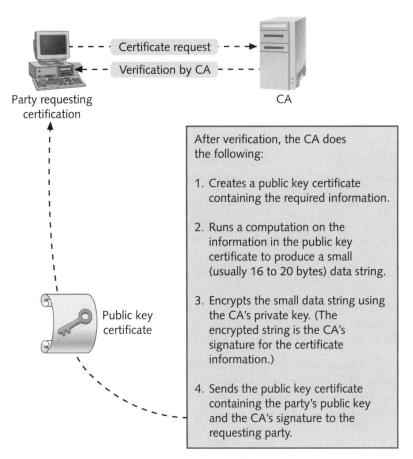

After verification, the CA does the following:

1. Creates a public key certificate containing the required information.

2. Runs a computation on the information in the public key certificate to produce a small (usually 16 to 20 bytes) data string.

3. Encrypts the small data string using the CA's private key. (The encrypted string is the CA's signature for the certificate information.)

4. Sends the public key certificate containing the party's public key and the CA's signature to the requesting party.

Figure 11-22   Creating a public key certificate

VeriSign, your public keys will be trusted by any Web browser, thus making e-commerce transactions easier and less risky for users.

On the other hand, obtaining signed public key certificates from external CAs can be expensive and time consuming. Most NOSs, including NetWare, Windows 2000/2003, and Linux, include CA software that the server uses to issue X.509 certificates to clients. Internal CA services run on a local server and can be used to automatically issue and sign public key certificates for applications and services available to authorized network users. For example, transactions between OneNet utilities and Web Services on a NetWare 6.5 server take place by using public key certificates issued and signed by the internal Novell Certificate Server, discussed in the following section.

NOTE

RSA Data Security maintains Public Key Cryptography Standards (PKCS) for using public key cryptography on the Internet, and PKCS-compatible CAs use the X.509 standard to format certificates for encrypting and decrypting data. There are PKCS standards for different encryption needs. For example, PKCS#7 is an extensible message format representing the results of cryptographic operations on data. PKCS#12 is often used for encrypting login requests and is included as a NetWare 6.5 login option.

Using Novell's Certificate Services

As you have learned, a critical part of offering services across a public network, such as the Internet, is providing security. In previous chapters, you have learned how Novell's file system security and eDirectory security use trustee assignments to grant users rights to access data and manage network objects and to prevent unauthorized access. Novell's Certificate Services is an additional measure for authenticating users and encrypting data transmissions.

Novell Certificate Server, included with NetWare 6.5, integrates public key cryptography services into eDirectory and enables administrators to create, issue, and manage user and server certificates. It helps network administrators meet the challenges of public key cryptography with the following functions:

- Creating an Organizational CA in the eDirectory tree that allows the certificate server to issue user and server certificates without going to an external CA, thereby reducing costs and the time needed to set up Net Services

- Storing key pairs in the eDirectory tree to provide security against unauthorized access and tampering yet make public keys available to all network entities

- Allowing centralized management of public key certificates by using ConsoleOne snap-ins

- Supporting commonly used e-mail clients and Web browsers

Novell Certificate Server consists of PKI.NLM and a snap-in module for ConsoleOne that administrators use to request, manage, and store public key certificates and their associated key pairs in the eDirectory tree. Using Novell Certificate Server, administrators can establish an Organizational CA that's specific to the eDirectory tree. Because **Novell International Cryptography Infrastructure (NICI)** is used to support all cryptography and signature functions, a single version of Novell Certificate Server can be used throughout an organization's intranet. NICI must be installed on both the Novell server and client to provide secure, two-way communication between applications using public key cryptography. NICI can be installed on the client from the Novell client CD or by downloading the NICI file from the Novell Web site.

Novell Certificate Server is installed by default on the first NetWare 6.5 server installed in a tree. If an eDirectory tree already contains an older version of Novell Certificate Server, you need to upgrade the existing certificate server to the latest version before installing NetWare 6.5 Open Enterprise Server. Common tasks that network administrators need to perform using Novell's Certificate Services include the following:

- Create a Server Certificate object for the NetWare server

- Create trusted root certificates

- Create a user certificate

- Create trusted root containers and objects

Creating Server Certificates

When NetWare OES is installed, all the necessary certificate security objects are created automatically, including an Organizational CA and the key pairs needed to support cryptographic activities. During installation, two server certificates are created: one for the DNS service and one for other IP services. These certificates are used to create secure SSL connections with client computers. You can use the following steps in iManager to create server certificates for special third-party services you install on the NetWare server:

1. Start iManager and log in with your eDirectory administrative user name and password.

2. Expand the Novell Certificate Server heading, click the Create Server Certificate link, and enter the following information:

    - *Server*—Specify the server that will own the certificate being created.

    - *Certificate nickname*—Enter the name of your server certificate. The name you enter is combined with the server name to create a unique name for the Server Certificate object.

    - *Creation method*—Select the Standard method to use default certificate parameters. Select the Custom method to define the following parameters manually:

        - Name of the CA that will sign the certificate (default is your Organizational CA)

        - Key size (default is 2048 bits)

        - Key type (default is SSL)

- Algorithm for creating the certificate (default is SHA-1)
- How long the certificate will remain valid (default is two years)
- Certificate root (default is your organizational certificate)

Creating Trusted Root Certificates

Trusted root certificates provide the certificates from other organizations that your server will trust automatically. You can use iManager to add trusted root certificates to your eDirectory tree in the specified container by clicking the Create Trusted Root link and entering the following information:

- *Name*—The eDirectory object to be assigned to this trusted certificate
- *Container*—The name of the eDirectory trusted root container to store the trusted certificate object
- *Certificate file*—The path of the certificate file you have received from the CA

Creating User Certificates

For users to make use of a Public Key Infrastructure application, such as an e-mail system, they need key-pair certificates assigned to their user accounts. In the following activity, you use iManager to create user certificates in eDirectory.

Activity 11-6: Creating User Certificates

Time Required: 15 minutes

Objective: Use iManager to access and manage user certificates with the Novell Certificate Services.

Requirements: A Windows XP or SUSE Linux 10 computer

Description: Eric is planning to set up an e-mail system that uses PKI to encrypt user e-mail transactions and wants you to create certificates for users in the IT Department. In this activity, you use iManager to create certificates for all users in your IT OU.

1. If necessary, log on to your local computer, start your Web browser, start iManager, and log in with your administrative user name and password.

2. Click to expand the **Novell Certificate Server** heading and then click the **Create User Certificate** link to display the Create User Certificate Wizard.

3. Click the **Object Selector** button next to the Create a new certificate for the following users text box, navigate to your **IT** OU, and then click to add IT users to the Selected Objects list box.

4. Click **OK**, and then click **Next** to display the Certificate Details window.

5. Enter **Email service** in the Certificate nickname text box, verify that the Standard creation method is selected, and then click **Next** to display the summary window. Record the signing CA, signature algorithm, and expiration date:

   _____

6. Click **Finish** to create the user certificates and display the Results window.

7. Click **Close** to return to the iManager main window, and exit iManager. Leave your system running for the next activity.

Encryption Protocols

A number of encryption protocols can be used to secure data and passwords transmitted across networks. Most protocols can be configured to use symmetric or asymmetric cryptography, depending on security and performance needs. When exchanging keys isn't necessary, symmetric protocols require less processing overhead, so they are often used to encrypt data transmitted on private networks, and keys for each user can be stored in a directory service on the server.

Public systems that allow access by users who are unknown to the server often use asymmetric cryptography in the encryption protocol to exchange keys securely. Some protocols use a combination of symmetric and asymmetric cryptography, thus taking advantage of the security of asymmetric cryptography to exchange a key that a symmetric protocol then uses to encrypt and decrypt data packets. The following sections introduce some common protocols for securing network transmissions and access to the NetWare 6.5 server console.

IP Security Protocol (IPSec)

Data transmitted across the network can also be secured by performing data encryption at layer 3 (the network layer) of the OSI model, which eliminates the need to encrypt passwords. The IP Security (IPSec) protocol, developed by the Internet Engineering Task Force (IETF), secures the network layer by using Encapsulating Security Payload (ESP) to perform encryption and decryption at the IP packet level. Either symmetric or asymmetric encryption can be used. Because IPSec packets have a standard TCP/IP header, they can be routed through the network with standard devices that might not be IPSec aware. The main disadvantage of IPSec is the additional processing time needed to encrypt and decrypt all IP packets. Security systems that work at a higher level in the OSI model can selectively encrypt sensitive data packets, thereby improving network performance.

Secure Sockets Layer and Transport Layer Security

Secure Sockets Layer (SSL) and Transport Layer Security (TLS) are widely used protocols for securing message transmission across the Internet. Originally developed by Netscape, SSL and TLS are also supported by Microsoft, Novell, and many other Internet application developers. Although TLS is essentially the latest version of SSL, it's not as widely available in Web browsers.

SSL and TLS use a hybrid of symmetric and asymmetric encryption to encrypt data packets. First, the sending computer uses the receiver's X.509 certificate (covered earlier in "Using Novell's Certificate Services") to verify the receiver's identity. Next, the sender's computer randomly picks a symmetric key and encrypts it using the public key from the receiving computer's digital certificate. The sending computer then sends the encrypted key to the receiving computer, which decrypts the data packet with its private key. After the sender and receiver identify the secret symmetric key, the computers can use this shared key to perform standard symmetric encryption of data packets more efficiently than using the asymmetric technique to encrypt and decrypt each data packet.

The length of the symmetric key also plays a role in secure transactions. Web browsers that use 40- and 56-bit keys are considered to have weak encryption because these key sizes can be cracked in a short time (one week on average) by using commonly available processing power and specialized software. The 40- and 56-bit browsers are common because of U.S. government regulations on exporting strong (128-bit) cipher keys.

 NOTE   Key lengths aren't the sole characteristic that makes key security weak or strong; the security of a key also depends on the encryption algorithm. Short keys based on certain encryption algorithms can be 10 to 20 times stronger than long keys based on a weaker algorithm.

Secure Hypertext Transfer Protocol

Secure Hypertext Transfer Protocol (HTTPS) is a secure communication protocol designed to transfer encrypted information between computers over the Web. HTTPS is essentially an enhancement of HTTP that uses SSL/TLS for secure data transmission. The major difference between HTTPS and SSL/TLS is that SSL/TLS is used to encrypt a persistent connection; HTTPS uses SSL to encrypt a single page. After a digital certificate is installed on a Web server, an SSL–enabled Web browser can connect to the Web server with HTTPS and exchange information securely. (You might notice the "https" in your browser's address box when accessing Novell Web Services from your Web browser, for example.) HTTP combines with SSL/TLS in the following process to enable secure communications:

1. By accessing a URL with HTTPS, the client requests a secure transaction and negotiates an encryption algorithm.

2. The server sends the client the server's digital certificate containing the public key and a list of supported ciphers and key sizes in priority sequence.

3. The client compares the certification authority (CA) that issued the certificate to a list of trusted CAs and verifies that the certificate hasn't expired.

4. The client generates a secret symmetric key based on the list of ciphers and then encrypts the key with the server's public key and sends it to the server.

5. The server then decrypts the new symmetric session key using its own asymmetric private key.

6. After the symmetric key has been identified, both the server and client use that key along with the negotiated algorithm to secure all further communication.

Message Digest Security

Another important aspect of securing data transmitted across the Internet is ensuring that data hasn't been tampered with or changed since it left the sender. Data transmissions can be secured against tampering by using a hashing algorithm to create a fixed-length message called a message digest, as shown in Figure 11-23.

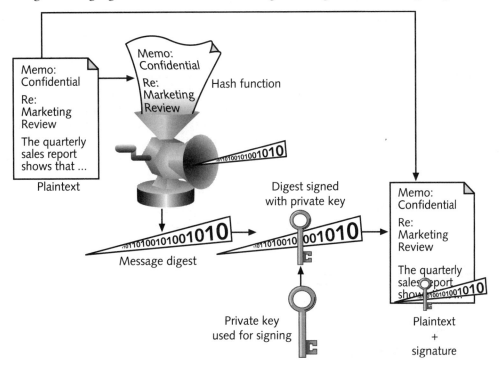

Figure 11-23   Creating a message digest

The message digest is signed with the user's private key and added to the end of the message transmission. The receiver opens the transmission and uses the sender's public key with the hash algorithm to compute a message digest from the original message. If the message digests match, the receiver knows that no bits in the message have changed since the sender signed it. Two major hashing algorithms are in use in message digests today. Secure Hash Algorithm 1 (SHA-1), developed by the National Security Agency (NSA), produces 160-bit message digests and is considered the most secure. Message Digest 5 (MD5), developed by RSA Data Security, produces 128-bit digests and has been placed in the public domain. Because it requires no licensing, as of this writing MD5 is the most commonly used hashing algorithm, but cryptography experts fear it has flaws that could cause it to be broken in the future.

Working with the Secure Shell Protocol: OpenSSH

Many users and network administrators of Linux-based systems are familiar with utilities such as Telnet, Rlogin (remote login), and FTP to access servers and transfer files. However, these utilities have the disadvantage of transmitting information across the local network or Internet unencrypted. With NetWare 6.5 OES, Novell has integrated an open-source solution to this problem by including OpenSSH. OpenSSH offers the same functions as Telnet, Rlogin, and FTP but includes encryption to protect data and passwords from eavesdropping, connection hijacking, and other attacks. Using OpenSSH, Novell developers and administrators can access data on NetWare servers securely by using Novell International Cryptographic Infrastructure (NICI), as described earlier. With the Secure Shell protocol (SSH), you can gain remote access to any server in the network running the OpenSSH service. OpenSSH includes the following utilities:

- SSH, which replaces Rlogin and Telnet
- SCP, which replaces RCP
- S/FTP, which replaces FTP
- OpenSSH Manager, which can be accessed via a Web browser and used to view SSH connections, change the Sshd.config file, and set log preferences; enables any user who is a member of the Ssh admin Administrators group in eDirectory to modify the configuration of OpenSSH servers

SSH is used with remote login and file transfer programs, such as Telnet and FTP, to provide an encrypted link between the client and server. SSH uses public key cryptography to establish an encrypted, secure connection between the user and the remote system. After the secure connection is established, user names, passwords, and all other data can be transmitted securely over the connection. Because of its popularity, many network applications and OSs, including NetWare 6.5, now support SSH ports, and free clients are available for logging on to an SSH-compatible server. In the following activity, you learn how to install OpenSSH on your NetWare 6.5 server.

If you're using a shared classroom server, your instructor might perform this activity as a class demonstration.

NOTE

Activity 11-7: Installing OpenSSH

ACTIVITY

Time Required: 10 minutes

Objective: Use the NetWare server's graphical console to install the OpenSSH service.

Requirements: A dedicated NetWare 6.5 server

Description: To allow users to download files securely from the FTP site, Eric wants to use S/FTP. In this activity, you Install OpenSSH on your server console.

1. At the NetWare 6.5 server's graphical console, click the **Novell** button and then click the **Install** option to display a list of installed services.

2. Insert your NetWare 6.5 Products CD 2 into the server's CD-ROM drive, and then click the **Add** button.

3. Click the **browse** button, navigate to the **NW65PROD** CD, and click it to display the Postinst.ni file. Click the **Postinst.ni** file and click **OK** to see a list of product options.

4. When the product list window is displayed, click the **Clear All** button, and then scroll down and click to select the **OpenSSH** check box.

5. Click **Next** and then click **Copy files** to copy the files and complete the installation. If requested, log in with your administrative user name and password.

6. After the installation is finished, click the **Reset Apache** button to reload your Apache administrative server.

7. At the server console, press **Ctrl+Esc** to display the console list. Type **1** and press **Enter** to switch to the server console.

8. At the server console, type **SSHD** and press **Enter** to start the OpenSSH service, which replaces the less secure Rlogin (remote login) and Telnet services.

9. Type **SCP** and press **Enter** to start the SCP (remote console) service. Then type **SFTP** and press **Enter** to start the S/FTP service.

10. To return to the graphical interface, press **Ctrl+Esc** key, type the number for the X Server - Graphical Console option, and press **Enter**.

Using the OpenSSH Secure FTP (S/FTP) Service

Originally, FTP didn't ensure secure encrypted data transmission between client and server. As a result, several attempts have been made to fix FTP's security shortcomings, but they haven't been widely adopted. The most common file transfer program that provides encrypted security is Secure File Transfer Protocol (S/FTP). S/FTP is not a rework of FTP; it's a new component of SSH with the same command syntax as FTP, but it conducts all operations over an encrypted transport. S/FTP can also use SSH features, such as public key cryptography and compression. Novell has included S/FTP with OpenSSH in NetWare 6.5 to offer the following advantages over the traditional FTP service:

■ Because S/FTP uses the underlying OpenSSH protocol, it offers strong authentication through a variety of methods, including X.509 digital certificates.

■ By using OpenSSH, all authentication information, commands, and data transferred between the S/FTP client and the Novell server are encrypted and secured.

■ S/FTP uses a single TCP connection port, making it easy to configure on a firewall. On the other hand, the older FTP service uses two connection ports: the initial connection that uses port 21 and a second reverse connection that opens a random high port number. Assigning a random port number for the second connection makes firewall configuration more difficult.

Many networks use NAT to route packets between a secured private network and the Internet. S/FTP makes NAT configuration easier because it doesn't need to negotiate a separate IP address for the data connection, as with traditional FTP clients and servers.

Activity 11-8: Using the OpenSSH S/FTP Protocol

Time Required: 10 minutes

Objective: Use OpenSSH to access the S/FTP protocol.

Requirements: OpenSSH installed on the server and a Windows XP computer with Internet access

If you don't have Internet access, your instructor will need to provide a copy of the S/FTP software.

Description: In this activity, you use S/FTP to download a file from the FTP site.

1. If necessary, start your Windows XP computer and log on with your local administrator user name and password.

2. Use Windows Explorer to create a **Downloads** folder at the root of your C: drive.

3. Start your Web browser, and enter the URL **http://www.chiark.greenend.org.uk/~sgtatham/putty/download.html**. Download the PuTTy FTP client (Psftp.exe) to your Downloads folder. (Note that the URL might have changed since the time of this writing, in which case you can use *www.google.com* to do a search for the client.)

4. Download the PuTTy SSH client (PuTTy.exe) to your Downloads folder from the same site.

11

5. Open a command prompt window. To switch to your Downloads folder, type **cd \Downloads** and press **Enter**. To run the Psftp.exe software, type **psftp *IPaddress*** (replacing *IPaddress* with the IP address of your server) and press **Enter**.

6. Type your eDirectory administrative user name and press **Enter**.

7. Type **y** to cache the server's key in the Registry and press **Enter**.

8. To display the contents of the SYS volume, type the password for your administrative user name and press **Enter**.

9. Type **help** and press **Enter** to get a list of commands.

10. Type **ls** and press **Enter** to list the directory contents.

11. Type **cd public** and press **Enter** to change to the Public directory.

12. Type **dir *.EXE** and press **Enter** to display all executable files.

13. Type **get FLAG.EXE C:\Downloads\FLAG.EXE** (using this exact capitalization) and press Enter to download the Flag.exe program to your Downloads directory.

14. Type **exit** and press **Enter** to end your OpenSSH session. Leave your system running for the next activity.

Using the OpenSSH Service

Because Novell includes OpenSSH with NetWare 6.5, you can use one of several client programs to access the NetWare 6.5 server console securely. One popular choice is the PuTTy utility, which you can download from several sources. In the following activity, you learn how to use PuTTy to access your NetWare 6.5 server's console securely.

 If you're using a shared classroom server, your instructor might perform Activity 11-9 as a demonstration. If you're using a dedicated NetWare 6.5 server, you should perform this activity to install and then test the OpenSSH service.

NOTE

Activity 11-9: Using the OpenSSH Service

ACTIVITY

Time Required: 15 minutes

Objective: Use OpenSSH and PuTTy to access the NetWare 6.5 server console securely.

Requirements: A copy of the PuTTy utility or access to the Internet to download it as well as a user account that has rights to the server console; completion of Activity 11-8

Description: Because you need to access the server console periodically to perform server maintenance, you have downloaded the OpenSSH PuTTy utility and plan to use it to access the UASHOST server console.

1. From your desktop, open the SSH-compliant client by running the PuTTy utility and performing the following steps:

   a. In the Host Name text box, enter the IP address of your NetWare 6.5 server, and then click the **SSH** option button to change the port to 22.

   b. To begin the session, click **Open**. If necessary, click **Yes** twice to trust the host and continue with the connection.

   c. Enter your administrative user name and password at the "login as:" prompt. The server console screen should then be displayed on your desktop.

   d. Explore how the SSH session works by using the following keyboard commands: **Ctrl+Z** to display the screen list and **Ctrl+Q** to display the SSH keyboard commands help screen.

2. Press **Ctrl+X**, type **y**, and then press **Enter** to exit the SSH session and close the PuTTy utility.

BACKING UP NETWORK DATA

An organization's data plays a critical role in today's highly competitive and rapidly changing world of business and industry. A company robbed of its information would certainly suffer major losses and could even be forced out of business. Therefore, as a network administrator in an organization that relies on the network for data storage and retrieval, you become responsible for much, if not all, of your organization's critical data files. Management counts on your knowledge to provide a reliable storage system, secure from unauthorized access and protected from accidental loss. In this chapter, you have learned how to protect an organization's data from attacks by unauthorized entities and malicious viruses. Despite your best efforts, however, data could still be damaged or lost because of equipment failure, unauthorized access, operator error, or natural disasters. In this section, you learn how to use the Storage Management System to implement a disaster recovery plan that includes backing up and restoring data.

The Storage Management System

NetWare includes the **Storage Management System (SMS)** for backing up even complex networks consisting of data stored on multiple file servers and DOS and OS/2 workstations. The NetWare server that runs the backup program and has the attached tape or other backup medium is referred to as the **host server**. Other servers and client computers being backed up are referred to as **target servers**. When using SMS, the term "parent" refers to a data set, such as a directory or subdirectory, and the term "child" refers to a specific subset of a data set, such as a file or program. SMS uses NetWare Loadable Modules on the host server to communicate with modules on target devices, read the information from the target devices, and send it to the backup medium, as shown in Figure 11-24.

11

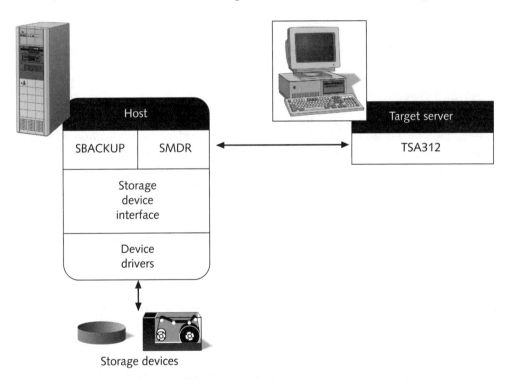

Figure 11-24   The SMS backup process

SMS consists of the following software components that can be run on NetWare servers as well as DOS or OS/2 workstations:

- Storage device drivers are loaded on the host server and control the mechanical operation of storage devices and media, such as tape drives.

- The enhanced SBCON utility is the main NetWare-provided software, which runs on the host server. It works with the SMDR module to control the backup process and transfer data to and from the host server's backup device.

- Target Server Agents (TSAs) are loaded on target servers and communicate with the backup program running on the host server. The purpose of the TSA is to get information from the target server's volumes and send it to the SBCON utility running on the host server. A server can act as host *and* target by running both SBCON and TSA software.

- Workstation TSAs run on DOS or OS/2 workstations to back up data on local drives across the network.

In addition to the SBCON Storage Management Engine (SME) that ships with NetWare 6.5, a number of other companies offer specialized SME software packages with several features and benefits. The most common third-party backup systems are ARCserve and Backup Exec.

Establishing a Backup System

Having a reliable and tested backup system is one of the best medicines a network administrator can have to ensure a goodnight's sleep, so spending some extra time planning and testing the backup system is well worth it. Establishing a successful backup system involves six steps:

- Determine your network's storage needs.
- Determine a backup strategy.
- Assign a backup user.
- Run the backup software on a scheduled basis.
- Test the backup.
- Develop a disaster recovery procedure.

In the following sections, you learn how Eric applied these steps to setting up the backup system for Universal AeroSpace.

Determining Storage Needs

The first step in establishing a backup system for your network is to calculate how much data needs to be copied to the backup tape on a daily basis by determining which volumes and directories you plan to back up. If possible, you should try to obtain an SMS-compatible tape backup system with enough capacity to store your daily backup on one tape cartridge. In a single-file server environment, the file server acts as both the host and target devices, requiring you to load the SBCON and TSA modules on the same server. An advantage of having a file server as both host and target devices is that a file server backing up its own data runs almost four times faster than a host file server backing up data across the network from another target server. As a result, when using SMS in a multiple-file server environment, you should plan on making the server that stores the most data the host system.

Determining a Backup Strategy

Depending on your backup storage needs, one of the three backup strategies shown in Table 11-3 are normally used.

Table 11-3 Backup strategies

Type of Backup	Data to Back Up	Status of Archive Attribute
Full	All data, regardless of when or if it has been previously backed up	Cleared
Incremental	Files created or modified since the last full or incremental backup	Cleared
Differential	All data modified since the last full backup	Not cleared

With the **full backup** strategy, all data is copied to the backup tape each night. This backup strategy will work well for Universal AeroSpace because the current size of files to be included on the backup doesn't exceed one tape cartridge. The advantage of the full backup strategy is that if a crash occurs, only the previous day's backup needs to be restored. The disadvantage is the need for a large tape capacity and the time required to perform backups.

The **incremental backup** strategy takes the least amount of time for each backup because only the data files that have changed that day are copied to the backup tape. When using the incremental backup strategy, a full backup is made at the beginning of the week, and an incremental backup is made each day. The disadvantage of this strategy is that all incremental backup tapes must be restored if data is lost. For example, if a crash occurs on Thursday, you need to restore the Monday full backup first, followed by the Tuesday and Wednesday incremental backups.

A compromise between the full backup and the incremental backup is the **differential backup** strategy, in which all files that have changed since the last full backup are copied to the backup tape. That means the size of the tape backup increases as the week progresses. The advantage of the differential strategy is that if a crash occurs later in the week, only the full backup and the last day's differential backup need to be restored.

Currently, Universal AeroSpace is using the full backup strategy to make a complete backup of all data and the eDirectory database each day. In the future, as UAS's data storage requirements grow beyond the space of one tape cartridge, Eric recommends using the differential backup strategy to reduce the backup time and eliminate the need for someone to change tapes in the middle of the night.

Assigning a Backup User

Although you can log in as Admin to perform a backup, most network administrators prefer to create a separate user account for backups. Creating a separate user account has the advantage of allowing you to assign other people to perform the backup and limits the number of times you need to log in to the network as Admin. The user account you create to perform the backup must have the following access rights and privileges:

- To back up the file system, the user account needs to have Read, File Scan, and Modify rights to the volumes and directories included in the backup. The Modify right is necessary for the backup program to reset the Archive attribute after backing up data files. When assigning these rights to the directory, you need to be aware of any IRFs (Inherited Rights Filters) that might block these rights from a subdirectory you want to back up.

- To back up the eDirectory database, the backup user account needs to have the Browse entry and Read attribute rights to the containers included in the backup.

- The person performing the backup needs to know the password used on the host server and the passwords assigned to any target servers or clients.

Running the Backup Software

After you have decided on a backup strategy and created any necessary user accounts, the next step is to test the SMS installation by backing up your server data and then testing the backup by restoring selected files from the backup tape. The following steps outline the process of using SBCON to back up files:

EXAMPLE

1. Install Storage Management System (SMS) on your NetWare 6.5 server. To start, insert the NetWare 6.5 Products CD into the server's CD-ROM drive and then click the Novell button in the graphical interface to select the Install option.

2. Attach the backup device and load the appropriate drivers, as described in the backup device installation instructions.

3. Start SMS on the NetWare 6.5 server by typing SMSSTART from the server console and pressing Enter. The SMSSTART command loads the following modules:

- The SMDR.NLM data requester module automatically creates an SMS_SMDR Group object in the server's container. This object contains each server and computer to be backed up by the host server.

- The TSAFS.NLM module enables you to back up data files and directories from this server.

NOTE   You can also insert the SMSSTART command in the server's Autoexec.ncf startup file. (See Chapter 2 for a description of using the server startup files.)

4. In addition, you should also load the SMSDI.NLM module in the Autoexec.ncf startup file by typing LOAD SMSDI.NLM and pressing Enter. This command loads the SMS device module interface used to let the SBCON program communicate with the backup device.

5. Load the SBCON program on the host server by typing SBCON from the server console and pressing Enter to display the menu shown in Figure 11-25.

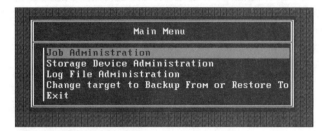

Figure 11-25   The SBCON main menu

6. You can use the Job Administration menu item to display the Select Job screen, which you can use to perform backup and restore tasks, as shown in Figure 11-26.

Figure 11-26   The Select Job screen

7. Select Backup to display the Backup Options screen shown in Figure 11-27. You can use this screen to select the target server to be backed up, the directory or volume to back up, and the device or medium to use.

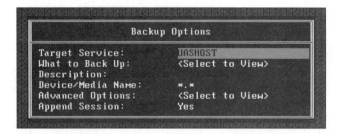

Figure 11-27   The Backup Options screen

8. Select Advanced Options to select the backup type and time (see Figure 11-28).

9. You can use the Backup Type option to select a full, incremental, or differential backup. After making your selection, press Esc to submit the job and then return to the Select Job screen.

10. Press Esc again to return to the SBCON main menu. The backup job is then started at the time specified in the Advanced Backup Options screen.

```
                    Advanced Backup Options
Backup Type:                     Full Backup
Subsets of What to Back Up:      <Select to View>
Scan Options:                    <Select to View>

Execution Time:                  12-21-2005 8:53:18 PM
Scheduling:                      <Select to View>
```

Figure 11-28   The Advanced Backup Options screen

NOTE
Performing an SMS backup requires having a backup device and driver installed on your server.

Testing the Backup

After completing a successful backup, the next step in testing your backup system is to try restoring selected files from the backup media. Doing a complete restore is often not feasible because of time constraints and the possible loss of data if the restore process fails. As a result, before doing a major restore, you should restore test files that aren't needed or files that have been copied to another disk storage device. To restore selected files, select the Restore option from the Select Job screen in the SBCON utility and then enter the path to the working directory you used when the backup tape was created. Next, select the option Restore from session files, and select the session you named previously when the backup was created.

Next, start the restore process. The selected files should then be copied back to their appropriate directories. When the restore process is finished, log in from a user computer and verify that the files have been restored correctly.

Developing a Disaster Recovery Procedure

After the backup system has been tested, the next step in implementing a reliable disaster recovery plan is to develop a tape rotation procedure and backup schedule. Having a multiple-tape rotation procedure that enables you to save certain backups for a long time is an important part of a disaster recovery plan because it gives you a way to go back to an earlier backup to recover files and to be able to store backup tapes outside the building. Sometimes you must be able to recover a file from an earlier backup if it becomes corrupted by a virus, an operator error, or a software bug, and the damage to the file is not discovered for several days or weeks. If you were rotating your backups between just a few tapes, by the time the error was discovered, the original backup with the valid file would have been overwritten by a backup copy of the corrupted file. To help prevent this problem, Eric has recommended a tape rotation system consisting of 20 tapes, as shown in Figure 11-29.

Four tapes are labeled Monday through Thursday and are rotated each week. Four tapes are labeled Friday1 through Friday4, with Friday1 used on the first Friday of the month, Friday2 on the second, Friday3 on the third, and Friday4 on the fourth. In addition, 12 tapes are labeled January through December. These tapes are rotated each year and can be used on the last Friday of each month by replacing the Friday# tape with the correct monthly backup. Another alternative, if someone is available to change the tape, is to make the monthly backup on the last Saturday of each month. Storage for backup tapes is also important in case of a fire or damage to the building; many administrators store weekly backups in a fireproof vault and keep monthly backup tapes off-site in a secure location, such as a safety-deposit box.

The final step in implementing the backup system is to set up a time for the backup to be performed and ensure that no users are logged in during the backup process. To prevent interference with user work schedules, many network administrators like the backup to start each night at 12:00 a.m. To keep night owls from working late and to prevent users from leaving their computers logged in during the backup, all user accounts, except the user account used to back up the system, should have a time restriction to prevent accessing the network between 12:00 a.m. and 5:00 a.m. This five-hour interval should be enough time to create your backup. If you need extra time, you can set the backup to begin at 11:00 p.m. or perhaps to end at 6:00 a.m., as long as the user time restrictions are also set for the longer backup period.

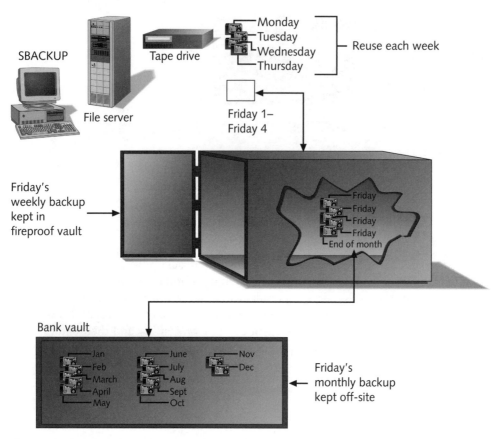

Figure 11-29 Tape rotation procedure

Chapter Summary

□ An essential part of Novell's strategy is to provide Internet services that enable clients and servers using diverse operating systems to be managed and accessed as one network. To do this, Novell has developed Web Services and Net Services. Net Services components include iFolder, NetStorage, iManager, Remote Manager, iPrint, and iMonitor. Because Net Services is written to run on top of the open-source Apache Web Server, the services can be used on other network operating systems, such as Windows 2000, Windows NT, and Linux.

□ Web Services includes Apache Web Server and FTP Server, which can be installed and customized to supply information and Web pages to the Internet and local intranet. The NetWare Web Manager portal is used to configure and manage Apache Web Server and FTP Server. Typical Web server management tasks include specifying the primary document directory, creating virtual Web sites, setting document preferences, and specifying public and restricted access to Web content. FTP configuration tasks include setting the default FTP directory, providing anonymous access, and restricting user access to the FTP server.

□ Internet security involves protecting Web and Net Services from threats such as information theft, intrusion, and computer viruses. An Internet security plan should include a firewall to isolate the internal network from the Internet and implement a virus protection and data recovery plan. Firewalls should be configured to detect denial-of-service attacks, such as the ping of death, SYN packet flooding, oversized UDP packets, teardrop attacks, and land attacks.

❏ Using public key cryptography to encrypt data transmission and provide authentication with digital signatures is a vital component of securing information transmission on the Internet. Public key cryptography uses public and private keys to create digital signatures and to encrypt and decrypt data transmissions. Clients use the public key to encrypt data, which can be decrypted only by the public key owner's private key.

❏ Certification authorities (CAs) issue public key certificates for verifying that the public key belongs to the entity distributing it. Clients receiving the public key certificate can then verify the owner's identity by trusting the CA's digital signature.

Key Terms

circuit-level gateways — Firewall devices that inspect packet heading information, including type of service, port number, user name, and DNS name.

denial-of-service attacks — A form of network attack that overloads the server with packets to shut down network services.

differential backup — A backup strategy in which only files that have changed since the last backup are copied to the backup medium.

firewalls — Hardware or software components that act as a point of access between an organization's internal private network and the Internet, used to filter packets and reduce the risk of unauthorized access or malicious attacks on the network system and services.

full backup — A backup strategy in which all data is copied to the backup medium daily, regardless of when it changed.

host server — The NetWare server that runs the backup program and has the attached tape or other backup medium.

incremental backup — A backup strategy in which only the files that have changed that day (the ones with the Archive attribute enabled) are backed up. The Archive attribute is then reset on all files that are backed up.

information theft — A form of network attack that uses wire taps and sniffer software to illegally intercept data.

intrusion — A form of network attack that involves gaining unauthorized and illegal access to an organization's information, usually through obtaining a user's account and password.

Java servlets — Applications written in the Java programming language to run on a Web server.

Net Services — A set of hardware and software components that work together to provide access to information services across the Internet or company intranet.

Novell International Cryptography Infrastructure (NICI) — Novell's implementation of the public key cryptography system that uses a combination of public and private keys to encrypt data and passwords transmitted across the network.

Novell Portal Services (NPS) — A Net Services component running on a NetWare server that provides customized pages or portals for users based on users' rights and style specifications.

packet filtering — A process performed by a screening router to determine whether a packet is from a trusted, untrusted, or unknown network.

private key — The digital key code used in public key cryptography that is kept solely by the owner and used to decode data and create digital signatures.

proxy services — Firewall services that work at the application level to give clients on a network both incoming and outgoing access to Internet services.

public key — The digital key code used in public key cryptography for clients to encrypt data being sent to a host and to verify a host's digital signature.

public key cryptography — An Internet security system that uses public and private keys to encrypt and decrypt data and create digital signatures for authenticating users.

spoofing — A method of illegally accessing network resources or attacking a network service by creating falsified packets that appear to come from an authorized entity.

11

Storage Management System (SMS) — The NetWare backup service that includes several NetWare Loadable Modules along with software that enables the host server to back up data from one or more target servers.

target servers — Servers with data that has been backed up by the host server.

trusted network — A network with an IP address range that's known to be safe or can be controlled and monitored by your organization.

unknown network — A network that's not specified as a trusted or untrusted network in a firewall. Firewalls treat unknown networks as untrusted networks.

untrusted network — An IP address range that might contain attackers or other malicious entities. Packets from networks listed as untrusted are inspected by the network firewall.

virtual private network (VPN) — A trusted network that sends packets over an untrusted network, such as the Internet.

viruses — Self-replicating programs that can be embedded in software to propagate between computers and can eventually be triggered to affect computer performance or destroy data.

Web Services — A set of hardware and software components that provide World Wide Web and FTP information services to clients on the Internet or company intranet.

REVIEW QUESTIONS

1. Which of the following is an example of a Web Services component? (Choose all that apply.)
   a. FTP Server
   b. Apache Web Server
   c. iFolder
   d. NetStorage

2. Tomcat is an example of which of the following?
   a. Web server
   b. Java servlet
   c. servlet engine
   d. FTP server

3. Which of the following does NetWare 6.5 use to provide Net Services?
   a. Enterprise Web Server
   b. Apache Web Server
   c. Tomcat
   d. Web Manager

4. Which of the following provides customized Web pages to users based on their access rights and privileges?
   a. Web servers
   b. Novell Portal Services
   c. iManager
   d. Remote Manager

5. Java servlets require which of the following to run?
   a. Enterprise Web Server
   b. FTP Server
   c. NetWare Web Manager
   d. Tomcat

6. Which of the following is an example of a Java servlet?

    a. Tomcat

    b. Enterprise Web Server

    c. Novell Portal Services

    d. iFolder

7. The _____ tab in the FTP Server Administration window is used to configure anonymous user access.

8. In public key cryptography, which of the following keys is digitally signed by a CA?

    a. public

    b. private

    c. digital

    d. certificate

9. In public key cryptography, which of the following keys is used to decrypt data packets?

    a. public

    b. private

    c. digital

    d. certificate

10. In public key cryptography, the CA is responsible for which of the following? (Choose all that apply.)

    a. creating public and private keys

    b. encrypting data

    c. verifying that users are who they claim to be

    d. signing and issuing public key certificates

11. Which of the following attacks involves sending large Echo packets?

    a. ping of death

    b. SYN packet flooding

    c. teardrop

    d. land

12. Which of the following attacks involves a failure to send ACK packets?

    a. ping of death

    b. SYN packet flooding

    c. teardrop

    d. land

13. Which of the following is a form of firewall packet filtering that uses port numbers and service types?

    a. proxy filtering

    b. circuit-level gateway

    c. packet filtering

    d. echo filtering

14. Which of the following is a form of firewall security that checks only packet source IP addresses?

    a. proxy services

    b. circuit-level gateway

    c. packet filtering

    d. echo filtering

15. Which of the following acts as an independent program that does not replicate but can infiltrate legitimate programs to alter or destroy data?

    a. worm

    b. polymorphic virus

    c. stealth virus

    d. Trojan program

16. Which of the following is not classified as a denial-of-service attack?

    a. land attacks

    b. oversized packets

    c. Trojan program

    d. SYN packet flooding

17. Which of the following is a firewall application that examines destination and source addresses to determine whether a packet is from a trusted network?

    a. packet filtering

    b. circuit-level gateway

    c. proxy service

    d. VPN

18. Which of the following firewall technologies is the best choice for Universal AeroSpace to control the type of information sent between the network and clients?

    a. proxy service

    b. circuit-level gateway

    c. NAT

    d. VPN

19. Eric is concerned about maintaining a secure channel when using the Internet to connect to servers at the AeroDyn facility. Which of the following technologies should he use?

    a. NAT

    b. circuit-level gateway

    c. packet filtering

    d. VPN

20. Which of the following firewall technologies can hide client IP addresses on a private network from the Internet?

    a. packet filtering

    b. circuit-level gateway

    c. NAT

    d. VPN

21. Which of the following is a basic component of public key cryptography? (Choose all that apply.)

    a. VPN

    b. CA

    c. public and private keys

    d. certificate signing

22. Which of the following is *not* a firewall technology?

    a. packet filtering

    b. NAT

    c. VPN

    d. virus scanning

CASE PROJECTS

Case Project 11-1: Identifying Net and Web Services

11

In Table 11-4, identify each type of server as a Web Services or Net Services component and supply a brief explanation of what makes it that type of service.

Table 11-4   Service identification table

Service	Type of Service	Explanation
iFolder		
Apache Web Server		
FTP Server		
Web Manager		
Novell Portal Services		

Case Project 11-2: Developing a Security Plan for AeroDyn

The AeroDyn facility is planning to use FTP Server so that users can download files. In this project, you develop a plan to secure the AeroDyn facility from outside attacks. Your plan should include a diagram of the following network components and a brief description of what type of attacks you plan to prevent:

- Router
- Firewall
- AeroDyn internal private network

Case Project 11-3: Developing a Virus Protection Plan

Luke McMann wants you to research the antivirus software listed in this chapter, and then make a recommendation that includes the vendor, product, and price for a 30-station network. Your recommendation should include two antivirus software packages and explain why you think this antivirus software would be a good choice for the AeroDyn network.

HANDS-ON PROJECTS

Hands-on Project 11-1: Creating a Web Site

Eric wants you to create a demonstration Web site for the Engineering Department. He plans to use it at the next management meeting to show managers how to use the Web server to access other Web pages by supplying the Web site's name after the Universal AeroSpace URL. The Web site should simply consist of a heading and a simple graphic in the IT\Web\Engineer directory. Follow these steps:

1. If you're using a shared classroom server, ask your instructor for the path to your virtual document directory. If you're using a dedicated server, create a virtual document directory by following these steps:

   a. Start your Web browser, and enter the URL **https://IPaddress:2200** (replacing *IPaddress* with the IP address of your server). If necessary, click **Yes** to close the security alert message box and open the Login window. Enter your administrative user name and password and then click **Login**.

   b. Click to expand the **Open Source** heading on the left, and then click the **Apache 2.0** link. Click **Administer Single Apache Server** under the Apache 2.0 Links heading on the right to display the Server Status window.

   c. Click the **Content Management** button, and then click **Additional Document Directories**.

   d. Enter **Engineering** in the URL prefix text box. (If you're using a shared classroom server, precede "Engineering" with your assigned student number.)

   e. Enter the path to your CORP:IT\Web\Engineer directory in the Map To Directory text box.

   f. Click **Save** to open the Save and Apply Changes dialog box. Click **Save and Apply** to apply your changes to the Httpd.conf file and display the Success! message box. Click **OK** to return to Apache Manager.

2. Copy the **Radiance.jpg** file from the C:\WINNT\Web\Wallpaper directory to your CORP: IT\Web\Engineer directory.

3. Create a simple HTML document that displays the Radiance.jpg file with the heading "Universal AeroSpace."

4. Save the document as **Index.html** in your CORP:IT\Web\Engineer directory.

5. Test the Web site by starting your Web browser and then entering the URL **http://IPaddress/Engineering** (replacing *IPaddress* with the IP address of your server and preceding "Engineering" with your assigned student number if you're using a shared classroom server.

6. After your test document is displayed, have your instructor check your work.

12

INSTALLING AND WORKING WITH SUSE LINUX

After reading this chapter and completing the activities, you will be able to:

♦ Describe the steps in preparing for a SUSE Linux installation

♦ Perform a SUSE Linux installation

♦ Use various tools to configure SUSE Linux

In Chapter 1, you were introduced to the common network operating system environments, including NetWare, Linux, and Windows. Novell Open Enterprise Server (OES) includes both NetWare 6.5 and a customized version of SUSE Linux Enterprise Server 9. In previous chapters, you have been working with the NetWare 6.5 system to set up and secure network services. The Novell version of SUSE Linux included with OES can implement most of the Novell services you have learned about in preceding chapters. In this chapter, you learn how to plan for and perform an install of a SUSE Linux system. In later chapters, you learn how to configure the SUSE Linux server to use Novell network services.

PREPARING FOR SUSE LINUX INSTALLATION

To install a network operating system successfully, you must know its hardware requirements and how to configure its disk system to create a server environment that meets your organization's needs. In this section, you learn how to prepare for a SUSE Linux installation.

Hardware Compatibility

Novell Linux OES is compatible with a wide range of hardware devices and interfaces. At a minimum, the server should meet the following hardware specifications for satisfactory performance:

- A Pentium III 750 MHz or faster processor
- 256 MB RAM (512 MB preferred)
- 4 GB hard drive (8 GB preferred)
- CD drive
- VGA adapter and monitor
- Network interface card

Linux systems are composed of three basic components: the Linux kernel, the input/output system, and the X-Server. (SUSE Linux currently uses XFree86 for the graphical X-Window environment.) Of these components, the Linux kernel and X-Server depend the most on hardware configuration. In the early days of Linux, hardware compatibility was more difficult to achieve because of the lack of driver software for the Linux kernel. Until recently, documentation from hardware suppliers needed to write driver software for Linux wasn't readily available to developers. With the rise of Linux popularity and market share, most hardware manufacturers are now making documentation and open-source code available to Linux developers. With these resources, Linux developers can modify drivers for the Linux kernel and keep drivers updated if the hardware manufacturer drops a product or goes out of business.

The graphical X-Window environment depends on display hardware and devices. Changing a display monitor or graphics card in a Linux system might require installing new drivers to run the graphical user interface (GUI). Because the Linux kernel is independent of the GUI interface, you can use the **command-line interface (CLI)** to start the system and update the driver software. During Linux installation, you have the choice of installing in text or graphics mode. If your system's adapter and monitor aren't recognized during the XFree86 startup process, you need to install SUSE Linux in text mode and then configure the display driver after the OS is installed and running.

Network Configuration

To prepare for SUSE Linux installation, you also need to consider how the disk system will be partitioned and whether the system will be multibooting. The space on a hard disk is divided into one or more partitions, as shown in Figure 12-1.

Partitions make it possible to divide hard disk space into smaller functional units that can be formatted to meet the needs of a specific file system, thereby allowing multiple OSs to share the same disk drive. The partition table provides information on the starting and ending locations of up to four physical partitions.

To avoid the limitation of only four partitions, each partition can be divided into multiple logical partitions. In the Microsoft partition scheme, one of the physical partitions can be designated as the extended partition. The extended partition can be further subdivided into four logical partitions, allowing for a total of seven partitions (three primary and four logical). Linux extends this scheme by allowing up to 60 logical partitions to be created within a physical partition.

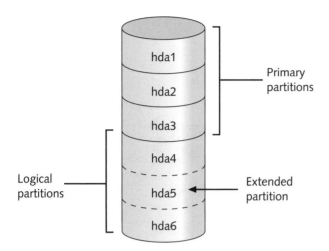

Figure 12-1   Hard disk partitions

Before installing Linux, you need to define the partitions and their corresponding sizes for your computer's hard drives. For example, Figure 12-2 shows Windows XP Professional and SUSE Linux sharing the same hard disk.

12

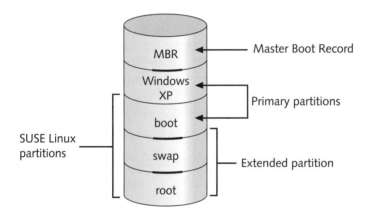

Figure 12-2   Linux disk partitions

As shown in Figure 12-2, SUSE Linux typically uses a minimum of three partitions when installed on Intel-based computers:

- The **boot partition** is a small partition containing only the essential system files Linux needs to load into memory. Although this partition can be as small as 20 MB, Novell recommends that the boot partition for SUSE Linux be 75 to 100 MB so that multiple Linux kernels can be installed simultaneously.

- The **swap partition** is used to page areas of memory called "program segments" in and out of memory. The size of this partition varies based on the server's memory capacity and function. At a minimum, the swap partition should equal the size of the system memory. For example, if the server has 1 GB of RAM, the swap partition should be 1 GB.

- The **root partition**, also denoted by just a "/" character, is where all other Linux OS files and utilities are stored. Novell recommends that this partition be at least 4 GB to ensure that it can store all necessary files and utilities. User and organizational data should be kept on separate partitions or disk drives, not on the boot partition, to ensure backup and system reliability.

The advantages of multiple partitions include the following:

- Separating system directories across multiple partitions results in faster performance, making network access more responsive.

- With multiple partitions, there's a limit on file and directory size, which improves system security because less information is stored in one location.

- Because Linux disk quotas are set on a partition basis, using multiple partitions gives you more options when setting up disk quotas.

Partitions in the Linux system are named based on the disk drive type, drive number, and partition number, as shown in Table 12-1.

Table 12-1 Linux partition names

Disk Drive Type	Partition Name	Description
IDE drive	hda1	Partition 1 on the first IDE drive
	hda2	Partition 2 on the first IDE drive
	hdb1	Partition 1 on the second IDE drive
SCSI drive	sda1	Partition 1 on the first SCSI drive
	sda2	Partition 2 on the first SCSI drive
	sdb1	Partition 1 on the second SCSI drive

Multiboot Configurations

Although most production Linux servers aren't configured for multibooting, educational and test servers and some user desktop systems might need to include multiple OS options. As shown in Figure 12-2, the first track of a hard disk contains a special area called the **Master Boot Record (MBR)**. The MBR stores a small program that determines how to start the OS. When the computer first starts, the system's BIOS initializes devices on the computer and then passes control to the loader program stored in the MBR. Normally, the MBR loader program is responsible for starting the process of loading the OS into the computer's memory. The MBR loader program does this by passing control to the **boot manager** program located in the active partition's boot record, as shown in Figure 12-3.

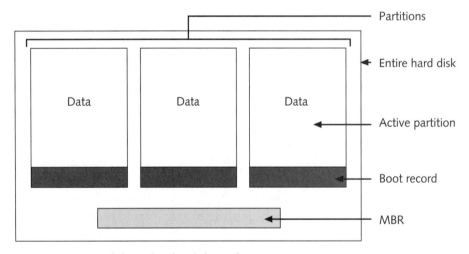

Figure 12-3 Multiboot loader disk configuration

Dual-boot configurations are created by installing an MBR loader program that enables you to select the partition record to boot from. Linux has two boot manager programs: LILO and GRUB. GRUB is newer and has more configuration options. You learn more about LILO and GRUB in the "Installing SUSE Linux" section later in this chapter.

When you install an operating system, the installation program stores its boot loader program in the hard drive's MBR. Multiboot loader programs, such as those in Windows and Linux, are designed to display a list of operating systems to load. The Microsoft boot loader lists only Windows OS boot options. Therefore, when you're building a multiboot system for both Windows and Linux, you should install Linux last so that the Linux boot loader can replace the Microsoft boot loader, thus providing a list of all bootable OSs. The Linux boot loader allows the system to boot from Windows or Linux; the Windows boot loader doesn't recognize the Linux OS. In the following section, you learn how to perform a basic installation of SUSE Linux Enterprise Server 9.

INSTALLING SUSE LINUX

The SUSE Linux installation process is flexible and can be performed from CD, from the hard disk, or over a network connection. The installation is controlled by the Yet Another Setup Tool (YaST) utility, which has a number of installation methods, including text-based, GUI, and AutoYaST. The YaST text-based process, the original SUSE Linux installation method, is still used on systems that don't have a video driver compatible with the YaST GUI. Beginning with SUSE Linux 6.3, the GUI-based installation became the standard. In addition to the manual installation methods, SUSE Linux offers an automatic or scripted installation process with AutoYaST. The SUSE Linux 10 installation process consists of two major steps: base installation and configuration, described in the following sections.

The Base Installation Phase

When you start your computer from the installation CD, the welcome screen appears with the installation options shown in Figure 12-4. If you don't select an installation option within 20 seconds, the first entry in the list (Boot from Hard Disk) is selected automatically. To stop the countdown, press the down arrow or Tab to select an option.

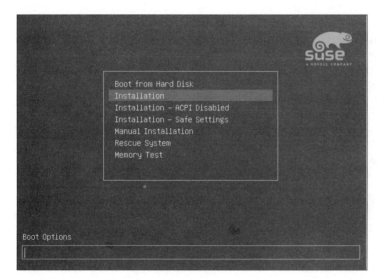

Figure 12-4   SUSE Linux Welcome screen

The following list describes the most important options:

- *Boot from Hard Disk*—Starts the computer using the OS currently installed on your hard disk. If there's no other OS on the hard disk, you see the message "Failed to boot from hard disk" and the welcome screen is displayed again.

- *Installation*—Starts the normal installation process.

- *Installation - ACPI Disabled*—Some older computers don't have Advanced Configuration and Power Interface (ACPI) power management, which could lead to problems during a normal installation. This option disables the ACPI power management features of the SUSE Linux installation, allowing SUSE Linux to be installed on these systems.

- *Installation - Safe Settings*—Older computers might not have any kind of power management or hard disk acceleration, which can cause installation problems. If you have problems related to these factors, retry the installation process using this option.

For most systems, you should select the Installation option and press Enter to load the Linux kernel. During the loading process, the installation program checks your hardware and attempts to detect your video driver and monitor. If you don't have at least 256 MB of RAM, the system displays an error message and stops the installation. In addition, if the detected display driver doesn't support the graphical interface, you see a warning message and have the option to continue installing in text mode. Whether you're installing in graphical or text mode, the base installation process works much the same way. If you're using the text version of YaST, after the SUSE Linux installation is finished, you can configure the video system to support the graphical interface. If your system supports the graphical installation, the graphical YaST utility is loaded.

The first installation screen asks you to accept the SUSE Linux Novell software license agreement. After you do, the installation language screen is displayed next, where you select the language used only for installation prompts and messages; this selection isn't necessarily the language SUSE Linux uses after installation. SUSE Linux supports numerous languages on the standard installation CDs. Next, your system hardware devices and configuration are analyzed, and you choose installation settings, as described in the following section.

Choosing Installation Settings

After the hardware analysis is finished, the Installation Settings screen shows the detected hardware and default disk partitioning settings (see Figure 12-5). As you have learned, disk drives and partitions in Linux are named with the hda# designation for partitions on the first IDE hard drive and sda# for partitions on the first SCSI drive. Following that notation, notice in Figure 12-5 that by default, SUSE Linux creates a 502 MB swap partition named /dev/sda1 on the SCSI disk drive and a second root partition named /dev/sda2 on the same SCSI drive.

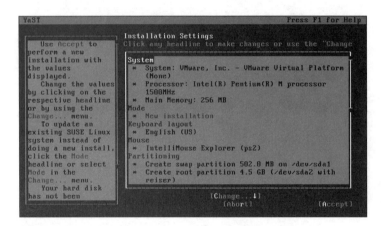

Figure 12-5   SUSE Linux installation options, part 1

To change the default partition sizes in the text-based screens, press Tab to highlight the Change option and press Enter. Then use the arrow keys to highlight the Partitioning option and press Enter. In the graphical YaST, simply click the Partitioning option to open the Suggested Partitioning dialog box and select the option to create a custom partition setup. After making changes, you can use the Back option in either YaST version to return to the Installation Settings screen.

Scrolling down the text-based screen displays additional settings, including software, booting, and time zone information (see Figure 12-6). You use the Software option to view and modify software packages to be installed on the SUSE Linux server. Because the server family of SUSE Linux comes with nearly 1000 packages, understanding the role of the Linux server in your network is necessary to determine which installation options to select. As a general rule, you should select only software packages that are required for system operation. Adding packages after installation is easier than removing unnecessary ones. Unnecessary software packages can decrease system performance, complicate troubleshooting, and cause security problems.

NOTE

You can select software packages during or after installation. You can also change the default installation options by scrolling down and using the Change option to display the Software Selection screen shown in Figure 12-7.

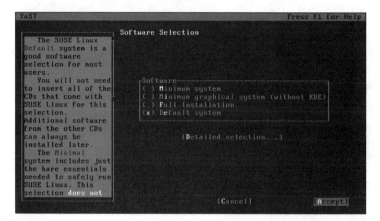

Figure 12-6   SUSE Linux installation options, part 2

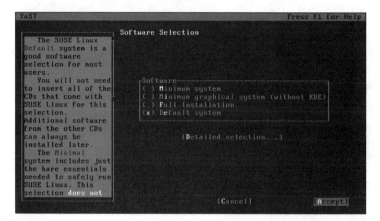

Figure 12-7   The Software Selection screen

You have the following options in the Software Selection screen:

- *Minimum system*—This option installs only the required SUSE Linux packages without a graphical system. You might select this option if you're building a special-purpose server (such as a Web server) or installing SUSE Linux on a computer where you want to keep hardware requirements to a minimum and don't need to use the graphical X-Server for any applications. With this option, server configuration needs to be done from the command prompt, as described in Chapter 13.

- *Minimum graphical system (without KDE)*—This option installs the required SUSE Linux packages and the basic window manager package, fvwm2. This option is useful when you want to keep the server as efficient as possible but still want to use a graphical interface for administration.

- *Full Installation*—This option installs most packages available on the SUSE Linux Server CDs. This option is used only on more powerful systems when you want to install a fully configured server for software development or testing purposes.

- *Default system*—This option installs a system with the most commonly needed software packages.

In the graphical YaST, click the Detailed selection button to display the window shown in Figure 12-8. To select additional packages or remove the default packages, simply click the corresponding check boxes next to the package names. The Package and Summary columns on the right show the software programs that are part of the selected package.

In the text-based YaST, press Tab to select the Detailed selection option shown in Figure 12-7 and press Enter to display the Detailed Selections screen. The default packages are indicated with a "+" symbol, as shown in Figure 12-9. In both YaST versions, you use the Filter option to select the software packages that are displayed. By default, the Filter option in the graphical YaST is set to display Selections; in the text-based YaST, the default is set to display the Amusements package.

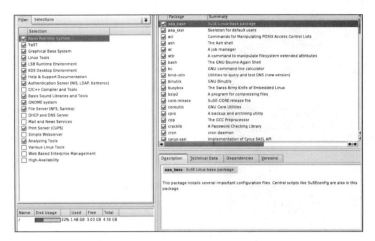

Figure 12-8 The Package Selection window

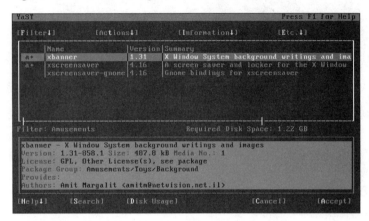

Figure 12-9 The Detailed Selections screen

To change the text-based filter to display software selections, press Tab to highlight the Filter option and press Enter. Then press the down arrow to highlight the Selections option and press Enter to display the Package Categories screen shown in Figure 12-10.

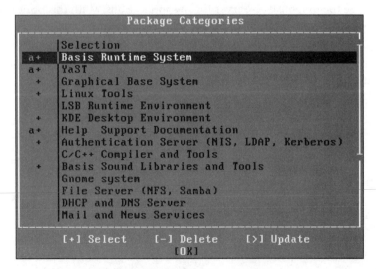

Figure 12-10 The Package Categories screen

In the text-based YaST, the "a" character indicates that the package is selected automatically. You can use the + and - keys to select or deselect software packages. When you select a software package and press Enter on the OK option, all components of that package category are displayed, as shown for the YaST package in Figure 12-11.

Figure 12-11   Components of the YaST package

You might also want to find specific products by name. You can do this with the Search option. To select this option in graphical YaST, click the Filter list arrow (shown at the top of Figure 12-8) and click Search. To select the Search option in the text-based version, press Tab to highlight the Filter option and press Enter to display the Filter list. Press the down arrow to highlight the Search option and press Enter. In either version, you then enter the name of the package and click Search or press OK. The details for any items found are displayed, and you can select which options to install by clicking the check box or pressing the + and - keys. After selecting or modifying the software selections, use the Accept option in either version to return to the Installation Settings screen.

When using the text-based YaST, you can select a check box by using the up or down arrow keys to highlight the check box, and then press the spacebar to place a check mark in the box.

TIP

The Booting section displays the boot loader type and location. By default, GRUB should be selected as the boot loader. GRUB is the most recent SUSE Linux boot loader and includes support for reading file systems, which means it can interactively load any kernel without the preconfiguration LILO requires. GRUB also has support for network booting, so it can boot the Linux OS from a server rather than the local hard disk. Network booting makes it possible to use SUSE Linux with diskless computers. If you have problems with your system booting from GRUB, you can try LILO, which might work better with some older systems because of its simplicity.

Use the Time zone section to set the system to your time zone. Scrolling down the Installation Settings screen further displays the default language and run level options. The run level is used to determine the environment in which Linux starts. For example, the default run level 5 provides a multiuser environment with a graphical user interface.

After configuring the installation settings, you can select the Accept option to display a message informing you that YaST has gathered all necessary information and is ready to start the installation. Select the Yes, install option to begin.

The installation process then formats your disk partitions and copies files. You are prompted to insert additional CDs as needed. Depending on your system performance and selected options, the copying process takes 20 to 30 minutes or more. Except for inserting the next disk when prompted, there's not much to do except take a short break. When the installation is finished, the system restarts and enters the configuration phase described in the next section.

12

The Configuration Phase

The SUSE Linux installation process restarts by entering the configuration phase. During server configuration, you're asked to enter a password for the root user, configure the network settings, perform online updates, configure services, configure OES, and specify device configuration settings. In the following sections, you learn about these tasks.

Set the Root User Password

In Linux, the superuser is named "root." Because this account has all administrative rights in the Linux system, you need to ensure that the root user has a secure password. The system administrator window contains fields where you enter and verify a password for root users. Passwords should be five to eight characters and contain both uppercase and lowercase letters as well as one or more numbers. In addition, the password should consist of random patterns and not be based on dictionary words, which makes it easier to break with password-cracking software. If your password is too short, consists of a dictionary word, or is all lowercase letters, you see a warning message asking whether you want to continue.

The root password is encrypted with one of the following encryption types:

- Data Encryption Standard (DES; Linux default)
- MD5
- Blowfish

For most installations, you should use the default DES encryption. If your Linux system needs to log on to other environments, such as Windows or UNIX, you might need to select MD5 or Blowfish. To change the default encryption, in the system administrator window, select Expert Options to display the Set password Encryption dialog box. Select the encryption method, and click or select OK. After entering your root password in the Enter and Reenter text boxes, click or select Next. If your password is too short or is based on a dictionary word, you see a "Password is too simple" message. Select Yes to continue using the simple password, or select No to return to the password entry screen.

Configure Network Settings

After entering the root user password and selecting Next, the installation process analyzes your system and displays the Network Configuration window with options for the network interface and for DSL, ISDN, modem, and proxy settings. An important configuration task is setting your SUSE Linux server's IP address and name. By default, the network card is set to get the IP address from DHCP and the server's name is set to Linux with no domain name. To change the IP address configuration and host name for your server in graphical YaST, you can use these steps:

EXAMPLE

1. In the Network Configuration window, click the Network Interfaces heading to open the Network cards configuration dialog box shown in Figure 12-12.

2. In the Already configured devices section, click the Change button to display the network card's name, device, and IP address.

3. Click the Edit button to open the Network address setup dialog box shown in Figure 12-13.

4. To set a manual IP address, click the Static address setup option button and then enter the IP address and subnet mask.

5. Click the Host name and name server button to enter the name of your SUSE Linux server and configure your DNS server's IP address. Click the Routing button to set the IP address of your network's default gateway. The Advanced button can be used to configure hardware settings, set DHCP client options, and enter additional alias addresses for your server.

6. After all configuration settings have been made, click Next to return to the Network cards configuration dialog box. Click Finish to save your changes and return to the Network Configuration window.

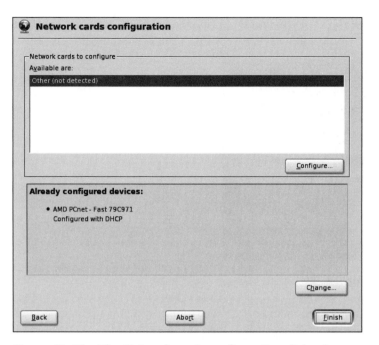

Figure 12-12   The Network cards configuration dialog box

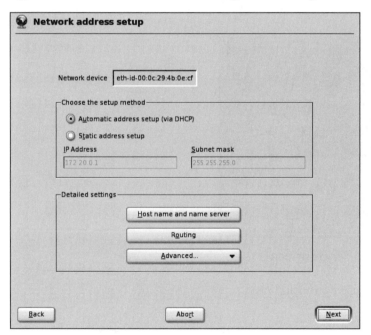

Figure 12-13   The Network address setup dialog box

As shown in Figure 12-14, the text-based YaST has the same options; however, the steps for selecting options are slightly different. For example, you would follow these steps to set the IP address of your network card:

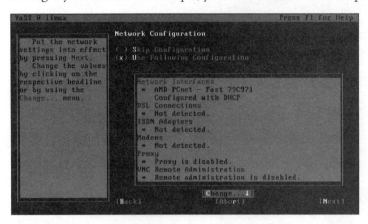

Figure 12-14 The Network Configuration screen

EXAMPLE
1. Press Tab to highlight the Change option and press Enter to display a pop-up menu containing the same configuration categories shown previously in Figure 12-14.

2. Press Enter to select the Network Interfaces category and display the Already configured devices screen (see Figure 12-15).

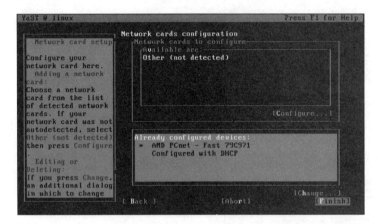

Figure 12-15 The Already configured devices screen

3. Press Tab to select the Change option and press Enter to display the Network cards configuration screen.

4. Press Tab to select the Edit option and press Enter to display the Network address setup screen shown in Figure 12-16.

5. Press Alt+T to select the Static address setup option.

6. Press Tab to select the IP Address option and enter the IP address to be assigned to your SUSE Linux server.

7. Press Tab and enter the subnet mask.

8. Press Tab to select the Host name and name server option, and press Enter to display the configuration screen.

9. Press Tab to select the Host name option and enter the name of your server.

10. Press Tab again to enter information in the Domain name and Name server fields.

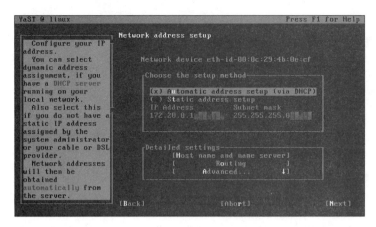

Figure 12-16   The Network address setup screen

11. If you're not using DHCP, press Alt+U to clear the Update name servers and search list via DHCP check box.

12. Press Tab to select OK and press Enter to return to the Network address setup screen.

13. Press Tab to select the Routing option and enter your default gateway configuration.

14. As in the graphical version, you can use the Advanced option to set another IP address for your machine or to configure DHCP client options and hardware settings. After finishing the configuration changes, press Tab to select Next and press Enter to return to the Network cards configuration screen.

15. Press Tab to select Finish, and press Enter to save your changes and return to the Network Configuration screen.

Perform Online Updates

After finishing the network card configuration, click or select Next to save your settings and display the Test Internet Connection dialog box. You can conduct a test of your Internet connection or skip the test and continue with the installation. If you select the default option to test your Internet connection, YaST attempts to download the latest release notes and checks for any updates. After the test is finished, a results message is displayed. You can use the View Logs option to view details, and then select Next to continue. If online updates are available, you can download and install them now, or skip the download and continue with the Service Configuration screen shown in Figure 12-17.

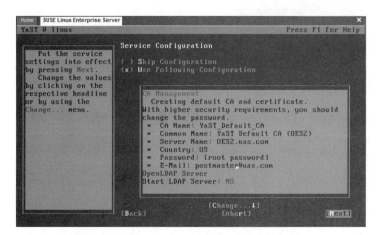

Figure 12-17   The Service Configuration screen

The Service Configuration screen contains options to create the certification authority (CA) and configure the LDAP service. The CA Management option is used to configure the CA services for encrypting passwords and other secure data transmissions between server and client. Notice that by default, the Start LDAP Server option is set to No. When configuring a SUSE Linux server for eDirectory, the OpenLDAP server is replaced by the eDirectory service and for most installations should not be used. For a standard OES Linux server installation, you should leave the Service Configuration options unchanged and click or select Next to create the CA certificate and update the system settings.

Open Enterprise Server Configuration

Next, you have the option to install the Novell Open Enterprise Server configuration. The Open Enterprise Server (OES) configuration includes eDirectory and several Novell services that make the SUSE Linux server perform most of the NetWare services you have studied in previous chapters. The default option is to install the OES configuration now by simply selecting Next to initialize the eDirectory configuration and display the eDirectory Configuration - New or Existing Tree window. Although you can add the OES Linux server to an existing tree, the default option is to create a new eDirectory tree by entering a unique tree name and then selecting Next to display the Admin user name and password fields. Enter the distinguished name for your administrative account (in this example, cn=Admin.o=AeroDyn) followed by the password you want to use for this account. After retyping the password in the Verify Password field, select Next to display a window for entering the server context and port information (see the text-based YaST screen in Figure 12-18).

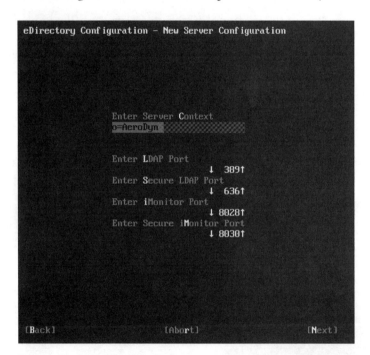

Figure 12-18 Entering the server context and port information

You should document the default port numbers for future reference, and then select Next to display the NTP and SLP configuration window. As described in Chapter 7, having the same time synchronized on all servers is important for replicating eDirectory changes throughout the network. In the Network Time Protocol field, you can select the local computer clock, or enter a DNS name or IP address of an Internet time server. The Service Location Protocol (SLP) is used to advertise services on an IP-based network so that client computers can locate network resources. On small to medium networks of fewer than 10 servers, you should select the Use multicast to access SLP option so that user agents running on client computers can find services without the need to configure directory agents. After setting the NTP and SLP configurations, select Next to perform the eDirectory configure and start the eDirectory service. This process might take several minutes; when it's finished, you see the release notes.

Specify Device Configuration Settings

NOTE

Review the release notes, and then click Next to display the Hardware Configuration window, similar to the text-based version in Figure 12-19.

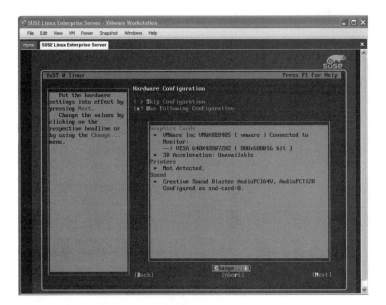

Figure 12-19   The Hardware Configuration screen

In text-based YaST, you can configure display settings by following these steps (or use similar steps in graphical YaST):

EXAMPLE

1. Press Tab to highlight the Change option and press Enter to display a menu with options to change graphics cards, printers, and sound and to reset defaults.

2. Press Enter to select the Graphics Cards option and display the SaX2: Extended X11 Configuration dialog box shown in Figure 12-20.

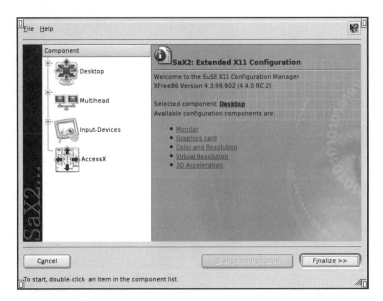

Figure 12-20   The SaX2: Extended X11 Configuration dialog box

12

3. Double-click the Desktop icon in the Component list on the left.

4. Click the Monitor option to display the Currently configured monitors dialog box showing any currently attached monitors and their settings.

5. With your current monitor highlighted, click the Change configuration button and then click Properties to open the xapi dialog box, similar to the one in Figure 12-21.

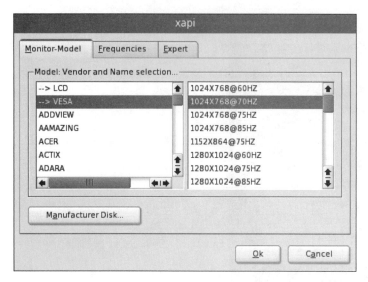

Figure 12-21   Configuring monitor settings

6. Notice that this dialog box has tabs to configure frequencies and other expert options and the Manufacturer Disk button for inserting a driver utility disk from the monitor manufacturer. In the section on the right, change your settings to a higher resolution (1024 x 768), and then click OK to return to the Currently configured monitors dialog box.

7. Click Finish to return to the SaX2: Extended X11 Configuration dialog box.

8. Click the Finalize button to open the SaX2 final steps dialog box with options to test, save, or cancel your configuration change.

9. Click the Test button to conduct a test of your new configuration settings. If the test displays the new configuration successfully, click Save and then click OK to return to the Hardware Configuration screen.

After making any further hardware configuration changes, select the Next option to configure devices and display the Installation Completed screen shown in Figure 12-22. Select the Finish option to restart your system and display the SUSE Linux login window. You learn more about logging in and working with your SUSE Linux system in the next section.

Activity 12-1: Performing a SUSE Linux Installation

Time Required: 50 minutes

Objective: Perform an installation of SUSE Linux Enterprise Server 9.

Requirements: A Windows XP computer running VMware Workstation 5 or a computer with at least 256 MB RAM and 5 GB free hard drive space (4 GB for the SUSE Linux OS and 1GB unpartitioned space) and the SUSE Linux OES DVD or CDs. This activity assumes a blank hard drive with no other operating systems installed.

Description: To take advantage of open-source software options and reduce licensing costs, UAS is planning to use SUSE Linux servers. In this activity, you perform an installation of SUSE Linux Enterprise Server 9 using a dual-boot computer or VMware. If you're using VMware, use the text-based installation and then configure your monitor for 1024 x 768 resolution.

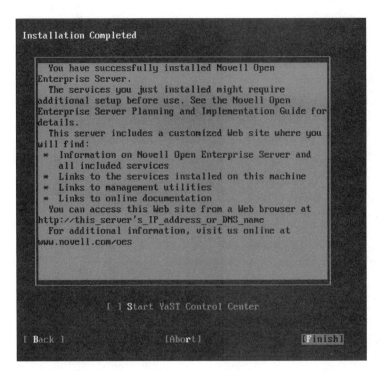

Figure 12-22   The Installation Completed screen

1. If you're using VMware, create a new virtual computer for the SUSE Linux server as described in Appendix C. If you're using a dual-boot computer, you should have Windows XP Professional installed and have at least 5 GB of unpartitioned space on your hard drive.

2. Insert the Installation CD 1 into the CD-ROM drive, and restart your computer or start your virtual machine. After a short time, the SUSE Welcome screen and installation options are displayed.

NOTE   If you're using VMware, click in the SUSE Linux window to pass keyboard and mouse control to your virtual Linux environment.

3. Press **Tab** to stop the 20-second timer.

NOTE   The VMware video environment might not be recognized by the SUSE graphical environment, which can cause an error message or an unreadable screen. If this happens, restart your virtual machine. When the Welcome window is displayed, click in the window, and then press F2 and select the Text Mode installation option.

4. From the installation menu, select **Installation** (and press **Enter**, if you're using the text-based installation) to display the license agreement screen. In the Novell Software License Agreement screen, select **I Agree** to display the installation language selection screen.

5. Verify that English is selected, and then select **Accept** to display the installation options.

NOTE   If you're using the text-based installation mode, press Tab to select an option and then press Enter instead of clicking an option button. You can also press Alt with the option's highlighted letter to select it. If you're using the graphical interface, your screens will be slightly different.

6. If necessary, select **New Installation** and then select **OK**. After a short detection process, the Installation Settings screen is displayed.

7. Make sure the correct keyboard layout, mouse driver, and video driver settings are displayed. If not, use the Change option to modify the settings.

8. Follow these steps to change the root partition's default size to provide at least 200 MB of free space that you can use to create additional partitions in Chapter 13:

    a. In the text-based screen, press **Tab** to highlight the Change option and press **Enter**. Then use the arrow keys to highlight the Partitioning option and press **Enter**.

    b. Select the **Base partition setup on this proposal** option to display the preset partitions and size information. Use the arrow keys to select the Linux native partition, and press **Enter**. In the End text box in the Size section, replace the current cylinder number with a "+" symbol followed by a size in GB for your native partition that will leave at least 250 MB free. For example, if the current partition is 4.2 GB, enter **+4.0GB** to create a 4 GB native partition leaving free space.

    c. In the graphical YaST, simply click the **Partitioning** option to open the Suggested Partitioning dialog box and select the option to create a custom partition setup.

    d. After making changes, you can use the **Back** option in either YaST version to return to the Installation Settings screen.

9. In the Change list, select **Software**.

10. Select the **Detailed selection** option to display the software configuration screen.

11. In the Filter list, select the **Selections** option, if necessary, and choose the following packages:

    ❑ LSB Runtime Environment

    ❑ KDE Desktop Environment

    ❑ Analyzing Tools

12. In the Filter list, select **Search**, enter **gettext** in the Search text box, and click the **Search** button. Next, select all the **gettext** application options. Click **Accept**, and then click **OK** to continue. (*Note*: You might see a message informing you that the system is adding other files based on your system dependencies. If so, click **Continue** to return to the Installation Settings screen.)

13. Follow these steps to set the time zone for your server:

    a. Click the **Change** button and then click the **Time zone** option to display the Clock and Time Zone Configuration window.

    b. Verify that your region is selected, and then click the corresponding time zone in the Time Zone pane.

    c. Verify that the time is correct; if not, click the **Change Time or Date** button to set your hardware clock.

    d. Click **Accept** to return to the Installation Settings screen.

14. Save the YaST installation options by selecting the **Accept** option.

15. Confirm the installation by selecting the **Yes, install** option. The installation process begins copying files. Insert additional CDs when prompted. This process takes 20 to 30 minutes, so you might want to take a short break after beginning the install or inserting a CD.

16. Specify a root password and record the password you use:

    _____

17. Select **Next**, and then confirm any warning messages by selecting **Yes**.

18. Enter the IP address and server name assigned by your instructor, confirm the network installation settings, and then select **Next**.

19. If you have access to the Internet from your computer, select **Yes, Test Connection to the Internet**; otherwise, select the **No, Skip This Test** option. Select **Next**.

Do *not* install any updates found at this time.

20. In the Certificate Service window, select **Next** to accept the default options and display the Open Enterprise Server Configuration - Now or Later screen.

21. Verify that the Configure Now option is selected, and then select **Next**.

22. If necessary, select the **New Tree** option. Enter the tree name your instructor assigned, and then select **Next** to display the New Tree information window. Enter **cn=Admin.o=AeroDyn** in the FDN admin name with context field, and enter a password in the Admin Password and Verify Admin Password fields. Select **Next** to display the server context and port information window shown previously for a text-based installation in Figure 12-18.

23. Verify that o=AeroDyn is shown in the Enter Server Context field, and select **Next** to display the NTP and SLP configuration window. Leave the NTP configuration set to your local computer clock, but change the SLP configuration to **Use multicast to access SLP**. Select **Next** to accept the default settings, and then select **Yes** to use the Multicast SLP Configuration and start the configuration phase.

24. Select **Next** to accept the default settings and configure iManager and the other Novell services. This process takes at least 15 minutes, so be patient. After all configuration is finished, the Release Notes window is displayed. Read the notes, and then select **Next** to analyze your system and display the Hardware Configuration window.

25. Read the hardware information, and then select **Next**.

26. When the installation is completed, select **Finish** to restart your SUSE Linux server. Congratulations! Your SUSE Linux Enterprise server is up and running.

12

WORKING WITH SUSE LINUX

When your computer boots to SUSE Linux, you see the SUSE Linux login dialog box shown in Figure 12-23. As described in the "Installing SUSE Linux" section, normally you shouldn't log in as the root user unless you need to perform major system tasks, such as installing new services. Most system administration and configuration tasks can be done while logged in as a normal user by switching user modes for specific commands or by entering the root user's password in the graphical YaST utility.

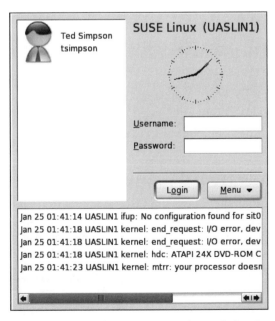

Figure 12-23   The SUSE Linux login dialog box

To log in to your SUSE Linux server, enter your user name and password and click the Login button. Remember that SUSE Linux passwords are case sensitive, so enter your password exactly the way you created it in the previous section. After you log in, the KDE desktop is displayed with a Kandalf's Useful Tips window (see Figure 12-24).

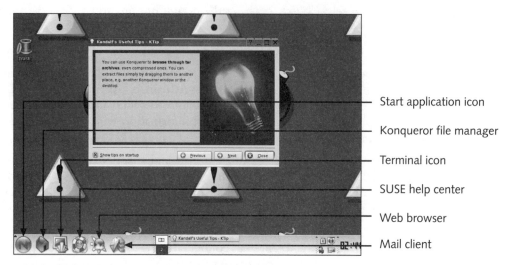

Figure 12-24   The default KDE graphical desktop

Review the tip and click Close (or Next for more tips). After closing the Tips window, you're in the KDE graphical desktop environment. In the following sections, you explore the SUSE desktop environment.

Using the KDE Desktop Environment

The default KDE desktop environment is composed of the following functional sections, described in the following sections:

- The desktop
- The KDE Control Panel (also called the Kicker)
- The KDE menu
- Virtual desktops

KDE Desktop

At first, only the Trash icon appears on the default desktop. If you don't like having the "bomb" symbol in the default background graphic, you can change it by following these steps:

EXAMPLE

1. Right-click the desktop and click Configure Desktop to open the Configure – Desktop dialog box.

2. Click the Background icon on the left to display the options shown in Figure 12-25.

3. Click the Picture list arrow to select another background graphic.

4. Click OK to save your settings and return to the KDE desktop.

As in Windows, you can move icons by dragging them with the mouse and place menu items on the desktop by dragging them from the menu to the desktop. For example, to place a calculator icon on the desktop, click the Start application icon in the Control Panel (described in the following section) to display all applications. Point to the Utilities option, click the Calculator application, and then drag it to the desktop. Release the mouse button and click Copy Here. The Calculator icon then appears on the desktop.

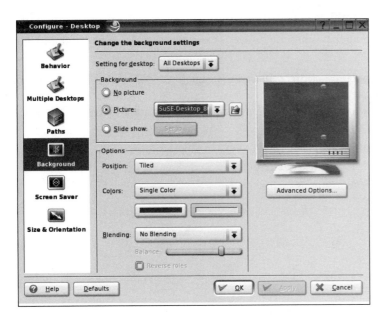

Figure 12-25   Configuring the KDE desktop background

12

KDE Control Panel (Kicker)

The KDE Control Panel (Kicker) is at the lower left of the KDE desktop and initially contains the following six icons:

- The Start application icon, a green button with a red "N," is used to display the KDE menu containing all configured programs and functions. This button is similar to the Start button on the Windows desktop.

- The Personal files icon (a blue house) is used to open the Konqueror file manager. You learn more about using Konqueror later in this section.

- The terminal icon, a seashell in front of a monitor, is used to open a command-line interface window. You learn more about using Linux commands later in this section.

- The lifesaver with a chameleon head is the icon for the SUSE help center. Use this option to get more information about using SUSE Linux.

- The globe with a gear wheel is the icon for starting the KDE Web browser.

- The "E" with an envelope leaning on it is the icon for starting the KMail e-mail application.

KDE Menu

The KDE menu is divided into the following sections (see Figure 12-26):

- *Most Used Applications*—This section contains the most frequently used applications and can be used as a shortcut.

NOTE

Because the KDE menu contains frequently used applications, your screen might not have the same options as Figure 12-26.

- *All Applications*—This section contains all configured applications. Options with submenus have a black arrow next to them. To open a submenu, move the mouse cursor over the menu and then click the submenu item.

- *Actions*—This section lists specific actions you can take, such as setting a bookmark or running a command. In addition, you can use the Switch Users option to log in with a common user name and then switch to the root user when you need to perform administrative functions. This option helps reduce the need to log in as the root user.

To log out, click the Logout option in the Actions section and then click the Logout button in the End Session message box. The SUSE Linux system logs out the current user and displays the login dialog box.

Figure 12-26   The KDE menu

Virtual Desktops

If you're working with several programs concurrently, the desktop can become cluttered with open windows, making it harder to find information. With Linux, you can prevent this problem by opening a second desktop environment. Each virtual desktop can host an almost unlimited number of applications, and they all share the same background and icons. By default, two virtual desktops are configured; however, you can use the KDE Control Panel to increase the number of virtual desktops to as many as 16. The gray and white boxes displayed in the Control Panel (shown in Figure 12-24) are used to change between virtual desktops. The white box represents the current desktop. To switch to another virtual desktop, click the gray box. In Activity 12-2, you get a chance to explore using the KDE desktop.

Konqueror File Manager

The Konqueror file manager is the primary graphical file-management utility. Nearly all work done on the file system can be performed with this utility. To start Konqueror, click the blue house icon in the Control Panel to display the opening window, similar to the one in Figure 12-27. By default, the Konqueror window displays the contents of a user's home directory, as shown in this figure for the root user.

The top section contains a menu bar, a toolbar, and the Location text box. Notice that the screen is split into a navigation bar on the far left and the main window. You can use the navigation bar for quicker navigation through the file system tree. When you select a directory in the navigation bar, the directory contents (the file view) are displayed in the main window.

You can navigate the file system in different ways. The three arrows at the far left of the toolbar are the simplest way to move up, backward, and forward through the file system. For example, to move from the root user's home directory to the beginning of the file system, click the up arrow to display all partitions that make up the file system. You learn more about the file system and using Konqueror in Chapter 13. In the following activity, you explore the KDE desktop and Konqueror.

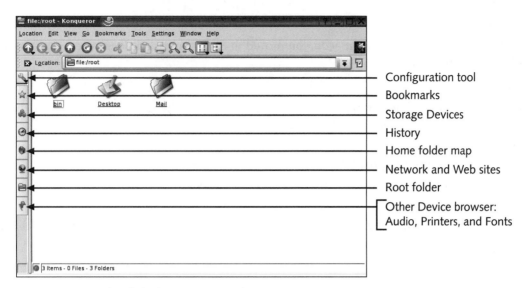

Configuration tool
Bookmarks
Storage Devices
History
Home folder map
Network and Web sites
Root folder
Other Device browser:
Audio, Printers, and Fonts

Figure 12-27 The default opening window in Konqueror

Activity 12-2: Exploring the KDE Desktop and Konqueror

12

Time Required: 10 minutes

Objective: Work with the KDE desktop environment.

Requirements: Completion of Activity 12-1 or access to a SUSE Linux server console with the root user's password

Description: Luke McMann wants you to give a demonstration of the KDE desktop to users in the Engineering Department. In this activity, you prepare for this demonstration by exploring the available features.

1. Log in to your SUSE Linux server with the user name and password you created for yourself in Activity 12-1.

2. Read the tip and then close the welcome window.

3. Follow these steps to change your desktop background:

   a. Right-click the desktop and click **Configure Desktop** to open the Configure – Desktop dialog box.

   b. Click the **Background** icon on the left to display the Change the background settings dialog box.

   c. Click the **Picture** list arrow, and select another background for your desktop. Record the name of the desktop you selected: _____

   d. Click **OK** to save your changes and return to the new desktop.

4. Follow these steps to copy the YaST shortcut to your desktop:

   a. Click the **Start application** icon (green circle with a red "N") in the Control Panel to display the KDE menu.

   b. Point to the **System** item in the All Applications section to display the submenu.

   c. Drag the **YaST** option to your desktop, release the mouse button, and click **Copy Here**.

5. Start Konqueror by clicking the blue house icon in the Control Panel.

6. Click the root folder icon (red folder) in the navigation bar at the left.

7. View the contents of the /etc directory by clicking **etc** in the main window.

8. Copy the **etc/DIR_COLORS** file to the **/tmp/** directory by clicking the **DIR_COLORS** file icon, dragging it to the /tmp icon, releasing the mouse button, and clicking **Copy Here**.

9. View the contents of the /tmp/ directory by clicking **tmp** in the main window.

10. Right-click the DIR_COLORS file icon you moved in Step 8, and click **Rename**. Enter the name **sample.txt**, and press **Enter**.

11. Close Konqueror.

12. Log out by clicking the **Logout** option in the Actions section of the KDE menu, and then clicking the **Logout** button in the End Session message box.

13. As with all operating systems, using the power off procedure when shutting down your computer is important. Make sure you use the following steps to restart your Linux server.

    a. Click the **Menu** button in the SUSE Linux login dialog box.

    b. Click the **Shutdown** option to open the Shutdown type dialog box.

    c. Click the **Restart computer** option button. (If you're shutting down the system, leave the default Turn off computer option selected.)

    d. Enter the root password you assigned in Activity 12-1, and then click **OK** to restart your computer.

Using YaST

In the "Installing SUSE Linux" section, you learned how to use the text-based and graphical YaST versions to manage the installation process. You can also use YaST for most SUSE Linux configuration tasks. The appearance and operation of the YaST interface depends on whether you use the GUI or the command line. In later chapters, you use YaST for many Linux administrative tasks, including managing user accounts and printers. In the following activity, you explore some YaST options by viewing your SUSE Linux server configuration.

Activity 12-3: Getting to Know YaST

Time Required: 15 minutes

Objective: Use the graphical YaST utility to view system configuration settings.

Requirements: Completion of Activity 12-1 or access to a SUSE Linux server console with the root user's password

Description: YaST is one of the major tools you use as SUSE Linux server administrator. In this activity, you use it to view some of your SUSE Linux configuration settings.

1. Log in to your SUSE Linux system with the user name and password you created in Activity 12-1. (Do not log in with the root user account.)

2. Click the **YaST** shortcut on your desktop. If necessary, enter the root user password to display the YaST startup window.

3. Follow these steps to check your display settings:

    a. Scroll down and click the **Hardware** icon on the left (see Figure 12-28), and then click the **Graphics Card and Monitor** icon on the right to display the Desktop Settings dialog box. Record your graphics card information:

    _____

    b. Click the **Change** button to open the SaX2 dialog box.

    c. Click **Monitor**, and then click **Properties** to open the xapi dialog box. Verify that your monitor vendor and resolution settings (1024 x 768) are correct.

If you're using VMware, make sure the monitor type is set to VESA or LCD.

NOTE

Figure 12-28 The YaST Hardware menu

d. Click **Ok** and then **Finish** to save your changes, or click **Cancel** if you want to leave the default settings.

e. Click **Finalize** and then click **Save** to save your settings and return to the YaST menu.

4. Follow these steps to set your network address:

a. Click the **Network Devices** icon on the left, and then click the **Network Card** icon on the right to display the Network cards configuration dialog box.

b. In the Already configured devices section, click the **Change** button to display the Network cards configuration dialog box.

c. Verify that your network card is selected, and click **Edit** to open the Network address setup dialog box.

d. Click the **Static address setup** option button and enter the IP address and subnet mask you're using for this computer.

e. If you're using a gateway or router to access the Internet, click the **Routing** button and enter the IP address of your default gateway. Click **OK** to save your changes and return to the Network address setup dialog box.

f. Click the **Host name and name server** button. If you see a resolver configuration file warning, click **Modify**.

g. If necessary, change your host name to **UASLinux##** and change the domain name to **UAS##** (replacing ## with your assigned student number).

h. Click to clear the **Change host name via DHCP** check box.

i. Click **OK** to save your changes and then click **Next** to return to the Network cards configuration dialog box.

j. Click **Finish** to save your changes and return to the YaST main menu.

5. Follow these steps to create a user account for yourself:

a. Click the **Security and Users** option and then click **Edit and create users** to display the User and Group Administration dialog box.

b. Click the **Set Filter** button and click the **System Users** option to display system user accounts. Record the first two user accounts:

_____

_____

12

    c. Click the **Set Filter** button and click the **Local Users** option. Are any user accounts listed?

    _____

    d. Click the **Add** button to open the Add a New Local User dialog box.

    e. Enter your full name in the Full User Name text box, enter a login name in the User Login text box, and then type a password in the Password and Verify Password text boxes.

    f. Click the **Create** button and, if necessary, respond to any password warning messages to create your user. You then return to the User and Group Administration dialog box with your new user name displayed.

    g. Click **Finish** to return to the YaST main menu.

6. Follow these steps to set your system date and time:

    a. Click **System** in the left pane and then click **Date and Time** in the right pane to open the Clock and Time Zone Configuration dialog box.

    b. If necessary, change the Time Zone setting.

    c. If necessary, click the **Change Time or Date** button to set the correct date and time, and then click **Apply**.

    d. Click **Accept** to save your changes and return to the YaST main menu.

7. Follow these steps to view the system log:

    a. Click **Misc** in the left pane and then click **View System Log** in the right pane to view system messages.

    b. After viewing the log, click **OK** to return to the YaST main menu.

8. Click **Close** to exit YaST and return the KDE desktop.

CHAPTER SUMMARY

❑ Although SUSE Linux Enterprise Server 9 is compatible with a wide range of devices, at a minimum it requires a Pentium III 750 MHz processor with 256 MB RAM.

❑ Linux systems consist of three major components: the Linux kernel, the input/output system, and the X-Server graphical window.

❑ Disk partitions make it possible to divide the hard disk into smaller functional units. At a minimum, a SUSE Linux server contains boot, swap, and root partitions.

❑ In Linux, partitions are named based on the disk drive type, the drive number, and the partition number. For example, the first partition on the first IDE drive is named hda1.

❑ The SUSE Linux installation consists of two major phases: base installation and configuration. The base installation contains options for partitioning the hard disk, configuring devices, and selecting software options. The configuration phase involves setting the root user password, configuring the network card, and installing eDirectory.

❑ YaST is the main SUSE Linux utility for installation and administrative tasks.

❑ The KDE desktop is divided into four functional areas: the desktop, the Control Panel (Kicker), the KDE menu, and virtual desktops. Virtual desktops make it possible to organize multiple applications into separate desktop environments. By default, the KDE environment is configured for two virtual desktop environments that share the same background and icon settings.

❑ Konqueror is the primary graphical file-management utility in Linux and can be used for a wide variety of tasks, including navigating the Linux file system and copying, moving, and deleting files.

KEY TERMS

boot record — A small area at the beginning of each partition that contains software to load the operating system.

boot partition — A small Linux partition that contains only the system files Linux needs to load the operating system kernel into memory.

command-line interface (CLI) — An interface with a screen for entering text-based commands and displaying text messages and data.

Master Boot Record (MBR) — The area of the hard disk that holds the boot record.

root partition — The partition that is the beginning of the file system where all other Linux operating system files and folders are stored.

swap partition — A Linux partition used to page program segments in and out of memory. Linux swap partitions should be at least twice the size of the system's RAM for best performance.

REVIEW QUESTIONS

1. At a minimum, SUSE Linux Enterprise Server 9 requires which of the following?
   a. Pentium II 700 MHz and 128 MB RAM
   b. Pentium III 750 MHz and 512 MB RAM
   c. Pentium III 750 MHz and 256 MB RAM
   d. Pentium IV 750 MHz and 512 MB RAM

2. Which of the following SUSE Linux components depends most on hardware configuration? (Choose all that apply.)
   a. kernel
   b. input/output system
   c. X-Server
   d. YaST

3. The _____ partition contains only essential system files.
   a. boot
   b. swap
   c. root
   d. MBR

4. The _____ partition must be large enough to hold all operating system files.
   a. boot
   b. swap
   c. root
   d. MBR

5. Which of the following contains the boot loader software?
   a. boot partition
   b. MBR
   c. root partition
   d. swap partition

6. The language selection screen displayed early in the installation process is used to select the language for the operational SUSE Linux server. True or False?

7. If your computer has 512 MB of RAM, by default Linux creates a
   _____ swap partition.

   a. 1.2 GB

   b. 512 MB

   c. 256 MB

   d. none of the above

8. As a general rule, selecting all the software options you might need during the installation process is better than waiting until later to install them. True or False?

9. In the text-based software selection screen, the _____ symbol indicates a software package is selected for installation.

   a. +

   b. *

   c. a

   d. X

10. Which of the following menu options in YaST determines which software packages are displayed during installation?

    a. Search

    b. Filter

    c. Package

    d. Locate

11. Which of the following can load any kernel interactively without using additional configuration files?

    a. MBR

    b. GRUB

    c. YaST

    d. LILO

12. In Linux, the default name of the administrator account is _____ .

    a. Admin

    b. Sysop

    c. root

    d. supervisor

13. In DES (the default password encryption algorithm in Linux), the maximum length of a password is _____ characters.

    a. 8

    b. 12

    c. 16

    d. 32

14. The name of the SUSE Linux server is entered in the _____ step.

    a. network configuration

    b. service configuration

    c. installation settings

    d. server configuration

15. The CA service is used to do which of the following?

    a. encrypt passwords

    b. authenticate users

    c. configure the LDAP server

    d. none of above

16. Which of the following can't be changed in the user account's Properties dialog box?

    a. default home directory

    b. shell

    c. group memberships

    d. default background

17. Settings for the graphics card and monitor can be changed during the _____ installation step.

    a. network configuration

    b. service configuration

    c. installation settings

    d. hardware configuration

18. The name "Kicker" is also used for which of the following?

    a. KDE desktop

    b. KDE menu

    c. KDE Control Panel

    d. Linux boot loader

19. All virtual desktops share the same background and icons. True or False?

20. Which of the following is the main KDE file-management utility?

    a. YaST

    b. Konqueror

    c. Control Panel

    d. Kicker

12

CASE PROJECTS

Case Project 12-1: Selecting a Linux Server

CASE PROJECTS

Wiggerts and Son Heating and Air Conditioning is planning to set up a network system based on a SUSE Linux server and has asked you to create specifications for the server. The manager wants to ensure a high level of protection from system and power failures and keep the total hardware cost under $5000. Write a brief report listing the minimum SUSE Linux requirements and recommending a system that you think will best meet the company's needs.

Case Project 12-2: Preparing for Linux Installation

CASE PROJECTS

In this project, document the essential steps for installing SUSE Linux on the server you identified in Case Project 12-1.

HANDS-ON PROJECTS

Hands-on Project 12-1: Using Konqueror

To get started using the system, Wiggerts and Son wants you to create the following directory structure on the new SUSE Linux server: a main directory called WHA and subdirectories called Shared, Accounting, and Marketing.

Use Konqueror to create this directory structure off the root of the file system. Copy a file from your local computer to the Shared directory, and have your instructor check the directory structure after you have completed it.

# CHAPTER 13

MANAGING LINUX ENVIRONMENTS

After reading this chapter and completing the activities, you will be able to:

♦ Create and manage Linux users and groups

♦ Work with command-line utilities from a Linux shell

♦ Manage Linux applications with run levels and RedHat Package Manager

♦ Work with the Linux file system, including file system permissions, partitions, and logical volumes

In Chapter 12, you learned how to perform a basic installation of SUSE Linux, including disk partitioning and working with the YaST and KDE graphical environments. In this chapter, you learn how to integrate a Linux desktop system into your network environment by creating local Linux user accounts, setting up file system security, accessing network resources, and installing software applications. You also learn how to use the YaST utility to manage system configuration and the command-line interface to run common Linux commands.

CREATING AND MANAGING LINUX USERS AND GROUPS

Because Linux is a multiuser system, you must log in with a valid user name and password before working with a Linux system. As you learned in Chapter 12, the root user has all rights to the Linux system; other user names can be given limited access permissions. If possible, you should avoid logging in with the root user account to reduce the risk of damaging the system or data accidentally. During the Linux installation, administrators can create additional standard user accounts for themselves and other users. As in NetWare, user accounts are often granted rights and permissions by being part of a group. In this section, you learn how to use the YaST utility and the useradd and groupadd commands to create and modify user and group accounts.

Local Group Accounts

In Linux, there are two major types of groups: local and system. Network administrators use **local groups** to assign rights and permissions to users, and the operating system uses **system groups** to grant rights to access certain system resources. To view local or system groups, use the Set Filter button in the YaST utility. Figure 13-1 shows an example of using YaST to view the default system groups.

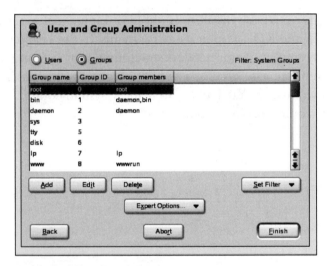

Figure 13-1   Default SUSE Linux system groups

The root group is important because it can be used to grant all rights to the Linux system. Notice that the root user is a member of the root group. You can use the root group to create a backup administrator account by making another user account a member of the root group.

Although a number of system groups are created during Linux installation, only one local group named users is created (see Figure 13-2) to give members of this group basic permissions to the system. In SUSE Linux, when a user account is created, it's assigned to a primary or default local group. The system defaults to placing new users in the users group, but network administrators can select another local or system group as a new user's default group.

Linux administrators often create other groups to grant users rights to certain files and resources. If you plan to create a number of new users who will belong to a special default group, creating that group before creating the user accounts is easier because you can simply select that group as the default group for user account creation instead of changing the default group assignment for all user accounts later. In Activity 13-1, you use YaST to create a new local group and then make it the default group for new users.

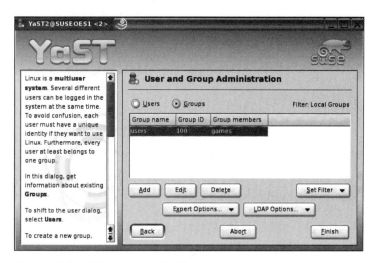

Figure 13-2 The default SUSE Linux local group

Local User Accounts

In addition to a user name and password, each Linux user account needs to be assigned a user ID (UID), a home directory, a default command shell, and password setting parameters. Because computers handle numbers more efficiently than alphabetic characters, all user accounts are assigned a UID number. The root user is assigned a UID of 0, and other user accounts are given randomly generated UIDs.

As in the NetWare and Windows environments, each user account in Linux should be given a home directory. When users log in, their default file system paths are directed to their home directories. During installation, a directory structure named /home is created in the root partition for the purpose of storing user home directories.

The Linux command-line interface (CLI) is referred to as the **shell**, which is actually a program that runs on the Linux kernel to provide a command-line environment for starting other programs. When you create a user account, that user is assigned a default command shell. Table 13-1 lists some common command shells that can be assigned to user accounts.

Table 13-1 Common Linux shells

Shell Name	Program Name	Description
Bourne shell	sh	The original UNIX shell, which has been replaced in Linux with the Bash shell.
Bourne Again (Bash) shell	bash	An enhanced and extended version of the shell created by the GNU project for use on many UNIX and Linux systems. Commonly referred to as the Bash shell instead of its full name. Bash is the default Linux shell.
C shell	csh	This shell, developed by Bill Joy in the 1970s, was the first to contain features such as history and tab completion. Because of its additional complexity, it's not as popular with users and developers as the Bash shell.
Korn shell	ksh	A proprietary (not freely available) shell written by David Korn. This revision of the Bash shell includes the interactive features of the C shell but maintains the Bash shell programming syntax.

Because the Bash shell is the default in Linux, it's used for command lines in this book's activities.

NOTE

Local user accounts are stored in two files named shadow and passwd in the /etc directory structure. The /etc/shadow file is used to store encrypted case-sensitive passwords, and the /etc/passwd file contains the user name, UID, home directory path, and default shell. All users can read the passwd file, but for security purposes, only the root user can read the shadow file. Figure 13-3 shows sample lines for the EKenton user account in the passwd and shadow files.

Passwd file entry for Eric Kenton

    ekenton:x:1001:100:Network administrator:/home/ekenton:/bin/bash

        User name
        Password ("x" means the password is in the shadow file)
        UID
        Primary group ID
        Comment
        Home directory path
        Default shell

Shadow file entry for Eric Kenton:

    ekenton:rSECmuZ.ht0qo:13061:0:99999:7:-1::

        User name
        Encrypted password
        Date of last change (# of days from 1/1/1970)
        Date after which password can be changed
        Date after which password must be changed
        How many days before password expiration user should be warned
        Number of days that password is valid after expiration (grace period)
        Day on which account is locked

Note: The information under each file entry describes the fields from left to right.

Figure 13-3   Passwd and shadow file entries

In the sample shadow file entry, the Date of last change field indicates when the password was last changed and is expressed using the number of days from January 1, 1970 (a date prior to Linux being released). The date after which the password can be changed and date after which the password must be changed are used to set password change restrictions. The "-1" entry for the day on which the account is locked means that the account hasn't been locked.

Activity 13-1: Creating User and Group Accounts in YaST

Time Required: 10 minutes

Objective: Use the YaST utility to create local user and group accounts.

Requirements: Completion of Activity 12-1, a local Linux user name created during installation, and access to the root user password

Description: Now that a SUSE Linux system has been installed in the Engineering Department, Eric Kenton wants you to create some local user and group accounts so that Engineering and Manufacturing users can share the Linux system. In this activity, you use YaST to create local group accounts and then add Engineering and Manufacturing user accounts.

1. If necessary, log in to your SUSE Linux server with the user name and password you created for yourself during the Activity 12-1 installation.

2. Start the YaST utility by clicking the **Start application** icon (a red "N" in a green circle) in the Control Panel, clicking **System**, and then clicking the **YaST** option.

3. Enter the password for your root user.

4. Scroll down the left pane and click the **Security and Users** option. In the right pane, click **Edit and create groups** to open the User and Group Administration window shown previously in Figure 13-2.

5. To set the filter to view local groups, click the **Set Filter** button to display the filter options shown in Figure 13-4.

Figure 13-4   Setting the filter for groups

6. Click the **Local Groups** option, and notice that the default group named "users" is the only group that's displayed.

7. Follow these steps to create a Mfg group:

   a. Click the **Add** button to open the Add a New Local Group dialog box shown in Figure 13-5. Notice that a default group ID of 1000 is already assigned to the new group. In the Members of this Group section, you can select group members from existing group and user accounts by simply clicking the check box next to the object's name. You can also assign an optional password to the local group.

Figure 13-5   The Add a New Local Group dialog box

   b. Enter **Mfg** in the Group Name text box and click **Next** to add this group to the User and Group Administration window.

8. Repeat the procedure in Step 7 to create a group named **Design**. Record the group's ID: _____

9. Follow these steps to create a Russ Pence user account for the Mfg group:

   a. Click the **Users** option button at the top of the User and Group Administration window.

   b. Click the **Set Filter** button, and then click the **Local Users** option to display any existing users.

   c. To add a new user, click **Add** to open the Add a New Local User dialog box shown in Figure 13-6.

   d. Enter **Russ Pence** in the Full User Name text box and **rpence** in the User Login text box.

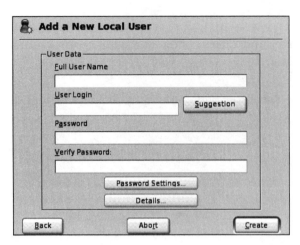

Figure 13-6   The Add a New Local User dialog box

    e. Enter **Pass01** in the Password and Verify Password text boxes.

    f. Click the **Details** button to open the Add/Edit User Properties – Details dialog box shown in Figure 13-7.

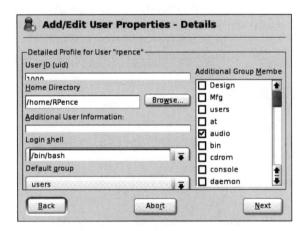

Figure 13-7   The Add/Edit User Properties – Details dialog box

    g. In the Additional Group Membership section, click to select the **Mfg** check box, and then click **Next** to return to the Add a New Local User dialog box for Russ Pence.

    h. Click the **Create** button to create the Russ Pence account and return to the User and Group Administration window.

10. Follow the procedure in Step 9 to create user accounts for **Lianne Jarka** and **Tony Rucci** and add them to the Design group.

11. Follow these steps to change password settings for the Russ Pence account:

    a. Click to select the **Russ Pence** user account.

    b. Click the **Edit** button to open the Edit an Existing Local User dialog box shown in Figure 13-8.

    c. Click the **Password Settings** button to open the Password Settings for User rpence dialog box.

    d. Change the setting in the Maximum number of days for the same password text box to **90**.

    e. Click **Next** twice to return to the User and Group Administration window.

    f. Click **Finish** to save your changes and return to the YaST main window.

12. Click the **Close** button to exit the YaST utility, and log off. Leave your system running for the next activity.

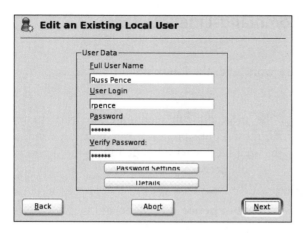

Figure 13-8 The Edit an Existing Local User dialog box

WORKING WITH THE BASH SHELL

In Chapter 12, you learned how to work with the KDE interface for a number of administrative and user-oriented tasks. Although Linux now has more graphical environments to make it user friendly, network administrators still need to be comfortable working from the command line. Linux system operation is controlled through text-based configuration files that can be modified directly from command-line utilities. GUI environments make it more convenient to access applications and change many of these configuration files, but certain configuration parameters and applications still need to be managed through text-based commands.

Accessing the Command-Line Interface

When a user first logs in to Linux, the user is placed in his or her home directory and given a command shell or GUI environment, depending on the run level specified for the system (explained in "Managing Linux Applications" later in this chapter). Because most systems are set to use a graphical run level, you need to open a terminal window to work with the command shell. Linux is a multiprocessing OS, so you can have several terminal windows open at once and switch to a virtual terminal via the graphical console or by pressing Ctrl+Alt followed by the function key you want to assign to the terminal session. Holding down Ctrl+Alt and pressing F7, for example, returns you to the graphical console. Each terminal window is identified by a number in its title bar. Using multiple virtual terminals can come in handy when you're working on different projects and want to switch between commands quickly. Table 13-2 lists several commands that you work with in the following activity.

Table 13-2 Common Linux commands

Linux Command	Description
ls	View directory contents.
cat	Display the contents of a text file.
cd	Change directory.
pwd	Display the current directory path.
su	Switch user; can be used to switch to the root user for certain administrative tasks.
id	Display user and group identification information about the logged-in user.
who	List all regular users logged in to the system.

Activity 13-2: Exploring the Linux Command-Line Interface

Time Required: 10 minutes

Objective: Use basic Linux commands to view and work with the Linux system.

Requirements: Same as Activity 13-1

Description: The Linux shell is probably one of the most difficult techniques to learn in the Linux environment. Fortunately for network administrators, most Linux processes can now be configured and managed in graphical utilities. However, at times the graphical environment might not be available, or command lines are needed to automate a process. In this activity, you practice a few common Linux commands, using the Bash shell from a Linux terminal window.

1. If necessary, log in to your SUSE Linux server with your **rpence** user name and password. (Don't log in with your root user account.)

2. Click the **Terminal** icon (next to the Home icon). If a Tip of the Day window opens, click **Close**. (*Hint*: If you don't want this window to open in the future, you can click the option to not show tips.)

3. Type **pwd** and press **Enter**. Record your current directory path:

   _____

4. Type **id** and press **Enter**. Record your ID information:

   _____

5. Open a second terminal session, and switch to the root user by following these steps.

   a. Type **su** and press **Enter**.

   b. Type the password for your root user and press **Enter**.

6. Follow these steps to display the contents of the passwd file:

   a. Type **cd /etc** and press **Enter** to change to the etc directory.

   b. Type **ls** and press **Enter** to display the directory contents.

   c. Type **cat passwd** and press **Enter** to display the passwd file contents. Record the last entry in the file:

   _____

   d. Type **cat shadow** and press **Enter** to display the shadow file. Record the last entry in the file:

   _____

7. Type **exit** and press **Enter** (once for each terminal session) to close both terminal sessions, and then log out. Leave your system running for the next activity.

Accessing Command-Line Help

As you learned in the previous section, Linux commands have many options that must be typed exactly to get the results you want. Remembering all the options for even common Linux commands would be next to impossible, however, so Linux includes a built-in manual or information pages for each command. You can access this information with the man or info command, as described in the following sections.

Using Man Pages

The man (short for manual) command provides detailed help information on specific commands in **man pages**. For example, to view the man page for the ls command, type the command "man ls" to get the results shown in Figure 13-9. You can use the Page Up and Page Down keys to browse through man pages. After you have finished viewing the man documentation, press Q to quit the manual and return to the shell prompt. Notice that the heading of each man page displays the command name at the left and right sides followed by the section number in parentheses to which the man page belongs. The default section number (1) in Figure 13-9 means that information on user command options is being displayed. Other section numbers can be used to display man pages on a variety of topics (see Table 13-3).

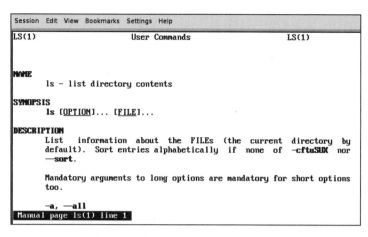

Figure 13-9 The man section (1) page for the ls command

Table 13-3 Section options for the man command

Section Number	Description
1	Executable programs and user shell commands; the default section number
2	System calls
3	Functions and library routines
4	Device files
5	Configuration files and file formats
6	Games
7	Macro packages and file formats
8	System administration commands

For example, to view the configuration files and file formats for the crontab command (see Figure 13-10), enter the command "man 5 crontab."

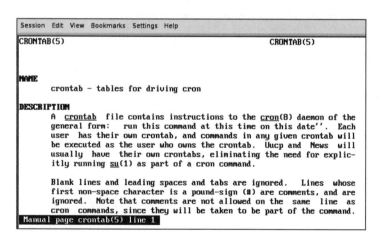

Figure 13-10 The man section (5) page for the crontab command

13

Using Info Pages

Linux has another source of command documentation called **info pages**, which often provide a more current version of command documentation and can be read by using the info command, as shown in Figure 13-11. In SUSE Linux, info files are stored in the /usr/share/info directory and have the following advantages over man pages:

- Info files use a standard structure in the documentation layout.
- Info files contain specific sections that can be accessed directly from the table of contents, compared to using section numbers with the man command.
- Info file sections can be linked to form a complete document.

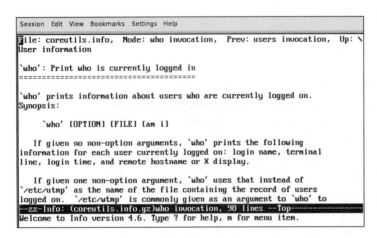

Figure 13-11   The info page for the who command

You can use several command keys, listed in Table 13-4, to move around info pages.

Table 13-4   Common info command keys

Command Key	Description
Spacebar, Page Down	Page down one screen
Backspace, Page Up	Page up one screen
b	Move cursor to the beginning of the info page
Tab	Move cursor to the next reference
h	Display help
q	Exit the info page

Creating Users and Groups from the Command Line

Most network administrators find it more convenient to create and manage user and group accounts with YaST, but the Certified Linux Professional (CLP) certification requires creating user and group accounts from the command line with the useradd and groupadd commands. Being able to use command-line utilities has certain advantages, such as creating users from script files and working on other Linux systems that don't have the YaST utility installed. Command-line utilities use parameters to specify additional information and options. Parameters usually take the form of a letter preceded by a hyphen. To learn more about parameters for command-line utilities, use the man command. For example, Figure 13-12 shows an example of using the man command to view information about parameters for the useradd command. In the following activity, you learn how to use the adduser and addgroup commands to create new local users and groups on your SUSE Linux server.

```
Session  Edit  View  Bookmarks  Settings  Help

useradd(8)                                           useradd(8)


NAME
       useradd - create a new user account

SYNOPSIS
       useradd [-D binddn] [-P path] [-c comment] [-d homedir]
               [-e expire] [-f inactive] [-G group,...] [-g gid]
               [-m [-k skeldir]] [-o] [-p password] [-u uid]
               [-r] [-s shell] [--service service] [--help]
               [--usage] [-v] account

       useradd --show-defaults

       useradd --save-defaults [-d homedir] [-e expire]
               [-f inactive] [-g gid] [-G group,...] [-s shell]

Manual page useradd(8) line 1
```

Figure 13-12   Parameters for the useradd command

Activity 13-3: Creating User and Group Accounts from the Command Line

Time Required: 10 minutes

Objective: Create local user and group accounts with command-line utilities.

Requirements: Completion of Activity 12-1 (Linux installation), a local Linux user account created during Activity 12-1, and access to the root user password

Description: Eric Kenton wants you to show him how to create user and group accounts with the Linux command-line utilities. In this activity, you use man and info pages to look up documentation on the useradd and groupadd commands, and then use them to create an ITMgrs group and user accounts for the IT Department.

1. If necessary, log in to your SUSE Linux server with the user name you created for yourself during Activity 12-1.

2. Open a terminal session.

3. Switch to the root user by typing **su**, pressing **Enter**, typing the password for your root user account, and pressing **Enter** again.

4. Type **man groupadd** and press **Enter** to display a man page on the groupadd command. Read the man page, and then type **q** to quit and return to the command prompt.

5. Enter a groupadd command to create a group named **ITMgrs** with the default options. Record the command you used:

   _____

6. Type **info useradd** and press **Enter** to display information on the useradd command. Read the info page, and then type **q** to quit and return to the command prompt.

7. Enter a useradd command to create a user account named **ekenton** that belongs to the ITMgrs group and has a home directory in the /home path. Include the -m parameter to create the home directory and the -c parameter to enter **Eric Kenton** as the full name. Record the command you used:

   _____

8. Type **cat /etc/passwd** and press **Enter** to display the contents of the passwd file. Notice that information for each user account is stored on a separate line. Record the line in the passwd file that shows the account for your ekenton user:

   _____

9. Type **exit** and press **Enter** to exit the su shell, and then type **exit** and press **Enter** again to return to the command prompt.

10. Use the procedure in Step 11 of Activity 13-1 to change Eric Kenton's password restriction to 90 days.

11. Exit YaST and log out. Leave your system running for the next activity.

13

Using Linux Online Help

Sometimes you need more detailed information about a command or procedure than the man or info command provides, or you want to learn how to perform an administrative task or solve a technical problem. The developers of Linux and other open-source software have always shared software documentation online for everyone's use. You can find a wealth of useful information online, but remember that software documentation is often written by developers who assume that you're familiar with the documentation available for other Linux commands. As a new Linux administrator, you should expect to see many details that you don't understand at first. Going through this chapter and reading additional material will help you clear up many of these details, however.

Matt Welsh started the Linux Documentation Project (LDP) in the early 1990s. The LDP was the first major effort to offer Linux documentation in a variety of formats. Currently, it has more than 6000 pages of information available free on the Internet. Many network administrators find the HOWTO documents to be the most helpful part of the LDP. These documents cover topics such as sharing files between Linux and Windows XP or accessing network printers. In addition, mini-HOWTO documents focus on narrower subjects, such as configuring a DHCP server. A good place to begin researching the LDP documentation is at *www.tldp.org*.

When you have a challenging Linux question, such as configuring a Linux driver, you can also try searching for the answer at the Google site. Entering "Linux driver Intel(R) PRO/1000 MT Mobil," for example, might return several messages from Linux administrators discussing how to use this network card driver. Table 13-5 lists some Web sites that you might find useful in learning more about the world of Linux. In the following activity, you investigate some of these sites to learn more about accessing online help with Linux.

Table 13-5   Linux documentation Web sites

Site	Description
www.linuxjournal.com	A companion Web site for the monthly magazine *Linux Journal* with additional Linux links and information
www.linuxmagazine.com	A technical companion Web site for the monthly *Linux magazine*
www.linux.sys-con.com	A business-oriented online magazine with interviews, links, and technical information
www.lwn.net	A collection of weekly news articles
www.linuxtoday.com	Recent Linux news items

ACTIVITY

Activity 13-4: Accessing Online Help

Time Required: 10 minutes

Objective: Find online help information.

Requirements: Access to the Internet

Description: Linux online documentation is a great resource for learning and working with the Linux OS. In this activity, you practice using some online sites to find information.

1. If necessary, log in to your SUSE Linux server with your user name and password.

2. Start your Web browser and explore the URLs listed in Table 13-5. Record your favorite site:

   _____

3. Exit your Web browser and log out. Leave your system running for the next activity.

MANAGING LINUX APPLICATIONS

To support users and manage the Linux server, you need to know how Linux works with applications. In this section, you learn how run levels are used to start the Linux server and how software packages can be added with the RedHat Package Manager (RPM) and YaST.

Working with Run Levels

Run levels determine the startup environment for a system and can be configured from the command line or in the YaST utility. Run level 5 includes graphical support through the **X-Window** interface, which other software packages, such as the KDE and Gnome desktops, draw on. Table 13-6 lists the run levels defined in SUSE Linux.

Table 13-6   SUSE Linux run level options

Run Level	Description
0	System wait
1	Single user mode
2	Local multiuser without remote network
3	Full multiuser with network
4	Free
5	Full multiuser with network and X-Window
6	System restart

The simplest way to manage run levels is with the YaST Runlevel Editor (see Figure 13-13). In the following activity, you have an opportunity to practice using it.

Figure 13-13   The YaST Runlevel Editor

Activity 13-5: Manage Run Levels in YaST

Time Required: 10 minutes

Objective: Use YaST to manage SUSE Linux run levels.

Requirements: Access to the root password

Description: Eric thinks that changing run levels when troubleshooting the Linux system could be useful and wants to know what options are available in YaST. In this activity, you use YaST to work with the available run level options.

1. If necessary, log in to your SUSE Linux server with your user name and password.

2. Start the YaST utility and enter the password for your root account.

3. In the left pane, click the **System** icon, and then click the **Runlevel Editor** option in the right pane.

4. Click the **Expert Mode** option button and record the default run level:

_____

5. Click the **Set default runlevel after booting to** list arrow, and record the run level options:

_____

_____

_____

6. Click the **Back** button twice to return to the YaST System menu.

7. Exit YaST, and stay logged in for the next activity.

RPM Package-Related Operations

Installing applications can require a number of steps, such as determining what support modules an application needs, decompressing software modules, performing the actual installation procedure, and then testing the application. Just as Windows has wizards to help with installation procedures, Linux offers several software package tools to help administrators install applications. The application tool that Linux administrators use most often is **RedHat Package Manager (RPM)**. RPM has the following features that make it an excellent software package manager:

- *Noninteractive, scriptable installations*—Provides a set of tools you can use to perform scriptable installations of software packages.

- *Verification of correct installation*—Includes several methods for verifying installed files so that administrators can verify that software is installed correctly and hasn't been modified since installation.

- *Dependency tracking*—With this feature, administrators can determine whether additional updates or modules need to be installed on the Linux server before installing the package.

- *Digitally signed packages*—Allows all packaged software to be digitally signed using public key technology so that you can verify the authenticity of software and help prevent installation of Trojan programs.

To use RPM to install a software package, first copy the package to a temporary work directory in the Linux file system. RPM software packages have a name in the following format: *name-version-release.architecture*.rpm. Each part of the RPM name describes the package component:

- *Name*—Indicates the software packaged in the .rpm file

- *Version*—Version number not required but can be used in the .rpm file

- *Release*—An optional component that specifies the revision of the version number

- *Architecture*—Indicates the computer platform the software package is written for; typical values include the following:

  - If86: The package can be used on any Pentium class or higher 32-bit CPU; default value for SUSE Linux.

  - I686: The package can be used on any 686-class 32-bit Intel-compatible CPU.

  - noarch: The package doesn't contain binary code.

  - nosrc: The package contains code and no source is available.

  - src: The package contains items such as the source code, patches, and spec file you need to build a binary package.

After you copy the file to a work directory, you can use the cdir command to change to the directory and then issue the rpm –i *package_name*.rpm command. You can also install rpm packages from a graphical interface by using YaST. In Appendix B, you have the opportunity to practice using the YaST utility and rpm command to install packages, such as iFolder.

MANAGING THE FILE SYSTEM

In Chapter 12, you learned how a disk is partitioned during Linux installation into boot, swap, and root partitions. The OS uses the boot and swap partitions for starting the computer and swapping memory pages to disk, and the root partition (represented by the / character) is used to store the OS software, applications, and data. In addition, the root partition is used as the starting place for the entire file system structure. All file systems on disk partitions, CDs, and other storage devices (even on other computers) are accessed from the root partition instead of with drive letters, as in the Windows OS. Partitions form disk areas that can be formatted and managed with a file system, as described in the following section. A disk can have up to four partitions, one of which can be an extended partition. A Linux extended partition can be used to create other "logical" partitions, thereby allowing you to have as many partitions as needed on a single disk drive.

Linux File Systems

A partition sets the physical disk area and size, but a disk partition must be formatted with a file system to be used by the operating system. File systems also provide a means of storing and retrieving data from a disk partition. Common file systems in the Windows world include FAT16, FAT32, and NTFS.

Linux file systems can be classified as traditional or journaling. **Journaling file systems**, such as NTFS and Novell Storage Services (NSS), keep a log of data transactions applied to a disk partition. Keeping a transaction log enables the OS to back off incomplete transactions in the event of a system crash, thereby preserving the integrity of the file system's data. Journaling file systems are more fault tolerant; the traditional FAT and FAT32 often have problems and have to be rebuilt following a system crash. A powerful feature of Novell OES SUSE Linux is its capability to use the NSS file system (discussed in more detail in Chapter 14). Tables 13-7 and 13-8 describe the traditional and journaling file systems supported by SUSE Linux.

Table 13-7 Traditional file systems supported by SUSE Linux

File System	Description
minux	The first file system supported by Linux is fairly limited compared to other file systems and is no longer in general use.
MS-DOS VFAT	The original DOS/Windows 9x file system with support for long file names can be mounted by Linux systems.
ext2	This inode-based file system most commonly used with Linux has been available for many years and is easily converted to ext3. By design, ext2 is almost as fast as ReiserFS (see Table 13-8) and isn't prone to fragmentation. Because Linux doesn't crash often, the lack of journaling in this file system hasn't been a major problem.

Table 13-8 Journaling file systems supported by SUSE Linux

File System	Description
ext3	Enhanced journaling version of the ext2 file system.
ReiserFS	First included in the official Linux kernel in January 2001, this high-speed system can handle a large number of small files efficiently.
NTFS	This Windows NT/Server 2003 file system is designed to be more robust and secure than MS-DOS VFAT.
NSS	Novell's main file system uses logical volumes and storage pools to store data on disk partitions. It uses Novell's access rights to provide file system security and can be mounted on SUSE Linux systems by using the Enterprise Volume Management System and installing .rpm files.

13

The most common file systems in SUSE Linux include ext2fs, ReiserFS, NSS, and NFS. Ext2fs is basically the same as the traditional UNIX file system and works best on computers with less processing power. The newer ReiserFS requires more processing power but is often preferred over ext2fs for the following reasons:

- Uses the more efficient balanced-tree system for organizing data blocks, resulting in faster file access and volume mounting.

- Uses a fixed block size of 1024 bytes, which requires less storage space for smaller files.

- Has almost no limit on file size (compared to ext2fs, with a maximum file size of 16 GB).

The Network File System (NFS) isn't actually a disk file system; it's a network server used to make data available on the network. With NFS, it doesn't matter which file system format is used on the local disk partition because the NFS server provides data to clients in the NFS format. You learn more about using NFS in "Sharing and Accessing Network Files" later in this chapter.

For a user or program, it doesn't matter which file system format is used. A standard interfacing system called the **Virtual Filesystem Switch (VFS)** sends user requests from a specific process to the file system to access data stored on a disk device, as shown in Figure 13-14.

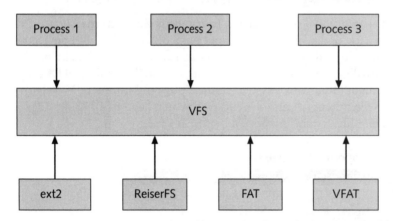

Figure 13-14   Accessing Linux file systems through the Virtual Filesystem Switch (VFS)

In all Linux file system formats, system file information is kept separate from the file's data through the use of inodes. An **inode** is a 128-byte record containing all the system information about a file, such as owner, access permissions, time of access, and links to data blocks.

Disk partitions and their associated file systems need to be mounted on the root partition before Linux applications can access the data. Although file systems can be mounted manually with the mount command, certain file systems are mounted automatically by placing the partition or device in the fstab (file system table) file. When Linux boots, it reads the fstab file and mounts the file systems listed in the / directory structure identified in the fstab parameters. Figure 13-15 shows an example of the fstab file created during Linux installation. Notice that the system partitions and common devices, such as the CD-ROM drive, are mounted automatically by using the information in the fstab file. In the following section, you learn how to create a new partition and mount its file system with the fstab file.

```
httpd                      passwd.old            zshenv
hushlogins                 pcmcia                zshrc
SUSEOES1:/etc # cat fstab
/dev/sda2       /                     reiserfs   acl,user_xattr      1
 1
/dev/sda1       swap                  swap       pri=42              0
 0
devpts          /dev/pts              devpts     mode=0620,gid=5     0
 0
proc            /proc                 proc       defaults            0
 0
usbfs           /proc/bus/usb         usbfs      noauto              0
 0
sysfs           /sys                  sysfs      noauto              0
 0
/dev/cdrecorder /media/cdrecorder     subfs      fs=cdfss,ro,procuid,nos
uid,nodev,exec,iocharset=utf8 0 0
/dev/fd0        /media/floppy         subfs      fs=floppyfss,procuid,no
dev,nosuid,sync 0 0
SUSEOES1:/etc # ▮
```

Figure 13-15 Sample fstab file contents

Creating and Managing Linux Partitions

Linux disk partitions can be created and managed in YaST or with the fdisk command. YaST includes the Expert Partitioner utility for displaying existing partitions (see Figure 13-16) and can be used for a number of operations. The partitions shown in the figure include the swap and root partitions created during Linux installation. Notice that both partitions are on the sda device (the first SCSI drive) and given the names sda1 (for the swap partition) and sda2 (for the root partition). This system has two drives: sda and sdb. Currently, the sdb drive is an empty disk containing no partitions.

13

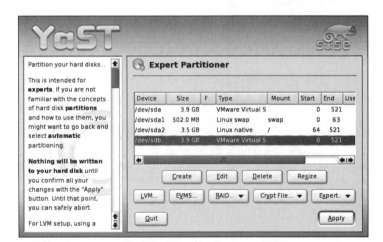

Figure 13-16 The YaST Expert Partitioner window

The Expert Partitioner utility includes a number of buttons for different tasks, described in Table 13-9. In the following sections, you learn how to use these options to create, format, and resize disk partitions.

Table 13-9 YaST Expert Partitioner buttons

Button	Description
Create	Create new primary or extended partitions.
Edit	Change partition settings or reformat a partition with a new file system.
Delete	Remove the selected partition. (Warning: Removes all data on the deleted partition.)
Resize	Change a partition size by specifying a new ending point. Note that the hard drive must contain additional unpartitioned space before you use this button to increase partition size.

Creating a New Disk Partition

To create a new partition in the YaST utility, you must start YaST with root user privileges. You click the System icon in the left pane, and then click the Partitioner option in the right pane. Next, you see a warning message stating that you should use this program only if you're familiar with partitioning hard disks. After clicking Yes to continue, you see the Expert Partitioner window. If unpartitioned disk space is available on a drive, you can create a new partition by clicking the Create button and following these steps:

EXAMPLE

1. If you have more than one drive on the system, select the drive where you want to create the partition.

2. Next, the "Which type of partition do you need" window displays options for selecting a primary or extended partition type. Click the option button to select a partition type, and then click OK.

3. If you're creating a primary partition, the Create a primary partition on device *DeviceName* window is displayed (see Figure 13-17). In the Format section, selecting the Encrypt file system check box encrypts all information written to the partition for stronger security. The disadvantages of this option are slightly slower access speeds and more difficult data recovery. If you click the Options button, you can select a hash function for sorting file names in a directory and select the version of ReiserFS to be used. Both options default to "auto" and should not be changed unless you're using the file system on older versions of SUSE Linux.

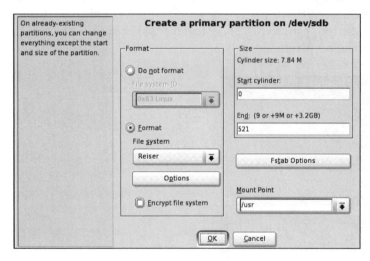

Figure 13-17   Creating a primary partition

4. In this section, you can also choose to format the partition with the selected file system or select a file system ID for the new partition. The default file system is Reiser, but you can click the File system list arrow to select another option (see Figure 13-18).

5. If you select the Do not format option button, you can select optional file system IDs, as shown in Figure 13-19. The 0x83 Linux and 0x0C Win95 FAT32 file systems can be formatted. Other file system types are used for specific purposes. For example, the 0x8E Linux LVM file system is used with logical volumes, as described in "Working with Logical Volumes" later in this chapter.

6. In the Size section (see Figure 13-19), you can set the starting and ending disk cylinders for the partition. By default, the disk partition takes all available space on the drive. To reduce the partition size, change the end cylinder number to produce a smaller partition size.

7. Click the Fstab Options button to enter information on how to mount the partition in the Linux file structure (see Figure 13-20). You can mount the file system by device or volume name and select options such as not mounting the partition at startup or mounting in read-only mode.

8. The last option in the Create a primary partition window is selecting the mount point. By default, the partition is mounted in the /usr structure. You can also create a directory in the root structure (the / partition), and then select that directory as the mount point.

Figure 13-18   File system format options

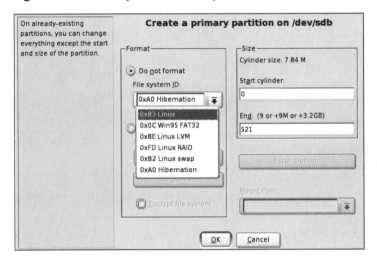

Figure 13-19   File system IDs

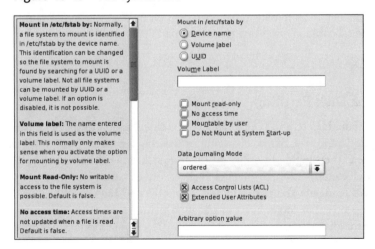

Figure 13-20   Selecting fstab options

You can also use the YaST utility to create an extended partition by following these steps:

EXAMPLE

1. Click the Extended partition option button to open the dialog box shown in Figure 13-21.

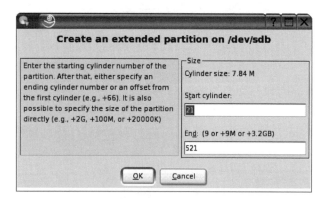

Figure 13-21 Creating an extended partition

NOTE

Only starting and ending cylinder values are available because extended partitions are used to contain logical volumes. After creating an extended partition on a disk drive, the next time you use the Create button and select that drive, you're given options to create a primary or logical partition. If you select a logical partition, you can then set format, size, and fstab options in the dialog box for a primary partition (refer back to Figure 13-17).

2. After creating the extended partition, click OK to return to the Expert Partitioner window. The extended partition is then displayed in the partition list.

3. Click the Apply button to display a list of all changes you have made. You can then click Apply again to save your changes and return to the Expert Partitioner window, or click Quit to return to the YaST System menu.

TIP

Remember to use the Apply button before performing other operations on the file system, such as creating a logical partition or resizing an existing partition.

Editing, Deleting, and Resizing a Disk Partition

The YaST Expert Partitioner utility has Edit, Delete, and Resize buttons for changing partition information, such as file system ID, format, mounting options, and size. Before changing or deleting a partition, you must unmount the partition from the file system. You can then highlight the partition and click one of the option buttons. You can use the Delete button to delete the selected partition. If you click Delete, you see a warning message to confirm deleting the selected partition. Click Yes to delete the partition and return to the Expert Partitioner window. Clicking the Edit button opens a dialog box that looks like the Create a primary partition dialog box shown previously in Figure 13-17. You can use this dialog box to change file system IDs, change mounting point and Fstab options, or reformat the partition with a different file system.

CAUTION

Changing the file system ID or format might delete information. Be sure you have a backup of the partition data before using any of the editing options.

The Resize dialog box shown in Figure 13-22 contains fields for setting new starting and ending cylinder numbers. In the following activity, you learn how to use the Expert Partitioner utility to create a new partition and then change its size.

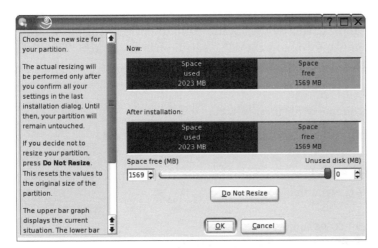

Figure 13-22   Resizing a partition

Activity 13-6: Creating and Editing Linux Partitions

Time Required: 10 minutes

Objective: Use the YaST utility to create and work with Linux partitions.

Requirements: Free or unpartitioned space on your disk drive

If you're using VMware, you might want to add another drive to your Linux system, as described in Appendix C.

Description: After installing the Linux server, often you need to create and work with partitions to set up the network file system. For example, Eric wants you to create another traditional partition to be used for storing Engineering Department CAD files. In this activity, you use the Expert Partitioner utility to create a new partition and then resize it.

1. If necessary, log in to your SUSE Linux server with your user name and password.
2. Start the YaST utility and enter your root password.
3. Click the **System** icon in the left pane, and then click the **Partitioner** option in the right pane. When you see the message asking whether you want to continue, click **Yes** to display the Expert Partitioner window.
4. Click the **Create** button. (If you're using VMware and have a second disk drive, you're asked which drive to use. Select the second drive and click **OK** to continue.)
5. Click the **Primary partition** option button, and then click **OK** to display the Create a primary partition dialog box.
6. Verify that the Reiser file system is selected in the Format section.
7. Enter a partition size of at least 50 cylinders, and record the mount point: _____
8. Click **OK** to create the partition.
9. Click **Apply** to write your changes and return to the YaST main menu, click **Apply** again if asked for confirmation, and leave YaST open for the next activity.

Working with the Linux File System

After a file system has been created and formatted, it must be mounted in the root partition before it can be accessed. As described previously, file systems can be mounted automatically in the fstab file or manually with the mount command. When mounting a file system, first you need to create a directory off the root partition where the file system will be located. You can specify this location and the partition name with the mount command or in the fstab file. For example, to mount the sdb1 partition in a directory named CorpData located off the root of the file system, you could use the following commands:

- su—Switch to the root user.

- mkdir /CorpData—Create a directory for the file system off the root.

- mount sdb1 /CorpData—Mount the file system in the CorpData directory.

After the file system is mounted, you need to know some common Linux commands, listed in Table 13-10, to work with the Linux file system. In the following activity, you use these commands to mount your file system and then create a simple directory structure.

Table 13-10   Common Linux file system commands

Linux Command	Description
ls	View directory contents
cp	Copy files
cd	Change directory
mkdir	Create a new directory
mv	Move or rename a file
rm	Delete the specified file
grep	Search for a specific string in a text file
tail	Display the last 10 lines of a text file

Activity 13-7: Creating a Linux Directory Structure

Time Required: 10 minutes

Objective: Use basic Linux commands to view and work with the Linux file system.

Requirements: Access to the root user password for your Linux server

Description: Eric wants you to create a directory in the root of the Linux server's file system to provide a mount point for the Engineering Department's partition. In this activity, you learn how to use command-line utilities to create a directory off the root of your file system that will be used to mount the Engineering partition in Activity 13-8.

1. If necessary, log in to your SUSE Linux server with your user name and password.

2. Open a terminal window.

3. Type **su** and press **Enter** to switch to the root user. Type the root user's password and press **Enter** again.

4. Type **cd /** and press **Enter** to change to the / (root) directory.

5. Type **mkdir EngData** and press **Enter** to create the EngData directory.

6. View your directories by typing **ls** and pressing **Enter**.

7. Type **exit** and press **Enter** twice. You can stay logged in and leave your system running for the next activity.

Working with Logical Volumes

In addition to traditional physical disks and partitions, SUSE Linux can manage logical volumes with the **Logical Volume Manager (LVM)** or **Enterprise Volume Management System (EVMS)**. Both volume management systems allow you to group physical partitions from one or more hard drives into volume groups from which logical volumes can be created, as shown in Figure 13-23.

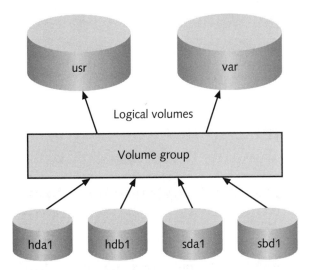

Figure 13-23   Volume groups

Volume groups in LVM correspond to the NSS storage pools described in Chapter 3.

Using volume groups enables administrators to increase disk space by adding hard disks or partitions to the volume group during system operation without needing to unmount the file system. In addition, logical volumes can be given meaningful names, such as AcctData instead of sda1 or sda2, which are used in the traditional partition system. Additional benefits of using logical volumes include the following:

- You can combine several hard disks or partitions into a large volume group.
- Hard disks can be added to the volume group in a running system if you have hot-swappable hardware.
- You can add logical volumes to a running system.
- You can use several hard disks in the RAID 0 (striping) mode for improved performance.

LVM works with the ReiserFS file system, but EVMS has the advantage of supporting NSS. However, because a disk can be assigned to only one volume manager, and the LVM utility is required for Linux system partitions, typically you need to assign a second hard disk to EVMS to support NSS volumes. In Chapter 14, you learn how to set up the NSS file system with EVMS.

Volumes are managed in YaST by using the LVM option of the System menu or clicking the LVM button in the Expert Partitioner window. When you first select the LVM option, you're asked to create a volume group named "system" that contains the swap and root partitions. Click OK to create the system volume group and display the window shown in Figure 13-24. In the following activity, you learn how to create a LVM partition, add it to a volume group, and then create a logical volume.

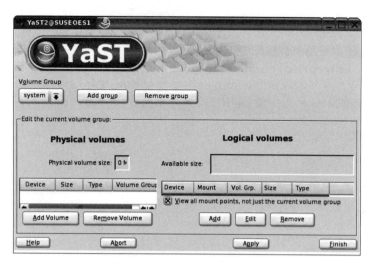

Figure 13-24   The YaST LVM dialog box

Activity 13-8: Creating a Logical Volume in the Logical Volume Manager

Time Required: 10 minutes

Objective: Use YaST to create logical volumes.

Requirements: Completion of Activity 13-7 and free or unpartitioned space on your disk drive

If you're using VMware, you might want to add another drive to your Linux system, as described in Appendix C.

Description: In this activity, you use the Logical Volume Manager to create a logical volume for hosting the Engineering Web site.

1. If necessary, log in to your SUSE Linux server with your user name and password.

2. If necessary, start the YaST utility and enter the password for your root account.

3. Follow these steps to create a partition for use with LVM:

   a. Click **System** in the left pane, click **Partitioner** in the right pane, and then click **Yes** to the message box to display the Expert Partitioner window.

   b. Click the **Create** button and, if necessary, select the drive that will hold the new partition.

   c. Click the **Primary partition** option button, and then click **OK** to display the Create a primary partition dialog box.

   d. Click the **Do not format** option button. Click the **File System ID** list arrow, and then click the **0x8E Linux LVM** partition type.

   e. Change the ending cylinder number to create a partition of at least 150 MB.

   f. Click **OK** to add the partition to the Expert Partitioner window.

   g. Click **Apply** to display the Changes window.

   h. Click **Apply** again to save your changes and return to the Expert Partitioner window.

4. Click the **LVM** button at the bottom. The first time you use the LVM option, you see the Create a Volume Group dialog box asking you to create a volume group named system (see Figure 13-25).

5. If you see this dialog box, enter **EngVols** in the Volume Group Name text box and click **OK** to display the Physical Volume Setup dialog box shown in Figure 13-26.

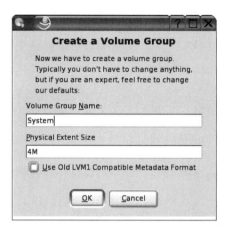

Figure 13-25   The Create a Volume Group dialog box

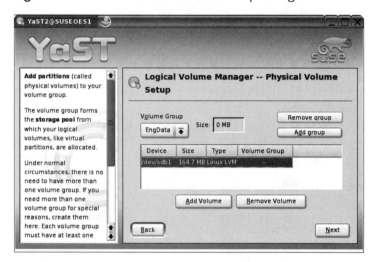

Figure 13-26   The Physical Volume Setup dialog box

6. If necessary, click to select the partition you created in Step 3, and then click the **Add Volume** button to add the space from that partition to the volume group. Click **Next** to open the Logical Volumes dialog box shown in Figure 13-27.

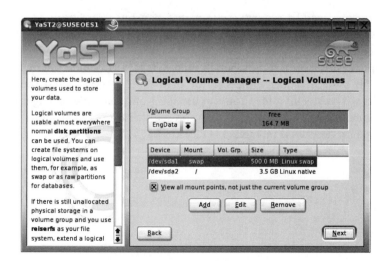

Figure 13-27   The Logical Volumes dialog box

7. Click the **Add** button to open the Create Logical Volume dialog box shown in Figure 13-28.

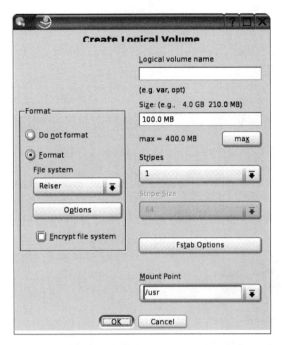

Figure 13-28   The Create Logical Volume dialog box

8. Enter **EngVol1** in the Logical volume name text box, and change the volume size to **100 MB**. Notice that the default file system is Reiser and the mount point is /usr.

9. Change the default mount point to **/EngData**.

10. Click **OK** to create the logical volume and return to the Logical Volume Manager dialog box.

11. Click **Next** to return to the Expert Partitioner window. Your new logical volume should now appear with the mount point of /EngData.

12. Click **Apply** to display the Changes window, and then click **Finish** to return to the YaST System menu.

13. Click **Close** to exit YaST. You can stay logged in for the next activity.

Setting File System Permissions

Every file system shared by multiple users needs a security system that prevents users from accessing or changing files they aren't authorized to use. In Chapter 6, you learned that Novell provides access to the NSS file system through user trustee assignments. The Linux file system has a rather simple security system that assigns rights to the file owner, a group, and other users. Rights are limited to read, write, and execute for these three trustees. When setting Linux file system security, the creator of the file is considered the owner. In addition, one group can be assigned as a trustee of a file. You can use the Konqueror file manager to view and set file system permissions (see Figure 13-29). You can also view and set file system permissions with the ls -l, chown, chgrp, and chmod commands, described in Table 13-11.

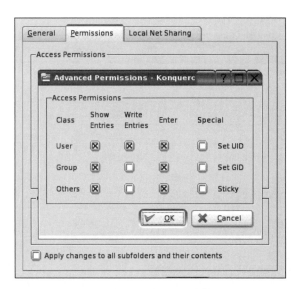

Figure 13-29 Setting advanced file system permissions in Konqueror

Table 13-11 Command-line syntax for file system permissions

Command	Syntax	Description
ls	ls -l	Displays all information about files, including the permission value
chown	chown *username filename*	Changes the file owner to the specified user name
chgrp	chgrp *groupname filename*	Changes the group assigned to the file
chmod	chmod *permissionvalue filename*	Changes the permissions set for the file owner, assigned group, and others to the specified value (see Table 13-12 for common values)

When working from the command line, permissions for each set of three trustees (owner, group, and others, in order from left to right) are indicated by using one octal digit per trustee. Each permission is represented by a single octal digit, which consists of three binary digits (bits) with possible values ranging from 0 (binary 000) to 7 (binary 111). A permission is assigned by placing a 1 in the corresponding binary position. The read permission is assigned a value of 4 (binary 100), the write permission is assigned a value of 2 (binary 010), and execute is assigned a value of 1 (binary 001). The value of the octal digit is computed by adding the numbers assigned to each permission.

For example, to grant the file owner all permissions, the assigned group read and execute permissions, and all others no permissions, you use the octal value 730, calculated as follows:

- The first octal digit 7 is calculated by adding the values of the read permission (4), the write permission (2), and the execute permission (1): 4 + 2 + 1 = 7.

- The second octal digit 3 is calculated by adding the values of the read and execute permissions (2 + 1).

- The final octal digit 0 means all others have no permissions.

The binary value of this assignment is 111011000:

- The first three bits (111) represent read, write, and execute permissions for the file owner.

- The second three bits (011) represent read and execute permissions for the assigned group.

- The last three bits (000) represent no permissions for all other users.

Table 13-12 shows the numeric value of commonly used file permissions. In the following activity, you use YaST to assign rights to the directories you created in Activity 13-8 and then use the ls command to view access permissions.

13

Table 13-12   Numeric values of commonly used file permissions

Permission	Description	Value	Corresponding Net-Ware NSS Rights
rwxr-xr-x	The owner has all three permissions, and the assigned group and all others have only read and execute rights.	755	Owner: Supervisor Assigned group: Read, File Scan Others: Read, File Scan
rw-rw-r--	The owner and the assigned group have read and write rights, and all others have only the read right.	664	Owner: Read, Write, Modify, Erase, File Scan Assigned group: Read, Write, Modify, Erase, File Scan Others: Read, File Scan
r-x------	The owner has read and execute rights, and the assigned group and all others have no rights.	500	Owner: Read, File Scan Assigned group and others: No rights
rw-r--r--	The owner has read and write rights, and the assigned group and all others have only the read right.	644	Owner: Read, Write, Modify, Erase, File Scan Assigned group and others: Read, File Scan
rwxrwxr--	The owner and assigned group have all rights, and all others have only the read right.	774	Owner: Supervisor Assigned group: Supervisor Others: Read, File Scan

ACTIVITY

Activity 13-9: Assigning File System Permissions

Time Required: 10 minutes

Objective: Use basic Linux commands to view and assign file permissions.

Requirements: Completion of Activities 13-1 and 13-8

Description: To access the newly created logical volume, Eric wants you to create two directories and then use Linux permissions to give the owner all rights, the associated group read and write rights, and all other users only the read right. In this activity, you use YaST to assign these permissions and then check them with the ls command.

1. If necessary, log in to your SUSE Linux server with your root user name and password.

2. Use the following commands to change to the EngData directory and create an EngWeb directory containing two subdirectories named products and facilities:

   ```
   cd /EngData
   mkdir EngWeb
   cd EngWeb
   mkdir products
   mkdir facilities
   ```

3. Use the following commands to assign the Design group to the products directory and to give the owner and Design group all rights and all others only the read right:

   ```
   chgrp Design products
   chmod 774 products
   ```

4. Use the procedure in Step 4 to assign the Mfg group to the facilities directory. Then give the owner and Mfg group all rights to facilities and give only the read right to all others.

5. Type **exit** and press **Enter** to end the terminal session.

6. Start the Konqueror utility and change to the EngWeb directory.

7. Follow these steps to record permissions for the products directory:

   a. Click the **products** directory and click **Properties** to open the Properties dialog box.

   b. Click the **Permissions** tab and record the permissions:

   _____

   c. Close the products directory window.

8. Use the procedure in Step 7 to record permissions for the facilities directory:

   _____

9. Close Konqueror, and leave your system running for the next activity.

Sharing and Accessing Network Files

As with any server operating system, one of the major functions of a Linux server is sharing data with client computers. In Linux, you can share directories with other Linux and UNIX systems by using the standard **Network File System (NFS)**. You can also share data with a Windows client by using the Samba service described in Chapter 14. In this section, you learn how to use NFS to share files on your Linux server.

Novell OES has NFS configured and ready to go. All you have to do is use YaST to start the service and add the directories you want shared on the network. To use YaST to enable NFS, use the following steps:

1. Start YaST and, if necessary, enter your root user password.

2. Click Network Services in the left pane to display the menu options. You can select NFS Client or NFS Server options. The NFS Server option is used to share directories, and the NFS Client option is used to mount remote directories.

3. To share a directory, click the NFS Server option in the right pane to open the Configuration of the NFS server dialog box.

4. Click the Start NFS server option button, and then click Next to display the Directories to export to the others dialog box (see Figure 13-30).

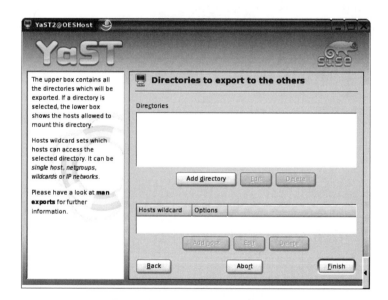

Figure 13-30   The Directories to export to the others dialog box

5. Click the Add directory Button and then use the Browse button to navigate to the EngData directory and then to the directory you want to share.

13

6. Click the directory to be shared, and then click OK to open the Hosts wildcard option dialog box, where you can change the wildcard symbol used when searching for files. In most cases, leave the default of the "*" character, and click OK to add the directory to the Directories to export to the others dialog box.

7. Click Finish to share the directory and return to the YaST Network Services menu.

Activity 13-10: Using NFS to Share a Directory

Time Required: 10 minutes

Objective: Use NFS to share and mount remote directories.

Requirements: Completion of Activities 13-1 and 13-9 and a partner to test your NFS shared directory

Description: To allow users in the Engineering and Manufacturing departments to access the Linux server directories from their Linux systems, Eric wants you to share them by using NFS. In this activity, you share your EngWeb directory structure and then try to mount another student's shared directory.

1. If necessary, log in to your SUSE Linux server with your user name and password.

2. Start YaST and, if necessary, enter your root user password.

3. Click the **Network Services** icon in the left pane, and then scroll down and click the **NFS Server** option in the right pane.

4. If necessary, click the **Start NFS server** option button, and then click **Next** to open the Directories to export to the others dialog box.

5. Click the **Add directory** button, and then click the **browse** button, click to select your **EngWeb** directory, and click **OK**.

6. Click **Finish** to save your changes and return to the Network Services window.

7. Follow these steps to mount your partner's NFS directory after he or she has finished Step 6:

   a. If necessary, start YaST and open the Network Services menu.

   b. Click the **NFS Client** option in the right pane to open the Configuration of the NFS client dialog box (see Figure 13-31).

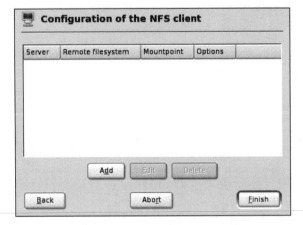

Figure 13-31   The Configuration of the NFS client dialog box

   c. Click the **Add** button to open the dialog box shown in Figure 13-32.

   d. Enter the IP address of your partner's server in the Host name of the NFS server text box, select the remote file system and mount point, and click **OK** to mount the remote file system.

8. Close all applications, log out, and leave your system running for the end-of-chapter projects.

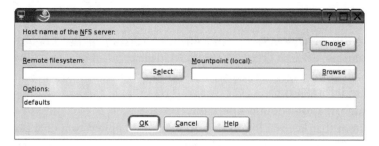

Figure 13-32   Entering information for the remote file system

Chapter Summary

- Linux is a multiuser operating system that requires users to have a valid user name and password to access the system. Groups are used to grant rights to users and can be defined as system or local. Local groups are used to give users rights to data and applications; system groups are used to grant users rights to the operating system.

- The root user account has full control of the system and is a member of the root system group. Other users can be superusers by making them a member of the root group.

- The shell gives users a command-line environment for starting programs. Common shells include the Bash, Korn, and C shells. Users are given a default shell when their user account is created.

- User and group accounts can be created and managed in the YaST utility or with the useradd and groupadd commands.

- The man and info commands are used to retrieve help information on Linux commands. You can also get online help from a number of Web sites.

- Run levels are used to set a user's default environment when he or she logs in. Run level 5 provides a multiuser, networked graphical environment, and run level 3 is used for text-based operations.

- RedHat Package Manager (RPM) is used to install and manage Linux applications from a compressed file. With RPM, you can determine software dependencies, install and test software, and perform automatic software updates.

- Linux supports a number of file systems, including ext2, ext3, and ReiserFS. ReiserFS offers the best performance for handling large numbers of small files and is the default file system in SUSE Linux.

- Disk partitions are the physical areas of the hard drive that are formatted to store data. Disk partitions are given names based on their disk drive and partition number.

- With logical volume management, disk partitions can be grouped into volume groups used to create logical volumes. Logical volumes are then mounted and used by the operating system.

- Volumes and other storage devices need to be mounted in the file system before they can be used. Logical volumes are mounted in the root partition of the file system, which is specified by a forward slash (/).

- The Linux file system has a simple security system that assigns rights to the file owner, associated group, and others. Rights include read, write, and execute. The read right is assigned a value of 4, the write right has a value of 2, and the execute right has a value of 1. These values are added to produce an octal digit representing the rights assignment.

- Linux directories can be shared with other Linux or UNIX systems by using NFS and with Windows systems by using Samba. NFS is a native Linux service that exports directories to the network. These exported directories can then be mounted in a remote computer's file system and accessed based on user rights.

KEY TERMS

Enterprise Volume Management System (EVMS) — An enhanced version of the Logical Volume Manager that supports Novell NSS volumes. *See also* Logical Volume Manager.

info pages — Command-line documentation pages viewed with the info command. Info pages are newer than man pages and often contain more information.

inode — An index entry containing information about a Linux file.

journaling file systems — A file system that keeps a log of data transactions applied to a disk partition.

local groups — Group accounts created by a Linux administrator and used to assign rights and permissions to users.

Logical Volume Manager (LVM) — A volume management system used to group physical hard drive partitions into volume groups for the purpose of creating logical volumes.

man pages — Command-line documentation pages viewed with the man command.

Network File System (NFS) — A Linux file system server that allows exporting files and directories to the network for remote access.

RedHat Package Manager (RPM) — A software installation file format used by the rpm command to install and manage software.

shell — A Linux command-line environment used to enter commands and start programs.

system groups — Group accounts that the Linux operating system creates to grant rights for accessing certain system resources.

Virtual Filesystem Switch (VFS) — An operating system interfacing system that sends user requests from a process to the actual disk file system.

X-Window — The interface used to provide graphical support that other software packages, such as the KDE and Gnome desktops, draw on.

REVIEW QUESTIONS

1. Which of the following system groups can be used to create a backup system administrator?
   a. admin
   b. root
   c. domain admin
   d. manager

2. The root user is assigned a user ID of _____ .
   a. 0
   b. 1
   c. 100
   d. 10

3. Which of the following is the default shell in SUSE Linux?
   a. Bourne
   b. Bourne Again (Bash)
   c. Korn
   d. C

4. Which of the following files does SUSE Linux use to store encrypted passwords?
   a. passwd
   b. system
   c. shadow
   d. password

5. Which command lists all users logged in to the system?

   a. who

   b. users

   c. stat

   d. su

6. Which of the following often provides a more current version of command documentation?

   a. man pages

   b. info pages

   c. root pages

   d. system pages

7. Run level _____ includes the X-Window graphical interface and support for network environments.

   a. 3

   b. 1

   c. 10

   d. 5

8. Which of the following RPM options indicates that the package doesn't contain binary code?

   a. i586

   b. noarch

   c. src

   d. bin

   e. nosrc

9. Which of the following is a journaling file system? (Choose all that apply.)

   a. FAT32

   b. NTFS

   c. ext2

   d. ext3

   e. ReiserFS

10. Which of the following file systems makes data available on the network?

    a. ext2

    b. ReiserFS

    c. NFS

    d. LVM

11. The first partition on the second SCSI drive would be named

    _____ .

    a. sda2

    b. sdb1

    c. db21

    d. db12

12. Which of the following is required to support Novell Storage Services?

    a. LVM

    b. EVMS

    c. ReiserFS

    d. ext2

13. Which file contains drive-mounting information?

    a. fileconfig

    b. mount

    c. system

    d. fstab

14. You need to dismount a partition before resizing it. True or False?

15. Which command is used to switch to the root user?

    a. admin

    b. root

    c. su

    d. grep

16. Which of the following works with the ReiserFS file system?

    a. LVM

    b. EVMS

    c. NSS

    d. LVM2

17. Which of the following commands gives all rights to the owner, read and write rights to the assigned group, and the read right to all other users for the EngData directory?

    a. chmod 764 EngData

    b. chmod 755 EngData

    c. chmod 975 EngData

    d. chmod 531 EngData

18. Which of the following is used to share directories with other Linux systems?

    a. Samba

    b. NFS

    c. NIS

    d. Share

19. The Linux command-line interface is also referred to as which of the following?

    a. system interface

    b. shell

    c. GUI

    d. terminal

20. Which of the following is used to install and manage Linux applications from a compressed file?

    a. YaST

    b. Samba

    c. RPM

    d. EVMS

CASE PROJECTS

Case Project 13-1: Comparing Volume Managers

Eric wants you to compare the LVM system to Novell Storage Services and explain their similarities and differences. Write a short paper comparing the components of LVM and NSS.

Case Project 13-2: Comparing File System Rights

Eric wants you to compare file system rights in Linux and NetWare. Write a short memo to Eric outlining the similarities and differences.

Case Project 13-3: Comparing Linux and NetWare Rights

Table 13-13 lists the NetWare rights for performing certain file system tasks. In the next two columns, enter the Linux permissions needed to carry out the operation and the octal value used to make the assignment.

Table 13-13   Rights required for common functions

Task	NetWare Rights Required	Linux Permissions	Octal Value
Read a file	Read		
View a directory listing	File Scan		
Change the contents of data in a file	Write		
Write to a closed file using a text editor that creates a backup file	Write, Create, Erase, Modify (not always required)		
Run a program file	Read		
Create and write to a new file	Create		
Copy a file from a directory	Read, File Scan		
Copy a file into a directory	Create		
Copy multiple files to a directory with existing files	Create, File Scan		
Create a subdirectory	Create		
Delete a file	Erase		

13

HANDS-ON PROJECTS

Hands-on Project 13-1: Creating Local Linux Users and Groups

You're adding the Business Division of Universal AeroSpace to your SUSE Linux server. Using the techniques you learned in this chapter, set up the following local groups and user accounts:

Managers group: Lynn Dai, David Heise

Accountants group: Terry Blackwell, George Perez, Amy Pan

Desktop Publishers group: Diana Brady, Julie Damrau

Hands-on Project 13-2: Creating and Mounting an LVM Directory Structure

Use the LVM option in YaST to create a logical volume named userdata that's mounted in the /usr structure. Have your instructor check your results.

PLANNING AND IMPLEMENTING NOVELL OES ON LINUX

After reading this chapter and completing the activities, you will be able to:

♦ Identify the Novell services included with SUSE Linux

♦ Create eDirectory objects and enable eDirectory users to access Linux services

♦ Use NetWare Core Protocol to enable access to Linux directories from Windows systems

♦ Create NSS volumes on a Linux server and enable access from Windows clients via Samba

♦ Describe the steps in setting up iPrint on a Linux server

In Chapters 12 and 13, you learned how to install a SUSE Linux server and work with the standard Linux environment. With Open Enterprise Server (OES), Novell has expanded the Linux operating system so that it can offer the Novell services you have become familiar with throughout this book, including support for eDirectory, NetWare Core Protocol (NCP), Novell Storage Services (NSS) storage volumes, iPrint, iFolder, and NetStorage. Running Novell services opens a world of possibilities for network administrators. Using Novell OES, an organization can take advantage of Linux-based services and applications yet still ensure that users have the convenience, security, and functionality of the NetWare environment. In this chapter, you learn how to set up Novell services on your SUSE Linux server and access it in much the same way as a NetWare 6.5 server.

Overview of Novell Services in SUSE Linux

When you install a SUSE Linux server with the default configuration described in Chapter 12, many Novell services are included automatically. The major Novell services that aren't installed include NSS, iFolder, and Novell Cluster Services. These services can be installed later in YaST, which can also be used to remove or reinstall Novell services. The following sections cover the Novell services in the order they appear under the YaST menu headings.

Services in the System Menu

In Chapter 12, you learned how to use the YaST Expert Partitioner and Logical Volume Manager (LVM) utilities to work with Linux partitions and volumes. In addition to Linux services, the YaST System menu contains the following Novell services:

- *Novell Cluster Services (NCS)*—With NCS, you can have multiple Linux servers providing access to network resources and services, such as disk partitions. Using NCS also improves performance and fault tolerance. For example, with two Linux servers providing access to a disk partition via NCS, data is available even if one server goes down.

- *Novell Storage Services (NSS)*—Installing NSS (explained in Chapter 3) on SUSE Linux servers enables network administrators to take advantage of Novell file system security and the speed and reliability of NSS disk volumes. Later in this chapter, you use this option to install and set up NSS volumes on your SUSE Linux server.

- *Storage Management Services (SMS)*—SMS provides backup capability for NSS volumes and can be used on SUSE Linux volumes.

Services in the Network Services Menu

The YaST utility has the following options for setting up and configuring network services:

- *eDirectory*—In Chapter 12, you installed the eDirectory service on the SUSE Linux system as part of the default OES installation. eDirectory provides authentication services for a number of platforms, including NetWare, Linux, and Windows. This option is used only if you uninstall eDirectory and need to reinstall it.

- *eGuide*—The eGuide service, installed as part of the default OES installation, is used to find and access user information in eDirectory. You can use this option to reinstall eGuide, if necessary.

- *iManager*—This utility is the primary management tool for administrative tasks in a Novell network. The iManager option is used only to reinstall the iManager utility.

- *iFolder*—The iFolder service, covered in Chapter 10, enables users to synchronize data with the NetWare server and can also be used on a SUSE Linux server. To allow additional volume configuration options, iFolder isn't installed during a default OES installation. For more information on using iFolder in SUSE Linux, see Appendix B.

- *iPrint*—The essential iPrint components (explained in Chapter 8) are installed on the SUSE Linux server as a part of the default OES installation, and you learn how to set up and configure iPrint on your SUSE Linux server later in this chapter.

- *Novell Samba*—With the Samba service, users working from the Windows client can access Linux files and directories by using the Common Interface File System (CIFS) protocol.

- *NCP Server*—NetWare Core Protocol (NCP) Server is enabled by default and provides access to the SUSE Linux server from Novell Client. NCP Server allows computers running Novell Client to access the Linux server as in a standard NetWare 6.5 server environment.

- *NetStorage*—This service, described in Chapter 10, enables users to access data and directories on NetWare volumes via a Web browser. NetStorage is included in a default OES installation to allow users to access data from Linux partitions via a Web browser.

Services in the Security and Users Menu

In Chapter 13, you used options in the Security and Users menu to create and manage users and groups. In this chapter, you learn how to use Linux User Management (LUM), which is also in the Security and Users menu, to synchronize eDirectory users with local Linux users stored in the etc/passwd file. In the following activity, you use YaST to find Novell service icons.

Activity 14-1: Exploring Novell Services in YaST

Time Required: 10 minutes

Objective: Use the YaST utility to find and view Novell services.

Requirements: Access to the root password for your SUSE Linux system

Description: Eric wants you to document all the Novell services available in the YaST utility. In this activity, you prepare a list of services in each YaST menu.

1. If necessary, log in to your SUSE Linux server with the user name you created for yourself during Activity 12-1.

2. Start the YaST utility and enter the password for your root user.

3. Record the Novell service options in the System menu. You can write more than one option per line:

   _____

   _____

   _____

4. Record the Novell service options in the Network Services menu. You can write more than one option per line:

   _____

   _____

   _____

   _____

   _____

5. Record any additional Novell services and their location in the YaST menu. You can write more than one option per line:

   _____

   _____

   _____

6. Exit the YaST utility, and leave your system running for the next activity.

eDIRECTORY SERVICES IN SUSE LINUX

Directory services play a critical role in authenticating users to the network and in finding and accessing network resources. eDirectory is a key component of Novell OES and is used by both NetWare and Linux for creating and managing eDirectory objects and configuring and managing OES components. As you learned in Chapter 12, during SUSE Linux installation, you also install eDirectory and place the server in an existing tree or create a new tree. You can then use iManager to create user and group accounts in much the same way as with a NetWare server. Novell services require users to have an eDirectory user account, but native Linux services use **Portable Operating System Interface (POSIX)** user accounts stored in the /etc/passwd file. Novell has developed a technology that enables eDirectory users to function as POSIX users on Linux servers: **Linux User Management (LUM)**. In the following sections, you learn how to use LUM to enable your eDirectory users to access Linux services.

14

Working with Linux User Management (LUM) Services

Users who access a Linux service can be defined as local or remote. Information on local users is stored in the /etc/passwd file, and data for remote user accounts is stored on computers outside the local system. With LUM, user accounts stored in eDirectory are allowed to access the SUSE Linux server through a process that enables them to function in the same manner as local POSIX users. To do this, eDirectory user accounts need to be enabled for LUM. Figure 14-1 shows how LUM controls access to the Linux server.

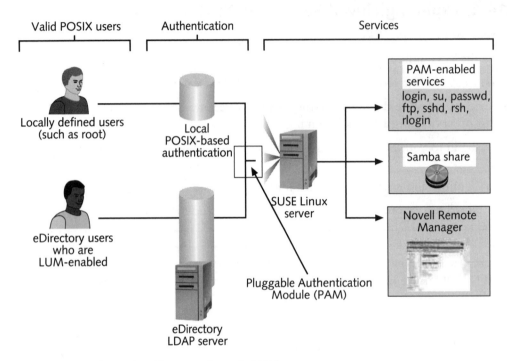

Figure 14-1   Accessing Linux services via LUM

As shown in the figure, the Linux server can authenticate login requests from local POSIX users (with accounts stored in the /etc/passwd file) or from an LDAP-compatible service (accounts stored in eDirectory). SUSE Linux uses LDAP to authenticate remote user login requests. LDAP login requests from eDirectory are processed by the **Pluggable Authentication Module (PAM)** architecture, which makes it possible for eDirectory users to authenticate with a SUSE Linux server.

The terms "LUM enabled" and "Linux enabled" describe the process of adding standard Linux attributes and values to eDirectory users and groups, thereby enabling them to function in the same way as POSIX users. Not all eDirectory users need to be Linux enabled to access the Linux server, however. For those using Novell Client, the NCP server handles access to the Linux server. Because of the NCP server's tight integration with eDirectory, users don't need to be Linux enabled as long as they're accessing data stored on NSS volumes. However, Novell Client users who need to access data on standard Linux volumes and partitions do need to be Linux enabled.

Three major types of Linux services and utilities require Linux-enabled access:

- *Core Linux utilities*—Core utilities and other shell commands that are specified for PAM-enabled access through LDAP, as shown in Table 14-1.

- *Novell Samba shares*—Windows workgroup users who need to access Linux directories must have Linux-enabled eDirectory user accounts because the Samba service requires POSIX authentication for access to network data.

- *Novell Remote Manager (NRM) on Linux*—Administrators can use the NRM utility to monitor and manage multiple Linux servers, but to do so, they must authenticate as one of these user types: the root user with all rights to the Linux server, a local user with access governed by POSIX access rights, or a Linux-enabled eDirectory user, such as Admin.

Table 14-1   PAM-enabled services controlled by LUM

Command	Task
ftp	Transfer files to and from the SUSE Linux server
login	Log in to the SUSE Linux server directly or through a remote session
passwd	Change the POSIX password
rlogin	Log in to the SUSE Linux server from a remote host
sshd	Establish a secure encrypted connection with the SUSE Linux server from a remote host

Creating Linux-Enabled User and Group Accounts

Users can be Linux enabled by being made a member of a Linux-enabled group. By default, the Admin user who installs the SUSE Linux server in the eDirectory tree is automatically Linux enabled by being made a member of admingroup. To enable other users, you use iManager or the nambulkadd command. Although this command can be useful when you need to enable several users and groups from a batch file, using iManager is usually easier and is the method you use in this chapter.

When you Linux-enable groups, you select the SUSE Linux servers that users in the group will be accessing. eDirectory objects for SUSE Linux servers have the name UNIX Workstation - *servername* (*servername* represents the DNS name of the Linux server) and are referred to as **Linux Workstation objects**. You can also select the **Linux Config object**, which stores a list of all SUSE Linux servers in the eDirectory tree. This object is a quick way to Linux-enable group members on all SUSE Linux servers at once. To Linux-enable a group, you can use these steps:

1. Log in to a local computer or your SUSE Linux server and start your Web browser.

2. Start iManager and log in with your eDirectory administrative user name and password.

3. Click to expand the Linux User Management heading and then click the Enable Group for LUM link.

4. Click the Object Selector button next to the Select a group to enable for LUM text box, click the group you want to Linux enable, and then click OK to display the Enable Group for LUM window (similar to the one in Figure 14-2).

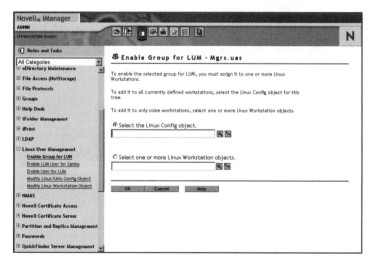

Figure 14-2   Configuring a Linux-enabled group

14

5. To enable group members to access all Linux servers, click the Object Selector button next to the Select the Linux Config object text box, and click the UNIX Config object. To Linux enable group members for selected SUSE Linux servers, click the Select one or more Linux Workstation objects option button, click the Object Selector button, and select only the Linux Workstation objects you want group members to access.

6. Click OK to enable the group and display the success message. Click OK again to return to the iManager main window.

In the following activity, you create a Linux-enabled group on your SUSE Linux server, create users, and then make one user a member of the Linux-enabled group.

Activity 14-2: Creating Linux-Enabled Groups and Users

Time Required: 10 minutes

Objectives: Use iManager to create Linux-enabled users and groups.

Requirements: Access to the SUSE Linux server with an administrative account and a Windows XP or SUSE Linux 10 computer; you can also perform this activity from the OES Linux Enterprise Server 9 console. If using Linux, use the Java-enabled Firefox or Mozilla Web browser.

Description: To test the SUSE Linux server, Eric wants you to create an eDirectory structure for the AeroDyn Division that contains a Users OU with two test users. In this activity, you use iManager to create a Users OU in the AeroDyn Division, and then create a Linux-enabled group and users so that Eric can test the server.

1. If necessary, start your Linux server and log in with the root user name and password. If you're working in Windows XP, log on to your Windows XP computer with your local user name and password.

2. Start your Web browser and start iManager by entering the URL ***https://IPaddress/nps/iManager.html*** (replacing *IPaddress* with the IP address of your SUSE Linux server).

3. Log in to iManager with your administrative user name and password.

4. Follow these steps to create a Users OU:
   a. Click to expand the eDirectory Administration heading, and then click the **Create Object** link.
   b. Scroll down and click the **Organizational Unit** object class, and then click **OK** to display the Create Organizational Unit window.
   c. Type **Users** in the Organizational Unit name text box.
   d. Click the **Object Selector** button next to the Context text box, and click your **UAS** container.
   e. Click **OK** to create the Users OU and display the completion message.
   f. Click **OK** to return the iManager main window.

5. Follow these steps to create a group and make it Linux enabled:
   a. Click the **Create Object** link to display the Create Object window.
   b. Click the **Group** object class, and then click **OK** to display the Create Group window.
   c. Type **LinuxUsers** in the Group name text box, click the **Object Selector** button next to the Context text box, and click the **Users** OU.

   d. Click **OK** to create the LinuxUsers group and display the completion message.

   e. Click **OK** to display the Enable Group for LUM window.

   f. Click the **Object Selector** button next to the Select the Linux Config object text box, and then click the **UNIX Config** object.

   g. Click **OK** to display the completion message, and then click **OK** again to return the iManager main window.

6. Follow these steps to create a user account named LUMUser:

   a. Scroll down, click to expand the **Users** heading if necessary, and then click the **Create User** link.

   b. Enter **LUMUser** in the Username text box and **LinuxUser** in the Last name text box.

   c. Click the **Object Selector** button next to the Context text box, click the **Users** OU, and then click **OK**.

   d. Enter a password in the Password and Retype Password text boxes.

   e. Click **OK** to create the LUMUser account, and then click **OK** again to return the iManager main window.

7. Follow these steps to Linux enable the LUMUser account:

   a. Under the eDirectory Administration heading, click the **Modify Object** link.

   b. Click the **Object Selector** button next to the Object name text box, navigate to the **Users** OU, and click the **LinuxUsers** group.

   c. Click **OK** to display the Modify Object: LinuxUsers.Users.UAS group window, and click the **Members** tab.

   d. Click the **Object Selector** button next to the Members text box, and then click the **LUMUser** account.

   e. Click **OK** to return the Members window, and then click **OK** again to save your changes and return to the iManager main window.

8. Follow the procedure in Step 6 to create a user account named **RegUser** but don't make it Linux-enabled.

9. Exit iManager, and log out.

NETWARE CORE PROTOCOL (NCP) SERVICES IN SUSE LINUX

As shown in Figure 14-3, the NCP service enables the SUSE Linux server to process requests from Novell clients. Windows computers running Novell Client can log in to the Linux server and access NSS volumes and NCP-enabled directories as though they were on a NetWare server. The default OES installation creates an NCP-enabled directory named sys in the /usr/novell directory that acts like the SYS volume on a NetWare server. This NCP-enabled sys directory contains Login and Public subdirectories to hold files that are available to all users. When a user logs in from Novell Client, the F: drive is mapped to the NCP-enabled sys directory, and the Z: drive is mapped to the Public subdirectory.

The NCP service and its directory shares are managed in the Novell Remote Manager utility. Figure 14-4 shows an example of the Manage Shares options in this utility. In the following activity, you create a Linux directory and then use Novell Remote Manager to share the directory as an NCP volume.

14

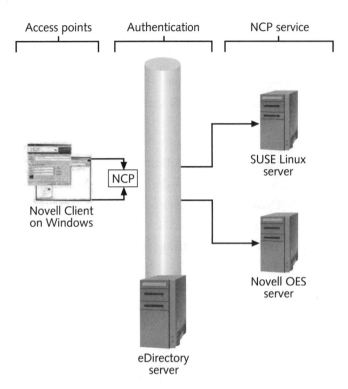

Figure 14-3   Using the NCP service in SUSE Linux

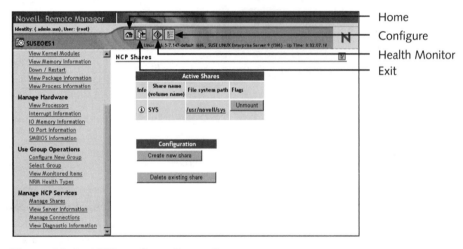

Figure 14-4   NCP configuration options

Activity 14-3: Creating an NCP-Enabled Directory

Time Required: 10 minutes

Objective: Use Novell Remote Manager to configure NCP services.

Requirements: Access to the SUSE Linux server with your administrative account, completion of Activity 14-2, and a Windows XP computer with Novell Client installed

Description: To complete the test environment Eric asked you to create, in this activity you use Novell Remote Manager to view NCP options and then create a Linux directory and share it as an NCP volume.

1. If necessary, start your Windows XP computer and log in to eDirectory with the **RegUser** account you created in Activity 14-2.

2. Open My Computer and record the network drive letters and their associated paths:

_____

_____

3. Open the **SYS** volume and record the directories:

_____

_____

4. Log off your Windows XP computer.

5. If necessary, log in to your SUSE Linux server with the root user name and password.

6. Follow these steps to create a directory named NCPTest on your SUSE Linux server:

   a. Open a terminal session.

   b. Type the following commands, pressing **Enter** after each one:

   ```
   cd /
   mkdir NCPTest
   ```

   c. Type **exit** and press **Enter** to end your terminal session.

7. From your SUSE Linux server, start a Java-enabled browser, and start Novell Remote Manager by entering **https://IPaddress:8009** (replacing *IPaddress* with the IP address of your SUSE Linux server).

8. Log in to Novell Remote Manager with your administrative user name and password.

9. To view NCP server information, under the Manage NCP Services heading, click the **View Server Information** link. Record the following information:

Server name: _____

NCP requests: _____

Open files: _____

10. Follow these steps to make the NCPTest directory an NCP share:

   a. Under the Manage NCP Services heading, click the **Manage Shares** link.

   b. Scroll down and click the **Create new share** button.

   c. Enter **NCPData** in the Share Name text box, and click **OK** to display the Path text box.

   d. Enter **/NCPTest** in the Path text box, and click **OK** to display the summary window.

   e. Click **OK** again to confirm the settings and return to the Novell Remote Manager main window.

11. Exit Novell Remote Manager.

12. Start iManager by entering the URL **https://IPaddress/nps/iManager.html** (replacing *IPaddress* with the IP address of your SUSE Linux server).

13. Log in to iManager with your eDirectory user name and password.

14. Follow these steps to create a login script for the Users OU that maps the N: drive to the NCPTest directory:

   a. Under the eDirectory Administration heading, click the **Modify Object** link.

   b. Click the **Object Selector** button next to the Object name text box, click the **Users** OU, and then click **OK** to display the Modify Object: Users.UAS window.

   c. Click the **Login Script** link.

   d. Enter the **MAP ROOT N:=NCPTest:** login script command.

   e. Click **OK** to save your changes and return to the iManager main window.

15. Exit iManager.

NOTE

The following steps require using a Windows XP computer.

16. If necessary, start your Windows XP computer and log in to eDirectory with your administrative user name and password.

17. Follow these steps in Windows Explorer to make the Users OU a trustee of the NCPTest directory with all rights except Supervisor and Access Control:

   a. Open My Network Places, and double-click the **Novell Connections** option.

   b. Double-click your SUSE Linux server to display all the NCP volumes.

   c. Right-click the **NCPTest** volume and click **Trustee Rights** to display the NetWare Services dialog box.

   d. Click the **Users** OU, and then click **Add** to add the Users OU to the Trustees list box.

   e. Click to select all the rights check boxes except the A check box.

   f. Click **OK** to save your trustee assignment.

18. Close all windows, and log off your Windows XP computer.

Activity 14-4: Testing NCP Access

Time Required: 10 minutes

Objective: Use NCP to access network files through a drive mapping.

Requirements: Completion of Activity 14-3

Description: In this activity, you complete the test environment Eric asked you to create by logging in as the test user and then verifying drive mappings.

1. If necessary, start your Windows XP computer, and log in to eDirectory with the **RegUser** account you created in Activity 14-2.

2. Use My Computer to check your drive mappings. Record the drive mappings here:

   _____

   _____

   _____

3. Start Notepad and create a simple text file containing your name and a short message.

4. Save the file as **message.txt** on your N: drive.

5. Log out.

6. Log in to eDirectory with your **LUMUser** name and password.

7. Use My Computer to check your drive mappings. Do you have an N: drive?

   _____

8. If you have a N: drive, open the **message.txt** file and make a change.

9. Save the file, exit Notepad, and then log out.

10. Log in to your SUSE Linux server with the root user name and password, and open a terminal session.

11. Use the following commands (pressing **Enter** after each command) to change to your NCPTest directory and view its contents:

```
cd /NCPTest
ls -l
cat message.txt
```

12. Record your results:

   _____

13. Close your terminal session and log out. Leave your system running for the next activity.

Storage Services in SUSE Linux

In addition to creating NCP shares, Novell offers other services to make data on Linux servers available to users. In this section, you learn how to use NSS volumes, NetStorage, and Samba to make Linux data available to users, no matter what client or network they are using.

Creating and Using NSS Volumes

The NSS file system offers several advantages over creating NCP shares from standard Linux partitions, including the following:

- The capability to mount the volume on a NetWare or Linux server
- Use of Novell access rights and attributes
- Compatibility with NCP applications

In this section, you learn how to install NSS on your SUSE Linux server and then create and access NSS volumes.

Installing NSS Services

Before using NSS volumes, in the following activity you use YaST to install NSS services on your SUSE Linux server. After NSS is installed, you can use it create NSS volumes that can be accessed with NCP, NetStorage, or iFolder.

Activity 14-5: Installing NSS

Time Required: 15 minutes

Objective: Use YaST to install NSS services.

Requirements: Access to the root user name and password and the Linux CD 2

Description: Eric thinks that using the NSS file system on the SUSE Linux server will be a good way to set up network files. In this activity, you use YaST to install the NSS service.

1. Log in to your SUSE Linux server with the root user name and password.
2. Start the YaST utility.
3. In the left pane, click the **System** icon, and in the right pane, click the **NSS** option.
4. After initializing the NSS configuration, click **Continue** to copy and install the RPM files. (This process takes several minutes, depending on your computer speed.)
5. When requested, insert the Linux CD 2, and click **OK** to display the Novell Storage Services LDAP Server Configuration window (see Figure 14-5).
6. Click the **Port Details** button and record the LDAP ports:

   _____

   _____

7. Enter your administrative password, and click **Next** to display the NSS Unique Admin Object window. Record the Admin object for your server:

   _____

8. Click **Next** to write your configuration settings and return to the YaST System menu.
9. Exit YaST, and leave your system running for the next activity.

Creating NSS Logical Volumes

As you learned in Chapter 13, NSS volumes require the Enterprise Volume Management System (EVMS) to manage the hard drive containing NSS components; traditional Linux volumes use the Logical Volume

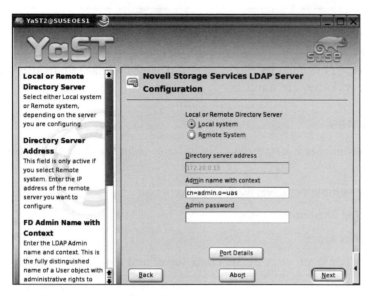

Figure 14-5   Installing NSS services

Manager (LVM). Because only one volume manager can control a hard drive, to use NSS you need a second hard drive on your SUSE Linux server.

NSS volumes on Linux consist of logical pools containing one or more disk partitions. NSS components on Linux servers are managed in iManager rather than Remote Manager, as on NetWare servers. With iManager, you can create NSS partitions, pools, and volumes. Figure 14-6 shows an example of using iManager to create an NSS partition in the Linux file system.

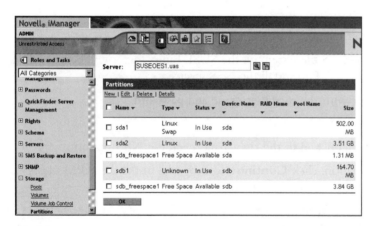

Figure 14-6   Using iManager to manage Linux partitions

Figure 14-6 shows the existing Linux drive and partition information with the partition-naming system you worked with in Chapters 12 and 13. Figure 14-7 shows an example of using iManager to create a storage pool on a SUSE Linux server. These options are much the same as the ones you learned about in Chapter 3. As in NetWare, when you create a NSS storage pool, an NSS partition can be created at the same time. In the following activity, you create NSS pools and volumes on a separate hard drive controlled by EVMS.

Activity 14-6: Creating NSS Components

Time Required: 15 minutes

Objective: Use iManager to create NSS components.

Requirements: A Windows XP or SUSE Linux 10 computer, completion of Activity 14-5, and a second hard drive on your Linux server. You can also perform this activity from the OES Linux Enterprise Server 9 console. If using Linux, use the Java-enabled Firefox or Mozilla Web browser.

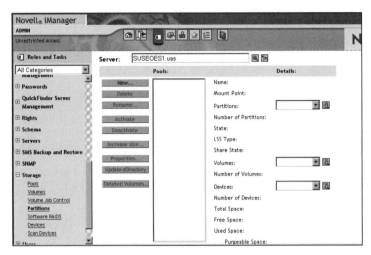

Figure 14-7   Using iManager to create an NSS pool

NOTE

If you're using VMware, you can add a second virtual hard drive by following the instructions in Appendix C.

Description: To further test the NSS file system on Linux, Eric has asked you to create a storage pool and volume for storing AeroDyn Division data. In this activity, you learn how to use iManager to create NSS components.

14

1. Log on to your Windows XP computer with your local administrator user name and password or log in to your SUSE Linux server with the root user name and password.

2. Start your Web browser, and then start iManager.

3. Log in to iManager with your administrative user name and password.

4. Expand the **Storage** heading and click the **Partitions** link.

5. Follow these steps to create an NSS partition:

    a. Click the **Object Selector** button next to the Server text box, and click your SUSE Linux server.

    b. In the Partitions section, click the check box next to an available area of free disk space, and click the **New** link at the top. When the message informing you that NSS creates partitions when you create a pool is displayed, click **OK** to display the Enter a name window.

    c. Enter **AEROPOOL** in the Name text box and click **Next** to display the Select device and space window (see Figure 14-8).

    d. Click to select the check box for your drive.

    e. Enter **500** in the Used Size (MB) text box, and then click **Finish** to create the pool and display the Pools window shown previously in Figure 14-7.

6. Follow these steps to create an NSS volume:

    a. Click the **Volumes** link under the Storage heading to display the Volumes window, similar to the one in Figure 14-9.

    b. Click the **New** button to display the Enter a name window.

    c. Enter **AEROVOL** and click **Next** to display the Select a pool and volume quota window shown in Figure 14-10.

    d. Click to select the **AEROPOOL** check box, and then click **Next** to display the volume attributes window (see Figure 14-11).

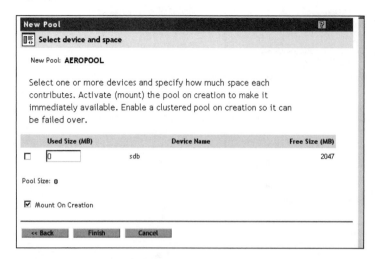

Figure 14-8 Selecting a device and the amount of space for an NSS pool

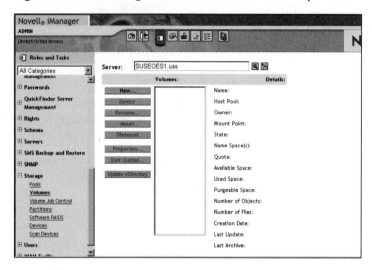

Figure 14-9 Using iManager to create an NSS volume

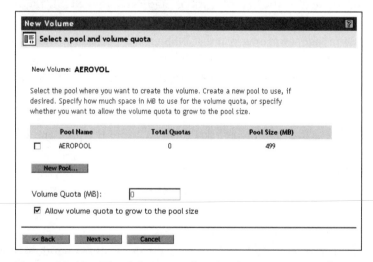

Figure 14-10 The Select a pool and volume quota window

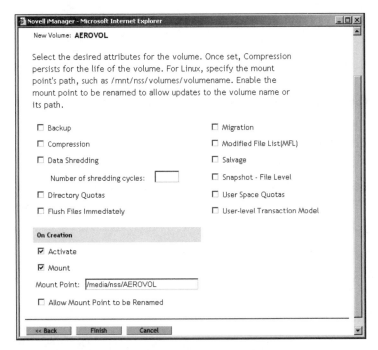

Figure 14-11 The volume attributes window

14

e. Click to select the **Directory Quotas**, **Salvage**, and **User Space Quotas** options, and record the mount point information:

f. Click **Finish** to create the volume and return to the Volumes window.

g. Click the **Mount** button to mount the AEROVOL volume.

7. Exit iManager, and leave your system running for the next activity.

Activity 14-7: Working with NSS Volumes

Time Required: 15 minutes

Objective: Map a drive to Linux NSS volumes and make trustee assignments.

Requirements: Completion of Activity 14-6 and a second hard drive on your Linux server

Description: To further test the NSS file system on Linux, Eric wants you to map a drive to the new AEROVOL volume and create an ISS directory that all users in the AeroDyn Users OU can access. In this activity, you create an ISS directory, grant rights to the AeroDyn Users OU, and create a login script.

1. From your Windows XP computer, log in to eDirectory with your administrative user name and password.

2. Open a command prompt window. Type the following commands, pressing **Enter** after each one, to map a drive to your AEROVOL volume and create an ISS directory:

```
F:
MAP G:=AEROVOL:
G:
md ISS
```

3. Type **exit** and press **Enter** to close the command prompt window.

4. In My Computer, double-click the **G:** drive. Right-click the **ISS** directory, and click **Trustee Rights**.

5. Click the **Users** OU, and then click **Add** to add the Users OU with Read and File Scan rights.

6. Click to select all rights except Supervisor and Access Control.

7. Click **OK** to save your changes.

8. Start iManager, and follow these steps to create a login script for the Users OU that maps a drive to the ISS directory:

   a. Click to expand the **eDirectory Administration** heading, and click the **Modify Object** link.

   b. Click the **Object Selector** button, and click the **Users** OU.

   c. Click **OK** to display the Modify Object window.

   d. Click the **Login Script** tab and enter the **MAP ROOT G:=AEROVOL:ISS** command.

   e. Click **OK** to save your changes, and exit iManager.

9. Log out, and then log back in to eDirectory with a user account you created in the Users OU.

10. Open My Computer and record your drive mappings:

    _____

    _____

11. Close any open windows, and log out.

Working with the Samba Service

Samba is open-source software that enables Microsoft clients to use CIFS to access data on Linux servers. Figure 14-12 shows using Samba on the SUSE Linux server. Notice that the Windows user account must exist in eDirectory and be Linux enabled. When the user attempts to access the Linux server using CIFS, the Samba service processes the request and uses eDirectory to authenticate the user's name and password. The user can then access Linux files and directories.

Before using Samba, you need to enable universal passwords in iManager as a password management option on your SUSE Linux server and create home directories for user accounts. In addition, the eDirectory accounts that will be accessing Linux files need to be enabled for Samba access. In the following activity, you learn how to use iManager to enable universal passwords and enable user accounts for Samba access.

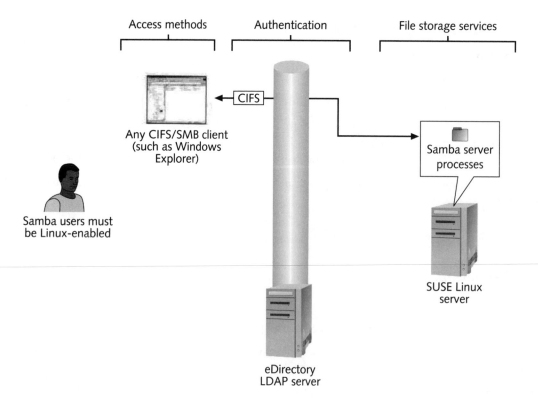

Figure 14-12   Using the Samba service in Linux

Activity 14-8: Enabling Universal Passwords and Samba Access

Time Required: 10 minutes

Objective: Use iManager to enable universal passwords.

Requirements: A Windows XP computer

Description: Several employees in the AeroDyn Division will be using Windows XP without Novell Client to access data on the SUSE Linux server. Eric wants you to test how this works by using Samba. In this activity, you prepare for this task by enabling universal passwords and enabling user accounts for Samba access.

1. Log on to your Windows XP computer.

2. Start your Web browser, start iManager, and log in to iManager with your administrative user name and password.

3. Expand the **Passwords** heading and click the **Password Policies** link to display the existing password policies (see Figure 14-13).

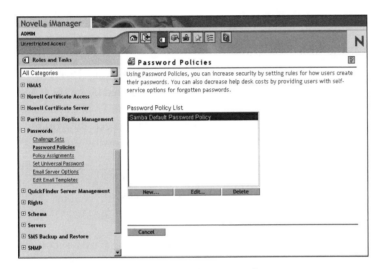

Figure 14-13   The Password Policies window

4. Click the **Edit** button to display the Policy Summary tab shown in Figure 14-14. Verify that all the Universal Password settings are set to true, except the Remove the NDS password when setting Universal Password option, which should be set to false.

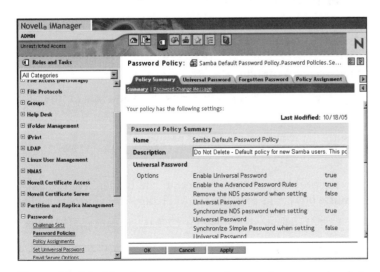

Figure 14-14   Viewing a summary of current password policies

5. Click the **Policy Assignment** tab.

6. If necessary, click the **Object Selector** button next to the Assign to text box. Click your **UAS** container, and then click **OK** to add this object to the policy assignments.

7. Click **OK** to save the assignment and return to the Password Policies window.

8. Now that you've made all your password policy changes, click **Cancel** to return to the iManager main window.

9. Follow these steps to enable user accounts for Samba access:

    a. Under the Samba Management heading, click the **Enable Linux User for Samba** link.

    b. Click the **Object Selector** button, and navigate to and click the **LUMUser** account you created previously.

    c. Click **OK** to enable the LUMUser account for Samba access and return to the iManager main window.

10. Exit iManager and stay logged on to your local computer.

11. Log out of your Windows computer.

Creating Home Directories for Linux-Enabled Users

Because Samba uses the Linux directory structure rather than NCP volumes, users accessing the Linux server from their Windows client need to be Linux enabled and should have home directories created by Linux. In Chapter 13, you used the adduser command with the -m parameter to create a new user account and a home directory for the user in the /home structure. Creating a Linux home directory for an eDirectory user account requires a different technique. To create a home directory for a Linux-enabled user, you can use the following steps:

EXAMPLE

1. Use iManager to create a new user account in eDirectory but don't create the home directory at this time. Home directories created with iManager are accessed through Novell Core Protocol and can't be accessed directly from Samba, which uses the Linux ReiserFS file system.

2. Use iManager to Linux enable the user account.

3. Use the Linux su command from the server console to switch to the new user account. The first time you use this command to switch to a Linux-enabled user account, the Linux system creates a home directory for that user in the /home structure.

In the following activity, you learn how to create home directories for your Linux-enabled users on the SUSE Linux server and then use the Windows client to test access to these directories.

ACTIVITY

Activity 14-9: Creating Linux Home Directories

Time Required: 10 minutes

Objective: Create home directories for Linux-enabled user accounts.

Requirements: Access to the SUSE Linux server console

Description: In this activity, you create home directories for your Linux-enabled users on the SUSE Linux server.

1. Log in to your SUSE Linux server with the root user name and password.

2. Open a terminal session.

3. To set the Linux system so that contents of the directories you create are hidden from everyone except the directory owner, type **umask 0077** and press **Enter** to change the directory rights mask.

4. To create a home directory for your LUMUser account, type **su LUMUser** and press **Enter**.

5. Switch back to the root user by typing **su**, pressing **Enter**, entering your root user password, and pressing **Enter** again.

6. To restore the Linux system to its default directory rights mask, type **umask 0022** and press **Enter**.

7. Verify the creation of the user's home directory by entering the following commands (pressing **Enter** after each command).

```
cd /home
ls -l
```

8. The user's home directory should now appear in the Linux /home directory. Type **exit** and press **Enter** to end your terminal session, and log off your Linux server.

 In the following steps, you use your Windows XP computer to test Samba by accessing the SUSE Linux server from My Network Places and storing a file in your home directory.

9. Follow these steps on your Windows XP computer to test Samba access:

   a. If necessary, start your Windows XP computer, click the **Workstation Only** check box, and log on to Windows with your local administrator user name and password.

   b. Click **Start**, **Run**, type the UNC name *IPaddress* (substituting the IP address of your SUSE Linux server for *IPaddress*), and press **Enter**.

   c. Enter your **LUMUser** user name and password and press **Enter** after typing each.

   d. Record at least two directories you can see:

      _____

      _____

10. Close all open windows and log out. You can leave your system running for the next activity.

Working with NetStorage

As with the NetWare operating system, NetStorage can be used to make Linux files and directories available across the Internet from any location or client via a Web browser and can also be used in SUSE Linux, as shown in Figure 14-15. Notice that the NetStorage service allows access to data through a number of protocols, including NCP for NSS volumes, Microsoft CIFS for Samba and NFAP shares, and SSH for traditional Linux volumes.

To use NetStorage, users must be Linux-enabled on the server hosting the NetStorage service. Another part of implementing NetStorage on Linux is making the directories or files available to the NetStorage service. On NetWare servers, NetStorage reads a user's login script and home directory information to determine what directories will be made available to the user when accessing NetStorage. On a Linux server, you make directories available to NetStorage by creating **Storage Location objects** in the eDirectory tree. These objects contain paths to the directories that will be accessible through NetStorage. In the following activities, you learn how to use NetStorage on the SUSE Linux server to enable file access from a Web browser.

14

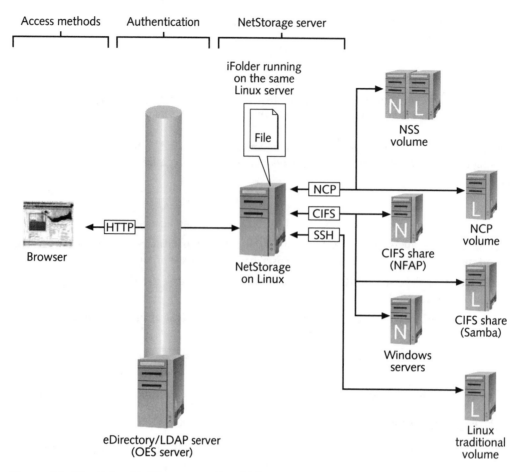

Figure 14-15   Using NetStorage on the OES Linux server

Activity 14-10: Creating Storage Location Objects

Time Required: 15 minutes

Objective: Use iManager to create a Storage Location object.

Requirements: Internet Explorer from Windows XP or Java-enabled Firefox from SUSE Linux 10

Description: Eric wants users to be able to access their home directories from NetStorage. In this activity, you make user home directories available by using iManager to create a Storage Location object for user home directories.

1. Log in to your Windows XP system with your local administrator user name and password or your SUSE Linux server with the root user name and password.

2. Start your Web browser, start iManager, and log in to iManager with your administrative user name and password.

3. Expand the **File Access (NetStorage)** heading and click the **New Storage Location** link to display the Storage Locations: Create Object window shown in Figure 14-16.

4. In the Object Name text box, type **storLoc_hostname** (replacing *hostname* with the name of the SUSE Linux server).

5. In the DisplayName text box, type **home**. This is the name that's displayed in the user's NetStorage window.

6. In the Directory Location text box, type **ssh:/IPaddress/home** (replacing *IPaddress* with the IP address of your SUSE Linux server).

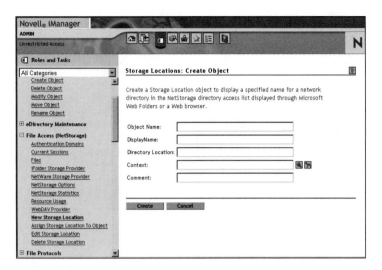

Figure 14-16   Creating a Storage Location object

7. Click the **Object Selector** button next to the Context text box, and navigate to and click your **UAS** container.

8. Click **Create** to create the object and return to the iManager main window.

9. Exit iManager and stay logged in for the next activity.

Activity 14-11: Accessing NetStorage

Time Required: 15 minutes

Objective: Use NetStorage to access the SUSE Linux server.

Requirements: Completion of Activity 14-8 and a Windows XP or SUSE Linux 10 computer

Description: In this activity, you test NetStorage by using your Web browser to log in with your LUMUser name and password.

1. If necessary, log in to your Windows XP system with your local administrator user name and password or your SUSE Linux server with the root user name and password.

2. Start your Web browser and enter the URL **https://IPaddress/NetStorage** (replacing *IPaddress* with the IP address of your SUSE Linux server).

3. Log in to NetStorage with your **LUMUser** user name and password.

4. List the files and directories you can see:

   _____

   _____

5. Exit NetStorage, and leave your system running for the next activity.

---

iPRINT SERVICES IN SUSE LINUX

The iPrint system can be used in SUSE Linux as well as NetWare 6.5, as shown in Figure 14-17. A printer can be installed on a Linux, Windows, or Macintosh computer using HTTP or the local operating system's native printer installation. When using HTTP, the Web browser on the computer directs the request to the printer page installed on the iPrint server. The OES server then uses the Driver Store object in Linux or the Broker object in NetWare to send the correct printer driver to the computer.

After a printer is installed, print jobs are sent via the IPP protocol to the Print Manager software, which uses a print spooler to direct the print job to a network-attached printer. The major difference between iPrint in

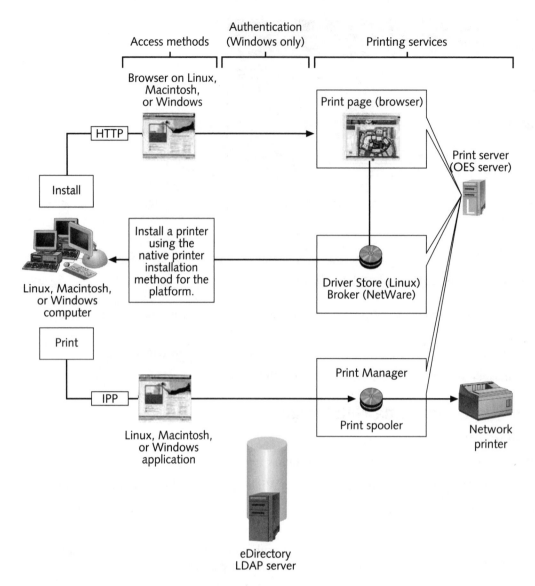

Figure 14-17   Using iPrint in SUSE Linux

Linux and NetWare is that you must create a **Driver Store** object on the SUSE Linux system for storing print drivers. This object replaces the Broker object used in NetWare. These are the basics steps for setting up iPrint in SUSE Linux:

1. Create a Driver Store.

2. Add print drivers to the Driver Store from the Windows platforms.

3. Create a Print Manager object.

4. Create iPrint printer objects.

In the following activities, you set up iPrint on your SUSE Linux system.

Activity 14-12: Creating a Driver Store

Time Required: 10 minutes

Objective: Use iManager to set up the iPrint service.

Requirements: Internet Explorer from Windows XP or Java-enabled Firefox from SUSE Linux 10

Description: The AeroDyn Division needs access to several network printers from both inside and outside the company network. In this activity, you learn how to create a Driver Store for setting up iPrint on the SUSE Linux server.

1. If necessary, log on to your Windows XP or SUSE Linux computer with your administrative or root user name and password.

2. Start your Web browser, start iManager, and log in to iManager with your administrative user name and password.

3. Follow these steps to create a Driver Store object for holding print drivers:

   a. Expand the **iPrint** heading and click the **Create Driver Store** link to display the Create Driver Store window shown in Figure 14-18.

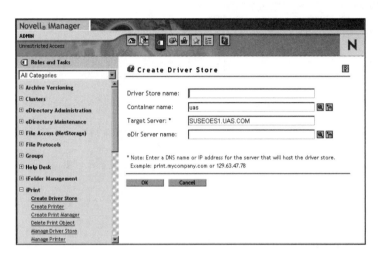

Figure 14-18 The Create Driver Store window

   b. If necessary, enter a container name by clicking the **Object Selector** button next to the Container name text box and clicking your **UAS** container.

   c. In the Driver Store name text box, type **UASPrint_Drivers**.

   d. Enter the IP address of your Linux server in the Target Server text box.

   e. Click the **Object Selector** button next to the eDir Server name text box, and click your SUSE Linux server.

   f. Click **OK** to create the Driver Store and display the completion message.

The following steps need to be performed from a Windows XP client.

NOTE

4. If necessary, use the following steps to install the iPrint client on your Windows XP computer. (If you installed the iPrint client in Chapter 8, you can skip to Activity 14-13.)

   a. If necessary, log on to your Windows XP computer and click the **Workstation Only** check box.

   b. Start Internet Explorer and enter the URL **http://IPaddress/ipp** (replacing *IPaddress* with the IP address of your SUSE Linux server).

   c. Click the **Install iPrint Client** link.

   d. Click the **Open** option to start the installation wizard.

   e. When the Install iPrint Client window is displayed, click **Next** to start the installation process.

   f. After the client is installed, click **Finish** to return to the iPrint window. Close your Web browser.

5. Leave iManager open for the next activity.

Activity 14-13: Creating a Print Manager Object

Time Required: 10 minutes

Objective: Use iManager to set up the iPrint service.

Requirements: A Windows XP or SUSE Linux 10 computer; completion of Activity 14-12

Description: In this activity, you learn how to create a Print Manager for setting up iPrint on your SUSE Linux system.

1. If necessary, expand the **iPrint** heading and then click the **Create Print Manager** link to display the Create Print Manager window (see Figure 14-19).

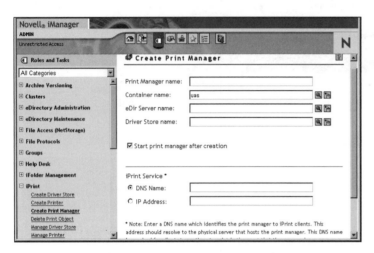

Figure 14-19   The Create Print Manager window

2. Type **OES_PMgr** in the Print Manager name text box.

3. Click the **Object Selector** button next to the eDir Server name text box, and click your SUSE Linux server.

4. Click the **Object Selector** button next to the Driver Store name text box, and click the **UASPrint_Drivers** object you created in Activity 14-12.

5. Click the **IP Address** option button, and enter the IP address of your SUSE Linux server in the text box.

6. Click **OK** to create the Print Manager object, and leave iManager open for the next activity.

Activity 14-14: Creating Printer Objects

Time Required: 10 minutes

Objective: Use iManager to set up the iPrint service.

Requirements: Completion of Activity 14-13

Description: In this activity, you learn how to create printer objects that can be used to set up iPrint on your SUSE Linux system.

1. If necessary, expand the **iPrint** heading and then click the **Create Printer** link to display the Create Printer window shown in Figure 14-20.

2. In the Printer name text box, enter **OES_P1**.

3. Enter the appropriate information for your printer, and click **Next** to create the printer object.

4. Close any open windows, and log off.

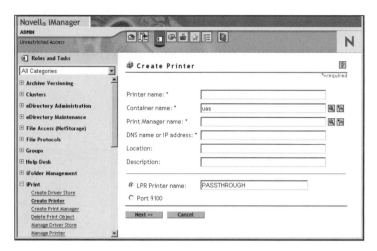

Figure 14-20   The Create Printer window

Now that you have learned how SUSE Linux can be used to provide Novell network services, in the end-of-chapter projects you apply what you have learned to setting up a simple system using the SUSE Linux server.

Chapter Summary

14

▫ SUSE Linux includes support for most Novell services, including NetWare Core Protocol, NetStorage, and iPrint. You can use the YaST utility to view and install Novell services on a SUSE Linux system, but iManager and Remote Manager are used to manage most services.

▫ For eDirectory users to access some Linux services, their user accounts must be Linux enabled by making them a member of a Linux-enabled group. This process makes their user accounts appear to the local Linux server as though they were POSIX users in the etc/passwd file.

▫ The NetWare Core Protocol (NCP) service enables users to access Linux directories and volumes with the standard Novell Client. User accounts don't need to be Linux enabled to use the NCP service.

▫ Storage services include Novell Storage Services, NetStorage, Samba, and iFolder. NetStorage and Samba require user accounts to be Linux enabled.

▫ iPrint is used in SUSE Linux in much the same way as iPrint on a NetWare server. The major difference is that in SUSE Linux, the Driver Store object replaces the Broker object used in NetWare.

Key Terms

Driver Store — An eDirectory object used to store print drivers.

Linux Config object — An eDirectory object used to store a list of all SUSE Linux servers in the eDirectory tree.

Linux User Management (LUM) — A method of storing Linux login information in eDirectory to make eDirectory users Linux enabled.

Linux Workstation objects — An eDirectory object used to store a list of all SUSE Linux computers in the eDirectory tree.

Pluggable Authentication Module (PAM) — A Linux software component used to interpret login requests from both local and LDAP users.

Portable Operating System Interface (POSIX) — An authentication method for user accounts stored in the passwd file on the local Linux server.

Samba — A service that allows Windows clients to access data on a Linux server by using the CIFS protocol.

Storage Location objects — eDirectory objects used to store paths to directories that will be available through NetStorage.

REVIEW QUESTIONS

1. Which of the following services doesn't require a user account to be Linux enabled?

   a. Samba

   b. NetStorage

   c. NCP

   d. PAM-enabled commands, such as ftp and passwd

2. Which of the following is required to set up Samba? (Choose all that apply.)

   a. Linux-enabled user accounts

   b. user home directories

   c. universal passwords

   d. NCP service

3. Which of the following is used to manage the NCP service?

   a. iManager

   b. YaST

   c. Novell Remote Manager

   d. su command

4. Which of the following is used to manage NetStorage?

   a. iManager

   b. YaST

   c. Novell Remote Manager

   d. su command

5. Which of the following iPrint components is not used in SUSE Linux?

   a. Broker

   b. Print Manager

   c. printer agent

   d. Driver Store

6. User home directories for Linux-enabled users are created on the Linux server with which of the following?

   a. iManager

   b. su command

   c. Novell Remote Manager

   d. YaST

7. In Linux, NetStorage uses which of the following to obtain directories to display? (Choose all that apply.)

   a. login scripts

   b. the passwd file

   c. Storage Location objects in eDirectory

   d. iFolder

8. The Samba service uses which of the following protocols?

   a. CIFS

   b. NCP

   c. HTTP

   d. NFS

9. The NetStorage service uses which of the following protocols?

    a. CIFS

    b. NCP

    c. HTTP

    d. NFS

10. Before creating a Print Manager for Linux, you need to create which of the following?

    a. Broker

    b. printer agent

    c. Driver Store

    d. a Printers OU

11. Which of the following do you use to install Novell Storage Services?

    a. iManager

    b. su command

    c. Remote Manager

    d. YaST

12. NSS volumes must reside on a disk managed by which of the following?

    a. LVM

    b. LUM

    c. EVMS

    d. NSS

13. To enable a user for Linux, you must _____ .

14. Novell Client is required to access iPrint printers. True or False?

15. Login scripts can be used with the NCP service for Linux. True or False?

CASE PROJECTS

Case Project 14-1: Planning a SUSE Linux System for Windows Access

The Wiggerts Heating and Air-Conditioning Company wants to use the SUSE Linux server and needs to access data files from a standard Windows system. As part of the planning process, you've been asked to explain the steps in setting up the file system for Windows users. For this project, list the steps you recommend that Wiggerts should follow.

Case Project 14-2: Planning for NetStorage

The Wiggerts Heating and Air-Conditioning Company wants to use the SUSE Linux server. As part of the planning process, you've been asked to explain the steps in allowing users to access data from across the Internet via a Web browser. For this project, list the steps you recommend that Wiggerts should follow.

Case Project 14-3: Planning for SUSE Linux Printing

The Wiggerts Heating and Air-Conditioning Company wants to use the SUSE Linux server. As part of the planning process, you've been asked to explain the steps in setting up a networking printing system that allows sharing two network-attached printers for local computers and computers used for the employee home location. For this project, list the steps you recommend that Wiggerts should follow.

HANDS-ON PROJECTS

Hands-on Project 14-1: Creating an eDirectory Structure in Linux

The Wiggerts Heating and Air-Conditioning Company wants you to create an eDirectory tree for its organization. Use what you've learned in this chapter to create the following tree structure on your SUSE Linux server:

- WHA Organization
- Users OU
- Printers OU

Hands-on Project 14-2: Setting up Linux-Enabled User Accounts

The Wiggerts Heating and Air-Conditioning Company wants you to create several eDirectory user accounts in the Users OU, some of which should be Linux enabled. In this project, create the following groups and user accounts in the Users OU:

Note that some users appear in more than one group.

NOTE

Managers group: Theodore Wiggerts (Linux enabled), Rosemary Simpson, Dora Christopherson

Accounting group: Timothy Bablick (Linux enabled), Peter LeJeune

Marketing group: Peter LeJeune (Linux enabled), Olie Iverson

IT group: Jason Novak (Linux enabled), Jarret Hamilton

Installation Managers group: Scott Theilig, Christopher Thompson (Linux enabled)

LinuxUsers group: Includes all Linux-enabled users

Hands-on Project 14-3: Setting up iPrint in Linux

The Wiggerts Heating and Air-Conditioning Company wants you to set up a printing system for its three network printers. In this project, create the necessary iPrint objects for this printing environment.

A

CERTIFICATION EXAM OBJECTIVES FOR OPEN ENTERPRISE SERVER

As you learned in Chapter 1, Novell has established a number of industry certifications to help ensure that people have the skills required to administer and troubleshoot network systems. Because Open Enterprise Server includes both NetWare and Linux network operating systems, having both the Certified Novell Administrator (CNA) and Certified Linux Professional (CLP) certifications enhances your employment options. This book covers all the objectives required to pass the NetWare 6.5 CNA exam 50-686 and several key objectives from the CLP exam. This appendix lists the objectives for both exams with the corresponding chapter and section (when applicable) covering information for each objective.

Novell CNA Exam 50-686 Objectives

Those pursuing CNA certification should have a fundamental knowledge of networking before learning the specifics of Novell networking. Novell strongly recommends having a CompTIA Network+ certification before pursuing CNA certification. In a recent survey, most Novell CNAs who had obtained the Network+ certification first rated the CompTIA knowledge as valuable to highly valuable in preparing them for CNA certification. The Network + certification ensures that you have a good understanding of network implementation, support, media, topologies, protocols, and standards—all necessary for completing CNA certification successfully. Table A-1 maps the Novell CNA 50-686 objectives to the chapter number and section title where exam objectives are covered in the book.

 In the objective-mapping tables, subsections are listed in parentheses.

NOTE

Table A-1 Novell CNA Exam 50-686 objective mapping

CNA Exam Objective	Chapter: Section
1 Identify NetWare 6.5 Features	Chapter 1: Introduction to Network Operating Systems
2 Describe How NetWare Works with Other Operating Systems	Chapter 1: Introduction to Network Operating Systems; Chapter 3: Implementing the NetWare File System (Implementing the Directory Structure); Chapter 4: Working with Novell Client
3 Identify Prerequisite Requirements	Chapter 2: Preparing for NetWare 6.5 Installation
4 Prepare the Existing Network	Chapter 2: Performing a NetWare 6.5 Installation (Upgrade an Existing eDirectory Network)
5 Prepare the Designated Computer	Chapter 2: Preparing for NetWare 6.5 Installation
6 Install NetWare 6.5	Chapter 2: Performing a NetWare 6.5 Installation
7 Describe the Novell Client	Chapter 4: Working with Novell Client
8 Install the Novell Client	Chapter 4: Working with Novell Client
9 Log in to eDirectory and the Workstation	Chapter 4: Working with Novell Client
10 Set Client Properties	Chapter 4: Working with Novell Client
11 Identify the Role and Benefits of eDirectory	Chapter 1: Introduction to Network Operating Systems (Directory Services); Chapter 4: Novell eDirectory Services
12 Identify How eDirectory Works	Chapter 4: Novell eDirectory Services
13 Identify and Describe eDirectory Components	Chapter 4: Novell eDirectory Services
14 Identify and Describe eDirectory Object Classes	Chapter 4: Identifying eDirectory Components
15 Identify the Flow and Design of the eDirectory Tree	Chapter 4: Planning the eDirectory Tree Structure
16 Identify eDirectory Tools and When to Use Them	Chapter 5: Introduction to NetWare Management Utilities
17 Describe the Admin Object	Chapter 4: Identifying eDirectory Components
18 Create User Objects	Chapter 5: Creating and Managing Users and Groups
19 Modify User Objects	Chapter 5: Updating Multiple User Accounts
20 Move Objects	Chapter 5: Deleting, Renaming, and Moving Objects
21 Delete User Objects	Chapter 5: Deleting, Renaming, and Moving Objects
22 Identify Network File Service Components	Chapter 3: NetWare File System Components
23 Identify Types of NetWare Volume Storage	Chapter 3: NetWare File System Components
24 Create Traditional and NSS Volumes	Chapter 3: Implementing the NetWare File System
25 Access Volumes Through Mapped Network Drives	Chapter 3: Accessing the NetWare File System
26 Identify Guidelines for Planning Network Volumes	Chapter 3: Implementing the NetWare File System

Table A-1   Novell CNA Exam 50-686 objective mapping (continued)

CNA Exam Objective	Chapter: Section
27 Identify the Content and Purpose of NetWare SYS Directories	Chapter 3: NetWare File System Components
28 Identify the Types of Directories Used for Organizing a File System	Chapter 3: NetWare File System Components
29 Evaluate Directory Structure Types	Chapter 3: NetWare File System Components
30 Identify the Types of Network Security Provided by NetWare	Chapter 1: Introduction to Network Administration and Certification
31 Identify How NetWare File System Security Works	Chapter 6: File System Security Components
32 Plan File System Rights	Chapter 6: Planning File System Security
33 Identify Directory and File Attributes	Chapter 6: Attribute Security
34 Describe eDirectory Security	Chapter 7: Working with eDirectory Security
35 Determine How Rights Flow	Chapter 7: Working with eDirectory Security
36 Block Inherited Rights	Chapter 7: Working with eDirectory Security
37 Determine eDirectory Effective Rights	Chapter 7: Working with eDirectory Security
38 Troubleshoot eDirectory Security	Chapter 1: Introduction to Network Administration and Certification
39 Identify the Features of NDPS	Chapter 8: iPrint Overview
40 Identify the Types of Printers	Chapter 8: Introduction to Network Printing
41 Describe NDPS Components	Chapter 8: iPrint Overview
42 Set Up NDPS	Chapter 8: iPrint Overview
43 Manage NDPS	Chapter 8: iPrint Overview
44 Implement Novell iPrint	Chapter 8: iPrint Overview, Configuring Printer Clients
45 Implement Novell iFolder	Chapter 10: Working with Novell iFolder
46 Describe Virtual Office	Chapter 10: Using Virtual Office
47 Install Virtual Office	Chapter 10: Using Virtual Office
48 Configure Virtual Office	Chapter 10: Using Virtual Office
49 Identify the Operating System Components of NetWare 6.5	Chapter 2: Preparing for NetWare 6.5 Installation
50 Use Server Console Commands to Manage NetWare 6.5	Chapter 2: Working with the Server Console
51 Use Configuration Files	Chapter 2: Working with the Server Console
52 Identify the Utilities to Remotely Manage NetWare 6.5	Chapter 2: Working with the Server Console
53 Internally Secure a Network	Chapter 1: Introduction to Network Administration and Certification
54 Troubleshoot Common Internal Security Problems	Chapter 5: Establishing Login Security; Chapter 6: Planning File System Security; Chapter 7: Working with eDirectory Security
55 Identify How to Provide External Network Security with a Firewall	Chapter 11: Securing Web Services, Working with Encryption Security

NOVELL CLP EXAM 50-686 OBJECTIVES

Complete coverage of the CLP exam objectives is outside the scope of this book, but information from several of the exam's key objectives is important for Novell administrators to know how to use Open Enterprise Server. If you want to obtain CLP certification, you should take an additional class for information and training in the remainder of the objectives. Table A-2 lists the CLP exam objectives along with the chapter number and section title where each objective is introduced in this book.

Table A-2 Novell CLP Exam 50-686 objective mapping.

CLP Exam Objective	Chapter: Section
1 Perform an installation of SUSE Linux Enterprise Server (SLES) 9	Chapter 12: Installing SUSE Linux
2 Navigate in the KDE and GNOME desktop environment	Chapter 12: Using the KDE Desktop Environment
3 Locate and use help resources in the Linux system	Chapter 13: Working with the Bash Shell (Accessing Command-Line Help, Using Linux Online Help)
4 Perform file management tasks in the SLES 9 system	Chapter 13: Managing the File System
5 Use the Linux command line shell	Chapter 13: Working with the Bash Shell
6 Use Linux text editors	Chapter 13: Working with the Bash Shell
7 Locate, view, and use SUSE Linux system information	Introductory coverage in Chapter 12: Working with SUSE Linux (Using YaST)
8 Administer processes	Introductory coverage in Chapter 13: Managing Linux Applications
9 Manage runlevels	Introductory coverage in Chapter 13: Managing Linux Applications (Working with Run Levels)
10 Schedule jobs	Not covered
11 Manage the kernel	Not covered
12 Manage GRUB boot loader	Introductory coverage in Chapter 12: Preparing for SUSE Linux Installation
13 Manage system and hardware settings	Introductory coverage in Chapter 12: Working with SUSE Linux
14 Manage the network configuration	Chapter 12: Installing SUSE Linux
15 Manage user and group accounts	Chapter 13: Creating and Managing Linux Users and Groups, Working with the Bash Shell
16 Manage and configure network printers	Chapter 14: iPrint Services in SUSE Linux
17 Manage and configure network file systems	Chapter 13: Managing the File System; Chapter 14: Storage Services in SUSE Linux
18 Manage resources on the network	Introductory coverage in Chapter 12: Working with SUSE Linux
19 Manage software packages using RPM	Introductory coverage in Chapter 13: Managing Linux Applications (RPM Package-Related Operations)
20 Enable Internet services	Not covered for Linux; Apache Web Server for NetWare covered in Chapter 11: Introduction to Novell Internet Services
21 Configure and use a DNS server	Not covered
22 Deploy and use OpenLDAP on an SLES 9 server	Not covered
23 Manage backup and recovery on an SLES 9 server	Introductory coverage in Chapter 13: Managing the File System
24 Create basic shell scripts	Not covered
25 Manage remote access	Introductory coverage in Chapter 13: Introduction to Managing and Securing SUSE Linux
26 Secure an SLES 9 server	Introductory coverage in Chapter 13: Introduction to Managing and Securing SUSE Linux
27 Find performance bottlenecks	Not covered

INTEGRATING SUSE LINUX CLIENTS

As a result of the increased popularity of Linux for servers and desktop computers, network administrators are more likely to be asked to integrate Linux into their existing networks. In Chapters 12 through 14, you learned how to install and configure the Novell Open Enterprise Server (OES) version of SUSE Linux Enterprise Server 9 in a network environment. This appendix focuses on techniques you can use to set up a SUSE Linux 10 client system as a desktop computer for administrative and user functions. First, you see how to download and install SUSE Linux 10, and then you learn how to use Novell Linux Desktop to perform administrative tasks via the Mozilla Firefox Web browser. Next, you're introduced to working with SUSE Linux as a user desktop environment by setting up iFolder. Finally, you learn more about the new Novell Client for Linux, which allows you to access NetWare Core Protocol (NCP) services via the Linux desktop in much the same way as from a Windows client.

DOWNLOADING AND INSTALLING SUSE LINUX

As of this writing, SUSE Linux 10 is the latest version of the SUSE Linux operating system offered by Novell. The product includes the stable, secure Linux kernel plus a complete set of desktop applications, including an office suite, the Mozilla Firefox Web browser, an instant messaging client, multimedia viewers, and graphical software. You can obtain SUSE Linux 10 directly from Novell's Web site (*www.novell.com/products/suselinux*) by selecting the free download or Buy SUSE Linux 10 options. SUSE Linux 10 currently costs less than $60 and comes on a bootable CD. The purchased product includes printed documentation plus 90 days of installation support.

Novell also has its own customized version of SUSE Linux called Novell Linux Desktop (NLD). As of this writing, it's based on SUSE Linux 9 and is available at *http://download.novell.com/Download?buildid=fMAfBuIXadQ~*. You can buy the full version for $35 or download a free 60-day trial version. Novell Linux Desktop includes a customized KDE desktop with utilities and options such as the Novell Client for Linux that make it easier to adapt to a Novell-based network environment. If you're using Novell Linux Desktop, you'll notice minor differences in the desktop environment and certain system utilities, such as YaST.

NOTE

Novell Linux Desktop is also available in a preloaded virtual machine format that can be run directly from VMware without performing a new installation. See Appendix C for more information on using VMware.

Installing SUSE Linux 10

The process for installing SUSE Linux 10 is similar to installing the OES Linux Enterprise Server 9 as explained in Chapter 12. If you're using VMware, create a virtual machine for the SUSE Linux operating system as described in Appendix C. The following steps summarize the process of installing a SUSE Linux 10 system that you can use to perform the activities in this book and appendix:

EXAMPLE

1. Boot your system from the SUSE Linux 10 CD. Accept the default language, accept the license agreement, and set your time zone.

2. Select the KDE desktop from the Desktop selection window to display the Installation settings window.

3. Click the Software link to display the Selections window (see Figure B-1).

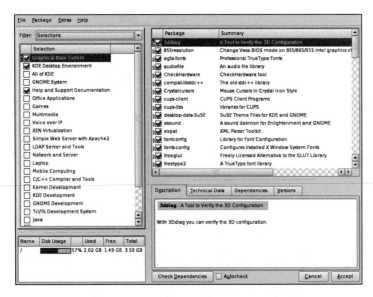

Figure B-1   The SUSE Linux 10 Selections window

4. Click the Network and Server check box in the left pane, and then click the ncpfs (Tools for Accessing Novell File Systems) option in the Package section.

5. Follow these steps to add software packages for supporting Novell Client for Linux:
   a. Click the Filter list arrow and click Search in the list of options.
   b. Enter gcc in the Search text box and click the Search button.
   c. Click to select the gcc (the GNU C Compiler and Support Files) option.
   d. Enter kernel-default in the Search text box and click the Search button.
   e. Click to select kernel-default (the standard kernel) and respond to the warning by clicking OK.
   f. Click Accept to accept your changes, and then click Continue to respond to the Changed Packages message box and return to the Installation Settings window.

6. Click Accept to accept the installation settings and then click to confirm any license agreements.

7. Click Install when you see the Confirm Installation window.

8. After files are copied, you're prompted to restart to continue the installation.

9. Insert the SUSE Linux CDs and click OK when prompted.

10. After all files have been copied, you're asked to enter a password for your root user. Enter a password of at least eight characters containing both uppercase and lowercase letters. Write down the password and keep it in a secure place.

11. Click Next to display the Network Configuration window.

12. Click the Network Interfaces heading and then click Edit to display the Network Address Setup window shown in Figure B-2.

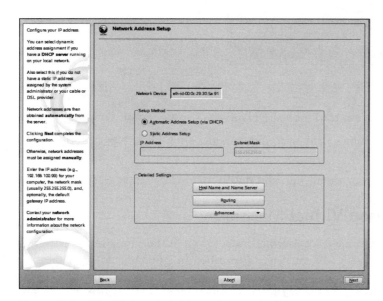

Figure B-2 The Network Address Setup window

13. Depending on your lab environment, select automatic or static address setup. If you click Static Address Setup, enter the IP address and subnet mask your instructor provides.

14. Click the Host Name and Name Server button to display the Host Name and Domain Name window

15. Enter a name for your Linux computer in the Hostname text box and a domain name in the Domain Name text box.

16. If you're using a DNS server in your lab, enter its IP address in the Name Server 1 text box, and then click OK to return to the Network Address Setup window.

17. Click Next to save your settings and return to the Network Configuration window.

18. Click Next to save the network configuration and display the Test Internet Connection window.

19. If your computer is attached to the Internet, click Next to test your connection. If not, click the No, Skip This Test option button, and then click Next to display the Authentication Method window.

20. Verify that the Local (/etc/passwd) option button is selected, and then click Next to display the New Local User window.

21. Create a new user for yourself by filling in the fields shown in Figure B-3. Click Next to create your user account and display the SUSE Linux 10 Release Notes.

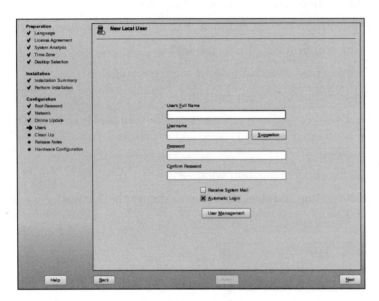

Figure B-3 The New Local User window

22. Read the notes and click Next to display the Hardware Configuration window.

23. Verify that the correct graphics card is configured, and then click Next to save the hardware configuration.

24. Click Finish to complete your installation and display the SUSE Linux 10 login window.

Using the Novell Linux Desktop Virtual Machine

The Novell Linux Desktop virtual machine is a convenient way to run SUSE Linux from VMware. First you need a copy of VMware Workstation or VMware Player (described in Appendix C), and then you install VMware on your computer. Next, you need to download a copy of Novell Linux for Desktop (the nld9_vmwarews5-vm.zip file) from *www.novell.com/downloads*. After you've downloaded the file, you can use the following steps to install it:

EXAMPLE

1. Click Novell Linux Desktop in the Product or Technology (optional) drop-down list, and click Search to display the products list.

2. Click the Novell Linux Desktop SP2 Evaluation product to display a list of files.

3. Click the nld9_vmwarews5-vm.zip file and log in to the Novell site. (You might be asked to create a user account at that time.)

4. Click the Download option and save the file to your local computer's hard disk.

5. Extract the file to your Virtual Machine folder.

The installation instructions for Novell Linux Desktop are at *www.novell.com/documentation/nld/esd/qrpnld9_eval.html*. You need to follow them carefully to use VMware and the supplied NLD 9 distribution.

After you have downloaded the VMware Workstation 5 Virtual Machine for Novell Linux Desktop 9, unzip the file (nld9-vmwarews5-vm.zip) to the directory on your Linux or Windows system where you keep your virtual machines. By default, it's home/vmware in Linux and My Documents\My Virtual Machines in Windows. When unzipping the file, make sure you re-create the folders in the .zip file.

Next, start VMware Workstation 5, open the virtual machine, and then power it on. At this point, you see a message asking whether you want to create a new identifier or keep the existing one. Keeping the existing identifier is strongly recommended. If you don't, you'll need to reconfigure the network card in the virtual machine.

In some circumstances, the X-Window system fails to initialize correctly on the virtual machine. If this happens, you see a text-based console repeated four times on the screen. To fix the problem, follow these steps:

EXAMPLE

1. Log in as root with the password "novell" (all lowercase letters).

2. Change to run level 3 by typing init 3 and pressing Enter.

3. Reset the X Server by typing sax2 –r and pressing Enter.

4. When the configuration screen prompts you to accept the configuration or change it, press OK to accept.

5. In the text-based console, start the X-Window system by typing init 5 and pressing Enter, or restart the system by typing init 6 and pressing Enter.

USING SUSE LINUX TO PERFORM ADMINISTRATIVE TASKS

Because Novell OES enables you to perform administrative tasks in iManager and Remote Manager via a Web browser, you can work in both SUSE Linux 10 and Windows XP. SUSE Linux 10 includes the Mozilla Firefox Web browser, which has been used to test chapter activities. The activities in the book that can be done with the Firefox Web browser are identified in the requirements section for each activity. This section describes how to access iManager and Remote Manager using the Mozilla Firefox Web browser and points out any differences you might notice when using Firefox instead of Internet Explorer.

Starting iManager and Remote Manager

To start iManager or Remote Manager via SUSE Linux 10 Mozilla Firefox, you need to know the IP address or DNS name of your OES NetWare or Linux server. You can use these steps to start either utility from your Firefox Web browser:

EXAMPLE

1. Start the Firefox Web browser. If you're not connected to the Internet, you might see a message stating that *www.novell.com* could not be found. If so, click OK to display the Firefox window shown in Figure B-4.

2. Enter https://*IPaddress*/nps/iManager.html (for iManager) or https://*IPaddress*:8009 (for Remote Manager) in the text box next to the home icon, and press Enter to open a secure connection.

3. Because Firefox doesn't recognize the certificate the OES server uses to establish a secure connection with SSL, you see the message box shown in Figure B-5.

4. To avoid seeing this message in the future, click the Accept this certificate permanently option button and click OK to continue. If you're using an IP address to access the OES server and the OES server has a DNS name defined, you see the Domain Name Mismatch error message (see Figure B-6).

5. If you like, click the View Certificate button to view the server's certificate, and then click OK to continue and display the login window. You can then log in to iManager or Remote Manager to perform administrative functions.

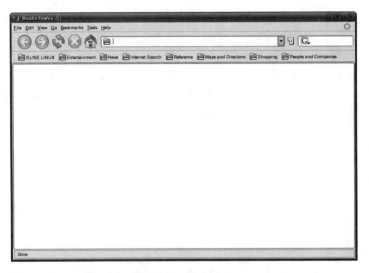

Figure B-4   The Mozilla Firefox window

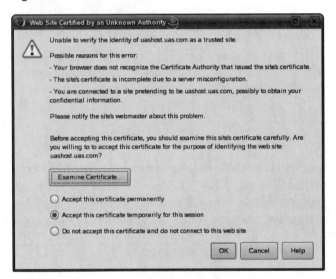

Figure B-5   Message about a Web site certified by an unknown authority

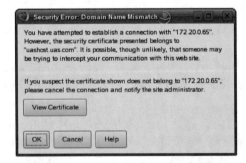

Figure B-6   The Domain Name Mismatch message box

Although most steps work the same in both Firefox and Internet Explorer, Firefox doesn't open files directly from Remote Manager. For example, in Activity 3-2 in Chapter 3, you won't be able to view the Hosts file as described in Step 9b. To view the Hosts file in Firefox, you need to perform the following steps in place of Steps 9a and 9b:

a. Click the ETC directory to display its contents.

b. Click the hosts file and then click OK to save it to your user home directory.

EXAMPLE

c. Open a terminal window.

d. Enter the cat hosts command to view the contents of the hosts file.

Using SUSE Linux for End User Tasks

To be productive, Linux system users need access to many of the same network resources and services that you work with in this book. In this section, you learn how to give Linux users access to iFolder data via the iFolder Linux client.

Installing the iFolder Client on Linux

In Chapter 9, you learned how to install iFolder on the NetWare server and set up the iFolder client on Windows XP. In this section, you learn how to set up an iFolder client on the Linux server, and then access iFolder files from both Linux and Windows platforms.

Downloading the iFolder Linux Client

Follow these steps to install the iFolder client on your Linux computer:

1. Follow the instructions in Chapter 9 to install iFolder on your Novell OES server.

2. Log in to your Linux client with the root user name and password.

3. From your Linux computer, start the Firefox Web browser and enter the URL https://*IPaddress*/iFolder (replacing *IPaddress* with the IP address or DNS name of the server running iFolder) to display the iFolder home page.

4. Click the Download Linux Client link to display the window shown in Figure B-7 asking what you want to do with the file.

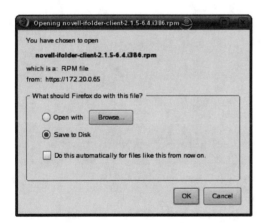

Figure B-7   Downloading the iFolder Linux client

5. Verify that the Save to Disk option button is selected, and then click OK to save the .rpm file to your root user's home directory.

Installing the iFolder Client

After the iFolder client's .rpm file has been downloaded, you can use the RedHat Package Manager (RPM) to install the iFolder client by following these steps:

1. Open a terminal session.

2. If you're not logged in as the root user, use the su command and enter the root user password to switch to the root user.

3. From the /root directory, type ls and press Enter to display the full name of the Novell iFolder client file.

You can press Tab after entering part of the file name to complete the entry. For example, enter "novell-ifolder" and press Tab to place the complete name of the .rpm file in the command line.

TIP

4. Next, type rpm –i *filename*.rpm –h –v and press Enter. The –i option is used to do a new install, the –h option displays a progress bar, and the –v (for "verbose" mode) option displays long messages.

5. After the installation is finished, type exit and press Enter to end the terminal session.

6. Create a new local user named ekenton on your Linux computer.

7. Log off.

Using the iFolder Client from Linux

To use the iFolder client, a user account on the iFolder server must be enabled for iFolder access as described in Chapter 9. Then you can perform the following steps to set up iFolder for that user on the Linux system:

1. Log in as the ekenton user.

2. Follow these steps to use Konqueror to run the iFolder application:

EXAMPLE

   a. Start Konqueror

   b. Enter a slash (/) to open the root directory.

   c. Browse to the opt/novell/ifolder/bin directory.

   d. Click the novell-ifolder-client file to open it and display the Novell iFolder Login dialog box (see Figure B-8).

Figure B-8   The Novell iFolder Login dialog box

   e. Enter the ekenton user name and password used on your iFolder server.

   f. Enter the IP address or DNS name of your iFolder server in the Server text box.

   g. Verify that the Place a shortcut to the iFolder on the desktop check box is selected, and then click Login to display the Novell iFolder Location dialog box shown in Figure B-9.

   h. Click OK to accept the default settings and display the Encryption dialog box.

   i. Verify that the Encrypt files check box is selected, and then click OK to display the Novell iFolder Get Pass Phrase dialog box (see Figure B-10).

   j. Enter a pass phrase you can remember along with a hint in case you forget.

   k. Click to select the Remember pass phrase check box, and then click OK twice to complete the iFolder setup.

   l. Close the Konqueror window. Your iFolder icon for ekenton should then appear on the desktop.

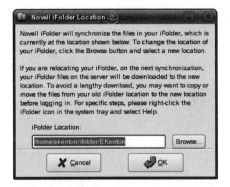

Figure B-9   Selecting the iFolder location

Figure B-10   Entering a passphrase for iFolder

3. Click the ekenton iFolder icon to display the contents of his iFolder. If you placed any files there in Chapter 9, they should be displayed.

4. Close the iFolder window and log out.

5. If you have iFolder running on a Windows XP computer, experiment with iFolder by placing some files from Windows XP in the iFolder.

6. Log in as ekenton again.

7. Click the iFolder icon at the lower right of the KDE desktop to display the Novell iFolder window shown in Figure B-11. Click the Sync button to synchronize your iFolder files.

8. View information in the Account Information and Preferences tabs.

9. Close the Novell iFolder window.

10. Click the ekenton iFolder icon on the desktop to access the iFolder files.

11. The files you placed in iFolder from Windows XP should now appear in Linux iFolder.

12. Close all windows and log out.

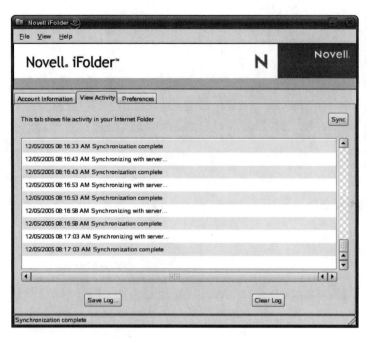

Figure B-11   Synchronizing files in iFolder

AN OVERVIEW OF NOVELL CLIENT FOR LINUX

A major component of Novell Open Enterprise Server is its capability to support open-source software through the use of Linux servers and computers. To allow network administrators to integrate Linux desktop environments into existing NetWare networks quickly and easily, Novell has released Novell Client for Linux, which offers the following features:

- Network login from the GUI interface and server console
- Support for container, profile, and user login scripts
- Mapped drives and home directory access from the GUI interface and server console
- Background authentication and authentication with universal passwords
- GUI and command-line tools
- Support for NetWare Core Protocol
- Name resolution through DNS, DHCP, Service Location Protocol (SLP), and NDAP
- Capability to perform file operations, such as viewing and managing file trustee rights, viewing file attributes, and performing purge and salvage operations
- Several command-line utilities, such as MAP, CX, RIGHTS, and FLAG
- Distributed File System junction support
- eDirectory multi-tree support

Although login scripts were originally created for use with Novell Client for Windows, Novell Client for Linux can take advantage of most functions available in login scripts. So the login scripts you created for Windows computers can also be used with Linux computers without having to modify them, and you have to manage only one set of login scripts.

As of this writing, Novell Client for Linux is in its beta form and should be released soon. Currently, Novell is planning to include Novell Client for Linux with Novell Linux Desktop. For more information and specific installation instructions, visit *www.novell.com/documentation/linux_client*.

C

WORKING WITH VMWARE WORKSTATION 5

VMware Workstation 5 gives you a way to run other operating systems on your Windows XP desktop by creating virtual computer environments. You can experiment with other OSs without having to create a system or disk partition and keep copies of older OSs for use in troubleshooting or testing software applications. In this book, you can use VMware Workstation to perform activities by installing and running Windows XP, NetWare 6.5, and SUSE Linux in virtual computers on your Windows XP desktop. With virtual machines in the classroom, you can have full administrative control of your virtual system without affecting the desktop environment. In addition, using VMware Workstation enables you to suspend your system so that you can continue work later or take a snapshot of your system if you need to return to a specific point because you made a mistake. Because virtual machines can communicate with each other, using VMware Workstation allows you to simulate the lab network on your desktop. In this appendix, you learn how to install VMware, create new virtual computers, configure virtual machine settings, and start and stop virtual machines.

INTRODUCTION TO VMWARE WORKSTATION

Virtual machine software works by emulating a computer's hardware environment, including the hard drive, memory, network interface, and peripheral devices (such as modems and LPT/COM ports), as shown in Figure C-1. VMware Workstation uses disk files on the desktop computer to emulate an entire disk drive for each virtual computer. For this reason, you can use virtual machines to install multiple OSs on your desktop without creating additional disk partitions.

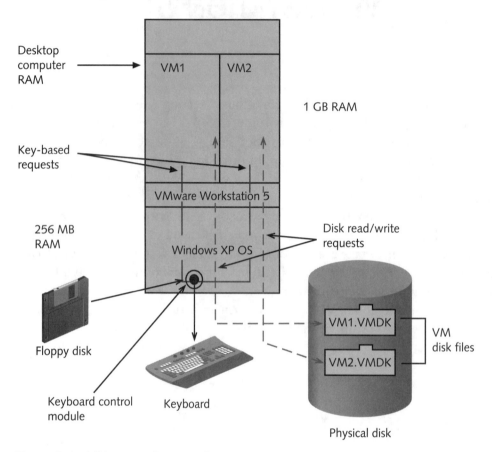

Figure C-1 VMware software architecture

In addition, a section of the desktop computer's memory is reserved for use by each virtual machine. Peripheral devices, such as network cards and USB ports, can be shared by the virtual computer and desktop OS. Certain peripherals, such as the keyboard and mouse, can be used by only one OS at a time. VMware solves this problem by allowing users to give control of the keyboard and mouse to a virtual PC.

VMware virtual machines are managed through the VMware Console, shown in Figure C-2. You can use this console to create new virtual machines, configure virtual machine settings, remove existing virtual machines, perform an OS installation, and start and stop virtual machines.

System Requirements to Run VMware Workstation

One of the major requirements for running virtual machine software is having a large amount of RAM on your desktop. You should have a minimum of 256 MB RAM plus at least 128 MB RAM for your XP virtual machine, 256 MB RAM for a SUSE Linux server, and 512 MB RAM for NetWare 6.5. The more memory you have, the better your virtual computers will perform.

You can use VMware to perform the activities in this book in two ways. First, work in teams with each team consisting of two computers: One computer should have at least 768 MB RAM to run the virtual NetWare 6.5 server, and the other computer should have a minimum of 512 MB of RAM to run the virtual

Figure C-2   The VMware Console

Windows XP or Linux client system. Second, work individually with a computer capable of running the NetWare 6.5 server and Windows XP computer simultaneously. This configuration requires at least 896 MB RAM (512 for the virtual NetWare 6.5 server, 128 for the virtual Windows XP client, and 256 for the desktop XP system).

Obtaining VMware Workstation Software

There are two major virtual machine software products: VMware and Microsoft Virtual PC. Microsoft purchased Virtual PC software from the Connectix company early in 2004. Before this acquisition, VMware was the major supplier of virtual machine software. A major advantage of VMware over Microsoft Virtual PC is VMware's capability of running a variety of OSs, including Windows, Linux, and NetWare. By contrast, Virtual PC software is intended to support earlier versions of the Windows OS to make migration and testing easier. Although running non-Windows OSs on Virtual PC is possible, it's not supported and could cause intermittent problems.

VMware offers a number of software products for using virtual machine technology in a variety of environments. The following sections describe a few of the most commonly used VMware products and their features. You can find more information on this product and download the trial version and VMware Player at *www.vmware.com*.

VMware Workstation 5

VMware Workstation is available in both full and Player editions. VMware Workstation and VMware Player are intended to allow software developers, testers, and students to run multiple OSs simultaneously on a single PC. The full edition is also available as a 30-day evaluation version. For the purpose of this book, you might want to download both the 30-day evaluation version and the free VMware Player. With this combination, you can perform all activities in this book without needing to purchase the full VMware edition. Some new features in VMware Workstation 5 include the following:

- The capability to take and manage snapshots of your operating system's state, which allows you to return to a saved state at any time
- A Snapshot Manager with a graphical view of all your system snapshots
- The capability to capture screens from virtual machines or create a movie consisting of multiple screen shots
- The capability to create teams consisting of two or more virtual machines interconnected across a LAN

VMware Player

The Player edition is free, but you can't use it to create new virtual machines, and its configuration options are more limited than VMware Workstation. For example, in VMware Player you can save the current machine state but you can't take snapshots. You learn more about setting up and using VMware Player in "Using VMware Player" later in this appendix.

VMware ESX Server

VMware ESX Server is a high-performance version of VMware Workstation that uses its own drivers to access the disk system directly, which increases access speed. It runs under Windows 2000 Server or Windows Server 2003 to provide a more powerful platform. VMware ESX Server is intended for use in data centers to implement multiple servers on a single high-performance computer system. Using ESX Server to run network operating systems, such as NetWare, Linux, or Windows, offers the following advantages over running these operating systems without VMware:

- ESX Server can increase utilization of costly computer hardware by running multiple server OSs on the same computer.

- A data center can dedicate servers to specific functions, such as DNS/DHCP servers, Web servers, database servers, and file servers, without the expense of buying additional computer systems.

- A data center can move a virtual server to another physical computer quickly and easily by simply copying the virtual machine files to the other system's hard drive.

- Because VMware isolates the virtual server from the physical hardware of the computer system it's running on, disaster recovery is simplified because you can restore a virtual computer's backup to another computer without having to reinstall the OS or change the hardware configuration.

VMware GSX Server

VMware GSX Server is similar to ESX Server except that it comes with its own kernel and doesn't require a host OS, such as Windows XP or Windows Server 2003. Using its own kernel gives GSX Server better performance and reliability when running servers in large data centers.

CREATING NEW VIRTUAL MACHINES

After installing VMware Workstation 5, your first task is creating a virtual machine environment for each OS version you want to install. Because the VMware Workstation 5 Player software can't be used to create new virtual machines, you need preconfigured virtual machine files from your instructor, or you must create the files on another machine running the full edition (or a 30-day evaluation version) of VMware Workstation 5.

If you're using preconfigured files from another computer, skip to the "Add an Existing Virtual Machine" section. If not, follow the procedure in the "Create a New Virtual Machine" section to learn how to use the full or 30-day version of VMware Workstation 5 to create new virtual machines for installing Windows XP, NetWare 6.5, and SUSE Linux. No matter which version of VMware Workstation 5 you're using, you should create a folder on the C: drive of your Windows XP computer to store virtual machines. For example, use Windows Explorer to create a folder named VMS on your C: drive. You can then place all your virtual machines in subfolders under this folder.

Create a Virtual Machine

To install a new OS, first you need to create a virtual computer environment that defines settings such as the OS version, the location of the disk file, and the amount of RAM. Use the following steps as a guideline for creating new virtual machines for use in this book's activities:

1. Start VMware Workstation by double-clicking the desktop icon to display the VMware Console shown previously in Figure C-2.

2. Click the New Virtual Machine icon to start the Virtual Machine Wizard, and then click Next to display the Select the Appropriate Configuration window.

3. Click the Custom configuration option button, and then click Next to display the Select a Virtual Machine Format window.

4. Verify that the New - Workstation 5 option is selected, and then click Next to display the Select a Guest Operating System window (see Figure C-3).

Figure C-3   The Select a Guest Operating System window

5. Select a guest operating system, click the version you're using in the Version drop-down list, and then click Next to display the Name the Virtual Machine window (see Figure C-4).

Figure C-4   The Name the Virtual Machine window

6. By default, the virtual machine folder is stored in the My Virtual Machines folder of My Documents. If you like, you can change the virtual machine name and location, and then click Next to display the Processor Configuration window. (If you're creating a Windows XP system, the wizard skips to the Memory for the Virtual Machine window.) Click Next to accept the default setting (one) for the number of processors and display the Virtual Machine Settings window (see Figure C-5).

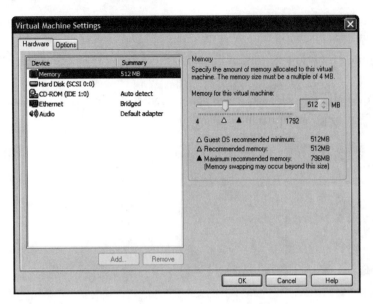

Figure C-5   Memory allocation for the virtual machine

7. Verify that the memory setting meets or exceeds the requirements for the operating system, and then click OK to display the Network Type window (see Figure C-6).

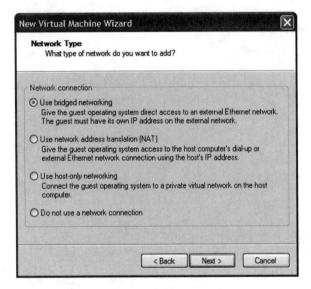

Figure C-6   The Network Type window

8. Verify that the Use bridged networking option is selected, and then click Next to display the Select I/O Adapter Types window.

9. Click Next to accept the default I/O adapter types and display the Select a Disk window.

10. Verify that the Create a new virtual disk option is selected, and then click Next to display the Select a Disk Type window.

11. Verify that the (Recommended) disk type is selected, and then click Next to display the Specify Disk Capacity window (see Figure C-7).

12. Change the Disk size (GB) setting to 1 GB above the default size, and then click Next to display the Specify Disk File window.

13. Click Finish to create the virtual machine and display a summary of settings for the new virtual machine (see Figure C-8).

Figure C-7   The Specify Disk Capacity window

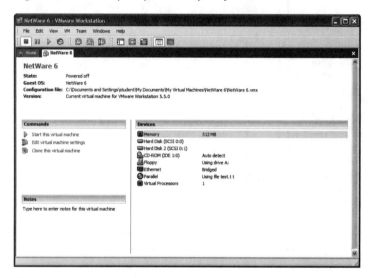

Figure C-8   Summary of settings for the new virtual machine

To verify the configuration of your network adapter and other virtual PC parameters, see "Configuring a Virtual Machine" later in this appendix. To prepare the CD-ROM drive of your new virtual machine for installing a new OS, follow these steps:

1. Insert the bootable CD for the operating system into your computer's CD-ROM drive.

2. Click the Start this virtual machine option and follow the instructions for installing that operating system.

EXAMPLE

Add an Existing Virtual Machine

You can use a virtual machine on multiple desktop computers by copying the virtual machine files from one desktop computer to another. For example, if you're using VMware Player, your instructor might provide a preconfigured NetWare 6.5 or Windows XP virtual machine that you can use for activities in this book. To use an existing virtual machine on your desktop, you need to copy the virtual machine files to your computer and then place the new virtual system in the VMware Console, as described in the following steps:

1. Copy the entire virtual machine folder from the source media or your My Virtual Machines folder.

2. Start VMware.

EXAMPLE

3. Click the Open Existing VM or Team icon to display the Open window.

4. Navigate to the folder containing your new virtual machine, and then double-click the appropriate *.vmx file to create a new tab in the VMware Console for the existing virtual machine.

5. To start the virtual machine, click the Start this virtual machine option.

CONFIGURING A VIRTUAL MACHINE

You can configure many settings in the VMware Console to customize your VMware system. Figure C-9 shows the Virtual Machine Settings dialog box that opens when you select the Edit virtual machine settings option.

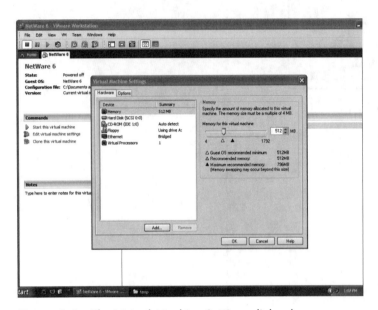

Figure C-9   The Virtual Machine Settings dialog box

Most settings (except the network care and CD-ROM options) require powering down the virtual machine to make changes. In the following sections, you learn how to use these options to customize your virtual machine.

Memory

You use the Memory option to set the amount of RAM the virtual machine uses. Increasing the memory available to a virtual machine can make it run faster, but you need to be sure you have enough memory available for your desktop (256 MB recommended) to prevent excessive paging, which slows down your entire system. In addition, each Windows virtual PC should have 128 to 256 MB RAM. To change the physical RAM, first power down the virtual machine and then double-click the Memory option shown in Figure C-9. Use the scrollbar to change the memory setting, and then click OK to save your changes and return to the VMware Console.

Hard Disk

With VMware, a virtual computer can have multiple virtual hard disk drives, with each hard disk drive mapping to a file on the local computer's physical disk drive. Having multiple disk drives is a great way to learn about disk management. For example, in Chapter 3, you might want to add another disk drive to your NetWare server to practice mirroring disk partitions. In Chapter 14, you need to add disk drives to your SUSE Linux system to practice creating NSS volumes. You can add a new hard drive to your virtual machine with these steps:

EXAMPLE

1. If necessary, start VMware to display the VMware Console.

2. Click the Edit virtual machine settings option to open the Virtual Machine Settings dialog box to the Hardware tab.

3. Click the Add button to display the Welcome to the Add Hardware Wizard window, and then click Next to display the Hardware Type window shown in Figure C-10.

Figure C-10 The Hardware Type window

4. Verify that the Hard Disk item is selected, and then click Next to display the Select a Disk window.

5. Click Next to create a new virtual disk.

6. Verify that the (Recommended) disk type is selected, and then click Next to display the Specify Disk Capacity window.

7. For your second disk, select a size of 2 GB or smaller, and then click Next to display the Specify Disk File window.

8. Click Finish to place the new disk file shown in the Disk file text box in the same folder as your virtual machine and return to the Hardware tab.

9. Click OK to close the Hardware tab and return to the VMware Console.

Your new hard disk can now be initialized and formatted by the guest virtual machine next time you start it.

CD Drive

You can use this option to configure which CD or DVD drive on your local computer is used by a virtual machine. By default, a virtual machine is configured to attach the CD or DVD drive to the secondary IDE controller. You can also have your virtual CD drive point to an ISO image of a CD-ROM by following these steps:

EXAMPLE

1. If necessary, start VMware to display the VMware Console, and click the Edit virtual machine settings option to open the Virtual Machine Settings dialog box to the Hardware tab.
2. Double-click the CD-ROM item to open the CD-ROM device dialog box shown in Figure C-11.

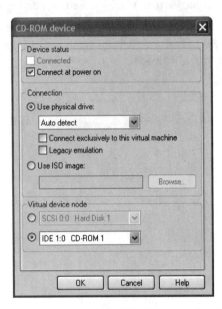

Figure C-11 The CD-ROM device dialog box

3. Click the Use ISO image option button. Click the Browse button to navigate to and double-click your ISO image file.
4. Click OK to save your changes and return to the VMware Console.

Floppy Disk

By default, VMware automatically detects the floppy disk drive and assigns it to the virtual machine. This feature can cause trouble, however, when multiple virtual machines and the desktop system need to use the floppy disk drive simultaneously. If your virtual machine won't be using the floppy disk drive, you might want to clear the Automatically detect floppy disk check box to prevent your virtual machine from taking control of this drive.

Ports

By default, a virtual machine uses no COM or LPT ports. If you want your virtual machine to send output to a printer attached to the local computer's LPT port or use a device attached to a serial COM port, you can add that port with the COM1, COM2, or LPT1 port settings. When adding a port, you can have the output sent to a text file on the local computer's disk drive. This option is handy when testing printer output because you can view the text file in Notepad on the local computer. You might want to try this option when testing printers in Chapter 8. You can use these steps to add an LPT port to your virtual machine:

EXAMPLE

1. In the VMware Console, click the Edit virtual machine settings option to display the Hardware tab shown previously in Figure C-9.

2. Click the Add button to display the Welcome to the Add Hardware Wizard window, and then click Next to display the Hardware Type window.

3. Click the Parallel Port item, and then click Next to display the Parallel Port Type window shown in Figure C-12.

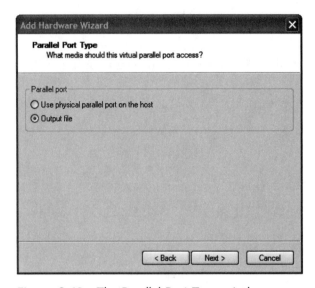

Figure C-12   The Parallel Port Type window

4. To send output from the virtual computer to a device attached to the host computer's physical LPT port, click Next to accept the default setting of Use physical parallel port on the host. To send output to a text file, click the Output file option button, and then click Next to display the Choose Parallel Port Output File window.

5. Use the Browse button to navigate to the directory where you want the file to be stored, enter a name for the file (such as LPTPort.txt) in the File name text box, and then click Save.

6. Click Finish and then click Yes to create the LPT port and return to the Hardware tab of the Virtual Machine Settings dialog box.

7. Click OK to save your changes and return to the VMware Console.

Network Card Settings

VMware provides for multiple virtual network adapters. Each adapter can be configured in one of the following ways:

- *Bridged*—You can select the local computer's network adapter to allow the virtual machine to communicate on a LAN. With this option, the virtual machine becomes another computer on the network and can be configured to communicate with other systems on the network, including printers, routers, servers, and other computers. Be sure to configure the virtual machine's TCP/IP settings to assign or obtain a unique network address.

- *NAT*—This option uses the VMware internal network, but it uses Network Address Translation (NAT) to share the host computer's Internet connection with the virtual network adapter. With this option, you need to set your Windows TCP/IP configuration to obtain its IP address settings automatically. With this option, VMware uses its own internal DHCP service to assign the virtual network adapter an IP address in its own range. You should use the NAT option when your virtual computer needs to be isolated from the LAN, yet you need Internet access for certain tasks, such as downloading patches. This option works only when your virtual PC is configured to get its IP address information automatically. If you have assigned your computer a manual IP address, you might need to temporarily change the IP address assignment to access the Internet.

■ *Host-only*—This option uses an internal network created by VMware that enables multiple virtual machines running on the local computer to communicate only with each other. With this option, the virtual network adapter doesn't communicate with the local computer's physical network adapter or with the local host computer. This option is ideal when you want to separate your virtual machines from the main network to prevent IP address conflicts or to test new network configuration settings.

You can change the setting of the virtual network card without having to power off your virtual machine by following these steps:

EXAMPLE

1. In the VMware Console, right-click the tab of the virtual machine you want to change and click Settings.

2. In the Hardware tab, double-click the Ethernet item to display the Network adapter dialog box shown in Figure C-13.

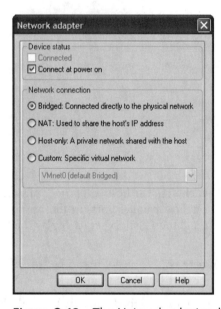

Figure C-13   The Network adapter dialog box

3. In the Network connection section, click to select the type you want to change to, and then click OK to save your setting.

WORKING WITH VMWARE

After you have configured your virtual machine, you can begin using it much like you would any physical computer. VMware offers a number of features that can enhance your use of the system, described in the following sections.

Starting and Stopping Virtual Machines

There are two basic ways to start a virtual machine. You can use the Start button on the VMware Console toolbar, or you can use My Computer to navigate to the folder containing the virtual computer files and then double-click the virtual machine configuration file (.vmx extension).

When a Windows XP system starts, you might be prompted to press Ctrl+Alt+Delete to display a logon dialog box. Because this key combination is intercepted by the local Windows XP OS, VMware uses the Ctrl+Alt+Insert keys to interrupt the virtual machine's operating system.

Before entering information such as your user name and password, click inside the virtual machine window to activate it. The local computer then passes all keystrokes and mouse activity to the virtual machine. To give control back to the desktop OS, press Ctrl+Alt while you move the mouse pointer.

Stop Options

The VMware Console's Action menu has three ways to end a virtual machine session: Power Off, Suspend, or Reset. The Suspend option is useful when you want to temporarily pause the virtual PC session while you perform other tasks. This option frees up processor and memory for other desktop applications. You can quickly resume a paused session by clicking the Start button on the VMware Console toolbar.

The Reset option is similar to using the reset or power off button on a physical computer. A reset operation immediately shuts down the virtual machine and initiates a restart. Normally, you should use the Reset option only when your virtual machine is "hung up" or not responding because you might lose data or corrupt the system's configuration.

If you have completed a virtual machine session, you might want to use the operating system's power off option to perform a normal powering-down process and return to the VMware Console. The Power Off option should be used only if the other two options do not work. Before using this option, you should attempt a shutdown of the Windows system by using the Start, Turn Off Computer procedure.

Working with VMware Views

VMware has a number of options in the View menu for viewing the guest operating system:

- *Full Screen*—Use this option to have your virtual machine use the entire monitor; in this view, you can't see your local desktop computer. To switch back to the VMware Console view, press Ctrl+Alt.

- *Quick Switch*—Use this option (or press F11) to hide the VMware menu and toolbar.

- *Current view*—Use this option to change between the Summary and Console views. The Console view is the default view showing the virtual machine's screen. The Summary view shows the system state and device list.

- *Autofit Window and Autofit Guest*—You use these options to adjust how the virtual machine's screen is displayed on the physical monitor. You can experiment to see which one works best for your virtual machine.

- *Go to Home Tab*—Use this option to display the Home tab shown previously in Figure C-2.

You can also use some key combinations, listed in Table C-1, to switch between virtual machine views.

Table C-1   Key combinations in VMware

Function	VMware Key Combination
Use the Ctrl+Alt+Delete combination used in Windows	Ctrl+Alt+Insert
Give keyboard control back to host computer	Ctrl+Alt
Switch between Full Screen and Console views in VMware	Ctrl+Alt

Installing VMware Tools

After you have installed the Windows OS on your virtual machine, you should install VMware Tools to gain the following benefits:

- Move the mouse pointer between the virtual machine and desktop computer windows. Without VMware Tools, you need to press Alt to move the mouse pointer outside the currently active window.

- Use the shared folders feature to copy files between virtual PCs and the desktop OS.

- Use higher screen resolutions.

Follow these steps to install VMware Tools on your virtual machine:

1. If necessary, open the VMware Console and start your virtual machine as described in the "Starting and Stopping Virtual Machines" section.

EXAMPLE
2. Log on to your operating system with your Administrator user name and password.

3. Press Ctrl+Alt to move the mouse pointer outside the virtual machine window.

4. Click VM, Install VMware Tools (see Figure C-14). Read the message and click Continue to start the InstallShield Wizard and display the VMware Tools welcome window.

Figure C-14 Options on the VM menu

5. Click Next to copy the files and start the installation, following any prompts, if necessary. When the installation is completed, click Finish and then click Yes to restart your virtual machine.

Using Snapshots

Snapshots allow you to save your virtual machine's current state so that you can return to it later. In earlier versions of VMware Workstation, you could have only one snapshot saved at a time. With VMware Workstation 5, you can save multiple snapshots and then use Snapshot Manager to return the machine to any saved state. To take a snapshot, choose VM, Snapshot, Snapshot Manager from the VMware Console menu to display the Snapshot Manager (see Figure C-15), and then click the Take Snapshot button.

To set your machine back to a previous snapshot image, simply click the icon for the state you want to return to, and then click the Go To button.

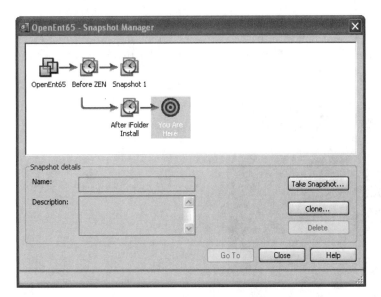

Figure C-15 The Snapshot Manager window

USING VMWARE PLAYER

As described earlier, VMware Player is a new product that runs pre-existing virtual machines and is available free for both Windows XP and Linux systems. VMware Player is limited in that it does not allow creating new virtual machines or taking snapshots and has limited configuration options. You can obtain a copy of VMware Player by downloading it from *www.vmware.com* or ordering the CD online. VMware Player includes the following features:

- Runs existing virtual machines created by VMware Workstation, GSX Server, or ESX Server
- Supports Microsoft virtual machines and Symantec LiveState Recovery disk formats
- Provides access to host PC devices, including CD/DVD drives, network adapters, and plug-and-play USB devices
- Enables you to copy and move text and files between a virtual machine and the host PC
- Includes multiple networking options that allow virtual machines to share the host network adapter (bridged and NAT) or be isolated from the network and host (the Host-only option).
- Supports 32-bit and 64-bit host and guest OSs (such as Novell NetWare, Microsoft Windows, Red Hat and SUSE Linux, and FreeBSD UNIX) so that you can run a wide variety of virtual machines simultaneously on the same physical system
- Enables you to adjust virtual machine memory for optimal performance
- Has configurable shutdown options, including an option to suspend the virtual machine when exiting VMware Player

In the following sections, you learn how to use VMware Player to run existing machines and perform basic configuration tasks.

Running VMware Player

Before starting VMware Player, you need to copy the directories containing any existing virtual machines you want to run to a hard drive attached to your local computer. You can place these virtual machine directories in the default My Virtual Machines folder that VMware Players creates automatically in your My Documents folder, or you can create a separate folder in another location to store the virtual machines. For example, you might want to run your virtual machines from a removable USB-based hard drive to move them between machines. This setup is handy when you want to work on projects both at home and at school.

When you first start VMware Player by double-clicking the desktop icon, the Browse for virtual machine configuration file window opens, where you navigate to the directory containing the virtual machine and then select the correct .vmx file. Then click the Open button to start the virtual machine and display the VMware Player main window shown in Figure C-16.

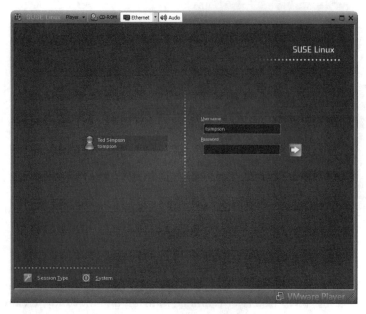

Figure C-16   The VMware Player main window

Notice that this window doesn't have tabs for multiple virtual machines. To run multiple machines on your desktop, you need to start separate instances of the VMware Player application. As in VMware Workstation, you use Ctrl+Alt to switch the keyboard between the virtual machine and the local operating system and Ctrl+Alt+Insert to represent the Ctrl+Alt+Del key combination on the virtual machine.

Configuring VMware Player

Notice in Figure C-16 that the menu bar at the top has a Player option and three icons representing the CD-ROM drive, the Ethernet adapter, and the audio player. You can use the CD-ROM icon to connect or disconnect the CD-ROM drive from the virtual machine and use the Audio icon to enable or disable the virtual machine's connection to your local computer's sound card. You use the Ethernet icon to change the type of network connection to one of the options shown previously in Figure C-13: Bridged, NAT, or Host-only.

You can use the Player menu to get help information, upgrade to VMware Workstation, determine the version of VMware Player, change the memory allocation with the Troubleshoot option (which opens a window similar to the Virtual Machine Settings dialog box), and set VMware Player preferences.

Choosing Player, Preferences from the menu opens the VMware Player Preferences dialog box shown in Figure C-17. In the Exit behavior section, you can determine how the virtual machine is shut down when you exit VMware Player. By default, the virtual machine is placed in a suspended mode. If you want to power down the virtual machine, you need to select the Power off the virtual machine option or use the guest OS's shutdown option.

You can also change some VMware Player settings, such as the amount of memory, by editing the virtual machine configuration file (a .vmx extension). Figure C-18 shows the Netware6.vmx configuration file viewed in Notepad. To change the amount of memory, first you'd power off the virtual machine and then change the memsize parameter from its current 512 setting.

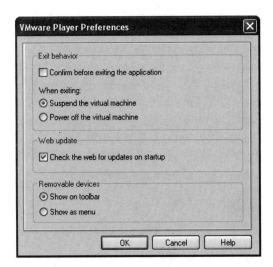

Figure C-17   The VMware Player Preferences dialog box

Figure C-18   A virtual machine configuration file

CAUTION   Before making any changes to the configuration file, you should be sure to make a backup copy so that you can restore your virtual machine settings if needed.

You can also use this file to set the CD-ROM device to use an ISO file. The current settings in Figure C-18 show the virtual device as ide1:0, the file name as "auto detect," and the ide1:0 device type is cdrom-raw. To use an ISO image file in place of the local computer's physical CD-ROM drive, you could change the settings as follows (with *image_name* representing the name of your ISO image file):

```
ide1:0.present = "TRUE"
ide1:0.fileName = "image_name.iso"
ide1:0.deviceType = "cdrom-image"
```

Save your changes and exit the text editor. You can then open VMware Player and start your virtual machine with the new settings.

Glossary

Access Control [A] right — An access right that allows a user to grant access rights for a directory to other users.

access control list (ACL) — A property of an object that lists other objects, such as users, groups, or containers, that have been made a trustee of the object along with the assigned entry and attribute rights.

access right — A file system permission that can be granted to users, groups, or containers. Access rights include Supervisor, Read, Write, Create, Erase, Modify, File Scan, and Access Control.

Add Self attribute right — A special case of the Write attribute right that allows trustees to add or remove their membership in a group.

address restrictions — Security restrictions that require a user to log in only from specified client IP addresses.

Admin user object — An important user object with Supervisor rights to the entire eDirectory tree.

alias object — An object used as a pointer to another object located in a different container of the eDirectory tree.

application directories — Directories that hold installation files needed to install or run software on users' computers.

application-oriented structure — This directory design provides a simple directory structure in which data and applications are arranged by type of use rather than by department.

Archive Needed (A) — A file attribute that indicates the file has been changed since it was last backed up.

attribute — A flag or code associated with files and directories to control what type of processing can be performed on them. *See also* property.

attribute rights — A group of eDirectory security rights used to define the rights granted to read and modify data in the properties of an object. Attribute rights include Read, Compare, Write, Add Self, Inheritable, and Supervisor.

authentication — The part of NetWare security that helps protect against attackers by validating each network packet to guarantee that it was sent from an authorized user.

authorization — The process of verifying a user's name and password to allow him or her to access network resources.

automatic load printers — *See* locally attached printers.

balanced trees (B-trees) — An indexing system that enables NSS volumes to be mounted more quickly and with less RAM than traditional volumes require.

binding — A process that connects protocol stacks to the LAN card driver.

block — The smallest unit of disk storage on a NetWare volume. NSS volumes use a block size of 4 KB; blocks in traditional volumes can be set from 4 KB to 64 KB.

boot partition — A small Linux partition that contains only the system files Linux needs to load the operating system kernel into memory.

boot record — A small area at the beginning of each partition that contains software to load the operating system.

Browse entry right — An eDirectory security right that grants the right to view an object.

cable system — The wiring that connects computers in the network.

Certified Novell Administrator (CNA) — An administrator who has passed the CNA certification test; the objectives for this test are covered in this book.

circuit-level gateways — Firewall devices that inspect packet heading information, including type of service, port number, user name, and DNS name.

client computer — The computer system that requests network services and accesses resources, such as shared files, printers, applications, or communication systems.

client-server applications — Applications that rely on software residing on both the client computer and the server.

command-line interface (CLI) — An interface with a screen for entering text-based commands and displaying text messages and data.

common name (CN) — The name given to an object in the eDirectory tree. A common name must be unique within the container that houses the object.

Compare attribute right — A special case of the Read right that allows trustees to find an object without viewing property information.

console commands — A command function built into the NetWare kernel Server.exe program, so it's always in memory.

container login script — A property of a container object that's run by all users in that container when they log in to the network.

container object — An eDirectory object used to store other objects.

context — The location of an object in the eDirectory tree.

controlled access printers — NDPS printers that exist as an object in the eDirectory tree. By default, only users in the same container as a controlled access printer can send output to it.

Copy Inhibit (Ci) — A file attribute that prevents Macintosh computers from copying the file.

Country container objects — A special type of container object used to group Organization container objects by country. Country containers must be assigned a valid two-digit country code and can exist only at the root of an eDirectory tree.

Create [C] right — An access right that allows users to create files and subdirectories.

Create entry right — An eDirectory security right that grants the right to create objects in a container.

current context — The default location of a client computer in the eDirectory tree.

Custom Device Modules (CDMs) — Software drivers used to manage disk drives through the HBA software. *See also* Host Bus Adapters (HBAs).

date variables — Login script variables that contain date information, such as weekday, month, and year.

dedicated server — A network server that can't be used as a client computer.

default login script — Commands stored in Novell Client that run when a user doesn't have a user login script.

Delete entry right — An eDirectory security right that grants the right to delete an object in a container.

Delete Inhibit (Di) — An attribute that protects a file or directory from being deleted.

denial-of-service attacks — A form of network attack that overloads the server with packets to shut down network services.

departmental structure — A directory design in which user home directories, shared directories, and applications are located within the departments that control them.

DFS junctions — eDirectory objects that contain a path to a NetWare volume.

directly attached printer — A printer that's connected directly to the network cable system.

Directory Access Protocol (DAP) — A protocol that handles formatting and transmitting data between the DUA and DSA.

directory database — A database used to store information about network objects.

directory entry table (DET) — A storage location at the beginning of each volume for storing information on files and directories, including name, size, location, owner, and access dates.

Directory Information Base (DIB) — The name of the X.500 directory database.

Directory Information Shadowing Protocol (DISP) — A special form of the DSP that's responsible for keeping multiple copies of the DIB synchronized.

Directory Information Tree (DIT) — A tree structure for the DIB containers that represents the hierarchical relationship between entries.

Directory Map objects — Objects in the eDirectory tree that contain a path to a volume and directory in the network file system.

directory schema — A set of rules for ensuring that information in the DIB is not damaged or lost.

directory service — Software that provides discovery, security, relational management, storage, and retrieval of directory database information.

Directory Service Protocol (DSP) — A protocol that handles communication between DSAs.

Directory System Agent (DSA) — Software running on a server that consists of a collection of services and protocols that manage specific portions of the DIB.

directory trustee — A user, group, or container object that has been granted access rights to a directory.

Directory User Agent (DUA) — Software that runs on the user's computer and acts as a client to send requests from the user to the directory service.

distinguished name — A name that uniquely identifies an object in the eDirectory database.

Distributed File System (DFS) — The NetWare 6.5 service that allows volumes to be moved to other servers without affecting user access.

Domain container objects — eDirectory containers used to store DNS information.

Don't Compress (Dc) — A file attribute that tells the operating system not to compress the file. When applied to a directory, none of the files in the directory will be compressed.

Don't Migrate (Dm) — A file or directory attribute that prevents files or directories from being migrated to a high-capacity storage device.

Don't Suballocate (Ds) — A file attribute that tells the operating system not to use block suballocation on the file.

dotted decimal notation — IP addresses consisting of 32-bit binary numbers, expressed as four bytes separated by periods.

drive pointer — A letter used to reference storage areas in the file system.

Driver Store — An eDirectory object used to store print drivers.

duplexing — A technique of increasing file service reliability by keeping two disks attached to separate controller cards synchronized on the server.

eDirectory — Novell's directory service; provides directory services to a wide range of network operating systems, including NetWare, Windows, and Linux.

eDirectory partition — A division of the eDirectory structure that starts with a single container and includes any subcontainers.

eDirectory tree — A hierarchical structure of eDirectory objects that places leaf objects within containers.

effective rights — A subset of access rights that controls which functions a user can perform in a directory or file.

Enterprise Volume Management System (EVMS) — An enhanced version of the Logical Volume Manager that supports Novell NSS volumes. *See also* Logical Volume Manager.

entries — Records in the directory database that store information on network objects.

entry rights — A group of eDirectory security rights used to control what a user can do with an object. Consists of Browse, Create, Delete, Inheritable, Rename, and Supervisor rights.

Erase [E] right — An access right that allows the user to delete files and remove subdirectories.

Execute Only (X) — A file attribute that can be applied to .com and .exe files to prevent them from being copied. Once applied, the Execute Only attribute can't be removed.

failover — The process of switching from a failed server to an operational server.

fault tolerance — The capability of a server or device to continue operations in spite of a component failure.

file compression — A NetWare technique to save disk space by automatically compressing files that have not been accessed for a specified time period.

File Scan [F] right — An access right that allows the user to view a directory of file and subdirectory names.

file trustee — A user, group, or container object that has been granted access rights to a file.

firewalls — Hardware or software components that act as a point of access between an organization's internal private network and the Internet, used to filter packets and reduce the risk of unauthorized access or malicious attacks on the network system and services.

Hidden (H) — A file or directory attribute that prevents standard DOS and Windows applications from seeing the associated file or directory.

home directory — A directory created for each user for storing his or her own files and documents.

host — The part of an IP address that represents a device attached to the network and must be unique for each network entity on the cable system.

Host Bus Adapters (HBAs) — Software drivers used to manage disk controller cards.

hot fix — An area of the hard disk that the NetWare file system uses to store data from damaged disk tracks.

hub — A central connecting point for computers attached to a star topology network.

identifier variable — A login script variable that represents information such as user login name, date, time, and DOS version.

iFolder — A NetWare service that enables files to be kept on a local computer (or one that's not attached to the network) and synchronized with the network.

Immediate Compress (Ic) — A file or directory attribute that tells the system to compress a large file immediately after it has been used.

info pages — Command-line documentation pages viewed with the info command. Info pages are newer than man pages and often contain more information.

information theft — A form of network attack that uses wire taps and sniffer software to illegally intercept data.

Inheritable attribute right — An eDirectory security right that enables leaf objects and subcontainers to inherit attribute rights in a container trustee assignment.

Inheritable entry right — An eDirectory security right that allows leaf objects and other subcontainers to inherit the trustee's assignments.

inherited rights — A group of entry or attribute rights that flow down to other containers or leaf objects.

Inherited Rights Filter (IRF) — A method of reducing inherited rights in a subdirectory or file by allowing only the access rights specified in the filter to be inherited.

initial installation phase — The NetWare 6.5 installation phase in which the installation language is selected.

inode — An index entry containing information about a Linux file.

installation startup phase — The NetWare 6.5 installation phase in which the disk and LAN drivers are loaded and the SYS volume is created.

Internet Printing Protocol (IPP) — An industry-standard system for installing and accessing network printers by using HTTP across the Internet.

intruder detection — A part of login security that works at the container level by setting a limit on the number of incorrect login attempts that can be made on a user account during a specified time period.

intrusion — A form of network attack that involves gaining unauthorized and illegal access to an organization's information, usually through obtaining a user's account and password.

iPrint — Novell's IP-based printing system that uses Internet Printing Protocol (IPP) through a Web browser to install and communicate with network printers from a local network or across the Internet.

Java servlets — Applications written in the Java programming language to run on a Web server.

journaling file system — A file system that keeps a log of data transactions applied to a disk partition.

leaf objects —eDirectory objects used to represent network entities, such as users, groups, printers, and servers. Leaf objects must exist within Organization or Organizational Unit containers.

Lightweight Directory Access Protocol (LDAP) — A simplified version of X.500 that makes it easier for compatible systems to exchange directory information.

Lightweight Directory Interchange Format (LDIF) — An ASCII text file format that uses a standardized syntax to add, change, or delete objects in LDAP-compatible directory systems.

Linux Config object — An eDirectory object used to store a list of all SUSE Linux servers in the eDirectory tree.

Linux User Management (LUM) — A method of storing Linux login information in eDirectory to make eDirectory users Linux enabled.

Linux Workstation objects — An eDirectory object used to store a list of all SUSE Linux computers in the eDirectory tree.

local area networks (LANs) — A high-speed communication system consisting of cables and cards (hardware) along with software that provides a means for different types of computers to communicate and share resources over short distances, such as within a single building or room.

local drive pointer — Drive letters that point to physical devices on the local computer, such as the floppy disk drive, hard drive, or CD-ROM drive.

local groups — Group accounts created by a Linux administrator and used to assign rights and permissions to users.

local printer — A printer attached to the server computer.

locally attached printers — Printers attached directly to a server's printer port or to a port on the client computer.

logging in — The process of being authorized to the eDirectory tree.

logging on — The process of being authorized to a Microsoft Windows system.

Logical Volume Manager (LVM) — A volume management system used to group physical hard drive partitions into volume groups for the purpose of creating logical volumes.

Login directory — The NetWare SYS volume directory that's available before a client logs in to the system.

login script — A list of commands that run when users first log in to the network. An important use of a login script is establishing initial drive pointer mappings.

login script variable — A reserved word in the login script language with a value that's unique to the user logging in. For example, the HOME_DIRECTORY variable contains the path to the user's home directory.

login security — The security system used to perform the authorization process. *See also* authorization.

man pages — Command-line documentation pages viewed with the man command.

manual load printers — *See* remotely attached printers.

Master Boot Record (MBR) — The area of the hard disk that holds the boot record.

Media Access Control (MAC) addresses — The binary hardware address of a network interface card. Each card is given a MAC address during manufacture, which it uses to send and receive data packets.

metropolitan area networks (MANs) — Networks that use fiber-optic or microwave towers to connect computers in the same geographical area.

Migrated (M) — A file attribute set by the system indicating that a file has been moved to an archive data medium.

mirroring — The process of automatically synchronizing the information on two partitions located on different disk drives attached to the same controller.

Modify [M] right — An access right that allows the user to change file and directory names—without changing the file contents—and use the FLAG command to change attribute settings on files or subdirectories.

Native File Access Pack (NFAP) — A protocol that enables diverse clients to communicate directly with a NetWare server by using their native protocol.

NDPS Broker — An NDPS component responsible for sending printer messages and notifications, using the Event Notification System (ENS), Resource Management Service (RMS), and Service Registry Services (SRS).

Net Services — A set of hardware and software components that work together to provide access to information services across the Internet or company intranet.

NetBEUI — A Microsoft nonrouting protocol stack commonly used on Windows.

NetBIOS — A standard protocol developed by IBM and used by Windows to find computers on the network by broadcasting the computer's name.

NetDrive — A Novell client service that uses NetStorage to map drive letters on the local Windows system to network drives by using HTTP.

NetWare Core Protocol (NCP) — A protocol NetWare uses to access services on a NetWare server.

NetWare Loadable Modules (NLMs) — Software modules that can be loaded in the server's memory to provide network services or perform administrative operations.

network attached printers — Printers that have their own network port, which allows them to be connected to the network cable without needing additional hardware.

network drive pointer — A letter, usually F: through Z:, used to represent directory paths and volumes in the network file system.

Network File System (NFS) — A Linux file system server that allows exporting files and directories to the network for remote access.

network interface card (NIC) — The network adapter that attaches a computer to the cable system.

network interface card (NIC) driver — The software driver that the operating system needs to communicate with the NIC.

network operating system (NOS) — The software that runs on servers to provide services to the network.

Network Time Protocol (NTP) — An industry-standard time synchronization protocol.

network-centric — A network operating system, such as NetWare 6.5, in which server functions run on a designated computer.

nondedicated server — A server that can also be used as a network client.

Normal (N) — A directory attribute that removes all other directory attributes.

Novell Distributed Print Services (NDPS) — A printing system developed by Hewlett-Packard and Novell to make network printer configuration and access more convenient.

Novell International Cryptography Infrastructure (NICI) — Novell's implementation of the public key cryptography system that uses a combination of public and private keys to encrypt data and passwords transmitted across the network.

Novell NetStorage — A WebDAV-compatible service that makes network files available by using HTTP via a Web browser.

Novell Portal Services (NPS) — A Net Services component running on a NetWare server that provides customized pages or portals for users based on users' rights and style specifications.

Novell Storage Services (NSS) — The file system used primarily by NetWare 6.5. In NSS, logical volumes are created from storage pools that consist of one or more disk partitions.

NSS volumes — Logical divisions of the NSS storage pool used to store system and user data.

OneNet — Novell's strategy of making multiple networks that consist of diverse clients and services work together as one network.

Organization container object — An eDirectory object used to group objects that belong to an organization. Organization objects can exist at the root of an eDirectory tree or within a Country container.

Organizational Role object — An object type that enables you to assign rights to a job position, for example, rather than a specific user.

Organizational Unit (OU) container object — An eDirectory object used to group leaf objects that belong to a subdivision of an Organization container. OU containers can exist within an Organization container or within another OU.

packet — A formatted set of bits transmitted across the network.

packet filtering — A process performed by a screening router to determine whether a packet is from a trusted, untrusted, or unknown network.

parallel port (LPTn) — A common printer port used on personal computers. Parallel ports require thicker cables to transmit several bits of information at one time.

partitions — Areas of hard disk storage formatted for a specific operating system. NetWare 6.5 uses NSS-formatted disk partitions to form storage pools.

password restrictions — Security restrictions that force users to use passwords that exceed or meet a minimum length and must be changed within a specified period.

path — The location of a file or directory in the network file system, often consisting of the server name, volume name, and directory name.

pattern selection phase — The NetWare 6.5 installation phase in which server installation options are selected.

peer-to-peer — A network operating system in which a computer can be both client and server.

Pluggable Authentication Module (PAM) — A Linux software component used to interpret login requests from both local and LDAP users.

Policy Package objects — eDirectory objects used in ZENworks for managing the way users access their computers and connect to the network.

Portable Operating System Interface (POSIX) — An authentication method for user accounts stored in the passwd file on the local Linux server.

primary time servers — Time servers that work in a time provider group with at least one other primary time server and a reference time server to distribute the correct time throughout the network.

Print Manager — The NDPS component that manages the printer agent for printers that don't have one embedded.

print queue — A network object representing a holding area where print jobs are kept until the printer is available. In NetWare, a print queue is a subdirectory of the Queues directory, located in the volume specified during print queue creation.

print server — A component of queue-based printing that manages network printers by taking jobs from print queues and sending them to the appropriate network printer.

printer agent — The software component of NDPS that transfers output from the client and controls the physical printer.

printer gateway — The NDPS component that works with the printer agent to send output from the printer agent to the network print device.

private key — The digital key code used in public key cryptography that is kept solely by the owner and used to decode data and create digital signatures.

profile login script — An eDirectory object containing login commands common to multiple users.

property — A field containing information about an object. Not all object types have the same properties.

protocol — A set of rules that define a communication procedure between computers.

protocol stack — Software that's responsible for formatting and routing packets of data between network devices.

proxy services —Firewall services that work at the application level to give clients on a network both incoming and outgoing access to Internet services.

public access printers —NDPS printers that are attached to the network but don't have an eDirectory object in the tree. Any user attached to the network can send output to a public access printer without having to log in to the network.

Public directory — A required NetWare-created operating system directory that contains NetWare utility programs and commands available to all users.

public key — The digital key code used in public key cryptography for clients to encrypt data being sent to a host and to verify a host's digital signature.

public key cryptography — An Internet security system that uses public and private keys to encrypt and decrypt data and create digital signatures for authenticating users.

[Public] trustee object — A special trustee object created during the NetWare installation that consists of all client computers attached to the network.

Purge (P) — A file or directory attribute that prevents files in a directory from being salvaged after deletion.

queue-based printing — A printing system originated in NetWare 3 that's designed to support simple printers and DOS-based applications.

Read attribute right — An eDirectory security right that includes the Compare right and allows the trustee to view values stored in an object's property fields.

Read Only (Ro) — A file attribute that prevents the contents of a file from being modified.

Read [R] right — An access right that allows the user to read files or run programs in a directory.

Read Write (Rw) — A default file attribute that allows the contents of a file to be changed.

RedHat Package Manager (RPM) — A software installation file format used by the rpm command to install and manage software.

reference time server — Similar to a single reference time server, except it's used in large network environments and participates in a time provider group that includes primary time servers.

regular drive pointer — A drive pointer assigned to a data directory on each volume.

relative distinguished name — A distinguished name that starts with the current context of the client but omits the leading period.

remote printer — A printer that's attached to another client computer.

Remote Printer Management (RPM) — Novell's system for using a Web browser to manage network printers.

remotely attached printers — Printers attached to the port of a networked computer and controlled by the print server.

Rename entry right — An eDirectory security right that grants the right to change the name of an object.

Rename Inhibit (Ri) — A file or directory attribute that prevents the name of a file or directory from being changed.

replica — A copy of the eDirectory database stored on a NetWare server.

Role Based Services (RBS) — The NetWare service used to assign users the rights needed to perform tasks in iManager.

Role Based Services (RBS) container objects — eDirectory container objects used to store iManager administrative roles.

root drive pointer — A regular drive pointer that acts as though it were the root of the volume.

Root object — An eDirectory object representing the beginning of the network's directory service tree.

root partition — The initial division of the eDirectory tree that starts at the root of the tree. In Linux, it's the partition that is the beginning of the file system where all other Linux operating system files and folders are stored.

[Root] trustee object — A special trustee object that represents all users defined in the eDirectory tree. All users who have logged in to the eDirectory tree are part of the [Root] trustee object.

Samba — A service that allows Windows clients to access data on a Linux server by using the CIFS protocol.

scalability — The capability to work with systems of different sizes.

search drive pointer — A drive pointer used to reference executable files and application directories via a DOS path.

secondary time servers — Time servers that get their time from a central time source and then distribute it to network clients.

Security container objects — eDirectory container objects used to store security objects, such as the server certificate.

security equivalence — A security assignment that grants an object rights equal to that of another object.

serial port (COMn) — A printer port often used to connect communication devices, such as modems and printers, to send signals over long cables. Serial ports send only one bit of data at a time, so serial cables can consist of only a few wires.

server — A computer that provides one or more network services.

server clustering — A setup in which two or more servers can share a common disk system, making the data available in case one of the servers has a hardware failure.

server configuration phase — The NetWare 6.5 installation phase in which you specify the server name, install eDirectory, and provide network settings.

Server Message Blocks (SMB) — The proprietary Microsoft protocol that clients use to access network services.

server-centric — A network system in which users must log in to a central server to access network services.

shadowing — The process of distributing and synchronizing the DIB among multiple locations.

Sharable (Sh) — A file attribute that allows multiple users to use a file at the same time.

shared directories — Directories that are available for multiple users to store and retrieve data files.

shell — A Linux command-line environment used to enter commands and start programs.

single reference time server — In the Novell default time server configuration, it's the first server installed in the eDirectory tree, and it distributes the time to secondary time servers and clients.

spoofing — A method of illegally accessing network resources or attacking a network service by creating falsified packets that appear to come from an authorized entity.

Storage Location objects — eDirectory objects used to store paths to directories that will be available through NetStorage.

storage pools — An NSS file system component used to group one or more partitions into a storage area that can be divided in one or more volumes.

suballocation — A feature of traditional volumes that divides blocks into smaller 512-byte increments so that multiple files can share the same block, thus saving disk space.

Supervisor attribute right — An eDirectory security right that grants all rights to a property unless blocked by an object's IRF.

Supervisor entry right — An eDirectory security right that grants all access privileges, including the Supervisor right to all the object's attributes or properties.

Supervisor [S] right — An access right that grants all rights to a directory and its subdirectories; this right cannot be blocked or reassigned at a lower subdirectory or file level.

swap partition — A Linux partition used to page program segments in and out of memory. Linux swap partitions should be at least twice the size of the system's RAM for best performance.

switch — *See* hub.

syntax — Rules to be followed when writing login script commands.

System directory — A required NetWare-created operating system directory that contains system software and commands available only to the server and Admin user, not to other users.

system groups — Group accounts that the Linux operating system creates to grant rights for accessing certain system resources.

System (Sy) — A file or directory attribute that flags a file or directory for operating system use.

threads — Web server processes that allow multiple CPUs to work on a Web application simultaneously to improve performance.

time restrictions — Security restrictions that allow users to log in to the network only during specified hours.

time variables — Login script variables containing system time information, such as hour, minute, and a.m. or p.m.

traditional volumes — Divisions of traditional NetWare partitions that use the older NetWare file system architecture. Traditional volumes can be used to store user and application data for backward compatibility with previous versions of NetWare.

Transaction Tracking System (TTS) — A system that protects the Transactional attribute, ensuring that all transactions are completed or left in the original state.

Transactional (T) — A file attribute used on database files to enable the system to restore the file to its previous state if a transaction is not completed.

Transmission Control Protocol/Internet Protocol (TCP/IP) — The protocol commonly used to format and route packets between computers; also used on the Internet.

trusted network — A network with an IP address range that's known to be safe or can be controlled and monitored by your organization.

trustee assignment — An entry in the ACL for a file or directory that makes the user a trustee of a directory or file.

typeful — A distinguished name that includes object type abbreviations (O, OU, and CN).

typeless — A distinguished name that assumes object type based on position instead of including the object type abbreviations.

uninterruptible power supply (UPS) — A backup power system that uses batteries to supply continuous power to a computer during a power outage.

unknown network — A network that's not specified as a trusted or untrusted network in a firewall. Firewalls treat unknown networks as untrusted networks.

untrusted network — An IP address range that might contain attackers or other malicious entities. Packets from networks listed as untrusted are inspected by the network firewall.

user login script — Personalized login script commands for a single user that are stored in the Login Script property of a user's eDirectory account. A user login script runs after any container or profile script commands are finished.

user template — A property that defines standard settings and configures restrictions for each user in a container.

user variables — Login script variables that allow users to enter parameters for their own login scripts.

Virtual Filesystem Switch (VFS) — An operating system interfacing system that sends user requests from a process to the actual disk file system.

Virtual Office — A Novell system that enables users to work in Virtual Teams and communicate and access data by using a Web browser interface.

virtual private network (VPN) — A trusted network that sends packets over an untrusted network, such as the Internet.

Virtual Team — A group of Virtual Office users who share common files and scheduling.

viruses — Self-replicating programs that can be embedded in software to propagate between computers and can eventually be triggered to affect computer performance or destroy data.

Volume Location Database (VLDB) — A DFS setting that identifies the server and volume containing the database that stores paths used in DFS junctions.

volume object — An eDirectory object used to represent physical NetWare volumes in the eDirectory tree; provides a link between the eDirectory system and the file system.

volumes — The major division of NetWare storage. All files are stored in volumes associated with a specific NetWare server.

Web Services — A set of hardware and software components that provide World Wide Web and FTP information services to clients on the Internet or company intranet.

wide area networks (WANs) — Networks that use carriers such as the phone system to connect computers over long distances.

workgroups — Units consisting of one or more computers used to share data in a peer-to-peer network.

workstation variables — Login script variables containing information about the computer's environment, such as machine type, operating system and version, and station node address.

Write attribute right — An eDirectory security right that includes the Add Self right and allows the trustee to change information in property fields.

Write [W] right — An access right that allows the user to change or add data to files in a directory.

X.500 — A set of recommendations created by the International Telecommunications Union that define directory services.

X-Window — The interface used to provide graphical support that other software packages, such as the KDE and Gnome desktops, draw on.

Zero Effort Networking (ZENworks) for Desktops (ZfD) — A Novell product that enables network administrators to centrally manage users' desktop environments.

Index